*A Stakeholder Approach to
Corporate Social Responsibility*

Long experience has taught me that the crux of my fortunes is whether I can radiate good will toward my audience. There is only one way to do it and that is to feel it. You can fool the eyes and minds of the audience, but you cannot fool their hearts.
Howard Thurston, master mason and magician

A Stakeholder Approach to Corporate Social Responsibility

Pressures, Conflicts, and Reconciliation

Edited By

ADAM LINDGREEN, PHILIP KOTLER,
JOËLLE VANHAMME AND FRANÇOIS MAON

GOWER

Gower Applied Business Research
Our programme provides leaders, practitioners, scholars and researchers with thought provoking, cutting edge books that combine conceptual insights, interdisciplinary rigour and practical relevance in key areas of business and management.

Published by
Gower Publishing Limited
Wey Court East
Union Road
Farnham
Surrey, GU9 7PT
England

Gower Publishing Company
Suite 420
101 Cherry Street
Burlington,
VT 05401-4405
USA

www.gowerpublishing.com

British Library Cataloguing in Publication Data
A stakeholder approach to corporate social responsibility :
   pressures, conflicts, and reconciliation.
   1. Social responsibility of business. 2. Corporations--
   Public relations.
   I. Lindgreen, Adam.
   659.2-dc23

   ISBN: 978-1-4094-1839-9 (hbk)
   ISBN: 978-1-4094-1840-5 (ebk)

Library of Congress Cataloging-in-Publication Data
A stakeholder approach to corporate social responsibility : pressures,
conflicts, and reconciliation / [edited] by Adam Lindgreen ... [et al].
   p. cm.
   Includes index.
   ISBN 978-1-4094-1839-9 (hardback) -- ISBN 978-1-4094-1840-5
   (ebook) 1. Social responsibility of business. 2. Corporations--Investor
   relations. 3. Risk management. I. Lindgreen, Adam.
   HD60.S676 2011
     658.4'08--dc23

                                                                    2011048045

Printed and bound in Great Britain by the
MPG Books Group, UK

Reviews for
A Stakeholder Approach to
Corporate Social Responsibility

In an era where companies have moved from CSR efforts as a "nice to do" to a "have to do", this anthology thoughtfully shares approaches on "how to do it well". In theory and practice, the authors dive deeply into stakeholder engagement essential for authentic and successful programs. Employee and NGO interactions are thoughtfully explored, with articles providing insights and actionable ideas. Other critical areas addressed: frameworks to effectively operationalize initiatives and the use of social media for stakeholder dialogue and engagement. This body of work is a critical companion for the practitioner and scholar desiring more effective business and social outcomes.

Ms Carol Cone, Global Practice Vice Chairman,
Edelman Business + Social Purpose, New York

I am pleased to recommend the new compendium, A Stakeholder Approach to Corporate Social Responsibility. Edited by a group of renowned scholars, this book features chapters from professors of marketing, business management, economics, business ethics, food technology, and risk management, among other fields. In addition to making significant theoretical contributions, this book provides practical advice to business managers, activists, government and NGO representatives, and others working across the business/stakeholder divide. Many chapters offer recommendations on how to improve the dialogue between industry representatives and their stakeholders. I wish all advocates working on the obesity issue would give careful consideration to the chapter on adversarial stakeholder interaction; the authors' findings are painfully eye-opening. The recommendations and managerial implications made in most chapters also have immediate relevance for students in public health, environmental protection, social marketing, social enterprise, and business management. For this reason, I have assigned several chapters to the doctoral students in my Public Health Policy and Practice seminar next semester.

Professor Carol Bryant, Distinguished USF Health Professor in Community and Family
Health,College of Public Health, University of South Florida

Companies the world over are moving past old business thinking to new strategies that merge the performance of the enterprise with the well-being of citizens and society. This calls for innovative perspectives on internal and external stakeholders. A Stakeholder Approach to Corporate Social Responsibility closely examines how these relationships are evolving, what they mean and how to create and analyze them. This important book makes a major contribution to understanding the impact of business and society.

Professor William D. Novelli, Distinguished Professor of the Practice, former CEO of the American Association of Retired People, Georgetown University

Future generations might perceive the current financial crisis as the historic turning point at which the decade-long dominance of shareholder value ideology was broken and replaced by a broader, stakeholder-oriented understanding of corporate responsibility. What does it mean to manage corporations with a stakeholder-view and what are the managerial consequences of such an enlightened understanding of responsibility? This highly innovative research anthology is a source of orientation for both practitioners and scholars. It is valuable for scholars who look for the most recent (trans-disciplinary) thinking in stakeholder theory and for practitioners who want to understand, how they can analyze and manage their stakeholder relations in times of growing complexity.

Professor Guido Palazzo, Professor of Business Ethics, École des hautes Études Commerciales (HEC), University of Lausanne

Contents

List of Figures

List of Tables

About the Editors

Adam Lindgreen

After graduating with degrees in chemistry, engineering and physics, Dr. Adam Lindgreen completed an MSc in food science and technology at the Technical University of Denmark. He also finished an MBA at the University of Leicester, as well as a one-year postgraduate program at the Hebrew University of Jerusalem. Professor Lindgreen received his Ph.D. in marketing from Cranfield University. He has been a professor of marketing (2007–2010) at Hull University's Business School (2010), at the University of Birmingham's Business School and (since 2011) at the University of Cardiff's Business School.

Professor Lindgreen has been a Visiting Professor with various institutions, including Georgia State University, Groupe HEC in France and Melbourne University; in 2006, he was made an honorary Visiting Professor at Harper Adams University College and is currently a Visiting Professor at Lincoln University's Business School. His publications include more than 90 scientific journal articles, 8 books, more than 30 book chapters, and more than 80 conference papers. His recent publications have appeared in *Business Horizons*, *California Management Review*, *Industrial Marketing Management*, *Journal of Advertising*, *Journal of Business Ethics*, *European Journal of Marketing*, *Journal of Business and Industrial Marketing*, *Journal of Marketing Management*, *Journal of the Academy of Marketing Science*, *Journal of Product Innovation Management*, *Psychology & Marketing*, and *Supply Chain Management: An International Journal*; his most recent books are *Managing Market Relationships*, *The New Cultures of Foods*, *The Crisis of Food Brands*, and *Market Orientation*. The recipient of the "Outstanding Article 2005" award from *Industrial Marketing Management* and the Christer Karlsson Award at the 2007 *International Product Development Management* conference, Professor Lindgreen also serves on the board of several scientific journals; he is the joint editor of *Journal of Business Ethics* for the section on corporate responsibility. *His research interests include business and industrial marketing management, experiential marketing, and corporate social responsibility.*

Adam Lindgreen has discovered and excavated settlements from the Stone Age in Denmark, including the only major kitchen midden—Sparregård—in the south-east of Denmark; because of its importance, the kitchen midden was later excavated by the National Museum and then protected as a historical monument for future generations. He is also an avid genealogist, having traced his family back to 1390 and published widely in scientific journals related to methodological issues in genealogy, accounts of population development and particular family lineages.

Philip Kotler

Philip Kotler is the S. C. Johnson & Son Distinguished Professor of International Marketing at the Kellogg School of Management, Northwestern University, Evanston, Illinois.

Kellogg is the "Best Business School for the Teaching of Marketing", and Professor Kotler has significantly contributed to Kellogg's success through his many years of research and teaching there. He received his Master's Degree at the University of Chicago and his Ph.D. at MIT, both in economics. He did postdoctoral work in mathematics at Harvard University and in behavioral science at the University of Chicago.

Professor Kotler is the author of *Marketing Management* (now in its fourteenth edition), the most widely used marketing book in graduate business schools worldwide; *Principles of Marketing*; *Marketing Models*; *Strategic Marketing for Nonprofit Organizations*; *The New Competition*; *High Visibility*; *Social Marketing*; *Marketing Places*; *Marketing for Congregations*; *Marketing for Hospitality and Tourism*; *The Marketing of Nations*; *Kotler on Marketing*; *Building Global Biobrands*; *Attracting Investors*; *Ten Deadly Marketing Sins*; *Marketing Moves*; *Marketing Insights from A to Z*; *Chaotics*; *Up and Out of Poverty*; *Winning at Innovation*; *Marketing 3.0*, and several other books. He has published over 150 articles in leading journals, several of which have received best article awards.

Professor Kotler was the first recipient of the American Marketing Association's (AMA) Distinguished Marketing Educator Award (1985). The European Association of Marketing Consultants and Sales Trainers awarded Kotler their prize for marketing excellence. He was chosen as the Leader in Marketing Thought by the Academic Members of the AMA in a 1975 survey. He also received the 1978 Paul Converse Award of the AMA, honoring his original contribution to marketing. In 1989, he received the Annual Charles Coolidge Parlin Marketing Research Award. In 1995, the Sales and Marketing Executives International (SMEI) named him Marketer of the Year. He has received honorary degrees from 14 universities.

Professor Kotler has consulted for such companies as IBM, General Electric, AT&T, Honeywell, Bank of America, Merck, Samsung and others in the areas of marketing strategy and planning, marketing organization and international marketing. He has traveled extensively throughout Europe, Asia and South America, advising and lecturing to many companies about how to apply sound economic and marketing science principles to increase their competitiveness. He has also advised foreign governments on how to develop the service quality of government agencies and how governments can support their domestic companies to prosper in the global marketplace.

Joëlle Vanhamme

Dr. Joëlle Vanhamme is Professor at the Edhec Business School. Professor Vanhamme has a bachelor's degree in business administration and two master's degrees (psychology and business administration), all from the Catholic University of Louvain. She also has been awarded the CEMS master degree from the Community of European Management Schools. Subsequently, Professor Vanhamme received her Ph.D. from the Catholic University of Louvain (Louvain School of Management). Her Ph.D. thesis examined the emotion of surprise and its influence on consumer satisfaction. Prior to joining Edhec, Professor Vanhamme was assistant professor of marketing at the Rotterdam School of Management, Erasmus University (2002–2009) and associate professor at IESEG School of Management, Catholic University of Lille (2009–2011). She has been a Visiting Scholar with Delft University of Technology, Eindhoven University of Technology, the University of Auckland and Hull University Business School. Dr. Vanhamme's research has appeared in journals including *Business Horizons, Industrial Marketing Management, Journal of Advertising, Journal of Business Ethics, Journal of Consumer Satisfaction, Dissatisfaction and Complaining Behavior, Journal of Customer Behaviour, Journal of Economic Psychology, Journal of Marketing Management, Journal of Retailing, Psychology & Marketing, Recherche et Applications en Marketing* and *Supply Chain Management: An International Journal.* She is the joint editor of *Journal of Business Ethics* for the section on corporate responsibility.

François Maon

Dr. François Maon is Assistant Professor of Strategy and Corporate Social Responsibility at the IESEG School of Management, Université Catholique de Lille. Dr. Maon received his Ph.D. from the Louvain School of Management, Université catholique de Louvain. He has been a visiting researcher at the Haas School of Business, University of California Berkeley. He has published in *California Management Review, International Journal of Management Reviews, Journal of Business Ethics,* and *Supply Chain Management: An International Journal,* among others. Dr. Maon's article "Developing supply chains in disaster relief operations through cross-sector socially oriented collaborations: a theoretical model" was nominated for *Supply Chain Management: An International Journal's* "Best Article 2009." His main research interests include corporate social responsibility, organizational culture, organizational change processes, and corporate branding. Dr. Maon serves on the review board of *Journal of Business Ethics.*

About the Contributors

Debra Z. Basil

Dr. Debra Z. Basil is an Associate Professor at the University of Lethbridge. Dr. Basil received her Ph.D. from the University of Colorado at Boulder. She has published in *Journal of Business Ethics*, *Journal of Business Research* and *Journal of Consumer Psychology*, among others. She edited *Social Marketing Advances in Research and Theory* (Haworth Press, 2007). Her research interests include cause-related marketing, charitable donations, corporate social responsibility, fear appeals and volunteerism. Dr. Basil serves on the board of *Journal of Social Marketing*. She has received major research grants from the Social Sciences and Humanities Research Council of Canada (SSHRC) and Imagine Canada.

David Boje

Dr. David M. Boje is Professor of Management at the New Mexico State University's College of Business. Dr. Boje received his Ph.D. from University of Illinois at Champaign-Urbana. He has published in the *Academy of Management Journal*, *Academy of Management Review*, *Administrative Science Quarterly*, and *Journal of Organization Studies*, among others. Among his most recent books are *Storytelling and Future of Organizations: An Antenarrative Handbook* (Routledge Publishing, 2011) and *Storytelling Organizations* (Sage Publications, 2008). His research interests include ontological-storytelling-inquiry, ethics and qualitative methods. Professor Boje is the founding editor of the *Tamara Journal of Critical Organizational Inquiry*, and for 13 years was editor of the *Journal of Organizational Change Management*.

Massimiliano Bonacchi

Dr. Massimiliano Bonacchi is Associate Professor of Accounting at the University of Naples "Parthenope" and Visiting Associate Professor at Baruch College, City University of New York. Dr. Bonacchi received his Ph.D. from Florence University. He has published in *Business Strategy and the Environment*, *European Transport*, and *Studies in Managerial and Financial Accounting*, among others. His research interests include corporate social responsibility, customer accounting, financial accounting and managerial accounting.

Maureen Bourassa

Dr. Maureen Bourassa is Assistant Professor of Marketing at the Edwards School of Business, University of Saskatchewan. Dr. Bourassa received her Ph.D. from Queen's School of Business. She has published in the *European Business Review* and *Journal of Public Policy and Marketing*, among others. Her research interests include corporate social responsibility, understanding the meaning and impact of respect in a marketing context and stakeholder engagement.

Timo Busch

Dr. Timo Busch is Lecturer in Corporate Sustainability at the Department of Management, Technology and Economics of ETH Zurich. Dr. Busch received his Ph.D. from ETH Zurich. He has published in *Business Strategy and the Environment, Ecological Economics, Journal of Business Ethics* and *Journal of Industrial Ecology*, among others. His most recent book, together with Paul Shrivastava, is *The Global Carbon Crisis: Emerging Carbon Constraints and Strategic Management Options* (Greenleaf Publishing, 2011). Dr. Busch's research interests include business and industrial ecology, climate change and sustainable finance. Before joining ETH, he worked at the Wuppertal Institute for Climate, Environment, and Energy focusing on corporate eco-efficiency and life-cycle analyses.

Robin T. Byerly

Dr. Robin T. Byerly is an Assistant Professor of Management at Appalachian State University's Walker College of Business. Dr. Byerly received her Ph.D. from the Florida State University. She has published in the *Business and Professional Ethics Journal, JONA's Healthcare Law, Ethics, and Regulation, Journal of Management, Journal of Management Issues,* and *Managerial and Decision Economics,* and is the author of a number of book chapters. Her research interests include business ethics, change, and restructuring, corporate-level strategy, and corporate social responsibility and sustainability. She serves as a reviewer for *Journal of Business Ethics* in the area of corporate social responsibility.

Tom Cooper

Dr. Tom Cooper is Assistant Professor at the Faculty of Business Administration, Memorial University. Dr. Cooper received his Ph.D. from the University of Warwick's Business School. He has published in *Greener Management International: The Journal of Corporate Environmental Strategy and Practice, Journal of the Academy of Finance* and *Workplace Review,* among others. His research interests include indigenous peoples' business issues, risk management, business ethics, strategic planning and commercial fisheries management. As part of his research with indigenous peoples, Dr. Cooper has worked with Ulnooweg Development Group, Atlantic Policy Congress of First Nations Chiefs and a large number of First Nations in Atlantic Canada.

Russell Craig

Dr. Russell Craig is Professor of Accounting and Head of the School of Accounting and Finance at Victoria University, Melbourne, Australia. Dr. Craig received his Ph.D. from the University of Newcastle, Australia. He has published in *Abacus, Accounting, Auditing, and Accountability Journal, British Accounting Review, British Journal of Management, Critical Perspectives on Accounting, Human Relations* and *Journal of Business Ethics*, among others. Among his most recent books are, with Joel Amernic, *CEO-speak: The Language of Corporate Leadership* (McGill-Queen's University Press, Montreal and Kingston, 2006). His research interests include accounting education, accounting history, financial accounting and reporting, international accounting, accounting and labour relations and the accountability discourse of executives. He serves on the boards of *Accounting, Auditing, and Accountability Journal* and *Issues in Accounting Education*; he is an editorial adviser to *Accounting Education: An International Journal*.

Peggy Cunningham

Dr. Peggy Cunningham is the Dean of the Faculty of Management at Dalhousie University and the R.A. Jodrey Chair. Dr. Cunningham received her Ph.D. from Texas A&M University. She has published in *California Management Review, Journal of Business Ethics, Journal of Advertising, Journal of the Academy of Marketing Science* and *Journal of International Marketing*, among others. She has co-authored numerous Canadian editions of *Principles of Marketing* (Pearson Publishing, third to ninth edtions) and *Marketing Management* (eleventh to fourteenth editions). Dr. Cunningham's teaching and research focus on ethics, corporate social responsibility and partnerships within the field of marketing. She serves on the editorial review boards of several journals and is the co-editor of *Journal of Historical Research in Marketing*.

Sally Davenport

Dr. Sally Davenport is Professor of Management at Victoria University of Wellington's Management School. Dr. Davenport received her Ph.D. in chemistry from Victoria University but, after a period in consulting, became an innovation management scholar. She has published in *British Journal of Management, Discourse Studies, European Journal of Marketing, European Planning Studies, Human Relations, International Studies in Management and Organization, Journal of Management Studies, Organization Studies, Research Policy, Science and Public Policy, Technovation* and *Technology Analysis and Strategic Management*, among others. Her research interests include the strategic management of innovation, commercialisation of research and the discourse of scientific organizations. She serves on the editorial boards of *Innovation: Management, Policy and Practice, Journal of Technology Transfer, R&D Management* and *Research Evaluation*.

Frank G. A. de Bakker

Dr. Frank G. A. de Bakker is Associate Professor at the Department of Organization Sciences, Faculty of Social Sciences, VU University Amsterdam, the Netherlands. Dr. De Bakker received his Ph.D. from the University of Twente. He has published in *Academy of Management Review*, *Business & Society* and *Journal of Business Ethics*, among others. His most recent book is *Managing Corporate Social Responsibility in Action* (Ashgate, 2007). His research focuses on processes of institutional change regarding corporate social responsibility and the role of social movement organizations and their networks therein. He serves on the boards of *Business & Society* and *International Journal of Sustainable Strategic Management*; he co-edits several special issues, including ones for *Journal of Business Ethics* and *Organization Studies*.

Gerard de Groot

Mr. Gerard de Groot is director and senior economist with the Development Research Institute of the Tilburg University. In 1974, Mr. De Groot received his MSc (*cum laude*) in economics from Tilburg University and since has worked and researched development-related issues in developing countries up to present. He has published in *International Journal of Human Resources Management and Development*, *Journal of Human Development* and *Journal of Supply Chain Management*, among others. His research interests include economic development, poverty, innovation, policy development and evaluation. At present, his professional activities encompass development research, consultancy and Ph.D. supervision.

Job de Haan

Dr. Job de Haan is Associate Professor of International Production Management at Tilburg University's School of Economics and Management. Dr. De Haan received his Ph.D. from Tilburg University. He has published in *International Journal of Production Economics*, *International Journal of Cleaner Production*, *International Journal of Production and Operations Management* and *Supply Chain Management*, among others. He has contributed to books such as *Entrepreneurship, Innovation and Economic Development* (Adam Szirmai, Wim Naude and Micheline Goedhuys, Oxford, 2011). His research interests include lean logistics, international supply chains, corporate social responsibility and innovation. He is a reviewer for several journals, member of the advisory board of *International Symposium on Logistics* and active in regional development agencies.

Frank den Hond

Dr. Frank den Hond is Associate Professor at the Faculty of Social Sciences of VU University, Amsterdam. Dr. Den Hond received his Ph.D. from VU University. He has published in *Academy of Management Review*, *Business & Society*, *Journal of Corporate Citizenship* and *Organization Studies*, among others. Among his most recent books are *Managing Corporate*

Social Responsibility in Action: Talking, Doing and Measuring (Ashgate, 2007) and *Pesticides: Problems, Improvements, Alternatives* (Blackwell Science, 2003). Dr. Den Hond's research interests include corporate social responsibility, institutionalization, NGOs and social movements. He serves on the boards of several journals including *Organization and Environment*; he is Senior Editor of *Organization Studies*.

Steven M. Elias

Dr. Steven M. Elias, who earned his Ph.D. in applied social psychology at Colorado State University, is an Associate Professor and Head of the Management Department at New Mexico State University. Although Dr. Elias is interested in several areas of organizational behavior, his primary research interests revolve around managerial influence, social power and self-efficacy. His research has been published in the *International Journal of Organizational Analysis*, *Journal of Applied Social Psychology*, *Journal of College Student Development*, *Journal of General Psychology*, *Journal of Management*, the *Journal of Management History*, *Social Influence* and *Southern Business and Economics Journal*. A past member of the *Journal of Management*'s editorial board, Dr. Elias is currently on the editorial board of *Journal of Applied Social Psychology*, *Journal of Organizational Behavior* and *PsycCRITIQUES*.

Matthias S. Fifka

Dr. Matthias S. Fifka is the Dr. Juergen Meyer Endowed Chair for International Business Ethics and Sustainability at Cologne Business School, Germany. Dr. Fifka received his Ph.D. from the University of Erlangen-Nuremberg, Germany. He has published in *Business Economics, Business Strategy and Environment, Journal fuer Betriebswirtschaft* and the *American Studies Quarterly*, among others. Among his most recent books is *Corporate Citizenship in Germany and the U.S.: Commonalities and Differences in the Civic Engagement of Businesses and the Potential for a Transatlantic Transfer* (Gabler, 2011). His research interests include business ethics, corporate governance, corporate social responsibility and sustainability; he is a reviewer for several journals and serves on the board for *Corporate Social Responsibility and Environmental Management*.

Peter Fleming

Dr. Peter Fleming is Professor in organization studies at the School of Business and Management, Queen Mary College, University of London. Dr. Fleming received his Ph.D. from Melbourne University. He has published in *Academy of Management Review, Human Relations, Journal of Management Studies, Organization Studies* and *Sociology* among others. Among his most recent books are *Contesting the Corporation* (Cambridge University Press, 2007), *Authenticity and the Cultural Politics of Work* (Oxford University Press, 2009), and *Charting Corporate Corruption* (Edward Elgar, 2009). His research interests include power at work, labour relations, business ethics, corporate corruption and workplace conflict. He serves on the board of *Organization Studies*.

Roberto García-Castro

Dr. Roberto García-Castro is Assistant Professor of Managerial Decision Sciences at the IESE Business School. His research interests include decision making in organizations, stakeholder management and metrics and corporate governance. His research has been published in *Business & Society, Journal of Business Ethics and Managerial and Decision Economics, among others*. Dr. García-Castro has been visiting professor at several European universities such as ESCP (European School of Management) in London, Universidad Carlos III in Madrid, and LMU (Ludwig Maximilians Universität) in Munich. Prior to academia, he worked for Arthur Andersen as auditor and consultant.

Georgios Georgakopoulos

Dr. Georgios Georgakopoulos is an Assistant Professor of Financial Accounting at the University of Amsterdam's Business School. Dr. Georgakopoulos received his Ph.D. from Strathclyde University. He has published in *Accounting, Auditing, and Accountability Journal, Accounting Forum* and *Agricultural Economics Review*, among others. His most recent book contribution was published in Hopwood, Unerman and Fries (eds) *Accounting for Sustainability: Practical Insights* (Earthscan, 2010). Dr. Georgakopoulos' research interests lie in the areas of assurance, capital markets, NGO accountability, corporate social responsibility, financial accounting and social and environmental accountability. He worked previously as a lecturer in accounting in the Kemmy Business School at the University of Limerick in Ireland, as a teaching assistant in accounting at Strathclyde University, and as an assistant economist in the Scottish Executive Environment & Rural Affairs Department in Scotland.

Robert L. Heath

Dr. Robert L. Heath is Professor Emeritus at the University of Houston. Dr. Heath received his Ph.D. from the University of Illinois. He has published in the *Australian Journal of Communication, Communication Studies, Communication Monographs, Communication World, Environmental Communication, Journal of Applied Communication Research, Journal of Communication, Journal of Marketing*, the *Journal of Mass Media Ethics, Journal of Public Affairs, Journal of Public Relations Research, Management Communication Quarterly, Public Relations Review, Public Relations Quarterly* and *Quarterly Journal of Speech*. Among his most recent books are *SAGE Handbook of Public Relations* (Sage, 2010), *Rhetorical and Critical Approaches to Public Relations II* (Routledge, 2009), *Strategic Issues Management* (2nd ed., Sage, 2009), and *Handbook of Risk and Crisis Communication* (Routledge, 2009). His peer research interests include issues management, risk communication, crisis communication, public relations, stakeholder participation, and organizational rhetoric. Professor Heath serves on the editorial boards of *Journal of Public Relations* and the *Public Relations Review*. He has performed research with Baker Oil Tools, ConocoPhillips, Schlumberger and Shell Oil.

Terry Hickey

Mr. Terence Hickey is the founder and principal consultant with Planning Resources Incorporated located in St. John's, Newfoundland. Mr. Hickey has worked in the area of Aboriginal economic, business and community development for over 20 years. Within the last five years, he was the primary author on a study of Aboriginal finance in Canada and was one of the lead consultants on a study of commercial fishing practices in First Nations in Atlantic Canada. As part of his consulting work with indigenous peoples, Mr. Hickey has worked with Ulnooweg Development Group, Atlantic Policy Congress of First Nations Chiefs and a large number of First Nations in Atlantic Canada.

Romy Kraemer

Ms Romy Kraemer is a Ph.D. candidate at the Rotterdam School of Management, Erasmus University. She has published in *Transnational Corporations*. Her research interests include transnational anti-corporate social movements (critical perspectives on), corporate social responsibility and the multinational mining and oil industry.

Shirley Leitch

Dr. Shirley Leitch is Professor of Corporate Communication and Deputy Vice Chancellor (Academic) at Swinburne University of Technology in Melbourne, Australia. Dr. Leitch received her Ph.D. from the University of Auckland. She has published in the *Australian Journal of Communication, Discourse Studies, European Journal of Marketing, Human Relations, International Studies in Management and Organization, Journal of Brand Management, Journal of Communication Management, Journal of Management Studies, Organization Studies, Public Relations Review* and *Science and Public Policy*, among others. Dr Leitch is a discourse scholar and her research has a strong interdisciplinary character. Her research is focused on public discourse and change, including science–society engagement and communication, particularly in relation to controversial science.

Adam Lindgreen

Dr. Adam Lindgreen is Professor of Marketing at the University of Cardiff's Business School. Dr. Lindgreen received his Ph.D. from Cranfield University. He has published in *California Management Review, Journal of Business Ethics, Journal of Product and Innovation Management*, and *Journal of the Academy of Marketing Science*, among others. Among his most recent books are *Managing Market Relationships* (Gower Publishing, 2008) and *Memorable Customer Experiences* (Gower Publishing, 2009). His research interests include business and industrial marketing, experiential marketing and corporate social responsibility. He serves on the boards of many journals; he is the joint editor of *Journal of Business Ethics* for the section on corporate responsibility.

François Maon

Dr. François Maon is Assistant Professor of Strategy and Corporate Social Responsibility at the IESEG School of Management, Université Catholique de Lille. Dr. Maon received his Ph.D. from the Louvain School of Management, Université catholique de Louvain. He has published in *California Management Review, International Journal of Management Reviews, Journal of Business Ethics* and *Supply Chain Management: An International Journal*, among others. His research interests include corporate social responsibility, corporate branding and organizational change processes. He serves on the review board of *Journal of Business Ethics*.

Stephanie Maynard-Patrick

Ms. Stephanie Maynard-Patrick is a Ph.D. candidate in the management program at New Mexico State University. She received her master's from the University of Illinois, Urbana-Champaign. Her research interests include efficacy, emotional labour, mentoring and commitment.

Katherine A. McComas

Dr. Katherine McComas is Associate Professor at Cornell University. Dr. McComas received her Ph.D. from Cornell. She has published in *Communication Research, Journal of Health Communication, Policy Studies Journal, Risk Analysis: An International Journal* and *Science Communication*, and among others. Her research interests include risk communication, environmental communication; public participation, trust, credibility and conflicts of interest in science. She serves on the boards of *Environmental Communication: A Journal of Nature and Culture, Journal of Risk Research*, and *Science Communication*; she is an associate area editor for Risk Perception/Risk Communication of *Risk Analysis: An International Journal*.

Michael J. Palenchar

Dr. Michael J. Palenchar is Associate Professor of Public Relations and Co-Director of the Risk, Health, and Crisis Communication Research Unit at the University of Tennessee's College of Communication and Information. He has published in the *Environmental Communication, Journal of Public Relations Research, Management Communication Quarterly, Public Relations Journal, Public Relations Review* and *Journal of Contingencies and Crisis Management*, among others. His most recent book is *Strategic Issues Management* (2nd ed., Sage Publications, 2009). His research interests include risk communication, crisis communication and issues management. Dr. Palenchar serves on the board of several journals, including *Journal of Public Relations Research* and *Public Relations Inquiry*.

Paolo Perego

Dr. Paolo Perego is Assistant Professor of Management Accounting at the Rotterdam School of Management, Erasmus University. Dr. Perego received his Ph.D. from the Radboud University of Nijmegen. He has published in *Abacus, Business Strategy and the Environment, European Accounting Review* and *Strategic Change*. His research interests are in the area of nonfinancial performance measurement with a particular focus on environmental accounting, sustainability performance measurement and control systems in the public sector. He serves on the board of *Business Strategy and the Environment*.

Jonatan Pinkse

Dr. Jonatan Pinkse is Associate Professor of Strategy at Grenoble Ecole de Management. Dr. Pinkse received his Ph.D. from the University of Amsterdam. He has published in *Business & Society*, the *California Management Review, Energy Policy* and *Journal of Business Studies*, among others. His most recent book is *International Business and Global Climate Change* (Routledge, 2009). Dr. Pinkse's research interests include business responses to climate change, corporate investments in clean energy technologies, and trade-offs in sustainability. He serves on the boards of *Business Strategy and the Environment* and *Organization and Environment*.

Stephanie Proutheau

Ms. Stéphanie Proutheau is a doctoral candidate at the Celsa Paris-Sorbonne and the French National Center for Scientific Research' Institute for Communication Sciences (ISCC). After a degree in international public law at la Sorbonne, she earned an MA at the University of Houston School of Communication. She is now part of the Scientific Expertise and Controversies research program at the ISCC, the CNRS's interdisciplinary institute where she conducts her doctoral work on the agricultural biotechnology controversy.

Rossella Ravagli

Ms. Rossella Ravagli is the Corporate Social and Environmental Responsibility Manager at Gucci in Florence, Italy. Prior to working with Gucci, she was the CSR Manager for two different certification bodies. Ms. Ravagli received an MSc in Statistics and Economic Sciences from Bologna University and master in Quality Assurance and Human Resource Development. She has published many interviews and articles about human rights, SA 8000 and social accountability. Among her most recent books are, with Molteni, Bertolini, and Pedrini, *CSR Manager* (Il sole-24 ore, 2007) and *Practical Guidance on the Social Responsibility* (SGS Training Center and De Qualitate, 1999).

Lúcia Lima Rodrigues

Dr. Lúcia Lima Rodrigues is Associate Professor of Accounting (with Habilitation) at the University of Minho, Braga, Portugal. Dr. Rodrigues received her Ph.D. from University of Minho. She has published in the *Accounting, Auditing, and Accountability Journal, Accounting Forum, Accounting Historians Journal, Accounting History, British Accounting Review, Business History, Critical Perspectives on Accounting, International Journal of Accounting, and Journal of Business Ethics*, among others. Her main research areas include accounting history, accounting for intellectual capital and intangible assets, corporate social responsibility, financial accounting and reporting. Dr. Rodrigues is editor of the refereed *Portuguese Journal of Accounting and Management* and European editor of *Accounting History*.

Nigel Roome

Dr. Nigel Roome is Professor of Governance, Corporate Responsibility, and Sustainable Development and Academic Director of the full time MBA program at Vlerick Leuven Gent School of Management. Dr. Roome received his Ph.D. from the University of Cambridge. He has published in *Business Strategy and the Environment, Human Ecology Review, Journal of Business Process Management, Organisation Studies* and *R&D Management*, among others. His most recent book is *The Ecology of the New Economy: Sustainable Transformation of Global Information* (Greenleaf Publishing, 2002). His research interests examine the relationship between business strategies, technological and management innovation and systemic changes arising from sustainable development, the internationalisation of business, and the credit crisis. Dr. Roome addresses how companies and managers understand and respond to these changes. He serves on the boards of many journals. He has worked closely with companies in the pulp and paper, chemicals, mining, power utilities, oil and gas, construction, banking, textiles and food sectors. He also has advised the American Association for Engineering Education, the European Commission and the governments of Belgium, Canada, Mexico, the Netherlands, Poland and the UK.

Mary Runté

Dr. Mary Runte is Associate Professor and the Director of Social Responsibility and Nonprofit Management at the University of Lethbridge. Dr. Runte received her Ph.D. from Saint Mary's University, Halifax, Canada. She has published in *Journal of Business Ethics, Journal of Business Research*, and *Human Relations*, among others. Her research interests include work–family interaction, critical theory, corporate social responsibility, cause-related marketing and volunteerism. She has received major research grants from the Social Sciences and Humanities Research Council of Canada (SSHRC) and Imagine Canada.

Sheldene Simola

Dr. Sheldene Simola is an Assistant Professor in the Business Administration Program at Trent University. Dr. Simola received her Ph.D. from Queen's University at Kingston. She has published in *Consulting Psychology: Research and Practice, Education + Training, Journal of Business Ethics, Leadership Quarterly* and *Society and Business Review*, among others. Her research interests include business ethics, corporate crisis management and leadership. Her research for this anthology was supported by a grant from the Social Sciences and Humanities Research Council of Canada.

Valérie Swaen

Dr. Valérie Swaen is Associate Professor of Marketing and Corporate Social Responsibility at the Louvain School of Management of Université Catholique de Louvain (Belgium) and at the IESEG School of Management (France). Dr. Swaen received her Ph.D. from Université Catholique de Louvain. She has published in the *International Journal of Management Reviews, Journal of Business Ethics, Recherche et Applications en Marketing* and *Corporate Reputation Review*, among others. Her research interests include consumer behavior, corporate social responsibility implementation and communication and customer relationship marketing.

Ian Thomson

Mr. Ian Thomson is Professor of Accounting at the University of Strathclyde Business School, Glasgow. He received his BA (Hons) from Heriot-Watt University. He has published in *Accounting, Auditing, and Accountability Journal, Accounting and Business Review, Accounting Forum, Critical Perspectives on Accounting* and *International Journal of Business Ethics*. His most recent publications include chapters in *Accounting and Sustainability: Practical Insights* (Earthscan, 2010), *Social Accounting and Public Management: Accountability for the Common Good* (Routledge, 2010) and *Sustainable Accounting and Accountability* (Routledge, 2007). In his research Mr. Thomson has worked with a range of organizations including the Prince's Charities, the Scottish Parliament and WWF Scotland. His research interests include carbon accountability, dialogic engagement and accountability social activism and sustainability accounting. He serves on the editorial boards of *Accounting, Auditing, and Accountability Journal* and *Accounting Forum*.

Rob Van Tulder

Dr. Rob Van Tulder is Professor of International Business-Society Management at Rotterdam School of Management, Erasmus University Rotterdam. He holds a Ph.D. degree (*cum laude*) in social sciences from the University of Amsterdam. He has been visiting professor in a number of universities and consultant to international organizations (such as the UN, the IMF and the European Union), multinational enterprises, nongovernmental organizations (NGOs) and ministries around the world. He is co-founder of the department of Business-

Society Management, one of the leading departments in the world studying and teaching about the contribution of business and leaders toward society. Dr. Van Tulder is presently academic director of the Partnerships Resource Centre (www.partnershipsresourcecentre.org) that studies the cross-sector partnerships between firms, NGOs and government for sustainable development. He has published in journals like *California Management Review, Journal of Business Ethics, Journal of International Business Studies* and *Journal of World Business*. His latest book publications include *Corporate Responsibilities in Turbulent Time* (China Economic Publishing House, 2010); *Skill Sheets: In Integrated Approach to Research, Study and Management* (Pearson International, 2007; www.skillsheets.com); *International Business-Society Management* (Routledge, 2006; www.ib-sm.org).

Jaap Voeten

Mr. Jaap Voeten is a Ph.D. Research Fellow at the Development Research Institute of Tilburg University. He is a development economist by education from Wageningen University and the University of Amsterdam. Mr. Voeten lived and worked in Vietnam and Yemen for years and was involved in a series of qualitative studies on economic development and small business. Over the years, he has published in books such as *Management Development: Perspectives from Research & Practice* (Routledge), *Entrepreneurship, Innovation, and Economic Development* (Oxford University Press), and in publication series of World Institute for Development Economics Research of the United Nations University (UNU-WIDER). His research interests include poverty alleviation, small business, responsible innovation and institutional economics. Mr. Voeten is member of the Academic Advisory Council of the African Studies Centre of Leiden University.

Duane Windsor

Dr. Duane Windsor is the Lynette S. Autrey Professor of Management at Rice University's Jesse H. Jones Graduate School of Business. Dr. Windsor received his Ph.D. from Harvard University. He has published in *Business & Society, Business Ethics Quarterly, Journal of Business Ethics, Journal of Corporate Citizenship, Journal of Management Studies* and *Public Administration Review*, among others. With L. E. Preston, he published the second edition of *The Rules of the Game in the Global Economy: Policy Regimes for International Business* (Kluwer Academic Publishers, 1997). He is editor (since 2007) of *Business & Society*.

Foreword and Acknowledgment

According to a recent McKinsey & Co. global survey, 95 percent of surveyed CEOs believe that "society has greater expectations than it did five years ago that companies will assume public responsibilities".[1] This increasing pressure on organizations demands that they adopt a broader perspective on their purpose—one that includes social and environmental considerations. In turn, corporate social responsibility has grown into a global phenomenon that encompasses businesses, consumers, governments and civil society and many organizations have adopted its discourse.[2] The various corporate social responsibility initiatives that organizations embrace range from the design and implementation of codes of conduct to triple bottom line reporting, collaborations with nongovernmental organizations and U.N. agencies and increased support for community development programs.

Yet despite this global spread, corporate social responsibility remains an uncertain and poorly defined ambition, with few absolutes.[3] First, the issues that organizations must address can easily be interpreted to include virtually everyone and everything.[4] Issues pertaining to corporate social responsibility can "vary by business, by size, by sector and even by geographic region",[5] relating to concerns about human rights, workers' well-being, environmental impacts, business ethics, community investments, governance and the marketplace. The vast range of such issues places enormous pressures on organizations.

Second, with their unique, often particular characteristics, different stakeholder groups tend to focus only on specific issues that they believe are the most appropriate and relevant in organizations' corporate social responsibility programs. Thus, beliefs about what constitutes a socially responsible and sustainable organization depend on the perspective of the stakeholder.[6] Stakeholders' corporate social responsibility expectations are not only inconsistent[7] but also inexorably evolve over time.[8] Thus, corporate social responsibility issues and practices require constant reassessments and dialog. Moreover, people tend to belong to multiple stakeholder groups at the same time.[9] For example, a consumer who evaluates a given product's sustainability might also be an employee of the organization that produces the product.[10] A financial investor with an economic interest in the organization might be a member of the local community in which the organization operates. Beliefs and expectations about organizations' corporate social responsibility programs thus differ not only among different stakeholder groups but also within the same stakeholder, depending on which hat they might be wearing at the time.

Third, in any organization, strategic, organizational and managerial implications associated with the design, development and implementation of corporate social responsibility commitments and policies differ across functional units and departments (e.g., supply and logistics, research and development, marketing, human resources, communication, finance). The beliefs of organizational members about their organization's social responsibilities thus vary according to their function and department, as well as their own managerial fields of knowledge.[11]

In summary, corporate social responsibility constitutes a complex notion for corporate and noncorporate actors, all concerned with the impact of business on society. The multiple lenses and perspectives of corporate social responsibility make it an intrinsically plural notion—one that seems almost irrelevant to approach from a single or narrow viewpoint. To approach corporate social responsibility in a comprehensive, responsible way, we must seek to understand the many-sided nature of organizations' relationships with business and wider society.

The overall objective of this research anthology is to provide a comprehensive collection of cutting-edge theories and research that can lead to a more multifaceted understanding of corporate social responsibility in its various forms, the pressures and conflicts that result from these different understandings and some potential solutions for reconciling them. The chapters in the research anthology thus consider:

- *Pressures* exerted by different external or internal stakeholders.
- *Conflicts* including within the same stakeholder, across different stakeholders and between the organization and its stakeholders.
- *Reconciliation* of the pressures that organizations confront and the different roles that stakeholders hold in the resulting conflicts.

The 21 chapters chosen for inclusion in this anthology have been organized into two broad sections, such that 14 chapters deal with empirical-based frameworks for understanding pressures, conflict and reconciliation, while 7 chapters in the second section address theoretical-based frameworks for understanding pressures, conflict and reconciliation.

Empirical-based Frameworks for Understanding Pressures, Conflicts and Reconciliation

The first part of the anthology has been divided into three sections: understanding stakeholder conflicts and mobilization; managing risks of stakeholder conflicts; and engaging with stakeholders and implementing a stakeholder approach to corporate social responsibility. In examining these three aspects of pressures, conflicts and reconciliation in a stakeholder approach to corporate social responsibility, the authors draw on a wealth of empirical findings from the following contexts: countries and populations, energy: oil and carbon, food and health, employee involvement and organization practices.

The first sub section—*understanding stakeholder conflicts and mobilization*—consists of five chapters. When Matthias S. Fifka chose to investigate "The impact of socioeconomic and political factors on stakeholder dialogs", he recognized the remarkable significance of stakeholder dialogs in modern, international business settings. Businesses seek feedback from stakeholders on past and current corporate social responsibility activities, input and suggestions for further projects, a platform for stakeholders to articulate their interests and a justification for their business agenda. Therefore, to determine if social, political, or economic environments in various countries affect stakeholder dialogs, he investigates the degree to which large businesses in Germany, France and the United States conduct stakeholder dialogs and identifies which stakeholder groups they include. The results of this empirical study, which features the 100 largest organizations in each country, reveal significant differences in the extent and inclusion of stakeholders in dialogs; these differences largely reflect unique socioeconomic and political factors across nations.

Whereas much research concentrates on stable forms of stakeholder management, Sally Davenport and Shirley Leitch investigate dynamic elements of stakeholder theory by asking "What makes a stakeholder act? Exploring the impact of the issue in the stakeholder relationship". Specifically, they assess how stakeholders respond to issues in their relationship with an organization over time and as the issue itself evolves. They also include the symbolic actions of identity-based stakeholders in their study, because few organizations are equipped to deal with such critical stakeholder responses. In the context of an organization that manages genetically modified organism approvals, the authors develop an issue–impact–action framework that offers suggestions for appropriate stakeholder management strategies for different stakeholder responses.

David Boje, Stephanie Maynard-Patrick and Steven M. Elias also deal with symbolic responses in "Swapping stories: how firms and stakeholders use blogs as narrative discourse to create efficacy and meaning for corporate social responsibility". Specifically, they analyze blog communications—including Walmart's and activist blogs—to explore how various stakeholders achieve different forms of efficacy through their storytelling.

In his second contribution to this anthology, Matthias S. Fifka revisits one of the most popular case studies in business literature: the intended deep sea disposal of the oil-storage buoy Brent Spar by Shell UK. Most studies address the core conflict between Shell, as the protagonist and Greenpeace, as the antagonist, but in "Brent Spar revisited: conflict and cooperation from a stakeholder perspective", Fifka notes the impact of other stakeholders too, including governments, the media, society and consumers. These various stakeholder groups exhibited various patterns of conflict and cooperation, beyond their more widely recognized interactions with Shell. By failing to recognize such patterns in its conflict management attempts, Shell doomed itself to suffering severe consequences.

In "Engaging with the enemy: understanding adversarial stakeholder processes and outcomes", Maureen Bourassa and Peggy Cunningham also address a wide range of stakeholders—public health officials, food marketers, parents, consumers—for whom obesity represents an increasingly important issue. The interactions among these groups tend to be adversarial, so the common research focus on positive stakeholder encounters offers little insight. To fill this knowledge gap, the authors use three years of participant observation data and in-depth interviews to develop a conceptual model, grounded in relationship marketing, social networks, stakeholder analysis, corporate social responsibility and ethics theory. Their model reveals in particular that disrespect and negative emotions drive defensive actions and power-building activities, which create barriers to collaborative outcomes.

The second sub section—*managing risks of stakeholder conflicts*—consists of three chapters. Romy Kraemer and Rob van Tulder borrow the notion of a "license to operate" from the oil and mining industry and reframe it as a measure for multinational enterprises. Specifically, in "A license to operate for the extractive industries? Operationalizing stakeholder thinking in international business", the authors apply a strategic, multilevel concept of license to operate to examples from the extractive industry, which offers a challenge to conventional wisdom about the global integration–local responsiveness trade-off by multinational organizations. That is, international business must go beyond a task focus when assessing the activities and location choices of multinational organizations. The authors thus recommend a shift from responsiveness to responsibility to improve the managerial sophistication of license to operate.

In "Risk management and communication: pressures and conflicts of a stakeholder approach to corporate social responsibility", the authors aim to extend the traditional paradigm of risk management, which focuses solely on direct communication between risk producers and the consumers who bear that risk. Therefore, Robert L. Heath, Michael J. Palenchar, Katherine A. McComas and Stephanie Proutheau review multiple product development and marketing stages to identify varying risk-based dialogs about the safety of products—particularly if their ingredients create scientific uncertainty. Through an infrastructural analysis of risk communication, this chapter reveals who is discussing which risk-related topics when, which should help managers communicate and manage risk perceptions more effectively, in cooperation with other stakeholders. This effort requires a commitment throughout the supply chain to safe products.

Food is a common context for risk considerations, as Georgios Georgakopoulos and Ian Thomson detail in "Risk conflicts and demands for social and environmental accounting: an empirical study" Using concepts proposed by the Risk Society, these authors clarify the relationships of social and environmental accounting processes and practices, stakeholder engagements, the emergence and perpetuation of risk conflicts, risk-governing structures and risk dynamics in the Scottish salmon farming industry. This industry has adopted accountability processes that extend beyond conventional social and environmental practices, which reflects its attempt to contest public perceptions of "legitimate" risk, define "real" risk and communicate and address risks overall. The diverse accountability practices led to further discussions about definitions of acceptable risks, as well as demands for greater social and environmental accountability by regulators before the industry could establish effective governance or accountability mechanisms.

The third sub section—*engaging with stakeholders and implementing a stakeholder approach to corporate social responsibility*—consists of six chapters. In a case study of one of the world's leading luxury fashion brands, Massimiliano Bonacchi, Paolo Perego and Rossella Ravagli describe key stages of corporate social responsibility-related initiatives in "The evolution of corporate social responsibility in Gucci: from risk management to stakeholder engagement". Gucci experienced a major shift that prompted its new awareness of incorporating corporate social responsibility into its strategic corporate agenda. For example, top management commitment, stakeholder engagement and stakeholder accountability led to the reconciliation of stakeholder interests. Accordingly, Gucci moved from a focus on reputation, adaptation to stakeholder pressures and risk management to an emerging stage that emphasizes innovation and reconciliation of stakeholder needs. The case offers insights for researchers who work to corroborate corporate social responsibility stage-development models, managers who need solutions to the conflicts among different stakeholders and the various groups that remain involved in practical stakeholder engagement.

Whereas current corporate social responsibility theory often seems to ignore how corporate social responsibility can attract, motivate and retain good employees, Peter Fleming argues that corporate social responsibility initiatives address a cultural and ideological purpose within the organization. Instead of adopting a functional perspective (i.e., does corporate social responsibility answer human resource management challenges?), "The working stakeholder: new perspectives on corporate social responsibility and the employee" offers a political view: corporate social responsibility can align employees' personal values with the pursuit of profit, even in controversial industries.

Mary Runté and Debra Z. Basil also investigate the effects of corporate social responsibility on employees in "Giving credit where credit is due: distributive justice and corporate volunteerism". Through interviews with 25 employees who participated in company-sponsored volunteering programs, these authors uncover the attribution of credit for such efforts, with distributive justice as a framework. Corporate support for employee volunteering can be well received when employees believe the organization truly contributes to the effort, in which case they are willing to share credit. However, the situation also can create tension and resentment if the organization takes credit without contributing itself.

If we accept the assertion that organizations should consider the interests of all constituents, then businesses that interact with indigenous peoples face a particular challenge to understand the long-term impact and risk of their actions on indigenous people's rights and livelihoods, according to Tom Cooper and Terry Hickey in "Indigenous peoples, stakeholders and corporate social responsibility". Integrating indigenous communities as instrumental stakeholders requires a precise understanding of risk and time horizons in indigenous cultures, as well as a recognition of the importance of full participation. The conceptual approach can help ensure organizations' effective engagement with indigenous stakeholders.

In "Resolving environmental and social conflicts: responsible innovation in small producers clusters in northern Vietnam", Jaap Voeten, Nigel Roome, Gerard de Groot and Job de Haan address another particular type of stakeholders: small Vietnamese producers. For these groups, Western-based corporate social responsibility and stakeholder practices have limited applicability, because the institutional setting relies on informally organized, small production clusters. With an inductive approach, this chapter derives a five-stage model of responsible innovation as a societal process, such that innovators acknowledge their responsibility to resolve conflicts that result from their innovations.

Despite relatively widespread agreement about the need for a climate strategy, Timo Busch and Jonatan Pinkse recognize that organizations have varying potentials for reduced carbon intensity. To help organizations choose an appropriate climate strategy, in "Reconciling stakeholder requests and carbon dependency: what is the right climate strategy?" these authors outline instrumental tools and propose four main strategies: increase internal efficiency, optimize the value chain, evade stakeholder pressures and maintain legitimacy. The strategies reflect different stakeholder requests and varying levels of carbon dependence. They also highlight essential steps to a low-carbon future.

Theoretical-based Frameworks for Understanding Pressures, Conflicts and Reconciliation

To begin the second part of the anthology, Frank den Hond and Frank G.A. de Bakker investigate "Boomerang politics: how transnational stakeholders impact multinational corporations in the context of globalization". Although globalization has allowed organizations to expand into different parts of the world, it has also opened those organizations to the complaints of non-traditional stakeholders, such that the vast multitude and complexity of global novel stakeholder relationships makes corporate responsibility increasingly "political." The authors suggest existing stakeholder theory is thus insufficient to explain the influence of nontraditional stakeholders, who lack a clear or direct stake in an organization. By proposing the terminology of "boomerang politics", this chapter acknowledges the challenges created by globalization and advances stakeholder theory to include nontraditional stakeholders.

The next chapter, "Using a dialectic approach to understand stakeholders' conflicts with corporate social responsibility activities", introduces another new concept, the corporate social responsibility dialectic. Lúcia Lima Rodrigues and Russell Craig propose this notion to depict corporate social responsibility activities as macro-dynamic phenomena emerging from large-scale human processes, according to Hegelian notions of thesis, antithesis and synthesis. For corporate social responsibility activities, synthesis depends on a process that reflects the complementary lenses of structural and institutional isomorphism, decoupling and Foucaultian power knowledge. The authors contend specifically that the synthesis of corporate social responsibility activities that becomes the institutionalized practice will reflect the belief system that gains momentum, the power and influence of structural and institutional isomorphism and the way organizational actors exercise power (e.g., imposing constraints, articulating rationales, formulating requirements).

Building on multidisciplinary literature about corporate social responsibility and organizational sensemaking, François Maon, Valérie Swaen and Adam Lindgreen present a generic descriptive model of corporate social responsibility development. In "'Make sense who may': corporate social responsibility as a continuous multi-stakeholder co-construction process" these authors emphasize four interdependent corporate social responsibility-related processes that social actors within and outside the organization experience: a convergent managerial sense-making process, a compounded managerial sense-giving process, a divergent stakeholder network sense-making process and a differentiated stakeholder network sense-giving process. By identifying key influence on these processes and their outcomes, this chapter extends existing corporate social responsibility conceptualizations and presents corporate social responsibility as a continuous, multi-stakeholder, inherently interactive notion.

In "A new institutionalism approach to stakeholder theory", Robin T. Byerly propose that new institutionalism theory can explain institutional pressures that encourage stakeholders to transform, be responsive and accountable to society and achieve greater responsibility. This integrative social theory also can help balance the competitive concerns of business organizations with their corporate social responsibilities to key stakeholders, as well as with heightened societal expectations. With this fresh perspective on the legitimization of stakeholder theory, this chapter suggests the potential for convergent acceptance of responsible attention to stakeholders.

Sheldene Simola takes a care ethics approach in "Enhancing the care-based resolution of corporate social responsibility-related, firm–stakeholder conflict: invoking the counsel of Mary Parker Follett". This chapter acknowledges that both corporate social responsibility and the stakeholder concept remain contested notions, surrounded by confusion regarding appropriate processes and conflict across frequently evolving stakeholder claims and with corporate practices. However, care ethics might provide a unified framework for responding to diverse challenges; work by Mary Parker Follett, a classic management scholar, might further enhance practical understanding of care ethics.

Also acknowledging the complexity and heterogeneity of corporate social responsibility, Roberto Garcia-Castro suggests thinking of different approaches to corporate stakeholders as a configuration of corporate social responsibility practices in "A configurational approach to corporate social responsibility–financial performance empirical research". That is, how corporate social responsibility affects an organization's bottom line depends on the corporate social responsibility approach adopted, as well as any contingencies between corporate social responsibility and other organization attributes. To measure these impacts, organizations need a methodology to uncover different corporate social responsibility configurations. This chapter proposes qualitative comparative analysis as a solution and provides an example of how it operates in practice.

Finally, Duane Windsor offers "A corporate social responsibility framework for managers and stakeholders". Arguing that managers cannot make corporate social responsibility decisions on theoretical grounds, without considering multiple salient stakeholders with conflicting perspectives, the author suggests a more logically structured assessment. The proposed framework helps managers and stakeholders evaluate specific corporate social responsibility decisions according to four neutral corporate social responsibility principles and a five-stakeholder structure, which can be adjusted in size and composition as necessary. Specifically, managers should (1) promote social welfare, (2) obey the law out of respect, (3) practice business ethics and corporate citizenship to advance the public interest and (4) have sufficient discretion to make corporate social responsibility decisions. These four neutral corporate social responsibility decision principles avoid adopting any particular corporate social responsibility perspective. The five salient stakeholders with influence on corporate social responsibility decisions are customers, employees, investors, at least one other impactee and at least one other influencer. This "advisory committee" should use six decision rules to evaluate any specific corporate social responsibility decision: market outcomes, prioritization of interests, aggregation (or voting), concession, balancing of interests, or some value principle. The chapter concludes with an application of the framework to three corporate social responsibility decisions.

Closing Remarks

We extend a special thanks to Gower Publications and its staff, which has been most helpful throughout the entire process. Equally, we warmly thank all of the authors who submitted their manuscripts for consideration for this book. They have exhibited the worthy desire to share their knowledge and experience with the book's readers—and a willingness to put forward their views for possible challenge by their peers. Finally, we thank Elisabeth Nevins Caswell for her editorial assistance.

There are organizations that have made corporate social responsibility the very heart of their existence and been remarkably successful. However, one clear message from all the chapters of this book is that not all organizations can or should proceed down the same corporate social responsibility path. For some organizations, it simply may be impossible to reconcile the pressures and conflicts they confront. Furthermore, there is still a lot we do not know about corporate social responsibility. We are hopeful that the chapters in this book fill many of the knowledge gaps readers suffer—but also that they stimulate further thought and action pertaining to corporate social responsibility issues.

Professor, Dr. Adam Lindgreen
Cardiff

Professor, Dr. Philip Kotler
Evanston

Professor, Dr. Joëlle Vanhamme
Roubaix

Assistant Professor, Dr. François Maon
Lille
February 1, 2012

Notes

1   Bielak, D.B., Bonini, S. and Oppenheim, J.M. (2007), "CEOs on strategy and social issues", *McKinsey Quarterly*, http://www.mckinseyquarterly.com, accessed April 2009.

2   Kotler, P. and Lee, N.R. (2005), *Corporate Social Responsibility: Doing the Most Good for Your Company and Your Cause*, *Wiley*, Hoboken, NJ.

3   Carroll, A.B. (1991), "The pyramid of corporate social responsibility: Toward the moral management of organizational stakeholders", *Business Horizons*, vol. 34, pp. 39–48.

4   World Business Council for Sustainable Development (2001), "Corporate social responsibility: Narrowing the focus", *WBCSD News*, 12 July, http://www.wbcsd.org, accessed April 2009.

5   Business for Social Responsibility (2003), *Overview of Corporate Social Responsibility*. http://www.bsr.org, accessed April 2009.

6   Zyglidopoulos, S. (2002), "The social and environmental responsibilities of multinationals: evidence from the Brent Spar case", *Journal of Business Ethics*, vol. 36, pp. 141–151.

7   Dawkins, D. and Lewis, S. (2003), "CSR in stakeholder expectations and their implication for company strategy", *Journal of Business Ethics*, vol. 44, pp. 185–193.

8   Jawahar, I. and McLaughlin, G. (2001), "Toward a descriptive stakeholder theory: An organizational life cycle approach", *Academy of Management Review*, vol. 26, pp. 397–414.

9   Fassin, Y. (2008), "Imperfections and shortcomings of the stakeholder model's graphical representation", *Journal of Business Ethics*, vol. 80, pp. 879–888; Post, J., Preston, L. and Sachs, S. (2002), *Redefining the Corporation: Stakeholder Management and Organizational Wealth*. Stanford Business Books, Stanford, CA.

10 Greening, D.W. and Turban, D.B. (2000), "Corporate social performance as a competitive advantage in attracting a quality workforce", *Business and Society*, vol. 39, pp. 254–280.

11 Maon, F., Lindgreen, A. and Swaen, V. (2008), "Thinking of the organization as a system: the role of managerial perceptions in developing a corporate social responsibility strategic agenda", *Systems Research and Behavioral Science*, vol. 25, pp. 413–426.

Empirical-based Frameworks for Understanding Pressures, Conflict and Reconciliation

Understanding Stakeholder Conflicts and Mobilization

1

The Impact of Socioeconomic and Political Factors on Stakeholder Dialogs

MATTHIAS S. FIFKA[*]

Keywords

Corporate social responsibility, Germany, France, stakeholder dialog, stakeholder participation, United States.

Introduction

Corporate social responsibility can only be successful if it is understood and practiced as an exchange and cooperation between a company and its stakeholders. One form of discourse that allows for the respective exchange is the so-called stakeholder dialog, which has received increasing attention during the last decade. From a management perspective, the possibility to improve long-term decision-making, continuous learning and innovation,[1] the preservation of the license to operate, and the utilization of external knowledge have been pointed out.[2] From the perspective of stakeholders, chances to move their ideas forward, to be involved in decision-making and monitoring processes and to raise credibility through cooperation instead of hostility have been put forward.[3] Finally, from a broader social perspective, the creation of social capital has been given as a reason for dialog.[4] Despite this substantial theoretical discussion and advocacy of stakeholder dialog, there has been only very limited empirical research on the actual dialog practices of businesses. It is the aim of this chapter to make a contribution towards filling this gap.

A stakeholder dialog can basically be understood as a "two-way dialogue on issues of corporate environmental and social responsibility, [which] is especially important in establishing stakeholder respect".[5] A broader definition that also considers the implications for businesses is offered by the World Business Council:

[*] Matthias S. Fifka, Dr. Jürgen Meyer Endowed Chair for International Business Ethics and Sustainability, Cologne Business School, Hardefuststrasse 1, 50677 Cologne, Germany. E-mail: m.fifka@cbs-edu.de. The author would like to thank Ms. Barbara Haefner, Mr. Martin Eirich, Ms. Stella Kraus and Ms. Svenja Heidemann for their suggestions and comments.

Stakeholder dialogue offers a tool to engage people in serious discussion, and a designed and facilitated process for groups to initiate dialogue with those persons and institutions that have a stake in their activities ... Dialogue is about communicating with stakeholders in a way that takes serious account of their views. It does not mean involving stakeholders in every decision, or that every stakeholder request will be met. It means that stakeholder input should be acknowledged and thoughtfully considered. It is about giving stakeholders a voice, listening to what they have to say, and being prepared to act or react accordingly.[6]

As pointed out, suggestions made by stakeholders usually do not have a binding character for the firm. Thus, stakeholder dialogs are considered to take place at the "consultative" level of stakeholder participation, exceeding the "informative" stage, but not reaching a "decisional" level as the highest stage of integration.[7] Moreover, stakeholder dialogs can be held in various forms such as traditional face-to-face conversations in a small group, but also as conferences, round tables, panel discussions, factory visits, open house days, etc. Regardless of the form, it is essential that the dialog is held on a regular basis and becomes institutionalized. This way, stakeholders frequently have the opportunity to voice their interests. Companies in turn are enabled to consider these interests on a continuous basis when planning their core business and corporate social responsibility activities, but they are given the opportunity to present and explain future undertakings to stakeholders as well.

Therefore, stakeholder dialogs can be regarded as a practical application of discourse ethics, as they intend to generate norms and consecutive actions which are acceptable to the actors involved. Steinmann and Löhr, as two of the major proponents of this approach, propose that the amicable resolution or prevention of conflicts should be the central aim of discourse ethics.[8] Based on these preliminary considerations, a stakeholder dialog will be defined here as the voluntary dialog between a firm and one or more constituent groups for the mutual understanding and benefit of all participants.

Before such a dialog can take place, it is necessary for the companies to identify the stakeholders to be included. This identification of the relevant stakeholders is not only a core necessity, it also provides a significant challenge for companies due to two reasons. First, there is a large, if not to say infinite, number of external stakeholders, and it is simply not feasible, especially under cost considerations, to identify them all. Second, a company has to evaluate which of the numerous groups are relevant. Therefore, the impact of the business activities on the various stakeholder groups as well as the stakeholders' potential influence on the business have to be assessed in order to identify the advantages or disadvantages which might arise from considering or not considering the respective interests.[9]

Unsurprisingly, a large body of literature on stakeholder identification has been developed,[10] also in the specific context of corporate social responsibility and corporate citizenship,[11] with the aim of making recommendations on how to select the crucial stakeholders. Mitchell *et al.* have suggested placing "an emphasis on the *legitimacy* of a claim on a firm, based upon, for example, contract, exchange, legal title, legal right, moral right, at-risk status, or moral interest in the harms and benefits generated by company actions"[12] in order to narrow the selection process. Additionally, they recommend considering the *power* a stakeholder group has to affect the company's behavior as well as the *urgency* of its claim. Falk and Helbich also point out that the potential influence wielded by stakeholders should be seen as the decisive selection criterion, but they refer explicitly to the influence on the cash flow of a company that groups can exert. They differentiate between groups that have a large influence (major suppliers and customers as well as managers), those groups which do not have a direct business relation but can still have a significant impact (e.g. the media), and groups of lesser importance that only have very sporadic contact with the company.[13]

While the identification of crucial stakeholders has been discussed intensively in the literature, either theoretically or prescriptively, little attention—as will be discussed in the literature review below—has been given to the empirical question of whether the dialog with specific stakeholder groups varies from country to country due to different political, social and economic structures. This is the central research question of this chapter. As countries for comparison, Germany, France and the United States were selected because they represent different economic and sociopolitical systems. The U.S. is often considered to be the prime example for a liberal market economy, with only minimal governmental intervention and a high degree of reliance on supply and demand as the central market mechanism. While Germany can also be considered a free market economy, governmental intervention is more extensive here, especially in order to guarantee a comprehensive social safety system through redistribution, commonly referred to as Social Market Economy. The degree of governmental coordination as a market mechanism is even higher in France due to the country's economic and sociopolitical history. Today, France is only ranked 64th in the "Heritage Index of Economic Freedom", finding itself among countries like Saudi Arabia, Thailand, and Turkey, while Germany and the U.S. are ranked 23rd and 8th, respectively.[14] Thus, the question arises of whether and how these "varieties of capitalism", as Hall and Soskice have called them, affect the inclusion of different stakeholder groups through dialog.[15]

This question will be discussed in the next chapter by first looking at the different business environments in the three countries and the results of existing studies. Based upon these observations and prior findings, it is hypothesized to what extent stakeholder dialogs with different groups will be held. These assumptions are then tested in an empirical study of the 100 largest companies in each of the three countries. With regard to the inclusion of the results of earlier studies to develop hypotheses, two important limitations must be pointed out, which make it difficult to compare their results to those of this study. First, earlier studies have usually analyzed the *importance* which was assigned to different stakeholder groups by businesses, but not whether *dialogs* with them were held. It is certainly possible to consider a specific stakeholder group as important, but not to voluntarily hold an institutionalized dialog with it, as, for example, in the case of shareholders who might be too numerous to be included. Second, the studies usually differ significantly with regard to the size and industry of the samples as well as the date of publication. The latter is especially crucial since it can be assumed that the attention given to stakeholders has increased considerably throughout recent years, although longitudinal studies that could prove that assumption do not exist.

Economic, Social, and Political Systems as Influence Factors for Stakeholder Dialog

As mentioned above, the economic, social and political environment for businesses differs substantially in the three countries of question. Throughout its history, the U.S.

has been a major proponent of economic liberalism with only a very limited degree of governmental interventionism, which only increased in times of social or economic crisis, such as the Great Depression, the reforms in the wake of the "Great Society" in the 1960s, and the latest financial crisis.[16] The social security system is rudimentary in comparison to Western European welfare states, thus the responsibility for individual well-being lies mostly with the private actors themselves. This has led to extensive charitable measures by American businesses, which partly compensates for the lack of social support through the government. Another important factor for the broad civic engagement of businesses is the puritan social ethos, because it propones the moral obligation of the more prosperous actors in society to help the ones in need.[17] Consequentially, social engagement has a long tradition in the U.S., but its specific design and extent are left to the companies themselves. Therefore, the nature of corporate social responsibility is mostly voluntary, aside from the economic responsibility to increase shareholder value. Other actors in society might be able to morally claim a consideration of their interests by businesses: a legal claim to social services provided by businesses, however, does not exist in most cases.

In this regard a profound difference to Germany and France exists, where the social responsibility of businesses is largely of a legal nature, as Maignan and Ferrell pointed out. They examined consumer perspectives of corporate social responsibility in Germany, France and the U.S., and found that European consumers placed a strong emphasis on legal compliance and social benefits, whereas economic responsibilities ranked high in the U.S.[18] Again, there are several reasons for this "European character" of corporate social responsibility. First, traditionally strong labor unions have fought for decades not only for specific workers' rights but also for social benefits provided by companies in general. Other than in the U.S., unions took the role of representatives of the working class in the French and German social systems, which were characterized by a deep-rooted class consciousness. Secondly and closely related, governmental interventionism has a strong tradition in both countries. Already in the late-nineteenth and early-twentieth century, governmental welfare programs, although initially very limited, were established and primarily directed at the working class in an effort to reduce social tensions. These systems have continuously been expanded over the decades until the 1990s. Today, this is reflected by the fact that government spending on welfare amounts to 52.5 percent in France and 43.4 percent in Germany, whereas in the U.S. it makes up only 38.6 percent of GDP.[19] In France, moreover, the belief in the government's ability to steer the social and economic development of the country (*dirigisme*) is even stronger than in Germany, resulting from the country's mercantilist tradition and elitist structures (*élitisme*) with a small but closely intertwined circle of political and economic decision-makers.

Considering these backgrounds, it is no surprise that France has the most extensive laws to compel "companies to inform their stakeholders on their social and environmental impact."[20] The "New Economic Regulations Law" of 2001, which is largely unique in its extent in Europe, requires all publicly listed companies to provide information on 32 elements of internal social data (e.g., workforce, safety, parity, etc.), 28 aspects of environmental performance (e.g., greenhouse gas emissions, use of natural resources, waste, etc.), and eight items related to the economic impact.[21] In Germany, the "Law on Accounting Reform" of 2004 also asks for the inclusion of "non-financial factors of performance" into annual reports, but does not specify those factors in any form and further reduces them to only those "which are relevant for the economic performance."[22]

As a result, that provision must be regarded as mostly ineffective. Finally, in the U.S., legal initiatives to promote corporate social responsibility reporting do not exist.

The regulatory framework in France—together with the general social, economic and political environment—can be assumed to generally promote stakeholder dialogs in comparison to Germany and especially the U.S. Thus we expect to see more stakeholder dialogs in general among the largest 100 French firms in comparison to their German and American counterparts. With regard to the 10 specific stakeholder groups examined (labor unions, political and administrative actors, environmental groups, human rights groups, customers, suppliers, employees, shareholders, the community, large charitable organizations) the following assumptions can be made.

Concerning labor unions, one can expect that their inclusion into stakeholder dialogs will be the lowest in the U.S. due to their traditionally weaker role, limited influence and dispersed organization, which is also reflected by current membership rates. According to the U.S. Bureau of Labor Statistics, union membership stood at 11.9 percent in 2010.[23] In France, union membership was even weaker at 8.1 percent. However, French unions are very well organized and exert considerable influence, especially through their high capability to organize strikes.[24] In Germany, finally, union membership amounted to 20.2 percent. Thus it can be assumed that stakeholder dialogs with unions will be most extensive there; also, unions play a strong role due to Germany's "tripartite" corporatist system, which calls for negotiations between government, employer associations and unions in all matters of significant political or social impact. This assumption is supported by a study by Holtbrügge and Berg who analyzed the importance of thirteen sociopolitical stakeholder groups—governmental as well as nongovernmental—for German multinational corporations (MNCs) in six countries, among them Germany, France and the U.S. They found that the companies examined assigned more relevance to unions in Germany than they did in France and especially the U.S.[25]

Due to the tripartite system, it can further be expected that large German companies practice intensive dialogs with political and administrative actors because of the country's strong fixation on the government to address social issues. For France, widespread consideration of governmental actors can also be assumed due to the strong influence of the government, although that influence has declined in recent years. In the U.S., the situation is different. While governmental interventionism is considerably lower, business traditionally interacts with government to a high degree in order to jointly address social and economic problems or to make voluntary concessions in order to avoid legal regulation. Thus stakeholder dialogs with governmental actors in the U.S. can be expected to be on approximately the same level as in both European countries. This assumption is also supported by Holtbrügge's and Berg's investigation, which demonstrated that German companies pay similar attention to the central government in France, Germany and the U.S., while state and local governments are of lesser importance in France.[26]

With regard to dialogs with environmental groups, significant differences between the countries can be assumed. Environmentalism has enjoyed increasing political and public importance in Germany since the mid-1980s. This has resulted in extensive regulation on environmental protection and a widespread environmental consciousness. In France, environmentalism is traditionally weak, but in recent years the French public has become increasingly aware of the problems and the Sarkozy administration has slowly stepped up regulatory efforts.[27] The passage of the "New Economic Regulations Law" of 2001 mentioned above also demonstrates the efforts made in the last decade. In the U.S., there is also increasing concern for the environment and Obama had made its protection at least a minor issue of his election campaign, but neither on the public level nor in the political arena has it reached a level equivalent to that of Western Europe. That is reflected in an empirical study by Maignan and Ralston in 2002. They investigated the home pages of 400 companies in four countries, among them France and the U.S., with regard to stakeholder issues mentioned. They found that environmental issues ranked considerably higher on the agenda of French than of American businesses.[28] Silberhorn and Warren found—in an empirical study on Great Britain and Germany—that protection of the environment was an important stakeholder issue for German companies.[29] Therefore, it can be assumed that environmental groups as dialog partners will be considered most often by German firms, followed by French and American ones.

Human rights groups in turn are likely to be considered most often by American companies due to the country's own history—especially with regard to African-Americans and Native Americans—and its traditional role as a major proponent of human rights globally. In Germany, the subject of human rights, due to the National Socialist past, also enjoys some public visibility, whereas in France it features less prominently. The Centre for Corporate Citizenship Germany (CCCG) demonstrated in an empirical study that "helping to safeguard civil or human rights" was an important issue for 21 percent of the large American companies surveyed, but only 3 percent of the respective German companies.[30] Rieth and Göbel support the finding that human rights do not rank high on the agenda of German companies.[31] Silberhorn and Warren discovered an average importance of human rights for German companies in their study.[32] Welford, in an empirical study on Asia, Europe and North America noted that "in Europe internal aspects of corporate social responsibility are well covered by policies with the exception of human rights."[33] He found that 57.1 percent of the German companies examined had a statement on the protection of human rights within their operations, while only 43.8 of the French companies did so. Moreover, Maignan and Ralston have shown that equal opportunities for employees, touching the issue of human rights, are addressed far more frequently by American than by French firms.[34]

Charitable organizations, as another stakeholder belonging to civil society, receive substantially more donations from the private sector in the U.S. than in Europe and enjoy significant importance there due to the absence of extensive social security provided by the state. However, it cannot be expected that American companies will perceive them as an important stakeholder for two reasons. First, charitable undertakings are seen to fall entirely within the company's own discretion. Second, charitable groups have hardly any possibility of retaliation if their interests are not considered. In Germany, the situation of charitable organizations like the Red Cross or Caritas is unique because they experienced an early professionalization already after WW I and have evolved into the major providers of social services of all kinds (hospitals, kindergartens etc.).[35] With 90 percent of their funding coming from the government, they can be considered "semi-governmental institutions". This results in a very low dependence on private donations, so it cannot be presumed that German corporations will consider them part of stakeholder dialogs to a high degree. In France, charitable organizations also receive government support, but it is less extensive than in Germany and they are more dependent on contributions from the private sector. In addition, it is crucial that corporations in France and Germany—unlike the U.S.—are seen to perform a social and not only an economic function.[36] Therefore, it can be assumed that in France charitable organizations will take part in dialogs more often than in Germany and the U.S., because they are more dependent on French corporations with regard to funding and act as a "social intermediary" for the corporations to some degree.

With regard to customers predictions of their inclusion into stakeholder dialogs are hard to make, because they are of vital importance to any business, irrespective of the country. However, Germany traditionally does not have a strong customer-oriented service culture as Witkowski and Wolfinbarger have remarked in comparison to the U.S.: "Instead of receiving the friendliness and courtesy ... new customers in numerous German stores, banks, or service desks encounter glares or, more commonly, a bored look of compulsory compliance."[37] American companies in turn place a significant emphasis on customer relations. Accordingly, German companies assume that corporate social responsibility is of no significant importance to their customers. Only 36.8 percent of the large German companies surveyed by the CCCG thought that corporate social responsibility mattered to consumers, whereas 53 percent of the respective American companies did so.[38] American companies in turn still fall behind French companies with regard to customer focus, as Maignan and Ralston have shown.[39] Thus it can be expected that French companies will place the most emphasis on customers as dialog partners, followed by American and German companies.

Regarding suppliers, the two studies just mentioned have demonstrated that neither German nor French or American companies extensively report about supplier relations.[40] Little difference in reporting on supplier issues was also found by Chen and Bouvain in their study of leading companies from the U.S., Germany, the U.K. and Australia. They conceded that these results were unexpected "since managing global supply chains responsibly has been a recurring theme in corporate social responsibility in recent years", and thus "further analysis"[41] was required. Although no prior empirical evidence exists for that assumption, it can be expected that dialogs with suppliers play a more important role than reporting on supplier relations. Moreover, it is assumed that French companies will practice stakeholder dialogs with suppliers most extensively due to the country's strong belief in economic coordination.

Predictions on the inclusion of employees are equally difficult. Employees in Germany and France enjoy more rights in relation to the employer and enjoy much better protection against dismissal than in the U.S. In Germany, through the system of "Mitbestimmung" (co-determination), worker representatives are members of the supervisory board of all listed companies with more than 2,000 employees, which gives them considerable influence. However, this guaranteed representation is perceived as a nuisance by many corporations, and thus might actually lead to a lower inclusion of employees in additional stakeholder dialogs of voluntary nature. In France "patronism" within the companies is strong and decisions are usually made top-down, but prior consultation with workers on lower levels is nothing unusual, which might also indicate widespread dialogs with employees. In the U.S., where top-down decision-making is strong, and workers neither enjoy guaranteed representation or are consulted when important decisions are made, stakeholder dialogs with employees are expected to be the lowest.

German and French companies are also likely to hold dialogs with shareholders more extensively than do American companies. At first, this might seem contradictory to the Friedmanesque concept that the "social responsibility of business is to increase its profits"[42] as well as to the traditional shareholder orientation of American companies, which is weaker in France and Germany.[43] However, the major reason for the assumption made is based less on the prevalent economic philosophy and more on the technical feasibility of dialogs. In Germany and France, large "blockholders"—banks, insurance companies, and owner families—are typical in comparison to the U.S., where share ownership is widely dispersed among small shareholders. That makes institutionalized dialogs with those groups extremely difficult. In Germany, for example, the median size for the largest shareholder for listed companies is 57.0 percent, in France it is 20.0 percent, whereas in the U.S. it amounts to only 5.4 percent.[44] Maignan and Ralston have shown that American corporations reported more extensively on shareholder issues than French corporations,[45] but it must be remembered that reporting to a wide audience is much easier than including it in a dialog. Thus, a comparison is hard to draw.

Significant differences can also be expected with regard to the inclusion of the community. In the U.S., the wide absence of government and the vastness of the country, which made centralization impossible, have led to a strong tradition of self-reliance and initiative by communities. The notion of community is strong and the interests of the community play an important role for its respective members. In Germany, on the contrary, such an understanding of community hardly exists: community is mostly perceived as an administrative unit. Accordingly, Chen and Bouvain have discovered that "German companies [make] little mention of community compared with US".[46] The importance of the community to American companies has also been shown by Holder-Webb and colleagues in a study on 50 publicly traded U.S. firms.[47] The CCCG has also shown that German companies only attribute minor importance to the exchange with the community. According to its study, 37 percent of all German companies considered "responding to community/interest groups regarding issues they care about" to be "not at all important", while only 6.3 percent of American companies did so.[48] With regard to France, Maignan and Ralston have found a stronger community orientation for American businesses than for French ones.[49] The inclusion of community representatives into stakeholder dialogs is stronger in the U.S. than in France and Germany.

The Study

METHODOLOGY

Freeman's definition of a stakeholder as "any group or individual who can affect or is affected by the achievement of the organization's objectives"[50] is widely accepted, although it permits consideration of an extremely wide variety of actors as stakeholders. Such broadness, however, was desired for the following study, which considers a large variety of stakeholders in order to have a wide basis for the analysis of stakeholder dialogs in comparative perspective. A limited selection of stakeholder groups could lead to the unintended exclusion of groups that might be important in one of the countries researched. Due to these considerations, customers, suppliers, labor unions, charitable organizations, environmental groups, human rights groups, political and administrative actors, the community, shareholders and employees were included. This is a broader set of stakeholders in comparison to those examined in previous studies which considered stakeholders in different aspects.[51] In turn managers, also often regarded as stakeholders, were not included because they are the ones usually holding or initiating the dialog with stakeholders on the part of the company. It should be noted at this point that we explicitly examined if a dialog as such was held. The frequency and the specific form of the dialogs were not investigated. Moreover, we did not consider how the companies translated the outcomes of the dialogs into specific actions. These aspects should be addressed by further studies as empirical literature on these aspects is scarce, the work of van Huijstee and Glasbergen, who investigated stakeholder dialogs from the perspective of stakeholders, being a notable exception.[52]

With regard to the research method, content analysis[53] was used. Since the late 1970s, it has become an established research method in the field of corporate social responsibility and has been applied in numerous studies.[54] Content analysis can be defined as "the study of recorded human communications, such as books, websites, paintings and laws."[55] In this study, the communications media analyzed comprised the most recent annual reports and nonfinancial reports (often being issued under the titles "Corporate Social Responsibility Report" or "Sustainability Report") published until 2009, as well as home pages provided by the companies in the sample. In the case of stakeholder dialogs, the underlying assumption was that companies that hold such a dialog will be inclined to report it because they assume or hope for a positive reception by the potential readers.[56] Moreover, it could also be assumed that the dialogs reported actually took place, and it would be too risky for a company to publicly claim they held a dialog with a stakeholder group when the respective group could easily reveal that the statement was a falsehood.

Concerning the compilation of data, the respective print and online publications were scanned for the relevant information by the author and a research assistant. This was done separately to provide for the possibility of cross-checking and validation. First, any dialog which was referred to as "stakeholder dialog" in the media examined was considered for analysis. Second, exchanges which were not explicitly "labeled" as stakeholder dialog were also considered if they enabled stakeholders to articulate their views and opinions through an institutionalized exchange provided by the company. Here, the following forms were taken into account: committees or work groups consisting of company and stakeholder representatives, conferences, panel discussions, round tables, surveys, interviews and feedback and evaluation processes.

SAMPLE

To examine the inclusion of stakeholders in Germany, France and the United States the largest 100 companies in each country were selected. The decision to examine large firms was made for three reasons. First, they are usually more likely to be the subject of stakeholder interest in comparison to small and medium-sized enterprises. Second, they also act as proponents of corporate social responsibility and its respective developments and thus take a pioneering role. Third, they are more inclined to provide information on their corporate social responsibility, as numerous past studies have shown.[57] Company size was determined according to revenue in 2008. The respective list for each country was provided by the *Süddeutsche Zeitung*, *L'Expansion*, and *Fortune* for the German, French and American companies respectively.[58]

With regard to the list for the U.S. and the one for Germany, modifications had to be made. As the initial list published by *Fortune* only contained corporations listed on the stock market, it was merged with the list of the largest nonlisted American companies offered by *Fortune* as well. The nonlisted companies which were larger than the smallest of the listed ones were inserted into the final list. Seven replacements were undertaken without changing the sample size of 100 companies. The original lists for Germany and

France already contained listed as well as nonlisted companies, so coherency in the samples with regard to listing status was guaranteed. However, the original list of the 100 largest German companies provided by the *Süddeutsche Zeitung* did not include banks and insurance companies, which had been ranked in a separate list. These lists were also merged into one using the method described above. Finally, in order to make the revenues of the American companies comparable to those from Germany and France, the dollar values were converted to euro, using the average exchange rate of $1.47/€ for the year 2008.[59]

The initial samples for each country were reduced somewhat because not all of the companies included provided information on their corporate social responsibility. However, that number was relatively small for two reasons. First, electronic as well as print reporting was examined. Second, only large companies were considered, for which the probability of providing information is high. In the case of Germany, 11 out of the 100 largest companies did not offer any information on corporate social responsibility, in France there were 18, in the U.S. only three (Table 1.1).

The three national populations differ substantially with regard to size and listing, as Table 1.1 shows. While the average revenue of the 100 largest companies in Germany (Top100-G) and France (Top100-F) is very similar at app. €20 billion, it is more than twice as much for the Top100-U.S. Among the Top100-G and the Top100-F, there are 44 and 39 companies, respectively, with revenues of less than €10 billion. Among the Top100-U.S., however, the smallest company had revenues of €17.7 billion. With regard to listing on the stock exchange, the differences between the Top100-G and the Top100-F are rather small again, with about half of the companies being publicly traded, whereas the share of listed companies is much higher among the Top100-U.S.

With regard to industries, five overall industry groups were defined, consisting of primary industry (agriculture, exploration and extraction, including oil companies), manufacturing, commerce (retail and wholesale), banking and insurance and other services. Companies active in more than one of these industry groups were allotted according to their dominant field of business. As Table 1.1 shows, there is one substantial

Table 1.1   Average size, stock listing and industry distribution of the samples

	Germany	France	U.S.
Initial population	100	100	100
Average revenue in billion €	21.3	19.9	45.8
% of companies listed	45	55	88
Primary industries (in %)	13	8	10
Manufacturing (in %)	45	36	33
Commerce (in %)	13	15	12
Banking and insurance (in %)	20	21	28
Other services (in %)	9	20	17
Excluded due to no reporting	11	18	3
Sample	89	82	97

difference between the three national samples: the service sector is strong in France and especially in the U.S., whereas manufacturing plays a significantly larger role in Germany.

RESULTS

In a first step, we examined what proportion of companies held a stakeholder dialog and how many different stakeholder groups were included. In France (Table 1.2), the number of companies that conducted a stakeholder dialog as well as the number of stakeholder groups included were significantly higher compared to Germany and the U.S., where the numbers were quite similar.

It should be noted at this point that size as well as stock market listing have a positive influence on the likeliness of a stakeholder dialog being held and the number of groups included, whereas industry does not. This holds true for all the national samples. In a logistical regression, using STATA, the correlation between size, stock market listing and industry as independent variables and holding a stakeholder dialog and number of groups included as dependent variables was conducted. As the analysis demonstrated, the likelihood of a stakeholder dialog being held increased by 17 percent in Germany, 8 percent in France and 4 percent in the U.S. with each additional billion in revenue. With regard to listing, companies traded on the stock market were 2.6 (G), 6.5 (F), and 4.2 (U.S.) times more likely to hold a stakeholder dialog than those which are not. In contrast, industry turned out to be of no significance and so will not be displayed here. The results are significant. Cragg & Uhlers R^2 stands at 0.369, indicating a solid explanatory power of the model. The Adj. Count R^2 has a value of 0.459 and must thus be judged as excellent.

Table 1.2   Extent of stakeholder dialogs and groups included

	Germany	France	U.S.
Sample considered	89	82	97
Companies holding a dialog (absolute)	54	80	48
Companies holding a dialog (in %)	61	98	49
Companies including (in %)			
Labor unions	20	55	2
Political and administrative actors	69	25	60
Environmental groups	25	8	10
Human rights groups	11	6	17
Charitable organizations	4	36	4
Customers	65	91	71
Suppliers	48	80	54
Employees	63	89	79
Shareholders	57	79	54
The community	48	84	71
Average number of stakeholders included	4.11	5.58	4.20

Given that the Top100-F are the smallest on average and the share of listed companies among them is only somewhat higher than among the Top100-G, but substantially lower than among the Top100-U.S., it can be observed that there is a much stronger tendency to hold stakeholder dialogs in France and also to include more groups.

In a second step, the participation of the ten stakeholder groups mentioned above was investigated (Table 1.2). Seven out of ten groups are included most often by French companies. Only political and administrative actors, environmental groups, and human rights groups are integrated more frequently into stakeholder dialogs by German and American companies.

DISCUSSION

The results of the empirical study are, to a large degree, coherent with the assumptions made. Nevertheless, some of the findings are substantially different from what was expected.

As projected, the French "New Economic Regulations Law" of 2001 seems to have a positive influence on the integration of stakeholders overall as it increases the pressure on corporations to enhance their social and environmental performance and thus the respective disclosures. The number of companies holding a dialog is by far the highest among the French firms in comparison to their German and American counterparts (Table 1.2). Moreover, they also include a larger average number of stakeholders, whereas the number for the German and American companies is almost similar. This reflects the notion that large firms in France are still seen and see themselves not only as profit-oriented organizations with economic responsibilities to shareholders, but also as social actors who have to contribute substantially to the material well-being of society at large.

With regard to labor unions, the results are not fully coherent with the assumptions made. On the one hand, it clearly holds true that they are of negligible importance for American companies. On the other hand, it is striking that contrary to expectation unions are included far more often in stakeholder dialogs by French than by German businesses. A possible explanation could be the mandatory negotiations with and representation of the unions through the corporatist system in general and the *Betriebsraete* in specific (workers' councils). In the eyes of German firms, the existence of these institutions, which we do not find in France, might make an additional voluntary exchange with unions unnecessary.

In the case of political and administrative actors, an extensive integration of these stakeholders was assumed for all countries. For Germany and the U.S. this holds true, as Table 1.2 shows, but French companies fall behind significantly despite the strong governmental interventionism with which they are confronted. There are three possible explanations for this phenomenon. First, the extensive transmission of governmental interests through legal and regulatory measures might make further voluntary dialogs unnecessary or even unwanted. Second, the fact that the French government is the sole owner for example of SNCF, or the majority owner, for example of Électricité de France, might also make voluntary dialogs with governmental institutions unnecessary since they can directly implement their interest. Third, the small number of dialogs could also be interpreted as an attempt by French companies to shake off governmental influence and to reduce *dirigisme*, which already is on the decline.

Stakeholders belonging to the civil society sector—environmental and human rights organizations and charitable organizations—play the least significant role as a partner in stakeholder dialogs and are considered less frequently than "traditional" stakeholder groups. With regard to all three groups, the results are in line with expectations. In Germany, environmental groups are given the possibility of participating in stakeholder dialogs more often than in France and the U.S., where environmental protection traditionally is of lesser importance. The consideration of human rights groups in turn is strongest in the U.S., where the discussion about human rights has always featured prominently, followed by Germany, which has also been confronted with major abuses of human rights in its past, and France. Finally, charitable organizations, also as expected, are invited to participate in dialogs more frequently by French companies, who consider them an important partner in fulfilling their social obligations.

The integration of customers is lowest in Germany, which is in line with the assumptions made, as service culture is traditionally weak there. It was also predicted that customer orientation would be somewhat stronger in France than in the U.S., in accordance with the study by Maignan and Ralston. The eventual difference between the two countries (Table 1.2), however, was bigger than expected, and it is hard to explain why the American firms hold significantly less dialogs with customers in comparison to French firms.

Regarding suppliers, first, the assumption that they play a more important role as stakeholders than previous studies have shown holds true. In all three countries they are among the top dialog partners, reflecting the increasing importance of the supply chain in economic, social and environmental matters, as Roberts has pointed out.[60] Moreover, the country's strong belief in long-term economic coordination could also be a reason why French companies hold more dialogs with their suppliers in order to facilitate procedures.

The findings on shareholders as dialog partners are also mostly in line with the assumptions made. The expected outcome that French and German firms would include this stakeholder group more often than American ones, because shareholder ownership is too widespread in the U.S. to organize an institutionalized dialog, has proven true. Considering that the number of companies listed on the stock exchange is by far the highest in the U.S., the results are even more striking and indicate that stakeholder dialogs may also depend on the technical possibility of organizing constituent groups.

Last, but not least, the results for the community as a dialog partner largely turn out as expected. Dialogs with the community as a stakeholder are much less common in Germany than in France and the U.S. This can be attributed to the fact that the community in Germany is seen primarily as an administrative unit. As a "communitarian body" serving to address local problems, it is of lesser importance. The assumption, however, that American firms would hold the most dialogs with community stakeholders has not proven true, as the community in France seems to play a bigger role than expected. Antal and Sobczak have noted a strong effort by French companies towards "legitimizing corporate activities for the community",[61] following the passage of the Law on Social Modernization of 2002, which intends to shift the focus away from the central government. This might explain the increasing tendency to include community stakeholders in dialogs, although the great extent remains astounding.

Conclusions and Implications for Business

We can conclude that the dialog with different stakeholder groups is dependent on the socioeconomic and political systems of nations and that notions of corporate social responsibility vary from country to country. In Germany, we find an understanding of corporate social responsibility that is mostly based on institutionalized dialog processes required by law as well as complying with the extensive social[62] and environmental obligations. Additional voluntary activities are often seen as an extra cost burden and thus as a disadvantage in international competition. This notion of a primary social function of the enterprise is also to be found in France, where "economic achievements [are viewed] as only secondary,"[63] as Maignan and Ferrell have noted. There is a strong belief that economic outcomes should be aligned with the general interest of society through governmental regulation. As a consequence, "[i]t is thus not surprising that the discourse and practice of corporate social responsibility in France has generated a body of legislation regulating business behavior corresponding with the culturally shared understanding of *roles* and *responsibilities*."[64]

They conclude that in France, as in Germany, businesses are expected to contribute substantially to the social welfare of the country, whereas economic performance is of lesser importance. Additionally, in France there is only little differentiation between the economic and social responsibilities of companies,[65] emphasizing the broad social function that business is perceived to have. In the U.S., due to social and economic liberalism, the voluntary component of social involvement by businesses is much stronger. Thus economic success is seen as the "enabler" of civic engagement, stemming from the puritan and Calvinist tradition.

These core understandings of corporate social responsibility are in line with the findings of the empirical study on stakeholder dialogs in the countries analyzed, so the following conclusions can be reached. In Germany, stakeholder dialogs are not held extensively because the consideration of many stakeholder interests already takes place through mandatory procedures. Therefore additional voluntary dialogs, which have been examined here, are often seen as unnecessary. In the U.S., stakeholder dialogs are held on a comparable level to Germany, but for different reasons. There is little or no legal or social pressure to include stakeholders, as the respective decision is made at the company's discretion. As a consequence, groups which are not considered to wield a significant amount of influence, such as environmental groups or the traditionally weak American unions, are hardly included. In France, finally, there is a lower level of legally mandatory consideration of stakeholder interests than in Germany, but very strong social and political pressure to do so due to public and political expectations. This leads to a strong integration, especially of those groups that are perceived to be directly dependent on a company: customers, suppliers, employees and the community. It is noteworthy that exactly these groups are considered more often as dialog partners by French firms than any other group in any of the three countries (Table 1.2).

For businesses operating abroad this means that a local adaption with regard to stakeholder inclusion is necessary. Groups that might not be influential in the home country or not even seek participation in a discourse might enjoy considerable power in another country and feel that they have a right to be included, and vice versa. Thus it is necessary for businesses to determine carefully what stakeholder groups they are confronted with abroad and which of those should be included in a dialog. Undoubtedly, this identification and inclusion of relevant stakeholders is even more difficult in less familiar environments, remembering that it is already far from easy on a domestic level. In order to facilitate that process, local companies in the respective host country can serve as examples as they are usually familiar with the relevant stakeholders and how to integrate them. Obtaining the relevant information should not be too difficult: large companies publish extensive information on their stakeholder dialogs, at least in industrialized countries. In developing and emerging countries, the situation is more complicated as stakeholder interests are often articulated and considered in a less formal way there. Moreover, it should not be forgotten that foreign companies are often perceived differently than domestic ones. Skepticism towards them is usually higher, so there is an even greater need to confer with stakeholders to reduce mistrust and confrontation.

The differing consideration of stakeholder groups by businesses in the three countries also indicates that a standardized universal approach to stakeholder management in different countries is bound to fail. It will not be possible to transfer the home country approach to host countries or to create a universally applicable procedure. The optimal solution, following Bartlett and Goshal,[66] lies in a transnational approach to stakeholder management which consists of a common code or guideline to foster stakeholder dialogs in all international subsidies of a firm and the headquarters alike, but leaves enough room to consider the specific characteristics of stakeholder groups in each country or region.

Finally, stakeholder dialogs are dynamic in nature: the relevant groups and their interests may vary over time on the one hand, just like the business goals on the other hand. These dynamics are easily altered by interactions between the stakeholders as they themselves are prone to cooperate in order to pursue their interests through alliances more forcefully.

Thus it is necessary for businesses to turn away from the traditional notion of stakeholder management as an isolated "bilateral" relationship and turn to a "multilateral" approach which considers stakeholders as a dynamic network. This approach might be especially helpful in foreign countries where a good relationship with one stakeholder group can be used to enhance relations with other, less familiar groups.

Overall, stakeholder dialogs should be seen as a constant learning process that lead to a better understanding and cooperation between the dialog partners and thus improve the situation of all of the actors involved.

Notes

1   Ayuso, S., Rodríguez, M.A. and Ricart, J.E. (2006), "Using stakeholder dialogue as a source for new ideas: a dynamic capability underlying sustainable innovation", *Corporate Governance*, vol. 6, no. 4, pp. 475–490.

2   Van Buren, H. (2001), "If fairness is the problem, is consent the solution? Integrating ISCT and stakeholder theory", *Business Ethics Quarterly*, vol. 11, no. 3, pp. 481–499.

3   Palazzo, B. (2010), "An introduction to stakeholder dialogue". In M. Pohl and N. Tolhurst (eds), *Responsible Business: How to Manage a CSR Strategy Successfully*, Wiley, Hoboken, NJ, pp. 17–42.

4   Habisch, A. and Moon, J. (2006), "Social capital and corporate social responsibility". In J. Jonker and M. de Witte (eds), *The Challenge of Organising and Implementing CSR*, London, Palgrave, pp. 63–77.

5   Wheeler, D. and Elkington, J. (2001), "The end of the corporate environmental report? Or the advent of cybernetic sustainability reporting and communication?", *Business Strategy and the Environment*, vol. 10, no. 1, pp. 1–14, see p. 2.

6   World Business Council for Sustainable Development, "The WBCSD's approach to engagement", http://www.wbcsd.org/DocRoot/xxBp16bdV46Ui2JpR1CC/stakeholder.pdf (accessed November 22, 2010).

7   Green, A.O. and Hunton-Clarke, L. (2003), "A typology of stakeholder participation for company environmental decision-making", *Business Strategy and the Environment*, vol. 12, no. 5, pp. 292–299.

8   Steinmann, H. and Löhr, A. (1994), *Grundlagen der Unternehmensethik* (Foundations of business ethics), Schäffer-Poeschel, Stuttgart.

9   Kaptein, M. and van Tulder, R. (2003), "Toward effective stakeholder dialogue", *Business and Society Review*, vol. 108, no. 2, pp. 203–224.

10 Freeman, R.E. (1984), *Strategic Management: A Stakeholder Approach*, Pitman, Boston; Jawahar, I.M. and McLaughlin, G.L. (2001), "Toward a descriptive stakeholder theory: an organizational life cycle approach", *Academy of Management Review*, vol. 26, no. 3, pp. 397–414; Carroll, A.B. and Buchholtz, A.K. (2003), *Business and Society: Ethics and Stakeholder Management*, South Western Publishing, Manson; Achterkamp, M.C. and Vos, J.F.J. (2007), "Critically identifying stakeholders", *Systems Research and Behavioral Science*, vol. 24, no. 1, pp. 3–14; Kaler, J. (2004), "Arriving at an acceptable formulation of stakeholder theory", *Business Ethics: A European Review*, vol. 13, no. 1, pp. 73–79; Kaler, J. (2002), "Morality and strategy in stakeholder identification", *Journal of Business Ethics*, vol. 39, no. 1/2, pp. 91–99.

11 Vos, J.F.J. (2003), "Corporate social responsibility and the identification of stakeholders", *Corporate Social Responsibility and Environmental Management*, vol. 10, no. 3, pp. 141–152; Davenport, K. (2000), "Corporate citizenship: a stakeholder approach for defining corporate social performance and identifying measures for assessing it", *Business and Society*, vol. 3, no. 2, pp. 210–219; Mitchell, R.K., Agle, B.R. and Wood, D.J. (1997), "Toward a theory of stakeholder identification and salience: defining the principle of who and what really counts", *Academy of Management Review*, vol. 22, no. 4, pp. 853–886; Branco, M.C. and Rodrigues, L.L. (2007), "Positioning stakeholder theory within the debate on corporate social responsibility", *Electronic Journal of Business Ethics and Organization Studies*, vol. 12, no. 1, pp. 5–15; Schwalbach, J. and Schwerk, A. (2008), "Corporate governance und corporate citizenship". In A. Habisch, R. Schmidpeter and M. Neureiter (eds), *Handbuch Corporate Citizenship* (Handbook of corporate citizenship), Springer, Berlin, pp. 71–85;

12 Mitchell, Agle and Wood, op. cit., pp. 854–876; see also: Agle, B.R., Mitchell, R.K. and Sonnenfeld, J.A. (1997), "Who matters to CEOs? An investigation of stakeholder attributes and salience, corporate performance, and CEO values", *Academy of Management Journal*, vol. 42, no. 5, pp. 507–525.

13 Falck, O. and Helbich, S. (2007), "Corporate social responsibility: doing well by doing good", *Business Horizons*, vol. 50, no. 3, pp. 247–254.

14 Heritage Foundation and *The Wall Street Journal* (2010), "2010 Index of Economic Freedom", http://www.heritage.org/Index/ranking (accessed December 5, 2010).

15 Hall, P.A. and Soskice, D. (2001), *Varieties of Capitalism: The Institutional Foundations of Comparative Advantage*, Oxford University Press, Oxford.

16 Hughes, J. and Cain, L. (2010), *American Economic History*, Prentice Hall, Upper Saddle River; Seavoy, R. (2006), *An Economic History of the United States: From 1607 to the Present*, Routledge, Abingdon.

17   For the cultural and religious background of CSR in the U.S. and Germany see also Palazzo, B. (2002), "U.S.–American and German business ethics: an intercultural comparison", *Journal of Business Ethics*, vol. 41, no. 3, pp. 195–216.

18   Maignan, I. and Ferrell, O.C. (2003), "Nature of corporate responsibilities. Perspectives from American, French and German consumers", *Journal of Business Research*, vol. 56, no. 1, pp. 55–67.

19   OECD (2008), *Economic Outlook 84*, OECD, Paris.

20   Delbard, O. (2008), "CSR legislation in France and the European regulatory paradox: an analysis of EU CSR policy and sustainability reporting practice", *Corporate Governance: An International Journal*, vol. 8, no. 4, pp. 397–405, see p. 400.

21   Delbard (2008), op. cit., p. 400.

22   Gesetz zur Einführung internationaler Rechnungslegungsstandards und zur Sicherung der Qualität der Abschlussprüfung (Law on the Introduction of International Accounting Standards and on Safeguarding the Quality of Financial Statements), December 4, 2004, referring to §289 (2)(2)(c).

23   U.S. Bureau of Labor Statistics (2010), "Union members summary", http://www.bls.gov /news.release/union2.nr0.htm (accessed March 3, 2011).

24   DARES (2008), "Le paradoxe du syndicalisme français: un faible nombre d'adhérents, mais des syndicats bien implantés" (The paradox of French syndicalism: a small number of supporters, but well implemented syndicates), http://www.laligue.org/assets/Uploads/NouveauxMilitants/ DARES.pdf (accessed March 3, 2011).

25   Holtbrügge, D. and Berg, N. (2004), "How multinational corporations deal with their socio-political stakeholders: an empirical study in Asia, Europe, and the US", *Asian Business and Management*, vol. 3, no. 3, pp. 299–313; see also: Holtbrügge, D., Berg, N. and Puck, J. (2007), "To bribe or to convince? Political stakeholders and political activities in German multinational corporations", *International Business Review*, vol. 16, no. 1, pp. 47–67.

26   Holtbrügge and Berg (2004), op. cit., pp. 299–313.

27   Bremner, C. (2007), "The next French revolution: Nicolas Sarkozy sets out his plans for a green future target", *The Times*, October 27, http://www.timesonline.co.uk/tol/news/world/europe/ article2726846.ece (accessed March 29, 2011).

28   Maignan, I. and Ralston, D.A. (2002), "Corporate social responsibility in Europe and the U.S.: insights from businesses' self-presentations", *Journal of International Business Studies*, vol. 33, no. 3, pp. 497–514.

29   Silberhorn, D. and Warren, R.C. (2007), "Defining corporate social responsibility—a view from big companies in Germany and the UK", *European Business Review*, vol. 19, no. 5, pp. 352–372.

30   Center for Corporate Citizenship Germany (CCCG) (2007), *Corporate Citizenship in Germany and a Transatlantic Comparison with the USA*, Center for Corporate Citizenship Germany, Berlin, p. 35.

31   Rieth, L. and Goebel, T. (2005), "Unternehmen, gesellschaftliche Verantwortung und die Rolle von Nichtregierungsorganisationen" (Companies, social responsibility, and the role of non-governmental organizations), *Zeitschrift für Wirtschafts- und Unternehmensethik*, vol. 6, no. 2, pp. 244–261.

32   Silberhorn and Warren (2007), op. cit., p. 359.

33   Welford, R. (2005), "Corporate social responsibility in Europe, North America and Asia", *Journal of Corporate Citizenship*, vol. 17, spring, pp. 33–52, see p. 42.

34   Maignan and Ralston (2002), op. cit., p. 506.

35   Roth, R. (2001), "Traditionen des bürgerschaftlichen Engagements in Deutschland" (Traditions of civic engagement in Germany). In Arbeitswohlfahrt Bundesverband e.V. (ed.), *AWO-Sozialbericht 2001. Ehrenamt im Wandel. Zum Internationalen Jahr der Freiwilligen*, AWO Bundesverband e.V., Bonn, pp. 9–15.

36   Matten, D. and Moon, J. (2008), "'Implicit' and 'explicit' CSR: a conceptual framework for a comparative understanding of corporate social responsibility", *Academy of Management Review*, vol. 33, no. 2, pp. 404–424; Hall and Soskice, op. cit.; Chen, S. and Bouvain, P. (2009), "Is corporate responsibility converging? A comparison of corporate responsibility reporting in the USA, UK, Australia, and Germany", *Journal of Business Ethics*, vol. 87, Suppl. 1, pp. 299–317; Hartman, L.P., Rubin, R.S. and Dhanda, K.K. (2007), "The communication of corporate social responsibility: United States and European Union multinational corporations", *Journal of Business Ethics*, vol. 87, no. 4, pp. 373–389.

37   Witkowksi, T.H. and Wolfinbarger, M.F. (2002), "Comparative service quality: German and American ratings across service settings", *Journal of Business Research*, vol. 55, no. 11, pp. 875–881.

38   CCCG (2007), op. cit., p. 30.

39   Maignan and Ralston (2002), op. cit., p. 506.

40   Silberhorn and Warren (2007), op. cit., p. 359; Maignan and Ralston, op. cit., p. 506.

41   Chen and Bouvain (2009), op. cit., p. 312.

42   Milton Friedman (1970), "The social responsibility of business is to increase its profits", *New York Times Magazine*, September 13.

43   Hartman, Rubin and Dhanda (2007), op. cit., pp. 373–389; Crane, A. and Matten, D. (2010), *Business Ethics*, Oxford University Press, Oxford, pp. 11–22.

44   Vitols, S. (2004), "Negotiated shareholder value: the German variant of an Anglo-American practice", *Competition and Change*, vol. 8, no. 4, pp. 357–374.

45   Maignan and Ralston (2002), op. cit., p. 506.

46   Chen and Bouvain (2009), op. cit., p. 307.

47   Holder-Webb, L., Cohen, J.R., Nath, L. and Wood, D. (2009), "The supply of corporate social responsibility disclosures among U.S. firms", *Journal of Business Ethics*, vol. 84, no. 4, pp. 497–527.

48   CCCG (2007), op. cit., p. 23.

49   Maignan and Ralston (2002), op. cit., p. 506.

50   Freeman (1984), op. cit., p. 46.

51   See for example Konrad, A., Steurer, R., Langer, M.E. and Martinuzzi, A. (2006), "Empirical findings on business–society relations in Europe", *Journal of Business Ethics*, vol. 63, no. 1, pp. 89–105; Chen and Bouvain (2009), op. cit., pp. 299–317; Holtbrügge and Berg (2004), op. cit., pp. 299–313.

52   Van Huijstee, M. and Glasbergen, P. (2008), "The practice of stakeholder dialogue between multinationals and NGOs", *Corporate Social Responsibility and Environmental Management*, vol. 15, no. 5, pp. 298–310.

53   For a methodological description of content analysis see Krippendorff, K. (2004), *Content Analysis: An Introduction to its Methodology*, Sage, Thousand Oaks; Weber, R.P. (1990), *Basic Content Analysis*, Sage, Newbury Park.

54   Bowman, E.H. and Haire, M. (1975), "A strategic posture toward corporate social responsibility", *California Management Review*, vol. 18, no. 2, pp. 49–58; Abbott, W.F. and Monsen, R.J. (1979), "On the measurement of corporate social responsibility: self-reported disclosures as a measurement of corporate social involvement", *Academy of Management Journal*, vol. 22, no.

3, pp. 501–515; Chan, J.L. (1981), "Corporate disclosure in occupational safety and health: some empirical evidence", *Accounting, Organizations, and Society*, vol. 6, no. 3, pp. 247–254; Dierkes, M. (1979), "Corporate social reporting in Germany: conceptual developments and practical experience", *Accounting, Organizations and Society*, vol. 4, no. 1–2, pp. 87–107; Chen and Bouvain (2009), op. cit.; Maignan and Ralston (2002), op. cit.

55   Babbie, E.R. (2010), *The Practice of Social Research*, Wadsworth, Belmont, p. 333.

56   This assumption is elaborated on by O'Riordan, L. and Fairbrass, J. (2008), "Corporate social responsibility (CSR): Models and theories in stakeholder dialogue", *Journal of Business Ethics*, vol. 83, no. 4, pp. 745–758.

57   Cowen, S.S., Ferreri, L.B. and Parker, L.D. (1987), "The impact of corporate characteristics on social responsibility disclosure: a typology and frequency-based analysis", *Accounting, Organizations and Society*, vol. 12, no. 2, pp. 111–122; Belkaoui, A. and Karpik, P.G. (1989), "Determinants of the corporate decision to disclose social information", *Accounting, Auditing and Accountability Journal*, vol. 2, no. 1, pp. 36–51; Esrock, S.L. and Leichty, G.B. (1998), "Social responsibility and corporate web pages: self-presentation or agenda-setting?", *Public Relations Review*, vol. 24, no. 3, pp. 305–319; Cormier, D., Gordon, I.M. and Magnan, M. (2004), "Corporate environmental disclosure: contrasting management's perceptions with reality", *Journal of Business Ethics*, vol. 49, no. 2, pp. 143–165; Cormier, D. and Magnan, M. (2003), "Environmental reporting management: a continental European perspective", *Journal of Accounting and Public Policy*, vol. 22, no. 1, pp. 43–62; Morhardt, J.E. (2010), "Corporate social responsibility and sustainability reporting on the internet", *Business Strategy and the Environment*, vol. 19, no. 7, pp. 436–452; Patten, D.M. (2002), "Give or take on the internet: an examination of the disclosure practices of insurance firm web innovators", *Journal of Business Ethics*, vol. 36, no. 3, 247–259; Stanny, E. and Ely, K. (2008), "Corporate environmental disclosures about the effects of climate change", *Corporate Social Responsibility and Environmental Management*, vol. 15, no. 6, pp. 338–348; Adams, C.A., Coutts, A. and Harte, G. (1995), "Corporate equal opportunities (non-)disclosure", *British Accounting Review*, vol. 27, no. 2, pp. 87–101; Brammer, S. and Pavelin, S. (2004), "Voluntary social disclosures by large UK companies", *Business Ethics: A European Review*, vol. 13, no. 2/3, pp. 86–99.

58   *Süddeutsche Zeitung* (2008), "SZ-Ranking: Die 100 größten Unternehmen" (SZ-Ranking: The 100 Largest Companies), July 10, http://www.sueddeutsche.de/wirtschaft/270/448004/ text/ (accessed April 20, 2009); *Süddeutsche Zeitung* (2008), "SZ-Ranking: Die 20 größten Versicherungen" (SZ-Ranking: The 20 Largest Insurance Companies), July 10, http://www. sueddeutsche.de/imperia/md/content/pdf/wirtschaft/top20.pdf (accessed April 20, 2009); *Süddeutsche Zeitung* (2008), "SZ-Ranking: Die 20 größten Banken" (SZ-Ranking: The 20 Largest Banks), July 10, http://www.sueddeutsche.de/imperia/md/content/pdf/wirtschaft/ top20banken.pdf (accessed April 20, 2009); CNNMoney.com (2008), "Fortune 1000", http:// money.cnn.com/magazines/fortune/fortune500/2008/full_list/ (accessed April 22, 2009); "Fiches Entreprises" (Company Data) (2008), *L'Expansion*, http://www.lexpansion.com/ classement/economie/entreprise.asp?typerec=1andcode_secteur1000=andtripalm=1andtrisect =0%7CTous+secteursandcodreg=0%7CToutes+les+r%E9gionsandpp=100 (accessed September 12, 2010).

59   Deutsche Bundesbank (2010), "Statistik, Zeitreihen, Euro-Referenzkurs" (Statistics, Time Series, Euro-Reference Rate), http://www.bundesbank.de/statistik/statistik_zeitreihen.php?lang=dean dopen=devisenandfunc=rowandtr=WJ5636 (accessed November 10, 2010).

60   Roberts, S. (2003), "Supply chain specific? Understanding the patchy success of ethical sourcing initiatives", *Journal of Business Ethics*, vol. 44, no. 2/3, pp. 159–170.

61   Antal, A.B. and Sobczak, A. (2007), "Corporate social responsibility in France: a mix of national traditions and international influences", *Business and Society*, vol. 46, no. 1, pp. 9–32.

62   Among all OECD countries, Germany ranks fifth in terms of nonwage labor costs behind Norway, Sweden, Belgium and Denmark; Institut der deutschen Wirtschaft (2008), "Industry labor cost, international comparison", *IW-Trends 3/2008*, Institut der deutschen Wirtschaft, Cologne.

63   Maignan and Ferrell (2003), op. cit., p. 64.

64   Antal and Sobczak (2007), op. cit., p. 13.

65   Maignan and Ferrell (2003), op. cit., p. 55–67.

66   Bartlett, C.A. and Goshal, S. (1989), *Managing Across Borders: The Transnational Solution*, Harvard Business School Press, Boston.

2 *What Makes a Stakeholder Act? Exploring the Impact of the Issue in the Stakeholder Relationship*

SALLY DAVENPORT[*] AND SHIRLEY LEITCH[†]

Keywords

Issue impact, stakeholder interests and identity, stakeholder mobilization, stakeholder relationship management.

Introduction

Corporate social responsibility and business ethics have achieved a high profile in organizational life of the early twenty-first century,[1] with calls for greater attention to be focused on the role of the corporation in society.[2] Stakeholder theory, which "begins with the assumption that values are necessarily and explicitly a part of doing business",[3] has become a central tenet in the inclusion of ethical approaches in organizations.[4] Stakeholder management, however, is more than simply an ethics tool for managers: it is a "neverending task of balancing and integrating multiple relationships and multiple objectives".[5] Organizations continue to face a far wider range of stakeholders, many of whom change from issue to issue.[6] Indeed, even the issue is not static and can change character over time, as can the position of the stakeholder.[7] Yet in a recent review of the stakeholder management literature, "stakeholder actions and responses" were found to be the least discussed theme.[8]

Like Wolfe and Putler, we believe that using a stakeholder lens can "facilitate our understanding of increasingly unpredictable external environments, thereby facilitating our ability to manage within these environments".[9] However, in order to do this, recommended stakeholder management strategies need to reflect the inherent complexity of the organizational environment, recognizing nuances in both the issue and the likely stakeholder response. As de Bakker and den Hond argue, the influence of stakeholders over organizations "is the temporary outcome of processes of action,

[*]   Sally Davenport, Victoria Management School, Victoria University of Wellington, PO Box 600, Wellington 6140, New Zealand. E-mail: sally.davenport@vuw.ac.nz.

[†]   Shirley Leitch, Swinburne University of Technology, PO Box 218, Hawthorn, Melbourne, Victoria 3122, Australia. E-mail: sleitch@groupwise.swin.edu.au.

reaction and interaction among various parties",[10] and it is these more dynamic aspects of the stakeholder relationships that we explore in this chapter. Using an example of a public sector organization which faced multiple and shifting stakeholder demands, we propose that introducing a focus on the impact of the issue that underpins an interaction between a stakeholder and the focal organization provides a useful addition to stakeholder relationship management.

After a review of stakeholder relationship management, we introduce the dilemmas faced by Bioreg,[11] an organization with a diverse range of stakeholders that it was mandated to serve. Second, we investigate aspects of stakeholder research that do exhibit dynamic aspects, such as that which addresses stakeholder group mobilization. We then suggest some likely implications regarding the impact of the issue on stakeholder mobilization and introduce an Issue-Impact-Action framework that can be used to identify and understand issue-based stakeholder action. We use the example of Bioreg and the dynamics of its stakeholder relationships to illustrate the implications. To conclude, we make suggestions regarding how the focal organization might respond with appropriate strategies to the different modes of stakeholder mobilization based on typical responses to the issue impact.

Managing Stakeholder Relationships

Stakeholder research is generally centred upon a focal organization and its dyadic relationships with stakeholders.[12] The stakeholder research tradition has at its core the purpose of describing and categorizing these organizational stakeholders using various frameworks.[13] As Donaldson and Preston argued, this description is usually coupled with (a) instrumental intent whereby making a connection with the stakeholder has the purpose of serving an objective such as profitability, and (b) normative intent to offer guidance in stakeholder management.[14] The resultant stakeholder descriptions, based upon questions such as "who are they?" and "what do they want?", are often static snapshots in time of relatively passive stakeholders, and rarely take into account shifts in these relationships.[15]

The potential for a changing relationship is, however, occasionally acknowledged. Mitchell *et al.* explicitly state that their model, based upon a legitimacy-power-urgency stakeholder typology, is dynamic because stakeholders can shift from one class to another by acquiring another attribute.[16] Jawahar and McLauglin introduced the evolving importance of different stakeholders by superimposing organizational life cycle concepts onto stakeholder theory but the implication remains that at certain stages in an organization's evolution, stakeholder relationships are stable.[17] Other than these examples, there appears to be little room in current stakeholder management approaches for intermittent variation in relationships and the factors that might drive sudden and possibly unexpected changes.

The purpose of this chapter, then, is to better understand what makes a stakeholder act in a certain way. There is no doubt that stakeholder relationships have a "steady state" for which the more static and descriptive elements of stakeholder approaches are perfectly adequate as a basis for "normal" stakeholder management. However, there is a finer grain of stakeholder interactions that we believe is not adequately captured in the models and frameworks currently available for stakeholder management. As Jawahar and McLaughlin state, a key question is "how an organization's management deals with stakeholders who vary in terms of salience" and we would add, how and why does that salience vary with each interaction?[18]

Research Approach

The research reported in this chapter was derived from a much larger five-year study on the sociocultural impacts of biotechnology in New Zealand funded by the New Zealand Foundation for Research Science and Technology (UoWX0227). This multidisciplinary study has involved hundreds of interviews and focus groups with individuals and representatives of organizations involved with biotechnology as scientists, policy managers, entrepreneurs, consumers, members of ethnic, cultural or religious groups, environmentalists and activists. The interview data was supplemented by a thematic analysis of Web sites, official documents, annual reports, promotional material, media material and other documents. They were also augmented by researcher observation of various events, such as conferences, seminars and workshops, staged by a wide range of actors with interests in biotechnology.

The catalyst for the line of enquiry reported in this chapter was our meetings with Bioreg's communications manager, after a critical review of Bioreg's stakeholder management, about her efforts to manage relationships with the wide range of stakeholders with which Bioreg was legally mandated to interact. Thus our research questions centred upon how various stakeholders respond to issues and what strategies might be developed to manage stakeholder mobilization. We drew primarily on interviews with members of Bioreg, ranging from the CEO to front-line analysts, and with representatives of typical "applicant" and "submitter" groups (see the Bioreg case to follow). We also gathered data from secondary sources produced by, or about, Bioreg and its stakeholders. Other secondary data sources included online information about, and media coverage of, the genetic modification (GM) approval applications made to Bioreg since 1996, when the organization began operating in its current form under the Hazardous Substances and New Organisms (HSNO) Act. The data was analyzed and categorized according to our interest in stakeholder mobilization around GM applications and Bioreg's approach to managing these stakeholders. This qualitative methodology adheres well with the recent call for "more fine-grained qualitative narratives", which "utilize interviews, direct observation of stakeholder gatherings and secondary sources" to inform stakeholder approaches.[19]

Bioreg and Stakeholder Mobilization

Even-handedness is part of the culture of Bioreg.

Bioreg CEO

Bioreg was charged with the regulatory oversight of biotechnology (including GM), new organisms and dangerous substances in New Zealand. It received applications for approvals from "applicants", which were usually scientific organizations (such as government laboratories or universities). Before making decisions, Bioreg received and took account of submissions made by "submitters" who were individuals or organizations (such as the advocacy groups Greenpeace and Mothers Against Genetic Engineering) that were often opposed to GM aspects of the application.

A 2003 review of Bioreg's capability to run the risk management processes associated with new organisms carried a statement that "a wide range of stakeholders, including some with excellent technical understanding of the applications under consideration", observed that Bioreg personnel "appeared to hold pro-approval views", that is, that it favoured scientific "applicants" over other stakeholders. In particular, Bioreg employees were perceived to disregard the beliefs of some submitters, for example, by expressing frustration with submitters' repetition of personal beliefs in the "wrongness" of GM, even referring to submitters as "the enemy".

It was the expectation of the public, the report stated, that Bioreg be even-handed in all its dealings even though it was deemed understandable that many staff and applicants would rather focus on the more familiar and specific (scientific) issues raised by the application and, therefore, turn a "blind eye" to ethical and "alternative science" considerations, or matters other than "hard" or "straight" science ("philosophy, ethics, spirituality, cultural awareness, social psychology, community values and the like"). Some staff and submitters had expressed concern that what they had thought were key issues in a particular application had been underreported. The review recommended that staff should be given training in dealing with conflicting information and with minority views.

At the centre of these concerns was the process for stakeholder relationship management around each application made to Bioreg. As a result of the apparent pattern of bias in favour of applicants, submitters (including many non-governmental organizations) had developed a reluctance to engage with Bioreg and, in turn, Bioreg felt that it had been given "the cold shoulder" by these stakeholder groups. The applicant community, however, felt that in contrast to the disciplined process they had to follow, submitters could raise any concerns they liked without being required to submit to a similar level of scrutiny. As their experience with the regulations improved, the applicant community also acted as submitters through representative bodies such as the Association of Scientific Organizations and the Biological Network.[20] It seemed to many staff that Bioreg could please none of its stakeholders!

The Dynamics of Stakeholder Interactions

For times when the "normal" stakeholder relationship is perturbed, we turn to those approaches that address stakeholder activism.[21] Most stakeholder approaches are based upon the prevailing assumption that stakeholders react to protect their interests, a proposition which is consistent with a rational choice, utility maximization perspective. However, stakeholders are not just interest-driven but also have identities and ideologies that influence whether, and in what manner, they will mobilize.[22]

In their attempt to answer the question "When do stakeholder groups attempt to influence the focal firm?", Rowley and Moldoveanu provided a description of stakeholder group mobilization that centered around a distinction between two different stakeholder group types—interest-based and identity-based.[23] Similarly, Wolfe and Putler argued that current stakeholder approaches place undue primacy on the role-based, self-interest of a stakeholder. Furthermore, they contended that even though it is difficult for an organization to respond to the breadth of expectations of heterogeneous groups, the assumption of stakeholder homogeneity, with role-based self-interest as the collective rationale, can have "powerful, unanticipated, and undesirable consequences".[24]

Observing that many stakeholders appeared to pursue actions that had negligible rational self-interest benefits (so-called "lost causes"), Rowley and Moldoveanu identified a second stakeholder group that was characterized by identity-based action. "An identity is a set of logically connected propositions that a person uses to describe himself or herself to himself/herself and to others, it is socially constructed and is verified or falsified by experiences".[25] For this stakeholder group, they argued, action was an expression of identity rather than a means to achieving more rational interests—the "act of acting" was the main objective. By expanding the range of behavioral motives that drive stakeholders, the authors proposed that stakeholder action be examined from both an identity-based and an interest-based perspective.

Although their research was focused on in-group heterogeneity, Wolfe and Putler also observed that, for some issues, "the circumstances are unlikely to result in self-interest being a dominant concern" and that "symbolic pre-dispositions will motivate individual's priorities".[26] Symbolic predispositions are "learned affective responses to particular symbols that are acquired relatively early in life ... but persist through adult life. These predispositions are central in forming basic values, feelings of nationalism, political party identification, racial prejudices, and other attitudes".[27] We would argue that a stakeholder's symbolic predispositions, which tend to be very stable over time, would be a major component of the concept of stakeholder identity.

Despite this expanded conception of stakeholder intentions, the question remains as to what makes a stakeholder act. It can be assumed that a stakeholder group will only mobilize when something has spurred it into action and that whatever is the trigger, it is perceived to be a threat to their interests and/or identity. We refer to this stakeholder mobilization trigger as "the issue".

Introducing the Mobilization Issue

The notion that it is an issue that mobilizes stakeholders and stimulates interaction with the focal organization seems to be mute in current stakeholder approaches, with most studies assuming homogenous or consistent actions no matter what the nature of the issue that has stimulated action. Mitchell *et al.* state that

> managers should never forget that stakeholders change in salience, requiring different degrees and types of attention depending on their attributed possession of power, legitimacy, and/or urgency, and that levels of these attributes (and thereby salience) can vary from issue to issue and from time to time.[28]

However, this aspect of their descriptive theory seems largely to have been ignored in subsequent stakeholder research.

Issues do make an appearance in the strands of stakeholder research that focus on social responsibility and environmental stakeholder management.[29] Hillman and Keim, for example, refer to "social issue participation" but define this as falling outside of the direct relationships with primary stakeholders and argue that this is negatively related to value creation through stakeholder management. Eesley and Lenox use the terminology "request" to refer to the issue between organizations and "outside constituencies" such as NGOs and advocacy groups.[30] Husted defines a social issue as:

- a controversial inconsistency based on one or more expectational gap;
- involving management perceptions of changing legitimacy and other stakeholder perceptions of changing cost–benefit positions;
- occurring within or between views of what is and/or what ought to be corporate performance or stakeholder perceptions of corporate performance; and
- implying an actual or anticipated resolution that creates significant, identifiable present or future impact on the organization.[31]

Husted then defined three types of social issue for an organization: type 1, when the issue is focused on disagreements about the nature of facts in a given situation; type 2, when there is a gap within the organization between "what is and what ought to be" to be resolved; and type 3, when there is goal incongruence between the firm and stakeholder perceptions about "what is and what ought to be".[32] Although Husted refers to the issue as being "social", we would propose that the "expectational gap", and other aspects described in the definition and typology, would apply to any issue between an organization and its stakeholders.

The presence of an "expectational gap" is also in line with legal usage of "issue" where it is defined as a matter of importance to be resolved; a matter or point in contention which remains to be decided, the decision of which involves important consequences; a choice between alternatives; a dilemma.[33] Translating this into a stakeholder framework we define "issue" (of whatever type) as a matter that is contentious to some degree (that is, there is an expectational gap) between the focal organization and the stakeholder, whether it be a decision, occurrence or event caused by, or that will affect, the focal organization and/or the stakeholder. When considering stakeholder mobilization, it is when an issue arises, even if that issue is only perceived as such by the stakeholder, that the stakeholder is mobilized into action.

The role of the issue in triggering stakeholder mobilization is inherent in Rowley and Moldoveanu's description but it is not made explicit that it is the impact of the issue that generates the interest or identity-based responses.[34] Making explicit the role of the issue leads us to propose that issues can have interest-based and/or identity-based impacts on stakeholders. Rowley and Moldoveanu argued that the desire to act and actual mobilization are "separated by the cost of organizing for such action". They proposed that the threshold for stakeholder mobilization with identity-based action is lower than that with interest-based action as the former do not have to go through the added step of evaluating either the impacts of the specific issue on their interests or the expected outcomes from action, as the desired outcome is mobilization itself.[35] Wolfe and Putler, referring to research on symbolic politics, noted that symbolic predispositions are often more important in forming attitudes and opinions than self-interest, and that self-interest is a dominant factor only in very specific cases.[36] A stakeholder's likelihood to respond to an issue will, therefore, depend on the specific issue and the ability of the stakeholder to assess the likely impact of that particular issue.

The Mobilization Issue and Bioreg

We turn now to illustrate the way an issue resonates with stakeholders and spurs action. In this case, stakeholder action takes place in response to an application for approval made by the applicants which is then notified to all stakeholders by Bioreg. When the application contains no GM aspects (such as applying to bring into New Zealand a circus animal that is new to the country) very little, if any, response from submitters is generated as the expectational gap between what the stakeholders expect Bioreg to do, and what Bioreg is likely to do, is insignificant. In Husted's terms, this is a "nonissue", in that both the organization and the stakeholders "agree with the factual representation of a situation, especially cause/effect relationships, and share similar interests, goals, and objectives".[37]

However, if the application concerned GM research, a raft of individual and group submissions was usually received. Thus the "issue" that drives the intermittent changes in Bioreg's stakeholder relationships is the content of the application to Bioreg and mobilization occurs as a result of that application. These issues are, in fact, a mixture of all three of Husted's types. First, a GM application is a type 1 issue in that there will be disagreement over the facts presented and their cause and effect relationships, for example, over scientific research that purports to prove that GM is not harmful or that there is no likelihood of transfer of genetic material if the GM organism is released into the environment. Secondly, a GM application is a type 2 issue in that there can be disagreement within Bioreg over how the organization should respond to the application. Lastly there is a range of type 3 aspects in that the interests, goals and objectives of the applicants and various submitters, and the stakeholder expectations of how Bioreg should respond to the issue, are often vastly different from those of Bioreg staff. Thus, it appears that issue type is not the most relevant factor because issues that are of a complex social, ethical or environmental nature are generally of mixed types and that categorising the issue by type might not be very useful for assisting the focal organization in its stakeholder management.

What is probably more important is the impact of the issue on the stakeholder and what type of mobilization response that impact is likely to generate. As is evident in the following quotations, the applicants exhibited interest-based action (at least initially) in response to the issue, as gaining approval had significant repercussions for the individual researcher and the (economic) costs and benefits were perceived by the applicants to be relatively clear. The applicants used scientific and economic arguments to support their applications because these benefits would accrue to the nation and were therefore perceived as the responsibility of the government, through Bioreg, to support. Negative outcomes would be a loss to the economy and the nation, as well as potentially the applicant's funding, if not livelihood. The applicants argued that their responses were "more rational", with clear benefits in relation to the critiques of submitters:

> We were also very clear that we weren't advocating open slather [of GM] and that it's not use of the technology without responsibility, it's use of the technology on a cautious, selective, careful basis to deliver benefits to New Zealand as a whole.

> GM is a good way to reduce humans' impact on the environment by increasing yields of key food crops, thus reducing the amount of land required and freeing it up for forests.

We've got to take a strategic point of view on that and we've got to be informed by knowledge not by emotion. (GM Researchers/Applicants)

The submitters, on the other hand, reacted against applications that they perceived as an affront to their values and their belief in the inherent "wrongness" of GM. While it was the particular application to which they were reacting, the submitters used similar arguments for each application no matter what the content because they had symbolic predispositions against the technology. They voiced concerns that the technology had potential negative repercussions for all humankind, not just the individual stakeholder, and that the degree of uncertainty was too high to risk introducing the technology into the food chain. Typical responses from submitters, such as a group of concerned mothers and some indigenous Maori groups,[38] included:

[I] fell in love with the clean, green image and thought it was a good place for children to grow up. [New Zealand] is like a little paradise, it is safe and relatively egalitarian. I don't think it is known yet if GM is safe or not. [It] should not be released until we know the effects on both children and adults.

The right to decide what we eat is fundamental.

The mixing of human and animal DNA is culturally and spiritually offensive to most New Zealanders.

Maori disagree with anything which tampers with the food chain, and with the knowledge of what went into the food chain. Maori have a different relationship with the environment than a lot of other people. We have a different world-view over what is considered tikanga, or right. (Submitters)

Submitters were motivated by identity-based concerns which led them to make a submission, sometimes the same submission, every time a GM application was lodged with Bioreg. It was these non-specific identity-based mobilizations that some staff of Bioreg found frustrating and difficult to accommodate within Bioreg processes.

Some Bioreg stakeholders exhibited a mixture of interest- and identity-based responses. In particular, indigenous Maori iwi (tribes) that farmed their own traditional land, and organic farmers, had both economic interests in the potential "contamination" of the source of their livelihoods and identity-based arguments against the technology more generally. Thus the costs and uncertainties were multilevel for these groups, resulting in mobilization that combined self-interest and symbolic predispositions. The following quotations exemplify the submissions received by Bioreg from these groups:

GM poses a risk to tribal gathering grounds ... We have given a great deal of consideration to this issue and oppose the granting of any applications for GMO development until we have the opportunity to determine the impact such developments would have on our values and social and cultural well-being. (Maori iwi/landowner)

What is commercial and what is non-commercial/philosophical? [We have] a passionate commitment to the ideal and to the practice ... to authenticity and integrity of product.

They will always try to denigrate organics—I always say YES we are a bunch of long-haired hippy dope-smoking-on-the-Coromandel[39] [farmers] AND the suit-wearing board members. (Organic farmers)

The Issue-impact-action Framework of Stakeholder Mobilization

The impact of an issue and the resultant stakeholder mobilization can be represented graphically in order to delineate between the types of action that are caused by the issue (Figure 2.1).

Inaction (quadrant 1): when the issue has a low, or no, impact on either the interests or the identity of the stakeholder, then they are unlikely to mobilize and inaction is the likely (non)response.

Interest-based action (quadrant 2): when an issue has a high impact on the interests of a stakeholder they will mobilize with action that supports or protects their interests, as in the arguments given above made by the GM researchers/applicants.

Identity-based action (quadrant 3): when an issue has a high impact on the identity of the stakeholder, the resultant mobilization mode will be identity-based, reflecting the need of the stakeholder to respond in a mode that is aligned with their identity-based values, as in the examples of responses from the submitters given above.

Interest and identity-based action (quadrant 4): when the issue has a high impact on both the interests and identity of a stakeholder, the action is likely to exhibit both interest and identity-based characteristics as is evident in the responses from some Maori iwi and organic farmers. The stakeholders mobilize both to support/protect their interests (e.g., as "a suit-wearing board member") as well as their identity-based values (e.g., as a "long-haired hippy").

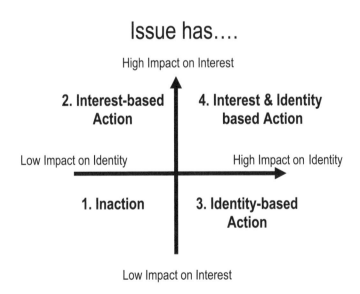

Figure 2.1   Issue-impact-action framework

Categorization of a stakeholder response using the Issue-Impact-Action framework does not imply that stakeholders will always respond in a set way to all issues, nor that stakeholders will necessarily confine their response on one issue to a singular mode. This latter point was observed in the Bioreg example in a changed response from the applicants, as a result of observing the submitters' arguments against their application. Some applicants expressed the view that their underlying scientific ethos and values, and therefore the existence of the scientific community, were being challenged. At this point, the issue would no longer result in mainly individual repercussions and greatly increased the uncertainty associated with the outcomes. Thus the nature of the issue shifted for these applicants to have both high interest and identity impacts. In comparison with the typical early responses of the applicants, the following quotation shows that the later response from one researcher had broadened away from solely focusing on the specific details of the application in question, to include a defence of the scientific research tradition in general:

> *Science is actually an international system and I don't use the word culture—[it] has to be regarded as an efficient form of communication rather than a cultural activity ... If it's a cultural activity in the same way that ethnic groups are of different cultures, then science should vary with the ethnic group but it doesn't, it's a bottom line. What is the bottom line— reproducible observation! (GM Researcher/Applicant)*

The observation that some stakeholders change mobilization mode as they observe other stakeholder actions and/or the issue evolving to have a different impact, leads us to propose that when interest-based stakeholders believe that their identity is threatened by the actions of other stakeholders in response to an issue, they might then mobilize with both interest- and identity-based action. This shift in impact and response mode is represented by arrow (a) in Figure 2.2.

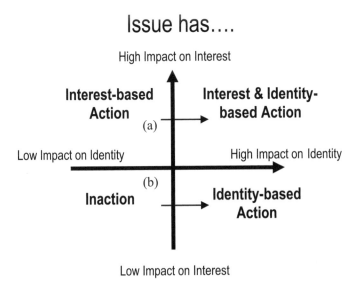

Figure 2.2   The dynamics of stakeholder mobilization

However, this group of stakeholders is not the only one that potentially could change their mode of mobilization. As described earlier, the impact threshold to exhibit an identity-based mobilization mode is lower than that for interest-based mobilization. In the Bioreg example, this threshold effect was observed in the initiation of mobilization in those that were previously inactive, particularly amongst those who did not perceive an interest-based reason to act. As part of its mandate, Bioreg was charged with "informing the public" about GM. However, by carrying out this educational role, Bioreg stimulated some of the previously relatively unconcerned "public" to feel motivated enough to express a stronger opinion when consultation regarding a GM application was carried out by Bioreg.[40] This "new" response, in the majority of cases, contained expressions of personal values rather than economic interests and, therefore, illustrated a move from the inactive mode to the identity-based mobilization mode, indicated by arrow (b) in Figure 2.2. This observation suggests that when inactive stakeholders are stimulated to respond to an issue, they are more likely to mobilize with identity-based action than with interest-based action.

The horizontal direction of the arrows in Figure 2.2, indicating likely changes in response mode, reflects that the dynamics of stakeholder mobilization are most strongly influenced by the identity perceptions of the stakeholders regarding an issue, than the interest concerns of stakeholders represented by the vertical axis. Although not found in this study, interest-based vertical shifts are a possibility, but the identity-based horizontal movement should be more common because of the lower threshold for identity-based stimulation in response to an issue. This observation has major implications for the way in which organizations develop strategies to respond to issue-inspired stakeholder mobilization.

Responding to Stakeholder Mobilization Modes

Organizational strategies for responding to stakeholder mobilization need to recognize the variety of ways in which a stakeholder might respond to an issue and also that the response will not necessarily be static but can change as the dynamics of stakeholder mobilization evolves. We propose that our Issue-Impact-Action framework is a useful way of identifying, understanding and following stakeholder responses to an issue that has arisen in the relationship with the focal organization, with the cautionary note that this impact and response can also be dynamic, so revisiting the framework for each issue and as an issue evolves becomes central to managing the dynamics of stakeholder relationships.

How might focal organizations such as Bioreg respond to the different modes of stakeholder mobilization? One of the problems for Bioreg was that many of its staff (another stakeholder group) identified more strongly with the applicant's interest-based mobilization, in that they were scientifically trained and understood economic rationale. There was also evidence that some staff felt that their own scientific identity was threatened by some of the identity-based submitter responses. For example, this is likely to have generated the response of Bioreg employees in framing submitters as "the enemy". Hence the staff would understandably have been most comfortable highlighting those interest-based arguments to which they were most sympathetic, at the expense of non-interest-based arguments, when preparing reports.

Savage *et al.* began to address issue-based stakeholder management when they asserted that the potential for stakeholder action is a function of how the focal organization acts on issues related to stakeholder interest.[41] Their framework was based on the potential for a stakeholder to either cooperate or threaten the organization, which resulted in a diagnostic typology with four categories of stakeholder: non-supportive (low potential to cooperate, high on potential threat), mixed blessing (high on both dimensions), supportive (high cooperation potential, low threat) and marginal (low on both dimensions). Savage *et al.* then suggested four strategies to match the type of stakeholder; defend, collaborate, involve and monitor, respectively.

While these authors constructed a typology of stakeholders rather than a typology of mobilization modes, appropriate stakeholder management response strategies could similarly be developed (Figure 2.3). By carefully observing the range of stakeholder responses and also by monitoring the dynamics of the mobilization modes, the focal organization might be better equipped to develop appropriate strategies to successfully manage stakeholder relationships when these are activated by an issue in that relationship.

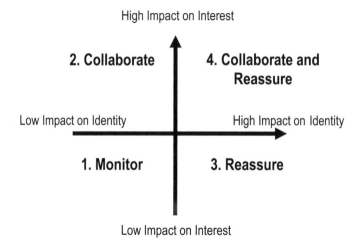

Figure 2.3 Response strategies for stakeholder mobilization

Monitor (quadrant 1): the "inaction" mobilization mode requires ongoing monitoring, as proposed by Savage *et al.*, as a response to "marginal" stakeholders, in case the impact of the issue on these stakeholders increases at a later stage. Even though the strategy appears to be similar, the motivation for the management strategy proposed here is quite different to that described for marginal stakeholders by Savage *et al.*, as they suggested that such stakeholders' interests tend to be narrow and should not have resources and effort "wasted" on them.[42] In contrast we would suggest that the monitoring of "inactive" stakeholders is of prime importance for focal organizations given the likelihood that stakeholders that do not appear to be acting could mobilize with identity-based action quite rapidly if they perceive the issue to now exhibit an impact upon their identity.

Collaborate (quadrant 2): those stakeholders that respond from an interest-based perspective are probably the group that is most straightforward to manage and the majority of standard stakeholder management techniques would apply. For our purposes, we use Savage *et al.*'s "collaborate" terminology for this response strategy, by which we mean "work closely with". Because these stakeholders are often the "easiest" to manage, there is a tendency for organizations to be perceived as taking these stakeholders' goodwill for granted. The risk of not collaborating extensively with such stakeholders is that they then perceive this lack of involvement as an impact on their identity as well as their interests, and move into the interest- and identity-based mobilization mode.

Reassure (quadrant 3): appropriate response strategies for identity-based action pose more of a conundrum. For many organizations, these stakeholders would be classified as Savage *et al.*'s "non-supportive" stakeholder type, for which a defensive strategy was proposed in order to reduce the dependence on that stakeholder, perhaps even to treating them like a competitor. However, there are dangers in such a strategy. Apart from the fact that many public sector organizations are not able to be defensive, in that they are legally mandated to take these stakeholders' concerns into account, the Bioreg example shows how identity-based mobilization that is perceived by interest-based stakeholders to be impacting on their identity can drive the latter group to also act in an identity-based mode. Thus the focal organization will need to respond in ways that reassure those stakeholders that mobilize in an identity-based mode that their concerns are being taken into account. It is likely that such responses will need to be centered on notions of fairness (which harks back to Bioreg's "even-handedness" goal) and procedural justice so that these stakeholders perceive that they are being treated appropriately.[43] Such a reassurance strategy is evident in the Bioreg example, when Bioreg's reviewers' recommended that the submitters' concerns be reflected in reporting and that Bioreg staff be trained to deal more effectively with these types of stakeholders. It was also reflected in the fact that many submitters were satisfied (and some "demobilized") when Bioreg staff visited the submitters personally and listened to their concerns, irrespective of whether or not Bioreg was able to act in response to these concerns.

Collaborate and reassure (quadrant 4): the most complex response strategies are required for stakeholders that mobilize when an issue impacts upon both their interests and identity. In such cases, the focal organization will need to collaborate with the stakeholders in order to allay concerns that their immediate (usually economic) interests are not in danger but will also need to make reassurances regarding any perceived affront to the stakeholder's identity. For Bioreg, the types of stakeholders that responded in this mode included applicants whose research projects and research livelihood were potentially threatened and whose worldviews were under attack by submitters. For all of these stakeholders a simple response from Bioreg regarding the specific application was not enough. Reassurance was needed about the robustness of the regulatory approval and risk management processes that underpinned Bioreg's legal obligations, but also more generally about Bioreg's intrinsic mandate to protect New Zealand's economic, environmental and social interests (and identity!).

Conclusions

Our intent in this chapter was to broaden discussions of stakeholder management away from stable "steady state" models to investigate the dynamic aspects of stakeholder management when complex issues are introduced into the relationship. As other researchers have identified,[44] the inherent bias of much stakeholder research towards a role-based, self-interest, "one size fits all" perspective on stakeholder management is one that is ripe for reconsideration, particularly given the increasingly complex nature of the issues that underpin stakeholder relationships and corporate social responsibility initiatives.

We propose that our particular contribution is that stakeholder management needs to consider the impact of the issue on a stakeholder group, and also to be aware that the impact will also be dynamic as the stakeholder interaction evolves. We canvassed the role of the "issue" in stakeholder theory and, in particular, built upon Rowley and Moldoveanu's stakeholder mobilization description, coupled with Wolfe and Putler's notion of symbolic predisposition, in order to understand the possibly sudden and intermittent changes that can occur in stakeholder relationships.[45]

Our research suggests that the impact of the issue will trigger four different modes of action depending on whether the issue has a high or low impact on either or both of the stakeholder's interests or identity, as captured in our Issue-Impact-Action framework. The dynamics of the relationships between Bioreg's staff and applicants and submitters have provided a useful context in which to illustrate the role of the issue impact in stakeholder mobilization and to make sense of the range of responses from Bioreg's stakeholder groups over GM applications. By framing stakeholder mobilization in this way, we hope that the Issue-Impact-Action framework will not only stimulate further research into the dynamics of stakeholder management, but also help focal organizations better understand the possible underlying drivers of, and therefore be able to tailor more appropriate and acceptable responses to, stakeholder mobilization over the arguably more complex issues that will challenge organizations in the future.

Appendix: Research Methodology

Research Phase	Activity	Task Detail	Output
Literature review: Stakeholder management in the public sector	Online search—source databases included *ProQuest, Web of Knowledge, Emerald Fulltext and Sage Journals Online* etc.	Guided literature search on terms such as "stakeholder-management", "-activism", "-mobilization", "issue management" etc.	Gap identified in public sector stakeholder management around controversial issues
Research design	Researchers discuss the literature review, formulate the research questions and methodological approach	Qualitative inductive approach applicable when research is reflecting upon existing theory in understudied areas[46]	Research questions, overall design, interview template
Research design	Minimizing limitations of methodological approach, particularly generalizability from "revelatory" single case study[47]	Follow recommended procedures for minimizing participant's perceptual and information limitations.[48] Factual secondary data gathered. All interviews attended by two researchers	Case study design
Data collection: primary data, internal Bioreg stakeholders	Interviews undertaken by both researchers with: CEO, communications manager (2 interviews at beginning and end of process) and senior analyst	Four semi-structured interviews conducted of about 1 hour in length. All interviews digitally recorded and transcribed in full	Transcripts (MS Word files)
Data collection: primary data, external Bioreg stakeholders	Interviews undertaken by both researchers with both applicant and submitter individuals and representatives of organizations, including related public sector organizations, scientific and farming (conventional and organic) organizations, individual scientists, activists and farmers	Twenty-seven semi-structured interviews conducted of about 1 hour in length. All interviews digitally recorded and transcribed in full	Transcripts (MS Word files)

Research Phase	Activity	Task Detail	Output
Data collection: secondary data, Bioreg	Electronic copies obtained of official Bioreg reports and reviews as well as selected internal reports of relevance to the research questions	Electronic files of six annual reports, six statements of intent, the stakeholder management review, Bioreg's stakeholder analysis/strategy, stakeholder awareness survey results and Bioreg's "Interested Person" submission to the RCGM[49]	Sixteen documents (MS Word or searchable pdf files)
Data collection: secondary data, other	Submissions to the RCGM by Bioreg's stakeholders, both organizations and individuals, either as interviewed or were identified by Bioreg as relevant stakeholders. Media articles related to Bioreg's stakeholder management, accessed through online archives such as *Index New Zealand, Newztext Newspapers* etc.	Ninety-three submissions (many less than one page) collated from the RCGM into one electronic file. Seventy-six media articles deemed to be relevant were collated into an electronic file	Two further files of data (MS Word or searchable pdf files)
Data analysis: wide thematic analysis	All data files read by both researchers to identify initial themes	Close reading resulting in a wide range of excerpts that fitted our categorization of indicating an impact on interest, identity or both	Two sets of independently coded files
Data analysis: narrow thematic analysis	Researchers swap files, discuss and agree on emerging themes	Key excerpts are extracted and categorized according to whether they illustrate interest and identity impact	Collation of illustrative excerpts
Framework development	Researchers develop 2 × 2 framework	Key excerpts are extracted to illustrate framework and dynamics over time	Draft research findings

Notes

1   Donaldson, T. (2003), "Taking ethics seriously: a mission now more possible", *Academy of Management Review*, vol. 28, no. 3, pp. 363–366; Freeman, R.E. (2000), "Business ethics at the millennium", *Business Ethics Quarterly*, vol. 10, no. 1, pp. 169–180; Husted, B.W. (2000), "A contingency theory of corporate social performance", *Business and Society*, vol. 39, no. 1, pp. 24–48; Lindgreen, A. and Swaen, V. (2010), "Corporate social responsibility", *International Journal of Management Reviews*, vol. 12, no. 1, pp. 1–7; Wicks, A.C. and Freeman. R.E. (1998), "Organization studies and the new pragmatism: positivism, anti-positivism, and the search for ethics", *Organization Science*, vol. 9, no. 2, pp. 123–140.

2   Kochan, T.A. and Rubinstein, S.A. (2000), "Towards a stakeholder theory of the firm: the Saturn partnership", *Organization Science*, vol. 11, no. 4, pp. 367–386; Laplume, A.O., Sonpar, K. and Litz, R.A. (2008), "Stakeholder theory: reviewing a theory that moves us", *Journal of Management*, vol. 34, no. 6, pp. 1152–1189.

3   Freeman, R.E., Wicks, A.C. and Parmar, B. (2004), "Stakeholder theory and 'The corporate objective revisited'", *Organization Science*, vol. 15, no. 3, pp. 364–369; see p. 364.

4   Gibson, K. (2000), "The moral basis of stakeholder theory", *Journal of Business Ethics*, vol. 26, no. 3, pp. 245–257; Jones, T.M. (1995), "Instrumental stakeholder theory: a synthesis of ethics and economics", *Academy of Management Review*, vol. 20, no. 2, pp. 404–437; Parmar, B.L., Freeman, R.E., Harrison, J.S., Wicks, A.C., Purnell, L. and de Colle, S. (2010), "Stakeholder theory: state of the art", *The Academy of Management Annals*, vol. 4, June, pp. 403–445; Whetten, D.A., Rands, G. and Godfrey, P. (2002), "What are the responsibilities of business to society?" In A. Pettigrew, H. Thomas and R. Whittington (eds), *Handbook of Strategy and Management*, Sage, London, pp. 373–408.

5   Freeman, R.E. and McVea, J. (2001), "A stakeholder approach to strategic management". In M. Hitt, R.E. Freeman and J.S. Harrison (eds), *Handbook of Strategic Management*, Basil Blackwell, Oxford, UK, pp. 189–207; see p. 194.

6   Husted (2000), op. cit.

7   Kochan and Rubinstein (2000), op. cit.; Mahon, J.F. and Waddock, S.A. (1992), "Strategic issues management: an integration of issue life cycle perspectives", *Business and Society*, vol. 31, no. 1, pp. 19–32

8   Laplume, Sonpar and Litz (2008), op. cit.

9   Wolfe, R.A. and Pulter, D.S. (2002), "How tight are the ties that bind stakeholder groups?", *Organization Science*, vol. 13, no. 1, pp. 64–80; see p. 64.

10   De Bakker, F.G.A. and den Hond, F. (2008), "Introducing the politics of stakeholder influence: a review essay", *Business and Society*, vol. 47, no. 1, pp. 8–20.

11   The name of the organization has been disguised, but we note that this case study augments the rare examples of stakeholder management research carried out on organizations other than large publicly traded corporations, Laplume, Sonpar and Litz (2008), op. cit.

12   Jawahar, I.M. and McLaughlin, G.L. (2001), "Toward a descriptive stakeholder theory: an organizational life cycle approach", *Academy of Management Review*, vol. 26, no. 3, pp. 397–414; Rowley, T.J. (1997), "Moving beyond dyadic ties: a network theory of stakeholder influences", *Academy of Management Review*, vol. 22, no. 4, pp. 887–910; Sundaram, A.K. and Inkpen, A.C. (2004), "The corporate objective revisited", *Organization Science*, vol. 15, no. 3, pp. 350–363.

13   For example, Mitchell, R.K, Agle, B.R. and Wood, D.J. (1997), "Toward a theory of stakeholder identification and salience: defining the principle of who and what really counts", *Academy of Management Review*, vol. 22, no. 4, pp. 853–886; Agle, B., Mitchell, R. and Sonnenfeld, J. (1999), "Who matters to CEOs? An investigation of stakeholder attributes and salience, corporate performance, and CEO values", *Academy of Management Journal*, vol. 42, no. 5, pp. 507–525.

14   For example, Donaldson, T. and Preston, L.E. (1995), "The stakeholder theory of the corporation: concepts, evidence and implications", *Academy of Management Review*, vol. 20, no. 1, pp. 65–91; Hillman, A.J. and Keim, G.D. (2001), "Shareholder value, stakeholder management, and social issues: what's the bottom line?", *Strategic Management Journal*, vol. 22, no. 2, pp. 125–139; Jones, T.M. and Wicks, A.C. (1999), "Convergent stakeholder theory", *Academy of Management Review*, vol. 24, no. 2, pp. 206–214.

15   Friedman, A.L. and Miles, S. (2002), "Developing stakeholder theory", *Journal of Management Studies*, vol. 39, no. 1, pp. 1–21; Frooman, J. (1999), "Stakeholder influence strategies", *Academy of Management Review*, vol. 24, no. 2, pp. 191–205.

16   Mitchell, Agle and Wood (1997), op. cit.

17   Jawahar and McLauglin (2001), op. cit.

18   Ibid, p. 400.

19   Laplume, Sonpar and Litz (2008), op. cit., p. 1174.

20   Disguised industry bodies that represented scientific organizations and/or pro-GE advocates.

21   Frooman, op. cit.; Rowley, T.I. and Moldoveanu, M. (2003), "When will stakeholder groups act? An interest- and identity-based model of stakeholder group mobilization", *Academy of Management Review*, vol. 28, no. 2, pp. 204–219.

22   Den Hond, F. (2010), "Review essay: reflections on relationships between NGOs and corporations", *Business and Society*, vol. 49, no. 1, pp. 173–178; Den Hond, F. and de Bakker, F.G.A. (2007), "Ideologically motivated activism: how activist groups influence corporate social change activities", *Academy of Management Review*, vol. 32, no. 3, pp. 901–924; Rowley and Moldoveanu (2003), op. cit.

23   Rowley and Moldaveanu (2003), op. cit.

24   Wolfe and Putler (2002), op. cit., p. 66.

25   Rowley and Moldaveanu (2003), op. cit., p. 208.

26   Wolfe and Putler (2002), op. cit., p. 68.

27   Sears, D. and Funk, C. (1999a), "The role of self-interest in social and political attitudes", *Advances in Experimental Psychology*, vol. 24, pp. 1–91; Sears, D.O. and Funk, C.L. (1999b), "Evidence of the long-term persistence of adults' political predispositions", *The Journal of Politics*, vol. 61, no. 1, pp. 1–28.

28   Mitchell, Agle and Wood (1997), op. cit., p. 879.

29   Bansal, P. (2003), "From issues to actions: the importance of individual concerns and organizational values in responding to natural environmental issues", *Organization Science*, vol. 14, no. 5, pp. 510–527; Buysse, K. and Verbeke, A. (2003), "Proactive environmental strategies: a stakeholder management perspective", *Strategic Management Journal*, vol. 24, no. 5, pp. 453–470; Hillman and Keim (2001), op. cit.

30   Eesley, C. and Lenox, M.J. (2006), "Firm responses to secondary stakeholder action", *Strategic Management Journal*, vol. 27, no. 8, pp. 765–781.

31   Husted (2000), op. cit., p. 28, citing Wartick, S. and Mahon, J. (1994), "Toward a substantive definition of the corporate issue construct: a review and synthesis of the literature", *Business and Society*, vol. 33, no. 3, pp. 293–311.

32   Husted (2000), op. cit., p. 32.

33   OED (*Oxford English Dictionary*) online 2010. http://dictionary.oed.com.

34   Rowley and Moldoveanu (2003), op. cit.

35   Ibid, p. 208.

36   Wolfe and Putler (2002), op. cit., p. 68.

37   Husted (2000), op. cit., p. 32.

38   In general Maori see interference by GM as irreconcilable with their cultural and spiritual beliefs. An in-depth discussion of Maori beliefs with respect to GM is contained in Ahdar, R. (2003), "Indigenous spiritual concerns and the secular state: some New Zealand developments", *Oxford Journal of Legal Studies*, vol. 23, no. 4, pp. 611–637.

39   The Coromandel is a region of New Zealand popular with those seeking "alternative" lifestyles.

40   Leitch, S. and Davenport, S. (2004), "Creating controversy through consultation", European Association for the Study of Science and Technology (EASST) Conference, Paris, August.

41   Savage, G.T., Nix, T.W., Whitehead, C.J. and Blair, J.D. (1991), "Strategies for assessing and managing organizational stakeholders", *Academy of Management Executive*, vol. 5, no. 2, pp. 61–75.

42   Ibid., p. 66.

43   Hosmer, L.T. and Kiewitz, C. (2005), "Organizational justice: a behavioural science concept with critical implications for business ethics and stake holder theory", *Business Ethics Quarterly*, vol. 15, no. 1, pp. 67–91.

44   Wolfe and Putler (2002), op. cit., p. 76.

45   Rowley and Moldoveanu (2003), op. cit., Wolfe and Putler (2002), op. cit.

46   Eisenhardt, K.M. (1989), "Building theories from case study research", *Academy of Management Review*, vol. 14, no. 4, pp. 532–550. Eisenhardt, K.M. and Graebner, M.E. (2007), "Theory building from cases: opportunities and challenges", *Academy of Management Journal*, vol. 50, no. 1, pp. 25–32.

47   Yin, R.K. (2003), *Case Study Research: Design and Methods*, 3rd edn, Sage, London.

48   Huber, G.P. and Power, D.J. (1985), "Retrospective reports of strategy-level managers: guidelines for increasing their accuracy", *Strategic Management Journal*, vol. 6. no. 2, pp. 171–180.

49   The Royal Commission on Genetic Modification (RCGM) commenced in New Zealand in April 2000 and completed its review in July 2001. Data from the RCGM process, covering transcripts of the deliberations, 10,904 public submissions to the review, including those of 292 individuals or organizations accorded "Interested Persons" status (entitled to make oral submission), were also available to the researchers. For more information on the RCGM see Leitch, S. and Davenport, S.J. (2007), "Strategic ambiguity as a discourse practice: the role of keywords in the discourse on 'sustainable' biotechnology", *Discourse Studies*, vol. 9 no. 1, pp. 43–61; Davenport, S.J. and Leitch, S. (2005), "Agoras, ancient and modern, and a framework for science–society debate", *Science and Public Policy*, vol. 32, no. 2, pp. 137–153.

3 Swapping Stories: How Firms and Stakeholders use Blogs as Narrative Discourse to Create Efficacy and Meaning for Corporate Social Responsibility

DAVID M. BOJE,* STEPHANIE MAYNARD-PATRICK[†] AND STEVEN M. ELIAS[‡]

Keywords

Antenarrative, sensemaking, stakeholder-efficacy, storytelling.

Introduction

Organizations face pressure from a variety of stakeholders to operate in a fair and socially responsible manner. In the twenty-first century, this pressure is magnified, because the internet has made it incredibly easy to share news of corporate misdeeds. Those that perceive they have been the victim of injustice at the hands of corporate America are no longer alone; through the use of the internet, one can reach others who have been victimized in the same way and rally other stakeholders to the cause. Further, stakeholders no longer have to champion their needs alone as one Web site or blog can serve as a portal for all stakeholders to come together with their issues and needs.

On blogs and Web sites, firms and stakeholders share their storytelling of organizational experiences which are read by people around the world. From the storytelling prevalent

* David M. Boje, New Mexico State University, College of Business, Las Cruces, NM 88003, USA. E-mail: dboje@nmsu.edu.

† Stephanie Maynard-Patrick, New Mexico State University, College of Business, Las Cruces, NM 88003, USA. E-mail: svmp@nmsu.edu.

‡ Steven M. Elias, New Mexico State University, College of Business, Las Cruces, NM 88003, USA. E-mail: selias@nmsu.edu.

in blogs, stakeholders may develop a sense of proxy efficacy. We theorize that online storytelling plays an important role in the proxy efficacy of stakeholders concerned about social responsibility. Some examples of these sites that we explore are Wakeupwalmart.com and Walmartwatch.com. Inherent to our theory of storytelling is that there are important differences between narrative, living story and antenarratives,[1] especially in organization and stakeholder communications. It is in the antenarrative aspects of storytelling that we theorize that proxy efficacy plays its role. In this chapter, we evaluate several blogs to see how proxy efficacy is formed, and how it helps reconcile stakeholder differences.

Creating Social Responsibility Through Storytelling

The definition of corporate social responsibility (CSR) is supremely vague, and has been for its entire history.[2] Therefore, each firm creates its own definition of what constitutes CSR. Firms communicate their definitions through corporate stories and narratives, which are shared with internal and external stakeholders via a number of media including Web sites, blogs, social networking sites, intracompany communications and strategies, shareholder reports and even through advertisements.

But an organization is not the only one who has a vision of what CSR should be. The stakeholders of the organization also create their own meanings of CSR based upon the different CSR activities and behaviors they value. However, the organization's multiple stakeholders each have different needs and desires for the organization, so each stakeholder group will have different definitions for CSR based upon those needs and desires. Through narratives and stories, organizational stakeholders create a discourse of direction to understand and influence one another's definitions and actions.[3] Internet blogs serve as the perfect forum for this discourse.

These differences in definition between the organization and its stakeholders must be managed in order to prevent conflicts that results in negative publicity, customer loss, lawsuits and even legislation. One of the ways organizations manage their human stakeholder relations is through the storytelling in various internal and external communications.

According to Boje[4] "storytelling is the preferred sensemaking currency of human relations among internal and external stakeholders". Stories stir emotions, arousing the physical and psychological states of both the storyteller and the audience through poetic elaboration of symbolic material.[5] Organizational leaders fashion stories that transplant, suppress, outweigh, or even complement existing stories as well as contemporary, oppositional counterstories[6] and counternarratives. These stories illuminate a firm's intentions, create credibility for their actions and attempt to create support for the firm.[7] By telling a "good story" an organization can create meaning[8] and increase the acceptance of the identity portrayed in those stories.[9] Effective storytellers achieve two fundamental outcomes: credibility and novelty. To do this, authors must convince readers or listeners that a narrative is plausible within a given context and bring about a change in reader perspective.[10] For many corporations, their goal is to manage the efficacy beliefs of its stakeholders. Firms want stakeholders to believe that the firm is always able, either now through its current activities or in the future, of acting in a socially responsible way. However, CSR proxy efficacy beliefs will vary from stakeholder to stakeholder, and it is not uncommon to see some firm stakeholders publishing statements that counter those of the firm in order to change the efficacy beliefs of other stakeholder groups. Therefore organizations must continually reconsider and rework stories to balance credibility, novelty, plausibility and impact.

However, when rewriting their stories many organizations reinterpret relationships to espoused values or corporate history, as well as editing the content to create the desired outcome and image. This creates a reified narrative that does not allow the audience to question the story or disagree.[11] As such, the living story that was a web of relationships to other living stories becomes reduced to narrative. Narrative is a form of meaning-making that captures the seemingly independent and disconnected actions and events as related parts of a whole,[12] creating a concrete past from a myriad of experiences.[13] de Certeau,[14] McCloskey[15] and Boje[16] make distinctions between narrative and living story processes in organizations. Thus narratives are reflective of the past, while stories capture the events going on in the present.[17] Another part of the living story webs that corporations use to maintain their petrified narratives is stories of justification. How an organization justifies its actions reflects how it interprets its relationships with stakeholders as well as how it views its broader responsibilities to society.[18] Over time, these justification stories may spiral through the organization, causing the firm to reflect and perhaps change the its position on an issue. Antenarratives explain how a firm plans to handle conflicts, predicaments and crises.[19] However, the actual outcomes of a crisis or conflict rarely match the organization's original intentions and purposes, and so antenarratives must be revised, becoming narratives that encompass acceptable representations of the past.

Stakeholder Efficacy

Efficacy beliefs have long been known to impact individuals' cognitions, affective states and behaviors.[20] These impacts can occur at either the individual (i.e., self-efficacy and proxy efficacy) or the group (i.e., collective efficacy) level. Regardless of the level such beliefs are operating on, efficacy functions in the same manner. The most widely accepted operational definition of self efficacy is "beliefs in one's capabilities to organize and execute the courses of action required to produce given attainments".[21] Proxy efficacy refers to an individual's belief that another entity has the ability to act on their behalf, and is most relevant to external stakeholders.[22] At the group level, collective efficacy refers to a shared belief among group members in their ability to perform the necessary tasks to accomplish goals.[23]

To further elucidate the three types of efficacy discussed above, let us assume an organization is going to implement an initiative that would be consistent with the notion of corporate social responsibility. Individual employees may be asked to partake in certain activities that are consistent with the firm's initiative. An employee's confidence in their ability to perform the required activities would be considered self-efficacy. If, for example, work groups are charged with implementing aspects of the initiative, collective efficacy would be the extent to which the group members believe their group has what it takes to successfully execute the task. A stockholder's belief in the CEO's ability to act on their behalf to ensure stockholder returns like increasing dividends or higher share prices would be an example of proxy efficacy. Each stakeholder group develops proxy efficacy beliefs based on its needs and definition of corporate social responsibility.

In terms of their determinants, self, proxy and collective efficacy share the same four sources.[24] In descending order of importance, these sources are mastery experiences, vicarious experiences, social persuasion and affective/physiological states. These sources of efficacy correspond to the different types of narratives and stories that organizations and stakeholders present to the world. The effects of efficacy beliefs on outcome expectations (regarding motivation, perseverance, effort and performance) can be seen in antenarratives. It is from these stories, narratives and antenarratives that researchers can evaluate firms and stakeholder efficacy beliefs.

Narrative and Efficacy

Most of the research regarding efficacy has been conducted through quantities data analysis. To date, research has seldom focused on understanding or assessing the sources of efficacy beliefs (mastery and vicarious experiences, social persuasion, psychological and physiological states). We assume this is because of the difficulty of measuring these sources empirically. Narratives and stories can convey much information about the experiences, expectation and states of individuals, groups and organizations. By analyzing narrative statements, researchers can examine the different sources of efficacy that are most meaningful to the subject as well as insight into the strength of each of these beliefs. In addition to assessing CSR-related efficacy beliefs, by analyzing the corporate narratives, stories and antenarratives researchers can attempt to determine which CSR areas and stakeholders are considered to be important or thought to have significant influence on the corporation. Table 3.1 summarizes narratives, stories and antenarratives and how these concepts can be integrated with efficacy.

Mastery experiences occur when an individual or group successfully completes a task. Retrospection of these experiences is the most important determinant of efficacy because it provides real-world knowledge that an individual or group has what is necessary to be successful. Contrarily, experiencing failure is the most effective means by which efficacy can be thwarted. These mastery experiences are communicated to others or oneself through narratives. Similarly, vicarious experiences are another source of efficacy with the main difference being success or failure observed in another individual, team, or organization rather than directly experienced. When models are successful, efficacy is enhanced, but when models fail, efficacy is undermined. Narratives are well suited for sharing vicarious experiences, as one can easily communicate to others the events and outcomes that one has experienced.

Social persuasion occurs when an individual's living stories spread and affect the efficacy beliefs of others. Efficacy is enhanced or weakened to the extent that others let someone know they believe he or she has what it takes to be successful via such processes as constructive or disparaging criticism. The last source of efficacy revolves around physiological and psychological states. When such states are interpreted positively during an activity, efficacy is likely enhanced. Contrarily, when such states are interpreted negatively, efficacy is likely thwarted. Because physical and psychological states can easily change, and may be different from one time to another, living stories that capture what is going on in the immediate present best reflect the thoughts and feelings inspired by these states.

Table 3.1   Relationship of narrative and storytelling with efficacy

Perspective	Description	Domain of time/sense-making	Relationship to efficacy
Narrative	A form of meaning-making that captures actions and events as related parts of a whole creating a concrete past from a myriad of experiences. Narratives have a clear beginning, middle, and end to the tale	Narratives are backward-looking, and use retrospective sense-making	Mastery experiences Vicarious experiences Social persuasion; may make references to mastery experience narratives
Living story	A way to process and understand the events going on at the moment, which may not allow for much time for in-depth sense-making	Captures events that are going on now, which might not have finished their course. Sense-making is in flux, as the outcome of events or actions have yet to happen and be evaluated	Physical and psychological states Social persuasion
Antenarrative	Antenarrative has a double meaning: "before" narrative finality sets in, and "bet" that a transformation, a shaping of the future, will take place	Antenarratives use prospective sense-making in an attempt to see the future	Motivation Perseverance Performance

Efficacy Through Blogging

Blogs serve as an avenue for people with similar interests, goals and concerns to come together. Individuals can share their living stories and vicarious experience narratives in a supportive community. When considering blogs and their potential to impact efficacy beliefs, vicarious experiences and social persuasion narratives are paramount. It is through blogs that employees will learn of their distant colleagues' successes and failures. When someone posts a blog in relation to accomplishing a goal, like the prevention of Walmart from entering a community, readers will likely experience a boost in efficacy as a result of the vicarious experience. Similarly, when a blogger reports on a failed attempt, readers will likely experience decreased efficacy. Because blogging is a form of storytelling discourse, readers can respond to postings in order to alleviate blows, or enhance gains, to a poster's efficacy through social persuasion. Here is a good example taken from an anti-

Walmart blog. This blogger picks up the story from other bloggers, capturing their post in a vicarious experience narrative.

> *A Houston blogger, ironically printed in the Chicago Sun-Times, pointed out that the superstore doesn't fit in with the area known in Houston as "Super Neighborhood 22." "It doesn't seem to fit in with their vision for the Washington corridor." Another blogger in Houston on Culture Maps warned Walmart that they are walking into a fight. "Well listen here, Walmart", wrote blogger Caroline Gallay, "you should heed the advice of Vizzini in The Princess Bride: 'Never fight a land war in Asia.' It would be a classic blunder. I know I'm not alone in my disdain for a company with a history of treating its workers horrendously, a cloying smiley-face mascot and products that aren't often anything to be proud of. Next to BP, Walmart may be the most hated company in America."*

> *Gallay says she's lived in the Heights her entire life—except for a sabbatical for college—"and in a neighborhood that values its independent coffee joints, unique boutiques and restaurants; fights hard for preservation; and has residents that sport bumper stickers like 'Friends don't let friends go to Starbucks,' I can tell you that Walmart's corporate icon isn't going to get a friendly welcome."*

> *"I'd bet money that no one who lives [in the Heights] will make themselves a patron. Even if convenience did persuade us to abandon our principles, we've got a massive Target just over I-10 on Shearn Street, and my family has always driven to the Costco on Richmond Avenue for the groceries Target lacks (when we want to buy in bulk). Most days we just head over to Houston's largest Kroger on 11th Street and Shepherd." "The way I see it", Gallay concluded, "Walmart's not offering a community that wouldn't be caught dead there anything they don't already have."[25]*

This post is a prime example of how blogs can impact efficacy beliefs by allowing them to be shared, and how it influences the readers of those blogs. By quoting this other blogger, it shows that her efficacy beliefs have been influenced by the poster. Further, it illuminates the feelings of communities nationwide towards Walmart stores and the company in general.

Limitations of Efficacy Narratives

Given the vast amount of blogs and blog postings, it is likely that one can find positive and negative postings in relation to any topic. This is in addition to the fact that organizations typically post their own version of the company's story. Indeed, companies frequently post sanitized or biased stories as a means to lessen or temper negative stories reported in the press and/or posted online and in blogs. However, it is doubtful that an organization will be successful at impacting the efficacy beliefs of its employees by publishing its own story. This is due to the mechanism through which vicarious experiences and social persuasion work. Specifically, these sources of efficacy function through a process known as modeling. Modeling is said to occur when one is impacted by "behavioral examples provided by influential models".[26]

The key to effective modeling is that the model is typically, in Bandura's words, influential. A model is considered influential when they are similar to the individual being influenced. The more similar the model is to the observer, the more impactful they will be. "The people with whom a person regularly associates delimit the types of behavior that he will repeatedly observe and hence learn most thoroughly."[27] As mentioned previously, blog postings can influence readers' efficacy beliefs. However, that a model needs to be similar to the observer in order to truly be influential has implications for just whose postings will have an impact. When information comes from people, like bloggers, which are thought of as being "just like me", there is a high probability that their postings will influence reader's efficacy beliefs. However, when content is posted by an individual (or organization) with which readers do not identify, the content is not likely to impact readers' efficacy beliefs.

So while the blogs are a forum for a variety of stakeholders, the impact of what is posted there may not affect everyone who reads the content. For instance, when reading anti-Walmart blogs, it is likely that anti-Walmart activists including unionizers, employees, suppliers and communities will see the greatest changes in efficacy, while the blogs will have little sway over stockholders' efficacy beliefs. Consumers fall into an ambiguous middle ground, as the company's "sanitized" narratives are pegged against the bloggers' counterstories, creating an internal struggle to define and redefine their beliefs.

The Internet as a Medium for Discourse

CONFLICTING BELIEFS YIELD CONFLICTING STORIES

Corporations present their desired face to the world through stories and narratives, and those actors that engage with the corporation on a frequent basis face events that the actors must reconcile by referring to the organization's stories. These stories help categorize the experience into the correct category, thereby enacting the thing that has been "described".[28] However, to those stakeholders that have a deeper relationship with an organization, one often sees or hears about activities that are true and a complete opposite to what the corporation has said. These "out-of-character" experiences, when shared with others, become counterstories, as they go against the predominant story regime.

As a result, the stakeholders must decide which stories and narratives to attend to, and thus incorporate into their efficacy beliefs. Based upon the efficacy modeling theory above, it is likely that the stories told by the organization are only effective to those that have a close relationship with the company, like stockholders. For stakeholders like employees, unions, suppliers, or activists, it is likely that the counterstories coming from other stakeholders will have a greater influence.

In the past it was easy for a corporation to bury the counterstory of an outraged and grieved stakeholder, as only major events like the 2010 BP oil platform spill make the national news. However, the internet has made it impossible to truly ignore the demands and counterstories of stakeholders. Blogs and Web sites have become tools for stakeholders to make their voices heard not only by the company but by the rest of the world. Blogs serve as an avenue for counterstory to be shared, and for stakeholders to come together in order to achieve their goals.

Walmart is one firm where stakeholders and corporate management often have different stories and efficacy beliefs. To illustrate the differences in the narratives and stories between a firm and its stakeholders, we have taken posts from two different blogs. For instance one blog reported:

> "Protecting our environment is simply the right thing to do," Wal-Mart vice president Mike Duke said in announcing the Acres for America deal. Under the deal, dubbed "Acres for America," Wal-Mart will donate this money—doled out over the next 10 years—to the National Fish and Wildlife Foundation, an outfit created by Congress that counts among its "partners" ExxonMobil and Alcoa. NFWF will use the funds to purchase land or secure conservation easements on wildlife habitat across the country. "Acres for America will permanently conserve at least one acre of priority wildlife habitat for every developed acre of Wal-Mart's current footprint, as well as the company's future development over the next 10 years," NFWF's press release said.

Yet absent in the press releases are the other sides of the stories, specifically, what impact Walmart stores have on the environment is not addressed in the release. So the blogger compiles other factual information that counters the positive story Walmart has put out in the media. She states:

> In Maine, even as Wal-Mart secures easements on northern forest land, it's also cutting down forest and filling wetlands elsewhere in the state. In the town of Scarborough, Wal-Mart plans to abandon one store—leaving a carcass the size of two football fields surrounded by acres of asphalt—and clear-cut a wooded site across the street to build an even bigger supercenter. The "old" Wal-Mart opened in 1993. But even more than the individual examples, it is the totality of Wal-Mart's impact on our environment that must be weighed against its $35 million donation. No other company has done more to make running our daily errands an ecologically hazardous activity. Wal-Mart has destroyed tens of thousands of neighborhood and downtown businesses. Situated in multi-story buildings that did not require acres of parking, these stores took up comparatively little space and provided goods and services a short distance from homes and apartments. Today, even the simplest of errands, like picking up a gallon of milk or a box of nails, often requires driving several miles to a big-box store. Indeed, American households log 50 percent more vehicle miles each year for shopping than we did in 1990.[29]

Stakeholders Coming Together Through Blogs

These blogs also serve as a venue for the different stakeholders to reconcile their different CSR needs and beliefs. Bloggers and readers realize that the overall stakeholder needs are the same: for the corporation to treat those that it interacts with respectfully and to strive for solutions that benefit all parties involved, whether it be employees, customers, suppliers and their employees, or the individuals in the communities it serves. It is imperative for the various stakeholders to reconcile the differences in their needs and to resolve conflicting desires in order to increase their influence and to increase the power of these counterstories to achieve their CSR goals.

The Wake Up Wal-Mart blog transcended cyberspace to help stakeholders with CSR interests in a variety of organizations come together to reconcile their differences at a social summit. Reported on the blog:

> This week Wake Up Walmart participated in the U.S. Social Forum, a movement building event that brought together more than 10,000 diverse people and groups working on issues from immigration to economic justice to food sovereignty. We brought a delegation of Walmart workers, union members, local activists, and local union staff members with us to spread the word about the work we're doing to change Walmart for the better, and create opportunities to work with other organizations.
>
> We discussed Walmart's impact on our jobs, communities, and environment, and our strategies for creating positive change. We had a panel of three Walmart workers who spoke about their experiences working at the giant retailer and why they believe they need to come together and support each other. They spoke of the lack of respect, the lack of adequate wages and benefits, and how Walmart has affected their communities. We also had a speaker from the Retail Action Project, a New York City retail store employee who helped his fellow workers win a union at his chain.[30]

This post shows how one stakeholder recognizes the impact on and the needs of other stakeholders, and calls for a further unification of the different groups. At this event, different stakeholders were able to share their mastery experience narratives, which likely enhanced the efficacy beliefs of those in attendance through the process of vicarious experience. At the same time, attendees likely experience a decrease in their sense of proxy efficacy toward the organizations they are trying to change.

Walmart: A Sample Case Analysis

In order to help illustrate how blogs create a forum for efficacy belief discourse and clarify the concepts we presented in the chapter, we conducted an analysis of the postings of several blogs revolving around Walmart. Walmart is a company of many facets, resulting in a myriad of demands from stakeholders, and is a master at using stories and narratives.[31] Kampf[32] investigated Walmart's CSR policies posted on several Walmart Web sites. At that time, Walmart was focused on environmental initiatives like sustainability and reducing its environmental impact. Additionally, Walmart's Web site focuses on its involvement in communities, providing stories on the different local projects that improved peoples' lives. Walmart has further been described by Beaver[33] as having built the image of a good corporate citizen, through tales of managers at the local level getting involved and providing contributions to charity. It is also noted that in the media Walmart does not fair so well, receiving negative press about unfair wages and aggressive competition. Walmart has chosen to respond to these criticisms by "getting more aggressive in telling its story" in advertising campaigns that focus on CSR successes.[34]

Indeed, when looking at another electronic media source, blogs, one sees a different picture than Walmart's narrative paints. Blog readers are shown a company that is primarily profit-focused, with a variety of stakeholders not having their needs met. Table 3.2 shows the various Walmart human stakeholders and their typical complaints. The reality of Walmart created by dissatisfied stakeholders is similar to that unearthed by Boje[35] of Walt Disney enterprises. Both firms seem to strive to hide the counterstory and ignore those stakeholders whose CSR definitions are incompatible with corporate goals and strategies, instead focusing on an audience of stockholders and customers spinning tales to warm the heart and loosen the purse strings.

Table 3.2   Some of the concerns held by Walmart stakeholders

Stakeholder	Complaint(s)
Employees	• Lay offs • Discrimination of female and minority employees • Poverty-level wages • Unaffordable and inefficient employee healthcare • Employee sick leave policies • Employee safety • Forcing employees to work through breaks • Not paying overtime when due
Suppliers	• Poor wages for supplier employees • Forcing suppliers to accept Walmart's contract terms
Customers	• Selling unsafe products • Customer safety at stores
Community	• Infringes on the sale of nonprofit organization products and does not share revenues • Desecration of national landmarks • Drives small business owners out of business • Depresses local communities' economies • Withholding taxes to local governments
Labor unions	• Banning union organization

Strategically, Walmart's focus is on minimizing costs so that it may offer products at lower prices than competitors, creating higher sales and trying to maximize revenues. With this in mind, when looking at the CSR activities that Walmart engages in and the areas from which it abstains, one sees a pattern. In 2010, Walmart has pushed the narrative that it is sustainable, and has been making changes that reduce environmental costs, but when evaluated critically one sees these changes also reduce costs for Walmart. Examples include working with suppliers to use less energy when producing goods, using semi-trucks that are hybrids and reducing the amount of packaging on products—all of which help Walmart spend less for the goods that it sells, which meets the needs of two particular stakeholders—customers and stockholders.[36]

Stakeholder issues that are not being met, like low wages for employees, are in direct conflict with the business plan. To increase employee wages means that costs will go up, and thus prices will have to rise, putting the image of Walmart as a "low price leader" in jeopardy. So for Walmart, its CSR activities are not driven by external demands but from the organization strategies and values which are embedded in the stories it tells. For stakeholders whose definitions of CSR are similar to Walmart's definition of CSR, these CSR activities will help maintain or increase the stakeholders proxy efficacy in the company to act socially responsible.

But now let us look into the other stakeholder narratives and counterstory webs told on some of the blogs. In September 2010, one blogger posted the following:

> If CEOs like Costco's Sinegal can work with their employees to find a better way, why wouldn't Walmart? Treating employees well doesn't seem to hurt Costco's stock price, a major concern at Walmart. And it hasn't hurt their reputation in the urban markets that Walmart wants to enter. Because no matter how much greenwashing Walmart does or how good their new logo makes television audiences feel, someone, like Justmeans, is always there to remind the public that they treat their employees poorly. That isn't how good business is done.[37]

This entry calls Walmart on its practices and the assumptions to which the company subscribes and utilizes when forming its strategic plan. It also provides evidence that other organizations can be successful at balancing conflicting stakeholder needs, as Costco, another big-box mass merchandiser, can pay its employees a fair living wage and still be profitable. Further, by appeasing one stakeholder group, Costco generates goodwill and possibly greater proxy efficacy in other stakeholders. Walmart's limited CSR behaviors, on the other hand, have made it so that stakeholders (with definitions of what is socially responsible that differs from Walmart's definition) in many communities across the United States are against the entrance of Walmart stores.

Implications for Theory and Practice

Various stakeholders can now come together to evaluate narratives, stories and antenarratives of a firm and share their efficacy beliefs with other stakeholders through the use of internet blogs. In addition, stakeholders on blogs can share their stories and experiences, which may counter the image and narratives put forth by the organization, to influence others efficacy beliefs. While currently underpublicized, these stakeholder blogs are slowly finding their way into the mainstream just as social networking sites have done in the last 10 years.

Executives must be mindful of the greater unification of stakeholders and may be forced to reprioritize which stakeholder concerns they attend to. By uniting on these blogs, stakeholders around the world gain knowledge, support and most importantly power for achieving their CSR objectives. As a result, most organizations cannot afford to ignore their stakeholders and instead may find it beneficial to come together in order to reach an acceptable compromise. It is advisable that firms monitor these blogs, because they can see how effective the stories and narratives it tells are, learn of what stakeholders are or are not satisfied, and how or why they feel their needs are not being met. It is not recommended that the firm hire a blogger to post the company's stories on these or other blogs as the individual will have no credibility and will not be effective. However, it may be possible for the firm to use the blogs as a forum for discourse with its stakeholders, as long as it is willing to listen to others' points of view and sincerely discuss the differences.

In this chapter we have provided a unique approach for evaluating how stakeholders share and develop their efficacy beliefs—evaluating the vicarious and social persuasion narratives and living stories posted on internet blogs. By analyzing these stories, one can see how organizations and stakeholders try to create legitimacy in order to affect individuals' efficacy beliefs and obtain greater positions of power and influence. The expectation is that by obtaining greater power and influence, these stakeholders can foster greater CSR among their organizations.

Notes

1   Boje, D.M. (2001), *Narrative Methods for Organizational and Communication Research*, Sage, London: Boje, D.M. (2008), *Storytelling Organizations*, Sage, London.
2   Sethi, S.P. (1975), "Dimensions of corporate social performance: an analytical framework", *California Management Review*, vol. 17, no. 3, pp. 58–64; Smith, N.C. (2003), "Corporate cocial responsibility: whether or how?", *California Management Review*, vol. 45, no. 4, pp. 52–76.
3   Barry, D. and Elmes, M. (1997), "Strategy retold: toward a narrative view of strategic discourse", *Academy of Management Review*, vol. 22, no. 2, pp. 429–452.
4   Boje, D.M. (1991), "The storytelling organization: A study of story performance in an office-supply firm", *Administrative Science Quarterly*, vol. 36, no. 1, pp. 106–126.
5   Gabriel, Y. (2000), *Storytelling in Organizations: Facts, Fictions, Fantasies*, Oxford University, Press, Oxford, England.
6   Gardner, H. (1995), *Leading Minds: An Anatomy of Leadership*, Basic Books, New York, p. 14.
7   Martens, M.L., Jennings, J.E. and Jennings, P.D. (2007), "Do the stories they tell get them the money they need? The role of entrepreneurial narratives in resource acquisition", *Academy of Management Journal*, vol. 50, no. 5, pp. 1107–1132.
8   Gergen, K.J. (1994), *Realities and Relationships: Soundings in Social Construction*, Harvard University Press, Cambridge, MA; McAdams, D.P. (1999), "Personal narratives and the life story". In L. Pervin and O. John (eds), *Handbook of Personality: Theory and Research*, 2nd ed., Guilford Press, New York, NY, pp. 478–500.
9   Ashforth, B.E. (2001), *Role Transitions in Organizational Life: An Identity-Based Perspective*, Lawrence Erlbaum Associates, Mahwah, NJ; Van Maanen, J. (1998), "Identity work: notes on the personal identity of police officers", paper presented at the annual meeting of the Academy of Management, San Diego, CA.
10   Barry and Elmes, op. cit
11   TwoTrees, K. (1997), *Seven Directions*, presentation at the International Academy of Business Disciplines Conference at Case Western Reserve, Cleveland, Ohio.
12   Polkinghorne, D. (1988), *Narrative Knowing and the Human Sciences*, State University of New York Press, Albany, NY.
13   Weick, K.E. (1995), *Sensemaking in Organizations*, Sage, Thousand Oaks, CA.
14   de Certeau, M. (1984), *The Practice of Everyday Life*, trans. by Rendall, S., University of California Press, Berkeley, CA.
15   McCloskey, D.N. (1990), *If You're so Smart: The Narrative of Economic Expertise*, The University of Chicago Press, Chicago, IL.
16   Boje (2001, 2008), op. cit.
17   Boje (2008), op. cit.
18   Basu, K. and Palazzo, G. (2008), "Corporate social responsibility: a process model of sensemaking", *The Academy of Management Review*, vol. 33, no. 1, pp. 122–136.
19   Gabriel (2000), op. cit.
20   Schwarzer, R. (1992), *Self-efficacy: Thought Control of Action*, Taylor and Francis, Abingdon, UK.

21   Bandura, A. (1997), *Self-efficacy: The Exercise of Control*, Freeman, New York, NY, p. 3.

22   Bandura (1997), op. cit; Elias, S.M. and MacDonald, S. (2007), "Using past performance, proxy efficacy, and academic self-efficacy to predict college performance", *Journal of Applied Social Psychology*, vol. 37, no. 11, pp. 2518–2531.

23   Bandura (1997), op. cit.

24   Bandura (1997), op. cit.

25   http://blog.wakeupwalmart.com/ufcw/2010/07/.

26   Bandura, A. (1973), *Aggression: A Social Learning Analysis*, Prentice-Hall, Englewood Cliffs, NJ.

27   Bandura (1973), p. 69, op. cit.

28   Tsoukas, H. (1994), *Beyond Social Engineering and Contextualism: The Narrative Structure of Organizational Knowledge*, Warwick Business School Research Bureau Paper, p. 69.

29   http://www.reclaimdemocracy.org/walmart/acres_america_greenwashing.php.

30   http://blog.wakeupwalmart.com/ufcw/2010/06/.

31   Boje, D.M. and Rosile, G.A. (2008), "Specters of Wal-Mart: A critical discourse analysis of stories of Sam Walton's ghost", *Critical Discourse Studies Journal*, vol. 5, no. 2, pp. 153–179.

32   Kampf, C. (2007), "Corporate social responsibility: Wal-Mart, Maersk and the cultural bounds of representation in corporate web sites", *Corporate Communications: An International Journal*, vol. 12, no. 1, pp. 41–57.

33   Beaver, W. (2005), "Battling Wal Mart: how communities can respond", *Business and Society Review*, vol. 110, no. 2, pp. 159–169.

34   Ethical Corporation (2005), "Watching Wal–Mart", pp. 16–17.

35   Boje, D.M. (1995), "Stories of the storytelling organization: a postmodern analysis of Disney as 'Tamara-Land'", *Academy of Management Journal*, vol. 38, no. 4, pp. 997–1035.

36   http://walmartstores.com/Sustainability/; Http://treehugger.com.

37   http://blog.wakeupwalmart.com/ufcw/2010/09.

4 *Brent Spar Revisited: Conflict and Cooperation from a Stakeholder Perspective*

MATTHIAS S. FIFKA*

Keywords

Brent Spar, Greenpeace, Shell, stakeholder alliance, stakeholder dialog, stakeholder mobilization.

Introduction

Without question, the occurrences around Brent Spar can be considered a landmark date with regard to business–society relations. It made evident the tremendous power that multinational corporations had increasingly acquired after the end of the cold war, paired with the decline of the nation state, but also reflected the formerly unknown possibilities of nongovernmental organizations to influence public and political opinion. Due to the scope and implications of the event, it is not surprising that the case of Brent Spar has attracted scholars from very different fields, such as business administration,[1] communications,[2] politics,[3] ecology[4] or business ethics.[5] They have consequently paid specific attention to the stakeholders relevant for their area of research, while the interplay between them has received less consideration.

Therefore this chapter aims at analyzing the occurrences around Brent Spar not only from the perspective of Shell, but also from the perspective of the important stakeholders involved: governments, consumers, the media and especially Greenpeace. Their interests and actions with regard to each other will be examined, as well as their different perceptions of what constitutes environmental responsibility. Specific attention will be given to the strategies that Shell and Greenpeace, as the two main antagonists, pursued during the conflict and how they interacted with the other stakeholders. Based on that, the chapter seeks to demonstrate that stakeholder relations are neither stable nor of an isolated bilateral nature between a company and the respective stakeholder, but

*   Matthias S. Fifka, Dr. Jürgen Meyer Endowed Chair for International Business Ethics and Sustainability, Cologne Business School, Hardefuststrasse 1, 50677 Cologne, Germany. E-mail: m.fifka@cbs-edu.de.

dynamic and network-like. The resulting implications for businesses will be discussed in the conclusion.

In the structure of the chapter a chronological approach is taken, because it helps to demonstrate the dynamic nature of stakeholder relations and how they multiplied during the course of events. Moreover, such an approach renders an additional historic account of events unnecessary and leaves more room for analysis.

The Stages of the Brent Spar Case

THE PREPARATIONS: DECOMMISSIONING THE BRENT SPAR

The Brent Spar was a loading and storage buoy located in the Brent oilfield, approximately 200 kilometers northeast of the Shetland Islands. It was jointly owned by Shell and Esso through a 50–50 joint venture called Shell Expro (Exploration and Production), but exclusively operated and managed by Shell UK since it had been put into service in 1976. Being one of the largest constructions of this kind, the Brent Spar was 147 m high and had a diameter of 29 m, weighing 14,500 tons with a storage capacity of 300,000 barrels of crude oil. Vividly speaking, its weight equaled that of 2,000 double-decker buses, while its capacity was equivalent to that of four Big Bens.[6]

In September 1991, Brent Spar was taken out of commission, and Shell began to consider several options for disposal (Figure 4.1), for which extensive research was conducted. These preparations were necessary to present a sound disposal plan to the British Government's Department of Trade and Industry (DTI) that was in charge of issuing the respective license. Two of six options, the large size of the buoy posing the central problem for all of them, were given closer consideration by Shell. The first possibility consisted of onshore dismantling, the cost of which was estimated at approximately £41m. Deepwater disposal formed the second option and, at £12m, was significantly cheaper.[7] Aside from cost considerations, the environmental risk was estimated to be substantially higher in the case of onshore dismantling as the fragile buoy might break up when towed horizontally into shallow coastal waters and taken out of it, where environmental damage would have been exponentially greater. Deepwater disposal, however, was not judged to be connected to severe problems as the buoy could be towed vertically and would neither have to be flipped horizontally nor lifted out of the water. While it was clear that the buoy would remain intact on the seabed for roughly 4,000 years, only little and gradual leakage was expected. That was confirmed by several studies,[8] among which an extensive one was conducted by the University of Aberdeen that also recommended deep sea disposal.[9]

After having internally decided on deep sea disposal, Shell contracted Fisheries Research Services, a Scottish governmental institution, to examine possible sites for disposal. These sites had to fulfill mainly three prerequisites: provide no hazard to shipping, have minimal environmental impact, especially with regard to fish populations, and be located in British waters. Having conducted the relevant studies, Fisheries Research Services eventually proposed the North Feni Ridge, which is located about 220 kilometers west of the northern tip of Scotland, and offered a depth of more than 2,000 meters, as a disposal site.[10]

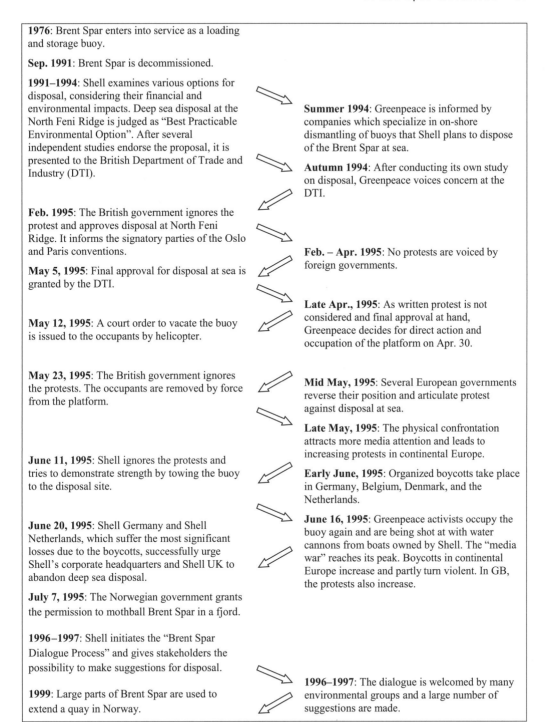

1976: Brent Spar enters into service as a loading and storage buoy.

Sep. 1991: Brent Spar is decommissioned.

1991–1994: Shell examines various options for disposal, considering their financial and environmental impacts. Deep sea disposal at the North Feni Ridge is judged as "Best Practicable Environmental Option". After several independent studies endorse the proposal, it is presented to the British Department of Trade and Industry (DTI).

Summer 1994: Greenpeace is informed by companies which specialize in on-shore dismantling of buoys that Shell plans to dispose of the Brent Spar at sea.

Autumn 1994: After conducting its own study on disposal, Greenpeace voices concern at the DTI.

Feb. 1995: The British government ignores the protest and approves disposal at North Feni Ridge. It informs the signatory parties of the Oslo and Paris conventions.

May 5, 1995: Final approval for disposal at sea is granted by the DTI.

Feb. – Apr. 1995: No protests are voiced by foreign governments.

Late Apr., 1995: As written protest is not considered and final approval at hand, Greenpeace decides for direct action and occupation of the platform on Apr. 30.

May 12, 1995: A court order to vacate the buoy is issued to the occupants by helicopter.

May 23, 1995: The British government ignores the protests. The occupants are removed by force from the platform.

Mid May, 1995: Several European governments reverse their position and articulate protest against disposal at sea.

Late May, 1995: The physical confrontation attracts more media attention and leads to increasing protests in continental Europe.

June 11, 1995: Shell ignores the protests and tries to demonstrate strength by towing the buoy to the disposal site.

Early June, 1995: Organized boycotts take place in Germany, Belgium, Denmark, and the Netherlands.

June 20, 1995: Shell Germany and Shell Netherlands, which suffer the most significant losses due to the boycotts, successfully urge Shell's corporate headquarters and Shell UK to abandon deep sea disposal.

June 16, 1995: Greenpeace activists occupy the buoy again and are being shot at with water cannons from boats owned by Shell. The "media war" reaches its peak. Boycotts in continental Europe increase and partly turn violent. In GB, the protests also increase.

July 7, 1995: The Norwegian government grants the permission to mothball Brent Spar in a fjord.

1996–1997: Shell initiates the "Brent Spar Dialogue Process" and gives stakeholders the possibility to make suggestions for disposal.

1999: Large parts of Brent Spar are used to extend a quay in Norway.

1996–1997: The dialogue is welcomed by many environmental groups and a large number of suggestions are made.

Figure 4.1   Overview of the most important events and actions of the parties involved

These prerequisites are interesting to look at with regard to stakeholders. Although there had not been any significant interaction with stakeholders at that stage, it can be seen that Shell did consider external interests. That consideration, however, had a purely legal basis as it only extended to the government itself and two groups that UK law identified as sea users: the shipping industry and the fishing industry. Especially the focus on British waters demonstrates that Shell was not interested in the involvement of other governmental stakeholders, though Irish waters, for example, would also have been a likely option for disposal. Thus, it must be assumed that Shell was confident of receiving the respective license from the DTI, when it submitted its proposal for the "Best Practicable Environmental Option" (BPEO) consisting of disposal in the North Feni Ridge.

The "Bipolar Phase": Shell and the British Government

This confidence resulted mainly from three considerations. First, Shell had previously worked with the DTI without any problems. Secondly, it was aware that the ministry also was interested in a less costly solution as high disposal costs would have significantly reduced Shell's tax burden.[11] This consideration on the government's side is reflected in a comment that Timothy Eggar, Minister for Energy and Industry, made in early 1995: "The abandonment of offshore installations and pipelines represents a large and costly exercise both for the operator and the Exchequer."[12] Here again, Shell calculated precisely with the interests of what it considered the most relevant stakeholder. Thirdly, neither Shell nor the DTI had any interest in expanding the set of stakeholders actively involved, seeking to avoid potential conflict and to remain exclusively in control of the bilateral negotiation process. Such negotiations between a corporation and the bureaucracy in a very specific policy field usually take place behind closed doors and receive little public attention, if any. As Jordan and Maloney have correctly observed, this interaction is characterized by "substantial agreement on problem definition, low public profile (visibility) of decisions … a small number of participants, and restricted access for dissenting perspectives".[13]

Due to this rather secluded policy process and the congruence of interests, the British government's announcement of February 15, 1995 approving the disposal suggested by Shell in the BPEO was an expected outcome. In accordance with existing treaties, the British government then informed the signatory parties—15 states and the European Community—of the Oslo and Paris conventions, which aimed at controlling the disposal of harmful substances into the northeast Atlantic and were officially replaced by the "Convention for the Protection of the Marine Environment of the North-East Atlantic" (OSPAR) in 1998.[14] Since within the following 60 days no objections were raised by the foreign governments, who only had little stakeholder interest in the proceedings at that point, the British government gave its final approval on May 5, 1995.[15]

However, this latter stage of the process did not take place behind closed doors: the British government had made its announcements publicly. Shell also had material in store in case of possible press requests, but there was no interest because, as Shell itself observed, "the media decided the story was boring".[16] This state of disinterest, which Shell and the government did not mind, was existent until Greenpeace entered the stage on a larger scale.

Enter Greenpeace: The Expansion of Stakeholder Interests

Greenpeace, founded in Vancouver in 1971, had long been fighting the disposal of industrial and nuclear waste at sea. It became aware of the planned deep sea disposal of the Brent Spar as early as summer 1994. Interestingly, the relevant information was provided by companies which dismantled used platforms and buoys on shore and thus were not happy with disposal at sea.[17] Here, a first weak form of cooperation between stakeholders becomes visible, as the dismantling industry saw Greenpeace as a welcome mechanism to transmit its interests.

Greenpeace itself feared that Brent Spar might become a dangerous precedent, as more than 50[18]—Greenpeace even spoke of 400[19]—other platforms were to be decommissioned in the years to come. They published a lengthy scientific report on deep sea disposal, which was produced by marine biologist Simon Reddy. Its title, *No Grounds for Dumping*, appropriately reflects the organization's position on the issue.[20] The report, however, did not specifically address the Brent Spar case, but oil and gas platforms in general, and was submitted to the DTI in December 1994, when the license for Shell was under consideration. Greenpeace's fear that Brent Spar could set a precedent was fully justified, as correspondence between the DTI and Shell shows. In a letter of January 1994, the DTI urged Shell to carefully examine the effects of toxic pollutants set free due to a disposal at sea, because this would be "an issue which is likely to feature in the abandonment of other offshore installations in the future".[21] Moreover, Greenpeace doubted that deepwater disposal was the best practicable environmental option and argued that financial rather than environmental considerations had been the primary guideline in its development.

Despite voicing concern, Greenpeace was not invited to participate in the talks between the DTI and Shell in early 1995, and one could actually speak of intentional "stakeholder exclusion". Neither of the two saw any advantage in cooperation with Greenpeace or considered the organization as an actor with a justified claim or the potential to threaten what had been a smooth and legally sound decision-making process until that point of time.

In reaction, Greenpeace decided that further formal protest would remain ineffective and that other measures would have to be taken. In a meeting between the British, Dutch and German branches of the organization—here it becomes apparent that Greenpeace had no intention of making this a purely British affair, as Shell had hoped it would be—it was agreed to resort to a technique that Greenpeace had applied successfully in the past: direct action on site. On April 30, the Greenpeace ship *Moby Dick* and some smaller vessels set out to the buoy, and twelve activists from the three countries just mentioned climbed the Brent Spar to protest against its planned disposal at sea.[22]

The action remained largely unnoticed at first, and neither Shell nor the British government—perhaps not even Greenpeace itself—assumed at this point that it would create a big impact. Although journalists were already present, media coverage was still limited.[23] However, as indicated above, on May 5 the British government went ahead and officially granted the license for deepwater disposal of the Brent Spar, and a dynamic process of "stakeholder multiplication" set in, which led to what Barbone has called "The Battle for the Brent Spar".[24]

The "Multipolar Phase": The Multiplication of Stakeholder Interests

As in any "battle", coalitions were now being formed. The "old" alliance on one side consisted of the two actors who had first been involved, Shell and the British government. The central coalition on the opposing site was formed by Greenpeace and the media—two actors that were fully dependent on each other. In contrast to Shell and the British government, who were sure to prevail on a scientific and legal basis, Greenpeace pursued a two-track strategy. One track consisted of challenging Shell based on scientific evidence. For this purpose, the team of protestors that occupied the buoy collected samples to calculate the amount of oil left in the tanks in order to demonstrate the environmental irresponsibility of deepwater disposal. However, Greenpeace was not sure it held the best cards for a scientific-based confrontation—with good reason, as became evident some weeks later. The amount of 5,500 tons of oil which could still be in the tanks, according to Greenpeace,[25] was greatly overstated. An audit by the independent Norwegian consultancy Det Norske Veritas later showed that only 150 tons had been left within the buoy.[26] Whether Greenpeace had simply miscalculated the amount or intentionally inflated it remains unknown, but it can be said that the organization was—in contrast to Shell and the British government—well aware that the battle might very likely not be won on scientific or legal arguments, but on emotions and the simple conviction that waste should not be thrown into the sea. To emphasize this notion, Greenpeace literally turned "disposal" into "dumping".

Therefore, Greenpeace's second strategy track consisted of garnering public attention and generating public and, consequentially, maybe even political protests. For what other reason would Greenpeace have occupied the buoy and brought along journalists and a satellite broadcasting unit?[27] It needed the media to distribute the pictures of the organization's effort on and for the high seas. For the media in turn the story was as good as it can be. It was a battle of a selfless David fighting for the righteous cause against an evil Goliath in the form of a MNC which did not seem to care about the natural environment and only strove for more profit. The effects of this image cannot be overestimated because they led to feelings of sympathy and support for Greenpeace which obviously needed the backing of other stakeholder groups to prevail against the mighty opponent.

Despite increasing media coverage, which certainly was not favorable for either Shell or the British government, they firmly maintained their stance, arguing on a scientific and legalistic basis. They continuously relied on scientific expertise and studies which had shown that deep sea disposal could be judged as the BPEO. From a legal standpoint, Shell and the British government also felt safe, because the respective rules and regulations had been observed. Shell had obtained all necessary licenses and the British government had notified all parties accordingly without objection being voiced within the required 60-day period.

This legalistic approach is also reflected by the fact that on May 12, a court order which Shell had obtained was delivered to the protesters on the platform by helicopter, demanding its immediate abandonment.[28] In retrospect, this act seems nothing less than grotesque. Why should the protestors, who were aware that their occupation was illegal in the first place, leave the platform now when their action was increasingly drawing attention? However, from their narrow perspective, Shell and the British government, having the law on their side, were confident that the respective legal procedures would put an end to the conflict. Fixed on that technocratic–legalistic dimension, they did not realize that the coalition which was forming against them was unified by a totally different dimension—one that was moralistic in nature and largely ignored law-based and scientific arguments. Chris Fay, general manager of Shell UK, later conveyed that mistake:

> We've perhaps done things too properly. We've covered all the scientific angles, we've covered all the technical angles, we've certainly very much covered all the legalistic angles, and maybe you could say, well, that was maybe a bit inward thinking, we hadn't taken into account hearts and emotions, you know, where people are coming from, which is in part today's debate.[29]

It is interesting to note that in this emotionally loaded atmosphere Greenpeace's legitimacy—legitimacy here being understood as a legal and political construct—to act as advocate of the environment or a presumed public interest was never posed. The organization had certainly never been given any public mandate, and its actions were based solely upon the decision of a small number of activists from the upper echelons of its hierarchy. While the question on the legitimacy of NGOs has been discussed extensively in the academic literature,[30] it only plays a minor role, if any at all, in public perception. NGOs usually claim a moral justification for their actions in order to compensate for a lack of a legal or political mandate.

Thus, Greenpeace forged the opposing coalition by emphasizing the simple conviction that "good 'citizens' did not casually throw unwanted goods away",[31] which strongly appealed to other stakeholders, especially the media and the public. While this coalition was not built to last, and it indeed dissolved rapidly after the conflict with Shell, it was effectively based on "emotional momentum" and focused on a concise issue, namely the disposal of industrial waste into the sea. With increasing media coverage public protests grew in intensity, which in turn led governments, who usually are very sensitive to voters' sentiments, to reconsider their position. While they had previously voiced their agreement with deepwater disposal or at least not voiced any disagreement, they now undertook a "realignment", which eventually left the British government largely isolated.

On May 9, the German government was the first to reverse its original position. Environmental Minister Angela Merkel from the conservative Christian Democratic Union now issued a formal protest against the planned deepwater disposal, although the German government had not articulated any objections only three months earlier when it had been notified accordingly by its British counterpart. In turn, the British government ignored Germany's protest because it came after the 60-day period called for by the Oslo–Paris Convention. It must be assumed that the German government reversed its position because it increasingly realized that disposing the Brent Spar at sea was not perceived as acceptable by the German public, as protests gradually became louder after May 5. Moreover, environmental protection was on the rise in Germany as well as in other European countries in the mid-90s, and governmental initiatives were numerous. Thus, demanding environmentally sound behavior from the citizens, but at the same time agreeing to the disposal of industrial facilities at sea, would have undermined the government's credibility, as Vidal correctly observed: "How can you tell 90 million Germans religiously to sort their rubbish and not expect them to cry foul when they see a global company fly-tipping its rubbish into the sea?"[32]

In the following days, other governmental actors also entered the arena as now active stakeholders condemned the disposal. On May 14, EU Environmental Commissioner Ritt Bjerregard voiced her opposition, and by May 17, the governments of Denmark, Iceland, Belgium and the Netherlands had also undertaken a realignment of their position and followed Germany's example. Finally, on May 18, the European Parliament adopted a resolution against the disposal.[33] Interestingly, it was mostly the British government as central stakeholder in favor of the disposal that took the heat from the other stakeholders at that stage, and not so much Shell itself. Critique also gradually increased on a domestic level. On May 16, the opposition parties in the British House of Commons realized their chance for an attack on the government and condemned the disposal.[34]

The British government and Shell, however, did not give in to the international and national protests and steered their course with a profound degree of short-sightedness, as the events to come were to show. On May 23, fifteen Shell employees and six police officers entered the buoy and removed the protestors by force. In retrospect, it is hard to understand how Shell and the British government could not have foreseen that this was exactly what Greenpeace and especially the media had wanted them to do. Now there were pictures of David being removed by a bullying Goliath by force, and their effects did not take long to show. Already on May 24, the youth organization of Germany's Christian Democratic Party, which usually takes rather business-friendly positions, called for a boycott of Shell gas stations. Greenpeace itself advocated a continental boycott of Shell, but focused its efforts on Germany, because of the country's economic weight and the widespread protests there, which seemed to provide a good basis for further action.

A few days later, Greenpeace commissioned a study conducted by EMNID, a large polling institute, on the willingness of German citizens to participate in a boycott against Shell. This was a remarkable step that reflects how carefully Greenpeace considered the interests of other stakeholders when planning its own strategy. As the study showed that 74 percent of Germans would be willing to participate in a boycott,[35] only one day later, on June 2, Greenpeace initiated direct action in the form of protests and issued leaflets to motorists at 300 Shell gas stations in Germany.[36] Actions of smaller scope were taken especially in the Netherlands, Belgium and Denmark.

Greenpeace had managed very well in setting the climate which would be decisive at the North Sea Ministers Conference on June 8 and 9 in Denmark. Not surprisingly, all countries bordering on the North Sea, with the exception of the UK and Norway,[37] agreed on a recommendation against the disposal of buoys and platforms:

> *The Ministers are aware that an increasing number of offshore installations in the North Sea are approaching the time of their decommissioning. Even if the offshore installations are emptied of noxious and hazardous materials, they might still if dumped or left at sea, pose a threat to the marine environment. Disposal of such installations on land by recycling recyclable materials and by ensuring safe and controlled disposal of unavoidable residues would be in accordance with generally agreed principles of waste management policy.*[38]

Despite the increasing pressure, now also from political stakeholders, Shell and the British government remained determined to dispose of the Brent Spar at sea. On June 11, Shell actually began to tow the buoy to its disposal site, accompanied by Greenpeace ship *Altair*, which also carried a number of journalists.[39] Inevitably, a further expansion of protests and boycotts followed. In Germany, a wide array of different groups—including, for example, labor unions, religious groups, the fishermen's union and other environmental groups—now began to protest against the "dumping", and parallel developments were observable in the Netherlands and Denmark. In addition to individual consumers, public authorities also urged their employees not to buy at Shell any longer, cancelled their contracts with Shell or threatened to do so. Protests also turned violent. Fifty Shell gas stations were damaged, two fire-bombed and one raked with bullets.[40] Eventually, Shell Germany reported a decrease in sales by as much as 50 percent by mid-June.[41]

On June 15, after a G7 summit meeting in Canada and further increasing political pressure on the UK, Prime Minister John Major publicly announced that he would not shift position on the issue and continue to back deepwater disposal of the Brent Spar. It is necessary to analyze why the British government as one of the central stakeholders did not rethink or reverse its stance. Certainly, a withdrawal of the legal permission for Shell would have severely damaged its own governmental authority, as permission had been granted in a regular administrative process and revoking it would have meant that there was no legal security when dealing with the British government. Moreover, it might have been perceived as a weakness which manifested in giving in to the influence of foreign governments and, even worse, to that of an NGO in what was legally, after having notified the relevant governments of disposal without objection, a purely British affair.

So while there was good reason for the British government to hold its position— although a less rigorous and more compromise-oriented behavior would undoubtedly have been helpful—Shell's inflexibility was short-sighted and eventually fatal. It had no reason to assume that Brent Spar would remain solely a British issue as soon as Greenpeace (with the help of the media) began to spread the protest to other European countries, where Shell also had operations. Technically, due to Shell's extensive matrix structure, Shell Germany, Shell Netherlands and Shell Denmark had no influence on what Shell UK was doing with regard to the Brent Spar, but it was naïve to assume that the public or the consumers would differentiate between individual country subsidiaries of Shell, as Zyglidopoulos has correctly observed:

> So, one can argue, that the subsidiaries of Multinational corporations, because they are "tied together" by a single name, and are seen by the public as a single entity, have to deal not only with the stakeholders in the country in which they operate.[42]

In fact, the subsidiaries in Germany, Denmark and the Netherlands felt the impact of Shell UK's actions more than the British subsidiary itself did. Protests in the UK were relatively mild in comparison to continental Europe and started much later, which might be another reason why Shell UK unflinchingly held on to its course, as can be seen in the events that followed.

On June 16, the battle for the Brent Spar reached its peak. Greenpeace activists managed to get onto the buoy once again, this time by helicopter, and Shell shot at the helicopter and the protestors with powerful water cannons—all in front of television cameras. Again, it is diffuclt to see how Shell did not have realized that this was exactly what Greenpeace and the media had wanted. As Mantow showed, June 16 was the day when media coverage around Brent Spar peaked. On German television alone there were 173 reports that day, and during the following days coverage was only marginally less.[43]

In the wake of Shell's violent action against the activists, protests in the UK also increased rapidly. A later sample showed that 61 percent of the respondents supported or at least agreed with Greenpeace, 27 percent claimed to have given money to the organization.[44] On June 20, well-known English actor and pop star Jerome Flynn conveyed in an article titled "We Shell not be moved" what most Brits felt by then: "I am disgusted by Shell. If I dumped my car in the sea, I would be arrested. It is shocking the [British] Government is allowing them to do this."[45]

On the same day, the British government in the person of John Major was defending deepwater disposal in the House of Commons, when at the same time Shell announced that it would not sink the Brent Spar. This was not only an embarrassment for the prime minister, it also showed the lack of coordination between Shell and its only ally among the stakeholders. Firm protests by Shell Germany and Shell Netherlands to Shell's headquarters and Shell UK finally caused the latter to abandon disposal at sea. Although it was internal pressure within the Shell conglomerate that finally led to a reversal by Shell UK, this pressure was only the consequence of extensive cooperation among Shell's stakeholders, an alliance that had been forged by Shell's main rival in the battle for the Brent Spar, Greenpeace.

The Aftermath

On July 7, Shell received permission by the Norwegian government to tow the Brent Spar to Erfjord, where it remained for several years until a decision was made as ro what to do with it. To come to this conclusion, Shell initiated the so-called "Brent Spar Dialogue Process", a process in which stakeholders could make suggestions on how to dispose of, dismantle or reuse the Brent Spar. The dialog itself was moderated by the Environment Council, an independent group which had considerable experience in designing that form of stakeholder engagement. The goal of the process, as described by the Council, was:

> to ensure that before key decisions on the future of Spar were taken, a much broader base of opinion was engaged. In doing so a better mutual understanding of the issues surrounding the solutions were evaluated. The issues surrounding the decommissioning of Spar covered technical risk, safety risk to personnel, environmental impacts to air, land and sea as well as economic considerations.[46]

Thirty to sixty representatives from different stakeholder groups had the opportunity to participate in one of seven sessions which were held in the UK, Germany, Denmark and the Netherlands. They discussed different proposals that had been presented as to what to do with Brent Spar. The representatives reported back to their groups and obtained feedback for future discussions.

Despite the open character of the process, Shell laid down three ground rules which, however, did not meet significant resistance from the stakeholders involved. First, the process was to assist Shell in finding a widely acceptable solution, but would not be binding and the final decision would remain exclusively with Shell. Secondly, the dialog would deal solely with issues concerning the Brent Spar and not the disposal of platforms or buoys in general. Thirdly, the benchmark for any proposal would be the BPEO that had been considered before, namely deep sea disposal in the North Feni Ridge.[47]

Throughout the process, which lasted throughout 1996 and 1997, the list of proposals was eventually reduced to six, which were independently evaluated by Det Norske Veritas for technical, safety and environmental aspects. The proposal that prevailed was one made by Stavanger Port Authority which suggested using most of the construction of the Brent Spar for extending a large quay at Mekjarvik, Norway.[48]

With regard to the regulatory environment, the campaign by Greenpeace also had its desired outcome. As we noted earlier, Greenpeace had always considered the outcome of the conflict around Brent Spar to be highly important because it would set a precedent for the disposal of oil rigs at sea. Almost immediately after Shell had reversed its decision, the regulatory body OSPAR agreed on a moratorium that banned the disposal of oil rigs and related devices at sea. Since it was only a moratorium, a follow-up decision had to be reached. Norway and the UK voiced strong reservations against a general ban of disposal at sea. It might very well be that Shell had intensively lobbied the British government against an outright ban, but proof for that cannot be found. Moreover, Shell was in a very difficult position after the Labour Party had won the general election in May 1997 and in October of that year Michael Meacher, the new UK Environment Minister, announced an end to the dumping of oil rigs at sea. Consequently, the respective OSPAR decision reached in 1998 generally prohibits disposal at sea, but provides for the possibility that companies may propose such disposal in exceptional cases. The OSPAR parties would then have to conduct an assessment of the ecological consequences. As the precautionary principle is strictly applied, however, it is extremely difficult to obtain the respective permission.[49] Thus, as far as it is known to the author, no major platform has been disposed in the North Sea until today.

Conclusions and Implications for Business

"Stakeholder management" is usually a term used in relation to companies. However, in the case of Brent Spar stakeholder management was not conducted by Shell but by its major rival, Greenpeace, who actually succeeded in managing or at least aligning most of Shell's stakeholders for its own goals. To achieve this, Greenpeace carefully considered the interests of the other stakeholders and catered to those needs where possible, for example when providing footage for the media. It also evaluated the positions and opinions of other stakeholders thoroughly and even conducted surveys before it took further action. This ensured that Greenpeace had a high certainty that the formal or informal cooperation which it initiated would turn out to be successful. The cooperation in turn was based on appealing to the common ground of very different stakeholders, on providing information to the media, politicians and consumers and on initiating protests and boycotts. Overall, the organization had an excellent understanding of the dynamics of stakeholder mobilization and the power which could be unfolded by the cooperation of the individual actors.

Shell, on the contrary, had fully underestimated this "coalition-building" among potential stakeholders, especially because its perceived set of stakeholders was extremely narrow. It had relied on its good relations with the British government, which could of course be regarded as the most powerful stakeholder. Shell certainly was aware of Greenpeace, but it did not consider Greenpeace a viable opponent, even after the activists had occupied the buoy. Heinz Rothermund, the general manager of Shell Expro at that time, later admitted that "Shell had not taken Greenpeace seriously. We should have done that from the very first day."[50] This judgment is interesting because in an isolated consideration Greenpeace was no significant threat: its written protests had no effect and neither did the first days of occupation. However, at the latest when media coverage began to make Brent Spar a public event, Shell should have acted and at least taken a position more open to compromise, but it did not.

Another point that is crucial here is that Shell fully relinquished control of the process to Greenpeace, which then was able to determine the agenda. From that point on, the battle of Brent Spar was decided on emotions and beliefs, not on legal and scientific issues where Shell had advantages or at least no disadvantages. This change is best reflected by the fact that the process from then on was described and perceived in the public as "dumping" rather than "disposal". Winning over the consumers who were the decisive group in the end provided no difficulty for the alliance of Greenpeace, continental European governments and the media.

Shell only began to consider the perspectives which the various stakeholders had on disposing the Brent Spar in the dialog process, which was initiated after the debacle. Had such an approach been taken before, the substantial damage to the company's image could have been avoided. In the dialog process, Shell gave the stakeholders the possibility of participating in the decision-making process without relinquishing the final decision to them. This, however, was unproblematic, as having the final say is not what stakeholders usually expect. Shell laid down ground rules which made it clear for both sides what they could expect. Nevertheless, the rules could be changed in an open process to a certain degree if needed. Shell exhibited no such flexibility during the battle for Brent Spar itself. Most importantly, the aim was to find a solution which was satisfactory from the perspective of most stakeholders and thus would gain wide acceptance.

One of the central implications for businesses is that key business decisions cannot only be regarded from the company's perspective, but must also be looked at from the various perspectives of potential stakeholders. Moreover, those stakeholders cannot be considered in isolation from each other. The traditional model of stakeholder management, which can be described as a hub and spoke model that centered on the company's "bilateral relations" to the individual stakeholders, is outdated. Businesses must consider the dynamic relation between the stakeholders themselves and their position towards the company. That position is subject to change, as we saw in the case of most of the governments involved.

Furthermore, stakeholder groups are not homogenous, especially not in an international context. While traditional models of stakeholder management regard governments, the media, consumers, etc. as homogeneous actors, a differentiation within those groups is necessary. Brent Spar is a perfect example of that necessity. While the British government was on Shell's side, most continental European governments were not. The media in Europe also portrayed things differently. The British press, for example, initially did not take much notice of what was going on, whereas the French and German press covered the occurrences almost from the start. The latter clearly portrayed Shell as a villain, just as the Dutch and Danish press did, the French press, however, depicted Greenpeace "as a greedy, war-engaging, militant 'guerrilla' organization".[51] Consequently, the French public was less inclined to actively voice concern, whereas citizens in Germany, Denmark and the Netherlands rapidly became involved in protests and even participated in boycotts.

This observation leads to another implication for businesses which operate on an international level. Even operations or procedures which are technically or legally limited to one country can easily gain an international dimension and involve stakeholders abroad, which in turn can enact significant pressure on multinational businesses.

These implications demonstrate the need for a dynamic and network-oriented stakeholder management instead of the traditional hub and spoke model of static nature. Without doubt such an approach is highly complex and thus less desirable, but it is inevitable for active and effective stakeholder management today.

Notes

1   Fombrun, C.J. and Rindova, V.P. (2002), "The road to transparency: reputation management at Royal Dutch/Shell". In M. Schultz, M.J. Hatch and M.H. Larsen (eds), *The Expressive Organization*, Oxford University Press, Oxford, pp. 77–96; Grolin, J. (1998), "Corporate legitimacy in risk society: the case of Brent Spar", *Business Strategy and the Environment*, vol. 7, no. 4, pp. 213–222.

2   Jensen, H.R. (2003), "Staging political consumption: a discourse analysis of the Brent Spar conflict as recast by the Danish mass media", *Journal of Retailing and Consumer Services*, vol. 10, pp. 71–80; Löfstedt, R. and Renn, O. (1997), "The Brent Spar controversy: an example of risk communication gone wrong", *Risk Analysis*, vol. 17, no. 2, pp. 131–136; Kruse, J. (2001), "Fantasy themes and rhetorical visions in the *Brent Spar* crisis: a comparative analysis of German and French newspaper coverage", *Argumentation*, vol. 15, no. 4, pp. 439–456.

3   Bennie, L.G. (1998), "Brent Spar, Atlantic oil and Greenpeace", *Parliamentary Affairs*, vol. 51, no. 3, pp. 397–410; Jordan, G. (1998), "Indirect causes and effects in policy change: the Brent Spar case", *Public Administration*, vol. 76, no. 4, pp. 713–740.

4   Gage, J.D. and Gordon, J.D.M. (1995), "Sound bites, science and the Brent Spar: environmental considerations relevant to the deep-sea disposal option", *Marine Pollution Bulletin*, vol. 30, no. 12, pp. 772–779.

5   Zyglidopoulos, S.C. (2002), "The social and environmental responsibilities of multinationals: evidence from the Brent Spar case", *Journal of Business Ethics,* vol. 36, no. 1/2, pp. 141–151.

6   Zyglidopoulos (2002), op. cit., p. 142.

7   Shell International (2008), *The Brent Spar Dossier*, Visual Media Services, London, p. 8; Jordan (1998), op. cit., p. 603.

8   Arts, B. (2002), "'Green Alliances' of business and NGOs. New styles of self-regulation or 'dead-end roads'", *Corporate Social Responsibility and Environmental Management*, vol. 9, no. 1, pp. 26–36, see p. 26.

9   Aberdeen University Research and Industrial Services (1995), "Brent Spar: decommissioning study," *CEMP News*, 1, 1.

10   Fisheries Research Services, *Case Study: Brent Spar*, Aberdeen, http://www.scotland.gov.uk/Uploads/Documents/AE07Brent2004.pdf, accessed October 10 2010.

11   Jordan (1998), op. cit., p. 605.

12   *The Times* (1995), February 17, cited in Neale, A. (1997), "Organisational learning in contested environments: lessons from Brent Spar", *Business Strategy and the Environment*, vol. 6, pp. 93–103, see p. 96.

13   Jordan, G. and Maloney, W.A. (1997), "Accounting for sub governments: explaining the persistence of policy communities", *Administration and Society*, vol. 29, no. 5, pp. 557–583, see p. 558.

14   OSPAR Commission, *History*, http://www.ospar.org/content/content.asp?menu=0035010808 0000_000000_000000, accessed October 5 2010.

15   Löfstedt and Renn (1997), op. cit., p. 132.

16   Cited in Jordan (1998), op. cit., p. 605.

17   Grolin (1998), op. cit., p. 214.

18   Grolin (1998), op. cit., p. 217; Zyglidopoulos (2002), op. cit., p. 143; a shorter but more detailed list on platforms that were about to be decommissioned was provided in Greenpeace, *Consequences of the Brent Spar Victory*, http://archive.greenpeace.org/odumping/noticeboard/reports/brent.pdf, accessed October 10 2010.

19   Greenpeace (2005), *Brent Spar und die Folgen* (Brent Spar and the Consequences). Greenpeace. Hamburg, p. 4.

20   Reddy, S. (1995), *No Grounds for Dumping*, Greenpeace, London.

21   House of Commons (1996), "Correspondence between DTI and Shell concerning Brent Spar", released February 21, 1996, cited in Grolin (1998), op. cit., p. 217.

22   Greenpeace (2005), op. cit., p. 16.

23   Kruse (2001), op. cit., p. 445–452.

24   Barbone, C. (1996), "The battle for Brent Spar", *Communication World*, vol. 13, no. 1, pp. 27–30.

25   Greenpeace (2005), op. cit., p. 19.

26   Shell International (2008), op. cit., p. 30.

27   Jordan (1998), op. cit., p. 613.

28   Greenpeace (2005), op. cit., p. 17.

29   Cited in Neale (1997), op. cit., p. 99.

30   The question of the legitimacy of NGOs has been widely addressed in the literature: Atack, I. (1999), "Four criteria of development NGO legitimacy", *World Development*, vol. 27, no. 5, pp. 855–864; Hudson, A. (2001), "NGOs' transnational advocacy networks: from 'legitimacy' to 'political responsibility'?", *Global Networks*, vol. 1, no. 4, pp. 331–352; Maragia, B. (2002), "Almost there: another way of conceptualizing and explaining NGOs' quest for legitimacy in global politics", *Non-State Actors and International Law*, vol. 2, no. 3, pp. 301–332; Collingwood, V. (2006), "Non-governmental organizations, power and legitimacy in international society", *Review of International Studies*, vol. 32, no. 3, pp. 439–454.

31   Jordan (1998), op. cit., p. 610.

32   Vidal D. (1995), "Agenda benders", *The Guardian*, June 22, quoted in Holzer B. (2010), *Moralizing the Corporation*, Edward Elgar, London, p. 36.

33   Grolin (1998), op. cit., p. 214.

34   Zyglidopoulos (2002), op. cit., p. 144.

35   EMNID (1995), *Bereitschaft zu Boykott von Shell-Tankstellen* (Survey) (Willingness to participate in a boycott of Shell gas stations), EMNID, Bielefeld.

36   Greenpeace (2005), op. cit., p. 17.

37   Norway was in a very similar position to the UK. It also had a significant amount of platforms and buoys in its waters and would also have been affected financially from high disposal costs.

38   Fourth Ministerial Declaration on the Protection of the North Sea, Paragraph 54, quoted in Greenpeace (2005), op. cit., p. 18.

39   Vowe, G. (2006), "Feldzüge um die öffentliche Meinung" (Campaigns for Public Opinion). In U. Röttger (ed.), *PR-Kampagnen: Über die Inszenierung von Öffentlichkeit*, VS Verlag für Sozialwissenschaften, Wiesbaden, pp. 75–94, see p. 77.

40   Zyglidopoulos (2002), op. cit., p. 144.

41   Grolin (1998), op. cit., p. 214.

42   Zyglidopoulos (2002), op. cit., p. 147.

43   Mantow, W. (1995), *Die Ereignisse um Brent Spar in Deutschland. Darstellung und Dokumentation mit Daten und Fakten* (The Events Surrounding Brent Spar in Germany. Presentation and Documentation with Facts and Figures), Deutsche Shell AG, Hamburg.

44   Cited in Jordan (1998), op. cit., p. 614.

45   *Daily Mirror* (1995), "We shall not be moved", June 20, quoted in Holzer (2010)., op. cit., p. 36.

46   The Environment Council, *The Brent Spar Dialogue Process*, http://www.the-environment-council.org.uk/index.php?option=com_contentandtask=viewandid=235andItemid=263, accessed November 29 2010.

47   Grolin (1998), op. cit., p. 220.

48   A detailed description of the process can be found at The Environment Council, op. cit.

49   Marr, S. (2003), *The Precautionary Principle in the Law of the Sea*, Martinus Nijhoff Publishers, The Hague, pp. 129–130.

50   Parts of the interview with Rothermund can be watched at Youtube, "Brent Spar, Greenpeace vs. Shell", http://www.youtube.com/watch?v=KToV-c8uvPc, accessed November 26 2010.

51   Kruse (2001), op. cit., p. 453.

5 Engaging With the Enemy: Understanding Adversarial Stakeholder Processes and Outcomes

MAUREEN BOURASSA* AND PEGGY CUNNINGHAM†

Keywords

Obesity, stakeholder, stakeholder engagement.

Introduction

A group of stakeholders—representatives from industry, government, and nongovernmental organizations (NGOs)—sits in a room packed with tables, listening intently to presentations about a pressing social and health issue: growing rates of obesity. While everyone in the room has been invited to discuss potential solutions and policy recommendations related to obesity, especially childhood obesity, "discussion" is not a word that captures the activity taking place. Instead, groups are drawing battle lines between themselves and others, and they are clearly lobbying for position and the right to speak on behalf of the public.

Activists quickly cast business as the enemy. They make claims that business is malicious and manipulative in its advertising aimed at parents and children. These activists claim that both young and old consumers, as a result of their exposure to advertising, are unable to resist the lure of high-fat, high-calorie foods. They hastily call for complete bans on advertising. Business representatives adamantly defend themselves, trotting out "evidence" about the ineffectiveness of advertising bans in Sweden and Canada. Activists counter, demanding tighter regulations like those recently introduced in the United Kingdom. Government representatives find themselves trapped in the middle, wondering if and how they should intervene. Disparaging comments come from all sides: "What a wing-nut she is!" The mood is one of hurt, anger and confrontation. Emotions run high. There is denial of others' positions, there is refusal to sit with someone from another sector, there is eye-rolling and name-calling, and there are questions about the accuracy of facts and figures presented by the warring groups.

*   Maureen A. Bourassa, Edwards School of Business, University of Saskatchewan, 25 Campus Drive, Saskatoon, Saskatchewan, S7N 5A7, Canada. E-mail: Bourassa@edwards.usask.ca.

†   Peggy H. Cunningham, Faculty of Management, R.A. Jodrey Chair, Dalhousie University, 6100 University Avenue, Halifax, Nova Scotia, B3H 3J5, Canada. E-mail: PeggyC@dal.ca.

This is not the stakeholder engagement one reads about in most books and academic papers. It is not collaborative and collegial—it is angry, hateful and adversarial. It is a battleground, but there is little in the extant literature that helps business, activists or government stakeholders understand and manage such a process. In this chapter, we intend to open the door on this type of engagement and shed light on the drivers of these stressful, nonproductive processes.

BACKGROUND

Successful stakeholder engagement is critical to the realization of most corporate social responsibility (CSR) initiatives, especially if one defines CSR as an organization's willingness to be accountable for the impact of its operations on stakeholders—employees, suppliers, competitors, communities, governments, the media and so on. We take this view. Traditionally, a stakeholder has been defined as anyone who has an interest in, or who may be impacted by, the actions of an organization,[1] and stakeholder engagement as "an organization's efforts to understand and involve stakeholders and their concerns in its activities and decision-making processes".[2]

Given that stakeholder engagement is a relatively new area of study, much of the extant literature, no matter what the field of study, is normative in nature. There is little rigorous empirical research that investigates the drivers of the stakeholder engagement process, the variables that affect success and failure and the various outcomes.[3]

The management literature typically views stakeholder engagement in a mechanistic fashion, with the firm positioned at the centre of a stakeholder network.[4] The firm is viewed as wielding power and strategically controlling the engagement. Illustrative of these approaches is work by AccountAbility, a United Kingdom NGO focused on setting standards for stakeholder engagement to promote sustainability. It describes the stakeholder engagement process as follows: "The overall purpose of stakeholder engagement is to drive strategic direction and operational excellence for organizations."[5] Under such perspectives, the fact that stakeholders influence each other is seldom acknowledged. Moreover, the focus is on successful, cooperative stakeholder relationships between a focal entity and its stakeholders where, for example, concepts from the trust–commitment model[6] of relationship marketing hold.[7]

While much of the existing research focuses on collaborative stakeholder engagement, our research, in which various stakeholders with unique interests and goals gathered around a common social problem, uncovered a very different process. The engagements we observed were anything but relational, collaborative and productive. While participants were firmly committed to their positions on the obesity issue, they showed little understanding or empathy towards representatives from other stakeholder groups. Trust was absent, emotions ran high and mutual respect was low. There was little cooperation and almost no willingness to work together to resolve the social issue.

Our research takes a network view and strives to uncover some of the complexity associated with adversarial stakeholder engagement. Networks of stakeholders coalesce around social issues and problems.[8] Within this perspective, stakeholder networks may be referred to as public policy networks,[9] multi-sector innovations,[10] social partnerships,[11] stakeholder networks,[12] issue networks,[13] cross-sector collaborations,[14] or multi-stakeholder interactions.[15] Regardless of the label, stakeholder networks are unique because (1) the focus shifts from dyadic relationships between firms and stakeholders to complex webs of relationships between multiple stakeholders, (2) the firm moves from occupying a central position to becoming one of the many stakeholders with an interest in the network's issue, and (3) any single stakeholder—including the firm—may or may not have power, credibility or legitimacy depending on the nature of the issue, its centrality in the network and the stance it takes with regard to the issue and other stakeholders. These networks are dynamic and in constant flux.[16] As stated by researcher Julia Roloff, "the major challenges of multi-stakeholder networks are to manage potential conflicts between participants and to understand and handle the problem in its full complexity".[17] Overall, little research has captured the dynamic, interactive, complex and nonlinear process of stakeholder engagement,[18] and the contribution of our work is that it sheds light on this underexplored area.

Within this network perspective, the definition of stakeholders and stakeholder engagement change because the firm is no longer at the center of the analysis. Instead, we define a stakeholder in this context as "any group or individual who can affect or is affected by the solution of the problem addressed by the network".[19] The concept of stakeholder engagement then becomes the organizations' efforts to understand and involve each other in solving the problem addressed by the network.

Other researchers acknowledge a lack of understanding around what both inhibits and promotes success in this kind of network-based stakeholder engagement. Because knowledge creation in this area of research is relatively new, much of the recent work draws on the case study approach, integrating the results of interviews, document analysis, and observation.[20] Other researchers in this area have used their findings to build models of the antecedents to collaboration within stakeholder networks.[21] We believe that, because these kinds of engagement often emerge in response to open conflict,[22] it is also important to understand the antecedents to conflict in this complex, multi-stakeholder field. Understanding the causes of conflict and the processes that arise as the result of this conflict provides an even greater understanding of what kinds of changes are required to move towards cooperation and collaboration.

The Stakeholder Marketing Consortium (Aspen Institute) recently recommended a pressing need for practitioners to gain insight into how stakeholder communication and dialog can be improved. To achieve this goal, a better understanding of adversarial relationships is also needed since such relationships may be more typical (at least initially) than collaborative stakeholder relationships. Even the press recognizes this problem. A recent newspaper article, for example, described the need for "a truce" between members of the forestry industry and environmentalists.[23]

To better understand and explain the dark side of stakeholder engagement, we focused our research on one major question: What are the factors that drive adversarial stakeholder engagement, and what processes and outcomes arise as a result of these factors? Our answers to this question helped us develop an illustrative model of the variables characterizing adversarial stakeholder engagement that may guide future research and theory development. We have also gleaned insights for managers involved in adversarial stakeholder engagement processes.

We chose the issue of obesity because it is timely and is of concern in all developed countries. The World Health Organization reports that:

Obesity has reached epidemic proportions globally, with more than 1 billion adults overweight—
at least 300 million of them clinically obese—and is a major contributor to the global burden
of chronic disease and disability. Often coexisting in developing countries with under-nutrition,
obesity is a complex condition, with serious social and psychological dimensions, affecting
virtually all ages and socioeconomic groups.[24]

Obesity has received increased attention from a range of stakeholder groups. Governments and regulatory bodies, national and international NGOs, academics, researchers, public health officials, consumers, the medical profession, health-based nonprofits, activists, lobbyists, educators, food manufacturers, fast food chains, grocery retailers and marketers are among the diverse groups embedded in the network engaging around this topic. Even creators of popular culture products have entered the fray with movies such as *Super Size Me*.

These diverse stakeholders have established strongly held positions on this issue. Many of the engagements among stakeholders are highly adversarial, with each party blaming the other for the problem. There are great differences in opinion about appropriate solutions, and there is considerable debate about what constitutes responsible action on the part of business, government, the public and consumers.

By exploring stakeholder engagement in this context, our research contributes to a more general understanding of the way in which urgent and important social problems are being addressed. Like obesity, other social, cultural, environmental and economic issues attract the attention of disparate stakeholders. Despite the perceived urgency and importance of these issues, however, stakeholders are often impeded from arriving at solutions because they cannot work together in a cooperative, collaborative manner. By achieving a better understanding of the adversarial situation characterizing many stakeholder engagements, we can better see the starting point from which stakeholder relationships have to evolve towards more collaborative stances.

Method

In order to explore stakeholder engagement from a network perspective, we used participant observation over a period of almost four years during which there was ongoing stakeholder engagement processes surrounding the issue of obesity. We participated in four major public conferences and two stakeholder engagement workshops. We were allowed to attend planning sessions in which aligned stakeholders mapped out strategies for dealing with opposing views as well as meetings and conferences which brought together the universe of stakeholders. We also participated in post-engagement meetings among two stakeholder groups who were involved in these events over a period of three years. These observations and interviews all form part of the same study. The processes we observed brought together food industry representatives, activist groups, nonprofit organizations, academic researchers, government representatives and policy-makers, medical practitioners and public health officials. Participants at the conferences were drawn from a number of geographies including the United States, the United Kingdom, Canada and Europe.

One of the researchers played an active participant role as a member of a food industry group. This role allowed for an insider's view of the overarching processes as well as the stance taken by industry members. To control for bias, the other researcher was largely an objective, outside observer.

Our ongoing involvement in these processes allowed for multiple observations of interactions among the numerous stakeholder groups focused on the issue of obesity. Many of the actors were common across various events and planning sessions; however, there was also considerable dynamism. New players entered as additional stakeholder groups engaged or people left due to changes in their roles. All of the events were focused on the issue of obesity, but they had different purposes. Some were a "call to action" with the stated purpose of controlling marketing to children. Others were focused on problem-solving: finding tactics that would help resolve the obesity issue. A third (much smaller) set were focused on building collaboration and trust among stakeholders involved in the issue. It is notable, however, that all of these engagements failed to achieve their stated objectives.

The various engagements provided us with data in the form of actual versus reported behaviors. At each event, we took extensive field notes to record observations about the setting, the social environment, planned programs and formal interactions, unplanned activities and informal interactions, language and nonverbal communications.[25]

To help familiarize ourselves with stakeholder engagement processes more broadly and to give a context to our findings from the participant observation processes, we also conducted 14 elite interviews using purposeful sampling[26] with managers involved in stakeholder engagement from a number of industries, including industries and fields related to obesity. We sought a diverse sample (e.g., small and large organizations, for profit organizations and NGOs, successful and unsuccessful stakeholder engagement efforts around obesity and other non-obesity related issues such as environmental protection issues) of representatives in different levels of their organizations. Four of our informants were involved in the stakeholder engagement processes we observed; ten were involved in other stakeholder engagement processes that we did not observe. Table 5.1 provides summary information about our informants.

We systematically analyzed all our data using thematic analysis, a method which guides the interpretation of data and the application of judgment to draw out themes that improve understanding and generate insights.[27] Themes can be constructed either deductively (directly from the phenomenon) or inductively (based on theory or prior research).[28] We used a hybrid approach, employing various theoretical lenses, but also allowed new insights to emerge. Each researcher analyzed the data independently, and then we met to discuss and debate themes. In reporting our data, we use quotations of typical responses where possible, as well as pseudonyms and fictitious company names to protect the privacy of the people we observed and interviewed. Our findings helped us develop a model of the factors driving adversarial stakeholder engagement.

Table 5.1   Interview participants

Pseudonym	Position	Sector	Obesity Network
Sharla	Senior VP, Public and Government Affairs	Industry (energy)	No
Heather	Senior Consultation Advisor	Industry (energy)	No
Ricardo	VP, Corporate Social Responsibility	Industry (mining)	No
Edward	VP, Environmental Leadership	Industry (mining)	No
Francis	Previous Manager of Northern Affairs	Industry (mining)	No
Lukas	Supervisor, Northern Affairs Office	Industry (mining)	No
Walter	Executive Director	Nonprofit	No
Allison	Director of CSR	Government agency	No
Jeffery	Principal	Education	No
Beverly	Community Liaison	Education	No
Samuel	CSR Director	Insurance	No
Norman	Assistant Director, Health Policy	Nonprofit	Yes
Natalie	Vice President, Children's Television	Media	Yes
Dominique	Senior VP, Public Affairs and Environment	Industry (Food mfg.)	Yes

Findings

While our interview informants (even those involved in adversarial processes) tended to talk about collaborative stakeholder relationships, our participant observations revealed a very different situation. In the interviews, it took considerable probing to begin a discussion of the darker side of stakeholder relationships. Adversarial processes were certainly acknowledged, but there was reluctance to admit failure with regard to stakeholder engagement processes. In fact, one manager expressed concern that she was the only one to experience such failure since the literature she had read suggested collaborative relationships were the norm. These findings point to the unique power of participant observation. Experts note the method gives the researcher an opportunity to see things that may routinely escape others' awareness, and the researcher learns things that people are not willing to talk about in an interview.[29] Thus, for the remainder of the discussion, we rely largely on what we observed and not only on what we were told.

Despite variance in the objectives of the various engagement events and planning meetings, all were focused in some manner on resolving the obesity problem (especially obesity in young people). Participants often approached the engagements with hope and optimism. One typical participant stated, "It is the respect, the honesty, the courage that people have shown by being here. This shows the level of willingness to move the agenda forward." Despite such statements and the fact that these events had a common goal, only a few processes showed any significant collaboration among stakeholder groups— most were highly adversarial across groups although there was consensus and growing entrenchment of positions within groups. In fact, despite the stated goal of seeking solutions, there appeared to be an underlying text where stakeholder groups struggled to own the issue and they vied to be seen as the legitimate spokesperson for obese children and adults.

The approaches to stakeholder engagement varied at the events we attended. There were standard conferences with presentations followed by question and answer periods, there were round tables and workshops, and there was one event where various groups presented their positions to a jury-like panel of media, Aboriginal, education, public policy, academic and arts representatives.

Even though the various stakeholder groups claimed that they were acting in the interests of obese adults and children, it is interesting to note that no obese consumers, parents or children were involved in the various engagements. In fact, there appeared to be an overall attitude of paternalism—members of the various stakeholder groups regarded themselves as the experts, as people who knew what was best for consumers. Consumers (both adults and children) were frequently discussed as a faceless, monolithic whole with few capabilities to make independent decisions.

Conflict and adversarial engagement were the norm. For example, when a coalition of food companies tried to present the positive initiatives they were taking to reduce fat, salt and calories in their products, an individual from a health-related organization was highly negative and introduced extraneous information to strengthen her case. She referred to the presentation as, "The hypocrisy of food companies promoting healthy living." Calling marketing "insidious" she made the following contention, "It is hard to find clothes without [marketers'] characters on them. You work to embed these characters in children's psyches." The use of such inflammatory statements and highly charged language was the norm more than the exception.

Our evidence suggests that conflict is not unusual in stakeholder engagement processes. When firms and other stakeholders come together around important issues, traditional assumptions that social agendas and profit goals are incompatible may surface. For example, Norman, one of our interview informants, explained that a benefit of stakeholder engagement is "minimizing opposition"—in other words, Norman assumed that stakeholders inevitably conflict. As a result of this conflict, one or both parties may perceive their very existence to be threatened.

From these observations, we were able to outline key insights that relate to lack of success. We identified a number of variables and patterns of behavior that characterize unsuccessful stakeholder engagement, as depicted in Figure 5.1. We identified lack of respect as a critical antecedent, and emotion as a consequence of respect. We believe that emotion also mediates the relationship between respect and two final outcomes: defensive actions and power building. Details with regard to each major variable are outlined in the subsequent sections.

Antecedents

LACK OF RESPECT

While respect is a term and concept frequently referred to in the CSR literature,[30] it is not often explored in great detail. We define respect as the perceived value or worth

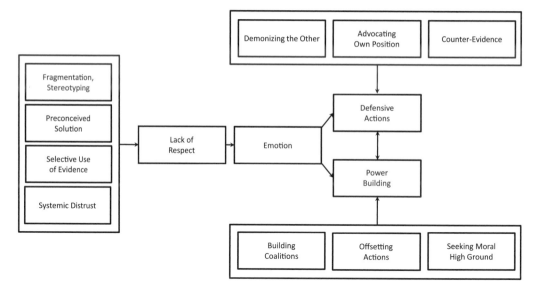

Figure 5.1   Patterns of behavior in adversarial stakeholder engagement processes

of another person. Respect is manifest in a number of behaviors related to stakeholder engagement such as taking the time to truly listen to others, considering others' thoughts and opinions, and treating others as unique individuals.[31]

The interviews supported our contentions about the importance of respect. Sharla made this point clear when she described a particular annual general meeting where a number of stakeholders were opposed to her company's direction. Sharla invited these stakeholder groups to have their own table at this meeting. She explained:

> *Why did I do that? It's very simply, they have a right to their opinion and if I can't see the fact that they have that right then they're going to be constantly telling me they have the right. If I acknowledge they have the right to that opinion then they're going to treat it in a more respectful manner. And they did. They came up to the microphone, they had their questions, there was no protesting, there was no screaming, there was no yelling. We had a respectful dialog and that was what we needed to achieve.*

We expected respect to be important given the controversial issue, the complexity of the stakeholder network, and the differences in stakeholder interests. We believed organizations would benefit from respecting diversity, individuality and alternative agendas. While we expected respect to be important, we were unprepared for the deep levels of disrespect we observed. For example, one health group member asked "Wouldn't you just like to slap her?" when referring to the statements made by an opposing presenter.

This lack of respect was underpinned by a number of behaviors and beliefs: assumptions of fragmentation and uniformity, preconceived solutions that blamed the other, selective use of evidence and systemic distrust across sectors. In turn, such lack of respect enabled the defensive actions and power building we observed, mediated by negative emotions. Overall, the lack of respect contributed to the lack of success we observed. There are similar findings in the existing literature, where relationships that lack respect experience more negative group conflict.[32]

FRAGMENTATION AND STEREOTYPING

Respect, because it is about the value and worth of another person, also entails regarding others holistically—in other words, taking a "whole person" perspective.[33] The notion of the "whole person" is a consideration for all aspects of a person—it ignores a split between mind and body, and acknowledges that people's lives are relational, spiritual, affective, physical and intellectual.[34] In the context of stakeholder engagement, this means acknowledging, for example, that a particular stakeholder is not just a company representative, but is also a parent, athlete, daughter, volunteer, community member and concerned citizen.

In contrast, the stakeholders we observed viewed others in a fragmented fashion—they rarely acknowledged others as whole persons but instead often only considered the professional identity (e.g., marketer, government representative, health official or activist). Moreover, many participants' understanding of other stakeholders was frequently based on positions, agendas, organizations or assumptions. For example, one woman was immediately labeled as "scary" and an "irrational basket case" because the advocacy group she worked with was known for its adversarial stance. A senior medical officer was labeled a "politician" when he took a stance against an industry group.

Respect implies that people and groups are not only regarded as whole, but also as unique. Rather than acknowledging individuality and variance of views, several presenters at the stakeholder meetings labeled all business people "evil" and did not distinguish between firms that had improved the nutritional quality of their products versus those that adhered to the status quo. This stereotyping is not surprising given the widely different worldviews of the various sectors. Norman, in his interview, suggested that differences in sector culture, differences in mission and differences in organizational culture impede engagement. In Norman's case, these perceived differences across sectors legitimize what would otherwise be seen as disrespectful behaviors, such as aggressiveness and bullying. Norman elaborated on these differences:

> A big piece of the difference between our [NGO] culture and the private sector culture is ... we have more flexibility in achieving our bottom line which is improving public health ... the corporate culture can possibly be more aggressive than it can be in ours ... the private sector could be successful because they could successfully bully some organizations in the charity sector ... I think we would probably assume some of the same tactics that they use.

PRECONCEIVED SOLUTIONS

The lack of respect was also underpinned by the fact that participants in the engagements did not take time to listen to or understand the other's position. As a result, they were forced to make certain assumptions. In addition, the stakeholders did not value each other, nor did they deem potential solutions offered by other stakeholders to be worthwhile. Such behaviors drove the groups we observed into distinct camps and put each camp on the defensive. Two industry participants expressed their frustration: "Industry is not being given any credit for the work that has been done over the last two years. It is shocking and alarming" (Helen). "This isn't surprising. Their minds are made up and they don't want to hear from us" (John).

Separate groups of stakeholders were forced to arrive at their own solutions to obesity and improper nutrition—solutions that often were viewed as viable only if the problem could be blamed on others. For example, the nonindustry stakeholders primarily blamed marketers for creating consumer demand for unhealthy food. As a result they took the stance that the nutrition content of food should be regulated and advertising of food, especially advertising aimed at children and youth, should be banned. In contrast, the industry stakeholders called for more education, especially around the need for exercise to balance food intake, and made the case that obesity resulted from a multitude of contributing factors.

SELECTIVE USE OF EVIDENCE

Voice is defined as both the opportunity to speak and the experience of being listened to, and is a fundamental entitlement in our society. Thus, when a person is denied voice, or when they are not listened to, they will feel that they have been treated unjustly or disrespected.[35] At the stakeholder engagement processes we observed, there was a significant lack of voice; the people chosen to present, as well as the contents of their presentations, appeared highly selective. In some cases, entire stakeholder groups (e.g., industry/consumer groups) were excluded from conference speaker lists. In addition, many of the materials used by speakers supported only the dominant position at the meetings. For example, at one meeting, a speaker used long outdated advertising to make her point that children's advertising was inappropriate and manipulative. In a similar fashion, an industry speaker focused solely on the positive role marketing can play in supporting healthy food choices and exercise regimes. In an interview, Dominique reflected the view that the panels had been handpicked to represent a particular point of view, such that no new information was being put on the table. Selective use of evidence is problematic, because stakeholders do not have an opportunity to become educated and fully informed around a particular issue. As Robert explained in his interview, people need expertise before they can fully engage in processes and exercise their voice.

SYSTEMIC DISTRUST

Stakeholders appeared to enter the process exhibiting high levels of distrust between sectors. There are questions about whether lack of respect causes lack of trust or whether the lack of trust causes lack of respect.[36] Our observations suggest, however, that lack of trust underpins lack of respect. The lack of trust was apparent in some of the presentations. One of the speakers demonstrated lack of trust in government when he stated, "I hope those who are still in Parliament will continue to support this bill [nutrition labeling] so we don't have to look under rocks to find out what we are eating." Another presenter implied distrust in suggesting that "marketers will do what they can get away with". The stakeholders not only lacked trust in each other, but also acted in a deceptive manner towards certain groups, which surely perpetuates this distrust. As Norman explained, "If we were working with an organization that was possibly a bit more of a bully [i.e., a business] we wouldn't be as transparent in our objectives, our agenda [because] we would lose our strategic advantage."

Mediator

EMOTION

Our data suggest that emotion is important,[37] yet it is not commonly discussed in the stakeholder engagement, CSR or even relationship marketing literature.[38] Research is starting to emerge, however, with regard to the impact of emotion on relationships[39] and the differential effects of positive and negative emotions.[40] Our research revealed that disrespect, in particular, resulted in strong negative emotional outcomes. Such emotions were physically manifested in actions such as name calling, raised voices, use of inflammatory language, disparagement of others, eye-rolling, facial distortions and turning away from other groups. Natalie explained that when it comes to some stakeholder groups, there is a real sense of "hate".

Inside the various stakeholder groups, each populated by like-minded people, respect was more dominant and more positive emotions resulted. Business stakeholders, for example, united and bonded, feeling they were under siege. Physical manifestations of such emotions included sitting closer together, making jokes at the expense of other stakeholders, exchanging notes, laughing and patting backs. On several occasions, nonindustry representatives collectively cheered for one activist representative, who had evolved into a charismatic spokesperson and information gatekeeper. Such in-group bonding, however, worked to increase disrespect across groups.

The importance of emotion is not surprising, given that the conflict between stakeholder groups resulted in perceived threats to legitimacy, personal credibility, authenticity and even organizational survival. Two major outcomes resulted from lack of respect and negative emotions: defensive actions and power building. We discuss these outcomes in the next sections.

Outcomes

DEFENSIVE ACTIONS

Given the anticipation of conflict and competing agendas, the interactions we observed were filled with several characteristic defensive actions. Rather than seeking to cooperate and develop joint solutions to the obesity epidemic—the task at hand—the stakeholders instead sought to defend and protect their own positions. While the various groups followed different tactics, defensive actions were common across groups and included: demonizing the other, advocating one's own position and establishing counter-evidence. It should be noted that while we have labeled these defensive actions, they were often colored with aggressive, bullying behaviors.

DEMONIZING THE OTHER

The discourse we observed revealed that stakeholders not only upheld their own positions, they also characterized others as untruthful, unbalanced, unfair, unjust, naïve, extreme and exploitative. One participant noted, "We have to be careful. There is a lot of dissemination of 'facts' that are not true." Each blamed others for actions that harmed the public. One informant, Natalie, described how the media "demonizes" food. War-like terminology was common. A typical sentiment was expressed as "divide and conquer" to break down perceived alliances.

ADVOCATING OWN POSITION

The stakeholders we observed were firmly entrenched in their own positions and clearly worked to advocate those positions. Key statements about position were repeated incessantly. In addition, during many question and answer periods, stakeholders did not ask questions, but instead took control of the microphone to give "lectures" that would reinforce their positions and build credibility. In one particular small group discussion, leaders appointed by the conference organizers quickly silenced those with opposing opinions, belittled them and prevented the sharing of other perspectives. In many cases, positions became increasingly entrenched. Participants re-stated and re-framed their positions to reinforce and protect their stances. A phrase heard commonly by industry stakeholders was, "We at the XYZ Company regard all food as healthy as long as it is part of a balanced diet and there is a balance between intake and physical exercise."

COUNTER-EVIDENCE

In each engagement we observed, there was a cycle of rebuttals with opposing groups presenting evidence and counter-evidence. To defend their position, each group claimed to use "scientific" evidence and reason to support their position, even though the language and tone of the presentations was often emotional and politically charged. In his interview, Norman described one stakeholder engagement experience where "buy-in" was achieved through "jointly listening to a lot of evidence from experts across the world". Another presenter was commended in the closing remarks for having an "amazing breadth of expertise" while another clearly stated that "strong science is fundamental" in combating nutrition issues. In extreme cases insignificant findings were reported as being significant. In one notable case, a doctor was challenged for presenting out-of-date material and inaccurate evidence. He replied, "Science can be used to prove many things, and given how harmful advertising is, I will use any facts it takes to prove it." To rebut such actions, a typical industry spokesperson expressed this opinion: "We are held to a higher level of accountability by the government than they [health advocates and activists] are. We must provide verifiable scientific evidence for our claims."

POWER BUILDING

Power is defined as "potential for influence".[41] In current research on CSR, stakeholders' power is viewed as predetermined given their potential impact on the firm, and the firm therefore places priority on stakeholders deemed most salient and powerful.[42] Under the network perspective of stakeholder engagement, however, power is dynamic and no single stakeholder is responsible for brokering power. Instead, all stakeholders have the potential to access or lose power as relationships co-evolve. As a result, power relations shift over time as some stakeholder groups gain credibility and legitimacy as spokespersons for important issues.[43]

Our evidence extends this contention. We found that power is not only distributed among network members, but it is also dynamic, negotiated and accrued as the network of stakeholders evolves. We observed three sets of actions the various groups undertook to build their perceived power: coalition building, offsetting actions and seeking the moral high ground. We discuss these next.

BUILDING COALITIONS

When relationships within the network are adversarial, stakeholders vie for power by forming coalitions. While the ideal outcome of a stakeholder engagement process is coalition building amongst all stakeholders around a common outcome, this was not the process we observed. Instead, coalitions were built with others who were perceived to be the most powerful at a particular point in time (e.g., government, the media), or they were built with like-minded stakeholders to amass power. One industry representative noted that partnering with a respected, like-minded nonprofit created "a shield for us".

At engagement events, this coalition building was physically manifested by the formation of physical groups and new sitting arrangements where people with similar views banded together. They would cluster together at coffee breaks often discussing how "misguided" other stakeholder groups were in their thinking and approach. In other instances, stakeholders would quote and reinforce each other's speeches in their own presentations to build the credibility of the in-group. After engagements, like-minded participants would also gather in closed meetings to debrief and to plan their defensive strategies. Coalitions would exchange e-mails re-stating their positions and disparaging others' viewpoints.

OFFSETTING ACTIONS

After being confronted with opposing views, stakeholder groups repeatedly pointed to other initiatives and "facts" that could be used to overcome criticism. When accused of inaction, public health officials pointed to programs designed to educate consumers and increase levels of physical activity. In answer to criticism about their supposed causal role in obesity, business stakeholders focused on a recent initiative supporting responsible advertising practices. To counter calls for advertising bans, a nonprofit group sponsored by food manufacturers advocated media literacy as a solution to the problem. While these actions were designed to increase the groups' voice, legitimacy and power within the network, they often became a flashpoint for criticism.

SEEKING THE MORAL HIGH GROUND

Our observations suggest that the ethics of positions were socially constructed, and that seeking the moral high ground was a tactic used to build power within the network. Each interest group advocated its own position as the "right" one. For example, an advertising ban advocate claimed, "We in the ABC Company believe it is morally wrong to exploit children for commercial gain." In seeking the moral high ground, stakeholder groups sought to position themselves as credible and legitimate spokespersons for the issue and the key constituency—young people. Dominique, in her interview, referenced a desire for the moral high ground when she explained that stakeholders tend to approach issues and interests "as if they were on the side of angels".

The various pressure groups did use ethical principles to support their arguments, but the principles employed differed. Public health officials and certain activist groups made use of the principles of "doing no harm" and "protecting the vulnerable", claiming that they are the most ethical because they care about public well-being and health. In contrast, industry representatives used principles like parents' and consumers' "right to choose" and "freedom of choice" as moral defenses for their actions. One informant, Natalie, reflected this thinking when she noted that consumers should decide for themselves whether they would like to comply with nutrition guidelines; therefore, the solution to obesity lies in educating people about balanced diets.

Summary of Findings

Overall, our research suggests that stakeholder engagement is a more complex process than the current literature acknowledges. Based on the processes we observed and our informants' narratives, we believe that respect and the lack thereof may be a fundamental driver of the nature of stakeholder interactions. As noted previously, respect is about valuing another person or party, and manifestations of respect generally include a willingness to listen to the other person, to hear what they have to say, and to understand their background and their point of view. Lack of respect is a critical barrier to successful engagement. If stakeholders do not value each other and therefore do not work to understand each other's position, they are left feeling threatened by opposing positions. In the face of this perceived threat, stakeholders engage in defensive actions to protect their own status and existence.

We anticipate that negative emotions mediate the relationship between lack of respect and defensive actions as well as lobbying for power. Previous research on respect in business-to-business interactions also found such mediation between respect and a number of outcome variables.[44] From a theoretical perspective, if a person senses they are not valued, this decreases self-worth and, according to appraisal theory, should make a person unhappy.[45] In observing the stakeholder engagement processes, we saw negative emotions were a conduit for lack of respect. They also drove the desire to defend positions and build the power essential to this defense.

While exploratory in nature, we believe our research makes a number of contributions. Our data enables us to derive a more complete picture of the variables that characterize adversarial stakeholder relationships. We extend stakeholder theory using a network perspective and demonstrate how disrespect and negative emotion incite a negative spiral of engagement. Our work provides a context where the traditional trust–commitment theory of relationship marketing theory does not hold. We developed a nomological network of variables that we anticipate will contribute to the development of a more complete model of stakeholder engagement. Our model includes testable relationships among important but underresearched variables (i.e., respect, emotion, dynamic power). By studying these variables in the context of stakeholder engagement, it expands our knowledge of adversarial relationships—a topic rarely approached in the literature.

Managerial Implications

Although most of the events we witnessed failed in terms of developing solutions or creating collaboration, there are lessons to be learned for managers. Training in dealing with conflict may be particularly helpful before entering stakeholder engagement processes. We witnessed three unsuccessful methods of dealing with conflict: denial and withdrawal, suppression of differences and seeking of power and dominance. We saw far less of the more productive methods of conflict resolution: compromise, integration and collaboration.[46] Our research suggests that beginning from a position where managers respect others, especially those highly different in their views, may be a better starting point to achieving the latter two conflict resolution methods. The ability to listen to positions without being defensive may also open the doors to greater collaboration.

If cooperation—"an orientation that reflects a spirit of willingness of one organization to work with another organization"[47]—is accepted as an indicator of successful stakeholder engagement, then there is already support from other literatures that respect could help to improve stakeholder engagement. In the social psychology literature, empirical studies have demonstrated that respectful relationships are more cooperative.[48] Research on respect in a marketing context has found that respectful interactions are more trusting, honest, cooperative and open. When there is lack of respect, conflict and an unwillingness to work together result.[49] Therefore, if managers can work to create a culture of respect within stakeholder engagement processes, there is an opportunity to move from conflict to cooperation.

In the absence of trust and commitment, managers must seek different paths to collaboration. We saw some indication that a focus on deeply cherished common values that all stakeholders could adhere to (e.g., the health and welfare of children) is more productive than a focus on differences. A search for commonalities could break down the adversarial cycle. One informant who was involved in a highly adversarial engagement noted how the process quickly changed when

> The focus evolved to one of "How do we promote children's health." This focus was hard to say no to. It helped keep us on track. When different people started taking the panel off track with their personal agendas, there was always a call to put these other issues on the shelf. Once on the shelf, they stayed there. The superordinate goal was very important and one that no one could take apart.

Bringing in credible facilitators and perceived expert but neutral sources with regard to the issue was also helpful in drawing the groups closer together. One facilitator was described as being "good at maintaining a balance and getting everyone's comments on the screen". A respected academic was instrumental in getting another group of stakeholders to think more creatively about potential solutions. One participant commented, "We heard you when you spoke of a 'third way'—you got through to them."

Repeating positions and constantly reiterating facts and figures, no matter how rational the argument, often failed to gain the attention of other groups. Key influencers must be engaged, often on a personal level. One particularly adept member of an industry association was determined to engage an activist who had adamantly opposed her position. She made a personal connection to help overcome the negative emotions that both had experienced earlier in the day. She noted her tactic as follows:

I just refused to let her put me off. She was giving me a hateful stare, but I just went over and sat down beside her. I figured she could ignore me, but it would be a long dinner for both of us if we didn't speak. She finally opened up and discovered I wasn't the devil after all. I listened before I talked, and we found a surprising amount of common ground.

Another manager found that small wins were important. Rather than confronting the opposition, he talked about a powerful small project that had an impact with regard to increasing exercise among children and reducing weight. His focus on the initiative attracted others and encouraged them to listen to other viewpoints.

Forming coalitions with credible third parties can help managers achieve greater power in the network. Mapping the network with an eye to alliance formation may help managers prepare for ongoing engagements. The alliance, in turn, can better acquaint them to the perspectives of opposing stakeholders and better inform them about the nature of the issue.

Conclusions

Even though adversarial stakeholder relationships occur frequently, and organizations struggle to find successful stakeholder engagement mechanisms, there has been little attention to the dark side of stakeholder engagement. Furthermore, the extant research does not account for the complexity which typified stakeholder networks. A network view of stakeholder engagement requires an understanding of processes which are nonlinear, multilevel and dynamic. Further research is therefore needed to better understand the dynamics we uncovered. In particular, questions need to be asked about the interventions to turn disrespect into respect, to turn defensive actions into cooperative actions, to convert perceived power differences into perceived equality and to integrate single-sector solutions into jointly supported actions. We observed that some stakeholder groups (e.g., consumers, children) who are central to the issue were not engaged in the stakeholder processes. There is, therefore, a need to understand how to manage those stakeholders who choose not to be engaged in such adversarial processes, or who have been purposefully excluded from the engagement. Finally, future research should explore the boundary conditions of this proposed model—specifically, in what contexts is this model most relevant, and under what conditions are the different components of the model most applicable (e.g., does respect matter more at the beginning of the process; do emotions become more relevant only over time).

Notes

1   Freeman, R.E. (1984), *Strategic Management: A Stakeholder Approach*, Pitman, Boston.
2   Partridge, K., Jackson, C., Wheeler, D. and Zohar, A. (2005), *From Words to Action: The Stakeholder Engagement Manual* (vols. 1 and 2), Stakeholder Research Associates Canada Inc., Coburg, Ontario, Canada; see p. 6.
3   Lockett, A., Moon, J. and Visser, W. (2006), "Corporate social responsibility in management research: focus, nature, salience and sources of influence", *Journal of Management Studies*, vol. 43, no. 1, pp. 115–136; Margolis, J.D. and Walsh, J.P. (2003), "Misery loves company:

rethinking social initiatives by business", *Administrative Sciences Quarterly*, vol. 48, no. 2, pp. 268–305.

4   Amaeshi, K.M. and Crane, A. (2007), "Stakeholder engagement: a mechanism for sustainable action", *Corporate Social Responsibility and Environmental Management*, vol. 13, no. 5, pp. 245–260; Rowley, T.J. (1997), "Moving beyond dyadic ties: a network theory of stakeholder influence", *Academy of Management Review*, vol. 22, no. 4, pp. 887–910.

5   AccountAbility (2005), *Stakeholder Engagement Standard*, http://www.accountability.org/ images/content/0/4/047/SES%20Exposure%20Draft%20-%20FullPDF.pdf, accessed December 28 2010, p. 9.

6   Morgan, R.M. and Hunt, S.D. (1994), "The commitment–trust theory of relationship marketing", *Journal of Marketing*, vol. 58, no. 3, pp. 20–38.

7   For example, Sisodia, R., Sheth, J. and Wolfe, D. (2007), *Firms of Endearment: How World-Class Companies Profit from Passion and Purpose*, Wharton School Publishing, Upper Saddle River, NJ.

8   Edelenbos, J. and Klijn, E.H. (2006), "Managing stakeholder involvement in decision making: a comparative analysis of six interactive processes in the Netherlands", *Journal of Public Administration Research and Theory*, vol. 16, no. 3, pp. 417–446; Frooman, J. (2010), "The issue network: reshaping the stakeholder model," *Canadian Journal of Administrative Sciences*, vol. 27, no. 2, pp. 161–173; Roloff, J. (2008a), "Learning from multi-stakeholder networks: issue-focused stakeholder management", *Journal of Business Ethics*, vol. 82, no. 1, pp. 233–250; Wheeler, D., Colbert, B. and Freeman, R.E. (2003), "Focusing on value: reconciling corporate social responsibility, sustainability and a stakeholder approach in a network world", *Journal of General Management*, vol. 28, no. 3, pp. 1–28.

9   Roloff, J. (2008b), "A lifecycle model of multi-stakeholder networks", *Business Ethics: A European Review*, vol. 13, no. 3, pp. 311–325.

10   Hansen, J.D. and Bunn, M.D. (2009), "Stakeholder relationship management in multi-sector innovations", *Journal of Relationship Marketing*, vol. 8, no. 3, pp. 196–217.

11   Wilson, E.J., Bunn, M.D. and Savage, G.T. (2010), "Anatomy of a social partnership: a stakeholder perspective", *Industrial Marketing Management*, vol. 39, no. 1, pp. 76–90.

12   Garriga, E. (2009), "Cooperation in stakeholder networks: firms' 'tertius iungens' role", *Journal of Business Ethics*, vol. 90, Supplement 4, pp. 623–637.

13   Frooman (2010), op. cit.

14   Murphy, M. and Arenas, D. (2010), "Through indigenous lenses: cross-sector collaborations with fringe stakeholders", *Journal of Business Ethics*, vol. 94, Supplement 1, pp. 103–121.

15   Van Huijstee, M. and Glasbergen, P. (2010), "Business–NGO interactions in a multi-stakeholder context", *Business and Society Review*, vol. 115, no. 3, pp. 249–284.

16   Handelman, J.M., Bourassa, M.A. and Cunningham, P.H. (2010), "Stakeholder marketing and the organizational field: the role of institutional capital and ideological framing", *Journal of Public Policy and Marketing*, vol. 29, no. 1, pp. 27–37.

17   Roloff (2008b) op. cit., p. 313.

18   Bowen, F. Newenham-Kahindi, A. and Herremans, I. (2010), "When suits meet roots: the antecedents and consequences of community engagement strategy", *Journal of Business Ethics*, vol. 95, no. 2, pp. 297–318.

19   Roloff (2008b), op. cit., p. 314.

20   Garigga (2009), op. cit.; Murphy and Arenas, op. cit.; Roloff (2008b), op. cit.; Wilson, Bunn and Savage, op. cit.; Van Huijustee and Glasbergen, op. cit.

21   Garriga (2009), op. cit.; Hansen and Bunn, op. cit.; Roloff (2008b), op. cit.; Wilson, Bunn and Savage, op. cit.; Rusche, T.M. (2010), "The European climate change program: an evaluation

of stakeholder involvement and policy achievements", *Energy Policy*, vol. 38, no. 10, pp. 6349–6359.

22   Roloff (2008b), op. cit.

23   Mittelstaedt, M. (2010), "For gutted forestry sector, green is the colour of hope", *Globe and Mail*, May 18 2010, http://www.theglobeandmail.com/report-on-business/for-forestry-sector-green-is-the-colour-of-hope/article1572795/, accessed May 19 2010.

24   World Health Organization Fact Sheet (2003), *Obesity and Overweight*, http://www.who.int/hpr/NPH/docs/gs_obesity.pdf, accessed December 23 2010.

25   Patton, M.Q. (2002), *Qualitative Research and Evaluation Methods*, 3rd edn, Sage Publications, Thousand Oaks, CA.

26   Patton (2002), op. cit.

27   Braun, V. and Clarke, V. (2006), "Using thematic analysis in psychology", *Qualitative Research in Psychology*, vol. 3, no. 1, pp. 77–10.

28   Boyatzis, R.E. (1998), *Transforming Qualitative Information: Thematic Analysis and Code Development*, Sage Publications, Inc., Thousand Oaks, CA.

29   Patton (2002), op. cit.

30   Ayuso, Rodriguez and Ricart (2006), "Using stakeholder dialogue as a source for new ideas: a dynamic capability underlying sustainable innovation", *Corporate Governance*, vol. 6, no. 4, pp. 475–490., op. cit.; Partridge *et al.* (2005), op. cit.; Svendsen, A.C. and Laberge, M. (2005), "Convening stakeholder networks: a new way of thinking, being, and engaging", *Journal for Corporate Citizenship*, vol. 19, Autumn, pp. 91–104.

31   Bourassa, M.A. and Cunningham, P.H. (2008), "Respect in business-to-business marketing relationships". In J.R. Brown and R.P. Dant (eds), *Proceedings of the American Marketing Association Summer Educators' Conference, Unleashing the Power of Marketing to Transform Consumers, Organizations, Markets, and Society*, vol. 19, pp. 86–87.

32   Jehn, K.A. and Mannix, E.A. (2001), "The dynamic nature of conflict: a longitudinal study of intragroup conflict and group performance", *Academy of Management Journal*, vol. 44, no. 2, pp. 238–251.

33   Sennett, R. (2003), *Respect in a World of Inequality*, New York: W.W. Norton and Company, see p. 13.

34   Ellerby, N. (2006), Personal interview, October 13 2006.

35   Miller, D.T. (2001), "Disrespect and the experience of injustice", *Annual Review of Psychology*, vol. 52, pp. 527–553.

36   Bourassa, M.A. (2009), "The meaning and impact of respect in the context of business-to-business marketing relationships", Ph.D. thesis, Queen's University, September, https://qspace.library.queensu.ca/bitstream/1974/5272/1/Bourassa_Maureen_A_200909_PhD.pdf, accessed November 2009.

37   Keane, T.P. (2006), "Exploring stakeholder emotional intelligence", *Management Research News*, vol. 29, no. 3, 128–138.

38   Bagozzi, R.P. (2006), "The role of social and self-conscious emotions in the regulation of business-to-business relationships in salesperson–customer interactions", *Journal of Business and Industrial Marketing*, vol. 21, no. 7, pp. 453–457.

39   Lazarus, R.S. (2006), "Emotions and interpersonal relationships: toward a person-centered conceptualization of emotions and coping", *Journal of Personality*, vol. 74, no. 1, pp. 9–46.

40   For example, Fredrickson, B.L. and Branigan, C. (2005), "Positive emotions broaden the scope of attention and thought–action repertoires", *Cognition and Emotion*, vol. 19, no. 3, pp. 313–

332; Han, S., Lerner, J.S. and Keltner, D. (2007), "Feelings and consumer decision making: the appraisal-tendency framework", *Journal of Consumer Psychology*, vol. 17, no. 3, pp. 158–168.

41   Frazier, G.L. (1999), "Organizing and managing channels of distribution", *Journal of the Academy of Marketing Science*, vol. 27, no. 2, pp. 226–240; see p. 228.

42   Maignan, I. and Ferrell, O.C. (2004), "Corporate social responsibility and marketing: an integrative framework", *Journal of the Academy of Marketing Science*, vol. 32, no. 3, pp. 3–19.

43   Svendson and Laberge (2005), op. cit.

44   Bourassa (2009), op. cit.

45   Bagozzi (2006), op. cit.

46   Queen's University Centre for Teaching and Learning (undated), "Conflict management", http://www.queensu.ca/ctl/goodpractice/help/common_dealing_conflict.html, accessed December 21 2010.

47   Payan, J.M. (2007), "A review and delineation of cooperation and coordination in marketing channels", *European Business Review*, vol. 19, no. 3, pp. 216–232, see p. 228.

48   Barreto, M. and Ellemers, N. (2002), "The impact of respect versus neglect of self-identities on identification and group loyalty", *Society for Personality and Social Psychology*, vol. 28, no. 5, pp. 629–639; De Cremer, D. (2002), "Respect and cooperation in social dilemmas: the importance of feeling included", *Personality and Social Psychology Bulletin*, vol. 28, no. 10, pp. 1335–1341; De Cremer, D. (2003), "Noneconomic motives predicting cooperation in public good dilemmas: the effect of received respect on contributions", *Social Justice Research*, vol. 16, no. 4, pp. 367–377.

49   Bourassa (2009), op. cit.

Managing Risks of Stakeholder Conflicts

6 A License to Operate for the Extractive Industries? Operationalizing Stakeholder Thinking in International Business

ROMY KRAEMER* AND ROB VAN TULDER†

Keywords

Extractive industry, integration-responsiveness grid, license to operate, local community, local embeddedness.

Introduction

In May 2002, Occidental Petroleum pulled out of its legally granted concession to explore and extract oil in U'wa territory, Colombia. The U'wa believe that the crude oil is the blood of their "mother earth": they did not consent to the extraction and were supported by international NGOs whose campaign led investors to sell their Occidental shares and ultimately resulted in the company's withdrawal.[1]

In 2003, following immense public and shareholder pressure, Canada's largest oil company, Talisman Energy, pulled out of its Sudanese investments because it had been accused by civil society groups of fuelling the rampant civil war through generating income for the Sudanese government.[2]

In April 2008, Shell reported an output loss of 169,000 barrels of crude per day due to sabotage of its main pipelines in southern Nigeria. Overall, violence in the southern Delta region has reduced Nigeria's total crude oil production by a quarter since January, 2006.[3]

In August 2010, after years of campaigning by a coalition of national and international NGOs and activists in support of the Dongria Kondh tribe, the Indian government denied UK mining company and major aluminium producer Vedanta Resources, environmental clearance for a bauxite mine on the ancestral land of the tribe.[4]

*   Romy Kraemer, Rotterdam School of Management, Erasmus University, Department of Business-Society Management, P.O. Box 1738, 3000 DR Rotterdam, The Netherlands. E-mail: rkraemer@rsm.nl.

†   Rob van Tulder, Rotterdam School of Management, Department of Business-Society Management, Erasmus University, P.O. Box 1738, 3000 DR Rotterdam, The Netherlands. E-mail: rtulder@rsm.nl.

Following the massive oil spill in the Gulf of Mexico caused by the explosion of BP's Deepwater Horizon, the US government—after strong pressure by, among others, local fishery communities—put a hold on all offshore drilling licensing until the safety requirements for this practice had been reviewed.[5]

The examples above illustrate the complex set of stakeholder pressures and their influence on the operations and location choice of corporations from the extractive industry (mineral and oil and gas). Growing awareness for the impact of business operations in other parts of the world in the home countries of large well-known European and North American multinational enterprises (MNEs) from contested industries has turned them into prime targets for attacks by alliances of non-governmental organizations (NGOs) and locally affected stakeholders. The influence of NGOs and local communities on MNEs operations is an interesting perspective on international business.[6] It adds to the traditional emphasis on the quality and availability of natural resources, liability of foreignness,[7] the bargaining power of the host country government[8] and the need for global integration[9] as relevant factors for extractive industry companies' investment decisions. Such theoretical ideas about the nature of the extractive industry and the pressures it faces stand in stark contrast to today's management reality where, beyond the industry's operational and location imperatives, the need to obtain a "License to Operate" (LtO) is central to managerial discourse:

> Chevron: Our approach to stakeholder consultations is designed to earn our license to operate … We believe in earning our license to operate and bringing benefits to communities where we operate.[10]

> BHP Billiton: We understand it is a privilege to operate in communities, and that our licence to operate is crucial to our continued success as a company.[11]

> Vedanta Resources: Being well knit in the social fabric of our communities has enabled us to nurture our social license to operate and to work hand in hand with the local communities and the environment.[12]

The risk of losing the LtO has been dramatically described as "probably the single greatest threat to mining operations throughout the developing world"[13] and its importance was likened to that of financial resources.[14] Such statements clearly point to the crucial nature of stakeholder relationships for corporate success and future expansion strategies in the extractive industries. At the same time, they highlight the need for a reassessment of classic international business theory and an expansion of current thinking to a focus beyond the internal drivers for investments onto the external conditions within which such investments are embedded.

However, despite its popularity among managers, too many questions still remain to be answered, for example which stakeholders actually grant the LtO and especially how it can be conceptualized. This chapter is an attempt to systematize and work towards a coherent perspective on the LtO in order to limit its rhetorical and strategic usage and improve its realistic and managerial use. The chapter therefore extends traditional notions of local responsiveness in international business theory towards an incorporation of stakeholder thinking. Departing from a description of the extractive industry as an ideal case to examine stakeholder pressures, we review the use of the LtO concept by industry representatives and stakeholders. Based on its use by managers in the industry and the available academic literature, a multilevel conceptualization of the LtO is proposed and applied to a discussion of examples from the minerals and oil industry. Going beyond the related concepts of "local embeddedness" and "responsiveness", we highlight how the LtO can extend current international business theory through a shift from traditional ideas about local responsiveness to the notion of stakeholder responsibility. We conclude with a critical discussion of the meaning and implications of the LtO as a concept-in-use and suggest directions for further research.

Stakeholder Pressures in the Extractive Industry

Multinational corporations from the extractive industry (EI) have been confronted with the most long-standing, the broadest, but at the same time also the most fragmented set of requests from a variety of stakeholders, especially when operating in developing countries. Due to the boundedness of their location choices to the availability of natural resources and the increasing need to explore earlier uneconomic and remote reserves, EI firms often operate under the most complex and challenging conditions, e.g. in politically tense conflict zones, under unstable regimes, in disadvantaged rural communities in developing countries and on the lands of indigenous peoples—often combining more than one challenge.[15] Conflicts and local resistance to extractive operations are more frequent than in any other industry and our opening examples show that extractive industry firms repeatedly had to involuntarily withdraw from investments that seemed viable from a purely operational and economical perspective. Responsiveness to local claims and circumstances is therefore crucial to avoid high transaction and sunk costs and is becoming a precondition for future expansion strategies.[16] The EI has therefore been at the forefront of debates about corporate responsibilities and the role of multinational corporations in development.[17] Mining and oil multinationals are also featured prominently in debates about the internationalization of MNEs from transition and developing countries, south–south investment, and the strategic and developmental implications of such developments in international investment patterns.[18] These corporations are thus a highly relevant example for the need to integrate non-market and non-profit dimensions into the study of MNEs. Nevertheless, they remain a relatively poorly studied subset of MNEs.[19]

Pressures from and conflicts with three main stakeholder groups have shown to be especially relevant for EI companies in the past. The first, and most directly affected stakeholder group are the *local communities* who are displaced by or located in the vicinity of mining and oil development. A MNEs' interpretation of "sustainable development" increasingly also means corporate community involvement and responsiveness to local needs.[20] Especially in the high-impact extractive business, some corporations acknowledge the multiple social, cultural, environmental and economic effects of mineral and oil extraction[21] and engage in a host of more or less successful local development projects, often carried out in collaboration with NGOs. The second stakeholder group entails *national and international NGOs*. They often support communities' claims and shape the public opinion about individual corporations as well as the entire sector. Greenpeace's role in the controversy about the sinking of Shell's Brent Spar oil platform is a well-known case in point.[22] NGOs are central in the escalation of conflicts around large-scale investments in contentious industries[23] and have been crucial in highlighting important issues for the EI such as revenue transparency, their role in climate change discussion and the environmental and human rights impact of EI operations.[24] The third stakeholder group are the *host country governments*. They have a high impact on the activities of EI multinationals, e.g. through their role in the granting of exploration and exploitation licenses, taxation and the threat of nationalization due to the strategic nature of the sector.[25]

The combination of an often demanding operational environment accompanied by conflicting stakeholder demands creates a unique challenge for EI corporations. Sparked by the controversy and high attention with which their operations are usually met, EI multinationals have been at the forefront of CSR activities and rhetoric and have been crucial in coining the LtO concept. This has motivated major NGOs like Oilwatch or Corpwatch to accuse the industry of "greenwashing" and highlight deviations from their stated CSR commitments. This chapter thus also faces the challenge to try to go beyond the rhetoric and develop the LtO into a more sophisticated concept in which the complex stakeholder relationships with host locations are realistically included.

Trends in the Practical Use of the LtO Concept

Extractive industry firms in particular have embraced the LtO as a leading paradigm for business conduct and the achievement of long-term profitability. How central the LtO concept has become is apparent in industry-specific conferences covering the topic, especially in Australia and Canada with titles such as "Social License to Operate 2010" or "Land Access Forum":

> *The perceived right to have a physical presence of place in a community is a core challenge to the resources industry. Some might say it is the biggest issue they are facing. Gaining regulatory approval for mining and petroleum projects and developing the necessary infrastructure is a challenging, time and money intensive process. But without a social license to operate in a region, these physical and administrative investments can be rendered worthless.[26]*

Table 6.1 lists additional material from a basic web search (using the terms "license/licence to operate" on Google.com and EI corporate websites). This quick review illustrates three general trends: first, community and society at large feature most prominently as grantors of the LtO. Secondly, the LtO, instead of being a tangible document, is used in a metaphorical sense. It is the perception of managers that the firm's presence and operations are accepted by the local population. Finally, despite this relative consensus, there remains considerable variance in terms of the antecedents, outcomes and nature of the LtO, as well as related concepts such as reputation or citizenship. The importance of community, however, indicates that contributing to sustainable local development is widely seen as the key to local acceptance.[27] The lower part of Table 6.1 further suggests that the notion of the LtO has also been taken up by NGOs, consultants and the general public when discussing issues relevant for the EI and its stakeholder relationships.

This characteristic of the LtO as a concept-in-use and its widespread use across industry actors without a clear consensus about its meaning, makes it comparable to the concept of "corporate citizenship", a term which also largely originated from American multinationals and EI corporations.[28] Practitioners seem to attach increasing value to the LtO as a means to operationalize stakeholder relationships, while local communities and stakeholders embrace the concept also as an argument in obtaining a better bargaining position in their negotiations with investors to achieve better preconditions for sustainable development. Like corporate citizenship before it, the LtO concept has been embraced by academics,[29] notwithstanding its conceptual and managerial ambiguities.

Table 6.1   Overview of the use of the license to operate (LtO) concept

LtO quote	SH group	Actor/institution
"Our license to operate in a country is only as good as the community's attitude towards us"	Community	(Eyton 2010, Head Research & Technology, BP)[30]
"Our licence to operate—it's our reputation as a partner of choice. Gaining and maintaining our licence to operate is critical to our business. We aim to ensure that the communities in which we operate value our citizenship"	Community	BHP Billiton website[31]
"Social license is the acceptance and belief by society, and specifically our local communities, in the value creation of our activities, such as we are allowed to access and extract mineral resources"	Community, society	(Pierre Lassonde, Newmont Mining Corp. in Reichardt 2006)
"Most companies recognise the far-reaching effects that health, safety and environmental issues can have on their business. Like us, they believe that long-term competitive success depends on being trusted to meet the expectations of society as well as those of shareholders and stakeholders"	Society, shareholders, stakeholders	Shell website[32] under the heading "Licence to operate"
"For international oil and gas companies like BP, our 'license to operate' depends on the consent of the societies in which we work. Mostly, we operate under license. We rarely work alone. Almost nothing we do is unregulated. To succeed, we have to be in step with society"	Society	(Rice, D. Director, Policy Unit, BP p.l.c 2002)
"The social license is intangible, renewable daily and granted by the people only when their needs are being met"	Community	(Kurlander, L. T., Senior Vice President Newmont Mining 2001)[33]
"A 'social licence to operate' is earned by acquiring free, prior and informed consent from indigenous peoples and local communities"	Community	*Australian Journal of Mining* online article[34]
"Due to the egregious number of safety violations and warnings; they should lose any license to operate within the United States at all"	Host government	Reader's comment on an article about the BP oil spill[35]
"If society gives business its license to operate, then surely society can demand that business takes responsibility for any significant negative consequences associates with its products"	Society	Blog entry on a business ethics consultancy website[36]
"At the level of an individual project the Social License is rooted in the beliefs, perceptions and opinions held by the local population and other stakeholders about the project"	Community	Definition of LtO on the website of a LtO consultancy[37]
"This effort would go a long way toward improving Chevron's relations with host communities and, in the long run, strengthening Chevron's capacity to obtain legal and social 'license to operate'"	Community	Ian Gary, Oxfam America in the Huffington Post[38]

A Theoretical Elaboration

CONCEPTUALIZING THE LTO AT THREE LEVELS

The LtO is sometimes also termed "social license" or "social license to operate". It has mainly entered the field of management studies as part of stakeholder theory:[39]

With respect to individuals and groups involuntarily impacted by corporate activity, in particular those subject to pollution, congestion, unwelcome cultural influences, or the like, the critical management goals have to be avoidance of harm, reduction of risk, and/or the creation of offsetting benefits, so that the continued operation of the individual enterprise—its "license to operate"—remains acceptable to all parties.

Like practitioner statements, the academic definitions focus primarily on corporation's impact on and relationships with community stakeholders (see also Table 6.2). Other work on the LtO has been done from a legal perspective in the pulp and paper industry[40] and, following a very hands-on industry approach, also in the mining industry.[41] Some authors have focused on firm internal factors that influence how the need for an LtO is perceived and what response strategies are chosen in the face of external stakeholder pressures. They argue that the LtO is constructed through a continuous interaction process.[42]

Despite the initial focus on communities, at the same time the LtO always also has a more broad societal component that resonates in many of the definitions and industry statements. At the most extreme, it is the stated requirement for the corporation to "earn its 'license to operate,' both locally and globally, by demonstrating its respect for people and its contribution to building a better world".[43]

Others have criticized this weakly developed notion of the LtO as an obligation in return for the special privileges and benefits conferred on businesses by society.[44] Considering these lines of contention, it is very likely that the LtO discussion will move into an intellectual stalemate comparable to the one on corporate citizenship. To

Table 6.2   Definitions of the LtO

Source	Definition
	"Demands on and expectations for a business enterprise that emerge from neighborhoods, environmental groups, community members, and other elements of the surrounding civil society"
	"Comprises a set of concepts, values, tools and practices that represent a way of viewing reality for the communities. It not only forms the foundation of the mine life cycle, it also permeates each and every phase from discovery to reclamation"
	"The degree to which the firm's conduct is accepted by society"
	"Indigenous peoples and other affected parties do have the right to participate in decision making and to give their free prior and informed consent throughout each phase of a project cycle. This consent should be seen as the principal determinant of whether there is a 'social license to operate'"

prevent such a situation, and in order to synthesize the existing literature and the ways in which the concept has been used by practitioners, we propose a concept of LtO that interrelates three levels: the societal/global, the legal/national and the social/local license (Figure 6.1).

Before explaining these levels, however, we need to clarify how the LtO relates to other concepts—most importantly the concept of legitimacy.[45] While legitimacy is primarily a theoretical construct,[46] the LtO clearly is a practitioner concept and strategically employed to create a societal perception of organizational acceptance in society. Moreover, legitimacy is usually described as the absence of challenges towards the object of legitimation and as a non-rival and homogenizing concept.[47] This is often interpreted and operationalized as a "negative duty" approach. The LtO approach departs from a more "positive duty" approach where practitioners emphasize the need for actively obtaining a license (and with it potentially also a competitive advantage) from local or state-level stakeholders, as well as society.

The LtO, as it is currently used, is more immediate and dichotomous (either present or absent) and granted at a micro level compared to the more abstract concept of legitimacy that grows over time and can increase with increasing numbers of legitimizing actors/institutions.[48] Legitimacy is a broader concept that relates to the general societal acceptance of, for example, the extractive industry as a whole. This will be further referred to below as the "License to Exist". The local LtO might thus be seen as a possible expression or benefit of a firms' overall legitimacy.[49] These ideas will be integrated into a theoretically informed operationalization of the practitioner's LtO concept in order to

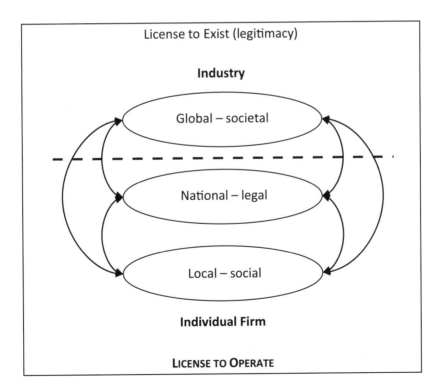

Figure 6.1 Multilevel conceptualization of the LtO

apply it to an analysis of the challenges faced by the EI and extend current thinking about local responsiveness and global integration later in this chapter.

The societal/global level refers to the broad acceptance of EI operations in general,[50] likened above to the overall legitimacy of the industry. Individual firms try to alter the image of the EI as a "dirty" industry and to align their values with those prevalent in the societies where operations take place in order to remain in business.[51] Joint EI company initiatives such as the "Mining, minerals, and sustainable development" initiative in 2002[52] are attempts to build public trust and contribute to the overall legitimacy of the industry, which we label the *License to Exist* because of its broad overarching industry-level implications. In moral theory this notion builds on the general "fiduciary duty" of corporations and has been operationalized as the compliance likelihood of codes of conduct and reporting strategies.[53]

The national level of the LtO is concerned with obtaining necessary governmental licenses and permits for a local operation and complying with, for example, emission and waste management guidelines. Past operating performance plays an important role here[54] in that it paves the way in the form of what has been labelled "reputation capital" by a Newmont Mining executive. However, the national license is not entirely legal in nature. If host governments decide that companies' activities are not benefiting the country enough, they might pull their support and withdraw the LtO through non-renewal of legal licenses, inviting competitors, or, in the worst case, nationalization of the industry. Governments need to trust firms for them to obtain prospecting rights and access to blocs of land for oil, gas or minerals exploration or to be accepted by the country as a retailer (e.g. selling refined petroleum). In the 1990s this was an issue for example in the opening up of Eastern European countries where not all foreign firms were equally successful in obtaining the licenses to operate gas stations from the local bureaucratic machine.[55]

The local LtO can be conceptualized in line with what many authors have referred to as the "social" LtO and portends to the management of relations with important local stakeholders—usually referred to as "the community" in the above quotes. Those are the stakeholders who could effectively prevent operations or increase transaction costs for corporations at the local level, e.g. through loss of production (strikes, blockades, land conflict), higher costs for security provision, costs for dispute resolution (community consultation, capacity building stakeholder meetings, employee/management time) and additional costs for data gathering and verification (e.g. environmental data, consultants).[56] This relates to the original meaning of corporate citizenship that requires corporations to be responsible members of the local community in which they operate.[57] The local LtO is not guaranteed by obtaining the support of the state and society and might not be equally persistent over time as a signed contract with the host country government. In that sense it is tied to "local needs" as referred to above by Kurlander (Table 5.1) and continuously negotiated. Reluctance of local governments to support firms in struggles with local stakeholders and normative expectations for good local relationships within and outside the enterprise (e.g. codes of conduct or policies such as ILO 169, World Bank Operational Directive 4.20) require firms to negotiate directly with local stakeholders and add to the need for obtaining a local LtO.[58] Additionally, the increasingly sophisticated organization of local communities and their expertise in linking up with international activists and campaigns makes it harder for firms to ignore those groups and practice what has been called a "right of way" policy,[59] where trespassing and land use issues were resolved with small cash payments to locals without any further consideration of their development needs.

Figure 6.1 also highlights the interconnectedness of the three levels and the two-way relationships among them. An industry's overall license to exist is influenced by the LtOs granted to individual firms all over the world at a national and local level and by the existence and public debate about universal standards or "hypernorms".[60] As for reputational effects,[61] it has been shown that deviance of individual firms and their loss of the LtO has negative spillover effects for innocent firms within the same industry and thus has implications for the overall legitimacy or license to exist.[62] Internationally operating activists and NGOs therefore raise broader questions about the legitimacy of the EI in general and have successfully influenced the relationships between MNEs and host country governments[63] as well as considerably change public awareness of the negative impact of the EI on host countries and communities. Likewise, national and societal challenges to the industry's or individual corporation's LtO can improve the chances of local communities in challenging individual EI corporations and motivate them to take local action.

Application to the Extractive Industries

The 2010 BP oil spill in the Gulf of Mexico and the subsequent congressional hearing with executives from ExxonMobil, Shell and Chevron highlights the threat of a loss of the License to Exist (LtE) for corporations following an individual corporation's malperformance. Likewise, the public debate about doing business in Sudan threatened the LtO of Western oil corporations in general and had an impact on individual firms such as Talisman Oil, who had to pull out of the country. In South Africa, the Black Economic Empowerment movement, supported by international NGOs, considerably affected the way individual mining firms now conduct their operations and engage in CSR by sparking a wider societal discussion.[64] The lawsuit of the inhabitants of Kivalina against Exxon Mobil and 23 other American oil producers because of their contribution to global warming and attempts to influence the public discourse threatens their overall LtE and would not have been possible without the current concern about climate change in the wider society. In general, calls for sustainable community development, that extend beyond the life cycle of the individual resource development project, would not be possible without the wide perception in society that long-term sustainability is a legitimate claim.

On the other hand, conflicts over natural resource development bring to light conflicts and deeper clashes of worldviews[65] and interests between different segments of society that are especially pronounced in industrializing countries and/or those with indigenous populations, ethnic or religious differences, and smouldering civil conflicts that are usually exacerbated by the prospect of resource rents. In countries like India or Brazil, the majority of the mainstream population supports the LtE of the mining and oil industry on the grounds that it is able to deliver income for national development, while the local LtO is routinely challenged by indigenous peoples and poor rural communities whose ways of life and subsistence base are threatened and who might not want or are unable to participate in the kind of development resource extraction might bring.[66] Faced with local resistance, EI corporations, claiming their legal rights and building on the national

LtO, often call in the government/police forces for support. The Sudanese government, for example, used heavy military force to "clear" areas for petroleum development and forestall local resistance to exploitation of resource wealth,[67] the Indian government has been accused of similar activities with respect to mining and the focus on fighting so-called Maoists in mineral rich states.[68]

The complexities of earning a national LtO have for example been felt by RioTinto operating in Guinea, where legal licenses stand and fall with the appointment of ministers. As a result of such turbulences, the company runs the risk of their right to exploit the largest known undeveloped iron ore reserve in the world being withdrawn and might incur sunk costs of $300 million.[69] In Russia, Shell lost half of its shares in the hugely profitable Sakhalin II project after signing an initially very beneficial production-sharing agreement with the government back in 1996. Ten years later, the technical ability of Gazprom to develop the reserve had increased and the Russian government, suddenly backing environmentalists' claims against the company, took over ownership in the enterprise. This is a prime example of a government (ab)using local level claims against a firm to increase its own bargaining power in negotiations about the national LtO.

The local LtO can be challenged or revoked at any time and the conditions under which it is granted are subject to renegotiation. If firms do not fulfil their obligations and promises for local development, local stakeholders will try to claim justice. In Mambia, Guinea, Russia's aluminum company Rusal signed an agreement with the local community in 1984 and by 2008 had failed to fulfil its promises regarding the provision of public services to affected communities. Two people were killed and several others injured during local protests,[70] only one example among many such incidences all over the world that make clear that EI corporations often fail to gain the local LtO.

Incorporating the LtO into International Business Theory: From Embeddedness and Responsiveness to Responsibility

LOCAL RESPONSIVENESS AND EMBEDDEDNESS

International business theory, though interested in the investment behavior of multinational corporations, has so far not paid much attention to the specific stakeholder pressures faced by the EIs and thus has not yet contributed to the concept of the LtO, a lacunae that we wish to address. Two core concepts have been introduced in the international business literature to research and prescribe management practices: responsiveness and embeddedness. Both concepts are relevant, but need updating and repositioning.

First, the integration-responsiveness (I-R) idea[71] belongs to the classic tenets of international business and strategy. It illuminates the tensions for multinational firms that arise from the need to balance responsiveness at subsidiary level with global efficiency, integration and headquarter control and has been widely applied at the level of the industry,[72] the multinational enterprise[73] and their subsidiaries.[74] Integration means exploiting cost and efficiency advantages and opportunities for standardization arising from multi-country operations, whereas local responsiveness is understood as reacting to domestic competition and host country demands while sufficiently differentiating operations to handle global competition. The classic international business thesis as formulated in the "integration-responsiveness grid"[75] portrays extractive industries as a prime example of "global industries" that combine a high pressure for integration and a low pressure for responsiveness (Figure 6.2).

Levitt's original work on globalization reinforced this impression: oil majors and mining companies serve global markets with relatively standardized products.[76] Pressures for integration and responsiveness vary not only across firms and countries, but also between functions within businesses, e.g. CSR and human resource management.[77] Previous studies however, favored the examination of pressures for global integration[78] and only more recent work tried to investigate the environmental, industry-structural, and firm-related factors that influence the local responsiveness of subsidiaries.[79]

The I-R model has been criticized for a number of reasons: for instance its lack of conceptual clarity which has lead to problematic empirical validation,[80] or its ambiguity as regards the nature of the pressure (exogenous, endogenous representing managerial choices) and its relationship with performance.[81]

Second, the concept of embeddedness[82] has also been widely applied in the international business literature, e.g. with respect to the integration of foreign subsidiaries into the local economy,[83] local clusters[84] and the potential of FDI to contribute to regional development.[85] Other studies examined institutional embeddedness,[86] the relationship between local embeddedness and employee attitudes,[87] or relational embeddedness between parent and international joint ventures.[88] Local embeddedness through connections and local networks is a source of information, knowledge and physical

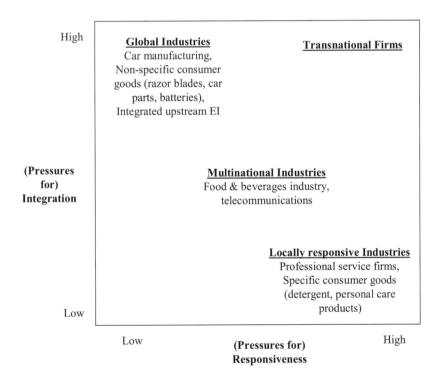

Figure 6.2   The traditional integration-responsiveness grid

resources, but also of power and legitimacy.[89] In terms of legitimacy, embeddedness created through corporate citizenship activities is said to help companies to overcome their liability of foreignness in a host country location.[90] What can be learned from those studies of firm networks is that embeddedness enables firms to obtain reliable information to categorize other actors in the network and inform decision-making regarding which players are important for the focal firm.[91] Applied to the EI context, higher embeddedness of Shell in local stakeholder relationships with local groups in the Niger Delta might have facilitated recognition of the importance of the oppositional movement led by Ken Saro-Wiwa, before it was too late for the company to take sensible action. Even 15 years after the original case materialized, the company is still struggling (in American and Dutch courts) with this issue.

Such local knowledge and learning issues have brought some authors to equate local embeddedness with local responsiveness, arguing that subsidiary managers possess crucial local knowledge that is needed at MNE headquarters and that knowledge and technology transfer to parents improves through embeddedness.[92] The local context is seen as a source of important information which headquarters are unable to obtain and that local responsiveness/embeddedness can thus deliver strategic advantages.[93]

Despite the prescriptions for local responsiveness and the seemingly high value of firm embeddedness into local networks, the international business literature is ripe with examples of under-adaptation of firms to their local environment, be it in marketing,[94] human resource management,[95] or internationalization strategy.[96] Similarly, for extractive industry operations, local adaptation is normatively seen as a specific success factor,[97] though it is often not reached in practice.

From Responsiveness and Embeddedness to Responsibility

Both the mainstream responsiveness and embeddedness approach have their limitations. The added value of the LtO concept to traditional international business theory is that it upgrades the idea of local responsiveness as mentioned in the I-R grid approach to include also the increasingly challenging stakeholder relationships that firms in the EI in particular face.

Local responsiveness as it is currently used is strongly biased towards market-seeking MNEs and their need to adapt products and services to suit host country markets and be responsive to local institutions and business cultures.[98] Pressures for responsiveness originate from customers and business partners: other local stakeholders are rarely considered in such a context. Our discussion of the LtO has shown the importance of a more diverse set of stakeholders that challenges the applicability of the classic I-R grid to the EI.

Due to the specific nature of the industry, responsiveness is not just a question of being able to "successfully confront cultures, markets, and business practices"[99] and of gaining some competitive advantage through exploitation of those differences. Local responsiveness in the EI often means securing the operability of a project or reducing transaction costs to a tolerable size. Current conceptualizations of local responsiveness do not account for this situation. Firms trying to obtain or maintain their local LtO usually do so with initiatives that are summarized under the label of corporate social responsibility. The traditional I-R framework (Figure 6.3) can thus be reformulated into an integration-responsibility (I-R$_2$) framework (Figure 6.3).

Figure 6.3 illustrates that the initial distribution of industries in the I-R framework changes considerably in the I-R$_2$ grid. Professional service firms, for instance, experience much less pressure for local responsibility than for responsiveness. Manufacturing industries (such as the car and chemical industries) have to be split up into a "low" and "high" polluting segment, in order to take into account pressures of responsiveness and responsibility. In this case it seems increasingly obvious that responsibility overrules responsiveness as an influencing factor for internationalization strategies. For specific consumer goods the pressure for local responsiveness (and adaptation) remains high. Building on this idea, C.K. Prahalad[100] developed the notion of the "bottom of the pyramid", which is basically a marketing approach built on responsiveness to the needs of billions of so far untapped customers at the lower end of the market. However, the claim that this strategy can be coupled with responsibility—in short that it might lead to alleviating poverty—is highly disputed.[101] Responsiveness and responsibility in consumer product markets are not the same.

With respect to the location of EI multinationals in the I-R$_2$ grid, we can see that it strongly depends on their position in the global value chain. The more vertically integrated and upstream and the bigger they are, the more they are prone to both pressures for integration and responsibility. While less integrated and smaller EI firms and those more active in downstream activities only face only one of these pressures, the former for responsibility and the latter for higher integration.

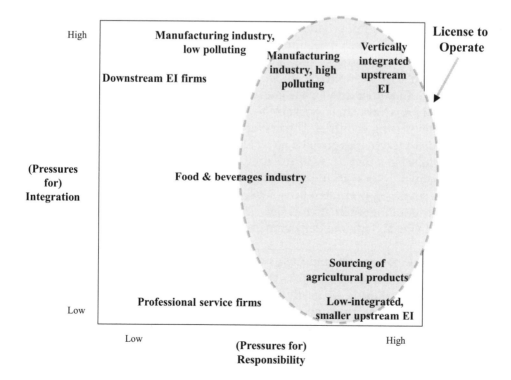

Figure 6.3   Adapted I-R grid: from responsiveness to responsibility (I-R2)

The LtO is most relevant in the area encircled by the dotted line. Firms outside this area benefit from low direct threats to their overall LtO. They might, however, as in the case of downstream EI firms, suffer from negative spillovers should the LtO of a firm from the same industry that is more vertically integrated be threatened. It is thus not the case that the LtO is irrelevant for all firms outside the oval. However, the direct threat to the LtO through a lack of responsibility is lower for these industries.

The need for a shift to local responsibility has also been emphasized elsewhere. From an international strategy perspective, London and Hart caution that "the transnational model of national responsiveness, global efficiency and worldwide learning may not be sufficient" and argue further that MNEs need to change their strategies in order to develop "a global capability in social embeddedness".[102]

Discussion and Conclusions

Our review of the specifics of the extractive industry, cases of failed or contested investments in this business and practitioner perspectives on how to confront this situation shows that natural resource development takes place in a complex and challenging stakeholder environment. We traced the emergence of the concept of the LtO among corporate executives and stakeholders of the extractive industry. The varieties of uses of the LtO concept suggests that, like sustainability or globalization, it is an "empty signifier", that takes on different meanings at different times and for different actors.[103] Nevertheless, we have tried to develop a first theoretical conceptualization of the LtO based on the scant academic literature and its current importance as a "concept-in-use". This conceptualization proposes three interconnected levels of LtO that highlight the local, national and societal requirements posed upon the extractive industry (and potentially also other industries). This approach combines the multiple ways in which the LtO has been selectively used into one overarching concept to highlight what has also been shown in a brief case review and application of the concept to the extractive industry (EI). EI firms have rarely been able to obtain the LtO at all levels, especially when operating in developing countries. Discussing the LtO at all relevant levels can help to unveil contradictory activities undertaken by EI firms when trying to reconcile the diverse stakeholder challenges they face. While they engage heavily in CSR and community initiatives to gain the "local license", these firms might at the same time demand support from the host country government in violently suppressing local resistance movements. Likewise, while funding alternative energy projects, many EI corporations have been accused of lobbying activities to deny climate change and maintain their overall license to exist.[104]

Despite failed investments and high sunk costs incurred by many EI firms, current thinking in international business on local adaptation has largely ignored this industry[105] and has evoked an illusion of nearly total discretion on the side of MNEs when it comes to investment decisions and the degree of local responsiveness.[106] Traditional approaches to local responsiveness and embeddedness of MNEs in their host locations do not take into account some of the specific challenges of the extractive industry. On the contrary, subsequent versions of the I-R framework have been simplified rather than being extended.[107] A reformulation of the traditional integration-responsiveness to an integration-responsibility grid was presented that captures the complexities raised by the notion of the LtO and might help save the original idea from its present critics.

The emphasis on local communities as a crucial set of local stakeholders strengthens the link between stakeholder theory and international business that has so far focused on MNEs' relationships with host governments[108] and, more recently, international NGOs.[109] The multilevel LtO concept highlights the importance of all three stakeholder groups and points out the increasing importance of the local license that, in interaction with the national and societal LtO, should be incorporated much more strongly in international management thinking. The emergence of the LtO rhetoric points to the fact that managers have realized this importance.

The I-R$_2$ grid points out that the "local license" is also relevant for other industries, and the multilevel LtO can potentially be applied to a wider set of corporations than has been done here. In the Indian state of Orissa for example, 11 out of 14 mega-investment projects in the mineral but also mineral processing and service industry (together nearly US$40 billion) are halted or delayed by community protests despite having been granted a national/legal license to set up business.[110] Likewise, after nearly two years of struggle, considerable sunk costs and the suicide of a number of farmers, Tata's Nano car plant was relocated from one Indian state to another.[111] These examples speak for the relevance of the multilevel LtO concept and the importance of including stakeholder considerations in international business theories about the investment behavior or MNEs. Future research should examine whether and how the LtO terminology is applied in other industries and what alternative concepts are being employed.

This contribution has also illustrated that the notion of the LtO, in particular the way it is currently used, needs to be critically examined. From an industry perspective, employing the LtO concept is a matter of "hegemonic strategizing"[112] in an attempt to shape the corporate responsibility discourse in favour of the extractive industries, to define what it means to gain a LtO and who is able to grant it. The risk is that, employing the LtO discourse, corporations interact with specifically selected stakeholders who are perceived to have the power to actually influence the firm's conduct to gain a LtO from this stakeholder group that then provides a tangible "insurance" against stakeholder activism. They might further use the LtO rhetoric to imply a continuous "license" equal to a legal license, which is the risk that lies in the use of such a term. Another risk is the ignorance of the role of the state in discussions that are focused on obtaining local licenses in the sense of a "right of way". This always carries the risk that individual licenses are "bought cheaply" from the local population with promises and CSR projects that ultimately often fail to produce the expected benefits.

Our multilevel conceptualization and discussion of the LtO is thus relevant, because it points out the three levels at which an LtO needs to be obtained and the tensions emerging from competing stakeholder claims. It also highlights the fact that the LtO is not some "thing" to be obtained or a one-time achievement that legitimizes the operations. The LtO is a process of ongoing negotiations between the corporation and its stakeholders who continuously evaluate corporate performance according to criteria they deem important and who influence and compete with each other. The terminology "license" in that sense seems not to fit the actual processes underlying it, but is now too deeply rooted in managerial discourse to be changed. A multilevel perspective on the LtO might counteract a tendency to apply the concept in a way that allows it to appear all too manageable and continuous. The level of the national LtO also emphasizes the role of the state and society in pressuring corporations to operate according to overarching principles, which avoids a situation where corporations only invest in social issues that might gain them a local LtO while ignoring issues of broader importance or claims of stakeholders that are not powerful enough to threaten their license. Our approach might help in safeguarding the LtO concept from its early supporters—who adopt a too superficial and strategic understanding of the concept, which would make it meaningless.

Future work should elaborate the preliminary conceptualization of the LtO presented in this contribution and further strengthen the link between International Business and stakeholder theory. In light of the increasing importance of EI multinationals for developing and transition economies,[113] that often function as shareholder-independent strategic extensions of their home country governments, future work should also examine the firm internal factors[114] that might influence differing perspectives among managers on the need to gain an LtO at all levels or how to obtain it. Although such corporations are less receptive to the traditional influence tactics of NGOs (e.g. shareholder divestments, public shaming), they too suffer from increased operating costs and the potential "inoperability" of a project due to local resistance and might forge even stronger alliances with repressive national governments than has been possible for shareholder-owned corporations.

With respect to the embeddedness of the MNE, some suggest the need of a "cultural embeddedness".[115] Our case discussion has shown that this seems hard to achieve. One could argue that even the hiring of local employees might not considerably improve this situation due to the clashing interests and worldviews, and the tensions within many developing countries that we have discussed above. Here it is the "relative power or powerlessness, accorded to various cultures and cultural practices"[116] that should be examined by management scholars instead of supporting a focus on corporations' embeddedness into dominant cultures.

Finally, the role of smaller EI corporations that are less globally integrated deserves further attention in light of the current discussion about local responsiveness/ responsibility. Due to their smaller size and focus on specific locations that are then crucial to the business success of the entire firm, such corporations have potentially more to lose from an unsuccessful investment and high sunk costs caused by local resistance. Although they might not have the funds available to implement large CSR or corporate citizenship programs, their need to embed themselves locally might be stronger and result in a more wise use of available funding. The success of such firms might prove the idea that it is (as often) not size that matters for the success of community investments.[117]

Notes

1   Idahosa, P. (2003), "Business ethics and development in conflict (zones): The case of Talisman Oi", *Journal of Business Ethics*, vol. 39, no. 3, pp. 227–246.

2   Aponte Miranda, L. (2007), "The U'wa and Occidental Petroleum: Searching for corporate accountability in violations of indigenous land rights", *American Indian Law Review*, vol. 31, no. 2, pp. 651–673.

3   Watts, M. (2007), "Petro-insurgency or criminal syndicate? Conflict and violence in the Niger Delta", *Review of African Political Economy*, vol. 34, no. 114, pp. 637–660.

4   Rahman, M. (2010), "India blocks Vedanta mine on Dongria Kondh tribe's sacred hill", *The Guardian*, http://www.guardian.co.uk/business/2010/aug/24/vedanta-mining-industry-india, accessed January 30 2012.

5   Dayen, D. (2010), "White House puts new offshore drilling on hold after BP disaster", http://news.firedoglake.com/2010/04/30/white-house-puts-new-offshore-drilling-on-hold-after-bp-disaster/, accessed January 30 2012.

6   Doh, J.P. and Teegen, H. (eds) (2003), *Globalization and NGOs: Transforming Business, Government, and Society*, Praeger, Westport, CT; Teegen, H., Doh, J.P. and Vachani, S. (2004), "The importance of nongovernmental organizations (NGOs) in global governance and value creation: an international business research agenda", *Journal of International Business Studies*, vol. 35, no. 6, pp. 463–483.

7   Zaheer, S. (1995), "Overcoming the liability of foreignness", *Academy of Management Journal*, vol. 38, no. 2, pp. 341–363.

8   Fagre, N. and Wells, L.T. (1982), "Bargaining power of multinationals and host governments", *Journal of International Business Studies*, vol. 13, no. 2, pp. 9–23; Grosse, R. (1996), "The bargaining relationship between foreign MNEs and host governments in Latin America", *The International Trade Journal*, vol. 10, no. 4, pp. 467–499; Ramamurti, R. (2001), "The obsolescing 'bargaining model'? MNC-host developing country relations revisited", *Journal of International Business Studies*, vol. 32, no. 1, pp. 23–39; Vernon, R. (1971), *Sovereignty at Bay*, Routledge, London.

9   Bartlett, C.A. and Ghoshal, S. (1989b), *Managing Across Borders: The Transnational Solution*, Harvard Business School Press, Boston, Mass.

10   McLeod, M. (2009), Manager Atlantic Canada, Chevron's growth strategy for Atlantic Canada, Expo Labrador.

11   Nasser, J. (2010), Chair BHP Billiton Plc., Speech at Annual General Meeting.

12   Vedanta Resources Plc. (2010), *Annual Report*, available at http://ar2010.vedantaresources.com/sustainability/sustainablecommunity.html, accessed May 12 2011.

13   Reichardt, C.L. (2006), "Due dilligence assessment of non-financial risk: prophylaxis for the purchaser", *Resources Policy*, vol. 31, pp. 193–203, p. 195.

14   Post, J.E., Preston, L.E. and Sachs, S. (2002), *Redefining the Corporation: Stakeholder Management and Organizational Wealth*, Stanford University Press, Stanford.

15   Coumans, C. (2008), "Realising solidarity: indigenous peoples and NGOs in the contested terrains of mining and corporate accountability". In C. O'Faircheallaigh and S.H. Ali (eds), *Earth Matters: Indigenous Peoples, Extractive Industries and Corporate Social Responsibility*, Greenleaf Publishing Ltd, Sheffield, pp. 42–66.

16   Reichardt (2006), op. cit.

17   Frynas, G.J. (2009), *Beyond Corporate Social Responsibility: Oil Multinationals and Social Challenges*, Cambridge University Press, Cambridge; KPMG (2005), *KPMG International Survey of Corporate Responsibility Reporting*, KPMG, Amsterdam; UNCTAD (2006), *World Investment Report: FDI from Developing and Transition Economies: Implications for Development*, United Nations, Geneva and New York; Van Tulder, R. and van der Zwart, A. (2006), *International Business-society Management*, Routledge, London; Zyglidopoulos, S.C. (2002), "The social and environmental responsibilities of multinationals: evidence from the Brent Spar case", *Journal of Business Ethics*, vol. 36, no. 1/2, pp. 141–151.

18   Athreye, S. and Kapur, S. (2009), "Introduction: the internationalization of Chinese and Indian firms—trends, motivation and strategy", *Industrial and Corporate Change*, vol. 18, no. 2, pp. 209–221; Aykut, D. and Goldstein, A. (2007), "Developing country multinationals: south–

south investment comes of age". In United Nations (ed.), *Industrial Development in the 21st Century: Sustainable Development Perspectives*, UN, Geneva, pp. 85–118; UNCTAD (2006), op. cit.

19 Jones, G. (2005), *Multinationals and Global Capitalism: From the Nineteenth to the Twenty-first Century*, Oxford University Press, Oxford.

20 Fortanier, F. and Kolk, A. (2007), "On the economic dimensions of CSR: exploring Fortune Global 250 reports", *Business and Society*, vol. 46, no. 4, pp. 457–478; Jones, I., Pollitt, M.G. and Bek, D. (2007), *Multinationals in their Communities: A Social Capital Approach to Corporate Citizenship Projects*, Palgrave MacMillan, Basingstoke; Kobeissi, N. and Damanpour, F. (2009), "Corporate responsiveness to community stakeholders: effects of contextual and organizational characteristics", *Business and Society*, vol. 48, no. 3, pp. 326–359.

21 Banerjee, S.B. (2000), "Whose land is it anyway? National interest, indigenous stakeholders and colonial discourses—the case of the Jabiluka uranium mine", *Organization and Environment*, vol. 13, no. 1, pp. 3–38; Evans, G., Goodman, J. and Lansbury, N. (eds) (2002), *Moving Mountains: Communities Confront Mining and Globalisation*, Zed Books Ltd., London; Whiteman, G. (2004), "Forestry, gold mining and Amerindians: the troubling example of Samling in Guyana". In F. Bird and S.W. Herman (eds), *International Businesses and the Challenges of Poverty in the Developing World*, Palgrave MacMillan, Houndsmills, pp. 181–205; Yakovleva, N. (2005), *Corporate Social Responsibility in the Mining Industry*, Ashgate Publishing Ltd, Aldershot.

22 Zyglidopoulos (2002), op. cit.

23 Skippari, M. and Pajunen, K. (2010), "MNE–NGO–host government relationships in the escalation of an FDI conflict", *Business and Society*, vol. 49, no. 4, pp. 619–651.

24 Levy, D.L. and Kolk, A. (2002), "Strategic responses to global climate change: conflicting pressures on multinationals in the oil industry", *Business and Politics*, vol. 4, no. 3, pp. 275–300; Utting, P. and Ives, K. (2006), "The politics of corporate social responsibility and the oil industry", *St. Anthony's International Review*, vol. 2, no. 1, pp. 11–34.

25 Vernon, R. (1981), "Sovereignty at bay ten years after", *International Organization*, vol. 35, no. 3, pp. 517–529; Wasserstrom, R. and Reider, S. (1998), Petroleum companies crossing new threshold in community relations", *Oil and Gas Journal*, vol. 96, no. 50, pp. 24–27.

26 Description of a Panel discussion on "Obtaining a social licence to operate" at the 2nd Annual Land Access Forum held in Brisbane June 22–23 2011, http://www.futureye.com/node/462, accessed January 30 2012.

27 Amaral, S.P. and La Rovere, E.L. (2003), "Indicators to evaluation environmental, social, and economic sustainability: a proposal for the Brazilian oil industry", *Oil and Gas Journal*, vol. 101, no. 19, pp. 30–35.

28 Van Tulder and van der Zwart, op. cit.

29 Gunningham, N., Kagan, R.A. and Thornton, D. (2004). "Social license and environmental protection: why businesses go beyond compliance", *Law and Social Inquiry*, vol. 29, pp. 307–342; Howard-Grenville, J., Nash, J. and Coglianese, C. (2008), "Constructing the license to operate: internal factors and their influence on corporate environmental decisions", *Law and Policy*, vol. 30, no. 1, pp. 73–107; Nelsen, J. (2006), *Social License to Operate: An Industry Survey*, paper presented at CIM Conference, Vancouver, Canada; Nelsen, J. and Scoble, M. (2006), *Social License to Operate Mines: Issues of Situational Analysis and Process*; Preston and Sachs (2002), op. cit.

30 Eyton, D. (2010), "Governance, innovation and service delivery", Stanford University Conference on Technology, Governance and Global Development, California, April 19.

31 http://annualreview.bhpbilliton.com/2007/company_overview/licence_to_operate.htm, accessed 20 December 2010.

32 http://www.shell.com/home/content/globalsolutions/products_services/licence_to_operate/, accessed 20 December 2010.

33 Kurlander, L.T., Senior Vice President Newmont Mining (2001), *Newmont Mining: The Social License to Operate*, paper presented at Global Executive Forum, University of Colorado, Denver.

34 http://www.theajmonline.com.au/mining_news/news/2010/april/april-22-10/other-top-stories/the-importance-of-maintaining-2018social-licence-to-operate2019, accessed 20 December 2010.

35 http://www.huffingtonpost.com/2010/07/27/bp-oil-spill-10-billion-tax-credit_n_661371.html, accessed 20 December 2010.

36 http://www.values.com.au/2010/05/14/the-ethics-of-oil-spills-bps-defining-moment/, accessed 20 December 2010.

37 www.sociallicense.com, accessed 20 December 2010.

38 http://www.huffingtonpost.com/ian-gary/will-chevron-heed-the-cal_b_589250.html, accessed 20 December 2010.

39 Post *et al.* (2002), op. cit., p. 21.

40 Gunningham *et al* (2004)., op. cit.; Gunningham, N., Kagan, R.A. and Thornton, D. (2003), *Shades of Green: Business, Regulation and Environment*, Stanford University Press, Stanford.

41 Nelsen (2006), op. cit.; Nelsen and Scobble (2006), op. cit.

42 Howard *et al.* (2008), op. cit.

43 Post *et al.* (2002), op. cit., p. 256.

44 Hopkins, M. (2007), *Corporate Social Responsibility and International Development*, Earthscan, London.

45 Deephouse, D.L. and Suchman, M. (2008), "Legitimacy in organizational institutionalism". In R. Greenwood, C. Oliver and R. Suddaby (eds), *The SAGE Handbook of Organizational Institutionalism*, Sage, Thousand Oaks, CA , pp. 49–77.

46 Ibid.

47 Ibid.

48 Ibid.

49 Bansal, P. and Roth, K. (2000), "Why companies go green: a model of ecological responsiveness", *Academy of Management Journal*, vol. 43, no. 4, pp. 717–736.

50 Cramer, J. (2002), "From financial to sustainable profit", *Corporate Social Responsibility and Environmental Management*, vol. 9, pp. 99–106.

51 Humphreys, D. (2001), "Sustainable development: can the mining industry afford it?", *Resources Policy*, vol. 27, no. 1, pp. 1–7.

52 MMSD (2002), *Breaking New ground: Mining, Minerals, and Sustainable Development*, Earthscan Publications Ltd, London.

53 Kolk, A. and van Tulder, R. (2005), "Setting new global rules? TNCs and codes of conduct", *Transnational Corporations*, vol. 14, no. 3, pp. 1–27.

54 Birley, M. (2005), "Health impact assessment in multinationals: a case study of the Royal Dutch/Shell group", *Environmental Impact Assessment Review*, vol. 25, pp. 702–713; Zinkin, J. (2004), "Maximising the 'license to operate': CSR from an Asian perspective", *The Journal of Corporate Citizenship*, vol. 14, pp. 67–80.

55 Knott, D. (1997), "European retailers scramble for market share in former communist bloc", *Oil and Gas Journal*, vol. 95, no. 25, pp. 35–39.

56 Reichardt (2006), op. cit.

57 Andriof, J. and McIntosh, M. (2001), *Perspectives on Corporate Citizenship*, Greenleaf Publishing, Sheffield, UK.

58 Wasserstrom and Reider (1998), op. cit.

59 Ibid.

60 Logsdon, J.M. and Wood, D.J. (2002), "Business citizenship: from domestic to global level of analysis", *Business Ethics Quarterly*, vol. 12, no. 2, pp. 155–187.

61 Fombrun, C.J. (2005), "Building corporate reputation through CSR initiatives: evolving standards", *Corporate Reputation Review*, vol. 8, no. 1, pp. 7–11.

62 Jonsson, S., Greve, H.R. and Fujiwara-Greve, T. (2009), "Undeserved loss: the spread of legitimacy loss to innocent organisations in response to reported corporate deviance", *Administrative Science Quarterly*, vol. 54, no. 2, pp. 195–228.

63 Kobrin, S.J. (2005), "Technological determinism, globalization and the multinational firm". In P.J. Buckley (ed.), *What is International Business?*, Palgrave Macmillan, Basingstoke, pp. 38–56; Ramamurti, R. (2004), "Developing countries and MNEs: extending and enriching the research agenda", *Journal of International Business Studies*, vol. 35, no. 4, pp. 277–283; Rugman, A.M. and Verbeke, A. (1998), "Multinational enterprises and public policy", *Journal of International Business Studies*, vol. 29, no. 1, pp. 115–136; Teegen, Doh and Vachani (2004), op. cit.

64 Hamann, R. (2004), "Corporate social responsibility, partnerships, and institutional change: the case of mining companies in South Africa", *Natural Resources Forum*, vol. 28, pp. 278–290.

65 Mander, J. and Tauli-Corpuz, V. (eds) (2006), *Paradigm Wars: Indigenous Peoples' Resistance to Globalization*, Sierra Club Books, San Francisco, CA.

66 Ali, S.H. and Behrendt, L. (2001), "Mining and indigenous rights: the emergence of a global social movement", *Cultural Survival Quarterly*, vol. 25, no. 1, http://www.culturalsurvival.org/publications/csq/csq-article.cfm?id=642, accessed May 7 2007; Young, E. (1995), *Third World in the First: Development and Indigenous Peoples*, Routledge, London.

67 Human Rights Watch (2003), *Sudan, Oil, and Human Rights*, Human Rights Watch, New York.

68 Roy, A. (2010), "The trickledown revolution", *Outlook India*, September 20, http://www.outlookindia.com/article.aspx?267040, accessed January 20 2012.

69 Ross, W. (2008), *Guinea turmoil threatens mine deal*, BBC, 12 October.

70 http://news.bbc.co.uk/2/hi/africa/7663573.stm, 11 October 2008.

71 Ghoshal, S. and Noria, N. (1989), "Internal differentiation within multinational corporations", *Strategic Management Journal*, vol. 10, no. 4, pp. 323–337.

72 Porter, M.E. (1986), "Competition in global industries. A conceptual framework". In M.E. Porter (ed.), *Competition in Global Industries*, Harvard Business School Press, Boston, pp. 15–60.

73 Bartlett and Ghoshal, op. cit.; Doz, Y.L., Bartlett, C. and Prahalad, C.K. (1981), "Global competitive pressures and host country demands: managing tensions in MNCs", *California Management Review*, vol. 23, no. 3, pp. 63–74; Ghoshal, S. and Nohria, N. (1993), "Horses for courses: organizational forms for multinational corporations", *Sloan Management Review*, vol. 34, no. 2, pp. 23–35.

74 Jarillo, J.C. and Martinez, J.I. (1990), "Different roles for subsidiaries: the case of multinational corporations in Spain", *Strategic Management Journal*, vol. 11, no. 7, pp. 501–512; Johnson, J.H., Farrel, W.C. and Henderson, G.R. (1995), "Mr. Porter's 'competitive advantage' for inner city revitalization: exploitation or empowerment?", *Review of Black Political Economy*, vol. 24, no. 2/3, pp. 259–289; Taggart, J.H. (1997), "An evaluation of the integration–responsiveness framework: MNC manufacturing subsidiaries in the UK", *Management International Review*, vol. 37, no. 4, pp. 295–318.

75 Bartlett, C.A. and Ghoshal, S. (1989a), *Managing Across Borders: The Transnational Solution*, Century Business, London; Doz, Y.L. and Prahalad, C.K. (1991), "Managing DMNCs: a search for a new paradigm", *Strategic Management Journal*, vol. 12, S1, pp. 145–164.

76 Levitt, T. (1983), "The globalization of markets", *Harvard Business Review*, vol. 61, no. 3, pp. 92–102.

77 Doz and Prahalad, op. cit.; Muller, A. (2006), "Global versus local CSR strategies", *European Management Journal*, vol. 24, no. 2–3, pp. 189–198; Rosenzweig, P.M. and Nohria, N. (1994), "Influences on human resource management practices in multinational corporations", *Journal of International Business Studies*, vol. 25, no. 2, p. 229.

78 Birkinshaw, J., Morrison, A. and Hulland, J. (1995), "Structural and competitive determinants of a global integration strategy", *Strategic Management Journal*, vol. 16, pp. 637–655; Kobrin, S.J. (1991), "An empirical analysis of the determinants of global integration", *Strategic Management Journal*, vol. 12, pp. 17–32.

79 Luo, Y. (2001), "Determinants of local responsiveness: perspectives from foreign subsidiaries in an emerging market", *Journal of Management*, vol. 27, pp. 541–477.

80 Venaik, S., Midgley, D.F. and Devinney, T.M. (2004), "A new perspective on the integration–responsiveness pressures confronting multinational firms", *Management International Review*, vol. 44, no. 1, pp. 15–48.

81 Devinney, T.M., Midgley, D.F. and Venaik, S. (2000), "The optimal performance of the global firm: formalizing and extending the integration–responsiveness framework", *Organization Science*, vol. 11, no. 6, pp. 674–695.

82 Granovetter, M. (1985), "Economic action and social structure: the problem of embeddedness", *The American Journal of Sociology*, vol. 91, no. 3, pp. 481–510; Polanyi, K. (1944), *The Great Transformation: The Political and Economic Origins of Our Time*, Beacon, Boston, MA.

83 Dunning, J.H. (1995), "Reappraising the eclectic paradigm in an age of alliance capitalism", *Journal of International Business Studies*, vol. 26, no. 3, p. 461.

84 Porter, M.E. (1998), "Clusters and the new economics of competition", *Harvard Business Review*, vol. 76, no. 6, pp. 77–90; Porter, M.E. (2000), "Location, competition, and economic development: local clusters in a global economy", *Economic Development Quarterly*, vol. 14, no. 1, pp. 15–34.

85 Lall, S. and Narula, R. (2004), "Foreign direct investment and its role in economic development: do we need a new agenda?", *The European Journal of Development Research*, vol. 16, no. 3, pp. 447–464; Pavlinek, P. (2004), "Regional development implications of foreign direct investment in central Europe", *European Urban and Regional Studies*, vol. 11, no. 1, pp. 47–70; Phelps, N.A., MacKinnon, D., Stone, I. and Braidford, P. (2003), "Embedding the multinationals? Institutions and the development of overseas manufacturing affiliates in Wales and North East England", *Regional Studies*, vol. 37, no. 1, pp. 27–40.

86 Choi, C.J., Raman, M., Usoltseva, O. and Lee, S.H. (1999), "Political embeddedness in the new triad: implications for emerging economies", *Management International Review*, vol. 39, no. 3, p. 257.

87 Newbury, W. (2001), "MNC interdependence and local embeddedness influences on perceptions of career benefits from global integration", *Journal of International Business Studies*, vol. 32, no. 3, p. 497.

88 Dhanaraj, C., Lyles, M.A., Steensma, H.K. and Tihanyi, L. (2004), "Managing tacit and explicit knowledge transfer in IJVs: the role of relational embeddedness and the impact on performance", *Journal of International Business Studies*, vol. 35, no. 5, p. 428.

89   Gnyawali, D.R. and Madhavan, R. (2001), "Cooperative networks and competitive dynamics: a structural embeddedness perspective", *Academy of Management Review*, vol. 26, no. 3, pp. 431–445.

90   Gardberg, N.A. and Fombrun, C.J. (2006), "Corporate citizenship: creating intangible assets across institutional environments", *Academy of Management Review*, vol. 31, no. 2, pp. 329–346.

91   Karamanos, A.G. (2003), "Complexity, identity and the value of knowledge-intensive exchanges", *The Journal of Management Studies*, vol. 40, no. 7, p. 1871.

92   Andersson, U. and Forsgren, M. (2000), "In search of centre of excellence: network embeddedness and subsidiary roles in multinational corporations", *Management International Review*, vol. 40, no. 4, p. 329; Hakanson, L. and Nobel, R. (2001), "Organizational characteristics and reverse technology transfer", *Management International Review*, vol. 41, no. 4, p. 395; Ling, Y., Floyd, S.W. and Baldridge, D.C. (2005), "Toward a model of issue-selling by subsidiary managers in multinational organizations", *Journal of International Business Studies*, vol. 36, no. 6, p. 637; Mu, S., Gnyawali, D.R. and Hatfield, D.E. (2007), "Foreign subsidiaries' learning from local environments: an empirical test", *Management International Review*, vol. 47, no. 1, p. 79.

93   Bartlett, C.A. and Ghoshal, S. (1986), "Tap your subsidiaries for global reach", *Harvard Business Review*, vol. 64, no. 6, pp. 87–94; Birkinshaw, J. (1997), "Entrepreneurship in multinational corporations: the characteristics of subsidiary initiatives", *Strategic Management Journal*, vol. 18, no. 3, pp. 207–229.

94   Dow, D. (2006), "Adaptation and performance in foreign markets: evidence of systematic under-adaptation", *Journal of International Business Studies*, vol. 37, no. 2, pp. 212–226.

95   Johnson, J.P., Lenartowicz, T. and Apud, S. (2006), "Cross-cultural competence in international business: toward a definition and a model", *Journal of International Business Studies*, vol. 37, no. 4, pp. 525–543.

96   Magnusson, P., Baack, D.W., Sdravkovic, S., Staub, K.M. and Amine, L.S. (2008), "Meta-analysis of cultural differences: another slice at the apple", *International Business Review*, vol. 17, no. 5, pp. 520–532.

97   Hamann op. cit. (2004).; Reichardt (2006), op. cit.

98   Harzing, A. (2000), "An empirical analysis and extension of the Bartlett and Ghoshal typology of multinational companies", *Journal of International Business Studies*, vol. 31, no. 1, pp. 101–120; Luo, op. cit.; Roth, K. and Morrison, A.J. (1990), "An empirical analysis of the integration–responsiveness framework in global industries", *Journal of International Business Studies*, vol. 21, no. 4, p. 541.

99   Luo (2001), op. cit.

100   Prahalad, C.K. (2006), *The Fortune at the Bottom of the Pyramid: Eradicating Poverty Through Profits*, Wharton School Publishing, Upper Saddle River, NJ.

101   Hopkins (2007), op. cit.

102   London, T. and Hart, S.L. (2004), "Reinventing strategies for emerging markets: beyond the transnational model", *Journal of International Business Studies*, vol. 35, no. 5, p. 350.

103   Laclau, E. (1996), *Emancipation(s)*, Verso, London.

104   Levy and Kolk (2002), op. cit.

105   Jones (2005), op. cit.

106   Shenkar, O., Luo, Y. and Yeheskel, O. (2008), "From 'distance' to 'friction': substituting metaphors and redirecting intercultural research", *Academy of Management Review*, vol. 33, no. 4, pp. 905–923.

107   Venaik, Midgley and Devinney (2004), op. cit.

108 Fagre and Wells, op. cit.; Vernon 1981, op. cit.

109 For example Doh, J.P. and Guay, T.R. (2004), "Globalization and corporate social responsibility: how non-governmental organizations influence labor and environmental codes of conduct", *Management International Review*, vol. 44, no. 2, pp. 7–29; Teegen, Doh and Vachani (2004), op. cit.

110 Bisoi, D. (2009), "11 out of 14 mega projects in Orissa lagging behind", *Financial Express*, September 18.

111 BBC (2008), *More protests hit Tata Nano plant*, September 3, http://news.bbc.co.uk/2/hi/business/7595422.stm, accessed October 22 2010.

112 Utting and Ives (2006), op. cit.

113 Hoyos, C. (2007), "The new seven sisters: oil and gas giants that dwarf the West's top producers", *Financial Times*, March 12, p. 15; UNCTAD (2007), *World Investment Report: Transnational Corporations, Extractive Industries and Development*, United Nations, Geneva and New York.

114 Howard, Nash and Coglianese (2008), op. cit.

115 Shenkar, Luo and Yeheskel (2008), op. cit.

116 Escobar, A. (2006), "Difference and conflict in the struggle over natural resources: a political ecology framework", *Development*, vol. 49, no. 3, pp. 6–13, p. 8.

117 Jones, Pollit and Bek (2007), op. cit.

7

Risk Management and Communication: Pressures and Conflicts of a Stakeholder Approach to Corporate Social Responsibility

ROBERT L. HEATH,* MICHAEL J. PALENCHAR,†
KATHERINE A. MCCOMAS‡ AND STEPHANIE PROUTHEAU§

Keywords

Corporate social responsibility, issues management, public affairs, risk communication, stakeholder participation.

Introduction

The discipline of risk management and communication began to evolve in the 1950s as discussants addressed daunting topics of health and safety relevant to nuclear energy, chemical hazards and public health (e.g., asbestos and tobacco). Iconic events such as the release of oil off the Santa Barbara coast of California, radiation at Three Mile Island, and methyl isocyanate (MIC) in Bhopal, India, focused attention on management practices in high-risk situations. These events featured the need for scientific and cultural (sociopolitical) interpretations of risk occurrence, magnitude and equity. This paradigm emerged again in 2011 in Japan when nuclear operating facilities were damaged so as to put workers and near neighbors at substantial risk. In such events, the quality of risk management and communication (before, during and after the event) centers on actions

* Robert L. Heath, University of Houston, 101 Communication Building, Houston, TX 77204-3002, US. E-mail: rheath@uh.edu.

† Michael J. Palenchar, University of Tennessee, 476 Communications Building, Knoxville, TN 37996-0343, US. E-mail: mpalench@utk.edu.

‡ Katherine McComas, Cornell University, Department of Communication, 313 Kennedy Hall, Ithaca, NY 14853, US. E-mail: kam19@cornell.edu.

§ Stephanie Protheau, CELSA–Sorbonne University and CNRS Institute for Communication Sciences (ISCC).

and statements to assess and manage risks primarily among plant operators, regulators and nearby neighbors and consumers.

In such cases, community relations occurring through stakeholder participation can be described as high centrality/high density. That means those engaged in the discussion of risks, the creators and potential sufferers of risk, may know one another and even engage interpersonally as they debate issues in shared public forums. The risk generators may be central as both a voice of and target of criticism. The interaction is dense because the persons and organizations are in a public arena of close time, space and communication contact.

However, what also deserves analysis is another risk management and risk communication context that features the roles and requirements needed in product development streams where ingredients of questionable safety are introduced from the start of the manufacturing, marketing and consumption chain. Using paradigmatic cases, this chapter investigates management and communication challenges that result when arguably unsafe chemicals and agrifood biotechnologies become part of products. Typical of such situations, scientific debates attendant to risk assessments mostly occur in confined arenas and publications, far from the attention of end users—consumers. As such, risk controversies are communication situations in which relevant fundamental science and scientific expertise unfold confidentially in scientific and regulatory institutions from which the consumer is easily alienated. Even so, scientific terminologies, demonstration canons and methodological assessment often maintain opacity to customers' evaluations. As such, infrastructures exist, or at least ought to be multiplied, to foster coexistence and dialog between science-based and culturally sensitive assessments, so as to protect the health, safety and welfare of customers who want and deserve safe products.

Relevant to such management decisions, considerable effort has been devoted to understanding how conflicting voices and competing standards of corporate social responsibility (CSR) become accepted as legitimate standards of business and public policy.[1] In such contests, CSR is not some fixed matter but rather socially constructed business operation standards. These are continually deliberated as competing interests by involved stakeholders. Especially in detail, controversies emerge as CSR guidelines are formulated. They center on issues relating to

1. standards and means by which those principles are relevant to stakeholder oversight in business activities;
2. government's and NGOs' consent on matters such as consumer health and safety as well as environmental impact;
3. scientific communities' risk expertise; and
4. public opinion that can affect consumer decisions.

Such CSR battles raise the prospect of the need for and advantages of effective stakeholder participation. Such participation calls for an infrastructural approach to risk communication characterized by robust, collaborative decision-making and deliberative democracy.[2] The principle of deliberative democracy recognizes public engagement that addresses conflicts of interest and marginalized stakeholders, which is central to legislative and regulatory decision-making. Such deliberation presumes that the quality of policy and business practice must occur in an arena where competing voices of the powerful and far less powerful are heard, understood and appreciated.

From this perspective, tensions occur when private sector businesses seek to operate from CSR standards that collide with those preferred by competitors and other industries, NGOs, government regulators and scientific experts, customers, and nearby residents affected by production, storage and transportation operations. These voices scrutinize what constitutes sound science as well as debate culturally sensitive judgments of risk magnitude and mitigation. Resolving differences is important so that CSR standards can provide the rationale for organizational legitimacy, reputation and brand equity. To demonstrate that it is responsible to others, an organization (or industry) is expected to know and prove that each product is not harmful or that benefits outweigh harms.

The business situation, however, becomes even more daunting when an organization designs or manufactures a product ingredient which some scientists claim passes a risk through business-to-business (B2B) marketing to retail marketers and consumers. Component manufacturing and marketing (whether chemical or biotechnology), thus, can create management challenges for retail marketing. Retailers' ability to manage risk through legitimate CSR standards can be challenged when consumers are legitimately concerned about a product's safety. Such challenges can harm the reputation of retailers as well as product lines. This situation occurs when scientists indict ingredients in basic products in ways that arouse concern on the part of other scientists, regulators and NGOs.

To address this management challenge, this chapter explores the literature on risk, stakeholder participation and market CSR integrity. It examines processes of public participation and stakeholder engagement, as well as substantive and instrumental perplexities of science-based and normative decision-making through risk management and communication. To blend these factors into a collaborative decision-making approach to CSR-based risk management and communication, two brief case studies explore the controversy over ingredients that find their ways to consumers, specifically bisphenol-A (BPA) and phthalates[3] and genetically modified organisms (GMOs).

In the first case, chemicals such as bisphenol-A are indicted as causing health problems, especially in children. Thus, companies that sell soft drinks become the target of consumer criticism that the bottles contain hazardous compounds. In this complex product chain, these companies bought the bottles from a manufacturer who obtained the chemicals from companies that developed them. The originating company (industry) is ultimately responsible for justifying and defending their safety or changing the ingredients. In such situations, the retailer may have little to say in the controversy, whereas activists and government agencies, and even scientists at times, speak with loud voices. The company whose name is on the product or the retailer who sells the product suffers risk outrage and loss of sales. The second and controversial case over genetically modified organisms (GMOs) serves to explain how international trade negotiations and food risk management disputes between European and American regulations intertwine and affect the emergence of international agrifood business practices and norms.

Thus, managements are wise to engage with stakeholders to help identify and address concerns about the design, production and retail use of such products. If constructive dialog fails to gain consensus regarding product safety, managements must adapt to protect the public interest.[4] Such dialog functions properly within what has been called a risk society to emphasize how CSR standards must be relevant to technological threats inherent to modern society. As will be discussed in the next section, stakeholder participation can be used constructively to minimize risk and protect market integrity.

Risk, Stakeholder Participation and Market Integrity

Risk management and its communication challenges are as old as humankind and constitute, as such, a key rationale to the sociopolitical organization and evolution of societies, as advanced by Mary Douglas and Ulrich Beck.[5] For the latter who focuses on contemporary specificities, our risk society converts/renews the inequities of the class struggle into risk exposure inequities. In any case, both authors and supporters of their positions reason that societies' raison d'être rests with the collective management of risk. Such matters can include risks created by nature (e.g., Hurricane Katrina or earthquakes/tsunamis in Japan, often entailing human intervention such as engineering and emergency response), personal health/safety choices (e.g., smoking, diet), and risks created by others (e.g., chemical manufacturing challenges for employee and near resident health/safety). Emergency management and numerous other topics, including the wisdom and efficacy of government regulation, are related challenges. Within such discourse, risk management provides a rationale for product design and positioning— "reduce the chance of heart attack" or "drive a safe car"—and cautions—"if symptoms persist, contact your physician".

As societal instruments of risk management, structures and functions are created to deliberate and thereby co-create standards to assess whether some ingredient, product, or action is sufficiently safe to be legitimate and condoned.[6] Discourse defines risk and determines its acceptability. A powerful outcome of such dialog is a platform for business activity that meets or exceeds stakeholders' expectations, today increasingly a common standard of corporate legitimacy.

A robust literature assesses matters of scientifically sound and normatively acceptable risk, as well as its management and communication.[7] This literature reflects battle lines drawn by key companies and industries, NGOs, government agencies, trade associations and inter- as well as intra-industry dialogs. Standards voluntarily adopted by business or imposed through legislation or judicial action guide management, manufacturing, marketing and communications. Savvy managements work to strategically implement a commitment to reflective and engaged risk management. To assist this effort, scholars delve into the topic of stakeholder identification, wanting to better understand which individuals and groups make a difference in the resource dependency of organizations.

These stakeholders are "any group or individual who is affected by or can affect the achievement of an organization's objectives".[8] Clarkson[9] defined stakeholders as individuals and groups that have an interest in a corporation, extending to activities, ownership and rights. These interests are debated and established through legal, moral, individual and collective interactions taken by or with organizations, even emergent and enduring narratives.[10] Foundations of stakeholder theory exist within reflective strategic management, including mission and vision, based on sound CSR principles achieved through issue-relevant dialog.[11]

Incorporation of stakeholders into consideration of operations brings new ideas to management and helps make organizational planning more reflective. One challenge of stakeholder theory is its orientation toward the equity of organizational relationships. Stakeholder theory assumes a constant interaction among stakeholders and organizations toward mutual outcomes, often devoted to assessment of risk.

Risk is traditionally defined by uncertainty: What can happen, at what probability, to which risk bearers, in what way and when and to what magnitude? Here lies the challenge of risk that demands applications of sound science sensitive to stakeholders' cultures. How such issues work themselves out can affect the image/reputation and product acceptance in marketing and public policy contexts. Sound deliberation depends on the ability of infrastructures to sustain and use discourse to society's benefit, rather than to some more narrow interest.

Thus, risk management, assessment and communication researchers debate what level of risk is safe enough,[12] which rapidly draws into the underlying question: how fair is safe enough?[13] These questions highlight the role of sound science and the cultural assessment of the norms of safety as a precursor to decisions regarding which organizations, products and processes deserve opposition or support.

The reality of this topic is that stakes are granted as reward or withheld as punishment for business transactions that are favored or opposed. Laying a foundation for a resource dependency approach to CSR, Mitchell, Agle and Wood[14] defined stake as

> something that can be lost. The use of risk to denote stake appears to be a way to narrow the stakeholder field to those with legitimate claims, regardless of their power to influence the firm or the legitimacy of their relationship to the firm.

Stakeholders' control is the ability to grant or withhold stakes from those who need the resources. Expectations relevant to such granting arise from prevailing CSR standards that might not differ as to principle (safety) but to its analysis (how safe, and how fair).

Within marketing, stakeholder theory and relationship management theory often are referred to as customer relationship management (CRM).[15] CRM is the infrastructure that enables the delineation of and increase in customer value, and the correct means by which to motivate valuable customers to remain loyal.[16] Knox and Gruar, among others,[17] have argued that CRM "places an emphasis on stakeholder collaboration beyond the immediacy of market transactions ... and views business as a coalition of stakeholders". The CRM literature demonstrates the need to take stakeholders' concerns seriously when conducting business. Relevant to providing insights to inform and guide such concerns, four approaches to risk management and communication have emerged, as will be discussed in the next section.

Approaches to Risk Management and Communication

Over the years, four paradigms (see Table 7.1) of risk assessment, management and communication have arisen. Each offers a foundational perspective that come together to support a view of risk as a societal matter. As such, societies create means (structures and functions) as well as normative protocols for assessing the legitimacy of risk managers.

One paradigm focuses on calibrating stakeholder views with expert views: the *mental models approach* (MMA).[18] MMA begins with scientists shouldering the challenge of getting the data correct to properly assess risks, determining the degree to which each stakeholder group agrees with that interpretation as a foundation for narrowing the gap between what scientists know and lay publics believe. This approach presumes a cost–benefit underpinning of risk perceptions.[19] MMA advocates champion risk communication anchored by scientific conclusions. Aside from problems inherent to scientists communicating with non-scientists, an additional obstacle occurs when stakeholders receive too much or contradictory data, which they find difficult to interpret and base decisions upon in meaningful ways.[20] It also wrestles with problems of conflicting results, inconclusive results, inconsistent findings, technical language and complex research methodologies.

Second, building on the foundations laid by Mary Douglas, researchers have advanced the *cultural interpretation of risk*,[21] and on those laid by Ulrich Beck, the *risk society approach*.[22] Advocates of these paradigms reason that those potentially affected by risks are (or must be) empowered to ask whose science and whose scientists are investigating and debating the levels and legitimacies of risk distribution. The concern is that the risk creators' scientists alone, or conspiring regulatory agencies, make the final decisions about the degree to which a risk exists and the determination of whether it is acceptable. This approach worries that business or government becomes privileged to determine risk probability acceptance and impact equity in hegemonic ways that short circuit stakeholder participation. This approach has long been seen as a decline of deference to the traditional corporate and scientific power structures of society and the presumption that they wisely and fairly interpret and manage risks in the public interest.[23]

A third paradigm, a *sociopsychometric approach*,[24] features the ways, often idiosyncratically sensitive to demographics, that recurring and predictable patterns of risk perceptions develop and affect individuals' judgments—including risk tolerance. For instance, risks that are perceptually associated with dreaded consequences, delayed effects and involuntary exposure (e.g., cancer resulting from long-term exposure to chemical residue) tend to be less tolerated than those associated with familiar activities or voluntary risks, such as driving/riding in an automobile.

The fourth paradigm, an *infrastructural approach*,[25] presumes that if stakeholder engagement is embedded in infrastructures it can foster perceptions of trust, fairness/equity and safety through collaborative public participation. It advances the premise that effective co-creation and enactment of transparent stakeholder engagement processes lead to more manageable risks, more fully explored and ethical allocations of risk–benefit ratios, and more widely accepted risk decisions. These rationales are often articulated as the normative, substantive, and instrumental arguments for stakeholder engagement.[26] The *normative argument* posits that engaging stakeholders is the ethically appropriate course of action. The *substantive* emphasizes the local expertise that stakeholders can contribute, which can improve the assessment and management of risks. The *instrumental* focuses on how stakeholder engagement can increase the acceptability and actual or perceived legitimacy of resulting decisions. Arguably, a well-designed and implemented engagement process can embody all three rationales. The effectiveness of the infrastructural approach depends, however, on having a representative sample of stakeholders, or their proxies or delegates, participate in the process. In other words, it is not adequate simply to offer opportunities to participate without also removing instrumental barriers to participation. Therefore, much work has sought to understand normative incentives and disincentives to engagement, which can range from the logistical (e.g., timing, location) to internal and external levels of efficacy (e.g., it is too confusing for me to understand, or my participation will not matter).[27] Along these lines,[28] it challenges society to aspire toward the Habermasian principle of deliberative democracy as the key to effecting sound risk management, although they may be difficult to implement in risk controversy situations where stakeholders benefit from unequal access to regulatory foray or scientific argumentations, for instance.

Table 7.1   Paradigms of risk assessment, management and communication

Mental models approach	Focuses on calibrating stakeholder views with expert; champions risk communication anchored by scientific conclusions
Cultural interpretation of risk/risk society	Reasons that those potentially affected by risks are (or must be) empowered to ask whose science and whose scientists are investigating and debating the levels and legitimacies of risk distribution.
sociopsychometric approach	Features the ways that recurring and predictable patterns of risk perceptions develop and affect individuals' judgments—including risk tolerance.
Infrastructural approach	Advances the premise that effective co-creation and enactment of transparent stakeholder engagement processes lead to more manageable risks, more fully explored and ethical allocations of risk–benefit ratios, and more widely accepted risk decisions.

The principle of deliberative democracy helps combine the four perspectives on risk, especially the infrastructural approach, to reveal the logic of stakeholder engagement and right to know, themes of the next section, as the rationale for dialog between risk creators, arbiters and bearers.[29] This theme underpins the principle of "community right-to-know" as CSR. The principle of deliberative democracy champions the ability of risk infrastructures to support and foster discourse where powerful voices do not dominate and drown out risk bearers' concerns. Relevant to advancing the quality of such infrastructures, stakeholder theory arose and became joined to the CSR literature to justify how and why managements must engage collaboratively with their myriad stakeholders, the central theme of the next section.

Stakeholders and CSR Battles: Striving for Mutual Benefit and a Fully Functioning Society

The basic idea of CSR is simple: because firms are social entities enfranchised by social contract, they have "obligations to society".[30] As a foundation for understanding the legitimizing influence of social capital, Freeman and Gilbert[31] reasoned "effective strategy will be formulated and implemented if and only if each player successfully puts himself or herself in the place of other players and endeavors to see the situation from the others' perceptions". Reflective management through CSR fosters actions taken by individuals or a group that further social good beyond the self-interest of the firm and required by law.[32]

Such challenges call for effective stakeholder participation to know, respond to and solve risk challenges in ways that conform to or exceed stakeholders' CSR expectations. By this logic, organizations either are expected to help manage risks they create or those other forces generate. Literally at stake is the ability to understand and bring to bear conditions, such as consumer safety, needed for legitimate business activities.

Stakeholder analysis advanced into systematic management theory with the seminal book by Freeman.[33] Rather than a mere strategic adjustment, a point Freeman never supported, by 1988, it had become a search for ethics.[34] By introducing "ethics" into the fray in an era of robust discussion of CSR responsiveness and rectitude,[35] Freeman helped join stakeholder analysis with efforts to define and implement CSR. As such, leaders in operations science and management theory have realized that a clear understanding of CSR is necessary for defining the limits, tensions and responsibility for legitimate stakeholder participation.[36]

Although most authors feature the legitimacy challenges associated with meeting stakeholder CSR expectations, critics have argued that champions of CSR can be irresponsible to shareholder interests,[37] or that companies' CSR proclamations constitute a smokescreen whereby empty claims and assurances divert criticism from corporate misjudgment.[38] Munshi and Kurian[39] suggested that CSR has become the go-to public relations strategy for many corporations to manipulate a more positive image of their environmental, social and cultural responsiveness as means to preserve their legitimacy and maintain power. Such paradoxes suggest that the terrain of stakeholder participation and CSR is rocky, steep and even treacherous.

Within this domain, risk challenges are among the most difficult to reconcile because the information shared is often technical, difficult to communicate, polarizing and fraught with risk–benefit options. Questions of blame and outrage linger at the surface. By every point of view, risk generators deserve and receive continual societal scrutiny.[40]

This discussion of stakeholder participation acknowledges that the topic can be approached in descriptive, normative, instrumental and managerial fashions.[41] From whatever perspective, and shaped by different motives, the challenge of stakeholder participation addresses a universal theme: to determine what factors shape the quality of relationships between and among various organizations, corporations and governmental agencies. Through the stakes that are at play and the manner in which decision-making and adaptation occurs, various interests compete, negotiate and collaborate in ways that shape markets, sociopolitical policies, economies and politics.

In this regard, process counts but so does co-created meaning. In the best sense, processes are developed and meaning fostered and applied to align interests as stakes are sought, held and granted in ways that foster mutual advantage rather than serve more narrow interests. As Donaldson and Preston[42] advised, "Stakeholder management requires, as its key attribute, simultaneous attention to the legitimate interests of all appropriate stakeholders, both in the establishment of organizational structures and general policies and in case-by-case decision making." Heath[43] summed up this perspective as defining a fully functioning society.

> A society—people and organizations—learns from mistakes. As a profession, public relations, marketing communication, and other professional forms of external rhetoric, can serve society by solving these mistakes, understanding problems, and offering solutions that invite thoughtfulness and willingness to overcome restraints to corrective actions.

One of the advances in co-creating meaning resulted through the logic of risk democracy as the right to know. Simply, people whose welfare is put at risk have the right to know that fact.

Right-to-know and Stakeholder Expectations

Deliberative democracy has been an incentive as well as victim of efforts to understand and practice sound risk communication. The asbestos crisis of the 1960s established the legal principle of failure to warn. Numerous events in the past century encouraged near residents and consumers to understand, assess and participate in managing health, safety and environmental risks—the right-to-know. For example, the 1969 blowout of the offshore drilling rig Alpha off Santa Barbara, California, launched the first oil clean-up and wildlife rescue effort in the United States—efforts that were demanded by nearby residents and activist groups.[44] Far from an isolated event, such problems were widespread, as demonstrated by 7,000 accidents involving toxic and hazardous materials that were registered between 1980 and 1985.[45]

Communities started to fight risk injustice using information, advocacy and activism to challenge risk-generating organizations. Such grassroots activity resulted in citizens' right-to-know as the key standard of risk democracy.[46] Right-to-know—also known as regulation through revelation—is based on principles of self-governance requiring public participation in decision-making.[47] Right-to-know as a political philosophy presumes a citizen's right to be educated about the purposes and actions of risk generating organizations. Following Hadden's[48] definition, people's right-to-know is a mechanism to empower people with knowledge they need to watch over their governments and industries in order to improve the quality of their lives.

The struggle for the right to know found a political and academic place in environmental and risk communication.[49] In the sociological tradition, Giddens[50] and Beck[51] pointed out the failure of exclusively market-based policies to provide just and desirable conditions for society as a whole. Beck proposed that, with the failure of established institutions to deal with the broad challenge of risk, society would need to turn to civic participation and self-governance for redress. For Beck, only through the inclusion of stakeholding publics into the decision-making process would governments be able to prevent and ameliorate risk problems.[52]

Ultimately right-to-know is critical to risk bearers' awareness of and potential understanding in regard to whether businesses produce contents in B2B marketing that are safe in end products. Right-to-know helps to create, foster, guide and manage robust infrastructures where scientific dialog encounters cultural and sociopsychometric interpretation. Such approaches to risk management conform to the challenge issued by[53] for corporations to achieve legitimacy through discourse. This approach moves beyond pragmatic, cognitive and moral legitimacy to connect "organizational legitimacy to a deliberative approach of political theory thus elaborating on the idea of a communicatively constructed corporate legitimacy" in the tradition of Beck.[54]

Stakeholder Engagement as Public Participation in Risk Decision-making

Work by Renn[55] has helped frame advances in public participation in risk management. It stresses the importance of social networks for societal risk assessment and mitigation. "Since stakeholder relationships do not occur in a vacuum of dyadic ties, but rather in a network of influences, a firm's stakeholders are likely to have direct relationships with one another."[56] However, stakeholders may not have direct and easy connections to the companies that design and manufacture product ingredients—and vice versa.

At least two factors are made relevant by this analysis. First, stakeholder participation is driven by collective expectations of what each stakeholder wants or desires from others and how each interprets the expectations voiced by others in the network. Secondly, density becomes a factor, at least because "dense networks furnish stakeholders with the capacity to monitor the focal organization's actions more efficiently".[57]

Density also predicts the ease of information exchange between stakeholders and how readily they create and use coalitions. In addition to density, centrality features each stakeholder's position in networks and its ability and willingness to relate to and influence, as well as be influenced by, others. Centrality is related to power and therefore predicts an organization's ability to resist stakeholder pressure. By this logic, Rowley[58] advanced the archetype driven logics that compromisers are typically found in high-density/high-centrality conditions, whereas commanders are high centrality but low density. Subordinates are in high-density networks but are low in centrality. Low-density and low-centrality networks characterize the solitarian. Stakeholder participation can also result in co-management of dysfunction. Social media increasingly give opportunity for the voices of the solitarians who are not part of high-density/high-centrality networks. A challenge to the organizations that create risk-creating chemical ingredients and biotechnologies is to avoid attempting to be commanders, which either results from their low-density connections with end users or leads to such low density. The liability of such a posture is that other players in the risk infrastructures either are or will become more central to and in a more dense relationship with the end users, the risk-bearers.

Instead of one exhibiting linear and sequential participation from product originator to end user, the infrastructure that can be identified in cases such as these is nodular. Each node is likely to center on some matter of deliberation regarding risk (how safe and how fair). Such infrastructures may be integrated in a way that fosters all voices coming together collaboratively. However, infrastructures can leave the originator of the risk invisible and out of the discourse. The discourse can be more sporadic or situational than coherently collaborative. A nodular infrastructure has groupings or configurations of participants that can be identified as densely centralized discussants, but the interconnections between nodes may be neither. This stakeholder participation configuration places extra strain on those organizations whose science is fundamental to risk management but whose voice does not appear in all nodes and actually may be denied in some. Table 7.2 illustrates the conceptualization of BPA nodes.

The peril to the retailer is that the user of the product containing BPA, for instance, is not engaged intellectually and evaluatively in any of the other nodes of the network. One prediction in such circumstances is that one or more NGO will become a risk arbiter affecting end-user perceptions of the degree to which the product puts them at risk.

Thus, consumer stakeholder participation is extremely difficult, and the voice affecting the consumers' views is often that of an NGO, which also might not be in the primary stream of sound science but rather consumes scientific conclusions and commentary politically. This discourse features what is culturally uncertain about safety, or even claims with certainty that the product in question is not safe. For that reason, the NGOs are likely to engage (especially on the Internet) with customer stakeholders in ways far more central and dense than is the case of those who design and manufacture

Table 7.2 **Proposed nodular infrastructure of stakeholder engagement in risk management**

Nodular infrastructure	Description
Scientific node A	A robust scientific discussion within each or several private organizations and the industry characterizes this node. Much of this discussion, at least at the start, is often treated as proprietary.
Scientific node B	Here independent scientists (university, NGO and regulator) enter the fray, often by finding something troubling and controversial about safety. This can occur privately as well as publically, as at conventions where science undergoes peer review.
Regulatory node A	Trade association scientists, NGO scientists and others report in various ways, including online, their conclusions, interpretations and recommendations. Controversies may grow, and claims become part of the discourse of popular culture. In such cases, myth and fiction can even trump fact.
Regulatory node B	Government regulatory and review bodies (and even litigation) discuss scientific findings. Such discussions can be and often are politicized based on various public policy cultures, including national cultures regarding risks and their tolerance. Such discussions are less specifically based on sound science than the normative and culturally sensitive assessments of key conclusions.
Marketing and public communication node	Marketing communication and news reporting/commentary can rely on and/or ignore scientific findings and discussion. As such, communication can either be that which is required by law or presumed to have marketplace impact.
Consumer node	Far removed from the scientific community, and only partially dependent on it, discussions among consumer publics, especially using peer contacts relevant to pyschodemographic conclusions. Relevant to BPA, phthalates and biotechnologies, the key "market decision-makers" are often mothers and grandmothers, women who my employ "hearth and home" decision heuristics that are skeptical of chemicals and biotechnology.

the foundational chemicals or design and produce the biotechnologies that enter the marketing stream.

In this regard, a heavy burden can fall to retailers and end users of these chemicals and biotechnologies to weigh acceptability of a risk, even though the ultimate responsibility for high CSR standards folds back to the chemical manufacturers and biotechnology companies. How they communicate with other stakeholders, through trade associations such as the American Chemistry Council, becomes important. They may define and explain known risks associated with such chemicals but suffer at least in the mindful interpretation of some stakeholders as offering biased, pro-chemical or pro-biotechnology interpretations (making them commanders).

As argued by the cultural and infrastructural approach to risk, stakeholding consumers may not be central to the infrastructure as a whole, but can be densely engaged with other consumers (especially today with social media). They may hold different standards of risk acceptance. Sound science and risk/benefit analysis can reason that X level of risk is tolerable to gain Y benefits. Stakeholders who are risk-bearers often demand a zero tolerance of risk. As the sociopsychometric approach has shown, risk perceptions are damaging when the risk manifestation is delayed, has dreaded consequences, affects children and has no apparent compensating benefit to the bearers. The next section extends risk–benefit analysis is a rubric of the precautionary principle's application to BPA, which may lack apparent and significant benefits to offset risks. At least safety was a counterbalance to harm in the case of phthalates.[59]

Bisphenol-A: Another Risk to "be Borne"

Discourse regarding Bisphenol-A (BPA) is offered as a brief case to amplify the points made above. It is an industrial ingredient chemical used in many hard plastic bottles and metal-based food and beverage cans since the 1960s. It is used to make polycarbonate plastic resins, epoxy resins and other products. These uses of BPA are subject to premarket approval by the U.S. Food and Drug Administration (FDA) as indirect food additives or food contact substances.[60]

BPA (as has been phthalates) is scrutinized because of its ubiquity and alleged health hazard. One major kind of plastic bottle is that used to market water, fruit juice and carbonated beverages. Baby bottles and other containers used in the feeding of infants have become the target of consumer concern. Millions of tons of BPA have come to define lifestyles (such as ubiquitous bottled water); however, evidence suggests links between BPA and a host of negative health effects.

BPA, however, has positive attributes. It is an ingredient in the plastic used to line cans that contain acidic foods, such as tomatoes. That plastic inhibits deterioration of the metal that leads to food contamination. As such, BPA exemplifies the classic risk management paradox: a product used in B2B marketing that poses harms and offers benefits—the paradox of the precautionary principle. These attributes (risks) are at the center of pressures and conflicts among stakeholders about competing standards of CSR.

Numerous stakeholders' voices are readily available online, engaged in discussing the risks and responses to them for BPA. It is important to note that the Internet might be the most dense and central network available to concerned consumers and other stakeholders, including the industry and companies, as well as regulators and other governmental and health agencies.

A range of voices is readily engaged in discussing BPA risks. One site, "Bisphenol-A", is sponsored by the Polycarbonate/BPA Global Group, which is organized regionally by the American Chemistry Council, PlasticsEurope and the Japan Chemical Industry Association. The site featured these claims:

This website is a comprehensive resource for environmental, health and safety information about bisphenol A (BPA). Bisphenol A is an industrial chemical used primarily to make polycarbonate plastic and epoxy resins—both of which are used in countless applications that make our lives easier, healthier and safer, each and every day. On this site you'll find the latest information about bisphenol A and a wealth of scientific data and resources to answer most any question you might have.[61]

The American Chemistry Council operates its own site on this topic and provides similar and redundant information to BPA Facts.

Other stakeholders involved in the debate are the local, state and federal agencies that conduct and support medical research. The National Institute of Environmental Health Sciences of the National Institutes of Health offers information including (as was the case for phthalates) that BPA is an endocrine-disrupting chemical. This site includes a scientific statement issued by The Endocrine Society in 2009. This Society sets its mission as investigating, reporting and advising on matters relevant to endocrinology. Key documents featured this theme:

> There is growing interest in the possible health threat posed by endocrine-disrupting chemicals (EDCs), which are substances in our environment, food, and consumer products that interfere with hormone biosynthesis, metabolism, or action resulting in a deviation from normal homeostatic control or reproduction. In this first Scientific Statement of The Endocrine Society, we present the evidence that endocrine disruptors have effects on male and female reproduction, breast development and cancer, prostate cancer, neuroendocrinology, thyroid, metabolism and obesity, and cardiovascular endocrinology.[62]

The FDA[63] shares the perspective of the National Toxicology Program that "recent studies provide reason for some concern about the potential effects of BPA on the brain, behavior, and prostate gland of fetuses, infants and children". The FDA[64] also recognizes "substantial uncertainties with respect to the overall interpretation of these studies and their potential implications for human health effects of BPA exposure".

A third, and very predictable, voice is the NGO activist, concerned consumer, consumer advocate. Some of these voices are highlighted news stories of concerned citizens, consumer groups and local government agencies, including the news story that "Maine Regulators Consider Bisphenol-A Ban". Within the mix of articles, one could find ads for legal council. RightHealth[65] offered the opportunity to learn more, blog and access reference material including physician-reviewed guides. Treehugger (treehugger. com), the self-proclaimed king of green blogs, featured the theme: "Get bisphenol a out of the grocery store (Are you listening, Whole Foods?)."

How this dialog achieves safety is uniquely demonstrated in the approach the FDA is taking in regard to discussing, researching and ultimately changing standards and enforcement of regulations related to BPA. As a result of scientific uncertainties (often resulting from complex methodological and scientific assessment of risk dose exposure), the FDA[66] is taking the following steps: (1) supporting the industry's actions to stop producing BPA-containing baby bottles and infant feeding cups for the U.S. market; (2) facilitating the development of alternatives to BPA for the linings of infant formula cans; and (3) supporting efforts to replace BPA or minimize BPA levels in other food can linings.

The FDA is also supporting a shift to a more robust regulatory framework for oversight of BPA, and is seeking further public comment and external input on the science surrounding BPA. At the same time, the FDA "is not recommending that families change the use of infant formula or foods, as the benefit of a stable source of good nutrition outweighs the potential risk from BPA exposure".[67] In this sense, decisions and interpretations often result from different and even conflicting premises and frames, a reality that has also been discussed under the umbrella of the precautionary principle as relevant to biotechnology.

International Trade Rules and GMOs: Decision Dysfunction

In addition to chemicals in the market chain, parallel analysis addresses risk and biotechnology, specifically GMOs, as they impact the agrifood industry's quality norms. This case offers the opportunity to explore specific difficulties of stakeholder participation in risk-regulation forums seeking to integrate scientific considerations, CSR standards, market dynamics and co-created meaning into productive risk dialogs on the basis of which normalize globalized risk regulations. Globalization has both stemmed from and given leeway to multinationals' activities. Stakeholders have initiated various attempts to bring social and environmental considerations for CSR to the United Nations, the World Trade Organization (WTO) and the Organization for Economic Cooperation and Development. This situation offers an opportunity to look at how culture-based attitudes toward the relationship between scientific knowledge and civilization progress influence the quality of stakeholder participation in multilateral risk decision-making forums.[68] The biotech case at the WTO (2001–2007) demonstrates a high-profile international dispute that has had implications for corporate behavior regarding the traceability of GMOs in food products.

The biotech case constitutes a case for analyzing the emergence of competing perspectives on scientific uncertainty—such as different precautionary principles.[69] Policy-making challenges raise the attendant problem of creating *fully functioning decision systems*, within and among institutions, through discourse that leads to productive ends. One productivity measure in such decision-making is to align interests and vocabularies that (1) bridge rather than exacerbate differences, (2) translate science into shared rather than privileged interpretations, and (3) balance scientific methodology with cultural perspectives of precaution that fully address whether safe is fair enough.[70] Although deliberation can maximize a dialog's outcome, issue combatants can allow inertia to frustrate and even serve their purposes. These paradoxes led to the creation of the concept of precautionary principles for risk management. On the one hand, precaution reasons that, in the absence of compelling evidence that risks are tolerable, caution is advised to cause no harm. On the other hand, the substantial equivalence principle reasons that GMOs are not different from non-modified ones, until proven otherwise. Schematically, the biotech case at the WTO constituted an open conflict between the precautionary and the substantial equivalence principles, endorsed respectively by the European countries and the United States, the latter advancing that their opponents were in fact acting upon protectionist motives and were as such pushing for excessively strict food production quality norms without scientific risk-evaluation foundations.

International trade rules, as embodied by the WTO agreements, are not easily compatible with CSR standards, for their purpose and mission do not initially lay with social and environmental objectives but with trade liberalization. Specific dispositions in the WTO agreements make provisions for these exceptions, based on the current state of scientific knowledge needed to demonstrate that risks do exist and justify trade barriers. GMO importations can be opposed, for instance, on the assumption that each current state of knowledge cannot deliver certainty as to their safety, thereby reversing the burden of proof from a sound scientific point of view. A sound scientific point of view would argue, in contrast, that excess of precaution in GMO risk policy design can impede agricultural capacities in developing nations, as well as the capacity to feed a rapidly growing population. The spectrum of positions is wide and nuances highly complex to grasp; the two positions aforementioned constitute the two ends of the continuum. The GMO dispute constitutes an instance of the emergence of competing perspectives on scientific uncertainty, such as diverging variations of the precautionary principles identified by Maguire and Ellis,[71] against the substantial equivalence principle. Numerous stakeholders endorse and transform perspectives while they become visible as GMO risk-regulation advocates within and around the WTO.

The European Union (EU) is a key stakeholder in the GMO dispute at the WTO. European countries have tailored over the past decade a mandatory labeling policy for GM food products that stipulate a traceability rule to reduce consumers' uncertainty as to what lies on their plate. The EU Food Law holds strong implications for corporate supplier chain and labeling policies in the agrifood business. By contrast, the U.S. government has no incentive to impose these dispositions on its agrifood sector. It has invoked protectionism on the part of the EU that led to a trade dispute case and over seven years of proceedings.

Although the notion of CSR cannot be easily tailored to international institutions, the gap can be bridged by recourse to their participation values in traditional multilateralism and endorsement of sustainable development values.

As the BPA and GMO cases illustrate, the chain of stakeholders (infrastructure) plays out in a variety of ways, ultimately including the retailer, consumer, government public health agencies and environmental/public health activists. As our analysis draws to conclusion, we offer thoughts directed to managers (business, government and NGO) about the type of risk infrastructure. Primary responsible for the safety and health of consumers rests on the shoulders of the management for companies that develop chemicals and technologies that are incorporated into the consumption stream. They are responsible for seeing that their ingredients sustain scientific review, not only by their researchers but also by those of independent scientists, government scientists and those relied on by NGOs committed to public health and safety. If the originating industry presumes a commander role, it is likely to lack the legitimacy to reach and convince stakeholder consumers who can and do vote with their consumer dollars. Thus, and this note is very relevant to the managers along the product development and consumption stream, especially retailers, they are encouraged to press the originators to assure the reasonable safety of product and packaging ingredients. As reasoned in this chapter, standards of CSR and principles of stakeholder participation offer insights into the dialogs and management assurances along the route of the infrastructure. At every step, the scientific battles that often occur in such cases call for vigilance and sustained engagement.

The managers that provide basic chemicals and biotechnologies can hold different CSR standards of product safety. Other managers and consumers are likely to attribute the science of the originating industry as being profit-centric rather than consumer-centric in their communication philosophy and CSR standards. In addition, the manufacturers of the risky product ingredients are often several links removed from consumers in the product manufacturing and utilization chain. The relationship is often stronger (central) and more dense between consumers and the industry, especially retailers, that provides the product containing BPA or GMOs than with the companies that manufacture or engineer it as an ingredient.

These two cases illustrate a management challenge, especially for companies that design, develop, and market basic ingredients that find their way into the consumption stream. In this context, the chain of stakeholders (infrastructure) plays out in a variety of ways, ultimately including the retailer, consumer, government public health agencies and environmental/public health activists. If the originating company or industry presumes a commander role it is likely to lack the legitimacy to reach and convince stakeholder consumers who can and do vote with their consumer dollars. It needs to realize and appreciate that as "negative" interpretations get into the dialog, they tend to persist and even resist subsequent scientific findings. Part of that outcome results because consumers hold different standards (CSR) of product safety and attribute the science of the industry as being profit-centric. Basic science and peer review may be fostered by the industry but can be and often is not fully independent. Conflicting interpretations of facts, different evaluative protocols and dense networks of peers make such voices daunting, especially if findings either do not support or contradict those of the originating industry. As organizations aspire to networks and infrastructures of stakeholder engagement as effective and ethical means for risk communication, they are not easy to create and operate in such profit-centric contexts. The manufacturers of the risky product are often several links removed from consumers in the product manufacturing and utilization chain. The relationship is often stronger (central) and more dense between consumers and the industry that provides the product containing BPA or GMOs than with the companies that manufacture or engineer it as an ingredient.

Conclusions

The specific aim of this chapter is advance theory, research and management practice beyond the risk management and communication context where risk-creator and bearer are engaged in a public arena characterized by close time, space and communication contact. The context discussed here poses management challenges to companies that create basic ingredients that arouse concern regarding the health impact on consumers. The chapter does not propose to single out and point a critical finger at companies that create and provide basic product ingredients that might or do create harm through market chains. Rather the purpose is to offer a theory and research-based rationale for their continued and positive engagement in discourse: a commitment to openness and collaboration rather than an attempt to achieve command and control of product ingredient and design. As managers require legitimacy for their products and operations, they need to support infrastructures characterized by deliberative democracy.[72] If the safety of product ingredients cannot be established from the start of manufacturing and production, then risk merely falls on other's shoulders. At risk is the legitimacy of the product and the quality of relationships with end users, as well as regulators and critical NGOs. Marketplaces become corrupted by distrust and litigation, as well as ruinous assaults on products and retailers. Merely issuing assuring messages is insufficient in such matters since in various ways, and to various degrees, other voices will judge and even condemn those messages. Badly managed risk can harm the relationship between retailer and consumer, which can imperil the integrity of the marketplace. As Douglas, Renn, Beck, Palazzo, Scherer[73] and others have argued, such commercial practices are not merely matters of economic legitimacy but also of political legitimacy.

Notes

1   Heath, R.L. and Palenchar, M.J. (2009), *Strategic Issues Management*, 2nd edn, Sage, Thousand Oaks, CA; Palazzo, G and Scherer, A.G. (2006), "Corporate legitimacy as deliberation: a communicative framework", *Journal of Business Ethics*, vol. 66, pp. 71–88; Scherer, A.G. and Palazzo, G. (2007), "Toward a political conceptualization of corporate responsibility: business and society seen from a Habermasian perspective", *Academy of Management Review*, vol. 31, pp. 1096–1120.

2   Scherer and Palazzo (2007), op. cit.

3   Colborn, T., Dumanoski, D. and Myers, J.P. (2006), *Our Stolen Future: What are Phthalates and Why are there Health Concerns*, http:www.ourstolenfuture.org/newscience.

4   Beck, U. (1992), *Risk Society: Towards a New Modernity*, Sage, London; Beck, U. (1999), *World Risk Society*, Polity Press, Cambridge, MA.

5   Beck (1992, 1999), op. cit.; Douglas, M. (1992), *Risk and Blame*, Routledge, London.

6   Giddens, A. (1999). "Risk and responsibility", *The Modern Law Review*, vol. 62, pp. 1–10; Scherer and Palazzo (2007), op. cit.

7   Heath, R.L. (2010), "Stakeholder participation". In J.J. Cochran (ed.), *Wiley Encyclopedia of Operations Research and Management Science*, John Wiley and Sons, Boston, MA, pp. 5115–5123.

8   Rawlins, B.L. (2006), *Prioritizing Stakeholders for Public Relations*, Institute for Public Relations, Gainesville, FL, p. 2.

9   Clarkson, M.B.E. (1995), "A stakeholder framework for analyzing and evaluating corporate social performance", *The Academy of Management Review*, vol. 20, no. 1, pp. 92–117.

10   Gephart, R.P. Jr., (1984), "Making sense of organizationally based environmental disasters", *Journal of Management*, vol. 10, no. 2, pp. 205–225.

11   Heath and Palenchar (2009), op. cit.

12   Fischhoff, B., Slovic, P., Lichtenstein, S., Read, S. and Combs, B. (1978), "How safe is safe enough? a psychometric study of attitudes towards technological risks and benefits", *Policy Sciences*, vol. 8, pp. 127–152.

13   Rayner, S. and Cantor, R. (1987), "How fair is safe enough? The cultural approach to technology choice", *Risk Analysis*, vol. 7, no. 1, pp. 3–9.

14   Mitchell, R.K., Agle, B.R. and Wood, D.J. (1997), "Toward a theory of stakeholder identification and salience: defining the principle of who and what really counts", *Academy of Management Review*, vol. 22, no. 4, p. 857.

15   Johnson, J. and Zawawi, C. (2009), *Public Relations: Theory and Practice*, Allen and Unwin, Crows Nest, NSW, Australia, p. 72.

16   Dyche, J. (2002), *The CRM Handbook: A Business Guide to Customer Relationship Management*, Addison-Wesley, Saddle River, NJ.

17   Knox, S. and Gruar, C. (2007), "The application of stakeholder theory to relationship marketing strategy development in a non-profit organization", *Journal of Business Ethics*, vol. 7, no. 2, pp. 115–135, p. 115; Gummesson, E. (1999), "Total relationship marketing: experimenting with a synthesis of research frontiers", *Australian Marketing Journal*, vol. 7, no. 1, pp. 72–85; Miller, R.L. and Lewis, W.F. (1991), "A stakeholder approach to marketing management using the value exchange model", *European Journal of Marketing*, vol. 25, no. 8, pp. 55–68.

18   Fischhoff, B. (1995), "Risk perception and communication unplugged: twenty years of process", *Risk Analysis*, vol. 15, pp. 137–145; Morgan, M.G., Fischhoff, B., Bostrom, A. and Atman, C.J. (2002), *Risk Communication: A Mental Models Approach*, Cambridge University Press, New York.

19   Starr, C. (1972), *Benefit–Cost Studies in Sociotechnical Systems*, Committee on Public Engineering Policy, Perspective on Benefit–Risk Decision Making, National Academy of Engineering, Washington, DC.

20   Hadden, S.G. (1989b), "Institutional barriers to risk communication", *Risk Analysis*, vol. 9, pp. 301–308.

21   Rayner, S. (1992), "Cultural theory and risk analysis". In S. Krimsky and D. Golding (eds), *Social Theories of Risk*, Praeger, Westport, CT, pp. 83–115; Tansey, J. and Rayner, S. (2009), "Cultural theory and risk". In R.L. Heath and H.D. O'Hair (eds), *Handbook of Risk and Crisis Communication*, Routledge, New York, pp. 53–79.

22   Beck (1992, 1999), op. cit.

23   Laird, F. N. (1989), "The decline of deference: the political context of risk communication", *Risk Analysis*, vol. 9, no. 2, pp. 543–550.

24   Sjoberg, L. (2000), "Factors in risk perception", *Risk Analysis*, vol. 20, pp. 1–11; Slovic, P. (1979), "Rating the risks", *Environment*, vol. 21, no. 3, pp. 14–39; Slovic, P., Fischhoff, B. and Lichtenstein, S. (1987), "Behavioral decision theory perspectives on protective behavior". In N.D. Weinstein (ed.), *Taking Care: Understanding and Encouraging Self-Protected Behavior*, Cambridge University Press, New York, pp. 14–41.

25   Heath, R.L., Palenchar, M.J. and O'Hair, H.D. (2009), "Community building through risk communication infrastructure". In R.L. Heath and D.H. O'Hair (eds), *Handbook of Risk and Crisis Communication*, Routledge, New York, pp. 474–490; McComas, K.A. (2010), "Community engagement and risk management". In R.L. Heath (ed.), *SAGE Handbook of Public Relations*, Sage, Thousand Oaks, CA, pp. 461–476; Renn, O. (2009), "Risk communication: insights and requirements for designing successful communication programs on health and environmental hazards". In R.L. Heath and H.D. O'Hair (eds), *Handbook of Risk and Crisis Communication*, Routledge, New York, pp. 80–98.

26   Fiorino, D.J. (1990), "Citizen participation and environmental risk: a survey of institutional mechanisms", *Science, Technology and Human Values*, vol. 15, no. 2, pp. 226–243.

27   McComas, K., Besley, J. and Trumbo, C. (2006), "Why citizens do and don't attend public meetings about local cancer clusters", *Policy Studies Journal*, vol. 34, no. 4, pp. 671–698.

28   Scherer and Palazzo (2007), op. cit.

29   Palmlund, I. (1992), "Social drama and risk evaluation". In S. Krimsky and D. Golding (eds), *Social Theories of Risk*, Praeger, Westport, CT, pp. 197–214; Palmlund, I. (2009), "Risk and social dramaturgy". In R.L. Heath and H.D. O'Hair (eds), *Handbook of Risk and Crisis Communication*, Routledge, New York, pp. 192–204.

30   Freeman, R.E. and Gilbert, D.R. Jr. (1988), *Corporate Strategy and the Search for Ethics*, Prentice Hall, Englewood Cliffs, NJ, p. 89.

31   Ibid, p. 91.

32   McWilliams, A. and Siegel, D. (2001), "Corporate social responsibility: a theory of the firm perspective", *The Academy of Management Review*, vol. 26, no. 1, pp. 117–127.

33   Freeman, R.E. (1984), *Strategic Management: A Stakeholder Approach*, Pitman, Boston; Freeman, R.E., Harrison, J.S., Wicks, A.C., Parmar, B.L. and de Colle, S. (2010), *Stakeholder Theory: The State of the Art*, Cambridge University Press, New York.

34   Freeman, R.E. and Gilbert, D.R. Jr. (1988). *Corporate Strategy and the Search for Ethics*, Prentice Hall, Englewood Cliffs, NJ.

35   Freeman (1984), op. cit.

36   Heath (2010), op. cit.; Kotler, P. and Lee, N.R. (2005), *Corporate Social Responsibility: Doing the Most Good for Your Company and Your Cause*, Wiley, Hoboken, NJ; Post, J.E., Preston, L.E. and

Sachs, S. (2002), *Redefining the Corporation: Stakeholder Management and Organizational Wealth*, Stanford Business Books, Stanford, CA.

37   Friedman, M. (1970), "The social responsibility of business is to increase its profits", *New York Times*, September 13, pp. 122–126.

38   Reich, R.G. (2008, August 1), *The Case Against Corporate Responsibility: Statement*, Goldman School of Public Policy, University of California, Berkeley; May, S. (2008), "Reconsidering strategic corporate social responsibility: public relations and ethical engagement of employees in a global economy". In A. Zerfass, B. van Ruler, and K. Sriramesh (eds), *Public Relations Research: European and International Perspectives and Innovations*, VS Verslag, Wiesbaden, Germany, pp. 365–383.

39   Munshi, D. and Kurian, P. (2005), "Imperializing spin cycles: a postcolonial look at public relations, greenwashing, and the separation of publics", *Public Relations Review*, vol. 31, pp. 513–520.

40   Palmlund (2009), op. cit.

41   Donaldson, T. and Preston, L.E. (1995), "The stakeholder theory of the corporation: concepts, evidence, and implication", *Academy of Management Review*, vol. 20, pp. 65–91.

42   Ibid, p. 67.

43   Heath, R.L. (2011). "External organizational rhetoric: bridging management and sociopolitical discourse", *Management Communication Quarterly*, vol. 25, pp. 415–435.

44   Clarke, K. and Hemphill, J. (2001), "The Santa Barbara oil spill: a retrospective". *Proceedings From the 64th Annual Meeting of the Association of Pacific Coast Geographers*, Santa Barbara, CA.

45   Falkenberry, E.M. (1995), "The Emergency Planning and Community Right-To-Know Act: a tool for toxic release reduction in the 90's", *Buffalo Environmental Law Journal*, vol. 3, no. 1, pp. 1–36.

46   National Research Council (1989), *Improving Risk Communication*, National Academy Press, Washington, DC; Palenchar, M.J. (2009), "Historical trends of risk and crisis communication". In R.L. Heath and H.D. O'Hair (eds), *Handbook of Risk and Crisis Communication*, Routledge, New York, pp. 31–52.

47   Florini, A. (ed.) (2007), *The Right to Know: Transparency for an Open World*, Columbia University Press, New York; Hamilton, J.T. (2005), *Regulation through Revelation: The Origins, Politics, and Impacts of the Toxic Release Inventory Program*, Cambridge University Press, New York; Motta, B. (2009). *The Right to Know and the Fight Against Toxic Environments: The Emergency Planning and Community Right-To-Know Act Of 1986*, unpublished doctoral dissertation, Knoxville, TN, University of Tennessee.

48   Hadden, S.G. (1989a). *A Citizen's Right to Know: Risk Communication and Public Policy*, Westview Press, Boulder, CO.

49   Motta, B. and Palenchar, M.J. (2010), "Historical evolution of community right to know: implications on the development and practice of public relations", International History of Public Relations Research Conference, Poole, England.

50   Giddens, A. (1991), *Modernity and Self-Identity*, Stanford University Press, Palo Alto, CA.

51   Beck (1992, 1999), op. cit.

52   Motta (2009), op. cit.; Motta and Palenchar (2010), op. cit.

53   Palazzo and Scherer (2006), op. cit.

54   Beck (1992), op. cit., pp. 83–84.

55   Renn, O. (1992), "Concepts of risk: a classification". In S. Krimsky and D. Golding (eds), *Social Theories of Risk*, Praeger, Westport, CT, pp. 53–79; Renn (2009), op. cit.; see also McComas (2010), op. cit.

56   Rowley, T.J. (1997), "Moving beyond dyadic ties: a network theory of stakeholder influences", *Academy of Management Review*, vol. 22, pp. 887–910, p. 890.

57   Ibid, p. 897.

58   Ibid.

59   Colborn, Dumanoski and Myers (2006), op. cit.

60   U.S. Food and Drug Administration (2010, January), *Update on Bisphenol A for Use in Food Contact Applications*.

61   BisphenolA. (2010), *Bisphenol-a.org/FAQs*, from http://www.bisphenol-a.org/about/faq.html.

62   Since You Asked (2010), *National Institute of Environmental Health Sciences, National Institutes of Health*, www.niehs.nih.gov/news/media/questions/sya-bpa.cfm.

63   U.S. Food and Drug Administration (2010), op. cit., p. 3.

64   Ibid.

65   RightHealth. (n.d.). *Within the Mix of Articles, One Could Find Ads for Legal Council*, http://www.righthealth.com/topic/Within_the_mix_of_articles%2C_onecould_find_ads_for_legal_council?

66   Ibid.

67   Ibid., p. 1.

68   Proutheau, S. and Heath, R.L. (2009), "Precautionary principle and biotechnology: regulators are from Mars and activists are from Venus". In R.L. Heath and H.D. O'Hair (eds), *Handbook of Risk and Crisis Communication*, Routledge, New York, pp. 576–590.

69   Maguire, S. and Ellis, J. (2009), "The precautionary principle and risk communication". In R.L. Heath and H.D. O'Hair (eds), *Handbook of Risk and Crisis Communication*, Routledge, New York, pp. 119–137.

70   Proutheau and Heath (2009), op. cit.

71   Maguire and Ellis (2009), op. cit.

72   Scherer and Palazzo (2007), op. cit.

73   Beck (1992, 1999), op. cit.; Douglas (1992), op. cit.; Renn (1992, 2009), op. cit.; Palazzo and Scherer (2006), op. cit.; Scherer and Palazzo (2007), op. cit.

8 *Risk Conflicts and Demands for Social and Environmental Accounting: An Empirical Study*

GEORGIOS GEORGAKOPOULOS* AND IAN THOMSON†

Keywords

Accountability engagements, reflexivity, risk society, salmon farming.

Introduction

Our concern is that without effective social and environmental accountability mechanisms many of the hazards associated with contemporary Western societies to our ecosystems, society and economic well-being will remain uncontested and allowed to proliferate. In this chapter we report on the diversity of social and environmental accountability mechanisms observed in our research on salmon farming in Scotland[1] and discuss its relationship to stakeholder risk perceptions and risk conflicts. We discuss how Beck's conceptualization of risks and risk conflicts[2] help evaluate the effectiveness of social and environmental accounting processes, practices and expertise. Comprehending Beck's work can offer a number of important insights into how social and environmental accounting could contribute to social and environmental risk governance and effective stakeholder engagements. Risk conflicts are important engagement opportunities for stakeholders. They are also contexts where social and environmental accounts are extensively used. However, the social and environmental accounting processes and practices observed in salmon farming risk conflicts differed considerably from corporate social and environmental reporting.[3]

In the Scottish salmon farming arena there appeared to be a reflexive relationship between social and environmental accounting processes and practices, risk conflicts, stakeholder engagement dynamics and risk governance processes, practices and expertise. It was an arena characterized by intense, sometimes passionate debate amongst

* Georgios Georgakopoulos, Accounting Group, Amsterdam Business School, University of Amsterdam, Plantage Muidergracht 12, Amsterdam 1018TV, Noord Holland, Netherlands. E-mail: g.georgakopoulos@uva.nl.

† Ian Thomson, Department of Accounting and Finance, Strathclyde Business School, University of Strathclyde, 100 Cathedral Street, Glasgow G4 0LN, the UK. E-mail: i.h.thomson@strath.ac.uk.

stakeholders, trade organizations, NGOs, political institutions, regulatory authorities and voluntary certification bodies. This debate, although underpinned by economic and scientific evidence, was often played out in emotional language and amplified in the mass media. The history and diversity of resistance to salmon farming in Scotland has been characterized as a series of high-profile single-issue campaigns, which we argue has created a complex, fragmented approach to risk governance and the evolution of fragmented "single-issue" accountability processes, which were heavily influenced by the perceived power of stakeholders groups.

At any point in time there were a number of active risk conflicts involving polarized positions on the "legitimate" risks of salmon farming and contested discourses on the social, economic and environmental acceptability of the sector. The persistence and intensity of arguments over the risks posed by salmon farming created a complex network of voluntary and regulatory processes and practices across the salmon farming life cycle. These governance processes and practises evolved over time, normally in response to legitimacy crises in the industry and created extra regulation, surveillance and accountability obligations for salmon farming organizations. Despite these reforms certain stakeholder groups continued to believe these processes and practices were designed to protect the salmon farming business interests rather than the environment and society.

Stakeholders opposed to salmon farming practices and the associated risk governance regime combined scientific and economic evidence with risk dramatization to problematize the status quo, engage public support for their campaign and to provide a techno-scientific legitimacy for their interventions. Campaigning organizations used external social and environmental accounts[4] as part of their strategy to redefine acceptable risks and reform governance structures, processes, practices and expertise in alignment with their underlying values and mission.

This chapter will develop as follows. First we present our arena-based study into the risk conflicts, stakeholder engagements and social and environmental accounting in salmon farming in Scotland. Secondly, we develop our discussion of Beck's contribution to risk governance and its relationship to social and environmental accounting. Thirdly, we frame our findings within the context of a series of escalating risk conflicts. Finally, we conclude with our observations of the impacts of Beck's work on the development of a more effective social and environmental accounting in terms of stakeholder engagements and governing risks.

Researching Risk Conflicts in Scottish Salmon Farming

This project was influenced by arena studies into controversial social and environmental risk conflicts; particularly arena studies, such as nuclear power and genetic modification.[5] In our view this method offers a more holistic approach to exploring the relationships amongst social and environmental accounting, stakeholder engagements, media, political interventions, regulatory regimes and the organizations "creating" the risky situation.[6] The main elements of an arena study are represented in Figure 8.1.

An arena is a metaphor that describes the symbolic location of actions that influence collective decisions. It attempts to explain the process of policy formulation and enforcement in a specific context. It structures and represents the participants in a political arena, patterns of interaction, communication and decision-making processes. Within an arena, it is assumed that different actors use social resources to pursue their objectives. These resources include money, power, social influence and evidence. Resource accumulation may be the ultimate goal of an actor, but within an arena resources are more likely to be a means to an end. Success or failure of arena engagements are determined by participants' perceptions of their influence on decisions.[7]

Each arena is characterized by formal codified rules monitored by rule enforcers and informal rules that emerge from interactions between participants. Normally, these rules are external constraints for each participant but several participants may join forces to change rules. Rule enforcers ensure that participants abide by formal rules and may coordinate informal interactions and negotiations. Most rule enforcers are deemed to have powers delegated to them by political institutions via legislation.

Issue amplifiers (the mass media) play a role analogous to "theatre critics" observing actions on stage, communicating with the participants, interpreting their findings and reporting to others. Issue amplifiers can influence arena dynamics by mobilizing public support for particular factions within the arena. Their audience consists of other groups who may be enticed to enter the arena and individuals who may demonstrate their support or displeasure with participants.

Drawing upon an arena approach we assume that all the participants in our study (see Figure 8.1 and Table 8.4) would attempt to influence the outcome of a collective decision process in accordance with their values and beliefs. This outcome would not wholly be determined by an individual group but by structural rules and group interactions. Political organization and the reflexive impacts of participants' actions could lead to outcomes incompatible with the evidence and/or values of all or any participating group.

We see the arena framework as useful in representing, explaining and making sense of complex decision-making processes. It provides a structure to differentiate engagement activities that inform social and environmental discourses and describe the context of any

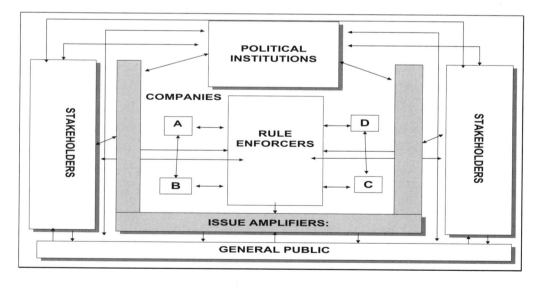

Figure 8.1 The arena model

Source: Adapted from Renn (1992: 190)

accounting disclosures. It recognizes a wider set of engagement routes than previously recognized in the social and environmental accounting literature, which is predominantly concerned with the unreflexive external transmission of corporate information to underspecified stakeholder groups. With a few exceptions[8] the literature does not explicitly consider the coexistence of alternate accounts, heterogeneous engagement activities or the co-evolution of these alternate accounts and diverse engagement dynamics within a particular empirical site.

In this light empirical data was collected on each of the key elements of the arena concept depicted in Figure 10.1. The main evidence was gathered using a semi-structured cascading interviewing process. In total 25 interviews[‡] were conducted with representatives from salmon farmers, government regulators, political institutions, rule enforcers and pro- and anti-fish farming stakeholder groups. This material was supplemented with an analysis of other relevant documents, accounts and reports. In addition evidence was gathered on the media representation of salmon farming of the main Scottish newspapers.[9]

Our research was designed to gather a diverse set of opinions from all elements of the arena model, as well as a range of views from within each element. For example we interviewed small-scale salmon farmers who developed in collaboration with the Soil Association (SA) organic salmon production as well as large-scale conventional salmon producers who were part of multinational corporations.

An important part of this study was to identify the different forms and uses of social and environmental accounts in this arena. Given the intensity, media visibility and persistence of opposition to salmon farming and farmed salmon we expected to find extensive use of social and environmental reports in order to demonstrate their social, environmental and economic acceptability. Our preliminary results were disappointing, in that there were very few annual corporate social and environmental reports or disclosures present in the arena, despite the high level of contested discourses over the many perceived risks, hazards and benefits of salmon farming (see Figure 8.3).

We then reflected upon what social and environmental accounting processes and practices would look like in the field. Following this period of reflection we adopted less restrictive definition of social and environmental accounting processes and practices[10] and extended our analysis to include accounts produced by all arena participants. This shift in research design uncovered extensive use of social and environmental accounts by all parties in the risk conflict arena (see Table 8.3).

These social, environmental and economic accounts appeared to be related to risk conflicts and power dynamics between all salmon farming arena participants. Each group had a privileged definition of "legitimate" risks that underpinned their involvement in the risk conflict. Each group was seen to publish their social and environmental accounts of the risks of salmon farming and to demand social and environmental accounts of salmon farming practices. Implicit in these accounts and demands for accounts were solutions intended to minimize or eliminate specific salmon farming risks.

---

‡ See Table 8.4 in the appendix for an overview of all the participants interviewed and the abbreviations used in this chapter. Note some of the names of the organizations have been changed to preserve the anonymity requested by certain research participants (also in Tables 8.1 and 8.2).

We will now develop our examination of how Beck's[11] notion of risks and Beck and Willms[12] risk conflict are linked with social and environmental accounting, prior to discussing in detail the results of our research.

Risk, Risk Conflicts and Social and Environmental Accounting

Of particular interest to our evaluation of social and environmental accounting processes and practices are Beck's observations on the links between science, political power, civic society, stakeholder activism, social legitimacy, profit and risk definitional powers. How a risk is established as a risk as worthy of government intervention is at the crux of Beck's work.[13] Risks, and their associated costs and liabilities, only exist in modern societies when there is irrefutable proof of a causal connection between an action and a hazard using modern scientific methodologies. Establishing socially acceptable levels of risk, however, requires the application of economics and accounting to value the cost–benefits associated with any scientifically legitimate risk.

Science, accounting and economics have become important technologies[14] to define acceptable levels of risks. Crudely, individuals, corporations or government institutions can only be held formally accountable for risks that can be scientifically attributed to a specific action. The extent to which they are accountable and to whom, is determined by economic and accounting methods. Science, accounting and economics are therefore important risk identifying and allocative technologies used by governments, regulators, stakeholders and civic society groups seeking transformation of conduct they consider unacceptable and/or illegitimate. Science, accounting and economics are also important risk denial or avoidance technologies utilized by powerful corporations or institutions to maintain their privileged positions in society.

Beck's work is grounded in the environmental movement and environmental politics in Europe and has been shaped by developments in the sociology of risk.[15] Environmental concerns and social activism originated from situations where the hazards were directly attributable to specific industrial sites, for example damage to human health through smoke, smog, polluted rivers and visible destruction of ecosystems. This made environmental regulation relatively straightforward because responsibility and liabilities were easy to assign. There was evidence of social and environmental accounts in nineteenth-century England associated with campaigns for social reform and environmental protection.[16] As these perceptible risks associated with industrialization were governed and mitigated, new technological developments created new forms of risks, imperceptible (to the human senses) undesired side effects of the production processes and products. Despite these risks being imperceptible to humans, through the application of scientific techniques and equipment they were able to be measured and scientifically verified. Once these risks were scientifically proven to exist then risk-reduction measures could be established as could "safe" levels of emissions and toxins.

However, in the 1980s there was a concern that regulatory processes of legitimating, identifying and managing risks were systematically ignoring significant hazards of industrialization. These included catastrophic risks and hazards with time-delayed effects. Beck argued that there has been a broad regulatory neglect and institutional failures of governing the hazardous consequences of industrialization. These risks were man-made, imposed on everybody regardless of circumstance, extending beyond geopolitical boundaries, not temporally bounded or attributable to any specific action of a specific organization. These risks were incalculable and unattributable in terms of the traditional rationale of insurance economics since the probability of their occurrence and potential damage is unknowable. Many of these risks are novel or have not yet caused measurable harm but their existence is based on predictions and models of things yet to come.

These risks fall outwith the capacity of modern science, economic, accounting and regulatory processes, practices and expertise. The objective levels of certainty required for science to prove a risk exists cannot be derived in modern postindustrial societies. Consequently subjective perception of risks becomes the dominant pattern for their description and definition. Assigning responsibility and accountability for risks by regulatory authorities is open now to challenge and contestation. Institutions and norm-based regulatory systems are considered incapable of dealing with these issues and are no longer automatically accepted as valid by civic society.

Civic society is becoming increasingly aware of the potential harm of those risks and willing to challenge risk-producing and risk-governing systems. This is evidenced by the emergence of grassroot community activism, growing numbers, power and reputation of campaigning NGOs. Civic society is acting as a new disciplinary force in society, in particular as a form of social control of the corporate sector. Civic society and stakeholder groups have created systems of extra-parliamentary monitoring, surveillance and alternative accountability processes that challenge the dominance of the political and corporate governing practices, processes and expertise. The defining and legitimating of the social acceptability of risks is no longer wholly in the hands of the state and determined by scientific institutions. Legitimate risks and acceptable risks are now potentially subject to contestation, conflict and challenge by any interested stakeholder and if we accept Beck's description of the risk society we are all stakeholders in all things.

Risks are no longer given but rather become socially constructed and emergent from risk conflicts. Beck and Willms[17] discuss the different stages and elements of a typical escalating risk conflict, which we have attempted to represent in Figure 8.2.

The first stage in a risk conflict is normally located around a growing concern, within a specific social group who perceive themselves to be suffering as a consequence of others' actions. These problems are developed and amplified by the media into tales of concern to consumers, especially to parents of small children. These media tales are normally met with official resistance by companies, rule-enforcing institutions and politicians. Despite this systemic institutional denial of these risks there is continuing coverage of these concerns over this reported threat that can transform these media tales into social facts.

Affected and/or worried groups consult "legitimate" scientists, to apply their expertise and judgment into their concerns. However, often rule-enforcing institutions' processes and practices are underpinned by processes, practices and expertise of the same "legitimate" scientists. This strategy by the affected/worried group can create scientific risk denial in addition to previous institutional risk denials, but it can also uncover competing theories and/or evidence as to the cause of the risk that has been suppressed, dismissed, or gone untested within the scientific community.[18] This can lead to the persistence of the social facts and a further amplification of the risks in the media fuelled by contradictory statements between experts, counter-experts, institutions, corporations and suffering individuals. The increased production and communication of knowledge on the "risk" does little to resolve the conflict but manufactures uncertainty;[19] rather than reducing risks this amplifies and transmits risk concerns.

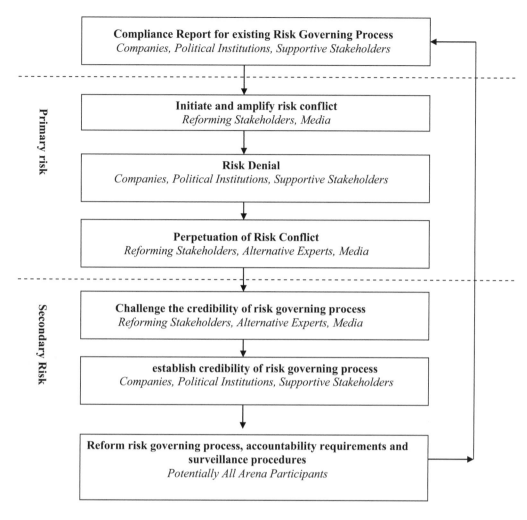

Figure 8.2   Overview of the risk conflict process

A major change in a risk conflict is when the epicentre of the risk conflict shifts from the problematic conduct to the legitimacy of those responsible for governing these risks.[20] This increases the stakes and entrenches those denying the risks and shifts the conflict from a first-order conflict (primary risk in Figure 8.2) to a second-order conflict (secondary risk in Figure 8.2). The concerned stakeholders may organize into a single-issue social movement or enter into coalitions with existing NGOs or campaigns that already possess social legitimacy and counter-expertise experience and resources.[21]

At this stage the risk conflict has moved away from a single factory, company or product to incorporate elements of legal systems, political systems, systems of science and mechanisms for the production of socially acceptable truth. The objective of the conflict may have mutated into campaigns for institutional reform, regulatory changes and the power to determine what is an unacceptable risk and who to blame. Second-order risk conflicts are characterized by clashing and compromising over regulations and power over the setting and enforcing of regulations. Existing risk-governing processes and practices have been shaped by past risk conflicts and thus perceived as reformable by future risk conflicts.

Beck argues that risk conflicts are not necessarily destructive, but rather are essential components of reflexive risk-governing processes. They can operate as mechanisms of quasi-revolutionary enlightenment.[22] Risk conflicts force different groups of stakeholders to communicate who would otherwise choose not to do so. Stakeholders who want to change rules and laws, redistribute costs, liabilities and obligations have to engage with those groups that benefit from the status quo and resist change. Often this engagement takes place in the full glare of the mass media. This forced public engagement is not enough to bring about change but would appear to be a necessary precondition to change. Beck and Willms[23] discuss a number of situations where risk conflicts have had a role in bringing about social transformations and a re-prioritization of societies' main concerns. First- and second-order risk conflicts involve multiple, at odds scientific, financial and social accounts[24] of potential harm. Legitimate evidence and how it is gathered, measured, presented, communicated and valued is critical to engagement processes and practices in risk conflicts.

The predominant theoretical approach to social and environmental accounting is that accounts are produced to legitimate an organization's past, present and future conduct to stakeholders. The account is part of an implied social contract between the organization and society and fulfils a legitimating role of proving the accounting entity is operating in a socially acceptable manner.[25] Typically this is done through the inclusion of social and environmental disclosures in the corporation's annual financial report and/or a stand-alone annual social and environmental responsibility report. There has been extensive criticism of the effectiveness of this type of social and environmental accounting processes and practices,[26] but we are not going to directly address these criticisms in this chapter. We rather look at Beck's notion of legitimacy and risk conflict to develop a broader understanding of how social and environmental accounting processes and practices are potentially formed and altered.

Drawing on insights from the risk conflict framework depicted in Figure 8.2 we would expect to find evidence-based accounts (in their broader sense) of perceived risks from all arena participants; accounts that are used to initiate and perpetuate risk conflicts, accounts that are used to escalate risk conflicts, accounts that are used to deny the existence of risks, accounts that demonstrate compliance with rules, norms and regulations, accounts that are used to delegitimate other arena participants, and accounts that are used to relegitimate specific arena participants. The giving, receiving and demanding for these social and environmental accounts can be seen to be integral to risk conflict and as a part of the struggle for legitimacy. Legitimacy on behalf of oppositional stakeholders for their desired transformation, and legitimacy on behalf of others to continue along the same trajectory.

The next section will present our empirical findings on how social and environmental accounting was related to the risk conflict processes observed in the Scottish salmon farming arena.

Scottish Salmon Farming, Risk Conflicts and Social and Environmental Accounting

The Scottish salmon farming arena comprised a large number of active participants and a history of intense risk conflicts, typically in the form of high-profile single-issue campaigns. This history has created a complex, fragmented approach to risk governance and a complex set of social and environmental accountability processes. These campaigns have covered almost every aspect of salmon farming and have targeted specific salmon farms, farming practices as well as second-order risk management issues that have challenged the legitimacy of the governing and regulation of salmon farming.

Figure 8.3 is our attempt to map out the types of risks that have been subject to conflict and contestation. These risks were derived from our thematic analysis of all the interviews conducted and relevant documents and reports.

Contested risks were mainly conflicts between oppositional stakeholder groups and coalitions of political institutions, supportive stakeholder groups and salmon farmers.

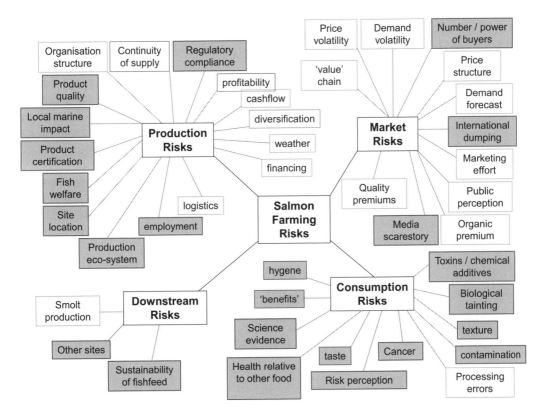

Figure 8.3   Map of thematic risks as formed from interview and document analysis

Note: Figure 8.3 tries to holistically depict the multiple dimensions of risk in Scottish salmon farming. It is a composite representation of different risks from different elements of the risk arena. No single institution/organization identified or accepted all of these risks as legitimate and in many cases they were explicit in denying the existence of certain risks. The shaded boxes represent the most contested risk claims

This coalition consistently challenged the legitimacy of the oppositional stakeholder's claims through framing them as emotional, irrational and misguided, for example "The industry has had a terrible press from a few people who are anti-fish farming campaigners. These are absolute nut cases" (Scottish Salmon Growers Association).[§]

As mentioned earlier, the salmon farming risk-governing regime was complex. Responsibility for governing salmon farming risks was dispersed across a large number of political institutions, statutory rule-enforcers and voluntary rule-enforcing bodies. For example:

> In the UK if you try to set up a farm you have to consult around 40 bodies from which 6 are statutory ... You have to do an Environment Impact Assessment which costs around £30,000 before you even apply for the license from the Crown Estate and if even one of those 40 bodies object you have £30,000 down the drain. (SSGA)

There was not an integrative institution or mechanism(s) that systematically governed the risks associated with salmon production, processing or consumption. Table 8.1 identifies the main rule-enforcers in the salmon farming arena. It is noteworthy that most of the supportive stakeholder groups in the arena (denoted by italics in Table 8.1) operated as voluntary rule-enforcers through anxiety-reduction strategies such as product certification or quality control enforcers.

Most farmers interviewed chose to submit themselves to these voluntary control regimes for two main reasons, price premiums and external legitimacy. Product certification, with its implied compliance with strict quality standards, led to marketing and price advantages. These regimes were more stringent and prescriptive than statutory regimes, but they conferred a visible product differentiation and attracted premium prices. However, the salmon farmers' freedom not to comply with these voluntary regimes was disputable, particularly in the case of the supermarkets. Supermarkets tend to forward-purchase at an agreed price, but reserved the right to withdraw from the contract based on any deviation from prescribed farming practises. Given that supermarkets controlled over 85 percent of salmon sold in the UK (Scottish Salmon Growers Association interview) and the lack of an efficient wholesale salmon market, it was difficult to regard the supermarkets as voluntary rule-enforcers.

This fragmented risk-governance regime dispersed across different institutions (with each institution possessing restrictive remits, either by legislation or by their organizational vision and strategy) is similar to those in other risk conflict arenas.[27] This fragmentation and dispersal was also observed in the oppositional stakeholder groups. This meant that each institution/organization involved in salmon farming risk conflicts had its own specific agenda as to risk prioritization, engagement strategies, compliance mechanisms, accountability processes and risk legitimization techniques.

[§]   See Tables 8.1, 8.2 and 8.4 (in the appendix with abbreviations) for information on the stakeholder groups that participated in this study.

Table 8.1   Scottish salmon farming arena political institutions and rule enforcers

Political institutions and rule enforcers
Scottish Environment Protection Agency (SEPA): the regulatory and enforcement authority for environmental protection and pollution control, covering discharges to air, land and water
Regional Authority (RA): democratically elected single, all-purpose local authority. It makes political decisions on policies, strategies as well as delivering services, enforcing statutes and regulations
Health and Safety Executive (HSE): responsible for the regulation of health and safety issues
Maritime and Coastguard Agency (MCA): develop, promote and enforce high standards of maritime safety and pollution prevention and to minimize loss of life amongst seafarers
Food Standard Agency (FSA): statutory food safety watchdog to protect the public's health and consumer interests in relation to food
Crown Estate (CE): political agency responsible for the management of the territorial seabed and foreshore between high and low tide mark
Veterinary Medicines Directorate (VMD): Executive Agency protecting public health, animal health and the environment, and promoting animal welfare by assuring the safety quality and efficacy of veterinary medicines
European Agency for the Evaluation of Medicinal Products (EAMP): EU agency to evaluate and supervise medicinal products for both human and veterinary use throughout the EU
Scottish Executive Environment and Rural Affairs Department (SEERAD): advises ministers on policy relating to agriculture, rural development, food, the environment and fisheries, and for ensuring the implementation of those policies
Regional Enterprise Network (REN): responsible for economic and community development across half of Scotland
Scottish Natural Heritage (SNH): Scottish Executive's statutory adviser on natural heritage and nature conservation matters
Soil Association (SA): an independent charity with the primary purpose is to promote organic agriculture. It is the main UK organic certifier
Supermarkets: dominate the retailing of salmon and impose strict product quality requirements as well as prescribing acceptable production regimes
Scottish Salmon Growers Association (SSGA): representative body of the salmon farming industry. SSGA plans the production of the industry on a collective basis, provides funding for various projects, public relations role for the industry
Scottish Quality Salmon (SQS) operates a quality product labelling scheme. Part of the Scottish Salmon Growers Association (SSGA)
Regional Quality Salmon (RQS) operating locally based labelling schemes. Part of the Regional Salmon Growers Association (RGA)

Source: Interview and document analysis

Table 8.2 summarizes the main stakeholder groups who participated in salmon farming risk conflicts and in general were opposed to existing farming practices and risk-governance regimes. These stakeholders were all observed to participate in both first- and second-order risk conflicts, however the larger, national or international stakeholder organizations focused most of their campaigning on second-order risk conflicts. Whereas the smaller regional stakeholder groups were more concerned with first-order risk conflicts.

Table 8.2   Oppositional stakeholder groups

Stakeholders
Royal Society for the Protection of Birds (RSPB): UK wildlife conservation charity with more than a million members
World Wide Fund for Nature (WWF): environmental nongovernmental network operating in more than 90 countries, concerned with survival of species, habitats, climate change, sustainable business and environmental education
Friends of the Earth Scotland (FOE): non-governmental network of environmental groups with representation in 68 countries and leading UK environmental pressure groups
Salmon Farm Protest Group (SFPG): small regional pressure group concerned with protecting the marine and freshwater environment from fish farm disease and pollution
Regional Fisheries Association (RFA): small regional producer organization concerned with protecting the interests of local marine fishing fleet
Regional Sea Trout Association (RSTA): small regionally based NGO concerned with maintaining public access for anglers and promoting a healthy aquatic environment

Source: Interview and document analysis

The use of scientific evidence was common to all the oppositional stakeholders as part of their campaigns to affect change and gain political legitimization for their risk perceptions. They engaged in risk conflicts by producing and promoting their independent scientific studies to add or challenge the dominant scientific position, by scientifically critiquing the basis of others' "legitimate" risk position or challenging the effectiveness of risk-governance regimes. Even the stakeholder most radically opposed to conventional salmon farming (Salmon Farm Protest Group) made extensive use of scientific evidence and scientific critique amplified via mass media channels.

This scientific evidence was often presented in what we would argue were in the form of external environmental accounts[28] designed to problematize and create opportunities to transform salmon farming and/or salmon farming risk-governing regimes.

Social and Environmental Accounting in the Salmon Farming Arena

The accounting demands by the risk-governing regimes on the salmon farmers are extensive.[29] Farmers were producing a considerable volume of mandatory and voluntary disclosures to a wide range of different external bodies in a variety of different modes. Each of these accounts tended to be very specific and customized to a single institution. The format, content and time frame of each account was contingent on the risk prioritization, engagement strategies, compliance mechanisms, accountability processes and risk legitimization techniques demanded by each institution. These social and environmental accounts took many different forms: including statistical returns, site inspections, compliance statements, questionnaires, face-to-face meetings, public meetings, press releases, newsletters, ad hoc communications, scientific reports, applications for public funds, environmental impact assessments, planning permission applications, policy consultations and Web-based disclosures. One salmon farmer even installed a Web camera under their salmon cages. Each account reported on a fragment of the social and environmental risks of salmon farming and consumption. In our research we could not find any evidence for the collation of these fragments into a systematic account of the social and environmental risk of salmon farming. A sample of the social and environmental accounts produced by salmon farming organizations is contained in Table 8.3.

Table 8.3   Examples of social and environmental accounts of salmon production process

Types of accounts	Intended recipient	Basis for disclosure
Application of medicines	Rule enforcers	Mandatory
Application of medicines	Product certifiers	Business case
Waste quantities/composition	Rule enforcers	Mandatory
Waste quantities/composition	Product certifiers	Business case
Production chemicals/additives	Rule enforcers	Mandatory
Production chemicals/additives	Product certifiers	Business case
Production regime details	Product certifiers	Business case
Noise, odors, visual/aesthetic impact	Rule enforcers	Mandatory
Fish movements	Rule enforcers	Mandatory
Fish traceability	Product certifiers	Business case
Fish-food—composition/source	Product certifiers/stakeholders	Business case
Compliance with licenses/consents	Rule enforcers	Mandatory
Economic impact of salmon farming	Political institutions	Voluntary
Annual salmon production volume and prices	Political institutions	Mandatory
Annual salmon import volume and prices	Political institutions	Mandatory
Disease notification	Rule enforcers	Mandatory
Disease notification	Product certifiers	Business case
Fish forecast harvests	Rule enforcers/supportive stakeholders	Voluntary
Changes in licenses/discharge consents	Rule enforcers	Mandatory
Plans for sea-lice treatments	Companies	Voluntary
Anti-predatory precautions	Stakeholders	Voluntary
Fish welfare	Stakeholders	Voluntary
Escaped salmon	Stakeholders	Voluntary
Impact on wild salmon population	Political institutions/stakeholders	Voluntary
Impact on marine environment	Stakeholders	Voluntary
Impact on other marine businesses	Stakeholders/companies	Voluntary
Salmon product labeling	Companies/public	Business case

Source: From Georgakopoulos and Thomson (2008: 1133)

The vast majority of the social and environmental accounts produced by salmon farming organizations and their supportive stakeholders were used to demonstrate compliance with existing mandatory and voluntary risk-governance regimes. This compliance was an essential component of their legitimacy claims and social acceptability of any risks associated with the production and consumption of farmed salmon.

However, these legitimacy claims were contingent on the perceived legitimacy of the risk-governance regime by all the stakeholders involved in the salmon farming arena. As described by Beck and Willms,[30] we observed stakeholders contesting the legitimacy of the risk-governance regime and problematized the notion that complying with existing regulation effectively dealt with salmon farming risks:

> The industry claims it is clean because it follows SEPA's regulations, but sea lice is not regulated by anyone and SEPA's models used for the monitoring of the discharges are too simplistic based on fjord-type systems, unable to grasp the complexity of the issues at least in our region ... so there is a lot of prescriptive inflexible regulation which does not relate a lot to what is happening. (RSTA)

We observed numerous instances of external social and environmental accounts produced by oppositional stakeholders, or perhaps more correctly press releases relating to these social and environmental accounts, used to initiate and/or perpetuate risk conflicts. These include 10 reasons to boycott Scottish salmon this year,[31] scientific papers/reports[32] and national newspaper articles.[33]

However, given the history and diversity of the risk conflicts in the Scottish salmon farming arena it was difficult to determine the actual initiation of any of the risk conflicts. As each "new" risk conflict emerged the discourse was soon conflated with past risk conflicts and empirically determining the origins of any of them was highly problematic. In our specific study we were unable to comprehensively differentiate between risk initiation and risk conflict perpetuation.

Nevertheless, we were able to clearly identify risk denial behaviors and the use of social and environmental accounts in this stage of risk conflicts. Salmon farmers and their supportive stakeholders expressed strong opinions on their lack of environmental risks and stressed the rigors of the risk-governance regimes they were subject to, pointing out how stricter regulations of perceived environmental risks could potentially put them out of business:

> The Salmon Industry is so environmentally friendly that it is choking itself to death ... Regulators only want to manage your disease problem for example and they do not care about the consequences this has on the profitability of the industry as a whole. (SMK—Small Salmon Smoking Firm)

We also observed institutional denial of risks by risk-governance institutions, as evidenced by the following quote from The Scottish Environmental Protection Agency (there was a similar comment from the Scottish Executive Environment & Rural Affairs Department):

> There is a potential risk for public health coming from the pigmentation of the salmon flesh. However, Scottish Salmon Growers Association estimated that the amount of salmon one needs to consume in order to develop a problem is not humanly possible to eat.

The Scottish Environment Protection Agency is the main regulatory body responsible for managing environmental risks in Scotland, yet in the above quote they appear to be relying on evidence produced by a stakeholder whose stated objective is to promote and develop salmon farming to dismiss health claims arising from legitimated scientific research publications.

However, as pointed out by Beck and Willms,[34] scientific research does not always support the status quo, nor do all scientists or regulators blindly follow institutional procedures. For example Regional Sea Trout Association (RSTA) described how they have informally worked in conjunction with government institutions:

> We are normally tipped off by politicians or scientists working for a "government research institute" to make noise about issues that they cannot officially comment upon, either because it is not their regulatory remit or because it opposes Scottish Executive Environment & Rural Affairs Department's general policy in salmon farming.

There was consensus amongst the oppositional stakeholders that the accounts produced by salmon farmers, or on their behalf, merely demonstrated compliance with problematic regulations rather than addressing their perceived notion of the "real" risk concerns.

There was an absence of significant disputes over legitimate risks between the farmers and the political institutions charged with governing their risks. The farmers viewed compliance with the regulatory regime as eliminating all significant environmental and social risks.[35] There was some evidence of resistance to the current risk-governing regime by salmon farmers and a sense that the balance of risk regulation was driven by the politics of the oppositional stakeholders. They were advocating a political strategy to take more control of their risk governance:

> As the industry becomes politically more self-aware it will start dictating to the rest of the regulators and certification bodies what should be done and not the opposite. (Tm1, UK Salmon Producer)

The political institutions generally expressed confidence in their methods of governing all the significant risks of salmon farming. External qualitative and quantitative reports of the regional or national social and environmental impacts of salmon farming were regularly prepared by political institutions and rule enforcers. Examples include annual salmon production reports,[36] economic impact of salmon farming,[37] pollution emissions data[38] and the Strategic Framework for Scottish Aquaculture.[39]

Challenging the Credibility of the Risk-governing Process

Oppositional stakeholders stated that they had attempted to engage constructively with regulators and political institutions but they also described their relationships as problematic and noted a lack of willingness of these institutions to listen to their concerns, particularly in relation to the effectiveness of their specific regulatory regimes: "The government until recently was refusing to accept that linkage between the industry and sea-lice" (RSTA).

Despite this reluctance to constructively engage with stakeholders on reforms to their regulatory practices and processes, regulatory institutions were happy to point out and identify gaps and inefficiency in other institutional practices:

A lack of co-ordination between the Regional Authority and SEPA. (SEPA, REN)

Risk for a clash between a local and a national policy on development/sustainability grounds. Co-ordination is needed with SEERAD. (RA, SEPA, REN)

Risks from the lack of clear planning remit between the Crown Estate and the local authorities. (SEPA, REN)

Regulatory risk for the sustainability of the fishmeal fisheries from the inability of the latter to meet the strict standards of international accreditation bodies. (SEPA)

Health risk for the public might exist from the presence of stuff in the fish feed. However, the official position is that the public should eat fish because it is healthy. (RA, REN)

There were also criticisms amongst different oppositional stakeholder groups over their engagement strategies and perceived collaboration with a flawed risk regulatory system. For example, The Soil Association (SA) were challenged by other stakeholder groups in that they were deemed to be propping up and legitimizing a problematic risk-governing system and their motives for creating the possibility for salmon farming to be organic were questioned. A common statement was that the SA was more concerned with empire-building than promoting sustainability and that organic production was not necessarily sustainable:

The so-called organic fish will affect in some way the pristine environment and it will have some kind of interaction with the wild fish. In that way organic salmon farming would be something similar to cutting down rain forests to grow organic coffee trees. (RSTA)

Stakeholders who were supportive of salmon farming made use of social and environmental accounts, amplified by media campaigns, both to discredit claims made against salmon farming and to regain legitimacy. This included supporting and maintaining the legitimacy of the existing risk-governance regime. Oppositional stakeholders responded to this by producing social and environmental accounts, amplified by media campaigns, both to discredit claims made against them and to regain their legitimacy.

There was a growing recognition that the risk conflict in the Scottish salmon farming arena was becoming more and more entrenched and polarized and potentially destructive to all parties. "The divergence of views makes constructive dialog impossible because they throw rocks at each other" (SEPA).

Political institutions were attempting to intervene and bring all the opposing parts together since they believed that a better understanding of the salmon farming practices would resolve many of the oppositional stakeholders' concerns. This appears to substantiate certain of Beck's insights on modern societies where political institutions seek to legitimate business practice and are concerned with their risk-reputation management[40] rather than resolving risk conflicts.

Reforming Risk-governing Processes

Oppositional stakeholders made many suggestions in their social and environmental accounts for reducing the risks associated with salmon farming and its risk-governing regime.[41] Typical examples included: moving operations to sites where environmental damage was less likely; scaling down of operations; vegetable protein usage for feeding purposes; more holistic approaches when, examining the treatment of discharges/ drafting Environmental Impact Assessments; introduction of sea lice regulation; less fragmentation in the regulatory structure; compulsory introduction of polyculture practices,¶ to name but few.

Concerns were also expressed about the lack of accountability of political institutions over their operations and how stakeholders could effectively engage in processes in order to bring concerns about salmon farming into the public discourse. The Scottish Executive (now Scottish Government) considered lack of any possible resolution of salmon farming risk conflicts as problematic and decided that a strong intervention and leadership was required. This came in the form of the Strategic Framework for Aquaculture.[42]

An important element of the strategic framework was the formation of the ministerial and tripartite working groups during the consultation stages. These working groups brought together regulators, salmon farmers and stakeholders as part of a structured, less antagonistic engagement process. During this consultation process levels of consensus on certain risks and agreement on changes in practices were achieved. The effectiveness of this consultation process was recognized by all parties and formed an integral part of the eventual strategic framework.

The Strategic Framework for Aquaculture attempted to establish a process to resolve the risk conflicts in salmon farming. It established a formalized structure for stakeholder engagements and a range of measures intended to regain legitimacy for the salmon farming risk governing regime. "The Strategic Framework for Aquaculture is the chance all stakeholders involved with the industry have to offer their views and help salmon farming progress in a sustainable manner into the future" (SEERAD).

The strategic framework created the potential for more cooperative stakeholder engagements and rick conflict resolution, similar to the reflexive approach suggested by Beck and others.[43] There was evidence of reduced antagonism, constructive engagement and mutually agreed changes in practice, e.g. voluntary agreements on the restricted use of anti-predatory nets, allowing stakeholder groups access to inspect fish farms, cooperation in the preparation of Environment Impact Assessments.

¶ Polyculture in agriculture refers to using multiple crops in the same space, in imitation of the diversity of natural ecosystems, and avoiding large stands of single crops, or monoculture. It includes crop rotation, multi-cropping, intercropping, companion planting, beneficial weeds and alley cropping. Polyculture, though it often requires more labor, has several advantages over monoculture: the diversity of crops avoids the susceptibility of monocultures to disease; the greater variety of crops provides habitat for more species, increasing local biodiversity (www.wikipedia.org). The term has a similar use in fish farming. It involves raising two or more complementary species in one pond. A successful polyculture operation will contain species that do not compete for food, mature at about the same rate and may complement each other's ecological habits (www.ehow.com).

However, it would be wrong to assume that all the risk conflicts had been resolved and some fundamental differences remained. Supportive stakeholders perceived the Strategic Framework as the way forward because they believed that once oppositional stakeholder groups understood fish farmers and their practices, they would realize the error in their stance and thus be more willing to compromise or withdraw their negative campaigning. The absence of these risk conflicts would then be extremely beneficial to the industry. For example, the Scottish Salmon Growers Association felt that there was a "risk for the industry not to take advantage of the Strategic Framework for aquaculture and turn it into a strategy which will attract foreign, indigenous, or multinational investment".

However, this engagement process also created legitimacy to other risks that the salmon farming risk-governing regime had previously denied or ignored. This had the potential to seriously escalate a number of risk conflicts, including genetically modified salmon, the cumulative impact of fish farms in a specific location and the sustainability of the salmon fish feed. The following quote from the World Wildlife Fund for Nature illustrates the risk conflicts that could seriously threaten future development in salmon farming:

> The consequences of the whole genetic mixing between farmed and wild salmon are unknown. At the bottom line, we do not know what is actually happening. There is not good monitoring of the escapees, we do not know where they go or the impacts they have.

Conclusions

We see the arena model and Beck's contribution as having helped to clearly describe what happened in the salmon farming sector in Scotland. A number of insights emerged from our study of this risk arena that resonated with Beck's work; insights into the emergence of risk conflicts, the role of governing structures and the behavior of actors. Risks were locally and temporarily emergent from engagements that formed part of a series of risk conflicts. At any point in time there were fundamental disagreements as to what were considered "real" risks, effective methods of dealing with these risks and effective methods of accounting for and communicating these risks to others. Legitimate salmon farming risks were shaped by a number of reflexively related factors such as risk legitimization processes, governance institutions, regulatory regimes, accountability mechanisms, stakeholder groups, media interest, new scientific evidence and campaign groups' strategies.

The giving, receiving and demand for social and environmental accounts was part of the struggle for legitimacy: legitimacy on behalf of oppositional stakeholders for the change they were proposing and legitimacy on behalf of the salmon farmers to continue with their business. Oppositional stakeholders were of the opinion that the risk-governance regime operated as legitimating processes and practices that justified rather than reduced the farmers' potential harm to the ecological and social environment. These groups provided social and environment accounts to support their claims of the unacceptability of the risk of salmon farming and the unacceptability of risk-governance regimes.

In our study we did, however, observe the reluctant revision of the definition of acceptable risks by salmon farmers, mainly through the creation of voluntary rule-enforcing institutions with the potential to reduce the risks of salmon farming practices. Social and environmental accounts produced by salmon farmers were instrumental in demonstrating compliance with mandatory and voluntary rule-enforcers and could be seen as a legitimating practice. These accounts changed as a consequence of the revised legitimacy of certain risks.

We consider that effective governance of salmon farming risks depends on establishing better interrelationships within the risk conflict arena and mechanisms to transcend these fragmented legitimate risks and to establish social consensus as to new legitimate risks. Greater consensus on legitimated risks is a prerequisite for constructing effective governance structures and accountability mechanisms. While the Strategic Framework for Aquaculture appeared to contain the potential for this process our evaluation was that it fell considerably short in terms of the level of reflexivity required to fully resolve salmon farming risk conflicts, if that could ever be possible given the polarized and entrenched positions observed.

A number of important issues emerged in relation to developing social and environmental accounting practices, processes and expertise. For instance recognizing that the demands for accounts are likely to be reflexively linked to regulatory regimes, contested discourses on risks; the diversity of risk legitimization practices, relative powers of arena participants, media amplifications and stakeholder engagements provides a richer more nuanced understanding of social and environmental accounting. Mapping the relationship between risk conflicts and emerging accountability routes and practices can also provide valuable insights into risk-governing processes, the legitimate risk perceptions of different parties and powers of different rule enforcers.

In examining social and environmental accounting an awareness of the interplay between formal regulatory systems and stakeholder engagements is important, particularly given that change is normally initiated driven by reforming stakeholders. Viewing certain social and environmental accounts as initiating and perpetuating risk conflicts is a new and important observation. Previously social and environmental accounts were viewed as intended to resolve risk conflicts and legitimate current business practices. If social and environmental accounting processes and practices are to form part of change processes they must both be sensitive to stakeholder strategies and engagement tactics, yet expressed in a way that can be considered legitimate by relevant political institutions.

Risks and risk conflicts problematizes the assumption of the business as the appropriate entity of social and environmental accounting. Many of the stakeholder groups were not concerned with first-order risk conflicts with individual companies, but rather with second-order conflicts targeted at regulators and rule-enforcers.** Rule enforcers, especially the political institutions, were perceived as potentially easier to change than individual companies who used compliance with rules as evidence of acceptable behaviour. Political institutions are, in theory anyway, subject to democratic accountability[44] control and reform. Stakeholder groups often created new accounting entities such as geographic areas, scientific institutions, regulators and the salmon farming industry as part of their second-order risk conflict. Most of the accounts in Scottish salmon farming[45] are linked to power struggles in order to determine the scope and levels of socially acceptable risks.

** In this light it could be argued that primary risks appear to exist in the centre of the arena (Figure 8.1), whereas secondary risks appear in all other routes and forms of engagement between all arena participants.

They also demanded greater social and environmental accountability of regulators and rule-enforcers as to the effectiveness of their operations. Establishing accountability of industry-level governing structures would appear to be a critical part of the social and environmental accounting project.[46]

A final point relates to the role of the media in the salmon farming risk arena. Despite the predominance of scientific and economic content in the accounts used in the risk conflicts, the importance of risk dramatization in initiating and maintaining media interest should not be understated. While risk conflicts have the potential to force different parties to engage the extent of this engagement appeared to be largely dependent on media amplification. Without media interest the potential of the conflict process to bring about emancipatory change is greatly reduced. Evidence (valid or legitimate) without dramatization through mass media channels did not appear powerful enough to drive change. However, in our study we did not explicitly examine the role the media played in this risk arena. Some preliminary content analysis was undertaken of associated newspaper reports. We view the role the mass media played as an area to return to and examine at greater length in the context of the salmon farming risk debate.

Appendix

Table 8.4   Overview of organizations from which representatives were interviewed and abbreviations

Salmon farming organizations	Regulatory rule enforcers/ political institutions	Supportive stakeholders
OS1: small family organic fish farm	SEPA: Scottish Environment Protection Agency	RGA: Regional Salmon Growers Association
OS2: small family organic fish farm	RA: Regional Authority. Democratically elected single, all-purpose local authority	FM1: Glasgow-based retail fishmonger, sole trader
ML1: subsidiary multinational group producing conventional and organic salmon	SEERAD: Scottish Executive Environment & Rural Affairs Department	FM2: Glasgow-based wholesale fish market, sole trader
ML2: subsidiary of multinational group producing conventional and organic salmon	Political institutions	FM3: Scottish-based wholesale/ retail group, UK company
TM1: subsidiary family-run group producing conventional salmon	REN: Regional Enterprise Network reports to Scottish Executive	Opposing stakeholders
MK: marketing company of TM1	Reforming stakeholders/ voluntary rule enforcers	RSPB: Royal Society for the Protection of Birds. Wildlife conservation charity
MM: large salmon-producing UK company	SA: Soil Association. Independent charity promoting and certifying organic agriculture	SFPG: Salmon Farm Protest Group. Regional pressure group concerned with protecting the marine and freshwater environment
SMK: a small salmon-smoking company	Supportive stakeholders/ voluntary rule enforcers	RFA: Regional Fisheries Association, represents sea fishermen
	SSGA: Scottish Salmon Growers Association	RSTA: Regional Sea Trout Association, sea fishing NGO
	SQS: Scottish Quality Salmon product-labeling scheme: part of SSGA	WWF: World Wide Fund for Nature Scotland: international environmental nongovernmental network
	RQS: Regional Quality Salmon labeling schemes: part of RGA	

Notes

1   Georgakopoulos, G. and Thomson, I. (2005), "Organic salmon farming: risk perception, decision heuristics and the absence of environmental accounting", *Accounting Forum*, vol. 29, no. 1, pp. 49–75; Georgakopoulos, G. and Thomson, I. (2008), "Social reporting, engagements, controversies and conflict in an arena context", *Accounting Auditing and Accountability Journal*, vol. 21, no. 8, pp. 1116–1143.

2   Beck, U. (1992a), *Risk Society: Towards a New Modernity*, Sage Publications, Thousand Oaks, CA; Beck, U. (1992b), "From industrial society to risk society: questions of survival, social structure and ecological enlightenment", *Theory, Culture and Society*, vol. 9, no. 1, pp. 97–123; Beck, U. (1994a), "The reinvention of politics: towards a theory of reflexive modernisation". In Beck, U., Giddens, A. and Lash, S. (eds), *Reflexive Modernisation: Politics, Tradition and Aesthetics in the Modern Social Order*, Polity Press, Cambridge; Beck, U. (1994b), "Self dissolution and self endangerment of industrial society: what does this mean?" In Beck, U., Giddens, A. and Lash, S. (eds), *Reflexive Modernisation: Politics, Tradition and Aesthetics in the Modern Social Order*, Polity Press, Cambridge; Beck, U. (1995), *Ecological Politics in the Age of Risk*, Polity Press, Cambridge; Beck, U. (1996), "World risk society as cosmopolitan society? Ecological questions in a framework of manufactured uncertainties", *Theory, Culture and Society*, vol. 13, no. 4, pp. 1–32; Beck, U., Giddens, A. and Lash, S. (1994), *Reflexive Modernisation: Politics, Tradition and Aesthetics in the Modern Social Order*, Polity Press, Cambridge; Beck, U. and Willms, J. (2004), *Conversations with Ulrich Beck*, Polity Press.

3   Global Reporting Initiative (GRI). (2007), *Making the Connection: The GRI Guidelines and the UNGC Communication on Progress*, United Nations Global Compact Office; The Prince's Charities. (2009), *Accounting for Sustainability*, Clarence House Publications; Hopwood A., Unerman J. and Fries J. (2010), *Accounting for Sustainability: Practical Insights*, Earthscan, London; www.globalreporting.org., accessed 14/3/11; www.sustainabilityatwork.org.uk., accessed 14/3/11.

4   Dey, C. (2003), "Corporate 'silent' and 'shadow' social accounting", *Social and Environmental Accounting Journal*, vol. 23, no. 2, pp. 6–10; Dey, C., Russell, S. and Thomson, I. (2010), "Exploring the potential of shadow accounts in problematising institutional conduct". In Osborne, S.P. and Ball, A. (eds), *Social Accounting and Public Management: Accounting for the Public Good*, Routledge.

5   Hilgartner, S. and Bosk, L. (1988), "The rise and fall of social problems: a public arena model", *American Journal of Sociology*, vol. 94, pp. 53–78; Jaeger, C. (1998), "Risk management and integrated assessment", *Environmental Modeling and Assessment*, vol. 3, pp. 211–225; Jaeger, C., Renn, O., Rosa, A. and Webler, T. (2001), *Risk, Uncertainty and Rational Action*, Earthscan, London; Lowi, T. (1972), "Four systems of policy, politics and choice", *Public Administration Review*, vol. 32, no. 4, pp. 298–310; Renn, O. (1992), "The social arena concept of risk debates". In Krimsky, S. and Golding, D. (eds), *Social Theories of Risk*, Praeger, Westport, CT; Rucht, D. (1990), "Campaigns, skirmishes and battles: anti nuclear movements in the USA, France and West Germany", *Industrial Crisis Quarterly*, vol. 4, pp. 193–222; Tierney, K. (1989), "Improving theory and research on hazard mitigation: political economy and organisational perspectives", *Mass Emergencies and Disasters*, vol. 7, no. 3, pp. 367–396; Wartburg, W.P. and Liew, J. (1999), *Gene Technology and Social Acceptance*, University Press of America, Lanham, MD.

6   Georgakopoulos and Thomson (2008), op. cit.

7   See Renn (1992), op. cit.

8   Adams, C. (2004), "The ethical, social and environmental reporting–performance gap", *Accounting, Auditing and Accountability Journal*, vol. 17, no. 5, pp. 731–757; Buhr, N. (1998), "Environmental performance, legislation and annual report disclosure: the case of acid rain and Falconbridge", *Accounting, Auditing and Accountability Journal*, vol. 11, no. 2, pp. 163–190; Gray, R., Dey, C., Owen, D., Evans, R. and Zadek, S. (1997), "Struggling with the praxis of social accounting: stakeholders, accountability, audits and procedures", *Accounting, Auditing and Accountability Journal*, vol. 10, no. 3, pp. 325–364; Harte, G. and Owen, D. (1987), "Fighting de-industrialisation: the role of local government social audits", *Accounting, Organizations and Society*, vol. 12, no. 2, pp. 123–141; O'Dwyer, B. (2005), "The construction of a social account: a case study in an overseas aid agency", *Accounting, Organizations and Society*, vol. 30, no. 3, pp. 279–296.

9   See Georgakopoulos and Thomson (2008), op. cit., for further details.

10   Dey, Russell and Thomson (2010), op. cit.

11   Beck (1992a), op. cit.

12   Beck and Willms (2004), op. cit.

13   Beck (1992a, b, 1994a, b, 1995, 1996); Beck, Giddens and Lash (1994); Beck and Willms (2004), op. cit.

14   Castel, R. (1991), "From dangerousness to risk". In Burchell, G., Gordon, C. and Miller, P. (eds), *The Foucault Effect: Studies in Governmentality*, Harvester Wheatsheaf, London, pp. 281–298; Ewald, F. (1991), "Insurance and risks". In Burchell, G., Gordon, C. and Miller, P. (eds), *The Foucault Effect: Studies in Governmentality*, Harvester Wheatsheaf, London, pp. 197–210; Foucault, M. (1984), "The politics of health in the eighteenth century". In Rabinow, P. (ed.), *The Foucault Reader*, Pantheon Books, New York, pp. 273–289; Foucault, M. (1988), "Technologies of the self". In Martin, L., Gutman, H. and Hutton, P. (eds), *Technologies of the Self: a Seminar with Michel Foucault*, Tavistock, London, pp. 16–49; Foucault, M. (1991), "Governmentality". In Burchell, G., Gordon, C. and Miller, P. (eds), *The Foucault Effect: Studies in Governmentality*, Harvester Wheatsheaf, London, pp. 87–104; Gordon, C. (1991), "Governmental rationality: an introduction". In Burchell, G., Gordon, C. and Miller, P. (eds), *The Foucault Effect: Studies in Governmentality,* Harvester Wheatseaf, London, pp. 1–52.

15   Lupton, D. (1999), *Risk*, Routledge, London; Matten, D. (2004), "The impact of the risk society thesis on environmental politics and management in a globalizing economy; principles, proficiency, perspectives", *Journal of Risk Research*, vol. 7, no. 4, pp. 377–398.

16   See for example Solomon, F.J. and Thomson, I. (2009), "Satanic mills?: an illustration of Victorian external environmental accounting", *Accounting Forum*, vol. 33, no. 1, pp. 74–87.

17   Beck and Willms (2004), op. cit.

18   Beck (1992a); Beck and Willms (2004), op. cit.

19   Giddens, A. (1994a), "Living in a post traditional society". In Beck, U., Giddens, A. and Lash, S. (eds), *Reflexive Modernisation: Politics, Tradition and Aesthetics in the Modern Social Order*, Polity Press, Cambridge; Giddens, A. (1994b), "Risk, trust and reflexivity". In Beck, U., Giddens, A. and Lash, S. (eds), *Reflexive Modernisation: Politics, Tradition and Aesthetics in the Modern Social Order*, Polity Press, Cambridge

20   Power, M. (2004). *The Risk Management of Everything: Rethinking the Politics of Uncertainty*, Demos, London.

21   Beck (1992a); Beck and Willms (2004), op. cit.

22   Beck and Willms (2004), op. cit.

23   Ibid.

24   Dey (2003); Dey, Russell and Thomson (2010), op. cit.

25   Deegan, C. (2002). "Introduction: the legitimising effect of social and environmental disclosures; a theoretical foundation", *Accounting, Auditing and Accountability Journal*, vol. 15, no. 3, pp. 282–311; Deegan, C., Rankin, M. and Tobin, J. (2002), "An examination of the corporate social and environmental disclosures of BHP from 1983–1997: a test of legitimacy theory", *Accounting, Auditing and Accountability Journal*, vol. 15, no. 3, pp. 312–343; Deegan, C. and Blomquist, C. (2006), "Stakeholder influence on corporate reporting: an exploration of the interaction between WWF–Australia and the Australian minerals industry", *Accounting, Organizations and Society*, vol. 31, no. 4/5, pp. 343–372; Deegan, C. (2007), "Organizational legitimacy as a motive for sustainability reporting". In Unerman, J., Bebbington, J. and O'Dwyer, B. (eds), *Sustainability, Accounting and Accountability*, Routledge, London, pp. 127–150; Milne, J.M. and Patten, M.D. (2002), "Securing organizational legitimacy: an experimental decision case examining the impact of environmental disclosures", *Accounting, Auditing and Accountability Journal*, vol. 15, no. 3, pp. 372–405; O'Donovan, G. (2002), "Environmental disclosures in the annual report: extending the applicability and predictive power of legitimacy theory", *Accounting, Auditing and Accountability Journal*, vol. 15, no. 3, pp. 344–371; O'Dwyer, B. (2002), "Managerial perceptions of corporate social disclosure: an Irish story", *Accounting, Auditing and Accountability Journal*, vol. 15, no. 3, pp. 406–436; O'Sullivan, N. and O'Dwyer, B. (2009), "Stakeholder perspectives on a financial sector legitimation process: the case of NGOs and the equator principles", *Accounting, Auditing and Accountability Journal*, vol. 22, no. 4, pp. 553–587; Suchman, C.M. (1995), "Managing legitimacy: strategic and institutional approaches", *The Academy of Management Review*, vol. 20, no. 3, pp. 571–610.

26   See for example Ball, A. (2005), "Environmental accounting and change in UK local government", *Accounting, Auditing and Accountability Journal*, vol. 18, no. 3, pp. 346–373; Ball, A., Mason, I., Grubnic, S. and Hughes, P. (2009), "The carbon neutral public sector: early developments and an urgent agenda for research", *Public Management Review*, vol. 11, no. 5, pp. 575–600; Cooper, C. (1992), "The non and nom of accounting for (m)other nature", *Accounting, Auditing and Accountability Journal*, vol. 15, no. 3, pp. 16–39; Cooper, C., Taylor, P., Smith, N. and Catchpowle, L. (2005), "A discussion of the political potential of social accounting", *Critical Perspectives on Accounting*, vol. 16, no. 7, pp. 951–974; Everett, J. (2004), "Exploring (false) dualisms for environmental accounting praxis", *Critical Perspectives on Accounting*, vol. 15, no. 8, pp. 1061–1084; Everett, J. and Neu, D. (2000), "Ecological modernization and the limits of environmental accounting?", *Accounting Forum*, vol. 24, no. 1, pp. 5–29; Gray, R. (2010), "Is accounting for sustainability actually accounting for sustainability ... and how would we know? An exploration of narratives of organisations and the planet", *Accounting, Organizations and Society*, vol. 35, no. 1, pp. 47–62; Gray, R., Dey, C., Owen, D., Evans, R. and Zadek, S. (1997), op. cit.; to name but few.

27   See for example: Beck (1992a, b, 1994a, b, 1995, 1996); Beck and Willms (2004), op. cit.; Castel (1991), op. cit.; Giddens (1994a, b), op. cit.; Kendall, G. and Wickham, G. (1992), "Health and the social body". In Scott, S., Williams, G., Platt, S. and Thomas, H. (eds), *Private Risks and Public Dangers*, Aldershot, Avebury, pp. 8–18; Lash, S. (1993), "Reflexive modernisation: the aesthetic dimension", *Theory, Culture and Society*, vol. 10, pp. 1–23; Lash, S. (1994a), "Reflexivity and its doubles: structure, aesthetics, community". In Beck, U., Giddens, A. and Lash, S. (eds), *Reflexive Modernisation: Politics, Tradition and Aesthetics in the Modern Social Order*, Polity Press, Cambridge; Lash, S. (1994b), "Expert systems or situated interpretation? culture and institutions in disorganised capitalism". In Beck, U., Giddens, A. and Lash, S. (eds), *Reflexive Modernisation: Politics, Tradition and Aesthetics in the Modern Social Order*, Polity Press, Cambridge; Lash, S. (2000), "Risk culture". In Adam, B., Beck, U. and Van Loon, J. (eds), *The*

Risk Society and Beyond: Critical Issues for Social Theory, Sage Publications; Lash, S., and Wynne, B. (1992), "Introduction". In Beck, U., *Risk Society: Towards a New Modernity*. Sage, London, pp. 1–8; Wynne, B. (1989), "Frameworks of rationality in risk management: toward the testing of naïve sociology". In Brown, J. (ed.), *Environmental Threats: Perception, Analysis and Management*, Belhaven Press, London, pp. 33–47; Wynne, B. (1992), "Risk and social learning: reification to engagement". In Krimsky, S. and Golding, D. (eds), *Social Theories of Risk*, Praeger, Westport, Connecticut; Wynne, B. (1996), "May the sheep safely graze? A reflexive view of the expert-lay knowledge divide". In Lash, S., Szerszinski, B. and Wynne, B. (eds), *Risk, Environment and Modernity: Towards a New Ecology*, Sage, London, pp. 44–83.

28 See Dey, Russell and Thomson (2010); Solomon and Thomson (2009), op. cit.

29 Georgakopoulos and Thomson (2008), op. cit.

30 Beck and Willms (2004), op. cit.

31 www.salmonfarmmonitor.org, accessed November 2003.

32 Friends of the Earth Scotland (FOE) (2001), *The One that Got Away: Marine Salmon Farming in Scotland*, Friends of the Earth Publications, Edinburgh, Scotland; Hites, R., Foran, J., Carpenter, D., Hamilton, M., Knuth, B. and Schwager, S. (2004), "Global assessment of organic contaminants in farmed salmon", *Science*, vol. 303, pp. 226–229.

33 *The Observer* (2004); *The Scotsman* (2004); *The Sunday Times—Scotland* (2004); *The Telegraph* (2004).

34 Beck and Willms (2004), op. cit.

35 Georgakopoulos and Thomson (2005), op. cit.

36 Fisheries Research Services (FRS) (1997–2004). *Scottish Fish Farms—Annual Production Survey*, Scottish Executive Environment and Rural Affairs Department publications.

37 Highlands and Islands Enterprise and The Scottish Office (1998), *Final Report: The Economic Impact of Scottish Salmon Farming*, Public and Corporate Economic Consultants (PACEC); Highlands and Islands Enterprise (HIE) (2002), *Eleventh Network Report*. Highlands and Islands Enterprise publications.

38 www.sepa.org.uk, accessed in November 2003.

39 Scottish Executive (2003), *A Strategic Framework for Scottish Aquaculture*, Scottish Executive publications, Crown copyright; Scottish National Heritage (SNH) (2002), *SNH's Vision of Sustainable Marine Aquaculture in Scotland*. Submitted as contribution to consultation on a strategic framework for aquaculture in Scotland.

40 Power, M. (2004), *The Risk Management of Everything: Rethinking the Politics of Uncertainty*, Demos, London.

41 Friends of the Earth, (2001); Scottish Executive, (2003); Scottish National Heritage, (2002), op. cit.

42 Scottish Executive (2003), op. cit.

43 Beck (1992a, b, 1994a, b, 1995, 1996); Beck, Giddens and Lash (1994); Beck and Willms (2004), op. cit.; Giddens, A. (1990), *The Consequences of Modernity*, Polity Press, Cambridge; Giddens, A. (1991), *Modernity and Self-Identity*, Polity Press, Cambridge; Giddens, op. cit.; Giddens, A. (2002), *Runaway World: How Globalisation is Reshaping our Lives*, Profile Books Ltd.; Lash (1993, 1994a, b, 2000); Lash and Wynne (1992); Power (2004); Wynne (1989, 1992, 1996), op. cit.

44 See Sinclair, A. (1995), "The chameleon of accountability: forms and discourses", *Accounting, Organizations and Society*, vol. 20, no. 2/3, pp. 219–237, for more information on different forms of accountability.

45 Georgakopoulos and Thomson (2008), op. cit.

46 Dey (2003); Dey, Russell and Thomson (2010), op. cit.

Engaging with Stakeholders and Implementing a Stakeholder Approach to Corporate Social Responsibility

9

The Evolution of Corporate Social Responsibility in Gucci: From Risk Management to Stakeholder Engagement*

MASSIMILIANO BONACCHI,† PAOLO PEREGO‡ AND
ROSSELLA RAVAGLI§

Keywords

Corporate social responsibility, organizational change, stakeholder engagement, stakeholder management.

I tell you that virtue is not given by money, but that from virtue comes money and every other good of man, public as well as private.

Plato, The Apology of Socrates

Introduction

In an increasingly resource-constrained and unequal world, luxury brands are normally expected to be more accountable in justifying the value of their products. Despite strong societal drivers for greater sustainability, the majority of luxury labels have traditionally

* We are grateful to Chiara Campione (Forest Campaigner at Greenpeace), Valeria Fedeli (President of the European Trade Union Federation of the Textile, Clothing and Leather sectors), Deborah Lucchetti (spokesperson and national coordinator at Clean Clothes Campaign Italy) for the time dedicated to the interview and in providing feedback on an earlier version of this chapter.

† Massimiliano Bonacchi, School of Economics, University of Naples "Parthenope", Via Medina, 40, 80133 Napoli, Italy. E-mail: massimiliano.bonacchi@uniparthenope.it.

‡ Paolo Perego, Department of Accounting and Control, RSM Erasmus University, P.O. Box 1738, 3000 DR Rotterdam, The Netherlands. E-mail: pperego@rsm.nl.

§ Rossella Ravagli, Corporate Social and Environmental Responsibility Manager at Gucci, Via Don Lorenzo Perosi 6, 50018 Casellina di Scandicci, Firenze, Italy. E-mail: rossella.ravagli@it.gucci.com.

been slow to recognize their responsibilities.[1] This chapter explores how one of the world's leading luxury brands exposed to CSR-related risks responded proactively to internal and external stakeholder expectations. Gucci decided to introduce CSR activities without being confronted by a CSR crisis or a request from its parent company. This voluntary move therefore anticipated many competitors in the fashion industry that were caught in CSR conflicts, such as unfair treatment of workers, lack of safety conditions, or use of child labor.[¶]

Relying upon the model of CSR stage development proposed by Maon, Lindgreen and Swaen (2010, hereafter MLS),[2] we document the shift from a stage focused on adaptation to stakeholder pressures and risk management (the value *protection* phase) to an emerging stage in which the emphasis is increasingly on innovation and reconciliation of different stakeholder needs (the value *creation* phase). The case analysis suggests that Gucci experienced a major change in knowledge, attitudes, structures and practices surrounding CSR issues, and emphasizes the importance of embedding a stakeholder engagement program in a firm's strategy.

The order of discussion is as follows. In the next section, we outline the theoretical background and the methodology used for this study. We then describe the key phases underlying the evolution of CSR activities in Gucci, with an emphasis on events that recently unfolded to reconcile the interests of the various stakeholders. The final section concludes with a summary of findings, theoretical and managerial implications, and some suggestions for further research.

Theoretical Background and Methodology

We refer to the stream of literature that draws upon core concepts from stakeholder theory to operationalize CSR principles and in particular to the definition of CSR provided by MLS (p. 23), i.e.

> *[CSR is] a stakeholder oriented construct which concerns the voluntary commitments of an organization pertaining to issues extending inside and beyond the boundaries of that organization and that are driven by the organization's understanding and acknowledgement of its moral responsibilities regarding the impacts of its activities and processes on society.*

This definition has the advantage of combining the two dimensions of CSR: one oriented toward the interaction between the firm and its stakeholders, and the other focused on the internal change processes required to integrate CSR principles into the firm's strategy and operations. We build upon the extant CSR development literature which proposes CSR as an evolutionary process in which several forces (such as cultural factors, industry dynamics, leadership and company culture) shape the CSR path within firms across stages.[3] Among the frameworks available, we apply the MLS model which revolves around three cultural *phases*: CSR reluctance, CSR grasp and CSR embedment. These phases further encompass development *stages* characterized by distinctive strategic and organizational

---

[¶]   *The Sunday Times* 12 August 2007 revealed "Topshop clothes made with 'slave labour'", Claire Newell in Port Louis, Mauritius and Robert Winnett, http://women.timesonline.co.uk/tol/life_and_style/women/fashion/ article2241665.ece; Thomas, D. (2007), *Deluxe: How Luxury Lost its Lustre*, Allen Lane, London.

dimensions. The CSR reluctance phase comprises only a so-called (1) dismissing stage; the CSR cultural grasp phase includes (2) a self-protecting stage, (3) a compliance-seeking stage, and (4) a capability-seeking stage; and the CSR cultural embedment phase consists of (5) a caring stage, (6) a strategizing stage and (7) a transforming stage.

We specifically examine how Gucci responded to and reconciled stakeholder pressures highlighting tangible changes in the *formal* dimensions of CSR development drawing on organizational economics (e.g. Brickley *et al.*, 2004) and management control systems (e.g. Merchant and Van der Stede, 2007) literature.[4] Table 9.1 shows the link between the dimensions originally formulated in the MLS model and the variables investigated in this case: corporate identity, strategy, structure, performance measurement and disclosure.

Table 9.1   Variables affecting corporate social responsibility development

MLS dimensions	Variables examined in this study
Knowledge and attitude	Corporate identity: a firm's mission, vision, values, or code of conduct
Strategic	Corporate strategy: a firm's rationale behind CSR initiatives Disclosure: extent and level of social and environmental voluntary disclosure across time
Tactical and operational	Organizational structure: formalization of CSR-related activities Performance measurement system: inclusion of CSR-related performance measures in management control systems

Case Study: Gucci

Founded in Florence in 1921, Gucci is one of the world's leading luxury brands.[**] With a world-renowned reputation for quality and Italian craftsmanship, Gucci designs, manufactures and distributes highly fashionable products, such as leather goods (handbags, small leather goods, and luggage), shoes, ready-to-wear, silks, timepieces and fine jewelry. In addition, Gucci manufactures and distributes eyewear and fragrances under license. Gucci is 44th in the "Top Global 100 Brands" ranking created by Interbrand, and the company's products sell exclusively through a network of approximately 327 (as of March 2011) directly operated boutiques and a small number of selected departments and specialty stores.[††] In 2010 Gucci reported €2.7 billion worldwide revenues. With over 7,000 employees (of which more than 1,000 are in Italy), Gucci products are manufactured in Italy (with the only exception of watches, manufactured in Switzerland) by more than 750 artisanal enterprises and their subcontractors, most of them family-owned companies that have worked for Gucci for more than a decade. The entire Gucci supply chain involves roughly 45,000 indirect workers.

We build our analysis on standard case study methodology[5] by collecting empirical evidence from several sources. Primary data stemmed from internal documents, archival

---

[**]   This chapter refers to the Gucci brand. Since 2001, the brand has been part of PPR, a group nurturing high-growth global brands distributed in more than 120 countries. Other luxury brands in the PPR stable include Bottega Veneta, Yves Saint Laurent and Alexander McQueen.

[††]   http://www.interbrand.com/de/knowledge/best-global-brands/best-global-brands-2008/best-global-brands-2010.aspx.

records, Web pages, press releases and promotional material at the corporate level. The discussion with the CSR manager of Gucci (co-author of this chapter and former SA8000 external auditor of Gucci for Bureau Veritas) helped us to integrate the primary data with a behind-the-scenes view of the evolution of CSR programs in recent decades. Lastly, to improve methodological rigor and enrich the case history, we additionally relied upon interviews with stakeholders such as representatives of trade unions and social-environmental NGOs. By taking into account their opinions we were able to critically describe stakeholders' tensions, conflicts and relative resolution.

Given the specific characteristics of Gucci, the MLS model has been properly adapted. In particular, the *dismissing* and the *self-protecting* stage, from one extreme of the continuum, and the *strategic* and the *transforming* stage on the other end, cannot be applied to our case study. However, this will not constitute a limit of the analysis because it still allows tracking the evolution as a continuum. We initially focus our attention on the transition from a compliance-seeking to a capability-seeking stage. We assume the compliance seeking stage as the first stage in the CSR grasp phase because, since its foundation, Gucci has continuously showed a commitment to high quality and ethical values in all aspects of the business (i.e. product quality, made in Italy, passion of people). As Patrizio di Marco (President and CEO of Gucci) emphasizes, CSR principles, although implicitly, have always been part of Gucci's heritage and values:

> Today, as in the days of the firm's founder Guccio Gucci, the critical success factors of our company remain the craftsmanship [of our products], their absolute quality, that they are made in Italy, and the passion of people who work for this company.‡‡

Further, we assume the caring stage as the current achieved stage. In fact, both the strategic and the transforming stage are still unfolding and represent a potential achievement for the future. For a summary of our main findings refer to Table 9.2.

---

‡‡   Press release for the signature of the "Agreement on the Sustainability of our Supply Chain", September 16 2009.

Table 9.2 Corporate social responsibility development in Gucci

CSR cultural Phase	Stage of CSR development	CSR formal dimensions				
		Corporate identity	Strategy	Structure	Performance measurement	Disclosure
CSR cultural reluctance	1. Dismissing	Cannot be applied to Gucci's case study				
CSR cultural grasp (2004–2009)	2. Self-protecting					
	3. Compliance-seeking	No formal reference to CSR. Social concerns in the supply chain addressed	Occasional activities for communities, employees, environment	No formal appointment of a specific organizational unit.	No need to measure CSR performance	No need to disclose CSR performance
	4. Capability-seeking	Formalization of the "Code of Business Practices" in the parent company. Social and environmental concerns addressed	CSR is part of the corporate strategy	Formal appointment of corporate social and environmental responsibility manager	Measures are collected, but a "plan–do–check–act" approach is not systematic	CSR activities are communicated in a nonsystematic way
CSR cultural embedment (2009–today)	5. Caring	Formalization of the "CSR policies" in Gucci. "Sustainability value" is the new mission	Embedding CSR as everybody's business: a cultural change	Enhance stakeholder dialog with a formal committee on relevant CSR issues	Associate key metrics to each stakeholder in order to monitor stakeholders' engagement and satisfaction	Sustainability report
	6. Strategizing	Potential achievement for Gucci				
	7. Transforming					

The Evolution of Corporate Social Responsibility in Gucci

In a world where leading brands are judged not just on the quality of their products and services, but also on the way they act in the community and towards the environment,[§§] Gucci is bringing a new business model of luxury to life: one where a central role is given to stakeholders' engagement and CSR is institutionalized as a day-to-day activity. Table 9.3 summarizes the challenges the company faces in reconciling stakeholder pressures and conflicts. The CSR initiatives and the relationships Gucci built with various stakeholders are explained in detail in the remaining sections and summarized in Table 9.4.

Table 9.3 Stakeholder pressures and conflicts

Internal stakeholders	Pressures and conflicts
Trade unions	Increase compliance with EHS and migrant workers regulation and at the same time preserve local employment
Suppliers/subcontractors	Increase compliance with EHS regulation while at the same time not compressing margins and preserving competitive advantage against cheaper illegal or delocalized productions
Customers	Increase compliance to ethical production standard
NGOs (national and international)	Pressure to make the luxury brands more transparent and accountable through stakeholder engagement initiatives
Artisan and industrial associations	Preserve know-how of the Florentine leather districts (financial crisis as background)

CSR Cultural Grasp Phase (2004–2009): Risk Management

In the past decade, human rights and environmental NGOs had targeted premium brand companies (such as Nike and Gap) for having infringed ethical or labor standards and for their high-profile visibility. This was not the case for Gucci, whose decision to pursue a CSR process was not spurred by a need to recover a damaged corporate image because of a company scandal. It was more the sense of responsibility and sense of purpose and a reputational risk concern, on one hand, and the pressure of the trade unions, on the other. In fact, trade unions were looking for increased compliance to Environmental Health and Safety (EHS) regulation, while at the same time not compressing margins and preserving competitive advantage against cheaper illegal or delocalized productions.

In this context, Gucci established its formal commitment to CSR in June 2004, when the company signed an agreement with the trade unions to adopt the SA8000 standard across the supply chain. SA8000 is an international standard from Social Accountability International aiming to help companies to develop and manage social accountability systems, with the objective of improving such CSR-related issues as child labor, health and safety conditions, compensation and working hours. This model is consistent with

---

§§ Retrieved from a recent press release by Patrizio di Marco: http://www.interbrand.com/en/best-global-brands/Best-Global-Brands-2010/Gucci-Patrizio-di-Marco.aspx

the requirements of the International Labor Organization conventions, The Universal Declaration of Human Rights and the UN Convention on the Rights of the Child.[¶¶] The innovation of the agreement lies in the creation of a "Joint Committee," which aims to ensure that practices at every point on the leather goods and jewelry supply chains comply with SA8000. Gucci's decision to pursue the SA8000 certification was prompted by its objective of developing a practical and certifiable CSR practice that could increase the monitoring activities of its supply chain, recognized as the largest source of reputational risk. In the period preceding the agreement, a significant interest around this theme was spurred by various institutional parties in Tuscany, the region that hosts most of Gucci's production. Among them, the trade unions were particularly keen on measures aiming to enhance labor and environmental standards in the leather and textile supply chains.

The early involvement of the trade unions in the SA8000 certification process (formally obtained in August 2007 for the leather and jewelry sectors and subsequently for other sectors; see Table 9.4) proved to be successful. It prompted a workable approach to realize CSR shared goals in consultation of employees, contractors and subcontractors. Just as Gucci secures commitment from its direct contractors to adhere to SA8000 requirements, the firm's suppliers commit to the same stringent agreement with their subcontractors. Such a strict monitoring system across the whole supply chain allows Gucci to identify areas of noncompliance, prioritize actions for improvement and eventually prevent future risks.

CORPORATE IDENTITY

Gucci initially shows an orientation towards CSR-related issues, but with no formal definition of corporate values or mission (the compliance-seeking stage). In fact, since its foundation in 1921, Gucci has been known for products of outstanding craftsmanship and quality. Even before seeking SA8000 certification, Gucci promoted sustainable values across the company through the adoption of nine key principles: business ethics, professional skills, environment, health and safety, cooperation, stakeholders, human rights, diversity and equal opportunities. While these principles formed the core of corporate identity, SA8000 certification provided the initial framework to make Gucci's standards around total quality fully actionable.

In the second stage (capability-seeking), the CSR identity becomes an explicit part of the corporate identity of Gucci's parent company PPR. In fact, the PPR group formalized the approach to CSR with seven key priorities.[***] They act as a common framework of reference for each brand and company in the group by distilling them into measurable objectives that suit their business, namely:

- Enhance employability through skills management and training
- Train each manager on diversity issues
- Integrate CSR criteria into the contractors' selection process
- Monitor and limit transport-related CO_2 emissions
- Reduce the environmental impact of stores and infrastructures
- Promote responsible products and usages

[¶¶] For more information see: http://www.sa-intl.org/.

[***] Retrieved from: http://www.ppr.com/en/commitments/7-csr-priorities#.

- Implement solidarity programs related to the company's business activity.

The definition of these PPR principles has been the framework for the "Gucci CSR policies" approved in 2010.

STRATEGY

During the cultural grasp phase, CSR-related issues evolve from compliance with a regulatory framework (i.e., SA8000, ISO14001) to commitment toward new categories of stakeholders with new CSR initiatives in place.

Gucci works in close partnership with its suppliers to improve their CSR processes by emphasizing:

- *Contractors and subcontractors mapping*: Gucci classifies in a database the characteristics of all the contractors using two dimensions: contractor heterogeneity (e.g. per industrial process and sector) and the importance of the relationship with Gucci. Using this database, Gucci classifies contractors as either high, medium, or low priority. High-priority contractors are monitored with a greater frequency;
- *Monitoring*: third-party audits of contractors and subcontractors are regularly conducted. Internal audits of subcontractors also take place, often without announcing them in advance. Monitoring of raw materials audits do not yet take place, although they might raise significant risks. Contractors are nevertheless actively involved, since they have to abide to Gucci's CSR principles. In total, 1,000 audits are normally carried out each year;
- *Training initiatives* (through workshops, information kits, and explanatory materials): approximately 400 contractors and subcontractors are trained in CSR through 20 half-day sessions.

It is worth emphasizing that Gucci chose to abide by SA8000 because the social accountability standard was functional to Gucci's specific CSR strategy and not because of a company scandal. Eventually, SA8000 became a powerful risk-assessment tool in which CSR factors started to be recognized as business-as-usual threats. In this phase, risk management is therefore an initial approach in which CSR is framed as a tool to create controls and countermeasures that minimize or eliminate disruption or damage to business operations.

Among the CSR initiatives taken with a long term strategic impact, the firm also became active in corporate philanthropic programs. For instance, it established a partnership with UNICEF that generated more than US$9 million in the last six years for its projects supporting disadvantaged children and women in sub-Saharan Africa.

Structure

During this phase, the formal event that indicates the evolution from the compliance-seeking to the capability-seeking stage was the appointment of a CSR manager. Prior to 2007, the responsibility for handling CSR activities was delegated to the Human Resources (HR) function, since this was traditionally the unit in charge of the contractual relationships with the firm's contractors. At that time, CSR in Gucci meant to ensure compliance with SA8000 at every point on the leather goods and jewelry supply chain. To help employees and contractors understand and adopt SA8000, the HR function developed a series of training seminars to instruct on regulation, occupational health and safety, maintenance procedures and so on.

In 2007 the responsibility of the CSR implementation shifted from the HR function to an officially appointed corporate social and environmental responsibility manager. Initially the CSR manager was a single person reporting to the HR function, but later, when CSR activities became more holistic than managing the implementation of SA8000, the CSR manager needed a major managerial role in the organization. Such a change was instrumental to improving communication across hierarchical levels with all other functions and processes of the organization, as well as to the creation of networks within the company. To reach this goal, a new organizational unit has been created.

Since the appointment of the CSR manager, CSR activities have begun to be perceived as strategic drivers able to differentiate Gucci from its competitors. Previously, a defensive approach characterized the first reaction towards CSR instances and requirements by stakeholders and NGOs in particular. The response "let's consult our corporate lawyers first" was typical of the underlying attitude around stakeholder engagement. Since the appointment of a CSR manager, Gucci has become more prone to listen to and dialog with its stakeholders. An internal CSR training program has been specifically designed for Gucci's middle management, with the objective of supporting them in making such a transition. A significant effort thus took place to change the attitude of the internal managers, employees and the external suppliers toward CSR.

PERFORMANCE MEASUREMENT

At the beginning, there were no direct metrics to gauge the implementation of CSR activities. The SA8000 certification was the first step in building a set of performance measures to monitor Gucci's internal production processes and external suppliers and subcontractors. However, such nonfinancial metrics were devoted more to compliance to regulation than to measurement of stakeholders' claims and reconciliation. Key CSR metrics were still hand-collected and remained constrained to tracking performance in areas strictly required by the certification process (SA8000 and ISO14001). For instance, to comply with SA8000, Gucci monitors indicators like on the job injuries, wage hours, strike hours and personnel turnover. The performance measurement system dedicated to the results of CSR activities is thus emergent and not systematic. Moreover, CSR metrics were not yet part of the internal report that periodically circulated among Gucci's top management, although some CSR-related information was available in the PPR financial report, in compliance with regulation on social information disclosure in France.

DISCLOSURE

During this phase, Gucci showed a low-profile approach when communicating its CSR commitment to the press and local communities. There was almost no voluntary disclosure about CSR activities. This attitude was consistent with the goal of implementing SA8000 as a risk-management tool. Also, later in the next stage, the disclosure was selective and not formalized.

The reasons for such attitudes can be explained by the fact that the approach to CSR has been fully voluntary and incremental, without being pushed by any stakeholder due to a scandal. Gucci management considers that, before opening up and publicly disclosing the CSR results, further milestones need to be achieved. Another important factor is that Gucci is a global brand that needs to be very careful about its disclosures: a little imprudence in external communication could transform the firm as the target of environmental NGOs and the media. Progressively, in the last two years, both the external as well the internal communication on these topics significantly increased (i.e. September 2009 agreement, CEO interviews, etc.).

Deborah Lucchetti of the Clean Clothes Campaign describes the disclosure attitude of Gucci as follows:

> I personally understand the communication strategy adopted by Gucci to focus mainly on brand value (Gucci's primary value as quality product and not as a "green" product). However, a firm's communication with more emphasis on sustainability-related aspects (for instance focusing on transparency and accountability along the whole supply-chain) would allow in my opinion a further appreciation of Gucci's brand as a whole.

CSR Cultural Embedment Phase (2009–today): Stakeholder Engagement

This phase, which aims to complete integration of CSR activities in Gucci's strategy and operating processes, is still in progress and it is therefore difficult to clearly distinguish the different stages of CSR development; however, it is relevant to analyze what has been done thus far and to point out the CSR challenges that are still awaiting reconciliation.

Gucci's top management is looking for a deeper involvement with stakeholders' needs, as well as more transparency in the internal and external communication of CSR results. Gucci aims to achieve a genuine process of stakeholder engagement, following the example of the Joint Committee where the trade unions (partner in this initiative) were a key player.

In particular, the scope of the Joint Committee was extended beyond the social issues linked to the SA8000 to encompass all aspects of sustainability. The Committee underwent a name change to "Joint Committee for CSR" and was given a more operative governance function, where the CSR manager is the *trait d'union* between the Committee and the top management. Every year, the Committee formulates new CSR targets that are verified in the annual management review. To reconcile the interests of Gucci, its employees and contractors, Gucci's senior management and the trade unions representatives appoint people with different backgrounds to the Committee.

Another innovation along the path of stakeholder engagement is the decision to form a committee on specific technical issues. For instance, the main event in this direction was the agreement signed in September 2009 between Gucci, the trade unions and two employers' associations. The innovation of the agreement lies in the necessity to work together to preserve the know-how of artisanal craftsmanship in the Florentine leather district and also to monitor the resilience of the Florentine leather district in coping with the financial crisis. One of the main goals of the agreement was to ensure that contractors get a fair margin to eliminate any incentive to subcontract to low-cost suppliers that do not comply with SA8000.

According to Valeria Fedeli (President of the European Trade Union Federation of the Textile, Clothing and Leather sectors):

> In the first year following the agreement, the Committee focused most of its attention on the processes of restructuring occurring at the sectorial level to cope with the global economic crisis of 2009, particularly to assess the needs for the retraining and requalification of personnel. These issues are not simple to address because none of the parties involved at the beginning of this process had a clear picture about either the financial viability or the requalification requirements of suppliers across the entire chain. The development of tools to map and monitor the financial and operational health of Gucci's supplier base is an excellent start and paves the way for future activities. In addition, the mere effort to enhance the communication of objectives and initiatives taken creates awareness across the entire production cycle, with an incentive for contractors to renew attention on decisions regarding product quality, productivity, and outsourcing to sub-contractors. Positive effects of such a process of "internalization" across the supply chain of Gucci's social and sustainability policy are already apparent at this early stage (V. Fedeli, email interview, December 28, 2010).

The path to a full stakeholder engagement has not been an easy one. The total transparency policy of sharing information in the supply chain generates two kinds of threats:

1. A financial threat due to the flexibility required by the production process. For instance, if a crucial subcontractor presents some irregularities and the firm is forced to make them public, the risk is to terminate the contract in a very short time, putting the production cycle in danger with negative financial consequences.
2. A reputational threat due to media exposure in case of information leakage about cases of noncompliance against Gucci's policies.

In the attempt to address these issues, the mediation of the CSR manager was insufficient to solve the conflicts, and a moral suasion of the CEO was necessary. The direct intervention of the CEO, who declared that transparency with the stakeholders is a firm's paramount value, came after several months of discussion between the CSR function and the other organizational functions involved. This is an example in which a stakeholder controversy is solved by applying a top-down approach, signaling a strong commitment of the top management in implementing CSR activities.

The company also enlarged the network of its secondary stakeholders to more effectively inform them about the changes in Gucci's production system. For instance, the company joined the Rainforest Action Network (RAN) in an effort to eliminate from its operations paper produced from Indonesian rainforests and plantations. This event can be seen as a first-mover choice to implement an industry-leading paper policy and signals the company's proactive engagement to address climate change. Lafcadio Cortesi, RAN Forest Campaign Director, commented:

> We are impressed with Gucci's actions to improve its environmental footprint. The company's decision to reduce its paper and wood consumption and only buy FSC certified products will

help protect Indonesian and other endangered forests around the world. It sets an example for other companies in the luxury sector.†††

Regarding the next steps in stakeholder engagement, new initiatives tackling specific CSR controversies and tensions were recently set up with different NGOs. Since these initiatives are still unfolding and are defined as confidential information, we limit ourselves to summarizing the players involved and the main issue at stake:

- Greenpeace: Gucci committed to the "Amazon Zero Deforestation" campaign that aims to tackle climate change and preserve biodiversity. The cattle sector in the Amazon is the single largest driver of global deforestation. With this campaign, Greenpeace wants to clean up the cattle trade. Although Gucci does not work with any bovine leather from Brazilian cattle, the firm opened a dialog with Greenpeace and strengthened its commitment to traceability by implementing a new requirement for suppliers to have official documentation accompanying all invoices of bovine leather used in the supply chain.
- Humane Society of the United States and Humane Society International (HSUS): Gucci is currently engaging HSUS in order to find a sustainable use of furs in its collections.
- Clean Clothes Campaign (CCC) for a campaign on sandblasting-free production processes to improve working conditions in the textile sector. Deborah Lucchetti of Clean Clothes Campaign declares:

From our point of view (CCC Italian branch), Gucci is the only company that showed a real and qualified commitment to cope with a problem emerging from society and not from the market. Gucci profiled itself as a serious and responsible counterpart regarding a complex problem that must be faced with a systematic approach. The firm's position on CSR issues has a broader scope that extends beyond the mere preservation of economic and reputational risks. CCC would like to observe with more frequency a similar organizational culture in our national context. The interesting and fundamental feature that characterizes Gucci is the integration of CSR into supply chain management. The rest is philanthropy or greenwashing (D. Lucchetti, email interview, March 22, 2011).

It is worth mentioning that the engagement of stakeholders, such as the above NGOs, has not been straightforward. Gucci has been progressively extended its disclosure on this subject. For example, during the summer of 2009, Greenpeace released a report linking deforestation in the Amazon to major consumer products including fast-food hamburgers, Gucci handbags and Nike shoes. However, Gucci and the Gucci Group do not work with any Brazilian cattle farms, leather suppliers, or any products that contain bovine leather from Brazilian cattle. After the report, Gucci learned its lesson and began a constructive dialog also with other NGOs, such as CCC, HSUS, and RAN.

The policy of full disclosure has been appreciated by the NGOs. For instance, Deborah Lucchetti from CCC commented:

The choices implemented by Gucci have been very positive in banning the use of sandblasting, as well as in spurring a dialog on workplace safety conditions in an open and constructive

---

††† Retrieved from: http://cms.ran.org/media_center/news_article/?uid=4834.

way. Moreover, they have paved the way toward establishing two essential requirements in any firm—stakeholder relationship, namely transparency in the supply chain and public accountability. We acknowledge the availability and commitment that always characterized Gucci in granting us full access to its subcontractors (D. Lucchetti, email interview, March 22, 2011).

Gucci has definitely moved from a defensive approach to a more open dialog with its stakeholders, although in reaction to NGOs' request (e.g., by Greenpeace against the deforestation in Amazonia). A current challenge is to further develop a proactive stakeholder engagement. There is an effort to make CSR policies part of common business knowledge in an attempt to push sustainability instead of being pulled from external forces (e.g., NGOs).

Corporate Identity

In 2010, Gucci formalized its CSR policies where it is clearly stated that Gucci's aspiration is to produce "sustainable value".‡‡‡ The document reflects a wider social and environmental orientation and addresses the following areas.

DEFINITION OF MISSION AND VALUES

Gucci's mission is to manufacture products of paramount quality following sustainable principles, both internally and in the supply chain. The concept of "sustainable value" is explicitly defined (i.e., combine long-term economic performance with fair and honest business practices towards partners and the environment in which they operate) and the importance of the measurement of CSR performance is stated.

WORKFORCE RIGHTS AND SUPPLY CHAIN ACTIVITY

Employees, contractors and subcontractors are considered internal stakeholders. They represent an important strategic investment for Gucci's success. The principles explicitly stated are the following:

- Human rights standards;
- Employees rights and equal opportunities;
- Health, safety, and well-being;
- Training and skill enhancement;
- Driving social and environmental standards through the supply chain;
- Building a control-and-promote system on CSR principles.

MARKETPLACE ACTIVITIES

Regarding its external stakeholders, Gucci management is inspired to fair and honest business practices, with full adherence to the laws and regulations applicable in all

---

‡‡‡ Internal document dated October 11 2010 and signed by the CEO Patrizio di Marco.

business areas. The company explicitly recognizes the right of the customer to know how the product is manufactured.

STAKEHOLDER ENGAGEMENT

Gucci recognizes that an effective CSR management must pay attention to stakeholders by adopting integrative strategic management processes, transparent reporting and communication.

COMMUNITY ACTIVITIES

Gucci states a commitment to engage and promote the development of local, national and international communities.

ENVIRONMENTAL ACTIVITIES

Gucci recognizes the importance of rethinking its technologies, its products and its services to offer an eco-friendly product.

Strategy

In this phase, CSR and sustainability are increasingly recognized as Gucci's competitive factors, a real element of differentiation. Globalization tends to standardize processes, therefore standing out in the market is essential. Gucci aims to "research innovative and competitive solutions for products" that are in line with the CSR policies and "identify and anticipate new environmental and social needs". CSR expanded from a focus on issues predominantly related to working practices and labor standards to a pervasive presence throughout the supply chain to embrace environmental sustainability. A clear example of a more strategic approach to CSR relates to the launch of a worldwide eco-friendly program designed to progressively reduce the company's impact on the environment. The centerpiece of this new initiative is a newly designed packaging to reduce materials, exclusively use Forest Stewardship Council (FSC) certified paper and to be 100 percent recyclable. Gucci is a leader in its segment for having complied with every requirement stipulated, as well as compelling all the company's contractors to be involved in the launch of the new FSC certified packaging. By the end of 2010, Gucci successfully saw to it that all of its purchases of nonrecycled forest products were FSC certified to ensure that no paper is being sourced from endangered forests. Furthermore, the company will continue to seek alternative fiber options to be used in its packaging products, including biodegradable bags made of corn, bamboo and cotton. Frida Giannini, creative director of Gucci, fully embraces this philosophy:

> This project proves that you sacrifice nothing creatively when working with environmentally friendly materials. The new packaging is very beautiful and evokes perfectly the combination of Gucci's values and the traditions for which it has become renowned since Guccio Gucci founded

the company in Florence nearly 90 years ago. I believe we have a collective responsibility towards future generations to minimize our impact on the environment.[§§§]

Another initiative consists of reducing the carbon footprint, with several actions being taken to decrease energy consumption in stores and the company fleet (refer to Table 9.4).

Structure

During this phase, the CSR organizational unit receives a more official structure with a direct assigned budget and employees to accomplish the certifications in process, the ongoing social and environmental projects, and to contribute to the various organizational arrangements around CSR issues. The evolution of the CSR structure is apparent when examining the 2011 CSR organizational chart (Figure 9.1).

With regard to the formal activity undertaken during this phase, the following seem the most relevant improvements:

- enhance the integration of CSR in decision-making processes and improving interfunctional coordination;
- improve the communication of CSR activities and results, organizing seminars in which to share experiences and knowledge across the organization;
- following the example of the Joint Committee with the trade unions, promote the creation of additional stakeholders' focus groups and their progressive integration in the formal decision-making process.

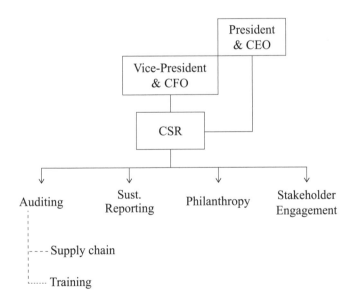

Figure 9.1   Corporate social responsibility organizational chart

§§§   PPR press releases June 5 2010, "Gucci announces the launch of a worldwide eco-friendly initiative aimed at reducing paper consumption and CO_2 emissions", http://www.ppr.com/sites/default/files/press-release/Gucci20EcoFriendly20Initiatives20FINAL_0.pdf.

The next challenge is to create a sort of stakeholder engagement platform to institutionalize the following initiatives: one-to-one interviews, submission of questionnaires and internet-based stakeholder dialog through a Web-based forum.

Performance Measurement

There is currently a need for a better alignment between Gucci's CSR strategy and the formal performance measurement system. Gucci's ambition is to build a measurement system able to measure, verify and report stakeholders' performance and satisfaction. The objective is to obtain timely feedback on CSR activities. The metrics should be the results of the stakeholder engagement process. In fact, the involvement of stakeholders is the best indicator of the credibility of CSR policies and plays a positive role in building trusting relationships with the interested parties. Such an enlarged set of metrics should then be used to set objectives and targets, periodically review performance and determine remuneration and career progression at various organizational levels.

The first result of this effort became evident in June 2010 when for the first time Gucci communicated the following company targets with the end of 2010 as a deadline:[¶¶¶]

- tons of reduction of plastic waste;
- tons of reduction of paper consumption (coming from the implementation of the new packaging, the replacement of a cardboard boxes with a recyclable bags and the optimization of paper consumption from catalogs and promotional materials);
- tons of reduction of CO_2 emissions;
- liters of reduction of gas and oil consumption.

This is a first step toward a systematic process of plan–do–check–act in CSR activities.

Disclosure

Internal communication about CSR goals and activities improved in this stage through a higher circulation of official documents, reports and training events across the various company levels. The extent and quality of CSR-related external disclosures, however, is still limited, with some exceptions related to initiatives with a larger marketing impact (such as the launch of the worldwide eco-friendly initiative). Gucci recognizes that a consequent step forward should align the internal reporting system with the firm's external disclosures. Gucci is considering the publication of a report on corporate sustainability, with the aim of accounting and representing, qualitatively and quantitatively, the implementation of its CSR practices.

[¶¶¶] PR press releases, June 5, 2010.

Findings

The Gucci case illustrates how CSR actions become progressively more systematic in addressing both internal and external stakeholders (see a summary in Table 9.4). Among the initiatives that were most instrumental in addressing the claims and pressures by internal stakeholders, the creation of the Joint Committee definitely represents an emblematic example of stakeholder engagement. In combination with the certification processes (SA8000 and ISO14001), the input provided by the trade unions and other stakeholders' representatives facilitated performance improvement across the supply chain, using an unadversarial and constructive model of industrial relations that is quite unique, especially in the luxury goods sector.**** In particular, the conditions of many suppliers in the sector of leather goods has meanwhile improved remarkably in terms of health and safety, and the third-party audits made by inspection agencies confirmed a significant improvement of working conditions. The Gucci approach of building a dialog with contractors and subcontractors on CSR issues suggests a potential mutual benefit to the whole chain.

Case evidence deviates significantly from the tenet that "the more interest stakeholders have in CSR (e.g., NGOs), the less important (economically speaking) they are to the company".[6] Because NGOs have the possibility of putting at risk the most valuable asset of a luxury firm, NGOs' priorities are taken very seriously by Gucci to strengthen the credibility and legitimacy of CSR internally and reinforce the value of reputational branding externally. In fact, compliance with the protocol imposed by the institutional certification bodies and opening up the supply chain to external observers (i.e., the Joint Committee) are costly decisions for those companies merely interested in philanthropy or greenwashing. It is no surprise that, despite the concerns surrounding the working conditions of contractors in the leather chain in the Tuscany region, so far Gucci has never been involved in any allegation. For instance, an investigation by Italian TV channel Rai-Tre screened in December 2007 addressed the manufacturing conditions of top brands. It reported that many bags and shoes were actually made in workshops where labor abuses occurred (such as using illegal or migrant labor paid morally insufficient wages, with workers forced to live in cramped conditions above the factory floor to be available to fulfil orders at any time). Gucci was able to prove that the illegal sweatshops were outside their official list of contractors.[7]

With regards to CSR issues raised by external stakeholders, brand reputation is an essential driver for a company operating in luxury goods because a greater proportion of their brand value is derived from empathy and trust. Compared to other sectors,[8] customers of luxury companies seem to be more sensitive to CSR-related topics. Customers not only can avoid purchasing, but also have the option to dissent and thereby support the call by NGOs (respectively "voice" and "exit" actions, to use Hirschman's labels) if they believe that a company is not behaving according to their expectations.[9] As emphasized by Anthony Kleanthous, Senior WWF Policy Adviser and co-author of the study "*Luxury labels brandish green credentials*": "Initially the companies were quite defensive, but now they are pushing environmental and social responsibility as a positive driver of brand

---

**** This consideration was confirmed by both NGO's representatives that we interviewed. In particular, Chiara Campione (Greenpeace) commented: "Gucci's position in its sector is definitely among the best performing firms. From our experience, not many firms in the fashion industry enforced CSR principles in their purchasing policies that were as strict as Gucci's" (C. Campione, email interview, March 21, 2011).

value."[10] What customers purchase in this segment is not merely the tangible product, but more importantly the intangible experience associated with the brand. This type of consumer is therefore concerned about the ethical consequences of its buying behavior, demanding more accountability about compliance to CSR minimum standards.

In sum, avoiding the reputational risks was initially the strongest incentive for Gucci to be transparent and certify its production processes along with the quality of its output (the value protection phase). In its current phase, however, the case documents an increased emphasis on innovation and reconciliation of different stakeholder needs (the value creation phase).

Moreover, the Gucci approach toward corporate social responsibility is very much related to the original meaning of the term (to be answerable and accountable)[††††] and significantly context-dependent, with specific historical and geographical reasons underlying the way CSR activities were shaped over time. Gucci's approach to incorporate sustainability is consistent with its critical success factors since Guccio Gucci established the company in 1921: "artisanal craftsmanship, paramount quality, made in Italy, and passion".[‡‡‡‡] The firm clearly capitalizes on a rich heritage of high-quality craftsmanship with a distinctive territorial dimension. Most of Gucci's contractors and subcontractors are located in the Florentine leather industrial district. These contractors have been manufacturing leather goods for centuries and tend to possess a kind of "leather culture and knowledge" that is hard to transfer. Using a metaphor, the district is like a forest that gives oxygen for Gucci to prosper. The health of the trees is crucial for Gucci and the market seems to recognize this mutual commitment and alignment of interests. According to Deborah Lucchetti (CCC):

> Currently global supply chains tend to delocalize their production activities instead of relying on the traditional vertical integration in one firm. To a certain extent, Gucci provides a special case of a firm that decides to maintain 100% of its operations in Italy. This approach gives the various stakeholders concrete opportunities for discussion. With regard to the campaign against sandbagging, CCC witnessed availability and openness for dialog by Gucci. The firm's organizational structure and its business operations were particularly functional to act upon issues like transparency, accountability, and stakeholder engagement. We cannot predict what could have happened if Gucci had a different business model, based upon a delocalized production structure. Probably CSR instances promoted by CCC would have been ignored or dismissed, as done by many other firms in the sector. After all, the path towards sustainability cannot be separated from core business decisions that have an effect on and are reflected in a firm's organizational culture (D. Lucchetti, email interview, March 22, 2011).

Gucci provides therefore an example of civil enterprise which does not pursue the mere objective of profit maximization;[11] rather it strives for the accomplishment of a long-term and sustainable business endeavour (cf. the idea of a company as a "project firm" theorized by Becattini).[12]

---

†††† Responsibility comes from the Latin word 'responses', past participle of the verb 'respòndere' (i.e., to answer).

‡‡‡‡ Press release for the signature of the "Agreement on the Sustainability of our Supply Chain," September 16 2009.

Table 9.4 Corporate social responsibility activities and stakeholder dialog at Gucci

CSR dimension	Stakeholder engaged	CSR issues	CSR actions put in place and target reached	CSR actions in progress
SOCIAL	Contractors and subcontractors represented by Trade unions (CGIL-Filtea) Industrial employers association (Confindustria) Artisanal employers association (CNA) Tuscany Region	Supplier selection Supply chain labor standards (e.g., labor rights, regulation of migrant workers)	Agreement on the sustainability of Gucci supply chain Innovative agreement signed between Gucci, Trade Unions, and two employers' associations (CNA and Confindustria). SA8000 certification successfully obtained for the following supply chains: • leather goods and jewelry in August 2007 • shoes in March 2009 • ready-to-wear (RTW) and silk in November 2009 • logistic platform in December 2009 Approximately 1000 contractors and subcontractors underwent third-party verification Training and seminars Approximately 20 half-day training sessions for about 400 contractors and subcontractors in: • leather goods (raw material) • packaging • shoes (60% of shoes subcontractors) • ready-to-wear and silk In July 2009 a special CSR workshop carried out, with the aim of launching the SA8000 certification for RTW and silk. About 300 supplier representatives attended	SA8000 certification of Italian stores Continue to carry out training and seminar for contractors and subcontractors Carry out audits "sustainable oriented" (social, environmental, and economics audit) New tools to carry out and manage the audit above will be in place
	Employees	Supply chain labor standards	Approximately 600 employees and managers trained in CSR design and implementation. CSR training programs in collaboration with Italian universities	Continuous training for employees and managers

Table 9.4 Continued

CSR dimension	Stakeholder engaged	CSR issues	CSR actions put in place and target reached	CSR actions in progress
ENVIRONMENT	National environmental NGOs (LAV, Greenpeace)	Supply chain environmental standards (e.g., waste, chemicals, waste water and water)	Environmental pre-audit against ISO 14001 for Gucci Spa and Gucci Logistics carried out in September 2009 ISO 14001 environmental audit carried out successfully in December 2010	Clean Clothes Campaign, for a pilot project on sandblasting free jeans
	International environmental NGOs (Rainforest Action Network, Greenpeace)	Materials sourcing (e.g., biodiversity; land use and deforestation; animal welfare) Product packaging (e.g., reduction, reuse, recycle and materials) Organic products Climate change (e.g., transportation; stores; value chain)	Certifications and audits New product packaging certified Forest Stewardship Council (FSC) in 2009 Certification Global Organic Textile Standard attained in May 2009 on the specific product of Alexander McQueen (Foulard Organic produced for Home Film event) Actions Concerning the packaging of leather products during the transportation from manufacturing plants to warehouse: eliminated cardboard boxes and replaced with biodegradable bags for 40% of leather products. This change also reduced the number of shipments "Go green" option for catalogues New recyclable mannequins, fully made in Italy, finished with water-based paints Realized the T-shirt Gucci (Home Film) using organic cotton Reduction of lighting of stores after opening hours and instalment of light detectors Switching to halogen lights and substitution of standard 50W halogen bulb with 35W in stores Initial replacement of company cars with a progressive shift from Euro 4 to Euro 5 to lower carbon emissions	Packaging across the whole range of Gucci's products will be FSC certified Future use in stores of composite stone instead of real marble/granite Incorporate LEED lighting and windows/night-time timers to reduce light consumptions in stores Replacement of company fleet Design of parking lot at corporate office with photovoltaic solutions Participation in "Amazon Zero Deforestation" campaign (Greenpeace)

Table 9.4   Concluded

CSR dimension	Stakeholder engaged	CSR issues	CSR actions put in place and target reached	CSR actions in progress
	Social Accountability International Responsible, Jewellery Council, SODALITAS	Industry membership, network for best practices in cooperation with international NGOs	Member of Social Accountability International since May 2009 Member of RJC (Responsible Jewellery Council) since November 2009 Member of SODALITAS (linked to CSR Europe) since November 2009	
COMMUNITIES	UNICEF, Film Foundation, China Children and Teenager's Fund FFAWN (Foundation for the Advancement of Women Now), Tribeca Documentary Fund, Ambulante Grant	Corporate philanthropy Social investment activities	Since 2004 Gucci established a partnership with UNICEF, which in the past six years has generated more than US$ 9 million for its projects supporting disadvantaged children and women in sub-Saharan Africa. Largest corporate donor to UNICEF's "Schools for Africa" that was established in 2004 by UNICEF, the Nelson Mandela Foundation and the Hamburg Society. Its goal is to increase access to basic schooling for all, with a special emphasis on children orphaned by HIV/AIDS and children living in extreme poverty Donation of $1.5 million to the Film Foundation for the restoration of classic Italian movies such as *Il Gattopardo* and *La Dolce Vita*. Local community initiatives: "Run for life", Meyer Children's Hospital	

Conclusions

In this chapter, we document the relevance of adopting a phase-dependent approach to better understand the linkages and the dynamic adaptation of cultural and organizational traits in CSR development. Using the MLS model across two cultural phases and three stages, we highlighted the main CSR-related challenges addressed by a company in the luxury industry, where several pressures to incorporate CSR in the business agenda are increasing. Our study illustrates that organizational culture shapes the context within which organizations design their strategies and policies. We specifically confirm the crucial role corporate leaders and internal champions play in influencing the nature and scope of an organization's responsiveness to stakeholder demands. Adding to previous evidence, our case underlines that the ability to embed intangible CSR values and beliefs in an organizational culture crucially depends on the adoption of formalized managerial control systems. Notwithstanding the peculiarities of Gucci (historical heritage as a civil enterprise and its territorial position), the case provides useful insights that can be generalized to other contexts.

First, the Gucci system signals the evolution of CSR from a rather unarticulated managerial discourse into a structured, business-as-usual management system. Leadership and corporate identity are necessary but not sufficient conditions to accomplish such a transition. Across the three stages of CSR implementation, the case highlights the central role played by a series of initiatives aiming, on one hand, at formalization (SA8000, ISO14001 systems) of CSR and at its codification (Code of Business Practices), and, on the other hand, to the engagement of stakeholders. It would be interesting to investigate across firms the consequences of various configurations (depth and span) of CSR activities on variables such as brand recognition, market share, or the company's cost of capital. As the Gucci case demonstrates, the transparency of CSR processes may be positively affected by the close scrutiny of NGOs. Further research is required to understand whether the relationship between CSR disclosure and firm performance depends on the scrutiny level by NGOs, provided that firms' can decide to enter partnership programs with NGOs at different engagement levels.

Secondly, the case emphasizes that the strategic integration of CSR in the business agenda requires some radical organizational arrangements in the responsibility structure, namely through the formal appointment of executives in charge of CSR programs. Such a change increases visibility at the board level, facilitates coordination among various organizational levels and establishes integration of CSR in the company's internal and external communications.

Thirdly, the case is emblematic of a firm that, while having consumers' individualistic values as its core business (luxury goods), at the same time seeks for active engagement with its suppliers, contractors and the trade unions to cope with complex CSR expectations. Gucci's example of the Joint Committee for CSR provides an interesting model of a multistakeholder dialog that might work just as well for other sectors, particularly in presence of increasing pressure for more transparent and collaborative business–society approaches. Further research could corroborate whether other firms across various sectors also combine a strategy of brand dominance with a relational or collectivistic identity as Gucci does, and how such strategies play out.

Lastly, on a more critical note, we observe that the level of sophistication with which CSR performance is defined, measured and disclosed currently suffers from several drawbacks when large multinationals like Gucci take steps to implement holistic sustainability policies. The lack of clear and international standards on CSR indicators often forces firms to start from scratch and makes it difficult to agree on common indicators and define benchmarks, particularly when supply chains are broad and opaque, as in the leather and textile sectors. Further research addressing the measurement and the disclosure of CSR performance in the luxury goods sector therefore seems warranted.

Notes

1   Bendell, J. and Kleanthous, A. (2007), *Deeper Luxury: Quality and Style when the World Matters*, http://www.wwf.org.uk/deeperluxury/report_download.html.

2   Maon, F., Lindgreen, A. and Swaen, V. (2010), "Organizational stages and cultural phases: a critical review and a consolidative model of corporate social responsibility development", *International Journal of Management Reviews*, vol. 12, no. 1, pp. 20–38.

3   Castelló, I. and Lozano, J. (2009), "From risk management to citizenship corporate social responsibility: analysis of strategic drivers of change", *Corporate Governance*, vol. 9, no. 4, pp. 373–385; Maon, Lindgreen and Swaen (2010), op. cit.; Mirvis, P. and Googins, B. (2006), "Stages of corporate citizenship", *California Management Review*, vol. 48, no. 2, pp. 104–126; Zadek, S. (2004), "The path to corporate responsibility", *Harvard Business Review*, vol. 82, no. 12, pp. 125–132.

4   Brickley, J.A., Smith, C.W. and Zimmerman, J.L. (2004), *Managerial Economics and Organizational Architecture*, McGraw-Hill/Irwin, Boston, MA; Merchant, K.A. and Van der Stede, W.A. (2007), *Management Control Systems: Performance Measurement, Evaluation and Incentives*, Financial Times/Prentice Hall, Harlow, England.

5   Eisenhardt, K.M. (1989), "Building theories from case study research", *Academy of Management Review*, vol. 14, no. 4, pp. 532–550; Yin, R.K. (2003), *Case Study Research: Design and Methods*, Sage Publications, Thousand Oaks, CA.

6   Steger, U. (2008). "Future perspectives of corporate social responsibility". In A. Crane, A. McWilliams, D. Matten, J. Moon and D.S. Siegel (eds), *The Oxford Handbook of Corporate Social Responsibility*, Oxford University Press, Oxford, pp. 561–567.

7   Lee-Potter, A. (2007). Designer labels' sweatshop scandal, *Sunday Mirror*, http://www.mirror.co.uk/sunday-mirror/2007/12/02/designer-labels-sweatshop-scandal-98487-20191613/; Thomas, D. (2007), *Deluxe: How Luxury Lost Its Lustre*, Allen Lane, London.

8   Steger (2008), op. cit.

9   Hirschman, A.O. (1970), *Exit, Voice, and Loyalty*, Harvard University Press, Cambridge, MA.

10   Bendell and Kleanthous (2007), op. cit.

11   Bruni, L., and Porta, P.L. (2003), "Economia civile and pubblica felicita' in the Italian Enlightenment", *History of Political Economy*, vol. 35, Supp. 1, pp. 361–385; Bruni, L. and Zamagni, S. (2007), *Civil Economy: Efficiency, Equity, Public Happiness*, Peter Lang, Oxford.

12   Becattini, G. (2003), *From Industrial Districts to Local Development: An Itinerary of Research*, Edward Elgar, Cheltenham, UK; Northhampton, MA.

10 The Working Stakeholder: New Perspectives on Corporate Social Responsibility and the Employee

PETER FLEMING*

Keywords

Authenticity, corporations, critical management studies, employees, values.

Introduction

The employee is a central feature of much stakeholder theory and corporate social responsibility (CSR) research and practice. It tends to be so in a manner that treats them as a salient stakeholder who has rights that ought to be observed by the firm. For example, health and safety, a fair wage, avoiding child labor within international commodity chains and so forth are central here.[1] Indeed, as Crane and Matten[2] have recently pointed out, when it comes to social reporting and social accounting the treatment of workers in terms of upholding labor standards is often primary, as is the perception of being deemed "a good employer". Not emphasized as much in the literature, however, is the internal role of CSR and business ethics programs—how they serve to deal with tensions between the values of workers and the unabashed pursuit of profit. This chapter serves to initiate a discussion in this area and will propose that CSR initiatives are not only driven by external stakeholders or a concern with labor standards and rights, but may also serve a cultural or even *ideological* purpose: to align employees' political and personal values with an aggressive business model, especially in industries that might be considered controversial.

The possible disconnect and subsequent attempt to realign the personal/political concerns of working stakeholders with the principles of commercialism represents a new terrain of stakeholder and CSR research. It builds upon a wider political understanding of the enterprise attuned to the way the interests of employers and employees (labor and

* Peter Fleming, School of Business and Management, Queen Mary College, University of London, Mile End Road, London, E3 2NS, the UK. E-mail: p.fleming@qmul.ac.uk.

capital) are often at odds with each other. What is good for the owners (and/or managers) is not always to the advantage of workers (and vice versa). Hence the prevalence of control and power indicative of modern firms. From this perspective, CSR might be seen as a vehicle for not only reconnecting the critical or conscientious worker with the for-profit firm, but as I shall argue below, also be used as a tool for capturing new ideas, products and skills among the workforce. The ironic result could be the commercialization of ideas that employees developed to overcome such commercialization in the first place. In order to unpack these propositions the chapter is organized in four parts. First, I begin with a short vignette to provide an empirical flavor of the phenomenon that stakeholder theory tends to downplay when considering the role of the worker. Secondly, I will survey mainstream management and consultancy literature to show how CSR is deemed a central instrument for attracting, motivating and retaining the working stakeholder. Third, a link will be made to the changing cultural politics of work in which a "holistic" human resource framework appears to be of crucial importance. This is typified by the firm inviting workers to "just be themselves" and express ostensibly nonworkrelated values and lifestyle indicators whilst on the job. The fourth section will argue that cultural or ideological integration is foremost here. How does a politically progressive, reflexive and socially sensitive individual reconcile themselves to a world of work that they feel at odds with? The discourse of CSR (e.g., consultancy firms supporting fair trade, tobacco multinationals giving lip service to biodiversity, etc.) may provide working stakeholders with a useful emotional safety valve to continue to labor in the "heart of the beast".

The Mysterious Envelope

The author had not previously given much thought to the way CSR might resonate with emergent problems relating to motivating, retaining and engaging employees. That was until the CSR Officer of a leading telecommunications firm approached him. Mary (a pseudonym) entered my university office, and beamed a happy and cheerful demeanor. The official reason for the meeting was to share ideas about the changing nature of business ethics and social responsibility in the telecommunications sector and to perhaps arrange a research project around achieving a sustainable business model. "So, what are some of the CSR issues that you are facing at the moment?" I asked. She replied swiftly and with more than a little apprehension. Her story is fascinating and rather disturbing.

The telecommunications firm—which I shall call Matrix—is a market leader in mobile phone technology in Europe. The UK national headquarters is based in a medium-sized city, and employs a substantial workforce consisting of marketing, technical and service workers. The key issue for Matrix was its association with the placement of mobile phone masts in urban and suburban areas. "We are extremely unpopular in some parts of the country because of the perceived controversy around mobile phone masts and radiation levels." I had vaguely heard about these concerns raised by scientists and neighborhood activists and probed for further information. She responded

> What these people do not understand is that the evidence concerning the risk of radiation exposure is pretty conclusive. It's a myth. What's more, they complain about putting a mast in a schoolyard or whatever, and then go home to use that very mast as if nothing was wrong. They're just complainers who have nothing better to do.

Mary shocked me regarding the lengths to which some concerned citizens went in order to convey the message that it was inappropriate to place mobile phone masts near schools, kindergartens and retirement homes. "Oh, we get all sorts of hate mail, crank phone calls and abuse." Apparently Matrix is now the target of such strong vitriol that it removed its company sign from their office building because a period of anonymity was thought best. Matters came to a head one day when a secretary received a large brown envelope with official markings, and a stamp reading "URGENT" on the front. Opening the envelope, the secretary smelt an awful odor, throwing it to one side and calling security. Covering their faces with large handkerchiefs and using two chopsticks seconded from the canteen, the security guards emptied the contents. Someone had sent human excrement wrapped in cling film, with a message: "this is how you treat our kids".

The incident Mary relayed was indeed shocking and not a little disgusting. But in a surprising turn, she smiled and said: "Oh, don't worry, we laughed about it in the end. It got sent to the glass cabinet, with all of the other crap that people send us. We use it to make fun of the weirdos out there." In my mind, the connection with CSR was quite obvious. The controversy about radiation posed a major brand-reputation problem. One of Matrix's key assets is its brand, and as any corporate reputation expert would tell us, brands gain their value not only through recognition, but also through *positive* recognition. And if Matrix is perceived by the consumer to be putting the health of children at risk and flagrantly disregarding the concerns of the community, then they might decide to question the legitimacy of that product or even worse, boycott it. As I prefaced the discussion with this brief summary of the issues, Mary quickly interjected with a look of confusion.

> No, it's not consumer confidence we have in mind with all this CSR stuff. Our focus is really about employee engagement. We need to worry about what they think and make sure they feel that they can work hard in the company, and be sure we do not go against their personal values.

As a result, Matrix spent a good deal of time and money on CSR initiatives that were not only driven by external stakeholders such as consumers, the government or concerned citizens, but by workers' values, both existing as well potential future employees. CSR for them—involving philanthropy, time off work to design more ecologically sound technological platforms, investment in biodiversity and various think-tanks that generate discussion and dialog pertaining to sustainable business models—was largely driven by how the firm relates to its workforce and vice versa.

The Importance of the Working Stakeholder

While most scholarly investigations of CSR focus on external stakeholders, there is a modest but growing stream of research that attempts to understand the internal impact of various types of business ethics initiatives.[3] Key concerns, for example, have been attracting new employees,[4] linking CSR to commitment and motivation[5] and analyzing the role human resource management in promoting CSR policies.[6] This research, however, does tend to be very functionalist in orientation. CSR is deemed an instrumental variable that may or may not enhance employee performance in the managerialist sense of the term. "Business as usual", the employer/employee power differential and capitalism more generally (with all of its controversial social outcomes) are largely deemed unproblematic and CSR is couched as something that might simply add value via higher employee productivity.

As might be expected, this functionalism is nowhere more evident than in the consultancy industry when it proclaims the importance of CSR for managing the employer/worker cultural interface. Even a brief survey of these companies and their services on the internet—using search terms such as "CSR and employee"—finds a variety of consultancies that are on hand to fine-tune this aspect of an organization's business ethics investment. The dominant discourse here centers on attracting, retaining and engaging staff. There are a number of administered surveys of varying quality and robustness that suggest employees are more willing to work for an organization that has a high-standing ethical record. One states, for example, in relation to a global survey that

> we found that CSR is the third most important driver of employee engagement overall. For companies in the US, an organizations' stature in the community is the second most important driver of employee engagement, and a company's reputation for responsibility is also among the top 10 drivers.[7]

Besides attracting high-calibre talent, for staff already part of the firm, maintaining an ethical presence is considered by some to be crucial if the enterprise is not to lose them to competitors.[8]

It must be said that the rationale used by many of these consultancies regarding the efficacy of this internal role of CSR does tend to be based on kitchen-sink psychology rather than substantive empirical observation. However, the key words evoked are nevertheless important. I propose that this interconnection of CSR and stakeholder management reveals a broader shift in the cultural politics of employment. As a number of commentators have noted, employees are now demanding to express and develop aspects of their self and identity that were once barred in the traditional workplace.[9] Rather than political views, self-ideals and lifestyle signifiers being prohibited at work, the "humane" postindustrial enterprise is often replete with people who are different, authentic and even idiosyncratic.[10] Indeed, the cultural make-up of the worker today makes for a tricky balancing act between corporate profit-seeking and personal principles. This is especially so among the emergent and inscrutable Generation-Y employee who believe that work "sucks", but nevertheless wants to enjoy a healthy salary.[11]

As opposed to the more mainstream functionalist literature and the consultancy proclamations outlined above, I suggest that a critical approach to understanding this facet of CSR would place the perennial contradiction between employers and employees or capital and labor at the heart of the analysis. In a cultural climate where workers tend to be cynical and even distrustful of business (while still feeling the necessity to participate), CSR could serve as a kind of ideological lure that allows doubting employees—who think capitalism and the corporation stands for everything wrong with the world—to continue working in the heart of the beast. Let us now examine how this might be so.

CSR and a Changing Management/Worker Interface

At one level, it is not too surprising that a firm like Matrix and others involved in so-called controversial industries might tailor well-wrought CSR policies to soften the emotional impact for conscientious workers. These scripted intimations to business ethics and environmentalism may pertain to the core competencies of the business (a petroleum company's views on sustainable energy) or may include broader statements that fall outside the core focus of the firm. The tobacco industry, for example, has long since given up on defending the serious health consequences of cigarettes. That battle was lost years ago and given the indomitable medical evidence coupled with immense governmental pressure (via taxes), they have changed tact. The key focus of its CSR policy is on workers' attitudes, with investments in charities, biodiversity and the rights of primary growers especially salient. Moreover, in an industry like this, which has a fortress-like culture, they offer inducements to workers typical of other "controversial" industries (guaranteed lifetime employment, higher than average salaries, etc.).

Employee-focused CSR initiatives in such industries is an important area of research that deserves more attention. I would argue that this trend extends to companies in a diverse range of industries and sectors in which CSR is utilized to align the worker with the principles of business and corporate life more generally. This is not only about the stigma of products that kill or harm, but also *the stigma of work itself*. In the context of a bank-led financial crisis, a post-Enron incredulity towards big business and a cultural climate that hardly ever portrays work in a favorable light (think of *The Office*, *Office Space* and the innumerable documentaries reporting on the shockingly gratuitous greed of large corporations) many workers now view "the job" with a jaundiced eye. I think these concerns resonate with some significant changes in the character of postindustrial employment and its attendant cultural politics.

The "Lifestyle Firm"

While the nature of work and the firm is still centered on profit maximization (via chains of exploitation, hierarchy and so forth) the ways in which this is achieved has undergone significant transformations. The emergence of knowledge-work, the service sector and the creative industries, for example, is illustrative of this. But what concerns me here are the major changes around the meaning of work and the implications this has for employee identity and self-understanding of both inside and outside the corporation. Indeed, shifts in the work–life balance, the increasing importance of diversity and difference pertaining to ethnicity and sexuality correlate with a growing class of workers who are reflective, politically engaged and ever so cynical about the value of old-fashioned business (especially in the post-Enron and post-crisis period in Western economies). This has meant that the cultural codes for interfacing the employee with work itself have also undergone some important changes. Put in this larger context, CSR might be seen as a human resource tool designed to align an otherwise apprehensive and conscientious workforce with an unsustainable corporate enviroment.

In the past, it was the staid "organizational man"[12] that prevailed in the large corporations of the Anglo-Saxon world. This individual was stripped of any uniqueness or idiosyncrasies that may have defined them outside of the office, and tended towards a homogenous grey obedience to the rules of the corporation. As Weber famously stated, the office is marked by a strict abnegation of all that might interrupt the smooth and impartial "machine" of the rational bureau.

In the last few years, however, as many commentators have observed, there has been something of a sea change in the corporate world regarding what it means to be at work. What has been called the rise of a more "holistic" approach to human resource management[13] and the "lifestyle firm"[14] has seen attempts to engage workers by allowing them to *just be themselves*, sometimes warts and all. The idea is that employees might be more engaged and motivated if they feel comfortable expressing, say, their gay identities or alternative political views at work, rather than hiding them from view for fear of chastisement. A good number of studies have noted how more "life" (that is to say, those features of us that were deemed more appropriate to be expressed outside of work) has become integrated into the corporate cultures of a diverse range of firms.[15] Consumer tastes, political sensibilities, sexuality and ethnicity and lifestyle associatives are (up to a point at least) now welcomed into the once impersonal offices of the enterprise. Moreover, the converse trend of expecting more from work *apropos* life outside of employment has deepened this process. As Hochschild[16] has noted, for example, a kind of "time bind" operates here where (mostly female) employees often find the space of employment an opportunity to escape the hierarchies of the home.

I see a connection here between the more general emergence of "holistic" management techniques in postindustrial workplaces (that both recognize and encourage the expression of the "whole person") and firm-level CSR policies that aim to align the working stakeholder with something they would otherwise find problematic (work itself, the business world, the corporation, etc.). Blowfield and Murray's[17] reading of CSR briefly touches upon this theme in a manner that may help us take the analysis further:

> *[some commentators] argue the commercial imperative is only part of effective corporate responsibility management and that it should also be linked to the personal values of individual managers. They point out that individual discretion allows personnel to introduce their values into corporate responsibility policies, whether through officially sanctioned actions, the unintended consequences of an individual resolving a problem by drawing people beliefs, or an individual's entrepreneurship in bringing values into the workplace.*[18]

This is certainly true. But what if these values the employee holds are distrustful or critical of corporate life, a disposition that is conveyed in innumerable films from the last decade including *Office Space*, *American Psycho* and so on? For sure, the cynical society has not looked kindly upon the world of corporatized work as the abundance of cultural references to anti-work attests.[19] From the workers perspective at least, it seems that the overall default view of business is one of (a) profound distrust following the post-Enron revelation that a whole generation of employees had been hoodwinked by overpaid corporate liars and its governmental lackeys, and (b) a feeling of unerring compulsion, the dull force of economic rationality whereby one feels little choice but to participate and make a living, especially in the expensive metropolises of the West. This critical and reflexive persona—especially among the unfathomable Generation-Y demographic—both hates the world of work and is nevertheless driven by the individualistic, self-serving goal of getting the most out of it.

CSR and the Disengaged Worker

In light of this pervasive culture of cynicism and disenchantment in the workforce, we might see CSR as an enterprise-led response to such concerns; for sure, concerns that for the most part are probably not vocally articulated, but are nevertheless shared by human resource managers, corporate executives and others in positions of authority who are certainly by no means immune to this economy of malaise. Indeed, in an article describing the new workplace as "feel good factories", Brammer[20] touches upon this important driver of CSR, which I want to discuss in a critical manner below:

> The overriding question, then, must be, why are employees beginning to care more about CSR? Its increasing importance to workers is part of a shift in wider social attitudes to the relationship between businesses and the societies they operate in. Employees are happiest when they associate themselves with organizations that behave ethically and have positive reputations, association with these organizations is consistent with their personal values and enhances their self-image.[21]

True, but what is *not* said in this statement is of more importance. Why would working stakeholders feel unhappy *without* CSR? Where does this preceding sentiment of dissonance originate that prompts CSR to be wheeled out in this manner? In the creative industries, for example, there is an unstated recognition that one is selling one's soul and becoming someone they are not as soon as their labor of love becomes a commodity to be exchanged on the market like a bar of soap or can of baked beans. In Ross's[22] excellent analysis of life in an IT firm in Boston, we see a new culture of business at play in a context where even the boss thinks work "sucks". Razorfish, the firm that was studied, carefully cultivated a climate of countercultural chic so as to retain a sense of amateurism and slacker underground cool. This in turn gave the job a sense of authenticity and integrity. Management manufactured this culture because many workers in the industry are driven by a passion for software development and even noncorporate values of shareware, hacking and an "IT communism" most notably summarized in the infamous *Hacker Manifesto*. As such, the company constructed a code that appealed to these creative, anti-commercial values. Strangely enough, leftwing and critical views of business and society were integrated into the official corporate discourse. As Ross[23] puts it, "giving the finger to corporate America ... was a big boost for recruitment and employee morale."[24]

Similarly, I propose that the language of business ethics can, at least partially, recuperate the emotional support of an otherwise disaffected postindustrial employee. Workers with values at odds with or contrary to conventional understandings of business can be motivated nevertheless through what we might call a *discourse of the social*, and it seems reasonable to suggest that CSR would be useful here. Obviously, this might especially be so among firms in industries generally associated with countercultural or even countercommercial values including the arts, journalism and so forth (also see Frank[25] in relation to the use of subversive motifs in the advertising world).

But it is not only in the crypto-subversive creative industries that we find this "discourse of the social" being activated as a human resources tool. Reporting on a study of two large international consultancy firms, Costas and Fleming[26] found an analogous use of CSR, this time to realign the disengaged employee with the objectives of humdrum office work and an aggressive business model. They observed a raft of CSR initiatives that had little to do with mustering the support of external stakeholders or clients. Fair Trade branding in the cafeteria and *pro bono* sabbaticals were favourites in one firm, "Y-International" (a pseudonym), an enterprise well-known in the industry for being exceedingly masculinist, culturally abrasive and sporting an impressive burnout rate. With many of its employees recruited from the humanities and some even proclaiming themselves "communists", the firm's CSR programme provided staff with an emotional mechanism to partially suture the disconnect between their critical views of business and their practical participation in the enterprise.

The Ideology of CSR and the Unhappy Worker

We can now unpack in more detail the various ways that CSR ideologically reconnects these widespread anticorporate values present among the workforce to the world of productivity, thus cultivating consent and reconciliation with the axiomatic principles of business. A central driver of this ideological moment is an interesting trend in contemporary management more generally. One of the more counterintuitive developments in business has been the appropriation of non-corporate or even anti-business rhetoric to motivate workers. Indeed, there has recently emerged a new discourse of management that is (prima facie at least) as "anti-management" as the radicals who deride the excesses of accumulation and consumerism. This peculiar co-optation of criticality has recently been studied by Boltanski and Chiapello.[27] They argue that the radical humanist critique of capitalism popular in the 1960s and culminating with the May '68 revolt in Paris and elsewhere is now a key feature in the parlance of the modern corporation. As employees demanded to express their authentic feelings on the job and no longer accepted their de-humanization, disenchantment and alienation as a matter of course, management responded by evoking the imagery of "spiritual freedom" to placate them. In other words, the "old" protestant work ethic of mental self-flagellation and denial of pleasure has been replaced with an ultra-liberal set of values under the rubric of "liberation management" and free self-expression. Of course, this was all in the name of saving and extending an exploitative corporate form. To do so, Boltanski and Chiapello suggest, management began to borrow and turn to its own use the very discourse of radicalism that it once deemed so dangerously subversive.

And might not CSR and its petition to noncapitalist principles also function as a kind of emotional alibi that inevitably serves to shore up unsustainable corporate activity? Might not the discourse of business ethics allow one to taste the "spirit" of a more moral world while becoming evermore enmeshed in an institutional enviroment that clashes with our moral values? For those working stakeholders who personally identify with the ethos of sharing, the enviroment, fair trade and egalitarianism, perhaps CSR helps quell the ethical anxieties that would otherwise arise from our participation in the commercial enterprise. In order to develop this argument further, I propose that there are two important ways that CSR may wed the anti-business values of the working stakeholder with the modern corporation.

Authenticity

Authenticity has seen a recent revival in the world of work.[28] With the growing popularity of the aforementioned management approach in which employees both demand and are invited to "just be themselves" (express their true feels, identities in all its difference and diversity in the workplace) the concept of authenticity becomes very significant. In relation to marketing and the CSR-branding process, for example, the quest for authentic products and service encounters has become big business.[29] The "authenticity marketing" movement is also popular in which consulting firms and various branding pundits aver that the corporation must avoid looking "fake", "superficial" or "phoney".[30] Online consulting depositories like "Authentic Business" and "Authentic Marketing Services" and texts like *The authentic brand* attest to this new trend. As Trosclair[31] argues in an online blurb regarding the virtues of authentice branding:

> *The premise is simple: Today's consumers are "longing" for authenticity because they find so many fakes and phonies in their lives. If people believe a company, product or service is authentic, they will buy and support it. If they think the company, its products and/or services are inauthentic, the firm is labelled a fake and is headed for failure. (www.advertising.suite101. com/article.cfm/authentic_marketing_strategy)[32]*

And the same sentiment might be said for the working stakeholder who enters the firm having been immersed in the critical consciousness of a post-Enron world of corporate crisis. In this cultural milieu the employee potentially finds themselves at odds with the world of work.[33] Indeed, this tension can also lead to a nagging feeling that we are inauthentic (or not being ourselves) and thus hypocritical because we do not "practice what we preach" when on the job. An extended analysis of the exact meaning of inauthenticity and its causes is beyond the scope of this chapter, but most research agrees that it is defined by the feeling of not being true to oneself.[34] That is to say, the lived contradiction between the personal values that we bring to the enterprise and the emotional and practical demands subsequently placed on us therein.

There are a number of examples in the literature to support this reading of CSR as a way of inspiring a sense of authenticity among employees with misgivings about the corporation.[35] Let's briefly discuss an "ideal" case, that of Google, since it represents an exemplar of how authenticity and business ethics intersect. As is well known, the founders of Google place much attention on Conway's Law that suggests the technological systems so vital for flexible and innovative design will tend to reflect the organizations' preexisting structure. Hence the importance of allowing people to be themselves (in ways that are productive of course) and the predominance of the ideology of authenticity in the enterprise. Here we see the discourse of the "new age" firm in its full glory, as stated on its Web site regarding the Google Philosophy:

> *We put great stock in our employees—energetic, passionate people from diverse backgrounds with creative approaches to work, play and life. Our atmosphere may be casual, but as new ideas emerge in a café line, at a team meeting or at the gym, they are traded, tested and put into practice with dizzying speed—and they may be the launch pad for a new project destined for worldwide use.[36]*

As Vise[37] has demonstrated, Google already had many of the cultural ingredients that would see a particular type of flexi-techno system emerge: youth, adherence to political autonomy, a do-it-yourself ethic and so forth. Crucial in the impressive array of progressive employment practices is the CSR policy that underpinned the founding of the firm, transforming it into a kind of social movement "for good". The Google Philosophy relentlessly reminds workers (and users alike) that its search engine rebuffs the heavy and exploitive advertising of rivals such as Yahoo and AoL, as well as the predatory competitive tactics of the giant Microsoft. While this policy was geared to impress customers, Google blurred its customers and employees into one image, following the principle that most IT workers are usually attracted to firms they purchase products from (and vice versa):

> Engineers who once longed to work for Microsoft came to see it as the Darth Vader of software, the dark force, the one who didn't play fairly. By contrast, Google presented itself as a fresh new enterprise with a halo, the motto Don't Be Evil, and a pair of youthful founders with reputations as nice guys.[38]

As similarly described by Ross[39] earlier in relation to Razorfish, perhaps the CSR campaign at Google is geared not only to customers, but working stakeholders themselves. Again, the typical rationale given by consultants is that this attracts, retains and engages staff—this might be true. But if we place such terms against a broader *political* backdrop of inauthenticty stemming from one's personal beliefs, the integrative aspect of the internally focused CSR project becomes evident. For in reality, Google is a capitalist firm that many of its IT workers realize is anathema to their beloved notions of open sourcing and hacker communism. The charge that it supported China's strict censorship policies, for example, flies in the face of open net democracy. So, what does the company do to allay trepidation among its workforce? The answer is *food*. The demographic of the typical Google employee is someone that would buy organic foodstuffs, support issues around biodiversity and place much importance on healthy living: something that sitting in front of a computer all day is not conducive to (the negative association between overwork in the office and overweight among employees has been nicely explored by Costas[40]). So they hired Grateful Dead chef Charlie Ayers to cook healthy meals for its workers. The negative experience of corporate life triggered by fast food and obesity was short-circuited through this "responsible employment" practice (also see Cederstrom[41] on the importance of the discourse of "health" in this context).

ENTER THE CORPORATE REBEL

The second way in which this dimension of CSR might culturally integrate the values of the working stakeholder (especially in a climate of anti-business sentiment) is via the discourse of resistance. Of course, resistance has strong connotations of labor fighting the powerful corporation to gain autonomy, fairer working conditions and so forth. I propose that CSR too conveys a level of criticality about the "greedy corporation", but more in a manner that resonates with Boltanski and Chiapello's[42] "new spirit of capitalism" discussed earlier. The themes of anti-exploitation and "being against the establishment" or "for the common good" are colonized by the CSR credo, thus redirecting a feeling of recalcitrance to precisely achieve key business objectives. Think how Starbucks has recently attempted to convey a sense of social responsibility among working stakeholders by "embracing resistance".[43]

On this count, I remind the reader that the motifs of radicalism such as emancipation, freedom, liberation and anti-authoritarianism are now key features of a new management discourse emerging in the wake of widespread cynicism about the corporate world. Rather than radicalism (in this abbreviated form at least) being barred as dangerous or illegitimate, it now enters the official rhetoric of the boardroom as an ally of "business as usual". Take this humorous observation by Frank[44] when describing how anti-establishment radicalism and the free market enterprise strangely joined forces to invent "liberation management":

> Beginning in 1991–1992 (when Nevermind ascended the Billboard charts and Tom Peters' Liberation Management appeared), American popular culture and corporate culture veered off together on a spree of radical sounding bluster that mirrored the events of the 1960s so closely as to make them seem almost unremarkable in retrospect. Caught up in what appeared to be an unprecedented prosperity driven by the "revolutionary" forces of gobalization and cyber-culture, the nation became obsessed with youth culture and the march of generations … In business literature, dreams of chaos and ceaseless undulation routed the 1980s dreams of order and "excellence".[45]

As also suggested by Brooks[46] in his discussion of Bobos (the bohemian bourgeoisie), management itself is taking on anarchic ideals, at least in a cardboard cutout fashion:

> If you want to find a place where the Age of Aquarius radicalism is in full force, you have to go higher up the corporate ladder into the realm of companies listed on the New York Stock Exchange. Thirty years after Woodstock and all the peace rallies, the people who talk most relentlessly about smashing the status quo and crushing the establishment are management gurus and corporate executives.[47]

In a similar manner, I want to propose that many senior human resource executives are now worried about how to deal with the army of nonchalant and sulky Generation-Y employees joining their ranks; here, CSR plays a fundamental role in re-scripting this underlying sentiment of dissent as something both manageable and potentially valuable for the firm (inspiring innovation, creativity and so forth).[48] Unlike earlier generations, employees today are less willing to suspend their countercultural values in the workplace. Moreover, the "permissive firm" is marked by the transposition of liberalist morals into the sphere of work: life, liberty and happiness are to be found in the formal rituals of the enterprise too and not just in the weekends or when one finally escapes into the leisure industry. Moreover, the pervasive skepticism about the legitimacy of the Anglo-US model of the corporate form must feature into this managerial shift as well. We all know that the modern corporation has suffered a remarkable legitimation crisis in relation to its politically regressive impact on the environment, employees in the Third World and so forth.[49]

So how does CSR and the working stakeholder fit into this? At a basic level, one is tempted to follow Žižek's[50] characterization of the "liberal communist" when he identifies a crucial moment when critics are able to reconcile their putatively anti-establishment ethics with a "business as usual" attitude. Take for example his description of George

Soros and Bob Geldoff (who incidentally is currently planning a £1 billion private equity venture in Africa):

> some of them, at least, went to Davos. What increasingly gives a predominant tone to Davos meetings is the group of entrepreneurs, some of whom refer to themselves as "liberal communists", who no longer accept the opposition between Davos (global capitalism) and Porto Alegre (the new social movements alternative to global capitalism). Their claim is that we can have the global capitalist cake, i.e., thrive as profitable entrepreneurs, and eat it too, endorse the anti-capitalist causes of social responsibility and ecological concern.[51]

There is much truth to this. But looking a little closer a more subtle psychological suturing operation is occurring. Like the question of authenticity mentioned above, CSR provides a medium for people to express their values (that reflect broader societal concerns about the effects of big business) and remain employed in firm with minimum emotional dissonance. A good example can be found in the theories of Meyerson[52] as she explores the "tempered radical" in large US corporations. Meyerson celebrates these everyday "radicals" who make quiet inroads into corporate power through micro-ethical campaigns, without rocking the boat too much. The tempered radical is defined in the following way:

> Tempered radicals are people who want to succeed in their organizations yet want to live by their values or identities, even if they are somehow at odds with the dominant culture of their organizations. Tempered radicals want to fit in and they want to retain what makes them different. They want to rock the boat, and they want to stay in it.[53]

For all intents and purposes, the tempered radical reflects a moment of reconciliation. Through acts of micro-resistance that do little to challenge the wider corporate hegemony in any meaningful manner, workers can nevertheless enjoy a "feel good" afterglow within an institutional setting they know is ethically dubious. Indeed, the activities of the tempered radical are further framed by Meyerson as employees "resisting quietly and staying true to one's self, which includes acts that quietly express peoples' different selves".[54] Subsequently, the working stakeholder who feels personally uncomfortable in a cutthroat business world is able to—via the discourse of business ethics and CSR—express their identities (even if *against the firm*) and continue to work very hard.

Conclusions

Even though the "employee as stakeholder" is much discussed in terms of labor rights and standards, the *ideological* function of CSR as an integrative tool requires more investigation. The practitioner literature suggests that CSR is important for attracting "talent", retaining staff and creating more engaged workers. This chapter has aimed to extend this investigation in a *critical* manner by suggesting that we need to delve further into the changing cultural make-up of the working stakeholder and societal values more generally. Given that many employees feel they are often "not themselves" when at work (surely exacerbated by the rising tide of cynicism and disappointment regarding business in a post-Enron and post-crisis corporate landscape), the CSR presence in a firm might operate as a political tool to smooth over the divide between capital and labor, employer and employee. This is especially so when the worker feels deeply at odds with their work role and the business world at large. That is to say, when someone thinks that they are compromising an important part of themselves when participating in the corporation. Here, CSR allows employees get by while in the heart of the beast.

Of course, not all workers feel alienated in their jobs or are cynical about big business. Moreover, not all CSR policies aim to integrate anti-work motifs in order to inspire its staff. But evidence has suggested a broader shift with respect to "liberation management" and the "new spirit of capitalism" that seems to resonate with the culture of criticism that is pervasive today. The working stakeholder today demands more from their places of employment, to express their personal values and political views that are often contrary to the world of unbridled free enterprise (today in crisis). And in the extreme case, corporations in controversial industries may rely upon CSR to insulate employees from the ethical anxieties they might have otherwise experienced. Because of the newness of this research area, the ideas posited in this chapter have largely been built from theorizing and evidence from other studies. So, more direct empirical research is needed to corroborate (or disprove) these claims. This could be done by analyzing the way CSR might feature in responses to the question: so if you hate capitalism, what do you get from working here?

The final aspect of this new perspective concerning CSR at work pertains to its more predatory nature (see Hanlon and Fleming[55] for an initial analysis in this regard). As we have seen above pertaining to the blending of a "lifestyle" human resource approach ("just be yourself") with an ameliorative CSR discourse the personal sphere becomes an important commercial resource. Indeed, much of the practitioner literature argues that CSR initiatives are particularly engaging if developed by workers themselves. This appeal to self-authored projects could be a way firms actively capture and enclose innovations generated by workers as they seek solutions beyond the confines of commercialism. For example, a CSR project might serve as a "key" for unlocking the personal skills, aptitudes and creativity of the worker. This is what Land and Taylor[56] found in their study of an ethical clothing company trading in organic (but high-priced) products. In order to give the job and products a veneer of authenticity, it captured the personal values and anti-business ethos of its employees (related to tattoos, surfing, skating, etc.) and fed them back into the branding process. As the authors point out:

> The company manufactured the Ethico brand by producing catalogues, a website, and other marketing communications. In order to establish the authenticity of the brand, this immaterial labour of brand management drew upon the recreational activities of employees. This inscription of employees' lives into the brand created the economic value of the company's products, situating their "lives" as a form of productive labour or "work".[57]

In other words, CSR might be conceptualized not only as a cultural suture, but also an instrumental foray into the social aptitudes of the workforce. Indeed, Blowfield and Murray's[58] argument supports this when they suggest that CSR unlocks the value-adding skills of the worker:

> individual discretion allows personnel to introduce their values into corporate responsibility policies, whether through officially sanctioned actions, the unintended consequences of an

individual resolving a problem by drawing people beliefs, or an individual's entrepreneurship in bringing values into the workplace.[59]

Again, more empirical research is required to clarify the exact nature of this kind of corporate capture of the personal sphere among working stakeholders and its connection to productivity (or otherwise).

The author hopes that this underexplored facet of stakeholder theory and CSR will prove fruitful for driving future empirical research. In particular, scholarship must place the working stakeholder within the context of a shifting corporate form and changing societal values about business. The tensions, conflicts and contradictions that result might be central for enhancing our understanding the ever-growing "business of business ethics" in contemporary organizations.

Notes

1   Jones, M. and Fleming, P. (2003), "Unpacking complexity through critical stakeholder analysis: the case of globalization", *Business and Society*, vol. 42, no. 4, pp. 430–454.

2   Crane, A. and Matten, D. (2010), *Business Ethics*, Oxford University Press, Oxford.

3   Bhattacharya, C.B., Korshun, D. and Sen, S. (2009), "Strengthening stakeholder company relationships through mutually beneficial corporate social responsibility initiatives", *Journal of Business Ethics*, vol. 85. no. 2, pp. 257–272; Gond, J.-P., El Akremi, A., Igalens, J. and Swaen, V. (2010), "A corporate social performance—corporate financial performance behavioural model for employees". In C. Bhattacharya, D. Levine, C. Smith and D. Vogel (eds), *Corporate Responsibility and Global Business: Implications for Corporate and Marketing Strategy*, Cambridge University Press, Cambridge, pp. 13–48.

4   Greening, D.W. and Turban, D.B. (2000), "Corporate social performance as a competitive advantage in attracting a quality workforce", *Business and Society*, vol. 39, no. 3, pp. 254–280; Turban, D.B. and Greening, D.W. (1996), "Corporate social performance and organizational attractiveness to prospective employees", *Academy of Management Journal*, vol. 40, no. 3, pp. 658–672.

5   Peterson, D.K. (2004), "The relationship between perceptions of corporate citizenship and organizational commitment", *Business and Society*, vol. 43, no. 3, pp. 269–319; Preuss, L., Haunschild, A. and Matten, D. (2009), "The rise of CSR: implications for HRM and employee representation", *International Journal of Human Resource Management*, vol. 20, no. 4, pp. 975–995; Collier, J. and Esteban, R. (2007), "Corporate social responsibility and employee commitment", *Business Ethics: A European Review*, vol. 16, no. 1, pp. 19–33.

6   Rupp, D.E., Gananpathy, J., Aguilera, R.V. and Williams, C.A. (2006), "Employees' reactions to corporate social responsibility: an organizational justice framework", *Journal of Organizational Behaviour*, vol. 27, no. 4, pp. 537–543; Wittenberg, J., Harmon, J., Russel, W.G. and Fairfield, K.D. (2007), "HR's role in building a sustainable enterprise: insights from some world's best companies", *Human Resource Planning*, vol. 30, no. 1, pp. 10–20.

7   Towers Watson (2008), "Corporate social responsibility: no longer an option", http://www.towersperrin.com/tp/showdctmdoc.jsp?url=Master_Brand_2/USA/News/Spotlights/2008/2008_07_30_Spotlight_Corporate_Social_Responsibility.htm.

8   Bhattacharya, C.B., Sankar, S. and Korschun, D. (2008), "Using corporate social responsibility to win the war for talent," *MIT Sloan Management Review*, vol. 49, no. 2, pp. 37–44.

9   Fleming, P. and Sturdy, A. (2009), "Just be yourself! Towards neo-normative control in organizations?", *Employee Relations*, vol. 31, no. 6, pp. 569–583.

10 Kuhn, T. (2006), "A demented work ethic and a 'lifestyle firm': discourse, identity, and workplace time commitments", *Organization Studies*, vol. 27, no. 9, pp. 1339–1358.

11 Fleming, P. (2009), *Authenticity and the Cultural Politics of Work*, Oxford University Press, Oxford.

12 Whyte, W. (1956), *Organization Man*, Simon and Schuster, New York.

13 Fleming, 2009, op. cit.

14 Kunh, 2006, op. cit.

15 Land, C. and Taylor, S. (2010), "Surf's up: life, balance and brand in a new age capitalist organization", *Sociology*, vol. 44, no. 3, pp. 395–413.

16 Hochschild, A. (1997), *The Time Bind: When Work Becomes Home and Home Becomes Work*, Henry Holt, New York.

17 Blowfield, M. and Murray, A. (2008), *Corporate Social Responsibility: A Critical Introduction*, Oxford University Press, Oxford.

18 Blowfield and Murray, 2008, op. cit., p. 110.

19 Svendsen, L. (2008), *Work*, Acumen, Durham.

20 Brammer, S. (2006), "The feel good factories", *The Guardian*, 21 January www.guardian.co.uk/money/2006/.../workandcareers.careers

21 Brammer, 2006, op. cit., p. 1.

22 Ross, A. (2004), *No-Collar: The Humane Workplace and Its Hidden Costs*, Basic Books, New York.

23 Ross, 2004, op. cit.

24 Ross, 2004, op. cit., p. 110.

25 Frank, T. (1998), *The Conquest of Cool: Business Culture, Counterculture and the Rise of Hip Consumerism*, University of Chicago Press, Chicago.

26 Costas, J. and Fleming, P. (2009), "Beyond dis-identification: towards a discursive approach to self-alienation in contemporary organizations", *Human Relations*, vol. 62, no. 3, pp. 353–378.

27 Boltanski, L. and Chiapello, E. (2005), *The New Spirit of Capitalism*, trans. G. Elliott, Verso, London.

28 Fleming, 2009, op. cit.

29 Potter, A. (2010), *The Authenticity Hoax*, HarperCollins, New York.

30 Gilmore, J. and Pine, B. (2007), *Authenticity: What Consumers Really Want*, Harvard Business School Press, Harvard.

31 Rosica, C. (2007), *The Authentic Brand: How Today's top Entrepreneurs Connect With Customers*, Noble Press, London.

31 Trosclair, A (2007), "Authentic marketing strategies", www.advertising.suite101.com/article.cfm/authentic_marketing_strategy, accessed 13 December, 2010.

32 Trosclair, 2007, op. cit.

33 Sennett, R. (1998), *The Corrosion of Character: The Personal Consequences of Work in the New Capitalism*, W.W Norton, London; Cremlin, C. (2010), "Never employable enough: the (im)possibility of satisfying the boss's desire", *Organization*, vol. 17, no. 2, pp. 131–149; Fleming and Costas, 2009, op. cit.

34 Fleming, 2009, op. cit.

35 Michelli, J. (2007), *The Starbucks Experience: 5 Principles for Turning Ordinary into Extraordinary*, McGraw-Hill, New York; Fleming, op. cit.; Cremlin, op. cit.

36 http://www.google.com/corporate/tenthings.html

37 Vise, D. (2005), *The Google Story*, Pan Books, New York.

38   Vise, 2005, op. cit., p. 96.

39   Ross, 2004, op. cit.

40   Costas, J. (2010), "Work-ing out: an analysis of sport, culture and identity in two management consultancy firms", paper presented at the Academy of Management Pre-conference Workshop on Bio-Power at Work, August 9, Montreal, Canada.

41   Cederström, C. (2011), "Fit for everything: health and the ideology of authenticity", *ephemera*, vol. 11, no. 1, pp. 27–45.

42   Boltanski and Chiapello, 2005, op. cit.

43   Michelli, 2007, op. cit.

44   Frank, 1998, op. cit.

45   Frank, 1998, op. cit., pp. ix–x.

46   Brooks, D. (2001), *Bobos in Paradise*, Simon and Schuster, New York.

47   Brooks, 2001, op. cit., p. 110.

48   Fleming, 2007, op. cit.

49   Parker, M. (2002), *Against Management: Organization in the Age of Managerialism*, Polity Press, Cambridge.

50   Žižek, S. (2008), *On Violence*, Profile Books, London.

51   Žižek, 2008, op. cit., p. 14.

52   Meyerson, D. (2003), *Tempered Radicals: How Everyday Leaders Inspire Change at Work*, Harvard University Press, Harvard.

53   Meyerson, 2003, op. cit., p. xi.

54   Meyerson, 2003, op. cit., p. 8.

55   Hanlon, G and Fleming, P (2009), "Updating the critical perspectives on corporate social responsibly", *Sociology Compass*, vol. 3, no. 6, pp. 937–948.

56   Land and Taylor, 2010, op. cit.

57   Land and Taylor, 2010, op. cit., p. 408.

58   Blowfield and Murray, 2008, op. cit.

59   Blowfield and Murray, 2008, op. cit., p. 110.

11 *Giving Credit Where Credit is Due: Distributive Justice and Corporate Volunteerism*

MARY RUNTÉ* AND DEBRA Z. BASIL†

Keywords

Corporate support for employee volunteerism, CSEV, distributive justice, volunteerism.

Introduction

Every weekend for the last two months, John has volunteered at the local library reading to young children as part of a literacy initiative of a local nonprofit charity. He found out about this initiative from his employer, who partners with the charity to buy books for the library and schools in their region. John is surprised to discover that his volunteer efforts are featured in a company report as evidence of the businesses' community orientation. John wonders how his company got to "take credit" for his volunteerism. (John, Marketing Representative, Manufacturing)

That companies will engage in prosocial behavior, frequently characterized as corporate social responsibility (CSR), has become a standard expectation. CSR presents a strategic opportunity, whether marketing to external or internal stakeholders, but successful development of a firm's CSR strategy requires an understanding of stakeholder expectations.[1]

CSR can take varied forms depending on the goals of the organization and the expectations of the salient stakeholders. One means of CSR enactment that explicitly engages the employee stakeholder group is corporate support for employee volunteerism (CSEV), the engagement of employees in volunteer charitable activity with the endorsement of, or under the direction of, the employer.[2] Basil *et al.*[3] identify that Canadian businesses support volunteerism both to satisfy CSR expectations placed upon them by external

* Mary Runté, Policy and Strategy, Faculty of Management, University of Lethbridge, Lethbridge, Alberta, Canada T1K 3M4. E-mail: mary.runte@uleth.ca.

† Debra Z. Basil, Centre for Socially Responsible Marketing, Faculty of Management, University of Lethbridge, Lethbridge, Alberta, Canada T1K 3M4. E-mail: debra.basil@uleth.ca.

stakeholders, and to improve employee morale. Commonly, businesses then promote the employees' activities as evidence of the company's general social engagement and of the businesses' CSR commitment to their communities.[4]

This chapter examines the evaluations made by employees in assessing the "fairness" of their employer using employee volunteer activities to satisfy the organization's CSR expectations. Volunteerism, which has traditionally been an activity undertaken during nonworking hours and with little or no employer involvement, offers the volunteer several benefits including the intrinsic reward of having "made a difference" and the extrinsic reputational benefits gleaned from the volunteer's service.[5] In the case of CSEV, however, the employer is claiming the reputational benefits of volunteerism, in whole or in part. This claim necessarily raises the question of whether the reputational reward for the good work of volunteerism is being appropriately distributed between the employee who engaged directly in the charitable activity, and the employer who, to varying extents, supported the effort. On the one hand employees may question why their employer is appropriating credit for their volunteer efforts, as was the case with John in the opening scenario; on the other hand, companies need to have their support for such volunteer activities acknowledged.

This question of credit allocation suggests that CSEV introduces potential tensions. One such tension relates to how the company chooses to position CSEV efforts. The company may be motivated to take credit for employee volunteering in order to gain favor with the public. Such credit allocation may however frustrate the employees who perform the volunteer service. A second potential tension, which is the focus of this chapter, relates to the internal tension an employee may experience when cognitively reconciling CSEV efforts. The individual may struggle with whether they as individuals deserve credit for volunteering, or whether they were simply representing the company in an employment capacity. The desire to be a "good employee" may conflict with the desire to receive personal recognition for one's efforts. This chapter examines the tension of credit allocation employees face when considering their CSEV efforts, with an eye toward discerning factors that create such internal tensions, and how they may be resolved.

We explore the ambiguity that may result when the previously personal activity of volunteerism is absorbed into the workplace. The emergence of CSEV as a CSR initiative requires employers to recognize the need to balance their own desire to present employee volunteering as part of their CSR scorecard, against the employees' desire to receive credit for their own efforts. For businesses to maximize both employee goodwill and the reputational gains available through CSEV they must first understand how employees assess the fair distribution of the "credit" for their good works under the conditions of CSEV.

This chapter begins with an overview of CSEV as an aspect of CSR and then positions CSEV within the perspective of volunteerism as an activity of individual and personal significance, traditionally rooted in a nonwork context. This research examines employees' experience of the blurring of these work and nonwork boundaries through the lens of "fairness" and presents justice markers used by employees when evaluating the distribution of the reputational benefits of the volunteer acts.

Theoretical Framework

CORPORATE SUPPORT FOR EMPLOYEE VOLUNTEERISM

CSEV is not a new phenomenon, although its profile and importance to business have grown significantly in recent years, perhaps as a result of being embraced as a CSR initiative. Although CSEV has a long history, it has only recently been subject to academic study. Within management literature, research has focused upon the organizational structuring of such programs[6] and the organizational benefit of CSEV.[7] CSEV can take several forms, from providing encouragement for employees to volunteer during nonworking hours, to the structuring of formal volunteer events held on company time; the larger the company, the more formalized the volunteer program tends to be.[8]

Companies may engage in CSR oriented programs, such as CSEV, to strategically reap the benefits associated with being prosocially engaged.[9] CSR benefits from CSEV programs have been identified in the literature.[10] Generally, customers respond positively to socially responsible company efforts,[11] although company motives may at times be questioned.[12] Canadian companies report a perception that these programs improve relations with the surrounding community.[13] A survey of American businesses conducted by the Points of Light Foundation and Allstate Foundation[14] demonstrated that a large majority of companies participating in that survey (83 percent) use CSEV strategically to aid public relations. A survey of Canadian consumers indicates that an overwhelming majority (74 percent) expect companies to perform socially responsible behaviors;[15] support for employee volunteering can help companies to meet these consumer expectations.

Extant research has focused less on the employee experience of CSEV and any conflicts that may develop between the expectations of employees and the employers, than on the structuring of CSEV programs. One exception is the research of Peloza, Hudson and Hassay[16] which focuses on the employee experience of CSEV; however, their orientation is the examination of the structuring of programs for external stakeholders and the development of organizational citizenship behaviors rather than employees' interpretation of the benefits received. Employees volunteer for a variety of reasons.[17] Previous research suggests that gaining job skills and credentials tends to be a strong incentive for younger employees participating in CSEV, whereas gaining social contacts is a strong incentive for older volunteers.[18] Recent research[19] indicates that the primary motivation for volunteerism, whether done with or without employer involvement, is the desire to contribute meaningfully to a cause of personal importance. Volunteerism is often characterized as a win–win proposition, with both the volunteer and the organization or cause gaining benefit. For the volunteer, this reward is often intrinsic,[20] although volunteer management literature is replete with advice on acknowledging volunteer contributions as a mechanism for gaining ongoing volunteer commitment. There is a developed body of literature examining the transfer of the extrinsic and knowledge-oriented intrinsic benefits from volunteerism to the worksite. Research suggests that company volunteerism increases several employee measures such as morale, productivity, retention and recruitment.[21] The research in this chapter examines the literature gap regarding the employee experience of the intrinsic benefits of CSEV when the perception of contribution is distributed between themselves and the employer. Employee assessment of fairness is determined through a justice evaluation: Is the organization claiming more than its just share of credit for the good work of the volunteers?

Distributive Justice

Employees' perceptions of organizational justice result from individuals' evaluations of whether their organization treats members fairly. Implicit in justice judgments is an evaluation of the entitlement or deservingness of recipients.[22] A referential structure is developed by the evaluator to determine who should be potential recipients of a resource allocation and who should be excluded as a recipient.[23] This structure involves both an evaluation of the reward distributions made or appropriate to be made, as well as an examination of the processes that led to those outcomes.[24]

Distributive justice, a component of justice theory, refers to the fair apportioning of rewards or penalties to recipients. Justice theory is most frequently applied at a micro level, with the employee assessing personal benefit level, such as pay or position, relative to a referent group. More recent research, however, has focused on a meso or macro level of assessment, whereby employees analyze group/team-based reward structures[25] or societal level distribution of compensation, such as perceived "fairness" of executive pay structure in a time of economic hardship.[26]

In the case of CSEV, which is treated by the organization as a CSR endeavor and publicized to stakeholders as such, employees will assess the fairness of the organization in the apportioning of credit for the volunteer activity to various recipients. Determining the extent to which they personally merit "credit" for the good work of volunteerism, the employees will also consider whether others merit such recognition.

Volunteerism that is supported in a work context can be organized in several different ways: sometimes volunteerism is a team effort; at other times it is an individual pursuit. In CSEV, regardless of how it is structured, there is always an additional partner, the employer. The employer's role may be expansive, as in the provision of paid time to volunteer, or limited to merely encouraging employees to be involved in volunteerism during nonwork hours.[27] Whether involved peripherally or directly, however, the employer has provided support or endorsement for the activity.

Justice theory identifies four key questions individuals assess when considering distributive justice processes based on principles of equity in the distribution of social and material rewards.[28] First, individuals form ideas of justice; in the distributive–retributive domain these are general ideas about what constitutes the just reward for each rewardee: in the case of CSEV, rewardees include the employer and employee-volunteer. Secondly, these ideas of justice may be used to help shape actual situations: for example, ideas of the just reward for volunteer efforts may play a part in an individual deciding to volunteer. Thirdly, individuals assess the justice or injustice of actual situations, often retrospectively, generating a justice evaluation: for example, they may judge that the employer claimed too much or too little of the credit for the volunteer activity creating a condition of inequity. Finally, the justice evaluation becomes an important determinant of further behaviors such as future engagement in CSEV or even other workplace activities. It is for this reason that employers and employees need to attend to this issue.

Perceptions of fairness have important implications for the employer. On the one hand, employees who perceive the workplace to be just express higher levels of satisfaction and commitment (including lower intention to leave), and more supportive behaviors. On the other hand, employees who perceive the workplace to be unjust have lower morale, lower job performance, higher turnover and may engage in retaliatory behavior toward the employer. In the context of CSR activities dependent upon employee engagement, such as CSEV, employees' participation in future volunteer activities will be determined in part by whether they feel that the employer was just in taking credit for their volunteer activities. Consequently, parties that anticipate future interaction generally benefit from fairness in exchange outcomes.[29]

Research Study

METHOD

The current study is drawn from a two-phase research program funded by Imagine Canada; the findings of the first phase are published elsewhere[30] and identify trends in CSEV in Canada from the employer perspective. The second phase examines the employee perspective of CSEV. Phase two draws on an employee sample generated from a leading international research panel operated by Market Facts, Inc. An online survey was conducted with 2,125 members of this research panel. Participants were all individuals currently or recently employed in Canada. The results of this quantitative survey are reported elsewhere.[31]

During the online employee survey, individuals were asked if they would be willing to participate in in-depth interviews. A convenience sample of 25 persons who agreed to this request was interviewed by one of the authors and results are reported here. All in-depth interview participants were from different organizations; the organizations vary in both size and mission. Participants held roles at various levels within their organizations; however none were part of the administration of CSEV for their organization.

The interviews were semi-structured and lasted an average of one hour. The interviews were transcribed verbatim and analyzed thematically; the information for this chapter was extracted from the participants' responses to queries on the distinction between corporate volunteerism as a personal charitable act and volunteerism as a work activity. Employees were asked to discuss their own experiences with corporate volunteerism and to respond to hypothetical examples.

Results

The analysis focuses on the relative justice of the CSEV experience, particularly emphasizing the allocation of credit for good works. Interview responses were analysed through the lens of distributive justice theory, with specific attention to the four key questions addressed regarding assessments of justice:[32] forming ideas of justice, determining whether to partake, assessing the actual situation and finally speculating about future participation. Responses from all participants were assessed and coded for common themes. Given the vast nature of qualitative data, only the most instructive and representative quotes are included below to demonstrate the extracted themes. Figure 11.1 demonstrates the process participants appeared to follow when making CSEV assessments.

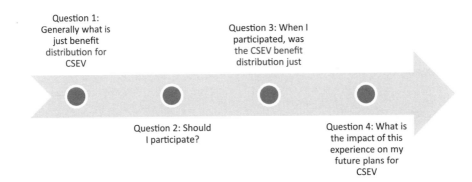

Figure 11.1 CSEV assessment process

Forming Ideas of Justice

Participants developed views of general fairness or justice for CSEV programs, regarding both company and individual responsibilities and benefits. Participants began by making a general judgment of the appropriateness of using volunteerism as a mechanism to satisfy societal CSR expectations:

> *Shouldn't the firm just do these things because it is the right thing to do? Why do they have to soil it all by advertising that they did it? (Peggy, Accountant, Public Accounting Firm)*

> *Guess that my company didn't really have to do anything at all. It is a bank after all, not a charity. So, if they want to look good, I shouldn't really be that critical. (Robert, Customer Service, Bank)*

> *Businesses these days are expected to do this kind of thing. I get that. I just don't like that I am the one doing the work and they get to look good. But, I guess that is how the game is played. All this talk about CSR really means that firms need to look good, not be good. And, if it helps the bottom line and they really did do what they claimed to do, they should get to tell people about it and get rewarded. (Stephen, Customer Service, Retail Chain)*

Implicit in this justice evaluation is a macro-level analysis of the role of charity in society and an assessment that engagement in charitable work for business gain is less honorable than engagement for more altruistic reasons. It appears that the employees who made this differentiation found the firm's subsequent portrayal of the charitable good work as CSR to external stakeholders was more acceptable, if not desirable, when the motivation was assessed to be "appropriate". Stephen, for example, who in the previous example stated that a firm seeking credit for CSEV effort was understandable, felt that this credit was more deserved if it was for a volunteer effort motivated by charitable intent:

> *But, really, it is better if it is done for the right reasons. Because they want to help. (Stephen, Customer Service, Retail Chain)*

It's fine with me that it makes them look good. I personally am happy to tell everyone what they do for [name of charity]. We need more companies like this one. Ones that care. (Walther, Health Care Worker, Hospital)

The interviewed employees then expanded upon this general assessment of CSEV by articulating criteria that, assuming any credit for CSEV engagement was warranted, would be employed to determine the apportioning of that credit amongst participants. Key among these criteria was the assertion that the company had to be an active participant in the effort in order for any credit to be assumed by the organization:

If they didn't do their bit, it would be using our work as advertising when it's not even them that's contributing to it. It's the employee who is volunteering. (Alura, Customer Service Representative, Food Services)

So they take the credit and do nothing. It is wrong. (Francis, Warehouse Manager, Retail)

Specifically, participants questioned whether a company expended sufficient effort or time to warrant consideration for merit:

Let's see … They (company) spend almost no time, buys a cake and some paper plates, and then wants to be seen like heroes. Seems like a bit of a song and dance to me. Do nothing and publicize yourself as being a good corporate citizen. Not really right, I think. (Robert, Customer Service, Bank)

When this requirement of the business regarding engagement was met, participants felt a company then would deserve at least some credit for their efforts:

The business deserves a share of the credit. (Scott, Manager, Consulting Firm)

I think that there is enough credit to go around. But only if my company actually did something to deserve the credit. If they did, then OK. We are partners. (Stuart, Engineer, Oil Company)

Views of CSEV justice were also based on the participant's assessment of employee contribution to the volunteer effort. Specifically, the participants felt that employees needed to make a sufficient contribution to be entitled to volunteering credit. For some, if one was being paid by the company they did not qualify as a "volunteer":

You shouldn't be paid to be a volunteer. (Terry, Manager, Public Service)

For others, the amount of expended effort or time, was salient. If the volunteer time commitment, for example, would be low for the employee then the activity didn't merit credit:

It seems a bit much patting people on the back like that, it really wasn't much. It wasn't really like I went out of my way or anything. (Tammy, Secretary, Resource Development Firm)

Determining Whether to Partake

Next, participants assessed how their general views of justice impacted their own decision to participate. Specifically, a general assessment of the ideal merit distribution for CSEV is followed by a particularistic appraisal of justice as employees determine whether they personally wish to engage in a volunteer effort or retrospectively assess former engagement. Most important in determining whether employees categorized their own behaviour as deserving a portion of credit was the intention driving the behavior.

Employees are aware of the benefits that they will receive for volunteering and consider these when making the decision. Sarah, a student, for example identified how volunteering for a community event sponsored by her summer employer, would help her forge more positive relationships within the firm and enhance her prospects for longer-term employment:

> *I know that there are better reasons for volunteering, but I did it in part because it would make me look good to the other employees. (Sarah, Student, institution unknown)*

Acknowledging this as her primary intent, led Sarah to dismiss her right to assume personal credit for the volunteerism. The decision to engage in a CSEV endeavor, therefore, does not necessarily mean that employees will categorize the event as volunteerism and deserving of acknowledgment or reward:

> *But, I wouldn't count it as volunteering then … Because I wasn't doing it for the charity, I was being selfish. I did it, but not for the right reasons. Not at all. So I wouldn't count it. (Sarah, Student, institution unknown)*

This sentiment was also expressed by Peggy who, when referencing the intent of others in her accounting firm, stated that some participated only to enhance their visibility in the firm:

> *Some would volunteer simply because it was a pet project of the managing partner. I'll give you the example of an AIDS walk. I volunteered for it because I wanted to support the partner and because it was an important cause. But a colleague of mine was disgusted by the whole AIDS thing and only did it because it would make her look good. I volunteered, she didn't. You have to care about the cause otherwise it is just work. (Peggy, Accountant, Public Accounting Firm)*

Although this assessment of the motivation of others did not diminish her willingness to engage in CSEV programming, Peggy did identify a possibility that such an effect was possible:

> *Do I feel less into volunteering because others were being so self-serving. I would say that it pisses me off and makes me feel like they were exploiting the charity, but I still would do it because it is the right thing to do. But, I can see how it would turn off others who are less into volunteering than I am. (Peggy, Accountant, Public Accounting Firm)*

The decision to engage in CSEV and to categorize the activity as volunteerism is linked to the intention of the participating employee and business. A commitment to the cause is a significant factor, both in motivating participation and in the anticipated apportioning of what is perceived to be a just distribution of merit. The anticipation of benefits from the sponsoring business may motivate participation in CSEV, but may diminish the employees' sense of entitlement to a portion of the credit for the good work.

Assessing the Actual Situation

Next, employees determined whether credit for the CSEV effort was justly distributed. The employees interviewed shifted their focus from a general assessment of the merits of CSEV to an appraisal of specific incidents of CSEV and the apportioning of credit for the volunteer effort linked to these specific events. Awarding the firm with credit for volunteering efforts was directly tied to the degree of contribution provided by the firm itself. Employees who felt that the firm was a deserving recipient group were very specific in identifying the type of contribution made by the employer and explicitly linked this contribution to their inclusion of the firm as a deserving recipient group:

> At the end of the day, I am volunteering because I want to help the charity. It is a plus that I get time off to volunteer, and my company deserves some of the credit for that, but it is about the charity, not about me. I would do it anyway. (Tammy, Secretary, Resource Development Firm)

A continuum of entitlement became evident in the analysis of the degree of contribution. Sara, an employee of a national bank, identified a high level of firm involvement:

> It wasn't just that the firm supported us volunteering. They made it happen. It wouldn't have happened without them. That is really cool. I was really proud to be part of a company that would put so much effort into organizing this event. (Sarah, Customer Service, Bank)

Sarah did not hesitate in granting the firm credit:

> I want people to know what a great bank I work for. When everyone talks about how greedy banks are, I tell them about how [Bank name] did this cool thing. (Sarah, Customer Service, Bank)

A much lower level of involvement resulted in an assessment that deemed the firm to be an undeserving recipient of reward. John, the marketing representative identified in the opening scenario, raised skepticism in terms of the firm as a deserving recipient group when he said:

> Telling me that opportunity exists for volunteering barely counts as having done anything towards making it happen. (John, Marketing Representative, Manufacturing)

The level of support provided by the company for the volunteerism must be assessed to be qualitatively and quantitatively substantive relative to other work functions, priorities or demands:

I would use work time to do some of the stuff ... but it isn't like it was much time and it wasn't like I didn't put in tons of unpaid overtime anyway. They owed me so much more for all I give them. (Peggy, Accountant, Public Accounting Firm)

OK, they give me a few prizes for a silent auction. They would have likely thrown them out anyway. It's not like they donated a car or something that would hurt their precious bottom line. (Amil, Drug Store Employee, Drug Store)

Peggy considered the firm's contribution of work hours towards her volunteerism to be insufficient to warrant their taking credit for her volunteerism because the firm's contribution of work hours did not offset what she saw as their otherwise extreme demands on her time. Likewise, Amil assessed the firm's contribution as less deserving because he believed that the cost to the firm had been negligible.

A firm's entitlement to be considered a recipient group for credit was also influenced by the involvement of the actual management team in supporting the volunteerism:

Everyone from the manager to the lowest level employee were volunteering. It wasn't like the managers were just there supervising us at work. (Alura, Customer Service Representative, Food Services)

Here, Alura has differentiated the volunteer activity from other work-related tasks using a criterion of equal status in participation coupled with the perception that the volunteer effort is of shared importance to the management team. Although she continues to identify that in a work context these individuals would be her supervisors, in the volunteer context she perceives them to be peers. Her later judgment of this activity as a volunteer endeavor with credit shared between the employer and herself reflected this aspect of her evaluation:

I don't know really how to explain this. But, it was like, by prioritizing it as much as they did, the management team was telling us that we really matter to them and that they are doing their share to make this event work. It's not just all on us hourly-paid, low-level staff doing all the work. It's the team. The company team. (Alura, Customer Service Representative, Food Services)

The participants thus all explicitly raised the question: Is the employer doing its share? This "share" may involve the volunteerism of senior management or the provision of resources, such as time, salary or financial donation to the charity. If the firm does not partner with the employees in serving the needs of the nonprofit, the employees may perceive that the employer is unfairly taking credit for what they perceive to be their personal volunteerism.

The type of support offered by the firm to the employee appears to be a critical determinant of whether employees feel it is "fair" for the employer to take credit for the charitable work. If the employee is paid for the volunteer hours by the employer, as is the case when volunteerism is done during regular work hours or for extra financial compensation, then a greater apportion of the credit is due to the firm rather than the volunteer:

I was paid, that they used my time that way means that they get the credit. (Terry, Manager, Public Service)

Interestingly, if the firm is contributing to the CSEV endeavor in ways other than paying for the employees' time (for example, by giving supplies, money or other tangible contributions to the charity), then the employees appear to see the credit for the volunteerism as more shared, rather than more heavily being apportioned to the employer. The more the employer provides, the more the employee feels the company deserves to share in the credit for their portion of the goodwork. They are "in it together" and credit is thus more equally distributed. The employee makes a more positive assessment of the relationship between him/herself and the company as partners in a collaborative engagement:

We (business and employees) were all in it together. The business supplied money, time, our hours, everything it could. I have never enjoyed a volunteer experience so much. (Jahil, retail manager, building supply company)

There are enough "brownie points" to go around; we all contributed. (Alura, Customer Service Representative, Food Services)

The reward of the volunteer contribution is shared between the two stakeholder recipients:

It's fine with me that they profile this volunteer work on the website. I'm proud of what I did and they should be recognized for what they did too. (Francis, Warehouse Manager, Retail)

As discussed in an earlier section, employees consider charitable intention in deciding whether or not to participate in CSEV programs. Similarly, an element in the apportioning of the reward to themselves as volunteers was the employees' assessments of their own motivations for participation in the volunteer work:

I remember crossing the finish line (at a charity race) and being handed my time sheet ... these were extra to normal hours; I knew that I would be paid when I volunteered, but that isn't why I did it. (Mike, Military, Public Service)

If they are doing something good, even if they have to be there, it isn't optimal, but at least people are helping others by helping out. But, do I think they are superheroes for doing it? No. (Iris, Office Administration, Manufacturing)

The employees also explicitly assessed the motivation of their employer in determining their right to a portion of the credit for the good work:

They (company) clearly did it for the right reason and I am impressed by that. They wanted to help the school. I don't doubt that it paid off in terms of their rep [reputation] but it isn't what drove the decision and that is cool. (Francis, Warehouse Manager, Retail)

> *In (organization) they really don't care where we volunteer, just that we are involved in our communities. It shows me that the intention is in the right place and people should feel good about (organization) because of that. (Mike, Military, Public Service)*

This sentiment was shared by Alura who stated:

> *Their heart was in the right place and they deserve to be acknowledged because of that. (Alura, Customer Service Representative, Food Services)*

Speculating About Future Participation

Finally, participants considered whether they would engage in future CSEV efforts. Consistent with justice theory, employees will use the justice evaluation as data when predicting or making determinations of future behavior. Employees feel a greater willingness to engage in future CSEV activities when they believe that the credit has been appropriately distributed. Employees seem particularly drawn to CSEV activities where the reward was shared between themselves and the employer:

> *I couldn't wait until the next event. It brought us all together. We were a team doing something more important. (Francis, Warehouse Manager, Retail)*

> *It's hard to explain. I have always volunteered but done so on my own. That event was different. It was nice, more than nice, to see my bosses out there. I want to be part of a company where this happens. (Walther, Health Care Worker, Hospital)*

Although most participants did not discuss contribution ratios explicitly, there appears to be some evidence that employees do not feel as equally engaged in CSEV if the employer contribution overshadowed their own sense of volunteerism. This lack of engagement was evident for some employees who volunteered during work hours and received pay for their time working on the CSEV event:

> *Would I do it again? Doubt it. It just meant that the rest of my job, my real job, didn't get done. I'll volunteer on my own time where I want to volunteer not where they tell me to. (Terry, Manager, Public Service)*

It appears that variables, such as the payment for the hours of volunteering (which counters the standard definition of volunteerism as an unpaid activity) diminished both the sense of entitlement for the credit of doing a good work as well as the interest in further participating in CSEV programs. This reluctance for ongoing participation may be ameliorated, however, by the opportunity to participate in volunteerism which is of personal significance or choice:

> *I didn't want to do the run. It was the senior partner's pet cause. Not mine. I am going to find an excuse next year not to participate. I might as well have been at the office working on an account. But ... if they are good with it, I would like to use the volunteer time that they allow us to take to do something else. I really want to work with kids. Always have. (Gail, Accountant)*

What was also notable in the interviews was the intensity of resentment engendered when the organization assumed any credit for activity that the employee assesses to be undeserved:

> I do the [volunteer] work and they take the credit. It is a form of theft. They are using me. It really pisses me off. It is like they own me 24 hrs a day now and nothing I do on my own time belongs to me anymore. (Robert, Advertising Sales)

> I don't mind that I did the volunteer work. I feel really good about that. What I don't feel good about is that they took credit for it. It looks to others like I did this [volunteerism] as part of my job when really they had almost nothing to do with it, except send out the email telling us about the charity run. I can thank them for that, but nothing else of this was their effort. (Janet, Lawyer)

Conclusions

Companies support their employees' volunteerism in a variety of ways, and this support can be quite valuable for the recipient nonprofit organizations. Potential tensions arise, however, as credit for the volunteering effort is attributed. For the company, taking credit for employee volunteerism can help to position the firm as socially responsible, a trait that is very important to today's consumer. A company claiming credit for employee volunteer efforts may however result in resentment on the part of the employee, thus damaging employee morale and respect for the firm.

Employees actively consider the ascription of credit for CSEV, often facing an internal tension whereby they must decide how much credit they deserve for their part of the volunteering effort, and how much should be given to their company. This evaluation can be quite complex. Both the quantity and nature of the company's efforts are assessed; additionally employees consider their own contribution not simply in terms of activities performed, but also in terms of intent and motive for volunteering. This complex web of issues must be integrated to develop an overall assessment of fair credit attribution.

Our results demonstrate a four-step process through which employees make this assessment of credit attribution. They first consider, overall, what would be fair. They then decide whether to participate in a particular event or program. After participating they assess their experience and the benefits they feel that they and the company received, and finally they determine whether or not to do it again. Notions of equity, assessed throughout the process, are fundamental to their future participation decisions.

These findings are consistent with the theories of distributive justice that outline employees' attempts to fairly apportion rewards based on perceived contributions by two stakeholders, in this case the employer and the employee. By assessing relative contribution, employees may perceive equitable or inequitable distribution of rewards.[33] The employees will generalize their learning from the labeling and judgment phases and follow-up on their assessment of justice with the question: "What am I going to do now that I assess this event as fair/not fair?" and "What are the implications next time I am in similar circumstances?" Perceptions of inequitable credit attribution can lead to negative employee perceptions, even creating alienation and animosity.

These issues are extremely important for the company. Given current consumer sentiment, companies face a strong need to demonstrate CSR to the public. Consequently, companies seek to highlight their CSR efforts in every way possible. The company's need to gain recognition for CSR efforts can create tension with employees. If companies inappropriately take credit for employee volunteering efforts, employee relations are likely to suffer. Companies face the challenge of balancing the expectations of these two critical stakeholder groups, employees and the public. Our findings suggest that the key to this tenuous balance is paying careful attention to whose effort was actually expended. In some cases the company may need to downplay volunteer efforts to the public, in order to avoid offending employees. In others, the company may benefit from marketing company efforts to employees themselves, so employees are aware of the company's own contribution to the effort.

Acknowledgment

This research was supported by Imagine Canada's Knowledge Development Centre, which is funded as part of the Canada Volunteerism Initiative through the Community Participation Directorate of the Department of Canadian Heritage.

Notes

1   Porter, M. and Kramer, M. (2006), "Strategy and society: the link between competitive advantage and corporate social responsibility", *Harvard Business Review*, vol. 84, no. 12, pp. 78–92.

2   Basil, D.Z., Runté, M., Basil, M.D. and Usher, J. (2011), "Company support for employee volunteering: does size matter?", *Journal of Business Research*, vol. 64, no. 10, pp. 61–66; Basil, D.Z., Runté, M., Easwaramoorthy, M. and Barr, C. (2009), "Company support for employee volunteering: a national survey of companies in Canada", *Journal of Business Ethics*, vol. 85, no. 2, pp. 387–398; Houghton, S., Gabel, J. and Williams, D. (2009), "Connecting the two faces of CSR: does employee volunteerism improve compliance?", *Journal of Business Ethics,* vol. 87, no. 4, pp. 477–494; Peloza, J. and Hassay, D.N. (2006), "Intra-organizational volunteerism: good soldiers, good deeds and good politics", *Journal of Business Ethics,* vol. 64, no. 4, pp. 357–379.

3   Basil *et al.* (2009), op. cit.

4   Basil *et al.* (2011), op. cit.

5   Clary, E.G., Snyder, M., Ridge, R.D., Copeland, J., Stukas, A.A., Haugen, J. and Miene, P. (1998), "Understanding and assessing the motivations of volunteers: a functional approach", *Journal of Personality and Social Psychology*, vol. 74, no. 6, pp. 1516–1530; Finkelstein, M.A., Penner, L.A. and Brannick, M.T. (2005), "Motive, role identity, and prosocial personality as predictors of volunteer activity", *Social Behavior and Personality: An International Journal,* vol. 33, no. 4, pp. 403–418.

6   Basil *et al.* (2011), op. cit.; Basil *et al.* (2009), op. cit.

7   Greenberg, J. (1987), "Reactions to procedural injustice in payment distributions: do the means justify the ends?", *Journal of Applied Psychology*, vol. 72, no.1, pp. 55–61; Houghton *et*

al. (2009), op. cit.; Peterson, D. (2004), "Recruitment strategies for encouraging participation in corporate volunteer programs", *Journal of Business Ethics*, vol. 49, no. 4, pp. 371–386.

8   Basil *et al.* (2009), op. cit.

9   Porter and Kramer (2006), op. cit.

10 Basil *et al.* (2009), op. cit.

11 Maignan, I., Ferrell, O.C. and Hult, G.T.M. (1999), "Corporate citizenship: cultural antecedents and business benefits", *Journal of the Academy of Marketing Science*, vol. 27, no. 4, pp. 455–469.

12 Ellen P.S., Webb, D.J. and Mohr, L.A. (2006), "Building corporate associations: consumer attributions for corporate socially responsible programs", *Journal of the Academy of Marketing Science*, vol. 34, no. 2, pp. 147–57.

13 Rostami, J. and Hall, M. (1996), *Employee Volunteers: Business Support in the Community*, Canadian Centre for Philanthropy, Toronto, and Conference Board of Canada, Ottawa.

14 Points of Light Foundation (2002), *Corporate Volunteering Overview*, Points of Light Foundation, Washington, DC.

15 Verschoor, C.C. (2002), "Canadian study shows wide support for corporate responsibility", *Strategic Finance*, vol. 83, no. 10, pp. 20–22.

16 Peloza, J., Hudson, S. and Hassay, D.N. (2009), "The marketing of employee volunteerism", *Journal of Business Ethics*, vol. 85, no. 2, pp. 71–386.

17 Clary *et al.* (1998), op. cit.

18 Peterson (2004), op. cit.

19 Runté, M. and Basil, D.Z. (2011), "Personal and corporate volunteerism: employee motivations", *International Journal of Business Environment*, vol. 4, no. 2, pp. 133–145.

20 Ibid.

21 Caudron, S. (1994), "Volunteerism and the bottom line", *Industry Week*, vol. 243, pp. 13–16; Geroy, G., Wright, P. and Jacoby, L. (2000), "Toward a conceptual framework of employee volunteerism: an aid for the human resource manager", *Management Decision*, vol. 38, no. 4, pp. 280–286; Peterson, D. (2004), op. cit.; Points of Light (2002), op. cit.; Smith, C. (1994), "The new corporate philanthropy", *Harvard Business Review*, vol. 72, no. 3, pp. 105–115.

22 Wenzel, M. (2000), "Justice and identity: the significance of inclusion for perceptions of entitlement and the justice motive", *Personality and Social Psychology Bulletin*, vol. 26, no. 2, pp. 157–176.

23 Cohen, R.L. (1991), "Membership, intergroup relations, and justice". In Vermunt, R. and Steensma, H. (eds), *Social Justice in Human Relations*, vol. 1, Plenum, New York, pp. 239–257.

24 Folger, R. and Konovsky, M.A. (1989), "Effects of procedural and distributive justice on reactions to pay raise decisions", *Academy of Management Journal*, vol. 32, no. 1, pp. 115–130.

25 Murphy-Berman, V., Cukur, C.S. and Berman, J.J. (2002), "Micro- and macro-justice in the allocation of resources between in-group and out group members, a cross-cultural comparison", *Journal of Crosscultural Psychology*, vol. 33, no. 6, pp. 626–633; Roberson, Q. (2006), "Justice in teams: the activation and role of sensemaking in the emergence of justice climates", *Organizational Behavior and Human Decision Processes*, vol. 100, no. 2, pp. 177–192.

26 Harris, J.D. (2009), "What's wrong with executive compensation?", *Journal of Business Ethics*, vol. 85, Supp. 1, pp. 147–159.

27 Basil *et al.* (2009), op. cit.

28 Jasso, G. and Wegener, B. (1997), "Methods for empirical justice analysis: part I framework, models, and quantities", *Social Justice Research*, vol. 10, no. 4, pp. 393–430.

29 Greenberg, J. (1987), op. cit.

30   Basil *et al.* (2009), op. cit.; Basil *et al.* (2011), op. cit.; Runté, M., Basil, D.Z. and Runté, R. (2010), "Corporate support for employee volunteerism within Canada: a cross cultural perspective", *Journal of Nonprofit and Public Sector Marketing*, vol. 22, no. 4, pp. 247–263.

31   Runté and Basil (2011), op. cit.

32   Jasso and Wegener (1997), op. cit.

12 Indigenous People, Stakeholders and Corporate Social Responsibility

TOM COOPER* AND TERRY HICKEY†

Keywords

Aboriginal, corporate social responsibility, Indigenous peoples, natural resources, projects, risk management, stakeholder engagement.

Introduction

Indigenous peoples have a stake or are in control of many of the major natural resource projects in the developed (and in some cases) developing world.[1] Corporations involved in the resource and other sectors have to appropriately engage with Indigenous peoples to ensure project, business and organizational strategic success. Otherwise, tensions will emerge and business objectives, strategies and plans will be put in jeopardy. The question then becomes how do organizations effectively engage Indigenous peoples and other stakeholders to ensure corporate social responsibility (CSR) objectives.

Governments, NGOs and other transnational bodies have recognized the importance of managing the tension between stakeholders and Indigenous peoples.[2] Stakeholder tensions often arise when addressing the risk-based approach of major development projects, including operational and financial risk.[3] Projects need to be done, on time and hopefully on budget. Failure to engage Indigenous peoples effectively as stakeholders may create significant project and overall strategic risk for organizations.[4] Issues emerge as stakeholder engagement in an Indigenous context may be different than the standard, formalized approaches to CSR and stakeholder management. Moreover, the aims and goals of corporate projects, government agencies such as the World Bank and other stakeholders are mismatched with the time horizon of Indigenous communities and their sometimes contrasting strategic goals.

* Tom Cooper, Faculty Of Business Administration, Memorial University, St. John's, NL, A1B 3X5, Canada. E-mail: tcooper@mun.ca.

† Terry Hickey, Planning Resources Incorporated, St. John's, NL, A1C 2N2, Canada. E-mail: terry@planningresources.ca.

Indigenous peoples have historically gained little from large-scale resource or business development on their traditional lands. Moreover, Indigenous peoples and communities have suffered from the negative consequences of business, specifically natural resource development projects, on their culture, economies and societies. In some cases, this has resulted in entire opposition to resource development and, in many others, a fundamental change has been sought in the distribution of benefits and costs.[5] How Indigenous people are treated as stakeholders as well as links to wider issues of CSR is therefore intriguing from both an academic and practitioner standpoint.

Research shows that good corporate community relations, stakeholder engagement and consultation, as well as efforts to meet particular community demands are means by which organizations seek to improve reputation among those with the ability to impact operations and thereby attain a social license to operate.[6] All of these issues are even more pronounced in dealing with Indigenous communities whereby CSR, risk- and project-management objectives complicate stakeholder engagement. When not handled appropriately, pressure and conflict among stakeholders dealing with Indigenous peoples and communities may arise. This pressure and conflict may deflect from wider CSR, community and economic development objectives among a wide range of stakeholders.

Indigenous peoples have utilized a range of approaches in addressing their own and other stakeholder concerns, including efforts to win greater recognition of rights in international forums. Approaches have included pressure for passage of national and state or provincial legislation recognizing Indigenous land rights and protecting their culture; litigation in national and international courts; and direct political action aimed at governments and developers, often in alliance with non-governmental organizations (NGOs).[7] How Indigenous peoples and the stakeholders engaging with them manage these wide range of tensions and risks in addressing their own and other concerns also puts forward lessons for those interested in engagement from a multitude of stakeholders' perspective, traditionally disadvantaged stakeholder groups, and how this should be attended to within a wider CSR context.

In this chapter, we explore the role of Indigenous peoples as stakeholders in the context of the development of business projects across the world. The basis of our exploration is our own experience as researchers and consultants in the Indigenous peoples' economic and community development field. We use the experience of over 30 projects we have been involved in during the last five years (please see Appendix A) to explore stakeholder management with Indigenous peoples, tensions that emerge and models to take engagement forward.

Indigenous Peoples

The United Nations Economic and Social Council contends that the dominant models of development have compromised Indigenous peoples in every aspect of their daily lives, including the imposition of large infrastructure projects on their lands without their consent.[8] This has generated poverty and severe inequality, massive environmental devastation and human rights violations. Moreover this development, pursued by the private sector, ignores Indigenous peoples' own governance, economic, social, education, cultural, spiritual and knowledge systems as well as the natural resources that have sustained them through the generations—specifically their human rights.[9] Indigenous peoples fall under the Universal Declaration on Human Rights implicitly because they are of a different national origin than most inhabitants of "settler" societies such as Canada and Australia. There are also important Indigenous peoples' rights enshrined national legislation such as Acts of Parliament.[10]

From a stakeholder perspective, the fundamental right conferred by the protection of human rights is identified in Article 2 of the Universal Declaration as freedom from discrimination of groups such as "race, colour, sex, language, religion, political or other opinion, national or social origin, property, birth or other status".[11] Ultimately Indigenous peoples are distinct in terms of their national or social origin within most "settled" and other societies. This makes them an important stakeholder group to be considered because they have different rights than other community groups[12] who may not hold the same obligations accrued from legislation or through the Universal declaration.

From the perspective of the right-based principles, in addition to the general human rights guidance rooted in internationally recognized UN declarations, covenants and treaties, captured in the United Nations Norms on the Responsibilities of Transnational Corporations and other Business Enterprises with Regard to Human Rights, there are also codes of conduct specifically for businesses that are rooted in the UN such as the Global Compact and the Voluntary Principles on Security and Human Rights that address, either explicitly or implicitly, Indigenous peoples. There are risk-based principles on dealing with Indigenous peoples including the International Finance Corporation's Safeguard Policies, related guidance documents and the Equator Principles. For example, the role of the World Bank in setting international standards and rules for engagements between mining companies and local Indigenous communities is significant and growing.[13] There are a multitude of stakeholders involved in the engagement of Indigenous peoples.

In this chapter, following on from Hindle,[14] we capitalize the word Indigenous as a mark of respect for its peoples. Most of our insights in this paper emerge specifically from Canada, although there are numerous case studies in the rest of North America as well as the Asia Pacific region[15] that have relevance to examining stakeholder management and Indigenous peoples.

Struggles by Indigenous peoples over resource extraction may be seen as a part of a broader fight to assert their right to self-determination and control over their lands, territories and resources. This struggle is globally organized through local, regional, national and international Indigenous organizations as well as through networks of stakeholders that may include non-Indigenous organizations.[16] A tension that emerges for stakeholders involved with Indigenous peoples is that it is sometimes unclear who they are, their goals and wider remit.

As described by the Secretariat of the Permanent Forum on Indigenous Issues in a 2004 workshop on data collection and disaggregation for Indigenous peoples by the United Nations, considerable thinking and debate have been devoted to the question of definition of "Indigenous peoples", but no such definition has ever been adopted by any United Nations system body.[17]

One of the most cited descriptions of the concept of the Indigenous was given by Jose R. Martinez Cobo, the Special Rapporteur of the Sub-Commission on Prevention of Discrimination and Protection of Minorities, in his study on the problem of discrimination against Indigenous populations.[18] In this study, he offered a working definition which stated that:

Indigenous communities, peoples and nations are those which, having a historical continuity with pre-invasion and pre-colonial societies that developed on their territories, consider themselves distinct from other sectors of the societies now prevailing on those territories, or parts of them. They form at present non-dominant sectors of society and are determined to preserve, develop and transmit to future generations their ancestral territories, and their ethnic identity, as the basis of their continued existence as peoples, in accordance with their own cultural patterns, social institutions and legal system.[19]

The tensions that emerge from the confusion as to whom Indigenous peoples are may be due to them not being a homogenous group. For example, the Canadian constitution recognizes three groups of Indigenous peoples: Indians (commonly referred to as First Nations), Métis and Inuit. These are three distinct peoples with unique histories, languages, cultural practices and spiritual beliefs. More than one million people in Canada identify themselves as an Indigenous person, according to the 2006 Canadian Census.[20] Natural resource companies dealing with Indigenous peoples as a homogeneous group for stakeholder management or CSR purposes may create issues. Tensions exist within and between communities as well as Indigenous peoples' ethnic groups.

Where and how to engage is also problematic. In Canada and elsewhere, Indigenous communities are located in urban, rural and remote locations, and include:

- First Nations or Indian Bands, generally located on lands called reserves;
- Inuit communities located in Nunavut, North Western Territories, Northern Quebec (Nunavik) and Labrador;
- Métis communities; and
- Communities of Indigenous peoples' people (including Métis, non-status Indians, Inuit and First Nation individuals) in cities or towns which are not part of reserves or traditional territories.

The relevance of exploring stakeholder engagement and management with Indigenous peoples as well as the tensions that emerge from the multitude of stakeholders involved is also timely.

Resource exploration and exploitation is rapidly expanding in remote regions of the world where large-scale projects have not taken place traditionally. The factors behind this rapid expansion include sustained high demand and prices for many commodities, not only minerals but also forestry, fishing and other natural resources; declining numbers of readily accessible lucrative natural resources; increased accessibility to equity and debt financing through public and private sources and international financial institutions; regulatory revisions in many countries that provide fiscal and regulatory regimes to different stakeholders, privileged access to land and advantageous ownership as well as profit repatriation provisions.[21] This creates tensions and strains between stakeholders with different goals and, in some cases, conflicting objectives.

For example, as mining companies move into areas such as the highlands of Papua New Guinea or the northern parts of Canada, they frequently encroach on lands and territories of Indigenous peoples.[22] Another example would be financial services firms who want to take advantage of a growing Indigenous sector but may also conflict with ownership and governance issues.[23] Corporations wanting to partner on tourism or leisure sector activities may also face barriers or issues in relation to cultural or spiritual elements of Indigenous communities. Finally, joint venture or partnership arrangements may suffer in the face of differing time, control and strategic objectives as well as legal/regulatory issues around Indigenous ownership.

For example, in a study we conducted on access to capital for Indigenous peoples, one community leader noted the following:

> *Capital, and access to it, is a key ingredient in economic activity. As we look to future economic development it is imperative that First Nations have ownership and control over such an essential lever of the economy. Alternatively, a nation which does not control the essential levers of its economy will always be subject to the influence of the external forces which do control these levers. The financial services industry which provides capital to our communities is an essential element for our future growth and development.*[24]

Issues of control and ownership have to be considered and included in any engagement with Indigenous peoples. Moreover, essential elements that are seen in a non-Indigenous context as bargaining points may be perceived or even enshrined as rights in an Indigenous one.

Indigenous peoples' economic development is a field that is exemplified by incomplete projects, partly realized partnerships, intercultural miscues, misunderstandings and expectations by stakeholders that "Indigenous peoples will simply, ultimately, be just like us, whoever and whatever 'they' are".[25] Misunderstanding and communication is also exemplified in the role of other stakeholders such as government; confusion and tensions emerging between the interests of corporations seeking resource rights on Indigenous lands and by self-interested governments who represent the "national" interest.[26] This conflicts with the representative interest of Indigenous peoples whose experience has been predominantly social, economic and cultural exclusion from the "national interest". Ultimately, appealing to national or regional interests or even corporate responsibility when engaging with Indigenous peoples further exacerbates existing tensions as to whose interest to promote and why.

Why is Engaging with Indigenous Communities as Stakeholders Important?

In "settler" societies such as Australia and Canada it is now commonplace for CSR commitments to be enshrined in legally binding agreements between companies and Indigenous landowners—a practice also increasingly common in some developing countries.[27] CSR, or at least a perception of it, is a key element of project or business success when dealing with Indigenous peoples. For example, experience has shown that if local Indigenous communities view a prospective natural resources company as an undesirable presence in their region, the company will face a longer development process and perhaps even find it impossible to operate in a hostile context.[28]

As a result, many of the organizations that undertake large-scale resource projects have sought to address concerns regarding the impact of their activities on Indigenous peoples by adopting CSR policies.[29] However, this may be only being done for reputational risk or ceremonial compliance purposes. Tensions emerge because CSR is being done in a manner that may be consistent with norms and expectations in larger non-Indigenous communities but not locally, regionally or in a manner that is consistent with Indigenous peoples' pillars of consent, participation and control.[30]

Indigenous communities and peoples are also not homogeneous in their experience of corporate policies and activities. There have been some very positive experiences— and some negative ones. Positive experiences would include the TD bank partnership with First Nations groups in Canada during the early part of this century.[31] Negative ones would be the nonengagement of seafood corporations with Indigenous fishers post the Marshall decision in Atlantic Canada since 1997.[32] While CSR agreements have important advantages, especially in establishing standards for company performance and corporate accountability, they may also bring about significant challenges to Indigenous groups.[33] The wider political, legal and administrative frameworks of CSR agreements may neglect to understand the context of Indigenous peoples and their communities, creating tensions and failure through ineffective stakeholder engagement.

Projects and organizations have to consider the impact of change that Indigenous peoples will have on business models. From a business perspective, opportunities are significant, timely and relevant. In Canada, for example, with help from billions of dollars in land claim settlements and joint ventures with established corporations, Indigenous groups are starting more businesses. For example, Indigenous peoples' own and control 20 percent of the Canadian land mass and this is expected to rise to 30 percent in the next 15 years.[34] Land rights are enshrined in government legislation[35] and this ownership will have a direct impact on companies' business models and plans. Government, NGOs and other transnational organizations (such as the World Bank) also have to consider the impact that Indigenous peoples will have on wider issues of CSR, environmental regulations and community development.

The Canadian experience shows that the Indigenous population is growing, on average per year, at a rate of 4.1 percent—more than five times the national average. In 2010, Indigenous people make up over 4 percent of Canada's population—over 1.3 million people. For example, this provides opportunity for firms in the financial services sector, as there is a rapid growth of the Indigenous population, increased access to resources and the emergence of a strong Indigenous business community all requiring increased access to capital.[36] As a result of this growth and power, corporations may take advantage of the opportunity to engage effectively with Indigenous peoples and their communities. Joint ventures may be proposed but then tensions may arise with regulators who want to ensure the same level of control and standards that a non-Indigenous organization may have. Stakeholder management and engagement is then further complicated as to whose interest to promote: the corporations, the regulators or the Indigenous peoples. Moreover, normative elements—what is the "right" thing to do for a retributive justice standpoint—may be in conflict with the business case for a particular decision as to how, when and where to engage.

Economic development needs for Indigenous communities are widespread and varied. Tourism, energy and community infrastructure projects are targeted as helping Indigenous communities address the systematic barriers around poverty and economic development.[37] Corporations and other stakeholders may engage with Indigenous communities to take advantage of a wide range of business models and projects. The diversity of projects with Indigenous peoples and their impact may also cause tensions for stakeholder engagement and CSR.

Opportunities for development have to be tempered with the reality that stakeholders are facing in dealing with Indigenous peoples and communities. In Canada, according to a 2004 study on equity capital and First Nations business development, First Nations in Canada "confront poverty, geographic and cultural isolation, infrastructure deficiencies, poor links to markets, low capacity for business development and growth as well as the flight of skilled human resources to urban centers".[38] These systemic barriers are reasons for business organizations and others to understand the CSR challenges in engaging Indigenous communities as stakeholders in the development and management of projects and joint ventures. Not understanding or addressing these barriers, as well as the impact on CSR policies in developing projects that affect Indigenous peoples as stakeholders, may be problematic. For example, internationally the risk-based lending policies of the World Bank explicitly recognize the importance of the effect of projects on Indigenous peoples. Not recognizing or engaging with Indigenous peoples in an effective manner to ensure that the consequences of projects are well understood and managed may cause problems such as not being able to access capital.[39] As a result, a wide range of stakeholder concerns have to be managed simultaneously when dealing with Indigenous peoples.

Stakeholders and Indigenous Peoples

The reason to understand how and why to effectively engage Indigenous peoples as stakeholders may also be found in theory. Freeman originally defined stakeholders as "any group or individual who can affect or is affected by the achievement of the organization's objectives",[40] but many view this definition as too broad to be workable,[41] especially when viewed from a project and Indigenous perspective. Perhaps surprisingly, little consensus from a theory perspective has been achieved on the question of which stakeholders managers should pay attention to on a project and risk basis, especially when it comes to engaging Indigenous communities.[42] Tensions emerge from a multitude of stakeholders and prioritization is difficult. Risk-based principles from one stakeholder, for example the International Finance Corporation's Safeguard Policies, in projects affecting Indigenous peoples may conflict with related guidance documents and the Equator Principles. The role of the World Bank in setting international standards and rules for engagements between resource companies and local Indigenous communities is also significant and growing.[43] There may be too many stakeholders with a multitude of competing priorities to be engaged when dealing with Indigenous peoples to use standard models and approaches.

As outlined by Maon and colleagues (2010),[44] stakeholder theory has emerged as crucial for understanding and describing the structures and dimensions of business and societal relationships. At its core, stakeholder theory helps to specify the groups or persons to whom organizations are ultimately responsible and provides a basis for legitimizing stakeholder influences on organization's decisions.

The moral philosophical foundation of stakeholder theory is routed primarily in deontological and/or social contract approaches whereby stakeholders cannot be treated merely as means to organizational ends, but rather are valuable in their own right and as ends in themselves.[45] Resorting to stakeholder theory commonly appears to be a necessary element in the normative process of managing CSR objectives,[46] especially when engaging with Indigenous communities.

From a strategic management standpoint, instrumental stakeholder theory links means and ends in addressing stakeholders.[47] In the management of stakeholders, organizational success is tied to the ability to manage stakeholders including ultimately their engagement. It may be possible then to argue that the ability of organizations to engage in a participatory stakeholder management approach with Indigenous peoples is validated by its instrumental validity.

Participants also needs to recognize that when engaging with Indigenous peoples, there may be a need to distinguish them as primary stakeholders,[48] even when a standardized approach to stakeholder engagement from an instrumental standpoint may not. This would be consistent with the approach of scholars who have suggested that organizations may have to adopt different approaches to engagement with primary stakeholders, including such strategies as proaction and accommodation.[49] As described in theory, proaction is to anticipate responsibility and accommodation is to accept responsibility.[50] More importantly for Indigenous peoples, a proaction strategy attempts to enhance the interests of a particular stakeholder without bargaining for concessions, as seen in the accommodation approach. Ultimately both strategies, from a theory standpoint, may make sense when dealing with Indigenous peoples yet little in the extant literature would indicate how or why to adopt either a proaction or accommodation strategy in an Indigenous context.

The trend in the stakeholder literature is also to include power relationships and the participatory nature of the relationships. As outlined by Jahansoozi,[51] academic interest in organization–stakeholder relationships stresses the need for organizations to understand, listen and develop a dialog with their important stakeholders such as Indigenous peoples. Ultimately a "conflict-reduction" approach away from a "revenue-generation" paradigm is based on the premise that important stakeholder groups, such as Indigenous peoples, preferred to be connected to organizations that invested in developing and maintaining relationships.[52] Jahansoozi further contends that focusing on relationships and a participatory approach moves the perspective away from the organization being viewed as the focal point in a stakeholder map. The actual interest instead lies with the relationships fostered by engagement considered essential for maintaining the organization's social license to operate.[53] In our experience, the development of these relationships (especially long-term ones) is crucial for any stakeholder engagement with Indigenous peoples.

Trust, commitment, satisfaction, control mutuality and dialog can all be considered to be essential to stakeholder engagement because without these critical success factors, the relationship would decline or no longer make strategic sense. For long-term relationships with extensive time horizons such as those necessary for engagement with Indigenous peoples, trust becomes even more important. It is only when trust has declined due to a crisis, or been eroded over time owing to perceived organizational practices such as failure to implement a benefits package for an Indigenous community, that transparency becomes an essential relational characteristic. When there is a lack of trust or a state of distrust exists in the organization–stakeholder relationship, transparency is a required condition for rebuilding trust and commitment in the relationship.[54]

Transparency is linked to openness and is described as being both a characteristic as well as an environmental condition for organizational processes. Transparency provides a number of outcomes that are beneficial for stakeholder engagement. As well as rebuilding trust, transparency can be viewed as promoting accountability, collaboration, cooperation and commitment. When an organization's decision-making and operational processes around stakeholder engagement are transparent accountability is possible. Internal and external stakeholders are able to see where (and how) the responsibility lies.[55]

Transparency as element of building trust is also important as stakeholders change throughout the life cycle of an organization or an issue such as a project with Indigenous peoples. Some stakeholders will become convinced in the future or only on certain projects[56]—however we have found that at the beginning of any project, venture, or engagement with Indigenous peoples, the element of uncertainty as to whether to engage is not an issue. Indigenous peoples as stakeholders must be engaged in a participatory manner.

In our experience, a pragmatic definition to facilitate the identification of stakeholders involved with an Indigenous project has been suggested by Nickols, who defines a stakeholder as "a person or group with an interest in seeing the endeavour succeed and without whose support the endeavour would fail".[57] Adopting a transactions-based perspective that emphasizes stakeholder contributions and inducements, Nickols argued that stakeholders "put something in and take something out" and must see value in the exchange.[58] This framing of the stakeholder approach can be usefully applied to the examination of the multitude of stakeholders involved in business and resource projects involving Indigenous communities. Nickol's definition is parsimonious and its focus on stakeholder value offers a useful point of convergence for comparing and aligning the interests of, and benefits to, the multitude of stakeholders involved with Indigenous peoples, business and resource projects. Specifically—what is being taken in—and what is being taken out.

The extant literature shows that managers need to accommodate the interests of strategic stakeholders because of their ability to provide or withhold resources needed by the organization.[59] Stakeholder theory also suggests that taking into account and accommodating stakeholder interests will lead to superior achievement of firm performance objectives and several studies have examined the validity of this claim.[60] The need for superior performance around objectives is especially true in engaging as well as managing the tensions emerging in the multitude of stakeholder interests in projects involving Indigenous peoples. Stakeholders are most likely to support the organization when they believe they have been fairly considered, fairly treated and fairly rewarded[61] and the same holds in an Indigenous context.[62] Building trust-based cooperative ties with stakeholders also enhances organizational legitimacy, producing stakeholder support and creating environmental stability, benefiting organizations over the long term.[63] The same should hold for ensuring that Indigenous people are engaged and tensions are managed when a multitude of stakeholders are involved.

Model of Stakeholder Engagement with Indigenous Peoples

In order to further the understanding of stakeholder engagement with Indigenous peoples, we now outline two related models to examine an approach through a number of critical success factors. Models for understanding Indigenous peoples have been explored in the literature at a macro level, especially in the economic development literature.[64] We attempt to take the analysis down to a lower level to assist in stakeholder engagement.

In order to effectively engage with Indigenous peoples, it is important to recognize that there are a number of critical success factors that must be identified, managed and controlled (Figure 12.1).

Stakeholders such as corporations, NGOs, governments and Indigenous communities have to recognize elements such as risk and time in any approach to stakeholder engagement. Moreover these elements have to be recognized as critical success factors for project and business model success.

The first critical success factor, *risk*, would include risk to the project or business model being proposed, and spiritual as well as cultural risk. [65] As with any risk, there are both upsides—if spiritual risk is identified and well managed then there may be better engagement with the Indigenous community—and downsides: if there is no recognition of cultural risk, in a proposed tourism project for example, then problems may emerge.

The second element to be considered is *time*. Our research and projects with Indigenous peoples have seen than the time horizons are different—usually longer— than when dealing with non-Indigenous stakeholders.[66] This means, for example, that time management issues are very complicated and have to be considered in any project or engagement process. Time also affects elements of ownership, control and governance. Indigenous peoples want to own (either full or partially) many of the business projects they are involved in on their own lands. Ownership gives them control over projects and outcomes and implicitly and explicitly brings forward issues around governance.[67] As a result, the process of governance needs to be very transparent in order to fully articulate benefits both in the short and long term.

Transparency and accountability, two of the main tenets of any approach to CSR, are also important parts of a stakeholder engagement model with Indigenous peoples. Stakeholders such as corporations, NGOs and government have to be transparent and

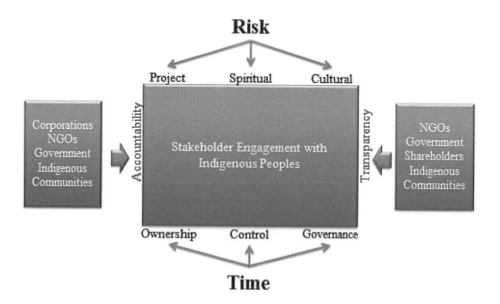

Figure 12.1 Critical success factors in stakeholder engagement with Indigenous peoples

accountable in their approach to Indigenous peoples—otherwise there will be non-effective engagement.

Our experience in working with Indigenous peoples, communities and other stakeholders has shown us that a participatory approach is essential when engaging with Indigenous peoples.[68] A participatory approach, in explicitly engaging and gaining consent, is critical in meeting Indigenous elements of time and risk as well as congruence with an organization's broader CSR strategy. A participatory approach, moreover, is recognizant of the multitude of stakeholder tensions and the heterogeneity within Indigenous peoples.

The concept of participation is consistent with a participatory research approach whereby research is done *with* rather than *on* people.[69] In the case of stakeholder engagement, this would involve engaging explicitly within an Indigenous context. It would also involve understanding the issues, opportunities and barriers facing Indigenous peoples before commencing with formalized stakeholder engagement.

For an effective approach to CSR and Indigenous peoples' stakeholder engagement, there needs to be both a participatory as well as a formalized stakeholder engagement process. The ideal strategy would be one whereby the approach is driven by consent, recognition of the risks involved in the approach and overall management of opportunities and benefits for Indigenous peoples and their communities.

An understanding of Indigenous stakeholder management can be best achieved through three concepts: control, participation and consent.[70] Ultimately these three concepts are consistent with most of the stakeholder literature. However, it is important to understand and reiterate these within an Indigenous content as issues such as rights management, appropriate cultural and spiritual risk as well as traditional knowledge all emanate from each of the different concepts.[71] Figure 12.2 outlines these three elements:

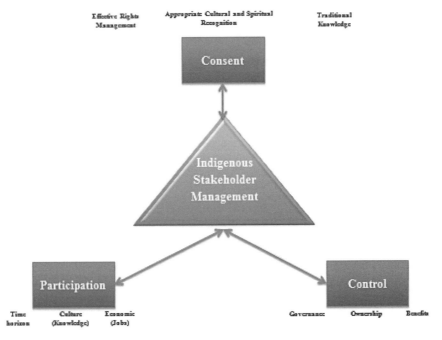

Figure 12.2 Elements of Indigenous peoples' stakeholder management

Consent

Consent is a key element of any Indigenous peoples' engagement activity and the notion of free, prior and informed consent is the basis of any stakeholder management. A number of specific issues emerge when considering consent as an element of Indigenous peoples' stakeholder engagement.

Effective rights management must be considered as a part of consent. The rights of Indigenous peoples' to natural resources—whether it be minerals, forestry or fishing—are usually enshrined in legal or regulatory bodies. In order to access these resources in a manner consistent with appropriate stakeholder engagement practice, consent must be given. How these rights will be protected and accessed by a wide range of stakeholders, including government, regulators, Indigenous and non-Indigenous communities, must be part of the engagement process.

Appropriate cultural and spiritual recognition is an also important issue and a vital consideration in any Indigenous peoples' business project.[72] The same holds true for aspects such as traditional knowledge, usually through the involvement of elders or other leaders in the community.

Participation

The second element of participation means that Indigenous peoples must believe and be actively shown they are participating as part of the stakeholder engagement process as well as the wider business or project. CSR agreements are being used more frequently to demonstrate this participation on behalf of corporations. CSR agreements can also offer preferential access to employment, training and business development opportunities for members of Indigenous groups or for Indigenous peoples' organizations. The reasons for ensuring that these CSR agreements are in place are important. Income levels tend to be considerably lower, and unemployment levels considerably higher, in Indigenous peoples' communities than in mainstream ones, and access to such opportunities can be critical in helping to overcome Indigenous peoples' economic disadvantages.[73] Agreements between Indigenous peoples and other stakeholders may also provide opportunities to be involved proactively, and on an ongoing basis, in managing the cultural, social and environmental impacts of business operations.[74] Participation may be explicit in terms of recording economic benefits accruing, or it may be implicit in that the stakeholder engagement is done in a manner consistent with cultural norms and expectations that are seen in Indigenous communities.

Control

The third element that must be considered in Indigenous stakeholder management is control. Issues of governance, by whom and how the venture will be governed, ownership of the project and finally the benefits that will accrue to the Indigenous peoples and communities, must be considered in addressing Indigenous stakeholder management. Organizations tend to fit stakeholder engagement and community relations into a much larger strategic picture than what may be occurring in a remote area of Canada or Papua

New Guinea. As a result, Indigenous peoples, leaders or communities may be ignored as part of the stakeholder engagement. The exclusion of Indigenous institutions (both representative and customary) from wider processes of decision-making (the board, the industry, processing and consumption sectors) may cause further stakeholder tensions to emerge.[75]

Understanding the three elements of consent, participation and control assists stakeholders in developing a more appropriate approach to Indigenous management and how it should be considered within a broader CSR strategy.

One of the challenges to corporations or other entities engaging Indigenous peoples is also understanding that they are coming from a different conceptual framework than mainstream institutions. This framework is influenced by their history, their experiences under legislation and regulations such as the Indian Act in Canada, prior experience with non-Indigenous cultures, an enduring collective memory and a communally based culture and lifestyle.[76]

Recognizing the need for an Indigenous peoples'-focused stakeholder framework is essential to effective engagement. A different conceptual framework would be manifest in a number of practical ways—experience and expectations of employment, the idea of personal and communal ownership of property, communication etc. Stakeholders that accept engagement at face value based on their prior experience in mainstream settings may find themselves dealing with unexpected situations. A participatory approach, as outlined in the previous models, would be more consistent with managing the multitude of stakeholders involved with engaging Indigenous peoples. Ultimately it may also help to minimize the occurrence of unexpected situations and help to develop more robust business models and projects.

Discussion and Conclusions

It is not only corporate organizations that have to recognize the challenges and pressures in engaging and managing stakeholder concerns with Indigenous peoples. For example, along with the systematic barriers facing Indigenous communities is the historic disregard for their rights by stakeholders such as government. In Australia, for example, Indigenous concerns were largely set aside by governments that actively pursued development of Hamersley Iron's Marandoo Mine, Century Mine in the Gulf of Carpentaria and the Jabiluka uranium mine in the Northern Territory.[77] Ensuring that all stakeholders, not just corporations, effectively engage with Indigenous peoples is important to ensure success.

The reason for understanding how and why noncorporate stakeholders such as governments engage with Indigenous communities is also important. Concerted government efforts to facilitate resource-based and other business projects, regardless of expressed opposition or concerns of local communities, deepens Indigenous peoples' disenchantment with formal structures and processes of government. Indigenous peoples and their communities may not recognize the role and/or authority of the non-Indigenous local government, which causes issues for corporations wishing to engage with Indigenous people through normal government routes.[78] Formalized or more specifically standardized approaches to stakeholder engagement may not work.

Ultimately, how government, corporations and other stakeholders engage with Indigenous peoples, as well as the role of NGOs and the communities themselves in promoting business projects, is vital—not only in the more timely execution of project milestones but also for the betterment of all. The numerous stakeholders involved in projects that engage Indigenous communities need reliable and comprehensive management consistent with a local and contextual understanding in order to secure benefits and opportunities for all the stakeholders involved.

Central to stakeholder theory is the notion that organizations should be managed in the interests of all their constituents, as opposed to solely the interests of their owners. In the case of business projects involving Indigenous peoples, this means not only understanding the profits that may accrue but also the long-term impact, risks and time horizons. Instrumental theory contends that organizations should achieve superior performance if their managers are able to balance the interests of stakeholders over time,[79] and the same is true in engaging Indigenous communities as stakeholders. However, an understanding of risk and time horizon is very much a balancing act that has to be achieved by a multitude of stakeholders, therefore creating many tensions in the engagement process.

The question then is how to achieve an appropriate balance and therefore better management of stakeholders' concerns when developing engagements models for Indigenous peoples? We hope that the models we have proposed within this chapter assist in the dialog as to how best to engage Indigenous peoples to ensure effective strategic and corporate objectives as well as wider CSR goals.

Recognizing that the time horizon and risk approach of Indigenous communities are different, and need to be managed, is an important element of any stakeholder engagement model, helping to develop better strategic approaches to CSR.

Increased formalization based on standardized approaches to a multitude of stakeholder engagement, involving processes of "stakeholder engagement", "communities relations programs" and formal agreement-making, can often serve to sterilize and limit the ability of stakeholders to engage with Indigenous peoples. The heterogeneity of Indigenous peoples, their experience with business and economic development and the number and type of stakeholders involved may ultimately constrain the issues that can be negotiated, restrict the time frame for issue resolution to a negotiation timetable, or exclude issues (or groups) that do not fit within the terms of negotiation set by the organization or relevant legislation.

While there is an increasing attempt to embed social and moral distinctions into a technical framework when engaging with Indigenous peoples, there is also a need to acknowledge that some elements exist in a space outside policies and procedures.[80] Having stakeholders be more participative in their approach to engaging with Indigenous peoples is a critical success factor in understanding elements such as consent and control that exist outside of normal policies and procedures. Recognizing the place and context of stakeholder engagement with Indigenous peoples becomes incredibly important.

The question that emerges when engaging with Indigenous peoples is, "Does stakeholder engagement have to be located in 'place', in real time, between people on the ground in order to be meaningful?" For example, bankers and finance executives investing in Indigenous peoples' territories have a different kind of engagement with communities. What does it mean for financial services professionals, managing risks and investments from their offices at Canary Wharf in London or Bay Street in Toronto to think about questions of Indigenous rights? Is the distance between their realities so great that the idea of meaningful engagement becomes unachievable? A single day of cross-cultural training cannot equip executives to deal with the complex issues or tensions emerging from Indigenous rights, histories of colonialism, the specificities of particular Indigenous cultures and peoples as well as the impacts of resource development projects on subsistence livelihoods.[81]

Developing appropriate models and methods for Indigenous peoples' stakeholder engagement can be a suitable approach to overcoming place relations and the impact of development projects on communities. Much may be learnt from dealing with Indigenous peoples because the business reasons for stakeholder engagement may not always be clear as is usually the case for developing formalized models grounded on issues of sustainability, triple-bottom-line reporting and CSR.

In dealing with Indigenous peoples there will not always be a clear business case from a CSR standpoint. Issues such as consent, control and participation may need to be considered outside the norms of the usual CSR and stakeholder engagement processes. Moreover, the lack of a standard business case may create further stakeholder tensions, especially with governments and NGOs. Tensions arise due to beliefs as to the profit motive, organizational effectiveness and project milestones that are subsumed under different cultural norms and rights-based issues when dealing with Indigenous peoples. Further complications may arise due to the number of stakeholders involved. Engaging with Indigenous peoples as well as the stakeholders involved in their community development is a complex area where a standard approach may not work or be appropriate. Contextual elements such as time and risk as well as the history of Indigenous peoples must be considered in the stakeholder engagement process.

Ultimately, pressures and conflicts emerge from a stakeholder perspective when dealing with Indigenous communities and these must be reviewed and considered as an important element in dealing with Indigenous peoples. Understanding the context of the engagement and the central pillars of consent, participation and control may assist in reducing tensions between stakeholder groups and lead to a more satisfactory outcome. Recognizing that Indigenous peoples may be different yet very important may also have salience to the process of engaging with other distinct or underrepresented groups in an approach to stakeholder engagement and CSR. However, much is to be done to further enhance the rights of Indigenous peoples and ensuring effective stakeholder engagement is one step in the process of enhancing these obligations.

Appendix A

A table of projects and research conducted by the authors with Indigenous peoples

Topic of project	# of projects	Main issues	Key actors involved
Governance	3	• How to ensure effective project governance in an Indigenous context • Appropriate level of Indigenous control and governance in joint ventures • Governance models that reflect an Indigenous context and priorities • Board and council planning—committees of the board, corporate governance issues etc.	• Government—provincial and federal • Joint venture partners • Indigenous communities • Natural resource companies • Stakeholders within Indigenous communities (elders, youth, council representatives)
Economic development	7	• Best practices to ensure effective economic development in an Indigenous context • Strategies and priorities in Indigenous community economic development—policy and procedure development • Approach to dealing with non-Indigenous partners in economic development • Securing government funding and programs to assist in economic development	• Indigenous communities • Joint venture partners • Suppliers and creditors • Stakeholders within Indigenous communities (elders, youth, council representatives) • Government (state and federal) • Financial services providers
Business development	6	• Indigenous business planning and development—social enterprises and "for-profit" businesses • Marketing and communication planning for Indigenous businesses and ventures • Sales strategies to Indigenous and non-Indigenous consumers • Training programs for Indigenous businesses and communities • Development of websites and other online material to promote culture and heritage • Development of management information systems for Indigenous training and skills assessment	• Indigenous business owners and social entrepreneurs (both reserve and off reserve) • Existing joint-venture partners and potential partners • Financial services firms • Indigenous community stakeholders (chief and council, youth, elders) • Local non-Indigenous communities • Indigenous groups (planning groups etc.)

Topic of project	# of projects	Main issues	Key actors involved
Strategic planning	5	• Strategic planning and development • Indigenous culture-focused strategic management frameworks • Strategic risk management model development in an Indigenous context • Risk assessments and review	• Indigenous communities (chief and council) • Government representatives • Natural resources companies • Financial services firms • Academia • Other Indigenous community stakeholders
Access to natural resources	6	• Review of specific Indigenous communities access to natural resources • Engagement models with natural resources companies and Indigenous peoples • Success factors in accessing natural resources	• Indigenous communities and organizations • Natural resource companies • Academia • Government • NGOs
Cultural and heritage protection and development	4	• Development of websites and other online material to protect culture and heritage • Development of management information systems for culture and heritage protection • Review and development of business models around culture and heritage development	• Various levels of government (including nonAboriginal affairs departments) • Outside suppliers • Indigenous communities and stakeholders within communities

Notes

1   O'Fairchellaigh, C. (2008a), "Introduction". In C. O'Fairchellaigh and S. Ali (eds), *Earth Matters: Indigenous Peoples, The Extractive Industries and Corporate Social Responsibility*, Greenleaf Publishing, Sheffield, UK, pp. 1–8.

2   Coumans, C. (2008), "Realising solidarity: indigenous peoples and NGOs in the contested terrains of mining and corporate accountability". In C. O'Fairchellaigh and S. Ali (2008), op. cit, pp. 42–67.

3   Akintoye, A., Bowen, P. and Van Wyk, R. (2008), "Project risk management practice: the case of a South African utility company", *International Journal of Project Management*, vol. 26, no. 2, pp. 149–163.

4   Cooper, T. and Ulnooweg Development Group (2010), "Risks and opportunities for indigenous peoples' financial services organizations". In J. White, J. Peters, P. Dinsdale and D. Beavon (eds), *Indigenous Peoples' Policy Research Volume 10: Research Methods, Justice, Governance and Politics*, Thompson Publishing; Ottawa, Ontario, pp. 197–217.

5   O'Fairchellaigh (2008a), op. cit.

6   Banerjee, S.B. (2001), "Corporate citizenship and indigenous stakeholders: exploring a new dynamic of organisational–stakeholder relationships", *Journal of Corporate Citizenship*, vol. 1, no. 1, pp. 39–55; Cragg, W. and Greenbaum, A. (2002), "Reasoning about responsibilities: mining company managers on what stakeholders are owed", *Journal of Business Ethics*, vol. 39, no. 3, pp. 319–335; Parker, C. (2002), *The Open Corporation*, Cambridge, UK, Cambridge

University Press; Trebeck, K. (2008), "Corporate social responsibility and democratisation". In O'Fairchellaigh and Ali (2008), op. cit., pp. 8–24.

7   O'Fairchellaigh (2008a), op. cit.

8   United Nations Economic and Social Council (2010), "Indigenous peoples: development with culture and identity: Articles and 32 of the United Nations Declaration on the Rights of Indigenous Peoples: Information Received from Government", *Permanent Forum on Indigenous Issues: Discussion on the Special Theme for the Year*, E/C/19/2010/1, New York: United Nations.

9   O'Fairchellaigh (2008a), op. cit.; Ulnooweg Development Group Inc. (2008). *Atlantic Aboriginal Financial Services Market Demand Study*. Leon Cooper, Virtual Ink Ltd, St. John's, Newfoundland.

10   Cooper, T., Faseruk, A. and Phillips, P. (2010), "Aboriginal finance and regulation—what are the regulatory impediments to establishing an Atlantic Canadian aboriginal financial institution?", *Workplace Review*, Fall 2010, pp. 64–80.

11   Cragg and Greenbaum (2002), op. cit.

12   Palenchar, M. and Heath, R. (2007), "Strategic risk communication: adding value to society", *Public Relations Review*, vol. 33, no. 2, pp. 120–129.

13   Coumans (2008), op. cit., p. 62.

14   Hindle, K. (2010), "How community context affects entrepreneurial process: a diagnostic framework", *Entrepreneurship and Regional Development*, vol. 22, no. 7, pp. 599–647.

15   Trebeck, K. (2007), "Tools for the disempowered? Indigenous leverage over mining companies", *Australian Journal of Political Science*, vol. 42, no. 4, pp. 541–562; Clydesdale, G. (2007), "Cultural evolution and economic growth: New Zealand Maori", *Entrepreneurship and Regional Development*, vol. 19, no. 1, pp. 49–68; Cahn, M. (2008), "Indigenous entrepreneurship, culture and micro-enterprise in the Pacific Islands: case studies from Samoa", *Entrepreneurship and Regional Development*, vol. 20, no. 1, pp. 1–18; Cornell, S. and Kalt, J.P. (2000), "Where's the glue? Institutional and cultural foundations of American Indian economic development", *Journal of Socio-Economics*, vol. 29, no. 5, pp. 443–470; Cornell, S. and Kalt, J.P. (2001), *Sovereignty and Nation-building: The Development Challenges in Indian Country Today*. Harvard Project on American Indian Development, Boston, Mass.

16   Coumans (2008), op. cit. p. 44.

17   http://whc.unesco.org/uploads/activities/documents/activity-496-6.pdf.

18   UN Doc. E/CN.4/Sub.2/1986/7 and Add. 1–4.

19   UN Doc. E/CN.4/Sub.2/1986/7, paragraphs 379–382.

20   http://www.ainc-inac.gc.ca/ap/index-eng.asp.

21   Coumans (2008), op. cit., p. 42.

22   Ibid.

23   Robertson, G. (2011), "First nations new focus for Canada's banks", *The Globe and Mail*, 15 June 2011, http://www.theglobeandmail.com/globe-investor/first-nations-new-focus-for-canadas-banks/article2062497/.

24   Ulnooweg Development Group (2008), op. cit., p. 3.

25   Howitt, R. and Lawrence, R. (2008), "Indigenous peoples, corporate social responsibility and the fragility of the interpersonal domain". In O'Fairchellaigh and Ali (2008), op. cit., pp. 83–104, see page 99.

26   Howitt, R. (1991), "Aborigines and restructuring in the mining sector: vested and representative interests", *Australian Geographer*, vol. 22, no. 2, pp. 117–119.

27   O'Fairchellaigh, C. (2008b), "Understanding corporate–Indigenous peoples' agreements on mineral development: a conceptual framework". In O'Fairchellaigh and Ali (2008), op. cit., pp. 67–82.

28 Trebeck (2008), op. cit.

29 O'Fairchellaigh (2008a), op. cit.

30 Cornell. and Kalt (2001), op. cit.

31 Ulnooweg Development Group, (2008), op. cit.

32 Cooper, T. , Hickey, T., Sock, L. and Hare, G. (2010), *Critical Success Factors in the First Nations Fishery of Atlantic Canada: Mi'kmaq and Maliseet Perceptions*, The Atlantic Aboriginal Economic Development Integrated Research Program, Cole Harbour, Canada.

33 O'Fairchellaigh (2008a), op. cit., p. 5.

34 Canadian Council for Aboriginal Business. http://www.ccab.com/.

35 Coooper, Faseruk and Phillips (2010), op. cit.

36 Ibid.

37 Ulnooweg Development Group (2008), op. cit.

38 National Aboriginal Risk Capital Association (2004), *Equity Capital and First Nation Business Development*, National Aboriginal Risk Capital Association, Ottawa, p. 4.

39 Cooper and Ulnooweg (2010), op. cit.

40 Freeman, R.E. (1984), *Strategic Management: A Stakeholder Approach*, Pittman: Boston, MA, p. 46.

41 Laplume, A.O., Sonpar, K. and Litz, R.A. (2008), "Stakeholder theory: reviewing a theory that moves us", *Journal of Management*, vol. 34, no. 6, pp. 1152–1189; Nickols, F.W. (2005), "Why a stakeholder approach to evaluate training", *Advances in Developing Human Resources*, vol. 7, no. 1, pp. 121–134.

42 Abednego, M.P. and Ogunlana, S.O. (2006), "Good project governance for proper risk allocation in public private partnerships in Indonesia", *International Journal of Project Management*, vol. 24, pp. 622–34.

43 Coumans (2008), op. cit., p. 62.

44 Maon, F., Lindgreen, A. and Swaen, V. (2010), "Organizational stages and cultural phases: a critical review and a consolidative model of corporate social responsibility development", *International Journal of Management Reviews*, vol. 12, pp. 20–38.

45 Evan, W.M. and Freeman, R.E. (1988), "A stakeholder theory of the modern corporation: Kantian capitalism". In T.L. Beauchamp and N.E. Bowie (eds), *Ethical Theory and Business*, Prentice Hall, Englewood Cliffs, NJ, pp. 97–106; Maon, Lindgreen and Swaen, (2010), op. cit.; Jawahar, I.M. and McLaughlin, G.L. (2001), "Toward a descriptive stakeholder theory: an organizational life cycle approach", *Academy of Management Review*, vol. 26, no. 3, pp. 397–414.

46 Maon, Lindgreen and Swaen (2010), op. cit., O'Fairchellaigh (2008a), op. cit.

47 Jawahar and McLaughlin (2001), op. cit.; Jones, T.M. (1995), "Instrumental stakeholder theory: a synthesis of ethics and economics", *Academy of Management Review*, vol. 20, pp. 404–37; Clarkson, M.B.E. (1988), "Corporate social performance in Canada, 1976–86". In L.E. Preston (ed.), *Research in Corporate Social Performance and Policy*, vol. 10, JAI Press, Greenwich, CT, pp. 241–265.

48 Clarkson (1988), op. cit.

49 Jawahar and McLaughlin (2001), op. cit.

50 Jawahar and McLaughlin (2001), op. cit.; Clarkson (1988), op. cit.

51 Jahansoozi, J. (2006), "Organization–stakeholder relationships: exploring trust and transparency", *Journal of Management Development*, vol. 25, no. 10, pp. 942–955.

52 Heath, R. (2001), "Shifting foundations: public relations as relationship building". In Heath, R. (ed.), *Handbook of Public Relations*, Sage, Thousand Oaks, CA, pp. 1–9; Jahansoozi (2006), op. cit.

53 Jahansoozi (2006), op. cit.

54 Jahansoozi (2006), op. cit., p. 943.

55 Ibid.

56 Kolk A. and Pinske J. (2004), "Corporate strategies for climate change", *European Management Journal*, vol. 22, pp. 304–314; Jawahar and McLaughlin, (2001), op. cit.

57 Nickols (2005), op. cit., p. 127.

58 Ibid.

59 Goodpaster, K.E. (1991), "Business ethics and stakeholder analysis", *Business Ethics Quarterly*, vol. 1, no. 1, pp. 53–73.

60 Donaldson, T. and Preston, L. (1995), "The stakeholder theory of the corporation: concepts, evidence, and implications", *Academy of Management Review*, vol. 20, pp. 65–91.

61 Hosmer, L.T. and Kiewitz, C. (2005), "Organizational justice: a behavioral science concept with critical implications for business ethics and stakeholder theory", *Business Ethics Quarterly*, vol. 15, no. 1, pp. 67–91.

62 Trebeck (2008), op. cit.

63 Heugens, P., Van Den Bosch, F.A.J. and Van Riel, C.B.M. (2002), "Stakeholder integration: building mutually enforcing relationships", *Business and Society*, vol. 41, no. 1, pp. 36–60.

64 Hindle (2010), op. cit.

65 Cooper and Ulnooweg (2010), op. cit.

66 Ibid.

67 Graham, J. and Edwards H. (2003), *Options for Commercial Enterprises in First Nations*, Institute on Governance, Ottawa, Ontario.

68 Cooper, Hickey, Sock and Hare (2010), op. cit.

69 Reason, P. and Rowan, J. (1981), "Issues of validity in new paradigm research". In P. Reason and J. Rowan (eds), *Human Inquiry: A Sourcebook of New Paradigm Research*, Wiley, Chichester, UK, pp. 239–252; Reason, P. and Bradbury, H. (eds), (2001), *Handbook of Action Research: Participative Inquiry and Practice*, Sage, London, UK; Reason, P. and Goodwin, J. (1999), "Toward a science of qualities in organizations: lessons from complexity theory and postmodern biology", *Concepts and Transformations*, vol. 4, no. 3, pp. 281–317; Reason, P. and Tortbert, W.R. (2001), "Towards a participatory worldview, Part 2", *ReVision*, vol. 24, no. 2, pp. 1–48.

70 Cooper, Hickey, Sock and Hare (2010), op. cit.; Coumans (2008), op. cit; Cooper and Ulnooweg (2010), op. cit.

71 Cooper and Ulnooweg (2010), op. cit.

72 Ibid.

73 Ulnooweg (2008), op. cit.

74 O'Fairchellaigh (2008a), op. cit.

75 Howitt and Lawrence (2008), op. cit.

76 Graham and Edwards (2003), op. cit.

77 Trebeck (2008), op. cit.

78 Trebeck (2007), op. cit.

79 Freeman (1984), op. cit.

80 Ibid., p. 88.

81 Ibid.

13 Resolving Environmental and Social Conflicts: Responsible Innovation in Small Producers' Clusters in Northern Vietnam*

JAAP VOETEN,[†] NIGEL ROOME,[‡] GERARD DE GROOT[§]
AND JOB DE HAAN[¶]

Keywords

Business clusters, developing countries, entrepreneurship, informal business, responsible innovation, sustainable development, Vietnam.

Introduction

Corporate social responsibility (CSR) and stakeholder analysis have increasingly become part of business operations as built-in, self-regulating mechanisms through which businesses monitor and ensure their adherence to the law, ethical standards and international norms. The idea of responsible business originated in the UK, Europe and the USA in the nineteenth century out of a sense that business inherently involves relationships between people and between people and resources.[1] Early academic writing on CSR and stakeholder analysis reflected concerns about the duty to respect direct stakeholders' environmental and social interests. These often focused around issues such as labor conditions and housing or funding local events, scholarships and clean-up campaigns.[2] However, until the 1990s, CSR and the stakeholder approach had only a

* The study was made possible by a grant for a research programme on responsible innovation from the Dutch Organization for Scientific Research (NWO) that was jointly carried out by Tilburg University and Hanoi University of Technology (Vietnam).

† Jaap Voeten, Development Research Institute (IVO), Tilburg University, Warandelaan 2, PO Box 90153 5000 LE Tilburg, The Netherlands. E-mail: j.voeten@uvt.nl.

‡ Nigel Roome, Vlerick Leuven Gent School of Management, Vlamingenstraat 83, 3000 Leuven, Belgium. E-mail: nigel.roome@vlerick.com.

§ Gerard de Groot, Development Research Institute (IVO), Tilburg University, Warandelaan 2, PO Box 90153 5000 LE Tilburg, The Netherlands. E-mail: G.A.degroot@uvt.nl.

¶ Job de Haan, Tilburg School of Economics and Management, Tilburg University, Warandelaan 2, PO Box 90153 5000 LE Tilburg, The Netherlands. E-mail: j.a.c.dehaan@uvt.nl.

limited influence on the private sector and relatively few business actors actually followed such practices.

In recent decades the world has developed into a global village. Brundtland[3] articulated the concept of sustainable development, which governments, multilateral organizations and civil society further consolidated into Agenda 21.[4] These reports advocated forms of development that would meet the needs of the present generation without compromising the ability of others around the planet—including developing countries, and future generations to meet their needs. Sustainable development therefore has a global perspective of integrating environmental, social and economic concerns. The central principles of this concept are those of anticipation, precaution and the recognition that, when scientific investigation has found a plausible risk, there is a social responsibility to protect the public from exposure to harm and avoid conflict.[5]

CSR has developed alongside the global changes of the past 20 years. During this time business actors have become more integrated in global value chains[6] and often transferred production to low-income countries that opened up for foreign investment. The formation of the Business Council for Sustainable Development, and its book *Changing Course*, signalled a business input to the debate on sustainable development.[7] This was followed by a series of emerging conflicts between business and social actors in the 1990s, such as Brent Sparr, Exxon Valdez, Enron and Nike. The idea that sustainable development is a valid concern for business too became more and more accepted.[8] The widespread adoption of information technologies capable of spreading information about societal impacts of businesses has allowed a broader public to become involved. Leading authors of that time argued that business—more than government or civil society—is best equipped to lead the world towards a sustainable world.[9] A business should not just behave responsibly in its home country; but also be concerned about the social and environmental interests of distant stakeholders, including those in developing countries. Prahalad[10] suggested that sustainable business offers opportunities for large companies as well as for the four billion poor people at the bottom of the pyramid. These evolving notions have led corporations to adopt a broader view of CSR and a greater concern for stakeholders than under the narrowly conceived interpretation of the firm as a pure economic actor. This implied some profound strategic adjustments to the modus operandi of companies in response to global environmental pressures, conflicts and changing societal expectations.[11]

Although the idea of stakeholders and the notion of CSR have gained ground, there is still confusion about the underlying concepts. Commentators today, both critics and proponents of the approach, often disagree about the nature and scope of CSR, partly because they share different perceptions and understandings of the role and purpose of the business in society.[12] CSR has become a heterogeneous concept which combines elements of sustainability, corporate governance and corporate accountability to stakeholders.

Despite the unclear understanding of what CSR actually means in theory,[13] there is a generally agreed and utilized set practices within the Western business community that aim to ensure corporate responsibility in activities, outcomes and communications. In general, these practices include the specification of a vision and mission of CSR for a company, the structuring of CSR activities from policy to practice within its organization, formulating measurable performance targets in terms of environmental and social aspects and communicating CSR reports to the public.[14] These activities may be accompanied by a process of stakeholder engagement that takes on any number of roles from defining the content of a CSR policy, reflecting on performance and reporting or helping the company foresee its future context. CSR thus involve an expert system, foresight studies and a predefined implementation process, responsibility protocols, goals outcome criteria and indicators. In practice, CSR and the stakeholder approach has become a "project" led by the corporations themselves as the central actors. An illustration of this type of such "projectification"[15] of CSR practice is the response of sports apparel producer Nike after it faced a storm of criticism in the 1990s over child labour practices in the soccer ball production of its Asian suppliers. The Nike Board set up a department focused on compliance and social responsibility. This department investigated the long-term implications of the company's product design and manufacturing decisions. It developed a new vision, targets, an in-house index to measure product design and operation and agreed on a code of conduct to ensure the transparency of its supply chain operations while developing standards for workplace conditions for overseas suppliers. Reports of Nike's corporate responsibility performance and strategy are openly communicated via various channels to the public and the stakeholders.

Operationalizing CSR in a global context, particularly in developing countries, implies the need to involve a much broader range of stakeholders with different agendas, cultures, ideas and normative reference frames than is the case for a domestic company. Some of these additional stakeholders are outside of the direct vision and "sympathy range" of the Western public. In developing economies the economic, social, environmental and governance context is often less familiar and seems more complicated and difficult to understand. Reports of the problems faced by Shell in Nigeria and the emerging environmental issues in China demonstrate the difficulties of operationalizing CSR in such contexts. Companies struggle to grasp the local agenda and incorporate it within their "licence to operate." Theories about CSR and stakeholder participation have usually been developed within formal business organizations operating within Western economies with relatively stable institutional and procedural systems. These CSR and stakeholder practices do not seem to involve approaches or perspectives that can automatically be applied in developing country contexts. Quazi and Kahn state that CSR is more relevant to corporations operating in developed countries due to elevated community expectations for socially responsible behaviour; societal expectations in the developing countries mainly centre on economic growth.[16] Visser observed that CSR in developing countries is most commonly associated with philanthropy or charity.[17]

That said, our recent research in Vietnam shows that there are institutional structures and mechanisms in place in developing countries that drive business owners to acknowledge their broader responsibilities and take environmental and social concerns into account, even though these do not readily correspond to the institutional structures or principles found in developed economies. We found evidence of these structures and mechanisms in our research into examples of innovations among a number of informally organized small industrial clusters in the Red River Delta in rural northern Vietnam.[18] These innovations improved the competitive position of producers and contributed to the economic development of these poor communities. The innovations also generated a range of outcomes or impacts that extended beyond the purely economic. These included both positive and negative effects on different members of the community. For example one beneficial effect of innovation was the use of less polluting and more energy-efficient technologies in manufacturing. On the negative side, small-scale producers and others living in the villages experienced new pollution problems and an uneven distribution of benefits arising from the innovations. During subsequent investigations, the innovators in some Vietnamese villages expressed how they acknowledged and then took some responsibility for the newly emerged problems resulting from the innovation, while innovators in other villages did not.

The Vietnamese cases show that while innovations by small businesses at community level in developing economies are often seen as desirable, because they contribute to development and the accumulation of wealth at the local level, they can also generate negative impacts in the community and its environment. The research presented in this chapter started with an interest in whether and how the innovators acknowledge responsibility within these informal contexts. Actually, these types of production systems run by poorer groups are highly representative of the small-scale economic production found in developing countries. Specifically, the aim of our research was to conceptualize the nature of *responsible innovation* in the Vietnamese small producers' clusters and understand the extent to which Western notions of CSR and stakeholders analysis theory and practice apply in these settings.

We applied *grounded theory*[19] as the research methodology to provide for the inductive exploration of a number of cases of innovation found at the community level in Vietnam. We opted for this research approach because it allowed us to conceptualize responsible innovation without being limited or steered by preconceived analytical frameworks, given the reservations discussed above about the applicability of projectified CSR and stakeholder theories in the institutional setting of developing countries. Moreover, grounded theory is not only a descriptive research approach; it is able to advance theoretical propositions around societal processes that are developed in more explanatory terms.[20] The empirical findings are organized and presented as case studies, as this allows rich investigation of contexts, perceptions, mechanisms, resources, conflicts, power relations and institutions.[21]

Through information-oriented sampling[22] we selected four cases of craft villages in northern Vietnam (Table 13.1). These cases shared several characteristics in common: they were all craft villages organized as small producers' clusters where the producers themselves had introduced small-scale low-tech innovations.[23] Moreover, the villages are all situated in the vicinity of Hanoi, and their demographic compositions, workforce, accessibility, policy, governance and administrative contexts are all similar to one another. Yet the cases are heterogeneous in the sense that they produce distinct types of craft products and introduced different types of innovations and these led to various environmental and social outcomes, which were differently perceived and addressed.

Table 13.1 Selected cases of craft villages in northern Vietnam

Case – village	Types of innovation	Social and environmental consequences
Van Phuc – silk	New marketing	Emerging environmental problems
Bat Trang – ceramics	New liquefied petroleum gas (LPG) oven technology	Less air pollution
Duong Lieu – cassava	New cassava-starch end products	Ignored environmental problems
Phu Vinh – rattan/bamboo	New export markets	Widening income gap among small producers

A team of Dutch and Vietnamese researchers collected data in the Vietnamese villages in November 2009 and May 2010. The research focused on the various innovation outcomes, the emerging conflicts and whether innovators acknowledged responsibility in conflict resolution. The team collected a broad array of quantitative and qualitative material through observations and open, in-depth interviews with 20–30 households per village. Additional interviews were held with local officials, clients and other resource persons in the villages and in Hanoi, including Vietnamese research institutes, NGOs and government agencies. The team combined positivist approaches and categories with more naturalistic and constructivist-based information that centered on the perceptions of the different actors on what was taking place. The data collection was an iterative exercise involving observations and interviews in the field, transcribing, discussing and interpreting the interview recordings and then further refining, coding and analysing the data before the second round of data collection, in line with the research procedures of grounded theory.

The following section presents the empirical part in four case descriptions. We subsequently carry out a comparative analysis and use this to develop a five-stage model that presents our conceptualization of responsible innovation as it took place in the case studies. We associate the model with a range of theoretical ideas so as to position the model in a broader theoretical context. The idea is not to use the theoretical associations to support the model, rather the theoretical embedding serves (i) to demonstrate the multifaceted nature of responsible innovation, (ii) to avoid reinventing conceptualizations that are insensitive to existing theories; and lastly, (iii) to provide pointers for framing further research. In the concluding remarks we underline the key differences between "projectified" CSR and the stakeholder approach and our understanding and interpretation of responsible innovation as a societal process in this developing country.

Case Studies: Four Small Producers' Clusters in Vietnam

VAN PHUC

Van Phuc is a silk craft village, west of Hanoi, with a long history of high-quality silk weaving. Historically, middlemen and later state-owned enterprises, handled the distribution of silk products to the domestic market. Following government reforms that introduced the free market economy in the 1990s, silk-weaving families started to open retail shops and benefit from the growing demand for silk products, spurred on by the increasing number of domestic and foreign tourists coming to the village. The retail shops have stimulated the silk industry in the village and brought prosperity, particularly between 2001 and 2008. The silk weavers and silk dye workshops enjoy higher and more stable incomes, but not to the same extent as the shop owners. The village administration receives more taxes and rent for land and this has increased the money available for public spending.

The coming of the retail shops has led to a change in the approach towards quality; there is now more demand for lower-priced silk, implying a lower quality. The lower prices and higher production volumes meant that the small household production units have had to increase productivity, but several of them were unable to do so. As a result, a number of household enterprises closed down. This was not considered to be such a big issue in the village since most weavers had specialized skills and swiftly found employment in the dominant and rapidly expanding workshops. The increased production volumes and new products—designs and colours—also meant an increased use of chemicals, particularly in the dyeing process. For years, the dye workshops have discharged untreated waste water from the dyeing process into the open sewage system. Today villagers, research institutes and the local administration have all expressed great concern about the surface water quality in and around the village. More and more people in Van Phuc consider the pollution as a serious threat to the village and associate it with the occurrence of more serious and fatal diseases. Most dye workshops owners are less concerned and see the pollution as a fact of life and an acceptable consequence of making money in the silk industry.

Villagers link the pollution to several textile-related companies around the village that discharge polluted waste water. However, the precise sources of the pollution—from the village and factories around—are not clear, and neither are the impacts on human health. Research institutes have examined the pollution and its impacts and produced several scientific articles on the matter. However, the villagers do not have access to straightforward and practical information about the origin and effects of the pollution or possible solutions to the problem.

There is a growing mood in the village that the pollution is a problem that violates people's right to live in a safe environment. However, the general attitude among small producers and shop owners is that the problem is an acceptable trade-off for increased economic prosperity. The dye workshop owners do not want to take any action to change their practices. As individuals, they consider themselves as small players in a larger complex. The small producers assume that pollution in Van Phuc—which comes from many sources—can only be addressed by the government and that it is the government's responsibility to do something about it. The villagers feel some sympathy for the dye workshop producers and do not blame them for the pollution. They recognize that these workshop owners are poor and trying to survive.

The richer shop owners do not see themselves as having a responsibility to solve the problem. The main street—where they have their shops—is some distance from the polluted areas. However, they do see that the pollution will eventually have an adverse effect on tourists coming to visit the village and that does worry them.

Small producers and other villagers are looking to the government for a solution. The village administration is assuming responsibility and developing plans to move the polluting workshops to a location just outside the village where they will be concentrated and provided with a waste water purification plant. The dye workshops, weavers, shop owners and villagers consider this to be a solution and do not feel the need to take further action. They also like the idea of developing new land outside the village, more—as they mention—because they are currently facing a shortage of land than because it will address the problem of pollution. While the local administration has developed plans, it is not evident how these will be implemented. The funding is not yet secured and there are complicated legal issues involved.

PHU VINH

Phu Vinh is a village south of Hanoi where household production units have produced rattan and bamboo products for more than 300 years. Until a decade ago they mostly produced household items, such as baskets and bins, for everyday use. These were mostly sold on the Vietnamese market. Before the end of the cold war and the collapse of the eastern European communist bloc, these products were exported to communist nations under bilateral trade agreements.

After the introduction of the free-market economy in Vietnam in the 1990s and the implosion of socialist cooperation, the government established new enterprise and export legislation, allowing private enterprises to enter into export contracts with Western countries without restrictions or government involvement. Entrepreneurs from the village and Hanoi saw new opportunities and started to establish export companies just outside the village. The business became prosperous, particularly between 2001 and 2009, with exports principally going to new and lucrative markets in USA, Canada, France and the Netherlands.

Once an overseas contract had been signed, the export companies outsource the work to middlemen in the village who in turn subcontracted the order to household enterprises scattered around the village. The small producers do the actual craft work (weaving) and deliver the semi-final rattan and bamboo products to the middlemen and export companies who then do the final colouring and varnishing, as the last step before shipment overseas.

While the export companies have enjoyed handsome profits the system has brought less prosperity for the small-scale producers. To maximize their profit in a free market system, the export companies have increasingly imposed lower unit prices on the small producers.

Today, the small-scale producers get only half the unit price for their rattan products that they did five years ago. Today a small-scale producer earns on average 20,000 VND/day (0.87 euro). This has created conflict between them and the export companies. The producers complain about the lower unit price and increasingly suffer from poverty. Today, 13 percent of the population in the village lives under the government-defined poverty line. Weaving is mostly done by older people and children, while young able-bodied workers look for employment elsewhere.

New environmental problems have also emerged. To meet international quality standards and design requirements, small producers, middlemen and export companies now use more chemicals to whiten, soften, colour and dry the bamboo and rattan. The waste water—containing high concentrations of chemicals—is usually discharged into the surface water with no concern or consideration about the effects. Nobody knows the exact level of pollution or what health impacts are to be expected.

Another emerging problem is the depletion of rattan and bamboo as a result of the increased production volumes of recent years. In the past, small producers, middlemen and export companies were not concerned about a possible depletion. Today the problem is evident for all to see and input prices have risen sharply. The small producers, middlemen and export companies involved did not do anything to address this issue until 2009.

The export companies take a hard-line business attitude and do not see that they have a role to play, or a responsibility to modify unit prices to reduce poverty. They see poverty alleviation as the role of the government. The small-scale producers have a different view and blame the export companies for offering such low prices, arguing that they could share more of their profits.

The village administration recognizes and sympathizes with the problems of poverty faced by the small-scale producers, yet is unable to interfere with the economic process and the free market price setting mechanism. In addition, they are closely connected— through family ties—to the export companies. In recent years, the export companies have helped the local authorities to construct a school and a medical clinic, have planted trees and provided tables and computers for the administration's offices. The local government has facilitated the procedures for renting land and completing export license procedures.

There are limited opportunities for interactions between these different actors. There are no village meetings where all the parties involved can come together to discuss the issues of poverty and the environment. The export companies receive government support to organize training for the small-scale producers (weavers) so that they can learn about new designs, but do not listen to their complaints about low prices. The small-scale producers have attempted to unite and to set up an association but this did not succeed due to the many conflicts of interest in the village.

DUONG LIEU

Duong lieu is a traditional craft village that has been producing cassava and canna noodles for decades. Within the village, production is divided into households that produce starch—an intermediate product from cassava and canna—and households that produce the noodles from starch.

Some 10 years ago, small-scale producers and medium-sized companies around the village started to look for alternative products to add more value. These alternatives included medicine pills, soft drinks, cardboard boxes and candy. Candy production has been particularly successful in helping noodle producers generate a better income.

Over the past seven years, these new products started to generate more income than noodles. Although not anticipated, people also found that the work was cleaner and lighter than noodle production. Moreover, these new products produce hardly any environmental pollution. By contrast, the starch producers in the village discharge vast amounts of organic solid waste from peeling the cassava and canna and discharge the waste water into the open sewage system. The amounts of waste have been increasing over past years as a result of the increased demand for starch for the new products. The starch waste is becoming an increasing source of debate and conflict. Many of the villagers—particularly the starch producers—ignore the problem and consider it as a trade-off for their livelihoods. But more and more villagers are bothered by the pollution and concerned about the health impacts and link the pollution to several diseases that have recently become more common. Research institutes and nongovernmental organizations (NGOs) have carried out environmental impact studies and negative reports about the environmental situation have been presented in the media. The villagers are worried and somewhat irritated about this as they think it will have a negative impact on demand for their products.

The household enterprises involved in producing the new products consider the waste issue to be the problem of the starch producers and do not see that they have any role to play in addressing this issue. They ignore the potential to allocate some of the wealth they create by producing candy to pay for the environmental damage it causes. The village administration has welcomed the idea of alternatives to polluting starch production, such as other types of economic activities that do not involve starch.

BAT TRANG

Bat Trang village, situated east of Hanoi, has been a traditional ceramics craft village for centuries. In the old days, small producers in the cluster produced a variety of ceramic items in traditional pottery kilns, fired with wood and coal. This resulted in severe air pollution: the roads and alleys in the village were covered in black dust from the kilns and a smoky haze hung in the air. By the 1990s, Bat Trang was reported as being one of the most polluted villages in the Red River Delta.

The inhabitants and village administration became aware of this environmental problem and were concerned about the many cases of lung diseases and other respiratory health problems. The small-scale producers worked together with the local authorities and NGOs to try to develop alternative firing methods. In 1997 the village administration and the German development agency organized a workshop on business development and the introduction of new kiln technologies that would improve quality, increase competitiveness, use less energy and produce less air pollution. Early innovators took up these ideas and purchased a liquefied petroleum Gas (LPG) kiln from Japan for initial trials. They also experimented with improved oven technology from South Korea and Taiwan. By 2001–2002 the LPG technology was working well. Today there are companies in Bat Trang assembling a modified version of the LPG kiln and two-thirds of the small producers in the village have switched to this technology.

Early innovators mention that personal profit was not the only reason for developing the technology. They also took the environmental situation into account and wanted to promote the image of Bat Trang as a ceramics village based on family traditions. The villagers, and particularly those involved in the ceramics industry, see that the introduction of LPG technology has brought a variety of positive outcomes. As expected, the innovation resulted in a better quality of ceramics and LPG uses half the energy of a charcoal oven, saving substantially on energy costs. The improved competitive advantage made it possible to access new (international) markets. Poverty in Bat Trang was a common phenomenon 20 years ago, but today poverty rates are below average for the province and far below the national average. According to the village's administration, the gap between rich and poor in Bat Trang has not widened, something which has had occurred in other craft villages in the Red River Delta.

The new technology also bought positive environmental outcomes which were quickly noticed. There was a dramatic improvement in air quality: much less smoke is emitted these days and black dust is now almost absent in the village. Villagers report, with satisfaction and a certain pride, that the village is now much cleaner and greener. Over the years a collective process of becoming more environmentally aware has been underway. Although the profit argument may have been dominant, the small-scale producers also mention that they took environmental considerations into account. Having seen the benefits of the LPG kilns in past years, they are convinced that they have made a difference in creating a cleaner environment for themselves.

The Ceramics Association, established in 2002, has played a prominent role in the introduction of LPG oven technology. Virtually all the small-scale producers in Bat Trang are members of the association. The association functions as a discussion and exchange platform and actively promotes LPG kiln technology, amongst others highlighting the environmental arguments. These discussions about the societal implications have come about naturally because the inhabitants of Bat Trang feel strongly connected through family ties and their shared history in ceramic production. In this sense the innovation process was a collective process and the villagers recognized their responsibility, rather than looking to the government for a solution. They have not sought much external assistance to help them move forward.

Interpretation of the Case Studies

The case study descriptions show that small-scale producers in all four clusters operate and manage their businesses without the use of preconceived CSR or stakeholder involvement practices prior to the innovation process. The innovations brought economic benefits and the inhabitants of the villages where the innovations took place experienced unexpected social and environmental side effects, sometimes positive and sometimes negative. The villages had varying levels of formal and informal systems and mechanisms to enable different actors to identify and discuss these social and environmental changes. In some cases the entrepreneurs were in denial about the effects of changing their practices and in others they thought that the trade-off between the benefits they experienced and the problems experienced by others was acceptable. In cases there was open conflict between actors due to the violation of de facto rights, unfair distribution of economic benefits, harming of others' economic interests and changes in power relations. Despite the lack of any formal deployment of notions derived from CSR or processes for stakeholder engagement, we did find evidence of societal processes enabling the community to address the negative environmental and social outcomes of innovation. In the following section we will compare and analyze the different cases, using a variety of theoretical associations to help us to conceptualize and position responsible innovation as a societal process.

Perception of Societal Change

The cases show that the societal process starts with the recognition by the community of a societal or environmental change. There are differences in how villagers perceived these. In the rattan bamboo case villagers are clearly aware of increasing poverty levels in some parts of the community over recent years and consider this to be unacceptable. In the ceramics case more or less all the villagers have experienced improved air quality. By contrast, the social and environmental consequences in the silk and cassava cases are less clear-cut and not commonly agreed upon. Some community members in these villages are aware of increased pollution and see serious health problems emerging, while others do not.

The concept of bounded rationality described in economic theory is useful here. It addresses the ways in which human beings perceive, interpret and understand the world around them. Simon[24] argued that the rationality of individuals is limited by available information, the finite amount of time that people have and their cognitive limitations in interpreting the complex environments in which they operate. In evolutionary economics, in which innovation plays a key role, the theory of bounded rationality is used to describe how human perceptions and understanding, decisions and actions are shaped through conformity to social rules; formal and informal institutions including local traditions, mental models, collective insights and conventional wisdom.[25] Despite the increasing evidence about pollution, the villagers in Duong Lieu (cassava) conform to a set of social rules which prevent them from complaining about the pollution. In such a case the intervention of outside parties can play a key role in changing perceptions within a community. A research institution, an NGO or government agency can promote public awareness about longer-term social or environmental impacts. Government extension programmes and campaigns often aim to inform people about harmful societal changes.[26]

Over the research period, we witnessed changing perceptions among the small-scale producers and community actors, due to them learning and developing new insights. Individuals, groups, or organizations perceive and react to changes in their environment through a process identified by Argyris and Schön[27] as single-loop learning. Experiential learning—the process of making meaning *through the transformation of direct experience*[28]—was particularly relevant in the daily reality of the case studies. Experiential learning can be both an individual, as well as a joint, process. It is referred to in the literature as a social learning process; as it is often beyond the capacity of any single actor to understand the nature of these emerging societal problems.[29] This process is evident among some of the small producers' clusters. The cases of Phu Vinh (rattan and bamboo) and Bat Trang (ceramics) are good examples of social learning and how a shared perception of a common problem developed. The "community of practice" literature is also relevant here. A community of practice is defined as "a group whose members regularly engage in sharing and learning, based on their common interests".[30] The Bat Trang Ceramics Association is a clear example of such a community of practice.

There are also differences between the cases regarding the extent to which the communities develop, or failed to develop, a "critical mass" of common perceptions. Once a shared understanding and perception of an issue takes shape among a community, a gradual development of a critical mass of concerned community members occurs; in this way the societal outcome becomes part of the community's "agenda". This occurred in Phu Vinh (rattan), where the majority of people in the community saw emerging poverty as a societal problem. In Van Phuc (silk) a growing critical mass of awareness about pollution looks set to emerge, but in Duong Lieu (cassava) the new pollution problems are mentioned by few individuals. The literature refers to such an accumulation of perceptions as a "tipping point". This concept was introduced by Gladwell[31] who defined it as "the moment of critical mass, the threshold, the boiling point—the levels at which the momentum for change becomes unstoppable". That tipping point is usually reached through an "information cascade", which occurs when people observe the actions/ conclusions of others and then arrive at the same perception.[32]

Linking Innovation with Societal Change

Once a critical mass of the community has perceived a harmful societal change the cases show that its members will go on to identify its cause. We found marked differences in the way in which the communities linked recent societal changes with innovations. In the rattan case, the community has no doubts that the lower prices offered by the export companies to local producers have resulted in more poverty among small-scale producers. Similarly in the ceramics case, there is general agreement in the community that cleaner air is a result of adopting a new technology. Conversely, the links are less obvious in the silk and cassava candy villages. The scattered workshops over the villages and other local sources of pollution make it difficult to trace who is contributing to the increased pollution and to what extent. Moreover, the innovators in the silk and cassava cases are not actually producing the pollution themselves. The cassava starch producers in Duong Lieu—who themselves did not innovate—pollute more due to the increased demand by the innovative households making new products. This is also the case in Van Phuc where the silk dye workshops pollute more due to increased demand by shop owners, the actual innovators. There is no clear agreement about the exact causes of the pollution because of the complexity of these environmental pathways.

External agencies, such as research institutions, the government and NGOs can also play a role in helping people to better understand the impacts of innovation. Innovation systems theory[33] is relevant here. This states that the innovation process takes place in a network of institutions in the public and private sectors whose activities and interactions initiate, import, modify and diffuse new technologies and research and development (R&D) outcomes. This process usually involves some mechanism to respond to the broader social and environmental consequences of the innovation.

As with perceptions of societal change, learning within the community is instrumental to developing an understanding of links between innovation and societal change. Learning may involve developing new insights into the origin of societal changes. The community has to question the issues that gave rise to the societal changes; if they are able to understand that they are related to an innovation (or another recognizable cause), then second-order or double-loop learning has taken place.[34] The social learning process may resolve information gaps or overload and filter the information required in order to understand whether or not there is a link. Through social learning, actors can begin to see different aspects of a problem and constructively explore their differences and search for solutions that go beyond their own limited vision of what is possible.[35]

Dissatisfaction With the Trade-offs

Once an innovation has been linked to a societal change a community can respond in different ways, as our case studies show. This is particularly evident in the different ways in which harmful changes are weighed against benefits such as prosperity, income, employment and stability, which is in fact a social cost–benefit analysis. For instance, in Phu Vinh (rattan), the small-scale producers are finding the new problem of poverty unacceptable and do not see any compensatory benefits. The result is dissatisfaction and an emerging conflict with the export companies. On the other hand, in Van Phuc (silk) there is a common perception that the new problems of pollution are sufficiently compensated for by the economic benefits of innovation and the community sees the pollution as an acceptable trade-off. A similar story emerges in the cassava candy case, where no overall conflict of interests has emerged about the harmful environmental consequences, which are both contested and sufficiently compensated by the economic outcomes.

Specific actors may not be able to weigh up the situation due to misinformation or limited information about the value of the innovation. This could be the result of the bounded rationality mentioned earlier or a deliberate attempt by the more powerful originators of a harmful societal change to cover up the level of value creation and keep this out of sight, a situation known in economic and contract theory as information asymmetry.[36] Actors that benefit directly from an innovation may keep this information hidden from the community, or suggest a misleading picture of the situation. Value-chain theory relates this issue to governance issues.[37] The dominant actors in the chain may have the power to hide information and sow discord in order to safeguard their appropriation of value. The export companies in Phu Vinh (rattan), who are reluctant to disclose information about their incomes and profits, are an example of this.

When harmful societal consequences are not compensated for by benefits, conflicts can emerge among people with differing interests and resources.[38] These can create social structures that reflect the unequal distribution of power and resources in society. In practical terms, these conflicts stem from the perception that one's own needs, interests, wants, or values are incompatible with someone else's.[39] They create a social situation in which a minimum of two actors are striving to acquire a set of scarce resources at the same time. Dissatisfaction provides the potential for conflict, also known as the "latent phase" in the process towards conflict.[40]

Glasl[41] shows how parties in a conflict lose the ability to cooperate in a constructive manner as they share fewer common and mutually beneficial experiences and lose the links that used to bind them in the past. He identifies several "points of no return" which contribute decisively to this escalation. Initially, there is a hardening of positions. The content of the conflict becomes the centre of attention, and each party trusts that it will be possible to solve the problem to their satisfaction. In subsequent stages further polarization and debate take place. Small-scale producers in the rattan village have reached the point where they no longer feel that it is productive to talk to the export companies. From this point on the behaviour of the parties towards one another is likely to become more negative, as will the images that each party have of each other. As the conflict escalates, the parties slide into a situation where each feels threatened and endangered by the actions of the other. In the last stage of the model, threatening begins and might lead to violent acts.[42]

Voluntary Acknowledgement of Responsibility

When actors in the community feel disadvantaged and conflict arises, innovators can react to these concerns in different ways. The innovators might be sensitive and exhibit altruism[43] or feel a sense of responsibility for the outcomes and arrange for some form of compensation within the community. Internal mechanisms within the community could push the innovators to acknowledge their responsibility in resolving the emerging conflict. In Bat Trang, where pollution was recognized to be a problem, the small-scale producers included environmental considerations in their assessment about whether or not to invest in LPG-fired kilns.

On the other hand, the innovators could intentionally not take responsibility, acting opportunistically and selfishly taking advantage of circumstances with little regard for principles or the welfare of others. Such behaviour involves misusing the ignorance of others by seeking self-interest with guile.[44] This situation can often escalate into a conflict. In the rattan case, the export companies lowered the price they offered and opted for opportunistic behavior, following the principles of the free market game.

Altruism and opportunism are discussed within the context of morality. Frederiksen[45] distinguishes several moral frameworks upon which CSR policies are based. These include moral egoists, libertarians (who believe in not violating anyone else's rights), utilitarians (who promote the best possible outcome), and supporters of common-sense morality. Most CSR and stakeholder literature contains the assumption of the societal interest of the entrepreneur as an individual or organization that is willing to accept responsibility and to redistribute benefits and important decision-making power to stakeholders.[46] These strands of CSR and stakeholder literature assume a variety of motives among dominant actors, once responsibility for outcomes is acknowledged.

While there are well-intentioned innovators who are willing to compensate others for harm caused, the scale and complexity of the problems, uncertain causality and bounded rationality may all make it difficult to know how to do so. Even if the causes are known it may still be difficult to establish the appropriate level or method of compensation. When there is proximity between the actors, as in the clusters in Vietnam, it should be easier for the innovators to arrive at acceptable compensation arrangements for the community.

Enforced Responsibility

In cases where there is no internal settlement of the conflict or voluntary compensation and the escalating conflict remains unsolved, innovators could be pushed by an external force or a new institutional arrangement to acknowledge responsibility and realize some form of resolution. In the silk village, the local administration sees its responsibility as addressing the pollution problem. If this does not happen the community is likely to end up with an unresolved and escalating conflict, as witnessed in the rattan case.

A third party, for example a court of law, can also be called in to intervene and to act as an arbiter. However, in many developing countries there is limited awareness of, or access to, *de jure* rights and poor people are often excluded from the formal legal system.[47] There are no or few formalized processes for local actors to claim their rights as a result of failing laws, judiciaries and other legal mechanisms.[48] An alternative is that resolutions might be arrived at through informal and multi-actor conflict resolution arrangements.[49]

A final difficulty here is that disadvantaged parties may lack the courage to fight a claim and therefore assume a position of powerlessness. This partly depends on the cultural patterns within the community. For example intimidation might play a key role in some countries. In the case of Vietnam, social mores about harmony, not complaining and accepting one's destiny are likely to be more decisive.[50] Some societies stress tolerance and are less inclined to engage in behavior that is seen as creating conflict.

The Societal Process Towards Responsible Innovation

In sum, based on the evidence developed from our cases we advance a suggestion to conceptualize responsible innovation. From the empirical material and theoretical insights drawn from the literature, we propose a five-stage model (Figure 13.1) of a societal process, depicted below. The process either ends in an unresolved conflict or moves into the zone of what can be termed responsible innovation; innovation that takes account of social, environmental or distributive issues and is acceptable for the community concerned.

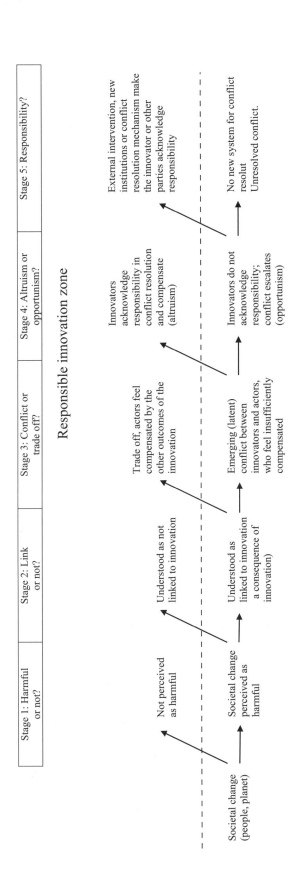

Figure 13.1 The societal process towards acknowledging responsibility

Concluding Remarks

We have considered the applicability of CSR theory and stakeholder perspectives in innovative small producers' clusters northern Vietnam. Our intent has been to develop a view of what constitutes responsible innovation in the context of a developing economy. Our conclusion is that there are limits to the extent to which projectified CSR practices can explain what happens on the ground in such a context.

We found that small producers in the cases in Vietnam do not consciously design procedures to anticipate or avoid environmental and social impacts. They work in a context that is characterized by risk, uncertainty, bounded rationality and weak formal institutional setting which implies high costs associated with information. Yet the innovation activities and societal consequences take place in the community in a direct and visible way. Unforeseen outcomes of innovations emerge and manifest themselves in the villages. Adaptive and informal institutional mechanisms may or may not enable the actors involved to react to these changes, whether through compensation or conflict. Experience and learning are critical in mediating and resolving the emerging conflicts. These can result in compensation or adaptations to the initial innovation. The assessment of societal impacts and the conflict resolution mechanisms do not involve external normative frameworks; rather people in the community decide what is important for, and fair to, them. However, the involvement of third parties seems essential for sharing information about the impacts, sorting out the understanding of complex situations and causality and in the mediation of conflicts. Although the processes do not follow the principles of the stakeholder approach or CSR practices, they do resemble the early origins of CSR which recognize the relationship between people and between people and resources.

An essential feature in this emergent and experiential learning-based mechanism is the quality of the process of human interaction. Quality concerns the community's ability to adapt and resolve conflicts so that they can enter the "responsible innovation" zone. Ideally, this involves an open and transparent discourse in which powerful actors do not seek to dominate the process to benefit their own interests. The actors affected by the innovation outcomes have a voice and are able to speak, which characterizes the deliberative and empowering capacity of a broad base of community members to achieve process justice and fairness. The quality of the process of human interaction is embedded and shaped in a specific institutional context. In sum, Table 13.2 lists the key differences we identified between the CSR and stakeholder engagement approaches and the societal process as analyzed and conceptualized in this chapter.

The factors that steer the societal model can be seen as embedded in a variety of theoretical associations, including bounded rationality, emergent learning, third parties and formal and informal institutions. The societal model proposed in this chapter does not explain the institutional context for a community to move towards a responsible innovation zone. It would be informative to explore why one case ended up in the zone of responsible innovation while others remained as unresolved conflicts. Further research could explore hypotheses regarding the role of institutional factors and the extent to which the nature of the innovation and the scale and complexity of the problems play a role. We believe that these Vietnamese case studies and our proposed "grounded view" of responsible innovation represent the reality facing many small producers and communities in developing countries.

Table 13.2 Key differences between CSR/stakeholder engagement and the societal process model

Projectified CSR/stakeholder approach	Societal process model
Planned project and foresight-based	Emergent and experience based
Quality of the analysis	Quality of the process
Expert system	Perceptions of community members
Predefined steps and procedures	Open process
One central actor	Multi-actor and social learning
Compliance with project framework that may include external values and norms	Community fairness
Dominance of the central actor	Empowerment of actors
Absolute outcomes	Compensation of outcomes

Notes

1   Halme, M., Roome, N. and Dobers, P. (2008), "Corporate responsibility: reflections on context and consequences", *Scandinavian Journal of Management*, vol. 25, no. 1, pp. 1–9.

2   Bowen, H.R. (1953), *Social Responsibilities of the Businessman*, Harper, New York; Carroll, A.B. and A.K. Buchholtz (2002), *Business and Society: Ethics and Stakeholder Management*, 5th edn, South-Western College Publishing, Cincinnati; Donaldson, T. and Preston, L. (1995), "The stakeholder theory of the modern corporation: Concepts, evidence and implications", *Academy of Management Review*, vol. 20, pp. 65–91; Frederick, W.C. (1960), "The growing concern over business responsibility", *California Management Review*, vol. 2, no. 4, pp. 54–61; Freeman, R. (1984), *Strategic Management: A Stakeholder Approach*, Prentice Hall, Englewood Cliffs, NJ.

3   Brundtland, G. (ed.), (1987), *Our Common Future: The World Commission on Environment and Development*, Oxford University Press, Oxford.

4   *Rio Declaration on Environment and Development* (1992), Report of the United Nations Conference on Environment and Development, Rio de Janeiro, 3–14 June 1992, UN report A/CONF.151/26 (vol. I).

5   O'Riordan, T. and Cameron, J. (1994), *Interpreting the Precautionary Principle*, Earthscan Publications Ltd, London.

6   Gereffi, G., Humphey, J. and Sturgeon, T. (2005). "The governance of global value chains", *Review of International Political Economy*, vol. 12, no. 1, pp. 78–104.

7   Schmidheiny, S. with Business Council for Sustainable Development (1992), *Changing Course: A Global Perspective on Development and the Environment*, MIT Press, Cambridge, MA.

8   Elkington, J. (1997), *Cannibals With Forks: The Triple Bottom Line of 21st Century Business*, Capstone, Oxford.

9   Hart, S. (2005), *Capitalism at Crossroads*, Wharton School Publishing, Upper Saddle River, NJ.

10 Prahalad, C.K. (2005), *The Fortune at the Bottom of the Pyramid: Eradicating Poverty Through Profits*, Pearson Education/Wharton School Publishing, New Delhi.

11 Jamali, D (2006), "Insights into triple bottom line integration from a learning organization perspective", *Business Process Management Journal*, vol. 12, no. 6, pp. 809–821.

12   Idemudia, U. and Ite, U. (2006), "Corporate–community relations in Nigeria's oil industry: Challenges and imperatives", *Corporate Social Responsibility and Environmental Management*, vol. 13, no. 4, pp. 194–206.

13   Roome, N. (2004), "Innovation, global change and new capitalism: a fuzzy context for business and the environment", *Human Ecology Review*, vol. 11, no. 3, pp. 277–279.

14   Hockerts, K. (2008), *An Overview of CST Practices Response Benchmarking Report*, INSEAD working paper 2008/67/ST, INSEAD, Paris.

15   Midler, C. (1995), "Projectification of the firm: the Renault case", *Scandinavian Journal of Management*, vol. 11, no. 4, pp. 363–375.

16   Quazi A., Rahman, Z. and Keating, B. (2007), "A developing country perspective of corporate social responsibility: a test case of Bangladesh", Conference proceedings, *Reputation, Responsibility & Relevance*, 3–5 December 2007, Australia and New Zealand Marketing Academy; Khan, A.F (1985), *Business and Society*, S. Chand & Company Ltd., New Delhi.

17   Visser, W. (2008), "CSR in developing countries". In *The Oxford Handbook of Corporate Social Responsibility*, edited by A. Crane *et al.*, Oxford: Oxford University Press, pp. 473–499.

18   Voeten, J., de Haan, J. and de Groot, G. (2011), "Is that innovation? Assessing examples of revitalized economic dynamics among clusters of small producers in Northern Vietnam". In A. Szirmai, W. Naudé, and M. Goedhuys (eds), *Entrepreneurship, Innovation, and Economic Development*, Oxford University Press.

19   Glaser, B. and Strauss, A. (1967), *The Discovery of Grounded Theory: Strategies for Qualitative Research*, Aldine Publishing Company, Chicago.

20   Birks, M. and Mills, J. (2011), *Grounded Theory: A Practical Guide*, Sage Publications, London.

21   Yin, R.K. (2003), *Case Study Research: Design and Methods*, Sage, Thousand Oaks, CA.

22   Bent Flyvbjerg, B. (2006), "Five misunderstandings about case-study research", *Qualitative Inquiry*, vol. 12, no. 2, pp. 219–245.

23   Voeten, de Haan. and de Groot (2011), op. cit.

24   Simon, H. (ed.), (1957), "A behavioral model of rational choice". In *Models of Man, Social and Rational: Mathematical Essays on Rational Human Behavior in a Social Setting*, Wiley, New York, pp. 241–261.

25   Dequech, D. (2001), "Bounded rationality, institutions, and uncertainty", *Journal of Economic Issues*, vol. 35, no. 4, pp. 911–29.; Nelson, R. and Winter, S. (1982), *An Evolutionary Theory of Economic Change*, The Belknap Press, Cambridge, MA.

26   Demirel, H. and Alkan, R. (2006), "Promoting environmental awareness: spatial information dissemination", *Fresenius Environmental Bulletin*, vol. 15, no. 8a, pp. 771–776.

27   Argyris, C. and Schön, D. (1978), *Organizational Learning: A Theory of Action Perspective*, Addison Wesley, Reading, MA.

28   Kolb, D. (1984), *Experiential Learning*, Prentice Hall, Englewood Cliffs, NJ.

29   Beers, P.J., Sol, J. and Wals, A. (2010), *Social Learning in a Multi-actor Innovation Context*, Ninth European IFSA Symposium, Building sustainable rural futures—the added value of systems approaches in times of change and uncertainty, Vienna, Austria, July 4–7 2010; Pahl-Wostl, C. (2006), "The importance of social learning in restoring the multifunctionality of rivers and floodplains", *Ecology & Society* vol. 11, no. 1, Art.10.

30   Lesser, E. and Storck, J. (2001), "Communities of practice and organisational performance", *IBM Systems Journal*, vol. 40, no. 4, pp. 831–841.

31   Gladwell, M. (2000), *The Tipping Point: How Little Things can Make a Big Difference*, Back Bay Books, Boston, MA.

32 Bikhchandani S., Hirshleifer, D. and Welch, I. (1992), "A theory of fads, fashion, custom, and cultural change as informational cascades", *Journal of Political Economy*, vol. 100, no. 5, pp. 992–1026.

33 Edquist, C. (1997), *Systems of Innovation: Technologies, Institutions and Organisations*, Pinter, London and Washington, DC; Lundvall B.-A. (ed.) (1992). *National Systems of Innovation: Towards a Theory of Innovation and Interactive Learning*, Pinter, London.

34 Argyris and Schön (1978), op. cit.

35 Beers, Sol and Wals (2010), op. cit.

36 Akerlof, G. (1970), "The market for 'lemons': quality uncertainty and the market mechanism", *The Quarterly Journal of Economics*, vol. 84, no. 3, pp. 488–500.

37 Gereffi, G., Humphrey, J. and Sturgeon, T. (2005), "The governance of global value chains", *Review of International Political Economy*, vol. 12, no. 1, pp. 78–104.

38 Mills, C.W. (1959), *The Sociological Imagination*, Oxford University Press, London.

39 Mayers, J. (2000), "Company–community forestry partnerships: a growing phenomenon", *Unasylva*, vol. 51, no. 200, pp. 33–41.

40 Brahm, Eric. (2003), "Conflict stages". In G. Burgess and H. Burgess (eds), *Beyond Intractability*, Conflict Research Consortium, University of Colorado, Boulder, posted September 2003, http://www.beyondintractability.org/bi-essay/conflict_stages/.

41 Glasl, F. (1999), *Confronting Conflict: A First-aid Kit for Handling conflict*, Howthorn Press, Gloucestershire.

42 Libiszewski, S. (1992), *What Is an Environmental Conflict?* Occasional Paper no. 1, Center for Security Studies and Conflict Research, Swiss Federal Institute of Technology, Zurich.

43 Schacter, M. and Marques, E. (2000), *Altruism, Opportunism and Points in Between Trends and Practices in Corporate Social Responsibility*, Institute On Governance, Ottawa, Canada.

44 Williamson, O. (1986), *The Economic Institutions of Capitalism*, Free Press, New York.

45 Frederiksen, C. (2010), "The relation between policies concerning corporate social responsibility (CSR) and philosophical moral theories: an empirical investigation", *Journal of Business Ethics*, vol. 93, no. 3, pp. 357–371.

46 Stieb, J. (2009), "Assessing Freeman's stakeholder theory", *Journal of Business Ethics*, vol. 87, no. 3, pp. 401–414.

47 Barendrecht, M. (2009), *Best Practices for an Affordable and Sustainable Dispute System: A Toolbox for Microjustice*, Tilburg University Legal Studies Working Paper no. 003/2009.

48 Buscaglia, E. and Ratliff, W. (2000), *Law and Economics in Developing Countries*, Hoover Institution Press, Palo Alto, CA.

49 Crowfoot, J. and Wondolleck, J. (1990), *Environmental Disputes: Community Involvement in Conflict Resolution*, Island Press, Washington, DC.

50 Warner, M. (2003), *Culture and Management in Asia*, Routledge, London.

14 Reconciling Stakeholder Requests and Carbon Dependency: What is the Right Climate Strategy?

TIMO BUSCH* AND JONATAN PINKSE†

Keywords

Climate change, carbon dependency, corporate strategy, stakeholder requests.

Introduction

Since the end of the 1990s, formulating a climate strategy has become a vital business practice for many companies.[1] The main incentive to pursue corporate activities in tackling this issue is the fact that scientists across the world are in broad consensus that climate change is a matter of fact and urgent action is needed. Furthermore, in many countries policy-makers are seeking to implement industry-specific climate change policies and a range of corporate stakeholders are making requests to companies to develop strategies and disclose information about their efforts to tackle this issue.[2] For industries that are highly dependent on fossil fuels climate change is of real strategic importance:[3] Fossil fuels are core to the business of the oil and gas and automotive industries for example, and their global presence makes them highly vulnerable to stakeholder pressure. While heavy industries such as steel and cement also depend on fossil fuels, they are less visible to outsiders and receive less scrutiny. For service companies and manufacturing companies producing food, clothing and electronics this issue is often part of broader efforts to advance corporate social responsibility (CSR). However, if for the larger part of business addressing climate change is merely a way of profiling socially responsible behaviour,[4] how seriously can we expect the corporate sector to truly contribute to curbing global greenhouse gas (GHG) emissions to the extent that is needed?

The reality is that most carbon management efforts have indeed contributed to increasing transparency with regard to corporate GHG emissions and corresponding accounting practices.[5] Nevertheless, in terms of the actual output of emissions the picture

*   Timo Busch, Department of Management, Technology, and Economics, ETH Zurich, Switzerland. E-mail: tobusch@ethz.ch.

†   Jonatan M. Pinkse, Grenoble Ecole de Management, France. E-mail: jonatan.pinkse@grenoble-em.com.

is rather bleak: despite a few examples of best practice the overall level of industrial GHG emissions has increased in recent years:[6] for instance, global GHG emissions increased by 70 percent between 1970 and 2004.[7] And this trend still continues: global carbon dioxide (CO_2) emissions from fossil fuel combustion, cement manufacture and gas flaring increased by 24 percent between 2000 and 2007.[8] This is in clear contradiction to the need for significant GHG emissions reductions as advocated by the Intergovernmental Panel on Climate Change[9] and other seminal reports such as the Stern Review.[10]

One potential explanation for this rather disappointing result so far is that, although climate change has gained in importance as a CSR topic, for the majority of industry and service companies it is still not an urgent issue that significantly affects day-to-day business. The time frame currently set by policy-makers is too far off and up to now established regulatory instruments in the form of cap-and-trade, such as the European Union emissions trading scheme (EU ETS), have been fairly toothless and failed to drive companies to radically change their business practices.[11] As a consequence, incentives for achieving real emissions reductions have been limited.

Nevertheless, this is only part of the story. While many regulatory efforts have proven to be too weak to date, there are clear signs that political efforts urging companies to curb their level of emissions are intensifying. For example, although the EU ETS might have had minimal impact during its first few years, emissions trading has become a legitimized means of regulating corporate environmental behavior within the EU. What is more, the trading scheme's financial impact on companies is likely to increase substantially in coming years because the cap on emissions is being lowered and more allowances are to be auctioned instead of being given away for free.

Furthermore, even in countries such as the US where strict regulation on the federal level is still lacking, requests from other stakeholders such as investors, suppliers and consumers are increasing, further compelling companies to take climate change into account within their business strategies.[12] It is therefore likely that climate-specific stakeholder pressure will only augment in coming years, thus fuelling a sense of urgency to go beyond efforts to increase carbon transparency alone and start considering more substantive ways of reducing GHG emissions. In other words, a wait-and-see approach which delays action until policy-makers in the global arena have reached agreement might not be tenable and, instead, the development of a proactive and effective climate strategy will become more important, even without a global policy framework in place. However, companies from different industries or even within the same industry differ quite substantially with regards both their dependency on fossil fuels and the kind and degree of stakeholder pressure they face. What then are the general options available in choosing an appropriate climate strategy?

Emerging Stakeholder Requests in the Climate Context

Although climate change will have a physical impact on companies due to changing weather patterns and an increase in extreme weather events,[13] for the vast majority of companies the impact has not yet become tangible due to the long-term nature of climate change. However, whether companies face physical consequences is not actually that critical; what currently tends to be more important is which stakeholders put climate change on the corporate agenda and in which way they do so.[14] Whether companies consider stakeholder groups differs depending on the specific attributes of the groups themselves. Clarkson, for example, differentiates between primary and secondary stakeholders. Primary stakeholders refer to a group "without whose continuing participation the corporation cannot survive as a going concern" and secondary stakeholders are "those who influence or affect, or are influenced or affected by, the corporation, but ... are not engaged in transactions with the corporation and are not essential for its survival".[15] Furthermore, primary stakeholders are perceived as having legitimate requests and the urgency and power to enforce them. Secondary stakeholders may also be perceived as making legitimate requests but lack the same level of urgency and power.[16]

It is not only the attributes of the stakeholder group that matter, however. The specific power relationships between a stakeholder group and the targeted company also play a role, as does the way in which the request is made.[17] When a company depends on a stakeholder for resources, a request from this stakeholder will more likely be given attention. However, even if a certain stakeholder group has power over a company due to the latter's reliance on the stakeholder for resources this by no means implies that a stakeholder will also take advantage of this power differential.[18] That is to say, while some powerful stakeholder groups will make their requests directly to a company, others may choose to do so in an indirect way, or not at all. This direct/indirect dichotomy purposely refers to the nature of the request, not the relationship of a stakeholder group with a company. Take for example a primary stakeholder who can be said to have a direct *relationship* with a company, because the company will not survive without the stakeholder's resources.[19] This does not mean, however, that this primary stakeholder will also use this direct dependency relationship to make direct *requests* to companies to change behavior. While the primary stakeholder has direct access to the company, it can nevertheless opt to make an indirect stakeholder request using some sort of intermediary. A case in point is the historically passive stance of institutional investors at shareholder meetings. These investors have a direct relationship with companies as they potentially have a very high impact on companies due to owning the bulk of the shares. Nevertheless, in the past they have only used this power sparsely. In those cases where a request was issued it was generally done so indirectly through nongovernmental organizations (NGOs), particularly with regard to social and environmental issues.[20]

Therefore it is a company's constant challenge to investigate its business environment with regard to emerging stakeholders making requests for corporate action to tackle climate change, and to assess the urgency of these requests based on whether they have been made in a direct or indirect way. In addition, when such direct or indirect stakeholder requests surface the company needs to ascertain whether and/or how to best start addressing these requests.

Direct Requests by Stakeholders

Until now the direct stakeholder requests companies receive to reduce GHG emissions have almost exclusively come from regional, national and subnational regulators in the form of climate change regulations using various policy instruments. Contrary to the deadlock that international climate policy still seems to finds itself in, regulatory stakeholders across the world have stepped up their efforts considerably within their own borders of authority. It must be noted, however, that the global economic crisis has had a dampening effect to some degree. On a regional level, the most prominent example is the European Union's emission trading scheme. The EU ETS limits the output of CO_2 emissions by requiring participating companies to render an emissions allowance for each tonne of CO_2 they emit. The scheme covers emissions from power generation, oil refineries, coke ovens, iron and steel, cement, lime, glass, ceramics and pulp and paper, as well as from other combustion plants with a thermal capacity of more than 20MW. If companies plan to emit more than the allowances they have been allocated, they either need to reduce emissions or purchase additional allowances. Consequently, the pressure to reduce CO_2 emissions rises as the allowance price is expected to increase over time.

In the US, the situation remains unclear—at least on the federal level. Thus far, the Waxman-Markey bill has been the most ambitious cap-and-trade bill. It is also the most successful, having been passed in the House of Representatives in June 2009. The Kerry-Boxer bill was also a cap-and-trade proposal, aiming for emissions reductions of 20 percent by 2020 and 83 percent by 2050. However, Senator John Kerry, one of its sponsors, abandoned it because he realized the necessity for debating a new bill. The future of these federal efforts is still uncertain. Nevertheless, on a State level climate change regulations have been put in place. For example, ten northeastern and Mid-Atlantic States have founded the Regional Greenhouse Gas Initiative, a mandatory market-based effort using cap-and-trade with the objective of reducing the CO_2 emissions of the power sector by 10 percent by 2018.[21]

A different form of climate change regulation is a carbon tax, which has by and large only been implemented on national and subnational levels.[22] In the US, such a tax—focusing on CO_2 emissions from electricity generation—was first introduced in 2007 in Boulder, Colorado.[23] Additionally, in Finland, Germany, Italy, Sweden and the UK carbon taxes were introduced throughout the 1990s and the early years of the twenty-first century. A more recent example is the Province of British Columbia in Canada, which introduced a tax that applies to the purchase or use of fossil fuels.[24] In July 2010 the tax equalled CAN$20 per tonne of CO_2 equivalent emissions and increases by CAN$5 per tonne each year for the next two years to CAN$30 per tonne in 2012.

These direct regulatory stakeholder requests to reduce GHG emissions can be expected to increase in relevance, especially on the international level. Although no mutual and effective global climate treaty was reached in Copenhagen and Cancun, this does not mean that international climate regulation efforts have been dismissed altogether. Undoubtedly, governments will seek to find new ways of reaching a treaty and spelling out a new international agenda for climate change, which will further increase pressure on the corporate sector. If and when these efforts result in actual and significant GHG reductions remains dependent on how such a global treaty is translated to lower levels, and thus the ensuing stringency of regional, national and subnational regulations. Beyond enforcement on these lower levels, companies also face direct requests in terms of reporting and disclosure standards. In February 2010 for example, the US Securities and Exchange Commission (SEC) released its disclosure guidelines with regard to business or legal developments on climate change.[25] Companies have to report on specific, climate-related areas if they constitute a material risk. They cover, for instance, the consequences of existing and pending US climate regulations, international accords and treaties.

Indirect Requests by Stakeholders

Companies also face indirect stakeholder requests to reduce GHG emissions, which are of a less coercive nature. We differentiate between three main types of powerful stakeholders in the climate change context: institutional investors, consumers and value-chain partners. These can currently be considered salient stakeholders making legitimate and urgent requests, but with a tendency to do so in an indirect way.

First, institutional investors increasingly demand data on companies' emissions and related reduction strategies.[26] However, these requests are typically indirect, not only because no attempt is made to force companies to reduce emissions but also because investors tend to use nongovernmental organizations as brokers to make the request on their behalf. The most prominent example of this is the Carbon Disclosure Project. Through this effort, investors do not individually hold a company's management accountable for their climate strategy. Instead, this project is based on a mutual effort of investors to obtain relevant information with a London-based NGO as acting intermediary.

Nevertheless, indirect requests can also put pressure on companies because achieving emissions reductions can be considered an underlying motive. Companies that are not disclosing emissions or those having very high emissions run the risk of losing investors. Investors increasingly consider climate change as a corporate risk factor.[27] If companies do not manage climate change appropriately, investors may interpret this as a reason for withdrawing from certain investments. This development is particularly reflected in the growing scope of the Carbon Disclosure Project, which asks more than 3,700 companies worldwide to disclose information on their GHG emissions and the implications of climate change in terms of business risks and opportunities. The number of institutional investors supporting the project soared from 35 in 2003 (representing assets worth US$4.5 trillion) to 534 in 2010 (US$64 trillion worth of assets).[28] As of 2010, 410 of the largest 500 global companies (based on market capitalization as in the FTSE Global Equity Index Series) have responded, a significant increase from 2003 when this number was only 235.

Other examples of pressures stemming from this stakeholder group are the Dow Jones Sustainability Index,[29] which explicitly addresses companies' carbon management efforts when assessing the sustainability performance of the companies to be included in the index, and the 'Investor Network on Climate Risk'.[30] As institutional investors base their decisions partly on such indices and assessments, they will push companies towards a strategic consideration of their GHG emissions. The consequences of such action can be substantial. For example, in the case of TXU, a Texas power company, the Environmental Defense Fund (a US-based nonprofit organization) pushed the investors Kohlberg Kravis Roberts and Texas Pacific Group to address the company's emissions. In response, among other measures, TXU withdrew its plans to build several new coal-fired power plants; instead the company doubled its investment in wind power.[31]

Secondly, many companies are under the impression that consumers are increasingly more concerned about the emissions generated by the manufacturing processes of products, although research findings show that ethical consumerism is still a predominantly niche phenomenon.[32] Such requests from consumers are also of an indirect nature as consumer organizations or other types of NGOs usually channel them. An example of corporate reaction to indirect stakeholder requests is the initiative of the UK-based retail chain Tesco. In cooperation with the Carbon Trust[33]—a UK-based nonprofit organization with the mission to accelerate the move to a low-carbon economy—Tesco started labeling products with the specific amount of emissions incurred over the course of their production. To date, 120 products have been labelled.[34] In addition, Tesco is aiming to reduce its own carbon footprint by cutting energy consumption in its retail stores around the world and has set and made public a target to reduce emissions by 50 percent by 2020. On its website Tesco states that these initiatives were triggered by its customers, who they demanded the company offer them ways to make it easy to identify the carbon footprint of shopping.

Thirdly, companies increasingly receive requests from their value-chain partners to report and address GHG emissions. With their specific emissions, each company within a supply chain contributes to the carbon footprint of the end product or service. A significant reduction in this footprint thus requires all companies along the entire supply chain to increase their efforts to curb emissions. Nevertheless, this is often an indirect request in the sense that it is not always clear what the real source of the request is. For example, a company might put pressure on its suppliers to pass on pending direct requests it is receiving itself, perhaps from the government. However, this does not necessarily prompt companies to change their behavior in a certain way or make clear what kind of effect providing such data will have. Some doubts can be raised regarding whether achieving emissions reductions is the actual aim of such requests; while companies could use the information further down the supply chain for labeling purposes, it could also provide grounds for termination of supplier contracts. One example in this context is the Carbon Disclosure Project Supply Chain Program. In 2009, the 44 member companies of this program sought to gather GHG emissions-related information from a total of 1402 suppliers:[35] 710 suppliers responded to this first request, which corresponds to 51 percent. The member companies declared the intention of continuing to monitor their suppliers' carbon performance. Furthermore, 56 percent stated that they expect to drop suppliers failing to meet formal carbon management criteria.

Companies' Carbon Dependency

In light of these existing and emerging stakeholder requests to reduce GHG emissions, companies are pressurized to search for adequate response strategies.[36] Although companies face a wide variety of economic and societal pressures that come and go, we consider climate change as a salient issue that will be persistent over time and calls for strategic responses. Climate change is a severe long-term issue and society has yet to start paving the way towards a low-carbon economy. This requires a long transition process. As in the past direct stakeholder requests have remained rather marginal, companies were not pushed to significantly reduce the level of their emissions. Nevertheless, the more new indirect requests arise, the more companies will feel pressure to move beyond providing transparency alone and may actually start addressing climate change-related stakeholder requests in a more substantive way where necessary. This requires companies to analyze their carbon utilization patterns and related reduction and optimization potentials. Recent research illustrates that the level of GHG emissions differs tremendously across industries.[37] Moreover, individual companies within one industry may have a different potential to substitute fossil fuels with cleaner alternatives or increase carbon efficiency in other ways. Companies therefore also vary considerably in their potential to reduce

GHG emissions. A way for companies to analyze their specific reduction potential is by determining their level of carbon dependency.[38]

A company's carbon dependency describes its potential to reduce physical carbon performance over time, i.e., the extent to which a company is able to actually reduce emissions. For this purpose, current carbon intensity needs to be assessed, i.e., the level of GHG emissions in relation to annual sales. As a next step a potential future state of carbon intensity needs to be determined, assuming that the company undertakes all economically feasible efforts to reduce the level of GHG emissions. Economically feasible efforts refer to investments in carbon optimization that are not in contradiction with normal business decisions. This is influenced by future price and market conditions, technological options and alternative production processes, and is based on the assumption that a company will realize all economically feasible carbon optimization potentials, such as efficiency improvements and substitution options (e.g. renewable instead of fossil fuel-based electricity). Comparing current and future carbon intensity enables individual carbon dependency to be derived.

A highly carbon-dependent company is hardly able to further reduce its carbon intensity over a considered time period. This would be the case, for example, when a cement company has already implemented best available technologies in terms of carbon efficiency. Further reductions are almost impossible as the chemical process of calcination necessary for cement production emits carbon dioxide, and consequently the company has a high carbon dependency. Thus, the information about a company's carbon dependency determines the range of available response options a company has. In the context of this chapter, it is particularly important to look at the differences in carbon dependency within an industry, that is, at the relative potential to reduce a company's carbon intensity compared to its competitors.

Choosing an Appropriate Climate Strategy

Based on several years of field research conducted by both authors in different research projects, the remainder of this chapter sets out key findings regarding the organizational process of climate strategy formulation. Our purpose is neither to test any theoretical models nor to suggest the one and only climate strategy all companies should pursue in an ideal world. Instead, we summarize—based on the insights we gained—how to define and implement an appropriate climate strategy. We start by giving some background information on the research we have conducted on this topic over the past few years. Subsequently, we describe each of the strategies that emerge when combining the dimensions of the nature of stakeholder requests companies receive and their level of carbon dependency. Finally, we reflect critically on current factors that seem dominant when companies choose the direction of their climate strategy. Based on this, we highlight steps that we believe are essential for a corporate contribution towards achieving a low-carbon future.

Through several research projects over the past few years, we conducted more than 30 interviews with representatives from different industrial sectors, including energy utilities, banks, automotives, cement and chemicals. These interviews predominantly involved the senior environmental managers of companies based in the Netherlands, Germany, Switzerland and Austria. In addition, content analyses of companies' answers to the Carbon Disclosure Project were carried out in several research settings. Based on the results of these analyses, we obtained a detailed understanding of how companies respond to climate change and the corresponding stakeholder pressures exerted on them. Finally, insights from a previously conducted global survey were utilized. Conducted in 2007, the survey covers companies from eight different carbon-intensive industries. In total, 21 climate-relevant questions were added to an annual questionnaire, which was sent out to companies included in the Dow Jones Sustainability Index. The survey asked companies about their GHG emission profile and related strategies and targets. Furthermore, the companies were asked how strong they perceived the pressures from different stakeholder groups for reducing GHG emissions to be, and queried about the extent to which they pursue specific responses. This survey yielded 199 responses revealing differences and similarities in the corporate responses to climate change.

Based on a wide variety of information and data sources, we discussed our experiences and observations from the different research settings. One central finding was that we observed significant differences in how companies respond to climate change, even within the same industry and institutional settings. We then sought to find interpretations and explanations for these differences, which we summarized by mapping them along two dimensions, resulting in the following climate strategy framework. As has become clear from the discussion above, in developing an appropriate strategy to deal with climate change two dimensions are particularly important: the exposure to direct or indirect stakeholder requests to reduce GHG emissions, and the potential to reduce carbon intensity which determines a company's carbon dependency relative to competitors. As Figure 14.1 shows, combining these two dimensions results in four cases exemplifying generic climate strategies: increase internal efficiency, optimize the value chain, evade stakeholder pressures and maintain legitimacy.

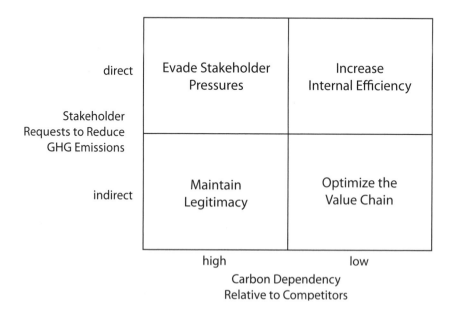

Figure 14.1 Strategic objectives of different climate strategies

Increase Internal Efficiency

The first case—increase internal efficiency—in the upper-right-hand corner of Figure 14.1 represents a condition where companies receive direct requests from regulatory stakeholders to reduce GHG emissions, but because they have a low carbon dependency there are still considerable opportunities to deal with the constraints set by the government. Since most policy instruments currently in place to regulate the output of GHG emissions are targeted at emissions generated within the boundaries of a company's production processes, a logical strategy for companies finding themselves in this situation is one of increasing the efficiency of internal processes. Such optimizations may aim at reducing the company's carbon intensity by substituting fossil fuels with cleaner alternatives or increasing energy efficiency. This strategy reflects the general concept of eco-efficiency[39] and the objective of reducing a company's environmental impact and its operational costs simultaneously. As a result, for companies that implement such a strategy any current or future GHG regulations and taxes will become less relevant compared to competitors that continue to generate a higher level of emissions.[40]

This strategy was undertaken by the international company CPH Chemie and Papier Holding AG[41] headquartered in Switzerland, whose activities include the development, production and sale of chemicals, paper and packaging films. In 2009, the company was able to reduce its CO_2 emissions by about 19 percent despite a higher production output. Furthermore, the company currently aims for a further GHG reduction of 10 percent per tonne of paper produced through the purchase of more efficient machines. This can be seen as a clear response to Swiss greenhouse gas regulations:[42] since 2008 companies have had to pay a CO_2 tax for emissions stemming from fossil fuels (in 2010 the tax was 36 CHF per tonne of CO_2). If a company commits to GHG reductions, it is exempt from paying the tax. The Swiss government assigns the amount of emissions allowances, reflecting the reduction target of the company. In the case of a surplus of allowances the company can sell the allowances on the Swiss allowance market. Two of CPH Chemie + Papier Holding AG's production sites obtained exemption from the tax, and the emissions reductions achieved were below the committed targets. Thus in 2009 the company was not only able to save on tax expenses, but could also sell the allowances and generate an additional income of 105,000 CHF.

Optimize the Value Chain

The second case—optimize the value chain—in the lower-right-hand corner of Figure 14.1 represents a condition where companies face indirect requests from various stakeholders, including investors, suppliers or consumers, to curb their GHG emissions. This is often brokered by NGOs. Due to the fact that these requests are made indirectly, the resulting pressure tends to be lower and, as a consequence, the corporate climate strategy can comprise a much broader range of reduction options. In the case where such pressures relate to a company's scope 1 emissions, management should focus on their own emissions within the value chain. This will result in strategies similar to those discussed for increasing internal efficiency. Thus, companies may have the opportunity to reconcile indirect and direct stakeholder requests by pursuing just one strategy. In the case where a lack of pressure exists regarding improving internal production processes, companies may focus on efforts that are targeted at other value chain-wide activities such as increasing the carbon efficiency of end products (downstream perspective) or engaging suppliers in proactive carbon practices (upstream perspective). This presupposes that either a company's end products have the potential for carbon reductions, or its supply chain bears a high potential to reduce carbon intensity and thus has a low carbon dependency. Furthermore, companies can explore low-carbon business niches by entering new business segments such as renewable energy technologies.

One example in this context is US-based retailer Walmart Stores Inc., which developed a sustainability index, intended to move its suppliers and retail competitors towards more sustainable business practices. Because Walmart is a retail company, opportunities to improve internal efficiency are very limited. Thus the company focuses on other value chain improvements. The company is implementing the index in three steps, starting with a survey to enable its suppliers to evaluate their own sustainability efforts. This survey comprises a set of questions for suppliers, the core components being the level of GHG emissions, corresponding reduction targets and energy costs. The intended purpose of this initiative is to first increase supply chain transparency, and to then make the necessary changes to foster life cycle-wide low-carbon production. Walmart's CEO stated that this initiative was triggered by customer requests: "The customer wants to know, wants transparency, and that's what this is all about."[43] In addition, the NGO Environmental Defense Fund has also engaged with Walmart on several issues since 2004; global warming being a central matter.[44] Walmart began this initiative as a consequence of indirect stakeholder requests, and has now pledged to eliminate 20 million metric tonnes of GHG emissions from their global supply chain by the end of 2015.[45]

Evade Stakeholder Pressures

The third case—evade stakeholder pressures—in the upper-left-hand corner of Figure 14.1 represents a condition where companies receive direct requests from regulatory stakeholders to reduce GHG emissions, creating very high pressure because companies have a limited potential to reduce carbon intensity. Such a high dependency places companies in a position in which they do not have many degrees of freedom in choosing how to deal with the constraints set by the government. Basically, under this scenario companies will be driven into a corner; not only are they highly carbon dependent, but they also have to respond to the stakeholder pressure somehow. Since there are no options that will not compromise business as usual in terms of production activities, companies typically rely on more politically oriented measures. In other words, instead of reducing emissions they will attempt to trim down the stakeholder pressure they face. There are two distinct directions in which a strategy aimed at evading stakeholder pressures can unfold.

On the one hand, a company may decide to divest or relocate carbon-intense business activities. In this case, the company reduces its exposure to governmental GHG regulation. When the regulation only has regional, national or subnational coverage, this leads to a phenomenon called "carbon leakage". Either the company itself or another company will fill the gap and continue production in a different regulatory environment. Experts on the EU ETS cap-and-trade system expected that emissions trading could prompt the relocation of industry and result in carbon leakage,[46] and this argument has also been used regularly by industry lobby groups to affect the way in which the trading scheme is implemented. However, since its introduction there is no evidence confirming that the EU ETS has triggered observable carbon leakage in sectors that are highly carbon-intense, such as steel and cement, and sectors requiring significant amounts of energy, such as primary aluminum.[47] One reason for this is the relatively weak reduction targets and free allocation of allowances of the first trading period from 2005–2007. It can be assumed that once the enforcement mechanisms are tighter, this situation might change.

On the other hand, a company may decide to lower stakeholder pressure by becoming active in the political arena. In this case, a company may seek to lobby policy-makers to avoid new regulations or shape new regulations in a way that does not result in market disruptions and loss of competitiveness. To illustrate, in 2007 numerous flagship companies such as Alcoa, Duke Energy and Du Pont formed the United States Climate Action Partnership,[48] a group of businesses and leading environmental organizations acknowledging the need for significant GHG emissions reductions. Essentially, the purpose of this partnership is to actively trigger new potential regulations, thereby contributing to emerging stakeholder requests and avoiding the situation that only their own business is exposed to new regulations. These efforts to steer the direction of regulatory developments are not only targeted at nationwide regulations, but sometimes also seek to push for a global climate change regime. An example of the former is a nationwide coalition in the US of more than 1,000 business leaders called "We Can Lead", which supports comprehensive, forward-looking energy and climate policies in the US.[49] A similar example on the international level is the initiative of more than 80 chief executive officers of leading global companies, who in 2008 published their collective recommendations to the G8 leaders for a future climate policy framework and for effectively combating climate change.[50]

Maintain Legitimacy

The fourth case—maintain legitimacy—in the lower-left-hand corner of Figure 14.1 represents a scenario where companies face indirect pressures to reduce their GHG emissions, but are highly carbon dependent and as such only have a low potential to actually reduce their carbon intensity. In contrast to the "evade stakeholder pressures" scenario, an immediate response to and/or interaction with policy-makers is not necessary. However, attempting to maintain control of the extent to which other stakeholders make indirect requests is considered prudent. The biggest risk for these companies is that the indirect requests will become direct requests over time, as many stakeholders also make requests to policy-makers to regulate industries that have remained unregulated until now. In other words, the main incentive to develop a climate strategy when a company finds itself in this situation is maintaining legitimacy to avert an escalating wave of stakeholder requests that might damage the corporate reputation. Nevertheless, companies in this scenario overall have more latitude in defining their response strategy and thus have a wide range of opportunities available in dealing with these stakeholder requests.

First, a company can conduct a carbon due diligence. This is an in-depth analysis of business operations, which may reveal thus far undiscovered GHG reduction potentials: even if these are minor they are often sufficient to satisfy stakeholder pressure. Notably, since the company does not face direct pressures such reduction efforts could be situated anywhere in the supply chain, even in the usage phase of the products. Secondly, a company may consider compensation of its GHG emissions. For example, the company could seek to become carbon neutral via voluntary offsetting projects. Similar to the Clean Development Mechanism (CDM), this requires reduction projects outside company boundaries (usually in a developing country) as a substitute for achieving internal efficiency gains within production processes. To actually boost legitimacy, such response strategies require further communication efforts. Customers can be informed about corresponding activities via green marketing campaigns and/or climate change labels on products. Financial markets, on the other hand, can be informed via the Carbon Disclosure Project or through participation in other NGO-led initiatives.

There are many prominent examples of companies aiming for a legitimacy-maintaining climate strategy. General Electric has invested significantly in its "Ecomagination" campaign to communicate its efforts in protecting the environment to stakeholders, especially with regard to their GHG emissions reductions.[51] Similarly, BP has created a low-carbon image through a rebranding campaign using the Helios logo and the "Beyond Petroleum" slogan, also offering website sections on renewable energies and an environmentally focused advertising campaign.[52] An example in the area of carbon neutrality is the logistics company DHL, which offers carbon-neutral package delivery to its customers by offsetting the incurred GHG emissions.[53] Furthermore, many companies engage in the current political debate on climate change via the World Business Council for Sustainable Development.[54]

Managing the Climate Challenge Ahead

In this chapter we have argued that in developing an appropriate strategy to deal with climate change two aspects are particularly important: the exposure to direct or indirect stakeholder requests and the relative carbon dependency compared to competitors. When combining these two dimensions, four cases exemplifying generic climate strategies emerge. In instances where a company has a high potential to curb emissions, the company can aim for win–win situations where, in the process of responding to stakeholder requests, competitiveness is protected and climatic impacts are reduced. The two cases "increase internal efficiency" and "optimize the value chain" in particular hold great promise in this regard. The strategy "evade stakeholder pressures", on the other hand, is not the most favorable one from a climate change perspective. When companies seek to maintain a business-as-usual scenario while at the same time influencing policymakers towards less stringent climate regulations global GHG emissions are likely to continue to increase further, as they have in recent years. In the case that a company chooses divesting instead, other companies outside regulatory boundaries would simply be prompted to fill the gap. The overall effect might even be worse because the offshoring of carbon-intense processes will typically occur in countries with lower environmental standards. Political lobbying might therefore be more favorable: even though the resulting regulations may be weaker than without lobbying, this outcome is still superior in terms of the reductions that can be achieved. Regarding a strategy of maintaining legitimacy, there is the risk that companies mainly focus on promoting their (often marginal) climate change or offsetting efforts instead of exploiting as much reduction potential as possible. Therefore, in light of the global climate challenge, it is important that companies prioritize their efforts: first by actually reducing their climate impact, and only then using the results for communication purposes.

A key question is whether companies may only embark on one strategy. We suggested that management could start to develop a climate strategy by considering the two dimensions suggested. However, this is just a starting point. Climate change is a complex issue and the same holds for corporate responses to it. Notably, companies do not usually only face pressures from a single stakeholder. Instead, it is likely that they face direct and indirect pressures from multiple sources simultaneously. As previously discussed, companies are able to reconcile direct and indirect stakeholder requests by increasing internal efficiencies. If companies have a high carbon dependency, however, it is unlikely that direct and indirect stakeholder requests can be reconciled.

Thus, companies may decide to start by focusing on one specific strategic option while also embarking on other options at a later stage in their carbon strategy. For example, the cement producer Holcim headquartered in Switzerland has formulated a strategy aimed at increasing internal carbon efficiency, even though the process of cement production is very carbon-dependent. To reduce CO_2 emissions the cement producer has increased its internal efficiency by focusing on product development (including composite cements), thermal energy efficiency (improving process technology) and the optimization of fuel composition (including use of waste as fuel).[55] Furthermore, the company substitutes clinker, a major raw material in cement production, with secondary materials like fly ash and blast furnace slag, so that the calcination process requires less fuel. As a consequence, when new emissions regulations are put in place, e.g., the introduction of a benchmark for emitted CO_2 per tonne of produced cement, the company is at the technological forefront. However, should the regulator pass a law targeting absolute emissions reductions, e.g., a carbon tax, the company would need to consider further options in addition. In anticipation of this, Holcim also seeks to evade stakeholder pressures through engagement in the Cement Sustainability Initiative, which is active in the political debate regarding international climate regulation in the context of sectoral approaches. Furthermore, Holcim participates in the World Business Council for Sustainable Development, which seeks to increase corporate environmental reputation, a precondition for maintaining legitimacy.[56] What the example of Holcim shows is that companies may not only follow one of the generic strategies, but also build in potential future contingencies; that is to say, besides reckoning with current stakeholder requests, proactive companies also envisage potential future requests.

Conclusions

In conclusion, there is no silver bullet solution to climate change. In light of intensifying climate change, it is of fundamental importance that both developed and developing countries acknowledge the necessity to curb GHG emissions. To find an appropriate corporate climate strategy, management may start by reconciling stakeholder requests and the company-specific carbon dependency. In the end, though, it will be essential that all companies seek to contribute as much as possible towards mitigating global climate change, independent of a new global climate treaty or stakeholder pressures. The times of the Global Climate Coalition and open corporate denial are over. In the corporate world climate change skepticism is not, at least officially, a big issue. This is a unique opportunity to combat climate change now.

Solving this overwhelming issue requires comprehensive and substantive action, accelerated by companies with proactive management of carbon issues targeted at curbing emissions internally and within their value chains to the greatest extent possible. This is reflected in our climate strategy matrix by the two strategic objectives "increase internal efficiency" and "optimize the value chain". Both require that companies be able to reduce their carbon intensity. Earlier we asked the question: how seriously can we expect the corporate sector to truly contribute to curbing global greenhouse gas (GHG) emissions to the extent that is needed? The answer is: we can expect a significant contribution, but this requires technological solutions and incentives for accelerated implementation. Only then can reductions in carbon dependency be realized. From the perspective of climate policy this implies that it is not only GHG regulation, which is important, but also active promotion and R&D in renewable and low-carbon technologies.

While we specifically focused on the issue of climate change in this chapter, the framework of potential response strategies could be extended to other contexts. Companies face direct and indirect stakeholder requests to deal with a great variety of social and environmental issues. What is specific about our framework, however, is the notion of carbon dependency as this sets limits on the range of available response options a company has. To apply the framework to different contexts it is therefore important to assess to what extent a company has the potential to reduce its dependency on specific human resources or natural resources compared to competitors. For example, if availability of cheap labor is one of the main drivers of competitiveness in an industry, this high dependency on less-educated human resources will probably reduce the options companies have in responding to stakeholder requests to deal with labor conditions. Equally, companies that make heavy use of natural resources which can only be extracted with high biodiversity loss face similar constraints. We thus argue that it is pertinent for companies to consider in what way competitiveness of the industry depends on specific human and/or natural resources related to the social or environmental issue on which stakeholders demand action.

Notes

1   Pinkse, J. and Kolk, A. (2009), *International Business and Global Climate Change*, Routledge, London.

2   Sprengel, D.C. and Busch, T. (2010), "Stakeholder engagement and environmental strategy: the case of climate change", *Business Strategy and the Environment*, vol. 20, no. 6, pp. 351–364.

3   Kolk, A. and Pinkse, J. (2008), "A perspective on multinational enterprises and climate change: learning from 'an inconvenient truth'?", *Journal of International Business Studies*, vol. 39, no. 8, pp. 1359–1378.

4   Devinney, T.M. (2009), "Is the socially responsible corporation a myth? The good, the bad, and the ugly of corporate social responsibility", *Academy of Management Perspectives*, vol. 23, no. 2, 44–56.

5   Kolk, A., Levy, D. and Pinkse, J. (2008), "Corporate responses in an emerging climate regime: the institutionalization and commensuration of carbon disclosure", *European Accounting Review*, vol. 17, no. 4, pp. 719–745.

6   The global economic crisis has pushed down GHG emissions, but this has largely been due to a slowdown in production activities instead of specific mitigation efforts.

7   IPCC (2007), *Climate Change 2007: Synthesis Report*, Intergovernmental Panel on Climate Change, Geneva.

8   In 2000, the estimation for global carbon dioxide emissions from fossil fuel burning, cement manufacture and gas flaring is 6738 million metric tons of carbon. After a continuous increase each subsequent year, the estimation for 2007 is 8365 million metric tons of carbon. This corresponds to an overall increase of 24 percent. Compare Carbon Dioxide Information Analysis Center, http://cdiac.ornl.gov/trends/emis/tre_glob.html.

9   IPCC (2007), op. cit.

10 Stern, N. (2006), *The Economics of Climate Change: The Stern Review*, Cambridge University Press, Cambridge.

11 Hoffmann, V.H. (2007), "EU ETS and investment decisions: the case of the German electricity industry", *European Management Journal*, vol. 25, no. 6, pp. 464–474.

12 Lash, J. and Wellington, F. (2007), "Competitive advantage on a warming planet", *Harvard Business Review*, vol. 85, no. 3, pp. 94–102.

13 Winn, M., Kirchgeorg, M., Griffiths, A., Linnenluecke, M.K. and Günther, E. (2010), "Impacts from climate change on organizations: a conceptual foundation", *Business Strategy and the Environment*, vol. 20, no. 3, pp 157–173.

14 Kolk, A. and Pinkse, J. (2007), "Towards strategic stakeholder management? Integrating perspectives on sustainability challenges such as corporate responses to climate change", *Corporate Governance*, vol. 7, no. 4, pp. 370–378.

15 Clarkson, M.B.E. (1995), "A stakeholder framework for analyzing and evaluating corporate social performance", *Academy of Management Review*, vol. 20, no. 1, pp. 92–117; citations on page 106–107.

16 Mitchell, R.K., Agle, B.R. and Wood, D.J. (1997), "Toward a theory of stakeholder identification and salience: defining the principle of who and what really counts", *Academy of Management Review*, vol. 22, no. 4, pp. 853–886.

17 Eesley, C. and Lenox, M.J. (2006), "Firm responses to secondary stakeholder action", *Strategic Management Journal*, vol. 27, no. 8, pp. 765–781.

18 Hill, C.W.L. and Jones, T.M. (1992), "Stakeholder–agency theory", *Journal of Management Studies*, vol. 29, no. 2, pp. 131–154.

19 Frooman, J. (1999), "Stakeholder influence strategies", *Academy of Management Review*, vol. 24, no. 2, pp. 191–205.

20 Sparkes, R. and Cowton, C.J. (2004), "The maturing of socially responsible investment: a review of the developing link with corporate social responsibility", *Journal of Business Ethics*, vol. 52, no. 1, pp. 45–57.

21 See http://rggi.org/home.

22 Attempts were made in the 1990s to implement a carbon tax on a European level, but after failing repeatedly the idea was abandoned altogether.

23 See http://www.carbontax.org/progress/where-carbon-is-taxed.

24 See http://www.fin.gov.bc.ca/tbs/tp/climate/A4.htm.

25 See http://www.sec.gov/news/press/2010/2010-15.htm.

26 Funk, K. (2003), "Sustainability and performance", *MIT Sloan Management Review*, vol. 44, no. 2, pp. 65–70.

27 Mercer (2011), *Climate Change Scenarios: Implications for Strategic Asset Allocation*, Mercer LLC, Carbon Trust, International Finance Corporation.

28   See http://www.cdproject.net.

29   The investment volume based on this index rose from about US$1 billion in 2000 to about US$6 billion in 2007. See SAM (2008), *Dow Jones Sustainability Indexes—Annual Review 2008*, Sustainable Asset Management, Zürich.

30   See http://www.incr.com.

31   Friedman, T.L. (2007), "Marching with a mouse", *The New York Times*, March 16 2007; Environmental Defense Fund (2007), "Ushering in a new era for coal", see http://www.edf.org/article.cfm?contentID=6025.

32   Auger, P., Burke, P., Devinney, T.M. and Louviere, J.J. (2003), "What will consumers pay for social product features?", *Journal of Business Ethics*, vol. 42, no. 3, pp. 281–304.

33   See http://www.carbontrust.co.uk.

34   See http://www.tesco.com/greenerliving/greener_tesco/what_tesco_is_doing/carbon_labelling.page.

35   CDP (2010), *Supply Chain Report 2010*, Carbon Disclosure Project, London.

36   Sprengel and Busch (2010), op. cit.

37   Trucost (2009), *Carbon Risks and Opportunities in the S&P 500*, Trucost, Boston.

38   Hoffmann, V.H. and Busch, T. (2008), "Corporate carbon performance indicators: carbon intensity, dependency, exposure, and risk", *Journal of Industrial Ecology*, vol. 12, no. 4, pp. 505–520.

39   Ehrenfeld, J.R. (2005), "Eco-efficiency: philosophy, theory, and tools", *Journal of Industrial Ecology*, vol. 9, no. 4, pp. 6–8.

40   Lash, J., and Wellington, F. (2007), "Competitive advantage on a warming planet", *Harvard Business Review*, vol. 85, no. 3, pp. 94–102.

41   See http://www.cph.ch/investoren/geschaeftsberichte.htm.

42   See http://www.bafu.admin.ch/co2-abgabe/05246/index.html?lang=de.

43   See http://www.pressreleasepoint.com/walmart-index-tout-ecofriendly-products.

44   See http://www.edf.org/page.cfm?tagID=2101.

45   See http://walmartstores.com/Sustainability/7673.aspx.

46   Reinaud, J. (2005), *Industrial Competitiveness under the European Union Emissions Trading Scheme*, International Energy Agency, Paris.

47   Reinaud, J. (2008), *Issues Behind Competitiveness and Carbon Leakage: Focus on Heavy Industry*, International Energy Agency, Paris.

48   See http://www.us-cap.org.

49   See http://www.wecanlead.org.

50   WBCSD and WEF (2008), *CEO Climate Policy Recommendations to G8 Leaders July 2008*, World Business Council for Sustainable Development/World Economic Forum, Geneva.

51   See http://www.ecomagination.com.

52   BP (2008), *Sustainability Report 2007*, British Petroleum, see http://www.bp.com.

53   See http://www.dpwn-gogreen.com/go.

54   See the section "Energy and Climate" at the WBCSD's web page http://www.wbcsd.org.

55   Busch, T., Klee, H. and Hoffmann, V.H. (2008), "Curbing greenhouse gas emissions on a sectoral basis: the cement sustainability initiative". In R. Sullivan (ed.), *Corporate Responses to Climate Change*, Greenleaf Publishing, Sheffield, pp. 204–219.

56   Doh, J.P., Howton, S.D., Howton, S.W. and Siegel, D.S. (2010), "Does the market respond to an endorsement of social responsibility? The role of institutions, information, and legitimacy", *Journal of Management*, vol. 36, no. 6, pp. 1461–1485.

Theoretical-Based Frameworks for Understanding Pressures, Conflicts and Reconciliation

15 Boomerang Politics: How Transnational Stakeholders Impact Multinational Corporations in the Context of Globalization

FRANK DEN HOND[*] AND FRANK G. A. DE BAKKER[†]

Keywords

Multinationals, social movements, stakeholders, transnational activism.

Introduction

As has recently been pointed out, stakeholder theory faces two closely related challenges in the light of globalization.[1] On the one hand, globalization has not only led many firms to explore and expand into different parts of the world, it has also—and perhaps consequentially so—created possibilities for nontraditional stakeholders to "knock on the doors" of firms and make their concerns heard. On the other hand, the context of the multitude and complexity of novel stakeholder relationships that were not usually considered in stakeholder mappings renders the issue of corporate responsibility even more "political"[2] than stakeholder relationships, at least in the context of specific issues, have always been.

However, exactly *how* such nontraditional stakeholders knock on the firms' doors has not been explored sufficiently in stakeholder theorizing,[3] even though there are some studies that focus on the characteristics of firms associated with the likelihood of them becoming targets of stakeholder group mobilization.[4] In a general sense, social movement studies have been suggested as providing useful concepts and theorizing for doing so.[5] Here, we build on this suggestion, more specifically on Keck and Sikkink's analysis of how transnational activist networks (TANs) are mobilized to remedy issues beyond the local situation where they occur.[6] Local issues become a cause for international mobilization

[*]   Frank den Hond, Department of Organization Sciences, Faculty of Social Sciences, VU University Amsterdam, the Netherlands. E-mail: f.den.hond@vu.nl.

[†]   Frank G.A. de Bakker, Department of Organization Sciences, Faculty of Social Sciences, VU University Amsterdam, the Netherlands. E-mail: f.g.a.de.bakker@vu.nl.

when local protesters seek support from international nongovernmental organizations (NGOs) and/or activist groups. This has been recurrent in various industries, notably the international garment and electronics industries where production chains have been globalized.[7] As firms in these and other industries have outsourced production to low-cost countries, concerns about the (lack of) regulation about the negative externalities associated with their production processes have also grown. Consequently, stakeholder mobilization has sometimes been substantial, focusing on issues of environmental degradation, occupational safety, child labor, forced labor, sexual harassment, wage-rates, etc.[8] Western firms have been challenged by Western stakeholder groups to improve their performance on these issues in their overseas production facilities.[9] Yet stakeholder theory appears to have difficulty in explaining the potential leverage that stakeholder groups *without* a clear and direct stake in a firm may exert over that particular firm.[10] The model Keck and Sikkink proposed could offer a way to overcome this shortcoming.

Although Keck and Sikkink's "boomerang model" was originally developed in the context of contentious politics—mobilization against state actors, as has traditionally been the focus of social movement scholars—the model can also be applied productively in the corporate context of "private politics", conflict resolution without recourse to the state or legal procedures.[11] Soule suggests that the separate study of contentious and private politics is an artifact of how research traditions in various fields have developed, and that in reality the two cannot really be separated.[12] Following her, as well as building on our own observations in the study of transnational mobilization against corporations, we propose to speak of "boomerang politics" as a general and overarching term in order to advance stakeholder theory in the light of the challenges from globalization by exploring how nontraditional stakeholders knock on firms' doors.[13]

In this chapter we will discuss the idea of boomerang politics and relate it to a less explored category of stakeholders, those *without* a clear and direct stake in a firm, and the way they could exert influence over that particular firm. In the next section we will explore Keck and Sikkink's boomerang model, expand it towards the area of private politics and illustrate it with some examples of what we refer to as "boomerang politics". We will highlight some reflections on the generalized model of boomerang politics and conclude our chapter with an indication of implications of this model for stakeholder theory, thus contributing to the objective of this volume.

Boomerangs in Contentious Politics

The boomerang model was developed in the 1990s by political scientists Keck and Sikkink in order to explain the mode of operating and success of what they called "transnational activist networks" (TANs). They used this term to highlight "the structured and structuring dimension in the actions of these complex agents".[14] Others defined such networks as "a collaboration of movement organizations in at least two countries that exchange information and experiences, provide mutual support, have at least a partially organized social base, and engage in joint strategic campaigns".[15] The boomerang effect explained, among other things, leverage politics: "the ability to call upon powerful actors to affect a situation, where weaker members of a network are unlikely to have influence".[16] Put briefly, the model thus makes clear how local protesters against a specific State A—the ultimate target—might be blocked, but could still be successful by mobilizing NGOs (international, or in State B) through TANs to stimulate State B—the primary target of the boomerang—to exert pressure on State A. When direct confrontation of the ultimate target is unproductive, some allies are sought that could pressure the primary target of the boomerang to compel the ultimate target to give in to demands. In Figure 15.1 this original boomerang model is depicted.

The model has been applied or cited in many different studies[17] in fields such as political science and sociology. Nevertheless, the model is of broader relevance than merely in its original focus on contentious politics. As the potential leverage that the model demonstrates is made possible through increased levels of communication and information exchange and transnational solidarity, resulting in mobilization within Western countries to the support of affected parties in other countries, it can be extended beyond state politics. This we point out in the next section.

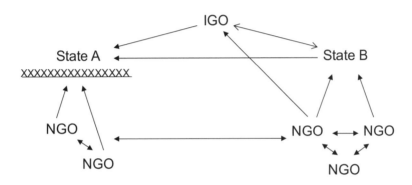

Figure 15.1 The boomerang effect (adapted from Keck and Sikkink, 1998).
Arrows indicate flows of information exchange, support, or pressure

Boomerangs in Private Politics

McAteer and Pulver were among the first to acknowledge the wider relevance of the Keck and Sikkink model for the domain of private politics. They proposed a "corporate boomerang model" to analyze international protest against multinational corporations.[18] Their model builds on the use of shareholder activism by two different TANs in their efforts to target oil companies. Both cases are set in the Ecuadorian part of the Amazon. In one case the TANs aimed to prevent Burlington Resources initiating oil extraction in two concession blocks; in the other to force Chevron Corporation to remediate the environmental damage caused by its earlier operations. In both cases the protest focused on environmental issues and the rights of indigenous people. The differences in outcome between the two cases are explained by variations in the cohesiveness of the respective TANs and by the relative vulnerability of the two corporate targets.

The model of McAteer and Pulver is a valuable extension of the original boomerang model because it explicitly focuses on the role of private politics and illustrates how these politics differ from state-focused activism. However, the problem with this conception is that is does not cover *all* possible pathways the boomerang effect could follow. We therefore extend their model by presenting different scenarios of how the corporate sector might be brought into the boomerang model some further, or of how private politics might intermingle with, or substitute for, contentious politics. To this end we explore the corporate boomerang effect from different angles to scrutinize its potential to understand the complex relationship between social movements, civil society, (multinational) corporations and state institutions. In the next section we present three examples of boomerangs in which corporations are involved.

Three Examples

In collaboration with various co-authors, we have been involved in empirical studies of interactions between activist groups and firms. Here, we summarize three of them: Gildan,[19] Nike[20] and multinationals in Burma/IHC Caland,[21] in order to present—in the next section—some reflections on boomerang politics.[22]

GILDAN, INC.

Gildan is a Canadian producer of sports apparel. It is one of the many Western multinationals in the garment industry that was challenged by activist groups over labor conditions in their overseas production facilities. When Gildan set up production facilities in Honduras in 1998, it had already adopted a corporate code of conduct. Unlike in other cases, in which the production plant is a subsidiary of another multinational, often under Chinese or Korean ownership,[23] the Honduras production facilities where under direct control by Gildan.

In the course of 2001–2002 two organizations, the Maquila Solidarity Network (MSN) and the Honduran Independent Monitoring Team (EMIH) jointly investigated the investment strategy and labor practices of Gildan in Honduras, Mexico and El Salvador. MSN is a Canadian network that had been involved in campaigns against several transnational companies; EMIH is an organization defending women's rights in the *maquilas*. Although Gildan claimed that working conditions in its factories were above local standards, a different picture was broadcast on January 22 2002, in the CBC television program *Disclosure*. It revealed a series of abuses of workers' rights in Gildan's El Progreso factory in Honduras: excessively high production quotas, wages insufficient to cover even basic needs, remuneration based on productivity, supervised breaks, 11-hour work shifts, poor air quality in the workshops, wrongful dismissals, mandatory pre-employment pregnancy tests for women and the dismissal of unionizing employees. MSN/EMIH demanded improvement of the working conditions and Gildan dismissed all allegations. The broadcasting transferred the conflict to Canada, and a campaign was born.

The case developed in several rounds of interaction. Gildan made several moves over time in first adopting the WRAP standard (an industry-based certification scheme), then seeking accreditation from the well-known Bureau Veritas, subsequently endorsing the FLA standard (a multistakeholder standard believed by many to be more stringent than WRAP),[24] then closing the plant, and finally reopening another plant while promising to preferentially hire workers from the previous plant. On their part, EMIH/MSN made clear that no progress was made, reiterated their claims and demands, expanded their network of support (Amnesty International, Oxfam, Solidarity Fund QFL—a socially responsible investment fund holding shares in Gildan), protested with FLA once Gildan was affiliated, and finally accepted a solution under tutelage of FLA although their preferred standard had been SA8000, an NGO standard deemed more stringent than FLA.

The Gildan case is a clear example of a corporate boomerang (Figure 15.2). After all, El Progreso workers could not solve their complaints with the local management, and hence sought support with EMIH in Honduras, and through EMIH, with MSN in Canada, thus creating a transnational activist network. MSN organized and kept pressure on Gildan until, eventually, the conflict was resolved.

Two characteristics make the case interesting. First is the recourse to labor standards and other external certifications, both by Gildan and MSN. Seeking refuge to such external solutions apparently strengthens both actors' position in their negotiation process, arguably in part by shifting the debate towards a discussion on the legitimacy of the external certification schemes rather than on what is actually being certified. The attention then focuses on the method of measurement instead of on what is being measured. Second is the observation of escalation in the conflict, prior to settlement, due to MSN expanding the network of supporters. Different modes of escalation are also observed in the next example.

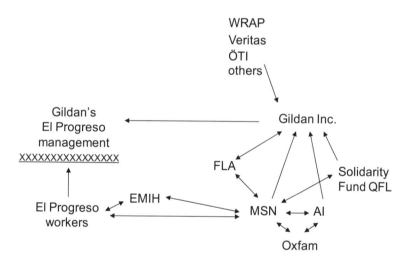

Figure 15.2 The Gildan case in a boomerang model

NIKE, REEBOK AND ADIDAS

Gildan is one of the many firms that were challenged for substandard labor conditions in its overseas production facilities. Other firms, such as Nike, Reebok and adidas, have experienced a wide variety of such challenges, relating to different production facilities in various countries. In each of these cases the protest model of the boomerang was similar, and need therefore not be repeated here. However, the recurrence of the protest led us to question whether and how such instances of protest might be related: do these protests have an impact on one another? Also, we were interested in gaining more insight into the patterning of protest tactics over time.

In order to address these questions we selected eight cases of protest against Nike, adidas and Reebok in different countries (Indonesia, Vietnam, China and Pakistan) that were thoroughly analyzed and well covered in publicly available documents (mostly academic articles and teaching cases). Notably, the anti-sweatshop campaign started with a case of Nike in Indonesia, which we included in our selection of cases. We focused our analysis on the right-hand side of the boomerang: the tactics employed by the activist groups in the TAN toward the company. Earlier on we presented a categorization of protest tactics, and argued that some tactics were only being used by activist groups when they felt that extra pressure was needed because of a lack of progress toward realizing their goals, i.e. escalation.[25] Following this typology of tactics, we coded for the observed tactics in each of the selected cases. We observed that the tactics used at the start of some of the cases resembled a stage of escalation. Hence we concluded that in order to understand how the activist groups in the TAN operate in each of the cases, we need to consider the collection of cases together rather than examining the cases individually.

We noticed escalation in corporate boomerangs along four dimensions. First in the choice of tactics: over time, as insufficient progress was made, activist groups would resort to tactics that make a larger impact on the targeted company. Secondly, in the intensity of employing tactics: over time there was an increase of the number of protest tactics being employed until the case would be more or less resolved, or for cases in China until the activist groups considered that no further progress could be made. Thirdly in the locus of protest: as little progress was made in the first case of Nike in Indonesia, protest was organized around allegations of substandard labor practices at other suppliers to Nike in different countries. Finally, the protest spread to targeting other firms in the industry, Reebok and adidas, as well as yet more firms. The latter two steps involve an upward "scale shift", "a change in the number and level of coordinated contentious actions to a different focal point, involving a new range of actors, different objects, and broadened claims",[26] in which the problem is redefined from a local mishap to one that is endemic for the industry. Hence, other elements of the corporate boomerang come into play here.

Multinationals in Burma

The third example is of a slightly different nature as the ultimate target here is a state. The Burma regime has long been considered to be an oppressive military dictatorship where the military controls large parts of the economy. Repressed social and political unrest in the late 1980s, and the rulers' refusal to acknowledge the results of the 1990 free elections, were instrumental in the setting up of expatriate activist groups and networks campaigning for a "Free Burma" in Western countries and Thailand. They argued that any foreign company setting up business in Burma needs to cooperate with the regime, and therefore these activists plead for a ban on novel, and the withdrawal of existing, investments by Western companies. The calls for boycott and disinvestment were endorsed by Aung San Suu Kyi, leader of the opposition and winner of the 1991 Nobel Prize for Peace. Many Western firms have hence experienced pressure to divest from the country. Consequently, many left the country, offering varying explanations, including protest threats, shifts in priorities and damage to their corporate reputation.[27] Levi-Strauss pointed out a moral argument, that doing business in Burma implies supporting the regime and hence its violations of human rights.

Other firms resisted the increasing activist pressure. IHC Caland, a Dutch specialist supplier in the offshore oil and gas industry, is one such company. It faced pressure when in the summer of 1998 one of its subsidiaries gained a contract for a project in Burma's territorial waters. The company refused to cancel the contract, providing various arguments, including that the company would need the turnover; that cancelling the contract would hurt the company's reputation as a trustworthy partner; and that other firms would take over the contract so nothing would change in Burma anyway. It also argued that unlike in the USA, where President Clinton had imposed a ban on further investment in Burma, there was no legal obligation in the Netherlands to refrain from doing business in Burma.

The Dutch Burma Coalition (BCN)—a pressure group set up by various development and environmental organizations and trade unions in order to coordinate the Burma campaign in the Netherland—staged protest events, for instance during and around the company's annual shareholder meetings, and mobilized public opinion, political parties and some of the firm's financers. It often did so in close collaboration with other organizations. Talks with the company were largely unproductive—actually, in 1999, the company accepted a second contract—but eventually, in 2003, IHC Caland's new CEO declared that the company would not accept new contracts with Burma and in finalizing its current contracts would adhere to OECD guidelines.

Multinationals in Burma can also be understood from the perspective of a boomerang model (see Figure 15.3 for the IHC Caland case), suggesting that States can be the ultimate targets of corporate boomerangs. In this example it is remarkable that there is no direct link between the TAN and the Burmese population although there is with their representatives in expatriate groups. A second point of interest is that when the activist coalition around BCN had difficulty in convincing the company to change its behavior, it sought to enrol yet other actors, such as political parties and banks financing the corporation, in its campaign. A second-layer or nested boomerang was thus created, as is depicted in the right-hand side of Figure 15.3.

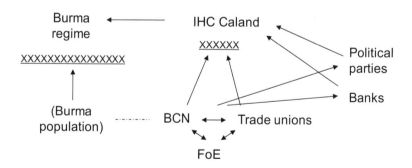

Figure 15.3 The IHC Caland case in a boomerang model

Discussion

As the examples have shown, boomerang models can be identified in both contentious politics and private politics, but as Soule suggests, the distinction is artificial. Nevertheless, in this chapter we applied this somewhat artificial distinction, if only because states can be the ultimate targets of boomerangs oriented toward corporations as is shown in the case of IHC Caland, and of Western multinationals in Burma more generally. Here, the "pressure path" is largely similar to the divestment campaign against firms having made investments in South Africa during the Apartheid regime—morally legitimized by the Sullivan Principles, and eventually supported by the USA government through legislation.[28] Hence, the boomerang model is a broader phenomenon than is acknowledged in either the Keck and Sikkink or the McAteer and Pulver models. We therefore propose to refer to "boomerang politics" as a general model in which NGOs and/or activist groups, on behalf of affected parties, exert pressure on primary targets in order for them to influence the ultimate target.

As shown in the examples, boomerang politics can be quite complex to unravel. They involve a dynamics of interaction, with parties acting and reacting to each other's moves. Standards and certification schemes may be involved. Escalation may occur along various dimensions: in the number of allies, in the choice of tactics and in the choice of where and when to challenge targets. Finally, boomerangs may become differentiated as a second layer of boomerang pressure is added to the primary target, as was the case in IHC Caland.

Beyond these observations on the intricacies of particular cases—which we expect to reflect more generalized patterns though—some further reflections on the generalized model of boomerang politics are warranted. Below, we focus on the nature and relationship of the different targets involved, their sensitivity to pressure and presence of intermittent organizations. These reflections provide an insight in who the targets are, why they are targeted, and how specific organizations can interfere in this process. We deliberately refrain from discussing the properties of the activists/NGOs because we focus on the specific tactic of boomerang politics, rather than on a broader overview of tactical choices such NGOs could make as discussed elsewhere in the literature.[29]

Nature and Relationship of Primary and Ultimate Targets

Both ultimate and primary targets can be states or firms or, for that matter, any authority.[30] We restrict our discussion here to states and firms. The situation in which both the primary and the ultimate targets are states is covered in the Keck and Sikkink model; it is the domain of international politics from which this model emanates. Here, the starting point is most often to assert that states are autonomous entities that have a prolonged existence. Although all sorts of (international) treaties and policy documents exist that formally bind states, the accompanying reinforcement mechanisms are usually weak. Hence, there are no hierarchical relationships between states. States are autonomous entities but all sorts of resource dependencies may attenuate their room to manoeuvre, as we will discuss in the next section.

However, the relationship between firms as primary and ultimate targets is quite different. As opposed to states, the long-term existence of firms is less certain as they may go bankrupt or cease to exist, for instance due to divestment. This is, in general, more likely for the ultimate targets as they are often (local) subcontractors or subsidiaries, than for primary targets who are more often multinational firms. The very existence of subsidiaries and subcontractors as ultimate targets might come to be at stake when the primary targets threaten to cease doing business with them. The threat is of course stronger to the extent that they are more dependent on a single client.

This brings us to a second major difference: the existence of a contractual relationship between the primary and ultimate target. The production facility, the ultimate target, is either part of the corporate hierarchy as a subsidiary, or is bound to the focal firm via contractual obligations. In the latter case, the relationship may involve several steps and can be discontinued once a conflict with stakeholders arises, enabling the contracting firm to deny responsibility for, say, social conditions in their contractors' production plants. This possibility of close down and potential replacement of production facilities weakens the position of these local firms, as well as of local workers and the coherence of TANs, as employers may pit workers against each other.[31] In such a situation, "gains made in one location may mean very real losses for workers elsewhere".[32] This possibility can be a threat to corporate boomerangs; activists' efforts to improve for instance working conditions might result in worsening circumstances for local workers as they could be put out of work.[33] Apparently the application of a corporate boomerang involves a careful balancing act, which might weaken its effectiveness and its attractiveness to activists.

Finally, whereas relations between states usually are permanent in nature, relations between firms are more temporal, or at least easier to sever. Of course, these relations are covered in contracts but a subcontracting firm may have contractual obligations to multiple firms which might mean that they are less dependent on one single firm.

Challenging states as ultimate targets through firms as primary targets—the situation in Burma—combines some of the above difficulties. After all, the very reason for which states might be challenged as ultimate targets is arguably related to the lack of a well-functioning pluralistic and democratic system, which would otherwise provide entry points for conflict resolution. Further, in the contractual relationship between the state as ultimate target and the firm as primary target, the balance of power is in most cases likely to lean toward the state. The state has concessions to sell and orders to grant, whereas the firm faces competition; other firms might step in and take the order, as the IHC Caland example illustrated.

Sensitivity to Pressure

Another important element in the comparison between state-focused and corporate boomerangs involves the differences in vulnerability of the respective targets. What makes a state or a firm sensitive to pressure?

The responsiveness of states as primary targets is relatively well understood—it is the domain of most of the social movement literature—and can be said to depend on the functioning of a pluralistic and democratic system.[34]

To exert influence over states as ultimate targets is more difficult, and likely to be related to resource dependencies as addressed in resource-dependence theory in organization studies.[35] For example, states can be dependent on other states or intergovernmental organizations (IGOs) for financial or military resources. Think of loans (either direct from other states, or through international institutions such as the International Monetary Fund [IMF], World Bank, or regional development banks), development aid (financial or material, from other states, through UN agencies such as FAO, WHO, or from relief NGOs), or defence capacity (delivery of equipment, training of forces, inclusion in security programs either bilaterally or through IGOs such as NATO). Such dependencies create power differences that can be used to exert leverage over the dependent party. Because of the autonomy of states, the possibility to opt for autarky (such as North Korea or Burma), or the presence of oppressive regimes, such resource dependencies need not always exist, or can turn out to be ineffective. Still, in many situations examples of such dependencies between states can be found.

Legitimacy is an important element in these discussions about sensitivity to external pressure.[36] To the extent that governments want to be perceived as legitimate (e.g., by being democracies, or by being members in good standing of IGOs such as OECD, ILO or other UN agencies), different types of pressure can be exerted upon them. In institutional theory often a distinction is made between cultural–cognitive, normative, and regulative elements that bring stability to social life.[37] Regulative elements often involve the force of law; cultural–cognitive elements are related to normative ideas about what constitutes moral legitimacy, to adhere to specific norms; and cultural–cognitive elements relate to what is perceived to be an entity in good standing. Obviously, the three elements are interrelated, and certainly not universal. For example, calling upon the Universal Declaration of Human Rights may be less effective in some Asian states or regarding Asian companies, as the very notion of human rights is contested across different cultures.[38] For coercive elements to be effective a government needs to accept the jurisdiction of international treaties, i.e. to acknowledge the underlying norms that are expressed in such treaties; only then can they be brought to the associated courts (think of the International Court of Justice, European Council of Human Rights or the European Court).

The vulnerability of firms as ultimate targets is implied in the contractual relationship with the firm(s) for which it produces. Michael Porter's framework nicely captures the dynamics of the relationship in case the ultimate target is in a supply relationship, rather than part of the corporate hierarchy of the primary target.[39]

Resource dependencies and legitimacy provide levers on firms as primary targets. Next to regulatory coercive pressure, several tactics can be applied to exert normative pressure.[40] Examples include:

1. Different forms of corporate governance, such as shareholder activism on social issues or socially responsible investments;
2. Attempts to influence operational costs and benefits, either in the marketplace or in public opinion (through a reputation effect); and
3. Through social alliances in which issues of corporate social responsibility can be influential.

The sensitivity to such pressure will vary across different industries and across different countries, but a combination of such tactics is likely to be applied by NGOs to invoke change at the level of the ultimate target.[41] The availability and nature of intermittent organizations is another element that is likely to influence the pressure paths.

Presence of Intermittent Organizations

Intermittent organizations can be important in boomerang politics. IGOs such as the United Nations, World Trade Organization, International Labour Organization or the European Union have a normative role, among other roles, in keeping up standards among their members. It is on this ground that they may have influence over State A, as it allows for symbolic pressure, and sometimes may legitimate coercive power. Thus, in Figure 15.4, IGOs may be approached by NGOs to pressurize State B to pressurize State A, or, NGOs and State B might seek to convince IGOs to pressurize State A. Sometimes NGOs may also have an observer status to these intergovernmental organizations and of course both firms and NGOs try to influence decision-making processes within these organizations, for instance via lobbying. IGOs make predominantly use of symbolic politics (exerting political pressure) and leverage politics (imposing sanctions).

Firms on the other hand may be adherents to multi-stakeholder initiatives (MSIs) which typically are independent from states, and in which NGOs may have a much larger say. In some cases NGOs are (co-)founders of multi-stakeholder initiatives, such as the Fair Labor Association or Social Accountability International, whereas in other cases they are partners in IGO initiatives, such as the UN Global Compact.[42] These MSIs predominantly make use of accountability politics such as certification or external verification. It should be noted that often Western firms are members of these MSIs, whereas their contract partners are typically not: this might be caused by a mix of higher vulnerability (reputation risks), slack resources or a stronger presence of NGOs in their immediate environment. Overall, the effectiveness of intermittent organizations is regularly debated with regard to both the state-focused and the corporate-focused ones.[43] With the increasing focus on private politics, their role nevertheless seems to become more and more important.

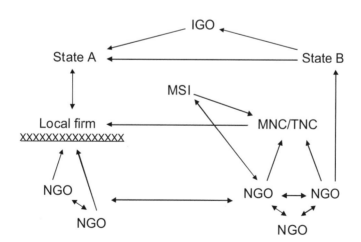

Figure 15.4 Intermittent organizations in boomerang politics

Implications for Stakeholder Theory

Having explored the notion of boomerang politics in some detail, we will now explore how this notion could contribute to stakeholder theory. In a recent review essay, De Bakker and Den Hond argued that the question of stakeholder influence over firms is a challenging one because activist groups are often considered as secondary stakeholders in the stakeholder literature.[44] Secondary stakeholders "are diverse and include those who are not directly engaged in the organization's economic activities but are able to exert influence or are affected by the organization".[45] As these stakeholders do not have a formal contractual bond with the firm and also lack direct legal authority over the firm, their position opposite firms is weaker and their salience often is considered to be relatively low. Being seen as less salient, they have received less attention in the literature but this is changing as the role of NGOs in impacting firms is receiving more and more research attention.[46] As Frooman already noted, these stakeholders may find indirect ways to develop power and legitimacy and thus enter the picture, working though allies.[47] As stakeholders, either primary or secondary, cooperate to get their claims attended to, they engage in collective action. They need each other to establish their objectives and they can build on each others' activities. To this end, it seems helpful not to view salience as a fixed attribute but as one that depends on the interaction between one or more stakeholder groups, the claim at hand and the firm to which it is addressed.[48] Boomerang politics can be helpful in understanding the pathways by which stakeholder groups that have for long been seen as more marginal can still be effective in the "politics of stakeholder influence".[49]

Stakeholders often do not operate in isolation. This is exactly where stakeholder theory could learn from social movement studies, as dealing with problems of collective action, allies and adversaries has been a central element of that branch of sociology. From a social movement studies' perspective, Whittier discusses various consequences that heterogeneity within a movement may have on that particular movement.[50] For example, it may result in the generation of new stakeholder groups that work on other themes, it may have spillover effects in the sense that stakeholder groups learn from each other in how to target firms effectively, or it may have consequences for their ability to change firm behavior.

Such heterogeneity may also be at stake within the TANs that apply boomerang politics. There may also be differences in interest, identity and ideology of local NGOs versus their international allies. According to McAteer and Pulver, a TAN can be seen as "an arena of convergence between widely different actors separated by cultural differences, geographic location, and access to resources".[51] These differences can be large, for instance on issues like power, culture, ideology or strategic interests.[52] The ways in which these transnational networks are able to cope with these differences in interests, identities and ideologies among their local member organizations will be important in the degree to which they can effectively exert pressure on corporations or states in both countries.

Although lessons might thus be learned from combining stakeholder theory and social movement studies, research combining both streams of literature is still relatively scarce. This might be caused by the different dominant foci of both domains: stakeholder theory traditionally considered (firm) management and stems from management studies, whereas social movement studies emphasized governments and society at large and stems from sociology. Interesting attempts to overcome this distinction between both approaches can be found in studies that focus on issues or issue domains. In such research on collaboration[53] stakeholders' issues have received quite some attention; increasingly concepts from social movement studies, such as mobilization and opportunity structures, are incorporated in such analyses,[54] for instance focussing on the formation of cross-sector social partnerships to deal with an issue. The current chapter, in which we combine several theoretical insights to understand a specific tactic, underscores the relevance of widening the scope of stakeholder theorizing—an important objective of this volume.

The stark analytic divide between collaboration and conflict that we applied in this chapter mainly served to outline the various positions actors in these boomerang politics can take. Although conflicts often are important in boomerang politics, the role of conflict should not be overestimated. The distinction between contentious and private politics is sometimes misguiding[55] in the sense that contentious and private politics in many cases are complementary. One can however expect that such interaction patterns will often be mixed and that next to conflict collaboration also can occur. It would be helpful to concentrate on interaction processes over time, including both collaboration and conflict, to understand the evolution of TANs' influence over time.[56] After all, if firms and states differ in the factors that affect their interests and reputations, as well as in the type of relationships they entertain with other actors, there might be some patterning in the evolution of protest (such as the sequencing of protest strategies), or there might be more or less effective or viable combinations of strategies like the simultaneous pursuit of both scale shift and insider tactics.

Concluding Remarks

In this chapter we discussed a specific application of stakeholder theory, thereby contributing to the objective of this edited volume to provide a multifaceted understanding of corporate social responsibility among different stakeholders and the pressures and conflicts that result from them. We present the notion of boomerang politics as a means to understand transnational stakeholder influence in the context of globalization. This notion generalizes Keck and Sikkink's state-focused boomerang model by including private politics, and thus making it relevant for stakeholder theorizing. As opposed to states, firms provide different leverage points for transnational stakeholder influence. Their commercial objectives make them more vulnerable for reputational damage, their contractual bonds provide them with different influence pathways opposite subsidiaries, and their stakeholders' calls for accountability require them to inform different audiences of their activities. All these characteristics provide a potential for boomerang politics. Taking these more complex pressure paths into account seems useful when trying to understand the ways secondary stakeholders try to impact their ultimate targets.

However, more work remains to be done to unravel these boomerang politics, both theoretical and empirical. First, following the combination of theoretical perspectives selected in this chapter, the links between stakeholder management and social movement studies could be explored further, for instance on issues like scale shift or transnational activism in a wider sense.[57] By contrasting state-focused and corporate boomerangs, we provide some angles for further empirical work on the links between social movements and corporations but we also call for a deeper examination. The growing literature on cooperation and focusing on issues or fields seem to offer valuable approaches to guide such empirical research. How are issues resolved? How are norms formed and transferred across fields? Detailed empirical work could help to paint a more nuanced picture of boomerang politics.

In addition, in this chapter we more or less neglected the variety in actors operating within TANs because we aimed to highlight the mechanisms at work in boomerang politics. Indeed, if one thing becomes clear in discussing boomerang politics it would be the variety of actors involved in these interaction processes and, therefore, the variety of different angles available to address this phenomenon. Tarrow, for instance, emphasized the domestic embeddedness of network members and the political opportunities that arise to shift scales.[58] In a case study of Oxfam researchers indeed claim that "existing scholarship has insufficiently identified the local or parochial nature of the identities of global civil society actors".[59] Other researchers do not focus on local protest movements in target countries; and yet others *only* consider such local movements or only focus on protest without examining other tactics such as framing or media use. Within empirical analyses of boomerang politics, is will be useful to investigate both TANs as a whole and the roles of individual organizations within them. When exactly do TANs opt for boomerang politics? What are the internal dynamics involved? And how do these dynamics develop over time? The examples provided in this chapter are based on a few studies that aimed to uncover parts of these processes, but more detailed information is needed.

Finally, it is important to note that in studying contentious and private politics the focus of analysis is often on the social movement, or maybe on the transnational stakeholder, thereby disregarding the responses by target firms and the way they connect, or not, to state policies. Corporate political activity[60] on issues like transnational activism is another area that should receive more attention. As Boris Holzer suggests, the lack of global enforcement of rules and standards makes these private politics, including corporate boomerangs, "indispensable to hold otherwise unfettered economic power in check".[61] The mechanisms outlined in this chapter provide some ways for transnational stakeholders to build or maintain such a system of checks and balances.

Notes

1   Jensen, T. and Sandström, J. (2011), "Stakeholder theory and globalization: the challenges of power and responsibility", *Organization Studies*, vol. 32, pp. 473–488.

2   cf. Matten, D. and Crane, A. (2005), "Corporate citizenship: Toward an extended theoretical conceptualization", *Academy of Management Review*, vol. 30, pp. 166–179.

3   de Bakker, F.G.A. and den Hond, F. (2008), "Introducing the politics of stakeholder influence: a review essay", *Business and Society*, vol. 47, pp. 8–20.

4   Hendry, J.R. (2006), "Taking aim at business. What factors lead environmental non-governmental organizations to target particular firms?", *Business and Society*, vol. 45, pp. 47–86. Rehbein, K., Waddock, S. and Graves, S.B. (2004), "Understanding shareholder activism: which corporations are targeted?", *Business and Society*, vol. 43, pp. 239–267.

5   King, B.G. (2008), "A social movement perspective of stakeholder collective action and influence", *Business and Society*, vol. 47, pp. 21–49.

6   Keck, M.E. and Sikkink, K. (1998), *Activists Beyond Borders: Advocacy Networks in International Politics*, Cornell University Press, Ithaca, NY.

7   cf. Levy, D.L. (2008), "Political contestation in global production networks", *Academy of Management Review*, vol. 33, pp. 943–963.

8   cf. Bartley, T. (2007), "Institutional emergence in an era of globalization: the rise of transnational private regulation of labor and environmental conditions", *American Journal of Sociology*, vol. 113, pp. 297–351; den Hond, F., de Bakker, F.G.A. and de Haan, P. (2010), "The sequential patterning of tactics: activism in the global sports apparel industry, 1988–2002", *International Journal of Sociology and Social Policy*, vol. 30, pp. 648–665; Frenkel, S.J. and Kim, S. (2004), "Corporate codes of labour practice and employment relations in sports shoe contractor factories in South Korea", *Asia Pacific Journal of Human Resources*, vol. 42, pp. 6–31.

9   Schepers, D.H. (2006), "The impact of NGO network conflict on the corporate social responsibility strategies of multinational corporations", *Business and Society*, vol. 45, 282–299.

10   In their state of the art overview, Freeman and colleagues (2010) do mention the issue of stakeholders and globalization but only refer to the UN Global Compact and to the Caux Round Table. That is, they point at the role of an international institution (the UN) and a form of dialog, neglecting other forms of interaction. Freeman, R.E., Harrison, J.S., Wicks, A.C., Parmar, B.L. and de Colle, S. (2010), *Stakeholder Theory. The State of the Art*, Cambridge University Press, Cambridge, MA.

11   Baron, D.P. (2003), "Private politics", *Journal of Economics and Management Strategy*, vol. 12, pp. 31–66.

12   Soule, S.A. (2012), "Targeting organizations: private and contentious politics". In D. Courpasson, D. Golsorkhi and J.J. Sallaz (eds.), *Rethinking Power in Organizations, Institutions, and Markets, Research in the Sociology of Organizations*, vol. 34, Emerald, Bingham, UK, pp. 261–285.

13   It should be pointed out here that we focus on situations of conflict between stakeholders and firms. We follow Pruitt and Kim (1998: 7–8) in defining conflict in a neutral way, as "perceived divergence of interest". Different routes are open to conflict resolution, varying between confrontation, negotiation and collaboration (Hardy, C. and Phillips, N. (1998), "Strategies of engagement: lessons from the critical examination of collaboration and conflict in an interorganizational domain", *Organization Science*, vol. 9, pp. 217–230). In the situations we discuss, negotiation and collaboration are no longer viable options, as is implied in the starting point out of which boomerangs emerge: the impossibility for affected parties to settle their conflict with the ultimate target. Of course, one outcome of boomerang politics might be to start negotiation or even collaboration. The literature on cross-sector partnerships and other forms of stakeholder engagement focus on situations in which there is a willingness on the part of the ultimate target, espoused or real, to collaborate with stakeholders in resolving their "perceived divergences of interest", or in which there is a perceived alignment of interests. For a review, see e.g., Selsky and Parker (2005). Pruitt, D.G. and Kim, S.H. (1998), *Social Conflict. Escalation, Stalemate, and Settlement*, 3rd ed., McGraw Hill, Boston, MA; Hardy and Phillips (1998), op. cit.; Selsky, J.W. and Parker, B. (2005), "Cross-sector partnerships to address social issues: challenges to theory and practice", *Journal of Management*, vol. 31, pp. 849–873.

14   Keck and Sikkink (1998), op. cit., p. 4.

15   Bandy, J. and Smith, J. (2005), "Factors affecting conflict and collaboration in transnational movement networks". In J. Bandy and J. Smith (eds), *Coalitions Across Borders. Transnational Protest and the Neoliberal Order*, Rowman and Littlefield, Lanham, MD, pp. 231–252.

16   Keck and Sikkink (1998), op. cit., p. 16.

17 In March 2011 Google Scholar indicated over 3,800 citations of Keck and Sikkink's book. An extensive overview of the application of this model is beyond the scope of this chapter.

18 McAteer, E. and Pulver, S. (2009), "The corporate boomerang: shareholder transnational advocacy networks targeting oil companies in the Ecuadorian Amazon", *Global Environmental Politics*, vol. 9, pp. 1–29.

19 Turcotte, M.-F., Bellefeuille, S. and den Hond, F. (2007), "Gildan Inc.: influencing corporate governance in the textile sector", *Journal of Corporate Citizenship*, no. 27, pp. 23–36.

20 den Hond, de Bakker and de Haan (2010), op. cit.

21 de Bakker, F.G.A. and den Hond, F. (2011), "A disputed contract: IHC Caland in Burma". In W. Dubbink, H. van Luijk and L. van Liedekerke (eds), *European Business Ethics Cases in Context. The Morality of Corporate Decision Making*, Springer, Dordrecht, the Netherlands, pp. 121–139.

22 For reasons of length, our representation of the various cases is obviously a simplification. The full stories can be found in the original publications.

23 Armbruster-Sandoval, R. (2003), "Globalization and transnational labor organizing. The Honduran maquiladora industry and the Kimi campaign", *Social Science History*, vol. 27, pp. 551–576.

24 WRAP is the Worldwide Responsible Apparel Production, now renamed Worldwide Responsible Accredited Production (http://www.wrapcompliance.org). FLA is the Fair Labor Association (http://www.fairlabor.org).

25 den Hond, F. and de Bakker, F.G.A. (2007), "Ideologically motivated activism. How activist groups influence corporate social change", *Academy of Management Review*, vol. 32, pp. 901–924.

26 McAdam, D., Tarrow, S. and Tilly, C. (2001), *Dynamics of Contention*, Cambridge University Press, Cambridge, MA, p. 331; see also Tarrow, S. (2005), *The New Transactional Activism*, Cambridge University Press, Cambridge, UK, p. 121.

27 Among the firms that have left Burma are Levi-Strauss (June 1992), PetroCanada (November 1992), Amoco (March 1994), Heineken (June 1996), Interbrew (October 1996), Philips Electronics (November 1996), PepsiCo (January 1997), Hewlett-Packard (November 1996), Ericsson (September 1998), Triumph (January 2002) and Premier Oil (September 2002).

28 Paul, K. (1989), "Corporate social monitoring in South Africa: a decade of activism", *Journal of Business Ethics*, vol. 8, pp. 463–469; Mangaliso, M. P. (1997), "South Africa, corporate social responsibility and the Sullivan principles", *Journal of Black Studies*, vol. 28, pp. 219–238.

29 den Hond and de Bakker (2007), op. cit., p. 23.

30 Snow, D.A. and Soule, S.A. (2009), *A Primer on Social Movements*, W.W. Norton, New York, NY.

31 Garwood, S. (1996), "Politics at work: transnational advocacy networks and the global garment industry", *Gender and Development*, vol. 13, pp. 21–33.

32 Garwood (1996), op. cit., p. 23.

33 Khan, F.R., Munir, K.A. and Willmott, H.C. (2007), "A dark side of institutional entrepreneurship: soccer balls, child labour and post-colonial impoverishment", *Organization Studies*, vol. 28, pp. 1055–1077.

34 Kriesi, H., Koopmans, R., Duyvendak, J.W. and Giugni, M.G. (1995), *New Social Movements in Western Europe: A Comparative Analysis*, UCL Press, London, UK.

35 Frooman, J. (1999), "Stakeholder influence strategies", *Academy of Management Review*, vol. 24, pp. 191–205; Pfeffer, J., and Salancik, G.R. (1978), *The External Control of Organizations. A Resource Dependence Perspective*, Harper and Row, New York, NY.

36 We refrain from elaborating on the relationship between factors derived from institutional and resource-dependence theories. They interact in various ways, as they may not only reinforce one another, but also oppose one another.

37 Scott, W.R. (2001), *Institutions and Organizations*, 2nd ed., Sage, Thousand Oaks.

38 Whelan, G., Muthuri, J., de Bakker, F.G.A. and den Hond, F. (2010), A Transnational Culture Clash: Human Rights Activism, Sudan and China National Petroleum Company, 26th EGOS Colloquium, Lisbon.

39 Porter, M.E. (1980), *Competitive Strategy. Techniques for Analyzing Industries and Competition*, Free Press, New York, NY.

40 de Bakker and den Hond (2008), op. cit.

41 de Bakker and den Hond (2008), op. cit.

42 cf. Kell, G. (2003), "The global compact. Origins, operations, progress, challenges", *Journal of Corporate Citizenship*, no. 11, pp. 35–49.

43 cf. Dijkzeul, D. and Beigbeder, Y. (eds) (2003), *Rethinking International Organizations. Pathology and Promise*, Berghahn, London, UK; Barnett, M.N. and Finnemore, M. (1999), "The politics, power, and pathologies of international organizations", *International Organization*, vol. 53, pp. 699–732.

44 de Bakker and den Hond (2008), op. cit. In the literature one can find many different names for these stakeholders, including secondary stakeholder, indirect stakeholders or fringe stakeholders. Here we use the term secondary stakeholders to highlight that these stakeholders are not directly impacting the primary process of a firm.

45 Savage, G.T., Nix, T.W., Whitehead, C.J. and Blair, J.D. (1991), "Strategies for assessing and managing organizational stakeholders", *Academy of Management Executive*, vol. 5, pp. 61–75, see p. 62.

46 Hendry, J.R. (2006), op. cit.; Lucea, R. (2010), "How we see them versus how they see themselves: a cognitive perspective of firm–NGO relationships", *Business and Society*, vol. 49, pp. 116–139. Schepers (2006), op. cit.; Van Huijstee, M. and Glasbergen, P. (2010), "Business–NGO interactions in a multi-stakeholder context", *Business and Society Review*, vol. 115, pp. 249–284.

47 Frooman (1999), op. cit.

48 Eesley, C. and Lenox, M.J. (2006), "Firm responses to secondary stakeholder action", *Strategic Management Journal*, vol. 27, pp. 765–781.

49 de Bakker and den Hond (2008), op. cit.

50 Whittier, N. (2004), "The consequences of social movements for each other". In D.A. Snow, S.A. Soule and H. Kriesi (eds), *Blackwell Companion of Social Movements*, Blackwell, Oxford, pp. 531–551.

51 McAteer and Pulver (2009), op. cit., p. 5.

52 Bandy and Smith (2005), op. cit.

53 Selsky and Parker (2005), op. cit.; Hardy and Philips (1998), op. cit.

54 Thanks to an anonymous reviewer for raising this issue.

55 cf. Soule (2012), op. cit.

56 den Hond, de Bakker and de Haan (2010), op. cit.

57 Tarrow (2005), op. cit.; Smith, J. (2005), "Globalization and transnational social movement organizations". In G.F. Davis, D. McAdam, W.R. Scott and M.N. Zald (eds), *Social Movements and Organization Theory*, Cambridge University Press, NewYork, pp. 226–248.

58 Tarrow (2005), op. cit.

59 Berry, C. and Gabay, C.B.A. (2009), "Transnational political action and 'global civil society' in practice: the case of Oxfam", *Global Networks—a Journal of Transnational Affairs*, vol. 9, pp. 339–358, p. 339.

60 Bonardi, J.P. and Keim, G.D. (2005), "Corporate political strategies for widely salient issues", *Academy of Management Review*, vol. 30, pp. 555–576; Hillman, A.J. and Hitt, M.A. (1999), "Corporate political strategy formulation: a model of approach, participation, and strategy decisions", *Academy of Management Review*, vol. 24, pp. 825–842; Schuler, D.A., Rehbein, K. and Cramer, R.D. (2002), "Pursuing strategic advantage through political means: a multivariate approach", *Academy of Management Journal*, vol. 45, pp. 659–672.

61 Holzer, B. (2010), *Moralizing the Corporation. Transnational Activism and Corporate Accountability*, Edward Elgar, Cheltenham, UK, p. 132.

16 Using a Dialectic Approach to Understand Stakeholders' Conflicts with Corporate Social Responsibility Activities

LÚCIA LIMA RODRIGUES* AND RUSSELL CRAIG†

Keywords

Activities, conflict, corporate social responsibility, dialectic, Foucault, Hegel, institutional theory.

Introduction

Throughout history, societies have expected organizations to act responsibly. Nonetheless, the term corporate social responsibility (CSR) is a relatively new one. In 1953, the seminal book *Social Responsibilities of the Businessman* by Bowen heralded a shift in terminology from the social responsibility of business to CSR. Renewed interest in CSR has motivated alternative (but related) concepts, including that of corporate sustainability.[1] In 1991, Carroll proposed a comprehensive and (subsequently) widely adopted definition of CSR:[2] one that included the idea that a corporation's obligations extended beyond economic and legal matters to also include ethical and discretionary (philanthropic) responsibilities.[3] Carroll argues that the four categories of CSR can be depicted as a pyramid, in which economic responsibilities are the foundation upon which all other responsibilities are predicated, and without which they cannot be achieved.[4] Discretionary responsibilities are at the apex. An important implication is that, contrary to common belief, "economic viability is something business does for society as well".[5] Although the scope and nature of CSR activities has developed and changed in recent decades, the concept entailed remains "embryonic and contestable".[6]

* Lúcia Lima Rodrigues, Department of Economics and Management, University of Minho, Gualtar Campus, Braga, Codex 4709, Portugal. E-mail: LRodrigues@eeg.uminho.pt.

† Dr. Russell Craig is Professor of Accounting and Head of the School of Accounting and Finance at Victoria University, Melbourne, Australia. E-mail: Russell.Craig@vu.edu.au.

We draw upon the lenses provide by Hegelian dialectic,[7] notions of *isomorphism* and *decoupling*, and salient features of Foucault's *concept of power-knowledge* to explain the development of CSR practice and stakeholders' conflicts with CSR activities. Using Hegelian terms, we regard argument that has been advanced to extol the merits of CSR to be the *thesis*. Militating against such argument is the *antithesis* or counter argument (such as the neoclassical view that any expenditure on CSR activities will disadvantage a company competitively). Such counter argument, debate and ensuing conflict lead to a third point of view that we refer to as the *synthesis*, in which the contradiction ceases to exist. We are consistent with Husted and Allen[8] in arguing that the specific processes of normative, coercive and mimetic isomorphism have strong potential to explain the dialectical process of adopting CSR policy and practices; and that structures of power and power-knowledge discourses are implicated in resistance or acceptance of CSR policy and practices. Syntheses achieved are facilitated by structural and institutional isomorphism; and are reinforced by power-knowledge beliefs. Using these analytical lenses, we seek to understand how companies avoid conflicts with stakeholders and how they minimize the risk and costs of boycotts, litigation and failure to obtain regulatory and societal licence to operate. Thus, we aim to provide better understanding of how CSR activities have evolved, how they have affected (and been affected by) institutional and social structures and how they might progress in the future.

Corporate Social Responsibility Dialectic

A dialectic perspective has strong potential "to provide a unique framework for understanding institutional change".[9] A dialectical view is one that is:

> *fundamentally committed to the concept of process. The social world is in a continuous state of becoming—social arrangements which seem fixed and permanent are temporary, arbitrary patterns and any observable social pattern is regarded as one among many possibilities. Theoretical attention is focused upon the transformation through which one set of arrangements gives way to another.*[10]

Hegel's theory of dialectic proposes that contradiction is the root of all change;[11] that one fact (*thesis*) works against another (*antithesis*) to produce a wholly new fact (*synthesis*); and that change is an inevitable and inherent component of worldly existence.[12]

Support for CSR activities can be regarded broadly as the thesis. However, this thesis contains an incompleteness that prompts opposition to CSR or a conflicting idea, an antithesis (that companies should not engage in CSR activities). As a result of the conflict, a third point of view arises, a synthesis (companies should have a certain level or type of CSR activities). The synthesis overcomes the conflict by reconciling the thesis and antithesis. Later, the synthesis becomes a new thesis. This, in turn, generates another antithesis, which then gives rise to a new synthesis. Hegel believed that, in such a fashion, an ongoing process of intellectual development was generated. The Hegelian dialectic process provides a convenient and dynamic model through which to understand current CSR activities (the process of *being*) and how those activities will develop in future years (the process of *becoming*). The process of becoming is influenced by isomorphism and power-knowledge beliefs.

Isomorphism occurs where one organization becomes similar to another by adopting (or moving closer to) the characteristics of the other organization. Proponents of new institutional theory are skeptical about whether organizations adopt practices or procedures for merely technical reasons. Rather, they contend that a crucial motive for isomorphic behavior is to achieve legitimacy and social acceptability from external stakeholder constituencies—even if potentially unsuitable practices have to be adopted. They allege that choice based on technical reasons often disguises high political and cultural influences. Viewed in this way, we can regard CSR practices as usually not adopted on grounds of efficiency, but almost always to enhance an organization's reputation with stakeholders for being rational, modern, responsible and legally compliant.[13] The basic premise of institutional theory is that organizations tend to conform to predominant norms and social influences or risk losing legitimacy.[14] This encourages convergence to homogeneous organizational structures and practices. Institutional theory explains this as *structural isomorphism*: that is, organizations become structures like each other.[15]

Also relevant is *institutional isomorphism*. This is the tendency of organizations to adopt the same practices over time in response to common institutional pressures exerted by similar organizations or industries.[16] Institutional isomorphism arises because other organizations are the "major factors that organisations must take into account".[17]

Several isomorphic processes are likely to prompt an organization to change its CSR activities.[18] DiMaggio and Powell[19] have identified three key forms of institutional isomorphism. These are particularly useful in understanding the development of CSR activities:

- *Coercive isomorphism* is driven by pressure from other organizations on which a focal organization is dependent (such as a parent company) and from pressure to conform to the cultural expectations of society at large (for example, norms and rules imposed by the State). Coercive isomorphism can occur as a consequence of a parent company pressuring subsidiaries to adopt CSR activities. The State can require State-owned companies to adopt CSR activities.
- *Mimetic isomorphism* occurs when organizations emulate (or "mime") the actions of similar organizations that are perceived to be more legitimate or successful in the institutional environment. In uncertain situations, organizational leaders may decide that the best response is to mimic a peer they perceive to be successful. If leading companies adopt CSR, other companies will tend to mimic them, because they believe that this will enhance their image and perceived legitimacy.
- *Normative isomorphism* is derived from formal education and legitimation of the cognitive base of a profession through discipline specialists in universities. It arises also from the elaboration of professional networks that span organizations and facilitate the rapid diffusion of new models and practices.[20] Normative isomorphism arises too through the advocacy by large international accounting firms of the benefits of preparing a sustainability report; the teaching of sustainability in university courses; and by professional bodies encouraging the need to disclose information about CSR activities.

Although institutional theory is useful in explaining how developments in CSR become institutionalized, sometimes a formally announced practice of an organization differs from its actual or informal practice. This gap between formal and informal practice is termed a *decoupling*:[21] it allows possible inconsistencies and anomalies of technical activities to remain hidden behind the façade of presumption that the formal structure is working as indicated publicly. Thus, although formal structures and systems can claim to have been adopted by an organization, such claims may be window-dressing. They may be divorced (or decoupled) from reality and be made simply to impress external stakeholders. When companies are pressed to adopt CSR activities to increase legitimacy, they often appear to overstate their level of CSR activities simply to impress stakeholders. This is decoupling: CSR activities have not increased by as much as is claimed. Although some organizations regard themselves as corporate social reporters, they do not behave in a responsible way concerning sustainability activities.[22]

The process of isomorphism is encouraged in historically specific circumstances and in particular contexts (consistent with Foucault[23]) in which belief systems (such as belief in CSR) gain momentum and power. This arises because more people accept, as common knowledge, the particular views associated with that belief system. When ideas begin to crystallize about what is right, wrong, normal and deviant, they are considered undeniable "truths". They define a particular way of seeing the world such that the way of life associated with such "truths" becomes "normal". Foucault sees forms of power-knowledge as being rooted in particular contexts and histories.

Power relations are important because they characterize the manner in which people are governed. But being "governed", according to Foucault,[24] is more a case of "disposition" than "imposition". The making of an assertive statement by a person does not constitute power. Rather, power is deemed to have been exercised when someone else takes the statement as true (or is disposed to accept it). Whether people are disposed to accept a statement is a function of their knowledge, which is evidenced through discourse. An important part of Foucault's power-knowledge nexus is the belief that those in power have specialist knowledge. In such cases, the production of knowledge and the exercise of administrative power are intertwined. Having specialist knowledge fosters unique power and control. The State, the professions and NGOs have power to diagnose a condition. If a person belongs to this specialist discourse, their word is considered authoritative and true. Hence, they have power. Thus, to understand knowledge, it is necessary to examine the institutions that produce discourse.[25] In the context of CSR, knowledge about CSR becomes power through discourse when firms and other parties are disposed to accept, as a taken for granted fact, that the world will be better if CSR practices are adopted. Sustainability discourses are adopted by the State and other actors and are accepted by companies.

Structural and institutional isomorphism and power-knowledge beliefs work together to resolve the conflict between the thesis and antithesis and to define the synthesis. When synthesis is achieved, contradiction ceases to exist. Although thesis and antithesis are opposite forces, the synthesis represents an understanding of the unity between the two apparent opposites.[26] Later, this synthesis will become the new thesis; and, in turn, contain an incompleteness that prompts a new antithesis. As a result of the opposition or conflict, a new synthesis will arise—one that will be a consequence of new power-knowledge beliefs and structural and institutional isomorphism at work in a specific historical context.

Thesis

The following arguments have helped to construct a belief, or a thesis, that CSR activities should be developed by companies and countries. The inherent arguments are statements that will become "power" if people are disposed to accept them as true.[27]

STAKEHOLDER MANAGEMENT THEORY

Stakeholder theory has two major branches. First, there is an ethical (or normative) branch that prompts managers to acknowledge the validity of diverse stakeholder interests and managers' moral requirement to respond to those interests.[28] Secondly, there is a managerial (or positive) branch that emphasizes the need to manage stakeholder groups, particularly those groups who control the resources required by an organization. Thus, the greater that the criticality of stakeholder resources is to the continued viability of an organization, the greater is the expectation that stakeholder demands will be addressed.[29] In the context of a *for profit* private sector enterprise, stakeholders include customers, suppliers, employees, community interest groups, the government (as the tax-raising authority) and financial institutions and shareholders (as providers of loan and equity capital). A widespread presumption is that stakeholders cooperate in a capitalist enterprise by applying different levels of economic effort to produce goods and services so all will benefit.

Stakeholder theory proposes a model of the firm in which all persons or groups with legitimate interests in the firm seek to obtain benefits. There is no prima facie priority of one set of interests and benefits over another.[30] Stakeholder theory gives rise to the view that companies engage in CSR after considering the impact of CSR activities on all constituents. Under stakeholder theory, management is given no direction on how to differentiate between the interests of different stakeholders. Thus, there is no best outcome, and no way of judging managers' performance.[31]

The stakeholder theory of the firm[32] widens the focus of management beyond merely using the resources of a company for the sole benefit of shareholders to one of using resources for the benefit of a much wider group of stakeholders. Furthermore, benefits to stakeholders can be increased through management's power to increase efficiency and to harness the creative and cooperative efforts of stakeholders for competitive advantage. For example, a company may aim to benefit stakeholders by supporting the construction of a community theatre complex, by reducing the pollution in a river system, by providing childcare facilities for employees and by producing cheaper and/or safer products for customers.[33]

Stakeholder theory suggests that stakeholders cooperate in generating and distributing profit. Such a view implies that better management will address the interests of all stakeholders more actively, and thereby, will increase benefits to all.[34] However, such a view has been challenged on the grounds that there are inherent conflicts between stakeholders in setting policy relating to matters of production and distribution.[35]

ENLIGHTENED STAKEHOLDER THEORY

The enlightened stakeholder theory proposed by Jensen[36] recognizes that any single-minded approach seeking to realize maximum value for shareholders (to the detriment of other stakeholder groups) is unlikely to succeed; and that no investment should be undertaken by a firm unless the present value to the firm of the associated incremental benefits exceeds the present value of the incremental costs.

In such a framework, investment in some CSR activities is likely to have a positive impact on the value of the firm, and thus is justifiable within Jensen's enlightened stakeholder theory. For example, paying minimum salaries to employees and requiring them to work in very poor conditions is likely to have a negative effect on productivity, offset any cost savings and reduce the value of the firm. Indeed, the capacity of a firm to generate sustainable wealth over time, and hence long-term value, should be recognized as determined by its relationships with critical stakeholders.[37] In this framework, it is highly possible that investment in some CSR activities will have a positive impact on the value of the firm and thus can be justified according to Jensen's enlightened stakeholder theory.

Expenditures on CSR activities can translate into increases in value for a firm[38] if they:

- Result in an immediate cost saving and increase the firm's market valuation. For example, a firm that decides to become more energy efficient will probably have a positive impact on the environment, reduce costs and boost profitability in the longer term;
- Bring reputational benefits (goodwill) and increase profitability and market valuation in the longer term. For example, decisions to improve product quality, or donations to medical research, might both initially reduce profitability. However, they may help improve the firm's market image and increase profitability and market valuation in the longer-term; and
- Dissuade government and other regulatory bodies from future actions that impose significant costs on the firm. For example, a firm that took action voluntarily to control pollution emission may have an initial cost. However, this initiative might dissuade government from introducing regulations and/or taxes that would impose greater costs on the firm and erode the firm's market value.

THE STAKEHOLDER ECONOMY

The notion of a stakeholder economy has been advocated widely by Tony Blair (former British Prime Minister) and Will Hutton.[39] Their broad claim is that all social groups have a stake in the well-being of corporations and the national economy, and that the welfare of all stakeholders is related strongly to the activities of corporations. They urge acceptance of the view that companies and the national economy need to cooperate to create wealth. Thus, the stakeholder economy is an ideological creation: it implies that all members of society contribute to economic prosperity and therefore all should receive their fair share of national economic wealth. By considering stakeholders as joint beneficiaries working in concert (and not as competing claimants) for the surplus produced by the enterprise, conflict is rendered unlikely. This view of stakeholding would support recruitment of trade union leaders into the management of a corporation, and the introduction of employee and consumer share ownership schemes. Adoption of a stakeholder economy viewpoint is claimed to be beneficial in driving costs down effectively and without dissent. This view of stakeholding gives the appearance of political liberalism and compassion while continuing and intensifying existing economic policies. In this conception of economic life, all stakeholders are included, and all are claimed to benefit.

To sum up, the thesis is that companies should develop CSR activities. Since management should use resources for the benefit of all stakeholders, CSR activities are likely to have a positive impact on the value of the firm. The welfare of all stakeholders is related strongly to the activities of corporations.

Antithesis

Cooper and Sherer[40] demonstrate many inherent conflicts between stakeholders. The antithesis to the thesis explained in the preceding section draws strength from the following arguments.

NEOCLASSICAL ECONOMICS

Neoclassical economists view the decisions of professional corporate management within a company as predicated solely on the objective of maximizing the corporation's long-term market value, and thus the wealth of company owners. The neoclassical view suggests that any expenditure on CSR activities will place a company at a competitive disadvantage and affect market performance negatively.[41] Despite this view, whether CSR activities have a positive or negative impact on a firm's financial performance has been the subject of considerable debate and conflicting results.[42]

According to Friedman[43] there is one and only one social responsibility of business. This is to use resources to engage in activities designed to increase profits—provided that such engagement is in open and free competition, and without deception or fraud. Friedman argues that managers of a public company are agents for shareholders and that the sole responsibility of managers is to act in shareholders' interests. This suggests that management has no right to expropriate shareholder wealth for the benefit of other stakeholders. Rather, Friedman contends that it is the role of government to consider the potential impact of companies on other stakeholders and to take these impacts into account when setting tax and regulatory rules governing the behavior of companies.

Thus, there are many areas of possible conflict for managers who are trying to balance the interests of shareholders with those of a broad spectrum of stakeholders. For example, in the environmental area, managers would be mindful that despite the recognition by security markets of the reputational benefits (and costs) flowing from CSR activities, those markets often discount the value of companies that have a strong commitment to environmental preservation.

CRITICISM OF "THE STAKEHOLDER ECONOMY"

Stakeholders are not joint beneficiaries for the surplus produced by the enterprise but are competing claimants. Conflicts between various stakeholders (especially the crucial conflict between employees and owners) are acknowledged infrequently.

The stakeholding debate can be illustrated by drawing on studies of privatized utilities. Typically, governments justify the privatization of utilities by arguing that "all would benefit: consumers, employees, the industry and the nation".[44] Thus, government rhetoric usually is that all stakeholders will be beneficiaries. However, rarely do governments acknowledge that all stakeholders are not homogeneous, but are likely to be in positions of conflict. Shaoul has drawn attention to this conflict:

> *management resolved the distributional conflict between the stakeholders of British Gas and British Telecom in favour of the owners and, to a lesser extent, the consumers ... at the expense of the workforce, in the case of the gas industry, the suppliers. In privatizations in the water industry, there was a different distributional conflict as a result of the investment requirements laid down by the EC. Management and the regulator resolved the conflict at the expense of the consumer, both present and future.*[45]

To sum up, the antithesis is that companies should not develop CSR activities. Since CSR activities will place a company at a competitive disadvantage, management should use resources to engage in other activities that will increase profits. The sole responsibility of managers is to act in shareholders' interests. Stakeholders are viewed as competing claimants for the surplus produced by the company. In Table 16.1 we provided some examples of how CSR has evolved using the lens of thesis–antithesis–synthesis:

Table 16.1 Conflicts with stakeholders and CSR dialectic

CSR dialectic	Customers[46]	Employees[47]	Community[48]
Thesis	Customers are a very important stakeholder. McDonald's fast food products should not be fat-laden, overloaded with calories, promote obesity or otherwise impair customer health.	Employees are a very important stakeholder whose interests should be considered. Nike should not exploit international labor markets to employ staff in Third World countries on very low wages under sweat shop conditions.	Communities in which companies operate are important stakeholders. Companies throughout the world, such as Morso (Denmark) and Harmon Stove (U.S.) should not make and sell old technology domestic wood burning fires in urban areas because such fires are a major cause of urban smog and respiratory problems.
Antithesis	There is no need to care about whether McDonald's fast food products promote good health and nutrition. It is more important to improve company profits and satisfy shareholders' interests.	There is no need to care about whether Nike employees work for very low wages. The practice of employing staff on low wages in developing countries lowers product cost, benefits shareholders and provides much-needed employment in host countries.	Old technology wood burners are used because they help to dispose of scrap wood and provide household heat. If they are cheaper, they should be used to increase profits and satisfy the interests of shareholders.
Synthesis	Although McDonald's still produces fat-laden products, low-fat, low-calorie product options are now offered too. Even if these product options are less profitable, they should be provided.	Nike pays higher wages, and provides better conditions of employment for employees in developing countries.	Many urban authorities throughout the world are progressively banning the use of old technology wood burners, regardless of the effect of this decision on company profitability.

Syntheses: Levels of CSR Activities

Below we outline several levels of CSR activities that have arisen (and will continue to arise) from several syntheses of thesis and antithesis. The syntheses achieved in each period are consequences of power-knowledge beliefs and the influences of structural and institutional isomorphism that are exerted by organizational actors (including the State and professions), affecting the level of CSR activities adopted. The extent to which isomorphic processes lead to more or less CSR activity will depend on the power-knowledge discourse that is produced by organizational actors.

NO CSR ACTIVITIES OR SOME CSR ACTIVITIES

Engaging in CSR activities is symptomatic of an agency problem between the interests of managers and shareholders.[49] There is no strong evidence that a lack of CSR, resulting in reputational damage, affects a company's share price significantly. In 2001 Frankental[50] argued that although UK company law offers legal protection for shareholders, it did not offer protection to any other stakeholder groups affected by a company's decisions. Thus, so long as the governance of companies reflects the interests of shareholders (and not any other groups in society) there is no compelling specific need under commercial law for businesses to be socially responsible. Frankental urged further legal embodiment of the stakeholder concept at the expense of a prime focus on the interests of shareholders. If this does not occur, CSR activities may be considered dubious or even illegal, thereby impeding the extension of CSR activities.

Sharfman[51] uses institutional theory to examine the evolution of corporate philanthropy from the time it was considered illegal through to the time it became legal and, indeed, expected behavior by businesses. He cites two US court cases dating from 1881 and 1905, respectively, in which the court considered that donations were unjustifiable since they did not affect the company's goals positively, and did not embody benefits for employees.

Attitudes to CSR activities have evolved in many settings, for example in the UK. Article 172 of the Companies Act 2006 evidences an evolution in UK company law: it now establishes that to promote the success of a company, a director must consider the interests of employees; foster the company's business relationships with suppliers, customers and others; be aware of the impact of the company's operations on the community and the environment; and maintain a reputation for high standards of business conduct. In Portugal, company law changed recently to incorporate the stakeholder concept. Article 64 of the Portuguese companies' code Código das Sociedades Comerciais (CSC) (regarding the responsibilities of directors) changed considerably between 1986 and 2006. In 1986 the CSC established that "managers or directors must act in the interest of the company, taking into account the interests of shareholders and employees". In 2006, Article 64 was extended. Article 64(1b) now states that "managers or directors must act in the interest of the company, given the long-term interests of shareholders and weighing up the interests of other stakeholders relevant for the sustainability of the company, such as employees, customers and creditors".

Extensive CSR Activities

If no legal restrictions exist, extensive CSR activities are more likely to happen. Using the theory of the firm perspective, McWilliams and Siegel[52] conclude that a public firm's level of CSR will depend on its size, diversification, research and development, advertising, government sales, consumer income, labor market conditions and stage in the industry life cycle. When expenditures on CSR activities have either a neutral or a positive impact on a company's market valuation, the extent of the actual conflicts for a management (drawn between the demands of shareholders and those of a wider circle of stakeholders) might be limited. Where no conflict exists there is likely to be a market solution that ensures the interests of a particular stakeholder are protected.

A compromise to resolve the conflict for any corporate management trying to decide whether to manage solely in the interests of shareholders or manage in the interests of stakeholders would be to reassure managers that it would be extremely unlikely to maximize shareholder value if the interests of other stakeholders were ignored. Under this enlightened approach, management should automatically take account of the interests of other parties before making their decisions, especially if this did not conflict with the interests of the company's shareholders. No legal constraint exists to doing this.

Some successful adopters of an enlightened stakeholder theory approach to CSR have been recognized recently. The SAM and Dow Jones Indexes[53] results of the Dow Jones Sustainability Indexes Review 2010 recognized the Portuguese company Energias de Portugal (EDP) as the top European Dow Jones utility company. This top classification was influenced strongly by a pilot project EDP is developing in Kakuma, Kenya that seeks to bring renewable energy and environmentally sustainable benefits for refugees.

Even if CSR Activities are Adopted Companies may need to Accommodate Stakeholders' Interests when there are Conflicts

A conflict exists when CSR activities have a demonstrably negative impact on earnings. In circumstances of conflict, management might compromise the interests of shareholders by taking account of other stakeholders so as to avoid conflicts and reputational risk. However, increasingly, stakeholder engagement is recognized as more than just a defensive response to criticism or imminent conflict. In some companies it has become an integral part of systematic risk management.

A turning point in the evolution of CSR activities occurred with Shell's partial metamorphosis in the mid-1990s.[54] Shell's plans to dispose of the Brent Spar oil platform at sea were foiled by Greenpeace. Shell was criticized internationally for its oil operations in Nigeria and its apparent cosy relations with the military junta. Shell was forced to rethink its strategy and to divert substantial resources into responding to widespread community concerns about its plans.

The conduct of the oil company BP seems likely to herald another turning point in CSR practices. BP was removed from the Dow Jones Sustainability Indexes (DJSI) on May 31, 2010. This was a consequence of *the extent of the oil-spill catastrophe in the Gulf of Mexico and its foreseeable long-term effects on the environment and the local population—in addition to the economic effects and the long term damage to the reputation of the company.*[55]

For several years BP was considered by many as engaging in best practice social responsibility behavior. The company topped the *Fortune* magazine ratings for CSR in 2004, 2005 and 2007; and BP subsidiaries in Russia and Malaysia won national awards for CSR in 2007.[56] Subsequently, BP reduced its investment in renewable energy to a negligible percentage of sales and profits. The company's focus has been on cutting costs, including through under-spending on safety. The *New York Times* suggested that BP could be vulnerable to takeover once all its liabilities for the spill in the Gulf of Mexico are accounted for.[57] So, as a consequence, BP has helped make environmentally sensitive companies more aware that under-spending on safety can have very substantial costs for society and for the company. This reinforces the thesis of the need to adopt CSR practices, and weakens the antithesis of cutting costs and improving profits for shareholders.

Discussion

Here we discuss why firms engage in CSR activities and how CSR activities develop.

CSR ACTIVITIES ARE A DIALECTICAL PROCESS OF THESIS, ANTITHESIS AND SYNTHESIS

As explained earlier, for each thesis related to CSR activity, an antithesis develops. When a thesis is negated by its antithesis, a new synthesis becomes a new thesis. The new thesis then, in turn, can be negated by a new antithesis. Thus, there is an ongoing Hegelian process of new thesis generation.

The current synthesis is that CSR activities should be adopted. The thesis of CSR is supported by multi-stakeholder organizations (like the Global Reporting Initiative [GRI]), several permissive legal environments (like that of Portuguese corporate law), sympathetic governments and big international accounting firms. GRI promotes and develops a standardized approach to reporting to stimulate demand for sustainability information. The extension of CSR activities in individual companies and over time is a consequence of a process of isomorphism; and whether knowledge about the discourse of CSR becomes power.

CSR ACTIVITIES AS A PROCESS OF ISOMORPHISM

Coercive isomorphism

Coercive isomorphism can be seen through parent company pressures on subsidiaries to adopt CSR and to make CSR disclosures. The legal environment of each country is important too: for example, Portuguese company law has evolved and now requires that directors consider shareholders' interests while also considering the interests of other stakeholders. Portuguese Companies' Code (Article 66) requires companies to disclose non financial information about environment and employees in the management report. This is also stimulating CSR practices and disclosure.

Additionally, governments can be coercive in imposing CSR activities on state-owned firms. For example, Resolution 49/2007 of the Portuguese Council of Ministers (Resolução do Conselho de Ministros 49/2007) recommends State-owned firms adopt governance models to achieve higher levels of performance. These models should contribute to the spread of good practices, including the adoption of sustainability strategies in economic, social and environmental domains. Publicly owned firms are obliged to inform stakeholders whether the firm's mission has been pursued, objectives achieved, social responsibility and sustainable development policies implemented and competitiveness safeguarded (for example, through R&D, innovation and integration of new technologies). The Portuguese Government's holding of shares in two major Portuguese companies (EDP and Portuguese Telecom) allows it to exert a positive influence on the CSR practices of those companies.

Normative isomorphism

Normative isomorphism can be seen in the advocacy, by large international accounting firms, of the benefits of preparing a sustainability report; in the teaching of sustainability in accounting and management courses in universities; and in the urgings by professional bodies of the need to disclose information about CSR activities. International accounting firms now are engaged in auditing sustainability reports. National and international bodies of auditors such as the Portuguese Auditors Association, Ordem dos Revisores Oficiais de Contas (OROC), have accepted recently that the auditing of sustainability reports is a responsibility of the auditing profession. In 2008, the Statutes of OROC were reviewed and the role of auditors expanded to include the auditing of environmental and sustainability reports (Decree-law 224/2008).

Frankental[58] argues that the best way to ensure markets reward ethical practice is to change accounting systems so that companies are audited not just according to their financial performance, but also according to a wide range of environmental and social indicators. If every company was audited accordingly, and the auditing system took greater account of the full impact of a company on society, CSR would be considered more favorably by companies. If companies are audited according to their environmental and social impact, and penalized in accord with principle of "polluter pays", then financial markets will begin to judge companies according to their wider impact on society.

Mimetic isomorphism

In most legal jurisdictions, CSR activities and sustainability reports are voluntary. Companies adopting CSR activities probably do not do so for competitive reasons, but to establish reputations for good citizenship, and to attain societal legitimacy. This tendency for companies to model themselves on organizations they consider to be more legitimate or successful can be regarded as mimetic isomorphism. This kind of isomorphism is expected to have a greater impact in the future, especially by institutions which believe it will enhance their image and perceived legitimacy.

Mimetic isomorphism in Portugal is encouraged by Portugal's Business Council for Sustainable Development (BCSD). This Council was created in October 2001 by three leading Portuguese companies (Sonae, Cimpor and Soporcel) all of whom are associated with the World Business Council for Sustainable Development (WBCSD). The BCSD Portugal aims to be a catalyst for sustainable development by promoting eco-efficiency in business, innovation and social responsibility. Membership of BCSD Portugal is claimed by the BCSD to add value to businesses. The BCSD's membership has increased rapidly since 2001 to 130 organizations.

Irrespective of whatever form of isomorphism is influential, the manner of effecting convergence will vary widely, influenced by local contexts and country-specific contextual factors.

CSR Activities are Likely to be Affected by Decoupling

Isomorphism is much more likely to occur in environments in which there are similar institutions. The more diverse the environment, the more likely it is that any two companies will operate differently, and that CSR will differ. Because companies are not consensual bodies, this can give rise to resistance, power struggles and contradictions. *Decoupling* seems likely to arise as a response of some companies to institutional pressures to adopt CSR activities and because of the unclear relationship between corporate disclosure and improved social responsibility.[59] Companies which contend that they are engaging in CSR activities may simply be engaging in a form of window-dressing to appease the community and stakeholders.

The Extent of CSR Activities will Depend on Whether Knowledge about the Discourse of CSR Becomes Power

Successive syntheses can be regarded as a consequence of knowledge-power relationships. CSR activities will increase in coming years if institutions believe such activities offer a good way forward and are conceived as being right and normal. During the last two decades, an increasing number of scholars and practitioners have adopted the discourse of CSR.[60] Political rhetoric, like the following statement by the Portuguese government is a "power-knowledge" discourse:

> Today, there is no question about the importance of sustainable growth and economic development ... there is no question about the need for companies to behave in a socially responsible way, especially in terms of equality of opportunities, and environmentally sound practices, which are consistent with sustainable growth and economic development. (Resolução do Conselho de Ministros 49/2007)

Whichever synthesis is observed in coming years will result from a belief system that will gain momentum and power. Such a belief system will influence the level of observed structural and institutional isomorphism (that is, coercive, normative and mimetic isomorphism). Belief systems that consider CSR activities as important are often motivated by concerns for stakeholder management. However, perhaps inevitably, a belief system will be constructed from taken for granted assumptions about what constitutes appropriate and acceptable CSR activities. Such a belief system will be important in determining future adoptions of CSR activities by companies, and will be constructed by organizational actors who support, oppose or strive to influence CSR activities. International and regional bodies, the State and professions, who were "the great rationalizers of the second half of the twentieth century",[61] will remain so in the first decades of the twenty-first century. They will exercise power by imposing constraints, articulating rationales and formulating requirements regarding CSR activities.

In sum, the extension of CSR activities in each company, and over time, will be a consequence of a dialectical process that depends on isomorphic pressures and power knowledge beliefs. Structural and institutional isomorphism of CSR activities (especially its coercive, normative and mimetic varieties) seems highly likely in coming years. The synthesis achieved about the desirable level of CSR activities will result from a belief system that will gain power and momentum. The evolution of such a belief system will be defined by decisive actors and will be a crucial influence on the future adoption of CSR practices.

As for further research, we suggest that the concept of CSR dialectic be tested in deep analytical case studies. Another avenue for research would be to map the evolution of syntheses over time.

Notes

1   Garriga, E. and Melé, D. (2004), "Corporate social responsibility theories: mapping the territory", *Journal of Business Ethics*, vol. 53, no. 1/2, pp. 51–71.

2   Carroll's famous definition comes from an article published in 1979: Carroll, A.B. (1979), "A three-dimensional conceptual model of corporate performance", *Academy of Management Review*, vol. 4, no.4, pp. 497–505. In 1991 he expanded this definition into its (pyramidal) conceptualization of CSR (see following note).

3   Carroll, A.B. (1991), "The pyramid of corporate social responsibility: toward the moral management of organizational stakeholders", *Business Horizons*, July/August, pp. 39–48, see p. 42.

4   Ibid.

5   Carroll, A.B. (1999), "Corporate social responsibility: evolution of a definitional construct", *Business and Society*, vol. 38, no. 3, pp. 268–295, see p. 284.

6   Windsor, D. (2006), "Corporate social responsibility: three key approaches", *Journal of Management Studies*, vol. 43, no. 1, pp. 93–114, see p. 93.

7   Hegel. G.W.F. (1975), *Hegel's Logic*, Oxford University Press, Oxford.

8   Husted, B.W. and Allen, D.B. (2006), "Corporate social responsibility in the multinational enterprise: strategic and institutional approaches", *Journal of International Business Studies*, vol. 37, no. 6, pp. 838–849.

9   Seo, M.-G. and Creed, W.E.D. (2002), "Institutional contradictions, praxis and institutional change: a dialectical perspective", *Academy of Management Review*, vol. 27, no. 2, pp. 222–247, see p. 222.

10   Benson, J.K. (1977), "Organizations: a dialectic view", *Administrative Science Quarterly*, vol. 22, no. 1, pp. 1–21.

11   Hegel, G.W.F. (trans. Miller A.V.) (1969), *Science of Logic*, Humanities Press, New York, NY.

12   Hegel (1975), op. cit.

13   Carruthers, B.G. (1995), "Accounting, ambiguity, and the new institutionalism", *Accounting, Organizations and Society*, vol. 20, no. 4, pp. 313–328, see p. 316; Meyer J.W. and Rowan B.

(1977), "Institutional organizations: formal structure as myth and ceremony", *American Journal of Sociology*, vol. 83, no. 2, pp. 340–363.

14 Carruthers (1995), op. cit.; DiMaggio P.J. and Powell, W.W. (1983), "The iron cage revisited: institutional isomorphism and collective rationality in organizational fields", *American Sociological Review*, vol. 48, no. 2, pp. 147–160.

15 Meyer, J.W., Boli, J., Thomas, G.M. and Ramirez, F.O. (1997). "World society and the nation state", *American Journal of Sociology*, vol. 103, no. 1, pp. 144–181.

16 DiMaggio and Powell (1983), op. cit.

17 Aldrich, H.E. (1979), *Organizations and Environments*, Prentice-Hall, Englewood Cliffs, NJ, p. 265.

18 Scott, W.R. (1987), "The adolescence of institutional theory", *Administrative Science Quarterly*, vol. 32, no. 4, pp. 493–511, see p. 498.

19 DiMaggio and Powell (1983), op. cit., p. 150.

20 DiMaggio and Powell (1983), op. cit., pp. 152–3.

21 Meyer and Rowan (1977), op. cit.

22 Moneva, J.M., Archel P. and Correa C. (2006), "GRI and the camouflaging of corporate unsustainability", *Accounting Forum*, vol. 30, no. 2, pp. 121–137.

23 Foucault M. (1991), "Governmentally." In Burchell G., Gordon C. and Miller P. (eds), *The Foucault Effect*, University of Chicago Press, Chicago, IL, pp. 87–104.

24 Foucault (1991), p. 102.

25 Cowton, C.J. and Dopson, S. (2002), "Foucault's prison? Management control in an automotive distributor", *Management Accounting Research*, vol. 13, no. 2, pp. 191–214, see p. 193.

26 Carr, A., (2000), "Critical theory and the management of change in organizations", *Journal of Organizational Change Management*, vol. 13 no. 3, pp. 208–220.

27 Rodrigues, L.L. and Craig, R. (2007), "Assessing international accounting harmonization using Hegelian dialectic, isomorphism and Foucault", *Critical Perspectives on Accounting*, vol. 18, no. 6, pp. 739–757, see p. 744.

28 Donaldson, T. and Preston, L.E. (1995), "The stakeholder theory of the corporation: concepts, evidence, and implications", *Academy of Management Review*, vol. 20, no. 1, pp. 65–91.

29 Roberts, R. (1992), "Determinants of corporate social responsibility disclosure: an application of stakeholder theory", *Accounting, Organizations and Society*, vol. 27, no. 6, pp. 595–612.

30 Donaldson and Preston (1995), op. cit.

31 Jensen, M.C. (2001), "Value maximization, stakeholder theory, and the corporate objective function", *Journal of Applied Corporate Finance*, vol. 14, no. 3, pp. 8–21.

32 Freeman, R.E. (1984), *Strategic Management: A Stakeholder Approach*, Pitman, Boston, MA.

33 Bird, R., Hall, A., Momente, F. and Reggiani, F. (2007), "What corporate social responsibility activities are valued by the market?", *Journal of Business Ethics*, vol. 76, no. 2, pp. 189–206.

34 Shaoul, D. (1998), "Critical financial analysis and accounting for stakeholders", *Critical Perspectives on Accounting*, vol. 9, no. 2, pp. 235–249.

35 Cooper, D.J. and Sherer, M.J. (1984), "The value of corporate accounting reports: arguments for a political economy of accounting", *Accounting, Organizations and Society*, vol. 9, no. 3/4, pp. 207–232.

36 Jensen (2001), op. cit.

37 Post, J.E., Preston, L.E. and Sachs, S. (2002), "Managing the extended enterprise: The new stakeholder view", *California Management Review*, vol. 45, no. 1, pp. 6–28.

38 Bird *et al.* (2007), op. cit.

39 Hutton, W. (1995), *The State We're In*, Jonathan Cape, London.

40   Cooper and Sherer (1984), op.cit.

41   Aupperle K.E., Carroll, A.B. and Hatfield, J.D. (1985), "An empirical examination of the relationship between corporate social responsibility and profitability," *Academy of Management Journal*, vol. 28, no. 2, pp. 446–463.

42   See, for example, Ullman, A.E. (1985), "Data in search of a theory: a critical examination of the relationships among social performance, social disclosure and economic performance of U.S. firms", *Academy of Management Review*, vol. 10, no. 3, pp. 540–557; Roman, R.M., Hayibor, S. and Agle, B.R. (1999), "The relationship between social and financial performance—repainting a portrait," *Business and Society*, vol. 38, no. 1, pp. 109–125; Mahon, J.F. and Griffin, J.J. (1999), "Painting a portrait—a reply", *Business and Society*, vol. 38, no. 1, pp. 126–133; and Orlitzky, M., Schmidt, F.L. and. Rynes, S.L. (2003), "Corporate social and financial performance—a meta-analysis," *Organization Studies*, vol. 24, no. 3, pp. 403–441.

43   Friedman, M. (1970), "A Friedman doctrine—the social responsibility of business is to increase its profits", *The New York Times Magazine*, September 13, pp. 32–33, and 123–125.

44   Shaoul (1998), op. cit., p. 241.

45   Shaoul (1998), ibid., pp. 244–245.

46   Anon (2004), "Big Mac's makeover: McDonald's turned around", *The Economist*, 16 October, vol. 373. no. 8397, pp. 63–65.

47   Knight, G. and Greenberg, J. (2002). "Promotionalism and subpolitics: Nike and its labor critics", *Management Communication Quarterly*, vol. 15, no. 4, p. 541.

48   Boman, B.G., Forsberg, A.B. and Jarvholm, B.G. (2003). "Adverse health effects from ambient air pollution in relation to residential wood combustion in modern society", *Scandinavian Journal of Work, Environment and Health*, vol. 29, no. 4, pp. 251–260. Bans on the use of old technology wood burners have been implemented in many cities around the world, including San Francisco, Vancouver, Montreal, Denver, Christchurch and Launceston.

49   Friedman (1970), op. cit.

50   Frankental, P. (2001), "Corporate social responsibility—a PR invention?", *Corporate Communications: An International Journal*, vol. 6, no. 1, pp. 18–23.

51   Sharfman, M. (1994), "Changing institutional rules: the evolution of corporate philanthropy, 1883–1953", *Business and Society*, 33, pp. 236–269.

52   McWilliams, A. and Siegel, D. (2001), "Corporate social responsibility: a theory of the firm perspective", *Academy of Management Review*, vol. 26, no. 1, pp. 117–127.

53   The Dow Jones Sustainability Indexes, launched in 1999, are the first global indexes to track the financial performance of leading sustainability-driven companies worldwide.

54   Frankental (2001), op. cit.

55   "BP removed from the Dow Jones Sustainability Indexes", http://www.sustainability- indexes. com/djsi_pdf/news/PressReleases/20100531_Statement%20BP%20Exclusion_Final.pdf, accessed September 10 2010.

56   Swaminathan S.A. (2010), "Corporate social responsibility can cloak irresponsibility", *The Economic Times*, 25 July, http://economictimes.indiatimes.com/news/news-by-company/corporate-trends/corporate-social-responsibility-can-cloak-irresponsibility/articleshow/6212519.cms.

57   Winston, A., Harvard Business Review, http://blogs.hbr.org/winston/2010/06/the-bp-oil-spill-top-5-lessons.html.

58   Frankental (2001), op. cit.

59   Shaoul (1998), op. cit.

60   Pederson, E. (2006), "Making corporate social responsibility (CSR) operable: how companies translate stakeholder dialogue into practice", *Business and Society Review*, vol. 111, no. 2, pp. 137–163.
61   DiMaggio and Powell (1983), op. cit., p. 147.

17 *"Make Sense Who May": Corporate Social Responsibility as a Continuous Multi-stakeholder Co-construction Process*

FRANÇOIS MAON,* VALÉRIE SWAEN† AND
ADAM LINDGREEN‡

Keywords

Corporate social responsibility, organizational sensemaking, stakeholder management.

The only way to make sense out of change is to plunge into it, move with it, and join the dance.

Alan Watts, author

Introduction

In the past two decades, many companies have adopted the corporate social responsibility (CSR) discourse and engaged in various CSR-related initiatives, ranging from the design and implementation of codes of conduct to triple bottom-line reporting, collaborations with nongovernmental organizations (NGOs) and U.N. agencies, and increased support for community development programs. For some companies, the pressures for more responsible corporate behaviors have prompted actual and important changes in their cultures, structures and daily activities, because they consider CSR "central to core business activities rather than a peripheral consideration associated with philanthropy".[1] Yet in

---

* François Maon, IESEG School of Management (LEM-CNRS), Université Catholique de Lille, 3 rue de la Digue, 59000 Lille, France, E-mail: f.maon@ieseg.fr.

† Valérie Swaen, Louvain School of Management, Université catholique de Louvain, 1 Place des Doyens, 1348 Louvain-la-Neuve, Belgium, & IESEG School of Management (LEM-CNRS), Université Catholique de Lille, 3 rue de la Digue, 59000 Lille, France, E-mail: valerie.swaen@uclouvain.be.

‡ Adam Lindgreen, Cardiff Business School, University of Cardiff, Aberconway Building, Colum Drive, Cardiff CF10 3EU, the U.K., E-mail: lindgreena@cardiff.ac.uk.

most cases, corporate responses to pressures mainly have resulted in CSR promises and activities that can be decoupled easily from the company's normal, ongoing activities.[2]

Potential explanations for the gap between CSR rhetoric and reality include the difficulties managers have making sense of the CSR concept and the complexities associated with making it operational.[3] Companies must approach the CSR concept in accordance with their specific context, culture and values.[4] Companies also assign their own meaning to the CSR concept to clarify the motivation that underlies their potential commitments and to make sense of the key societal issues they face. In addition, CSR demands the consideration of multiple groups of stakeholders, which may have different conceptions of a responsible company, such that the inconsistent CSR expectations inexorably evolve over time.[5] In turn, CSR demands constant and often challenging reassessments and dialog between the organization and its stakeholders.

In this chapter, we offer support for previous assertions that CSR understanding and implementation by a company should be considered a process of change that takes place through a process of sensemaking[6]—that is, the process by which people in organizations collectively grant sense to their environment.[7] A sensemaking approach on CSR might produce a more robust conceptual understanding of the socially constructive processes that underlie CSR development in companies.[8] Basu and Palazzo already have adopted such a perspective to provide a process model of CSR that insightfully emphasizes the main cognitive, linguistic and conative dimensions that characterize and influence the way companies make sense of their social responsibilities. However, their contribution focuses mostly on organizational actors and insiders, without addressing how collective processes of sensemaking and sensegiving might occur between the organization and its various stakeholders, as well as among different stakeholders that hold potentially conflicting views and perceptions of the nature of CSR-related issues and the way companies should address them.[9]

Building on previous sensemaking-oriented suggestions and CSR conceptualizations, we argue that CSR development in a company should be approached as a progressive creation and re-creation of "an internally and externally shared frame of reference in relation to CSR objectives, activities and results".[10] From this perspective, our conceptual chapter aims to offer a broader understanding of the interpretive and influence processes that characterize the creation of frames of reference, as well as the integration, development and communication of CSR by companies. In particular, we propose a dynamic, multi-stakeholder, descriptive model of how CSR unfolds in contemporary companies, based on four interdependent sensemaking and sensegiving processes that are influenced by key individual and organizational factors, including managers on the one hand, and internal and external stakeholders on the other. Specifically, we contend that CSR must be approached as an ongoing multipartite process by which internal and external stakeholders of the organization interactively construct and share sense through symbolic and empathetic dialog and actions about issues pertaining to the organizational activities that are interpreted in relation to the social good by one or several parties.

The descriptive model we propose contributes to academic literature and informs managerial practice in two complementary ways. First, this chapter extends existing sensemaking-based conceptualizations of CSR by considering the role and influence of external stakeholders. That is, our chapter resituates the unfolding of CSR in business organizations according to a more interactive perspective and thereby helps describe how the meaning of CSR for managers and the stakeholder network of an organization can be influenced by key individual and organizational factors, as well as co-created through confrontations of potentially conflicting viewpoints and the negotiation of meanings among diverse social actors. Second, we underscore and characterize the continuous and progressive nature of CSR development processes in organizations. The model we propose suggests that negotiations of meaning around CSR between managers and their environment, which take place through sensemaking and sensegiving processes, must be considered according to a longitudinal perspective. Sources of conflicts between managers and their environment in terms of CSR conceptions and CSR-related expectations cannot be identified and addressed once and for all; instead, they require recurrent efforts and continuous reassessments by managers who work to find a balance of the genuine concerns of the various influential actors.

Sensemaking and Sensegiving Processes at the Heart of (Inter-) organizational Life

Individual sensemaking is the interpretive process that people use to place equivocal and ambiguous environmental stimuli into defined cognitive schemas[11] or mental frames that allow them to make sense of the stimuli.[12] Sensemaking research emphasizes the temporary and circumstantial nature of the meanings people adopt to understand daily issues.[13]

Accordingly, organizational sensemaking is the process by which members make sense of equivocal and ambiguous situations in their organization by fitting them into existing schemas, based partly on their experience and socialization within the organization.[14] Organizational members often cope with confusing environmental stimuli by seeking others' interpretations, which enable them comprehend their environment and act collectively.[15] In this case, organizational sensemaking allows organization members to develop interactive, commonly shared meanings of the organization's vision, issues to target and solutions to propose. At the upper management level, sensemaking processes involve environmental scanning and issue interpretation, which influence decisions about the organizational image or rationales for organizational restructuring, development, or change.[16] At the middle management level, sensemaking processes influence the integration of strategic decisions and policies and the means used to cope with new corporate initiatives, as well as how managers construe organizational features and performance.[17] Finally, at lower levels, sensemaking processes dictate how employees conceive of their tasks and missions and help resolve the tensions between social interactions and the strategic and systemic realities of organizational life.[18]

Furthermore, organizational members at all levels endeavor to affect others' sensemaking processes through sensegiving—that is, "attempts to influence the sensemaking and meaning construction of others toward a preferred redefinition of organizational reality".[19] Sensegiving entails efforts to communicate one's own thoughts about organizational events and features and thereby increase support for this perspective through suggestive or persuasive language, as well as symbolic or empathetic actions.[20]

Theoretically, we can distinguish between sensegiving and sensemaking at any moment in time. Sensemaking aims to develop a mental model or vision of the environment, whereas sensegiving requires the articulation of that vision in an attempt to influence and persuade others. Building on this distinction, we conceptually approach interpretation-focused sensemaking and influence-focused sensegiving as sequential processes:[21] The outcomes of sensemaking inform sensegiving attempts, which influence subsequent sensemaking efforts. In practice though, sensemaking and sensegiving usually overlap.[22] The mutually dependent notions mirror each other and constitute, to some extent, two sides of the same coin.[23]

Existing research mainly focuses on sensemaking and sensegiving processes among organizational stakeholders only, leaving aside or neglecting external stakeholders of the organization. However, a broad variety of stakeholder groups make sense of issues and give sense to them through their own prisms, such that they can influence the way companies address and perceive issues and events. Maitlis describes the extent to which leaders and various stakeholders attempt to influence each other's comprehension of issues through their sensegiving processes,[24] and Gioia and Chittipeddi highlight the initiation phase of an organizational change initiative to emphasize the sequential, reciprocal cycle of sensemaking and sensegiving between managers and progressively expanding audiences, both inside and outside the organization.[25] In the model we propose, we emphasize a progressive, multipartite process that interactively co-constructs CSR meaning for the company through sensemaking and sensegiving efforts by managers and internal and external stakeholders of the company.

A Multipartite Sensemaking–Sensegiving Model of CSR

As depicted in Figure 17.1, we propose that CSR development in companies involves four interdependent processes: (1) a convergent managerial sensemaking process, (2) a compounded managerial sensegiving process, (3) a divergent stakeholder network sensemaking process, and (4) a differentiated stakeholder network sensegiving process. The managerial processes pertain to how upper and middle managers interpret the signals sent by the environment; design their organizational decisions; and maintain, nurture and advance their CSR commitments.[26] Conversely, stakeholder network processes refer to how diverse internal and external stakeholders comprehend, translate, and convey societal issues to the organization, as well as interpret and react to managerial discourses and actions.

Managerial CSR Sensemaking: A Convergent Process

Any CSR-related stimuli or issues (e.g., impact of business practices on local communities, emerging public concerns about a product component, potential new business opportunities at the base of the pyramid) require interpretation to translate them into knowledge, shared understanding and conceptual schemas, before the organization can determine whether and how to respond in a strategically relevant way. To make sense of the issues, as well as the pertinent environment, managers wade into the vast sea of stimuli and events that surround their organization to pursue an appropriate interpretation.[27] Yet managers inevitably perceive their environment and the virtually unlimited pool of CSR issues uniquely and imperfectly because of their specific individual and organizational characteristics.

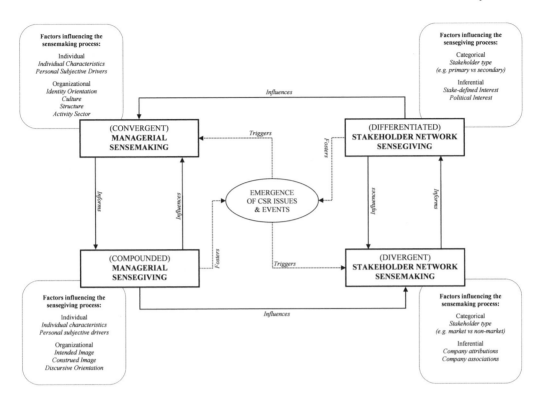

Figure 17.1 A sensemaking–sensegiving multipartite model of CSR development

On the one hand, individual characteristics, such as gender, age and level of education, influence how managers identify and interpret ethical or CSR-related issues.[28] More risk-averse managers also are less inclined to think about CSR-related marketing strategies,[29] whereas managers with more experience demonstrate a superior facility to consider how policies might address stakeholders' needs.[30] Personal values, affect and expectations also impinge on how managers make sense of their environment. For example, managers' personal values influence their inclination to take an interest in specific CSR-related stimuli and issues;[31] in particular, their dispositions toward self-transcendent values (i.e., universalism or benevolence) influence their propensity to notice ethical issues.[32] People's expectations further influence how they perceive cues and construct meaning, which can lead managers to overlook an ethical issue if their expectations at work do not include ethical criteria.[33]

On the other hand, the organization's characteristics powerfully shape members' collective interpretations of stimuli and issues.[34] For example, the sector of activity influences not only the nature of the CSR-related issues managers notice and attend to but also their perceptions of and attitudes toward those issues.[35] Because managers of highly visible fashion retailers have become preferred targets of social and environmental activists, they often exhibit more sensitivity and reaction to social and environmental issues in their supply chains than do managers of small, virtually invisible business-to-business service providers. The organization's identity orientation further influences the nature of the CSR-related activities that companies undertake:[36] Companies that adopt a firm-centered orientation tend to focus less on CSR than companies that embrace a system-centered or other-regarding orientation. Moreover, organizational culture provides storehouses of information, knowledge and know-how, which may support or detract from CSR understanding and efforts.[37] The stakeholder culture—"beliefs, values, and practices that have evolved for solving stakeholder-related problems and otherwise managing relationships with stakeholders"[38]—in particular critically influences managerial consciousness of and sensitivity toward CSR-related issues. Finally, organizational structure and functional characteristics might affect managers' sensemaking processes, notably by influencing who managers meet and which stimuli and issues they confront, as well as the way they address them.[39]

Ultimately, the individual features of managers can generate multiple and distinct CSR-related accounts across middle and upper managers in a single organization. However, organizational characteristics also support convergence across managerial accounts, thus contributing to collective understandings and "ways of seeing things" within organizations. Such progressive convergence in managers' views appears to result from regular interactions between and among managers, through both formal and informal processes and the creation of shared meaning. Yet even with high levels of cross-functional coordination, strong cultural and identity features and efficient intra-organizational dialog, diverging accounts might persist, especially between line managers and boundary spanners. In the long term, through CSR-related thinking and acting, more consensus should tend to mark the ambiguous CSR notion,[40] even if strictly uniform accounts do not exist. The formal and informal interactive processes that make this trend possible include multitudinous managerial sensegiving efforts.

Managerial CSR Sensegiving: A Compounded Process

As "sensegivers", managers promote certain understandings of CSR-related events to other internal and external stakeholders, while excluding or adapting other concepts. In particular, they may attempt to affect how other managers understand CSR-related issues by undertaking an internal "issue-selling process"[41] that introduces their own concerns and perceptions into the organization's collective awareness. They also might disseminate the organizational CSR vision and portray CSR initiatives to external stakeholders by informing, responding to, or even involving stakeholders in the development of these visions and initiatives.[42] However, whereas informing stakeholders implies a one-way sensegiving process, the two latter strategies imply both managerial sensegiving and sensemaking. With a stakeholder response strategy, the company attempts to change public attitudes and behavior but does not change itself; in the stakeholder involvement strategy, the company is more inclined to evolve through its interactions with stakeholders.

Both individual traits of managers and collective traits of the organization should influence how managers give sense to CSR-related stimuli and events. First, individual characteristics, such as functional or cultural backgrounds and acquired skills (e.g., education, training), affect the nature and level of managers' social involvement and commitment.[43] That is, managers' inclination to engage in CSR-related sensegiving efforts might depend on their own particular traits. Personal beliefs and motivational drivers also affect managers' propensity to influence the way others make sense of CSR-related stimuli and issues. In particular, motivation to sell an issue appears to be related to managers' beliefs about whether their efforts could succeed and benefit their image and credibility.[44] If managers perceive that their selling efforts will fail or regard CSR-related concerns as inappropriate in terms of current organizational goals or according to powerful organizational members, they might adapt their discourse or avoid engaging in CSR sensegiving altogether.

Second, the way managers give sense to CSR-related issues and events depends on various organizational elements, such as the construed and intended images of the organization. Managers collectively consider the associations they believe outsiders hold about the organization (i.e., construed image[45]) and determine other stakeholders' interpretations of the CSR issue to predict their reactions, once the issue catches the public attention. Then, depending on the mental associations that managers desire stakeholders to hold about the organization (i.e., intended image[46]), they endeavor to emphasize attributes that support that image for the organization.[47]

The discursive orientation of the organization represents another decisive factor that affects the nature and style of managerial sensegiving processes. Managers might use four different modes of justification to give sense to CSR actions.[48] With the legal mode, managers present officially accepted arguments that support initiatives to avoid any disapproval. Through the scientific mode, they rely on internal or external scientific expertise to rationalize corporate behaviors. The economic mode of justification implies that managers emphasize the substantial, constructive impacts of corporate actions on stakeholders. Finally, with the ethical mode, managers present cosmopolitan or higher-order interests that support corporate actions. According to the typical discursive orientation of the organization, managers thus will be more inclined to shape issues and messages in one way or another and thereby give sense to CSR issues and events in distinct manners.

Overall, managerial sensegiving for CSR usually consists of an arrangement of fairly similar, adapted processes, oriented toward other managers and stakeholders, which together constitute a compounded managerial sensegiving pattern. Similar to the managerial sensemaking process, homogeneous and collective managerial sensegiving efforts often progressively emerge among managers, supported by organizational factors such as the discursive orientation of the organization, leading to the progressive articulation of consistent, persuasive speeches and behaviors, even if some discrepancies might persist. However, when managers address messages to the company's environment, the sensegiving process and strategy adopted ideally should be adapted to communicate the intended and construed organizational images that appeal to each stakeholder group. It may be risky to convey totally different meanings about the same issues and initiatives to different stakeholders though; management instead may "color" its CSR sensegiving and frame its messages and signals accordingly,[49] depending on the perceived expectations and features of particular recipients.

Stakeholder Network CSR Sensemaking: A Divergent Process

Different stakeholder groups continuously interpret and reinterpret CSR-related issues and CSR initiatives proposed by the organization. They understand and interpret CSR-related stimuli in their own way,[50] which may differ substantially from the sense that managers make of or endeavor to give them. To help clarify the processes by which stakeholder groups variously make sense of CSR-related issues, associated initiatives and responses developed by companies, we begin by noting the importance of connecting the categorical and inferential factors that influence these processes.

Stakeholders can be classified into distinct categories, according to their business links with the organization. From this perspective, market stakeholders interact with the firm through some form of economic transaction; nonmarket stakeholders instead relate to the firm on a noneconomic basis. Stakeholder groups across categories typically are characterized by their own objectives and expectations of company behavior and social responsibility.[51] In contrast with many market stakeholders, nonmarket stakeholders tend to demonstrate higher interest in CSR issues and assess company performance through indicators other than profit.[52] Therefore, the intrinsic nature of the stakeholder category impinges on the way people perceive and interpret CSR-related issues.

We also suggest that stakeholders typically make sense of CSR stimuli using inferences, such as the motives they attribute to the companies' CSR activities. Stronger attributions of genuinely altruistic corporate motivations likely prompt more positive interpretations of CSR messages.[53] Similarly, a preexisting CSR reputation should positively color stakeholders' interpretations of CSR activities.[54] For example, consumers may hold a company less responsible for a product-related crisis if it already possesses a strong CSR reputation. Various stakeholders also share and discuss information about corporate reputations, such that their sensemaking processes depend on the intentions and influences of potentially wide groups. For many stakeholders who lack direct experience with the company, "when an issue arises, they will rely on others to supply information about the reputation of the firm and the industry".[55] Accordingly, the media play a central role in determining how stakeholders make sense of organizational realities, and reputation among employees appears to have a specific and direct impact on reputation among both customers and communities.[56]

Both categorical and inferential factors of influence can lead to situations in which CSR sensemaking in the organization's stakeholder network entails multiple and potentially conflicting accounts of CSR-related events and stimuli. The diverse stakeholders likely vary substantially in their interpretations of the same CSR issues and organizational responses. Because the constructions of sense thus tend to diverge, the organizational reality of CSR often emerges as multiple and fragmented. Nonetheless, distinct stakeholder groups progressively can develop fairly communal accounts of particular CSR-related issues or organizational initiatives. The Brent Spar crisis experienced by Royal Dutch Shell offers a pertinent example,[57] in which the initially conflicting views of NGOs, consumers, the media and public authorities gradually came into relatively close congruence. This alignment resulted from their engagement in sensegiving processes, as the different actors worked to influence others and ultimately produced fairly similar understandings.

Stakeholder Network CSR Sensegiving: A Differentiated Process

Finally, each stakeholder group typically develops distinctive sensegiving strategies to influence managers' and other stakeholders' sensemaking processes. In line with the previous section, we argue that the occurrence, nature and target of stakeholders' sensegiving efforts depend on the category of stakeholders involved, influenced by the inferences they make about the necessity, impact and reactions associated with their attempts.

In this setting, we can distinguish between primary stakeholders,[58] who have direct and well-established claims on company resources and whose continued participation is absolutely necessary for business survival, and secondary stakeholders, who are not essential for the company's survival but can "mobilize public opinion in favor of, or in opposition to, a corporation's performance".[59] This well-known categorization suggests the stakeholder groups differentially influence managers' and other stakeholders' CSR sensemaking: groups with clear, widely recognized, legitimate claims should be more prone to engage in direct influence strategies, whereas groups only indirectly engaged with the company and not essential for its survival typically use more indirect approaches.[60] Therefore, stakeholders may direct their CSR-related messages and behaviors directly toward managers (e.g., an investor questions company management about a CSR issue) or influence managerial sensemaking indirectly by addressing their messages to other parties in their network (e.g., a consumer association organizes a letter-writing campaign directed at the company).

In addition, stakeholder groups engage in CSR sensegiving depending on their inferences about the need to influence a company in their efforts to protect or support their particular interests, as well as on their expectations about the likely success of their actions.[61] However, stakeholders might choose to undertake sensegiving efforts, even if they perceive limited likely success, measured by a change in the target's sensemaking or behavior.[62] For example, to affirm an identity or reinforce its own position in a stakeholder network, a stakeholder group might engage in intense sensegiving processes directed at both managers and other stakeholders.[63] Similarly, stakeholder groups might adopt forceful sensegiving processes to form CSR coalitions that should "have more influence than a stakeholder alone".[64]

Because of their diverse natures, interests and political intentions, stakeholder groups are characterized by distinct CSR sensegiving processes. Each group, sometimes in coalition with others, develops strategies to influence managers' and other stakeholders' sensemaking processes. Managers thus face multiple, varied, tangible and symbolic messages, all aimed at altering their interpretation of and behavior toward CSR-related issues.

Discussion and Conclusions

The four interconnected interpretive and influence processes we emphasize in our proposed model simultaneously shape the social construction and meaning negotiation processes by which internal and external stakeholder groups attempt to interpret, explain, act and react to CSR-related stimuli and issues. These processes are interactive, concomitant and continuous.

By distinctly emphasizing sensemaking and sensegiving processes in the development of CSR in companies, as well as some of the underlying factors that influence them, our conceptual model contributes to existing literature and generates suggestions for managerial practice in two main directions. First, by explicitly integrating the role and expectations of stakeholders in CSR-related sensemaking and sensegiving processes, our proposed model overtly asserts that the meaning of CSR for managers and the stakeholder network of an organization gets co-created through confrontations of viewpoints, which reflect the organizational and individual characteristics, motivations and expectations of the various actors. Because managers and various stakeholder groups likely hold conflicting expectations and viewpoints about the nature or mere existence of CSR issues and the appropriate ways for companies to address them, managers must develop both formal and informal dialog processes to interact with their internal and external environments. Fostering such structures (e.g., boundary-spanning functions, stakeholder panels, multi-stakeholder collaborations and partnerships) can facilitate understanding and consideration of stakeholder motivations and expectations by managers, as well as encourage the co-construction of communal meanings and convergent conceptions of the company's mission and responsibilities with respect to CSR. This process should lead to constructive consensus—even if partial or imperfect—and support the design and implementation of constructive CSR policies and initiatives that contribute to the development of more responsible and efficient corporate practices, as well as greater goodwill toward and legitimacy for the company.

Second, our descriptive model adopts a longitudinal perspective to stress the unceasing cycles of CSR sensemaking and sensegiving and the continuous nature of CSR development. Our model thus exemplifies the evolution of perceptions and interactions among managers and their environment in the long term, which progressively establish CSR as an intrinsic part of the company's character, never just set once and for all. As sensemaking and sensegiving processes occur continually, they progressively typify the CSR fabric of the organization and—depending on their intensity and the key dimensions that affect them—define the company's dispositions at any moment in time to interpret CSR-related issues and events, address them and interact with and balance potentially conflicting expectations and influence attempts throughout its stakeholder network. The CSR character of the company moves on as managers' interpretive processes, understanding of stakeholders' viewpoints and expectations, and links with society's aspirations continuously get re-created.

Our conceptual inquiry is not exempt from limitations though. The complexity of organizational entities and organizational phenomena guarantees that rigorous models and theories cannot represent the entire range of real-life practices and situations; some of our suggestions require further discussion. The main factors we have briefly highlighted as key influences on the sensemaking and sensegiving processes of managers and stakeholders probably need to be complemented, perhaps with further investigations that pursue clearer empirical support, which offers suggestions for ongoing research. Nevertheless, we believe this sensemaking-based and multipartite CSR conceptualization, articulating key theoretical elements in a multidisciplinary perspective, represents an insightful, descriptive model of a central contemporary (inter)organizational phenomenon.

Notes

1   Bhattacharya, N.C., Smith, C. and Vogel, D. (2004), "Integrating social responsibility and marketing strategy: an introduction", *California Management Review*, vol. 47, no. 1, pp. 6–8.
2   Weaver, G.R., Trevino, L.K. and Cochran, P.L. (1999), "Integrated and decoupled corporate social performance: management commitments, external pressure, and corporate ethics practices", *Academy of Management Journal*, vol. 42, no. 5, pp. 539–552.

3   Grayson, D. and Hodges, A. (2004), *Corporate Social Opportunity! Seven Steps to Make Corporate Social Responsibility Work for Your Business*, Sheffield, UK, Greenleaf Publishing; Nijhof, A. and Jeurissen, R. (2006), "A sensemaking perspective on corporate social responsibility: introduction to the special issue", *Business Ethics: A European Review*, vol. 15, no. 4, 316–322.

4   Cramer, J., Jonker, J. and van der Heijden, A. (2004), "Making sense of corporate social responsibility", *Journal of Business Ethics*, vol. 55, no. 2, pp. 215–222; Van Marrewijk, M. (2003), "Concepts and definitions of CSR and corporate sustainability: between agency and communion", *Journal of Business Ethics*, vol. 44, pp. 95–105.

5   Dawkins, D. and Lewis, S. (2003), "CSR in stakeholder expectations and their implication for company strategy", *Journal of Business Ethics*, vol. 44, no. 2/3, pp. 185–193; Polonsky, M. and Jevons, C. (2006), "Understanding issue complexity when building a socially responsible brand", *European Business Review*, vol. 18, no. 5, pp. 340–349; Zyglidopoulos, S. (2002), "The social and environmental responsibilities of multinationals: evidence from the Brent Spar case", *Journal of Business Ethics*, vol. 36, no. 1/2, pp. 141–151.

6   Cramer, J.M., van der Heijden, A. and Jonker, J. (2006), "Corporate social responsibility: making sense through thinking and acting", *Business Ethics: A European Review*, vol. 15, no. 4, pp. 380–389; Nijhof and Jeurissen (2006), op. cit.

7   Weick, K.E. (1995), *Sensemaking in Organisations*, Sage, Thousand Oaks, CA.

8   Cramer *et al.* (2004, 2006), op. cit.; Nijhof and Jeurissen (2006), op. cit.

9   Gioia, D.A. and Chittipeddi, K. (1991), "Sensemaking and sensegiving in strategic change initiation", *Strategic Management Journal*, vol. 12, no. 6, pp. 433–448; Maitlis, S. (2005), "The social processes of organizational sensemaking", *Academy of Management Journal*, vol. 48, pp. 21–49.

10   Nijhof and Jeurissen, op. cit.

11   Schemas refer to the dynamic knowledge and internal structures of specific concepts, entities and events, which enable people to process and represent incoming information efficiently. They serve as mental maps that people use to orient themselves within their experiential terrain.

12   Starbuck, W.H. and Milliken, F.J. (1988), "Executives' perceptual filters: what they notice and how they make sense". In D.C. Hambrick (ed.), *The Executive Effect: Concepts and Methods for Studying Top Managers*, JAI Press, Greenwich, CT, pp. 35–56.

13   Luria, A.R. (1982), *Language and Cognition*, Wiley, New York, NY.

14   Weick (1995), op. cit.

15   Gioia, D.A. and Thomas, J.B. (1996), "Identity, image and issue interpretation: sensemaking during strategic change in academia", *Administrative Science Quarterly*, vol. 41, pp. 370–403; Maitlis (2005), op. cit.; Starbuck and Milliken (1988), op. cit.; Volkema, R.J., Farquhar, K. and Bergmann, T.K. (1996), "Third-party sensemaking in interpersonal conflicts at work: a theoretical framework", *Human Relations*, vol. 49, pp. 1437–1454.

16   Gioia and Chittipeddi (1991), op. cit.; Gioia and Thomas (1996), op. cit.; Gioia, D.A., Thomas, J.B., Clark, S.M. and Chittipeddi, K. (1994), "Symbolism and strategic change in academia: the dynamics of sensemaking and influence", *Organization Science*, vol. 5, no. 3, pp. 363–383.

17   Balogun, J. and Johnson, G. (2004), "Organizational restructuring and middle manager sensemaking", *Academy of Management Journal*, vol. 47, no. 4, pp. 523–549; Rouleau, L. (2005), "Micro-practices of strategic sensemaking and sensegiving: how middle managers interpret and sell change every day", *Journal of Management Studies*, vol. 42, no. 7, pp. 1413–43; Pratt, M.G. (2000), "The good, the bad and the ambivalent: managing identification among Amway distributors", *Administrative Science Quarterly*, vol. 45, no. 3, pp. 456–494; Wagner, J.A. and

Gooding, R.Z. (1997), "Equivocal information and attribution: an investigation of patterns of managerial sense making", *Strategic Management Journal*, vol. 18, no. 4, pp. 275–286.

18   Bean, C.J. and Eisenberg, E. (2006), "Employee sensemaking in the transition to nomadic work", *Journal of Organizational Change Management*, vol. 19, no. 2, pp. 210–222.

19   Gioia and Chittipeddi (1991), op. cit.

20   Ibid; see also Rouleau (2005), op. cit.

21   Gioia and Chittipeddi (1991), op. cit.

22   Gioia *et al.* (1994), op. cit.

23   Rouleau (2005), op. cit.

24   Maitlis (2005), op. cit.

25   Gioia and Chittipeddi (1991), op. cit.

26   See Child, J. (1972), "Organizational structure, environment and performance: the role of strategic choice", *Sociology*, vol. 6, no. 1, pp. 1–22; Hegarty, W.H. and Tihanyi, L. (1999), "Surviving the transition: Central European bank executives' view of environmental changes: a metamorphosis model of convergence and reorientation", *Journal of World Business*, vol. 34, no. 4, pp. 409–422; Mitchell, R.K., Agle, B.R. and Wood, D.J. (1997), "Toward a theory of stakeholder identification and salience: defining the principle of who and what really counts", *Academy of Management Review*, vol. 22, no. 4, pp. 853–886; Quazi, A.M. (2003), "Identifying the determinants of corporate managers' perceived social obligations", *Management Decision*, vol. 41, no. 9, pp. 822–831.

27   Daft, R. and Weick, K.E. (1984), "Toward a model of organizations as interpretation systems", *Academy of Management Review*, vol. 9, no. 2, pp. 284–295.

28   Deshpande, S.P. (1997), "Managers' perception of proper ethical conduct: the effect of sex, age and level of education", *Journal of Business Ethics*, vol. 16, no. 1, pp. 79–85; Van Maanen, J. and S.R. Barley (1984), "Occupational communities: culture and control in organizations". In B.M. Staw and L.L. Cummings (eds), *Research in Organizational Behavior*, vol. 6, JAI Press, Greenwich, CT, pp. 287–365.

29   Menon, A. and Menon, A. (1997), "Enviropreneurial marketing strategy: the emergence of corporate environmentalism as market strategy", *Journal of Marketing*, vol. 61, no. 1, pp. 51–67.

30   Thomas, A. and Simerly, R. (1994). "The chief executive officer and corporate social performance: an interdisciplinary examination", *Journal of Business Ethics*, vol. 13, no. 12, pp. 959–968.

31   Hemingway, C.A. and Maclagan, P. W. (2004), "Managers' personal values as drivers of corporate social responsibility", *Journal of Business Ethics*, vol. 50, no. 1, pp. 33–44.

32   Crilly, D., Schneider, S.C. and Zollo, M. (2008), "Psychological antecedents to socially responsible behavior", *European Management Review*, vol. 5, pp. 175–190.

33   See Moore, D.A. and Loewenstein, G. (2004), "Self-interest, automaticity, and the psychology of conflict of interest", *Social Justice Research*, vol. 17, pp. 189–202.

34   Van Maanen, J. and Schein, E. H. (1979). "Toward a theory of organizational socialization". In B.M. Staw (ed.), *Research in Organizational Behavior*, vol. 1, JAI Press, Greenwich, CT, pp. 209–264.

35   See Bhambri, A. and Sonnenfeld, J. (1988), "Organization structure and corporate social performance: a field study in two contrasting industries", *Academy of Management Review*, vol. 31, no. 3, pp. 642–662.

36   Basu and Palazzo, op. cit.; Agle, B.R., Mitchell, R.K. and Sonnenfeld, J.A. (1999), "Who matters to CEOs? An investigation of stakeholder attributes and salience, corporate performance, and CEO values", *Academy of Management Journal*, vol. 42, no. 5, pp. 507–525.

37   Doppelt, B. (2003), *Leading Change Toward Sustainability,* Sheffield, UK, Greenleaf; Maon, F., Lindgreen, A. and Swaen, V. (2010), "Organizational stages and cultural phases: a critical review and a consolidative model of corporate social responsibility development", *International Journal of Management Reviews,* vol. 12, no. 1, pp. 20–38.

38   Jones, T.M., Felps, W. and Bigley, G. (2007), "Ethical theory and stakeholder-related decisions: the role of stakeholder culture", *Academy of Management Review,* vol. 32, no. 1, pp. 137–155.

39   Maon, F., Lindgreen, A. and Swaen, V. (2008), "Thinking of the organization as a system: the role of managerial perceptions in developing a corporate social responsibility strategic agenda", *Systems Research and Behavioural Science,* vol. 25, no. 3, pp. 413–426; Sharma, S., Pablo, A.L. and Vredenburg, H. (1999), "Proactive corporate environmental strategies and the development of competitively valuable organizational capabilities", *Strategic Management Journal,* vol. 44, pp. 838–857.

40   Cramer, J.M., van der Heijden, A. and Jonker, J. (2006), "Corporate social responsibility: making sense through thinking and acting", *Business Ethics: A European Review,* vol. 15, no. 4, pp. 380–389.

41   Pater, A. and van Lierop, K. (2006), "Sense and sensitivity: the roles of organisation and stakeholders in managing corporate social responsibility", *Business Ethics: A European Review,* vol. 15, no. 4, pp. 339–351.

42   Morsing, M. and Schultz, M. (2006), "Corporate social responsibility communication: stakeholder information, response and involvement strategies", *Business Ethics: A European Review,* vol. 15, pp. 323–338.

43   Burton, B.K. and Hegarty, W.H. (1999), "Some determinants of student corporate social responsibility orientation", *Business and Society,* vol. 38, pp. 188–205; Thomas and Simerly (1994), op. cit.; Quazi (2003), op. cit.

44   Dutton, J.E. and Ashford, S.J. (1993), "Selling issues to top management", *Academy of Management Review,* vol. 18, no. 3, pp. 397–428.

45   Brown, T.J., Dacin, P.A., Pratt, M.G. and Whetten, D.A. (2006), "Identity, intended image, construed image, and reputation: an interdisciplinary framework and suggested terminology", *Journal of the Academy of Marketing Science,* vol. 34, no. 2, pp. 99–106.

46   Ibid.

47   Whetten, D.A. and Mackey, A. (2002), "A social actor conception of organizational identity and its implications for the study of organizational reputation", *Business and Society,* vol. 41, no. 4, pp. 393–414.

48   Basu and Palazzo, op. cit.; Ashforth, B.E. and Gibbs, B.W. (1990), "The double-edge of organizational legitimation", *Organization Science,* vol. 1, no. 2, pp. 177–194.

49   Mahon, J.F. and Wartick, S.L. (2003), "Dealing with stakeholders: how reputation, credibility and framing influence the game", *Corporate Reputation Review,* vol. 6, pp. 19–35.

50   Pater and van Lierop (2006), op. cit.; Schouten, E.M.J. and Remmé, J. (2006), "Making sense of corporate social responsibility in international business: experiences from Shell", *Business Ethics: A European Review,* vol. 15, no. 4, pp. 365–379.

51   Waddock, S.A., Bodwell, C. and Graves, S.B. (2002), "Responsibility: the new business imperative", *Academy of Management Executive,* vol. 16, pp. 132–149.

52   Baron, D.P. (1995), "The nonmarket strategy system", *Sloan Management Review,* vol. 37, no. 1, pp. 73–85.

53   Ellen, P., Webb, D.J. and Mohr, L.A. (2006), "Building corporate associations: consumer attributions for corporate socially responsible programs", *Journal of the Academy of Marketing Science,* vol. 34, no. 2, pp. 147–157; Sen, S., Bhattacharya, C.B. and Korshun, D. (2006), "The

role of corporate social responsibility in strengthening multiple stakeholder relationships: a field experiment", *Academy of Marketing Science Journal*, vol. 34, pp. 158–166.

54   Zagenczyk, T.J. (2004), "Using social psychology to explain stakeholder reactions to an organization's social performance", *Business and Society Review*, vol. 109, pp. 97–101; Klein, J. and Dawar, N. (2004), "Corporate social responsibility and consumers' attributions and brand evaluations in product-harm crisis", *International Journal of Research in Marketing*, vol. 21, no. 2, pp. 203–17.

55   Mahon, J.F. (2002), "Corporate reputation: a research agenda using strategy and stakeholder literature", *Business and Society*, vol. 41, pp. 415–445.

56   Carmeli, A. (2005), "Perceived external prestige, affective commitment, and citizenship behaviors", *Organization Studies*, vol. 26, pp. 443–464.

57   See Livesey, S.M. (2001), "Eco-identity as discursive struggle: Royal Dutch/Shell, Brent Spar, and Nigeria", *Journal of Business Communication*, vol. 38, pp. 58–91; Zyglidopoulos (2002), op. cit.

58   Clarkson, M.B. (1995), "A stakeholder framework for analyzing and evaluating corporate social performance", *Academy of Management Review*, vol. 20, pp. 92–117; Freeman, R.E. (1984), *Strategic Management: A Stakeholder Approach*, Pitman, Boston, MA.

59   Clarkson (19950, op. cit.

60   Frooman, J. (1999), "Stakeholder influence strategies", *Academy of Management Review*, vol. 24, no. 2, pp. 191–205.

61   Ibid.; Savage, G., Nix, T., Whitehead, C. and Blair, J. (1991), "Strategies for assessing and managing stakeholders", *Academy of Management Executive*, vol. 5, no. 2, pp. 61–75; Pfeffer, J. and Salancik, G.R. (2003), *The External Control of Organizations*, Stanford Business Books, Stanford, CA.

62   Rowley, T. and Moldoveanu, M. (2003), "When will stakeholder groups act? An interest and identity-based model of stakeholder mobilization", *Academy of Management Review*, vol. 28, pp. 204–219.

63   de Bakker, F.G.A. and den Hond, F. (2008), "Introducing the politics of stakeholder influence: a review essay", *Business and Society*, vol. 47, no. 1, pp. 8–20.

64   Vos, J. (2003), "Corporate social responsibility and the identification of stakeholders", *Corporate Social Responsibility and Environmental Management*, vol. 10, no. 3, pp. 141–152.

18 A New Institutionalism Approach to Stakeholder Theory

ROBIN T. BYERLY*

Keywords

New institutionalism, social contract, stakeholder engagement.

Introduction

A number of approaches to stakeholder theory have been offered over the past twenty-plus years with all subject to debate and various critiques. While the reality of the stakeholder idea is clearly flourishing,[1] tensions related to stakeholder theory continue to dominate its dialog.[2] These reflect in general the difficulty in integrating instrumental/economic theories of the business corporation with the normative/ethically oriented approaches used to justify business engagement with, and responsiveness to, society and stakeholders. It is often held that the two perspectives are antagonistic and largely incompatible as first, social duties present a trade-off problem to market-driven profit objectives and second, normative values are inherently difficult to morally and consensually justify.[3] As a result of these theoretical challenges, research orientations to stakeholder theory frequently do not entail solid integration of the two competing perspectives.

Increasingly in this age, business organizations are connected to and affected by larger systems of relations and thus play defining organizational roles in society.[4] Clearly, not every company is dedicated to stakeholder engagement or social responsibility, but many are establishing ambitious corporate social responsibility agendas, enhancing their roles as good global citizens and working to create better stakeholder relationships. This may be explained by new institutionalism theory which supports the notion of a reconceptualized business institution that is transformed materially and symbolically to bring society back in and recognize it as a critical allocating mechanism for the marketplace.[5] Further, new institutionalism theory deems corporate actors more accountable by focusing on how, within organizational fields, programs or rule systems come about which are neither imposed by legal pressure nor absorbed from the larger culture, but rather are built or created by system participants and as such, lead those actors to pursue collective goals.[6] It follows, then, that new institutionalism theory can be used effectively to explain

* Robin T. Byerly, Appalachian State University, Department of Management, P.O. Box 32089, Boone, NC, USA. E-mail: byerlyrt@appstate.edu.

institutional pressures to transform, be more responsive and accountable to society and in a collective fashion move toward greater stakeholder responsibility. It is considered here to be most useful as an integrative approach to balance the competitive concerns of the business organization, with its corporate social responsibility to key stakeholder constituents and increasing societal expectations. Moreover, it offers fresh perspective to the legitimization of stakeholder theory, and the possibility of a more convergent acceptance of how to integrate responsible attention to stakeholders.

This chapter is organized as follows: First, stakeholder theory is briefly reviewed in light of the tensions described above, including attention to extant research that has attempted to integrate the two positions. Next, three general problems associated with the operationalization of stakeholder theory are identified. New institutionalism theory is then discussed as it: (1) differs from traditional institutionalism, and (2) serves as a useful integrative approach to modern stakeholder theory by resolving to some extent the theoretical problems described. Subsequent to the development of this perspective, key stakeholder groups are brought into focus as illustrative examples—customers and employees. The new institutionalism approach to stakeholder theory is then summarized in the conclusion.

Stakeholder Theory—Three General Approaches: Descriptive, Instrumental and Normative

Three general approaches to stakeholder theory have been usefully described by Donaldson and Preston[7] as descriptive, instrumental, and normative. It is suggested that while these approaches differ, they are indeed mutually supportive, according to these authors, as stakeholder theory is intended to both explain and to guide an organizational entity to accomplish multiple, and not always congruent, purposes. The *descriptive* approach serves to describe or explain specific corporate characteristics and behaviors. Further, it reflects and explains past, present and future states of organizational affairs relative to corporate stakeholders. *Instrumental* approaches seek to identify connections, or the lack thereof, between stakeholder management and achievement of corporate objectives, such as profitability and financial performance. *Normative* approaches are generally prescriptive of what the firm ought to do and attempt to interpret function of, and offer guidance about, the investor-owned corporation, as determined by moral values or philosophical guidelines.

In a general sense, *normative* theory has sought to establish ethical justification for an enlarged view of the firm, its purpose, rights and responsibilities. Examples might entail philosopher Martin Buber's[8] notion of "I–Thou" human relations, or John Rawls'[9] conceptualization of justice, or Kant's prescription of categorical imperatives. It relies on an acceptance of implicit morality, either in the market itself,[10] in the moral personhood of the organization,[11] in the absolute existence of certain values[12] and in the responsibilities/duties associated with rights and claims of others.[13] These approaches are both *descriptive* about the nature of the firm and also involve either implicit or explicit moral and *normative* responsibilities for the firm that are separate and distinct from profit or self-serving concerns.

On the other hand, the *instrumental* approach has centered largely on finding a valid economic or rational justification for stakeholder engagement, such as Hall and Soskice's[14] discussion of varieties of capitalism and the institutional foundations of comparative advantage, or the occasional anecdotal piece that suggests business can do well by doing good.[15] But of particular importance in the evolution of stakeholder theory, many have sought to find meaningful, testable theoretical approaches that bridge the divide and integrate both economic and ethical approaches in an effort to avoid the purely normative rationale for business persuasion. In this regard, the contractarian approach to business ethics was initiated by Donaldson and Dunfee[16] and has served to invite much debate and theoretical discussion.[17] This stream of research has brought about any number of concerns and additional suggestions for development. The real implications of this debate are that reconciling the *normative* and/or *descriptive* with the *instrumental* is truly difficult to justify theoretically. These challenges notwithstanding, the quest continues as many stakeholder advocates hold that normative, descriptive and instrumental approaches must converge if they are to represent good, practicable stakeholder theory.[18]

Stakeholder Theory—Three General Problems

Visible progress toward responsible stakeholder management has been achieved despite three general sets of problems that have presented dilemmas as to the operationalization of stakeholder theory. First, as Milton Friedman[19] strenuously maintained, the purpose and nature of the business is economic and the achievement of its purpose is effectively enabled by economic freedom. The corporate duty is a fiduciary one—not social—and its overriding responsibility is to its primary stakeholder group, the owners of the firm. A conflict clearly emerges as the investment, time and the values associated with social initiatives must compete with that required to serve the primary purpose of the firm—making a profit and increasing shareholder value. The conflict between firm owners and the interests of societal stakeholders has indeed been the most prominent stumbling block in fashioning both theory and practice to truly embrace the notion of stakeholder engagement and response. For example, customer concerns regarding greater assurance of product safety or of sustainable business practice would likely be perceived as a cost trade-off to firm profitability initiatives and run counter to competitive concerns. Employee demands relevant to workplace conditions, pay, or job security may be regarded as either cost prohibitive or value-neutral to the owners and managers of the firm.

Secondly, in a pluralistic society and global marketplace, stakeholders represent a diverse and widespread set of concerns and petitions. How can the business organization attend to all, or make acceptable decisions about which to attend to, and why? While notions of supposed business social responsibility have generally included all stakeholders (all those parties affected or impacted in some way by business activities), frequently the legitimacy of many stakeholder claims, or their justification for corporate engagement, has generally been predicated on whether the stakeholder had the power to demand attention.[20] Further, stakeholder concerns may overwhelm the firm and many stakeholder demands may compete with each other. Evan and Freeman[21] equate such management to requiring the wisdom of King Solomon. Some duties toward others are more clearly warranted for prima facie moral reasons (e.g. reciprocity or justice),[22] while other stakeholder claims are more morally questionable or less guided by legal or clear obligation.[23] In short, even if the firm wishes to maintain a socially responsible reputation and actually engage with stakeholders, doing so can be formidable. Thus, responding to general societal concerns, or an array of stakeholder concerns, presents a pressure of considerable magnitude for even a large corporation. For stakeholder theory to have significance for the firm, of necessity, it typically involves a prioritization of relevant stakeholder groups, that is, identification of those groups that are most closely linked and of most importance to the organization, and fashioning a genuine engagement with those parties. Thus, a number of theorists suggest that a valid stakeholder approach must allow a legitimate partiality to certain groups. Gibson[24] suggests that the moral, or deontological, approach has the most promise as it narrows the scope of concern to those groups who are most easily understood as human moral agents.

Finally, a third general set of problems has to do with the nature of the business organization's relationships with stakeholder groups. Obligation to engage with and respond to stakeholders also relies on applying the notion of a hypothetical social contract, a model that has been used for centuries to argue the conditions for the legitimate exercise of power by government. This notion of an implied social contract endures and for more modern purposes, has been extended to include not only society and government, but also business. Although it has evolved over the centuries, its basic premise is still the same: to understand and determine what roles, relationships and responsibilities each of us has relative to the whole of society and its collective well-being. The contractarian approach to business ethics and the implied social contract, initially developed by Donaldson and Dunfee,[25] and extended by several others,[26] has sought to delineate the ethical, or normative, responsibilities of business, while integrating legitimate fiduciary, and instrumental, responsibilities. It is rooted in the concept of macro-social hypothetical agreements and, as such, it relies on rational agreement as to norms and presumes some set of understood societal obligations by institutions and the people who manage them. Donaldson and Dunfee[27] conceptualized a set of *hypernorms* that could render moral rationality and legitimacy to the definition of the macro-social contract. Conflicts naturally emerge regarding identification and agreement of norms or values that have not addressed context or biases,[28] or that may conflict.[29] Others have disagreed on the dynamic and changing nature of social norms,[30] and the process by which norms are derived.[31] To summarize in brief, contractarian approaches to managing stakeholders via a social contract struggle to articulate a theoretical framework that (1) fully integrates both fiduciary and ethical concerns, and (2) effectively establishes a set of moral standards that can be universally accepted.

Articulating a theoretical framework that effectively defines legitimate notions of stakeholder engagement while balancing the competitive and values-oriented approaches already established has indeed been contested and difficult. Nonetheless, what has endured and remains prominent in most approaches to stakeholder theory is a fairly clear recognition of *reciprocity*—that multiple parties have a stake in and can be impacted by business organizations' activities and that those parties can, as well, have an impact on business organizations. Theoretical notions of responsibility to those stakeholder groups are often supported with normative/moral approaches and also, in some cases, instrumental approaches. For example, Jensen[32] offers a melding of what he describes as "enlightened value maximization" and "enlightened stakeholder theory" and suggests that the long-term market value of an organization cannot be maximized without good treatment of important constituents, or stakeholders. Similarly, Wood[33] makes an instrumental argument for stakeholder engagement in that toxic consequences often accrue to businesses that ignore their institutional role of business in society. Moreover, she contends, a well-instituted program of stakeholder engagement offers a conceptual mechanism for better corporate self-control. These theoretical efforts, among others,[34] fashion stepping stones toward a more singular and integrated stakeholder theory.

The New Institutionalism—an Integrative Approach

Theory regarding business organizations has often relied on and borrowed from sociological theory (e.g., the population ecology of organizations, put forth by Hannan and Freeman in 1977, or the processes of decision-makers in organizations, developed by March in 1981). Institutional theory, initially developed by DiMaggio and Powell,[35] recognizes the strong normative pressures that emanate from other institutional agents and the persuasion toward mimetic behaviors that can influence related or similar institutions. As a result, much in business organizations is shaped by cultural, social and political pressures and in an even larger sense, *institutional* forces can shape organizational systems.[36] A half century ago, Parsons[37] emphasized that the correspondence of values pursued by organizations be congruent with wider social values if that organization was to be perceived as legitimate. Recognizing that responsible behavior of corporations must be influenced by wider institutional settings, social and political ideologies and collective expectations of norms and appropriate behaviors, several researchers have suggested an intersection of corporate social responsibility and institutional theory.[38] It follows that a melding of stakeholder theory and new institutionalism theory offers similar promise.

New institutionalism theory is a more modern development of institutional theory and reflects an analytical approach that is based on a theory of practical action, using a set of orienting principles that reflect cognitive turns in contemporary social values and attitudes.[39] New institutionalism is social in nature and focuses on developing a sociological view of institutions—the way they interact and the way they affect society. It provides a way of viewing institutions outside of the traditional views of economics by explaining why so many businesses end up having the same organizational structure (isomorphism) even though they evolved in different ways, and how institutions shape the behavior of individual members. An important contribution of new institutionalism is that it adds a cognitive-type influence that persuades individuals, instead of acting under rules or obligations, to actually act because of conceptions. Resultingly, organizations adopt new routines in many circumstances because other types of behavior are inconceivable; new behaviors are followed because they are taken for granted as "the way we do these things".[40] In short, it is designed to describe both how organizations become homogeneous in structure, culture and output (as in traditional institutionalism), and also how they increasingly do so in more creative and sustainable responses to society and contemporary social values and concerns (the new institutionalism).

Scott[41] identifies several general trends in the institutional analysis of organizations that help distinguish the "new" from the "old". He views these newer developments as constructive and contributing to the maturing of institutional theory. In one sense, new institutionalism reflects organizational change that is consequential and more enduring, as opposed to the traditional "ceremonial conformity" that was perhaps more superficial and short-lived. In other words, as institutional forces compel organizations to make structural changes, and new types of personnel are hired, business units become champions of the reforms, and sustainable changes become seen as being in the company's best interest.

He further suggests that traditional institutionalism, while focusing on change for both internal and external reasons, was still dedicated to achieving stability and convergent change. Whereas, new institutionalism responds to new logics that may come from foreign realms and challenge existing stable fields, resulting in deinstitutionalization processes, perhaps bringing about the collapse of existing institutions and their gradual reconstruction into new configurations. The implications of this theory for better understanding stakeholder engagement is inherently logical as it recognizes that business institutions are deeply embedded in their cultural, social and political environments and, practically speaking, the choices and behaviors they make should reflect that. Further, it is argued here that integrating new institutionalism and stakeholder theory serves to allay to some extent the three general problems identified earlier.

A NEW INSTITUTIONALISM APPROACH TO STAKEHOLDERS

Powell and DiMaggio[42] contend that individual business organizations, in efforts to deal rationally with the uncertainty and constraint of their competitive environments, move in the aggregate to homogeneity in structure, culture, and output, a process described as *isomorphism*. Institutional change becomes rational once rules and structures are adopted by large numbers, hence mimetic processes emanate and the likelihood of many institutions adopting new forms is enhanced. As social processes, obligations and actualities become commonly accepted, they take on a rule-like status in social thought and action. This presents a competitive and efficiency argument for organizations as the competition for social fitness actually has a decided payoff.[43] In short, business organizations that mimic others by engaging stakeholders and their concerns with more sustainable business practices or a better service warranty, etc. are, as a result, more competitively positioned. Similarly, an institutional employer that recognizes, not just the moral value of its human assets, but perhaps more significantly the benefits achieved by major competitors in recruiting and retaining valuable employees and building strong supportive organizational cultures, may smartly mimic those competitors by offering a more supportive work environment and benefit package.

Three types of mimetic behaviors are described by Powell and DiMaggio[44] to understand and operationalize this theory. Organizations compete not just for resources and customers, but also for political power and legitimacy, for economic success and for social fitness. In that quest, a variety of antecedents will influence their movement toward institutional isomorphic change. Political influence and the problem of legitimacy will influence what is called *coercive* isomorphism. *Mimetic* isomorphism results from standard responses to uncertainty, and concern regarding professionalization leads to *normative* isomorphism. As business organizations are influenced by moral, competitive and institutional pressures, newer proactive routines and behaviors toward key stakeholders are increasingly observed. Changing roles, structures, initiatives, etc. and the expanding nature of this phenomenon among large and small businesses may be explained as isomorphic institutional change.

COERCIVE ISOMORPHISM

Business organizations are persuaded to change when they are pressured by other organizations upon which they are dependent and by cultural expectations of the societies in which they operate. Such pressures may be felt strongly and lead to coercive isomorphism in which organizations join others in collusion to adopt new structural or policy changes. Organizational change may be a direct response to government mandate: civil rights legislation may reconstruct organizations' approach to hiring, promoting, or in recent cases in the U.S., extension of health care benefits for employees; new legal guidelines may result in stronger efforts to offer safe products with more extensive warnings to customers to avoid increased risk of liability. Similarly, legal and technical requirements emanating from national, state and/or local government or regulatory agencies may push organizations to follow each other in homogenous ways to ensure legitimacy, control and group solidarity.[45]

For example, the chemical industry is currently on edge over the United States Environmental Protection Agency's (EPA) efforts to make public some of the information companies claim as proprietary in submissions on commercial chemicals to that agency.[46] An EPA administrator has challenged manufacturers to voluntarily lift some of their confidentiality claims in health and safety studies previously sent to the agency. Activists have complained for years that too many of the public health and safety reports describe substances in overly broad, generic terms that are often meaningless. Stakeholders want to have honest and reliable information regarding the safety of chemical products. While some manufacturers are nervous and representatives of the American Chemistry Council are fighting back, many producers, including Proctor and Gamble, are voluntarily working with the EPA to develop a new form of classification. As coercive pressures mount, more are joining the voluntary efforts to improve health and safety accountability.

Coercive pressures that impose standard operating procedures and legitimated rules and structures may also come from outside the governmental area, particularly in strategic groups and industries, many of which are directed by trade organizations or leading business actors within those groups. Subsidiaries, suppliers, distributors and other business partners may be compelled to adopt compatible policies, as for example, attention to labor rights as required by powerful companies that outsource production to developing countries. Further, as large conglomerate corporations increase in global size and scope of operations, many will follow others in adopting global principles (e.g., Caux Round Table Principles for Business, the United Nations Global Compact, the CERES Principles, or the International Labour Organisation's [ILO] labour standards) resulting in certain standards being necessarily imposed upon subsidiaries. Coercive pressures have motivated businesses by the hundreds to voluntarily adopt many of these principles. As well, businesses are now encouraged to work collaboratively with citizen-sector organizations to approach large-scale issues which capitalize on complementary strengths to create both economic and social value.[47] Working with "The Natural Step" framework, companies like Nike have formed working relationships with numerous organizations dedicated to better serving stakeholders and the common good by adopting the CERES principles, endorsing The United Nations' Global Compact, partnering with the World Wildlife Fund and the Center for Energy and Climate Solutions, and The Global Alliance.[48]

Customers and employees as primary stakeholders have, in large part, always relied on such pressures to move producers and employers toward greater care in their policies and managerial approaches toward them. Formally (legally) granted rights establish clear affirmative and negative obligations for business organizations to attend to employee concerns regarding equal employment, workplace safety, fair wages, avoidance of discrimination or sexual harassment, etc. Rights granted to consumers obligate producers to provide safe products, honest and sufficient information, and to allow consumers to be heard. Over the past century, collective bargaining and the diligence of labor unions have pressured industrialized companies to improve working conditions and treatment of employees. As social issues have developed in the mainstream consciousness regarding worker safety, civil rights, rights of consumers for safe products and reliable information and environmental sustainability, governments have responded with laws and regulatory agencies that move business organizations in the aggregate to restructure accordingly.

MIMETIC ISOMORPHISM

Modern competitive environments may present significant uncertainty, a powerful force that encourages imitation. When technologies are poorly understood, goals are ambiguous, governmental regulation is threatening or international law is inadequate and/ or competition is hard to match, organizations may tend to model themselves on other organizations. Mimetic isomorphism may result as modeling is a common organizational response to uncertainty. As such, homogenous organizational responses may be influenced by consulting firms, industry trade organizations, or attempts to consciously innovate by imitating others. Organizations also tend to model themselves after others that are similar in their field that are perceived to be more legitimate or successful.[49] Finally, in today's rich media and socially connected world, many organizations are pushing social agenda frameworks, lending their expertise, sharing best practices and providing leadership for others that are pressured or generally moved to institutionalize and build in a more structured agenda that engages stakeholders.

Mimetic pressures may result from the ever-growing body of challenging, and some seemingly intractable, environmental problems related to natural resources, climate change, energy use, waste, water, etc., as these issues are characterized by much uncertainty.[50] As many businesses begin to pave the way to solutions, through innovation and more efficient processes, others are following their lead. Pressures are to operate more sustainably, to realize economic savings, to prepare in anticipation of more regulatory guidelines, but also to not be left behind competitively. The uncertainties associated with a global marketplace, differing cultures, legal systems, issues surrounding workers, sustainability and fair trade all present pressures to conform and to mimic others. Add to these uncertainties increasing societal pressures for business organizations to pursue good global citizenship, a worthy aspiration despite being rather nebulous in terms of how to achieve.[51]

An excellent example is seen in the successful efforts of the Interface Company, a global carpet manufacturer led by CEO Ray Anderson, to be the first company to become truly sustainable in all its operations.[52] In 1994, in response to employee and customer concerns about environmental degradation, Anderson challenged his company to pursue a bold new vision that would show the entire world, by its deeds, sustainability in all its dimensions: people, process, product, place and profits—and in doing so, become restorative through the power of influence. The Interface journey toward sustainability has been a momentous shift in the way Interface operates its business. Results include innovative new processes, elimination of waste, reduction of energy and water use, enormous cost savings, an improved reputation and an energized workforce. Further, the company has been a leader in teaching and motivating others to follow suit.

Primary stakeholders and their issues are better attended to as organizations mimic others in response to uncertainty. Kondra and Hurst[53] point out that mimetic processes may address uncertainty in the organizational links between inputs, outputs and rewards. In efforts to add legitimacy and stability to employment status, rewards and social belonging, institutional changes may work to build stronger, more supportive organizational cultures. Consumers may serve in uncertain environments to effect institutional social change with their demands for reliable corporate reputation, or ethical goods and services. The connection between consumers and corporations expands the significance of corporations in presenting as good citizens.[54]

NORMATIVE ISOMORPHISM

Normative isomorphic organizational change is influenced primarily by businesses' interpretation of professionalization. Conditions and methods of work, organizational design, incentive and reward systems are all defined in many ways by occupation.[55] Formal education, universities, professional networks and training institutions and certification programs all provide important influences in the development of organizational norms among occupational professionals and their staffs. Pressures for competitive efficiency, for status competition, organizational prestige and human resources are important in attracting and retaining qualified professionals. Regularly exchanged information among professionals helps contribute to a commonly recognized hierarchy of status that may be reinforced by government, professional and trade associations, representation on boards of other organizations, participation in policy development councils and other desirable professional affiliations.

Business organizations may be normatively pressured by what Scott and Meyer[56] identify as "societal sectors", in other words, bounded systems that are defined to include all organizations within a society supplying a given type of product or service together with their associated organizational sets, such as suppliers, financiers, distributors, regulators, etc. Although the concept of societal sectors is broader than that of industry and does include other organizations that support or constrain activities, a commonality of organizational characteristics tends to emerge.[57]

For example, companies in the sector of outdoor gear, equipment and clothing may collectively embrace values of environmental sustainability, leading to initiatives that appeal particularly to employees and customers, but also investors and other members of society (e.g., Timberland, Patagonia, REI, etc.). Companies in certain sectors such as health care or professional services may move in the aggregate to maintain postures dedicated to the public good. Social goals that address community needs or causes such as poverty, education, etc. may be commonly adopted by many firms in related sectors. Further, both coercive and mimetic inspired behaviors may become internalized to become normative behavior as any process that encourages the homogenization and internalization of organizational norms can be thought of as a normative process, or the "glue" that helps to hold an organization's social system together.[58]

The result of institutional responses to today's stakeholder expectations is a plethora of business organizations with social responsibility goals and programs, strategies, measurement and reporting procedures, and a much stronger engagement with primary stakeholders. Many businesses address key stakeholders and acknowledge responsibility to them in mission or vision statements which typically include strategic goals related to better practice and progress on key social issues that are most relevant to those stakeholder groups. In today's global marketplace, the institutionalized legitimacy of a global corporation may be defined as one developed in the climate of a truly global community, one characterized by global citizenship and moral responsibility to respect the concerns of the various cultures and communities in which it operates.[59] Primary stakeholders benefit as businesses are pressured by global awareness and concern for workers' rights and well-being, environmental sustainability in products and production processes and fair trade practices. While the pressures to conform to social and environmental responsibility are intense, the result of doing so not only gives greater care to primary stakeholders, but also lends greater legitimacy, control, risk aversion and competitive positioning to those businesses that institutionally conform.

New Institutionalism, Stakeholders and Three General Problems

To summarize, can the argument be made that a new institutionalism theoretical approach to stakeholder theory integrates competing perspectives and resolves the operational problems described earlier?

The first problem identified with operationalizing stakeholder theory has to do with competing arguments, fiduciary versus moral or normative duties. As discussed above, pressures for institutional change and collective response emanate from a wide array of coercive, mimetic and normative antecedents that, in effect, represent the multifaceted environmental, institutional, societal and competitive pressures surrounding today's modern business organization. Moreover, by virtue of institutional pressures for social efficacy, this theory allows economic organizational goals to be tied competitively to stakeholder and societal engagement and response.[60] Stakeholders become identified as those with true reciprocal characteristics, in other words, those most closely linked and those with genuine social/moral concerns.[61] Rather than posing confusion or conflict, the issues or concerns that invite business response are, in large part, institutionally determined.

A second problem recognizes that many stakeholders may present with issues and concerns, such that it may be prohibitive for any company to be able to respond to all. New institutionalism theory allows for business action and position to be directly responsive to the prevailing issues of society at any given time or that which is proximate. For example, Hoffman[62] examines organizational change in the U.S. chemical industry regarding environmental sustainability with the idea that organizational fields form around issues, not markets or technologies. In response to coercive pressure from federal regulators and trade journals, normative pressures from the public (this industry has been singled out in public opinion polls as posing the greatest environmental threat of all industries since the 1970s), and mimetic pressures as multiple chemical manufacturers began to evolve toward greater environmental management, many institutions in this and related industries were profoundly moved to make institutional changes.

The third problem identified has to do with stakeholder relationships and the social contract, particularly in light of theoretically determining what might constitute solid guidelines or values to uphold in a defined relationship with society. New institutionalism theory, as an integrative approach to stakeholder theory, is intuitive and one that balances values and morals, stakeholder concerns and issues with competitive and strategic organizational goals. It is open minded, creative and capable of responding intuitively with changes that become more established as values as they become institutionalized. As we are witnessing transcendental changes in corporate citizenship, stakeholder engagement and corporate social responsibility agendas, the increasingly collective manifestations of organizational responsiveness to stakeholder issues seems clearly framed by wider institutional settings, and by social and political influences.

Key Stakeholder Groups: Employees and Customers

Two stakeholder groups can be viewed as illustrative of new institutionalism theory because they are particularly vital to the business organization—customers and employees. Each is clearly of strategic importance. The stakeholder relationships that businesses must manage—particularly those that are external with customers and those that are internal with employees—have the distinct commonality of reciprocity. While each group has legal rights and certain ethical expectations of the business, each is of critical importance to the business. Indeed, each party can be viewed as a moral agent, but each is also a strategic factor with competitive implications for the business. Customers can follow their values or other concerns and transfer their allegiance to a competitor, and valuable employees who are not taken care of can find work elsewhere, all having the power to impact the firm economically. Some stakeholder theorists have made a distinction between primary and secondary stakeholders with primary designated as those who have a formal, official, or contractual relationship and all others as secondary stakeholders.[63] Customers and employees would naturally fall into the primary category and, according to theory, be most deserving of consideration, given the reciprocal power such stakeholders have.

Firm managers must consider pressure from shareholders/owners to please them with economic performance and return on their investment, while simultaneously managing pressure from customers to create and offer price/quality enticements in the firm's goods and services. While effectively pleasing customers will most likely translate into pleasing owners, *ceteris paribus*, theoretical conflicts have been voiced as to *how* that is actually done, given concerns regarding the inarguable nature of moral free space and ethical relativism that might be associated with the firm's individual values and choices and its response to the expectations of customers regarding health, safety, pricing, information, company reputation, etc. Further, satisfying customers and achieving organizational objectives cannot be achieved without the contributions of employees, a critical stakeholder group with its own issues, rights (perceived and legally granted) and expectations, particularly relating to health, safety, wages, privacy and other workplace concerns. Conflict, theoretical and real, may result as values related to prevailing views on how employees should be treated and economically managed diverge and are variously understood.

But this is where new institutionalism can bridge the divide. Foundational to the concept of stakeholder theory is the notion of *reciprocity*—stakeholders have a stake in and are impacted by the actions of business organizations and business organizations can be positively or adversely affected by those stakeholders. This is particularly so with primary stakeholders who are tightly connected through contract, formality, agency or in some official way, such as customers and employees. Stakeholder theory also relies on the premise of *legitimacy*—if stakeholder concerns are to be addressed, they must be perceived as valid, urgent and backed by authority; if businesses are to compete effectively in the global marketplace, they must be perceived by society and other institutions as conforming to expectations. New institutionalism theory lends support to stakeholder theory in both regards. Mutual engagement and response to stakeholders are inherently woven into this theory. It is, in fact, based on a notion of reciprocity to and from society and all its actors. Scott[64] holds that business organizations make choices among a narrowly defined set of legitimate options determined by a group of actors that comprise that firm's organizational field which includes a variety of loosely connected institutions. Indeed, other institutions can create powerful pressures for organizations to seek legitimacy themselves and strive for social conformity. Thus, the theory provides some convergence as pressures for isomorphism and collective change reflect a totality of social concerns, competitive positioning and collectively accepted practices.

Conclusions

New institutionalism reflects organizational response and practical action to pressures from other institutions, contemporary society, its stakeholders and government, including social values, attitudes and actual competitive concerns that are increasingly tied to stakeholder engagement. In today's society, a wide array of institutional pressures influence organizations to structurally and behaviorally respond. For several reasons, including the hypercompetitiveness of today's global marketplace, or the power engendered to information and media by technology, societal issues can develop to such widespread acceptance and prominence in the eyes of many that business organizations must take note, particularly so when issues are of paramount concern to primary stakeholders.

Real life examples and an abundance of anecdotal evidence suggest that businesses are indeed responding in a variety of new organizational and strategic approaches to the concerns that emanate from society and key stakeholder groups. Triple bottom-line and other institutional approaches reveal greater attention to human rights and societal values. Without legal requirement, many firms are making special provisions for same sex couples and their concerns, and providing better accommodations to facilitate work–family needs for their employees. They are responding to customer/societal concerns for sustainability and healthier/safer products. Businesses are playing a larger role than ever in their communities—local and global—by attending to social needs with marketing initiatives and employee volunteerism. Such initiatives are no longer only generated by a few—most large organizations are dramatically embracing stakeholder and societal concerns.

Are those who are genuinely attentive to stakeholders morally persuaded? Some are, but it can surely be argued that we are living in an age where values and competitive concerns are merging. The need for a convergence of a moral and pragmatic theoretical framework has never been greater. Many theorists agree that in our increasingly interdependent society, individual good is not possible outside the context of common good; moral principles simply cannot be separated from any approach to institutional behavior.[65]

Business organizations and societies are mutually interdependent; each has strategic and moral concerns and each has the power and legitimacy to impact the other. As the development of social capital in business organizations becomes increasingly important and firms pursue new ways of giving back to society, we see new focus on key stakeholders who play a vital part in achieving their organization's social goals.[66] Institutional initiatives include more attention to moral and supportive culture-building, more extensive benefit offerings, opportunities for employee flexibility and for volunteerism and others. As more business organizations mimic each other and homogeneously respond they benefit from enhanced legitimacy and from more satisfied and motivated employees. Recognizing that more and more customers care about others, have concerns about fairness and have increased awareness and commitment to causes,[67] new institutional approaches are seriously and systematically addressing their concerns related to human and worker rights, equitable trade, environmental sustainability, fair pricing, after sales service, corporate reputation and others. Again, the end result is better stakeholder engagement with customers, enhanced legitimacy in the marketplace and a stronger strategic position relative to competitors.

References

1   Agle, B.R., Donaldson, T., Freeman, R.E., Jensen, M.C., Mitchell, R.K. and Wood, D.J. (2008), "Dialogue: toward superior stakeholder theory", *Business Ethics Quarterly*, vol. 18, no. 2, pp. 153–190.

2   Margolis, J.D. and Walsh, J.P. (2003), "Misery loves companies: rethinking social initiatives by business", *Administrative Science Quarterly*, vol. 48, pp. 268–305.

3   Swanson, D.L. (1995), "Addressing a theoretical problem by reorienting the corporate social performance model", *Academy of Management Review*, vol. 20, no. 1, pp. 43–64.

4   Scott, W.R. and Meyer, J.W. (1991), "The organization of societal sectors." In W.W. Powell and P.J. DiMaggio (eds), *The New Institutionalism in Organizational Analysis*, The University of Chicago Press, Chicago, pp. 108–140.

5   Friedland, R. and Alford, R.R. (1991), "Bring society back in".In W.W. Powell and P.J. DiMaggio (eds), *The New Institutionalism in Organizational Analysis*, The University of Chicago Press, Chicago, pp. 232–263.

6   Galaskiewicz, J. (1991), "Making corporate actors accountable: institution-building in Minneapolis–St. Paul". In W.W. Powell and P.J. DiMaggio (eds), *The New Institutionalism in Organizational Analysis*, The University of Chicago Press, Chicago, pp. 293–310.

7   Donaldson, T. and Preston, L.E. (1995), "The stakeholder theory of the corporation: concepts, evidence, and implications", *Academy of Management Review*, vol. 20, no. 1, pp. 65–91.

8   Buber, M. (1937), *I and Thou*, Charles Scribner's Sons, New York (originally published in German, 1923).

9   Rawls, J. (1971), *A Theory of Justice*, Oxford University Press, Oxford.

10   Quinn, D. and Jones, T. (1995), "An agent morality view of business morality", *Academy of Management Review*, vol. 20, no. 1, pp. 22–42.

11   Gibson, K. (2000), "The moral basis of stakeholder theory", *Journal of Business Ethics*, vol. 26, pp. 245–257; Goodpaster, K. (1991), "Business ethics and stakeholder analysis", *Business Ethics Quarterly*, vol. 11, no. 1, pp. 53–74.

12   Evan, W. and Freeman, R.E. (1988), "A stakeholder theory for the modern corporation: Kantian capitalism". In T. Beauchamp and N. Bowie (eds), *Ethical Theory and Business*, Englewood Cliffs, Prentice-Hall, pp. 97–106.

13   Carroll, A. (1993), *Business and Society: Ethics and Stakeholder Management*, Southwestern Publishing, Cincinnati.

14   Hall, P.A. and Soskice, D. (2001), *Varieties of Capitalism: The Institutional Foundations of Comparative Advantage*, Oxford University Press, Oxford.

15   *The Economist* (2000), "Business ethics: doing well by doing good", April 22 2000.

16   Donaldson, T. and Dunfee, T. (1994), "Toward a unified conception of business ethics: integrative social contracts theory", *Academy of Management Review*, vol. 19, no. 2, pp. 252–284; Donaldson, T. and Dunfee, T. (1995), "Integrative social contracts theory: a communitarian conception of economic ethics", *Economics and Philosophy*, vol. 11, no. 1, pp. 85–112; Donaldson, T. and Dunfee, T. (1999), *Ties that Bind: A Social Contracts Approach to Business Ethics*, Harvard Business School Press, Boston.

17   Bishop, J.D. (2008), "For-profit corporations in a just society: a social contract argument concerning the rights and responsibilities of corporations", *Business Ethics Quarterly*, vol. 18, no. 2, pp. 191–212; Calton, J. (2006), "Social contracting in a pluralist process of moral sense making: a dialogic twist on the ISCT", *Journal of Business Ethics*, vol. 68, pp. 329–346; Cava, A. and Mayer, D. (2006), "Integrative social contract theory and urban prosperity initiatives", *Journal of Business Ethics*, vol. 72, pp. 263–278; Marens, R. (2007), "Returning to Rawls: social contracting, social justice, and transcending the limitations of Locke", *Journal of Business Ethics*, vol. 75, pp. 63–76; Phillips, R.A. and Johnson-Cramer, M.E. (2006), "Ties that unwind: dynamism in integrative social contracts theory", *Journal of Business Ethics*, vol. 68, pp. 283–302; Thompson, J.A. and Hart, D.W. (2006), "Psychological contracts: a nano-level perspective on social contract theory", *Journal of Business Ethics*, vol. 68, pp. 229–241; Wempe, B. (2004), "On the use of the social contract model in business ethics", *Business Ethics: A European Review*, vol. 13, pp. 332–341; Wempe, B. (2005), "In defense of a self-disciplined domain-specific social contract theory of business ethics", *Business Ethics Quarterly*, vol. 15, pp. 113–135; Wempe, B. (2007), "Four design criteria for any future contractarian theory of business ethics", *Journal of Business Ethics*, vol. 81, pp. 697–714.

18   Jones, T.M. and Wicks, A.C. (1999), "Convergent stakeholder theory", *Academy of Management Review*, vol. 24, no. 2, pp. 206–221.

19   Friedman, M. (1962), *Capitalism and Freedom*, University of Chicago Press, Chicago.

20   Freeman, R.E. (1984), *Strategic Management: A Stakeholder Approach*, Pitman, Boston.

21   Evan and Freeman (1988), op. cit.

22   Ross, W.D. (1930), *The Right and the Good*, Clarendon Press, Oxford.

23   Gibson (2000), op. cit.

24   Gibson (2000), op. cit.

25   Donaldson and Dunfee (1994), op. cit., Donaldson and Dunfee (1995), op. cit.

26   Bishop (2008), op. cit.; Cava and Meyer (2006), op. cit.; Marens (2007), op. cit.; Philips and Johnson-Cramer (2006), op. cit.; Sacconi, L. (2006), "A social contract account for CSR as an extended model of corporate governance: rational bargaining and justification", *Journal of Business Ethics*, vol. 68, pp. 259–281; Thompson and Hart (2006), op. cit.; Wempe (2004), op. cit.; Wempe (2005), op. cit.

27   Donaldson and Dunfee (1994), op. cit.

28   Cava and Meyer (2006), op. cit.; Thompson and Hart (2006), op. cit.

29   Reisel, W.D. and Sama, L.M. (2004), "Applying ISCT when norms are incompatible: the case of access to life-saving medicines in South Africa", Zicklin Center Conference, November.

30   Phillips and Johnson-Cramer (2006), op. cit.

31 Calton (2006), op. cit.; Rowan, J.R. (2001), "How binding the ties? Business ethics as integrative social contracts", *Business Ethics Quarterly*, vol. 11, no. 2, pp. 379–390; Hartman, L.P., Shaw, B. and Stevenson, R. (2003), "Exploring the ethics and economics of global labor standards: a challenge to integrated social contract theory", *Business Ethics Quarterly*, vol. 13, no. 2, pp. 193–220; Wempe (2007), op. cit.

32 Jensen, M.C. (2010), "Value maximization, stakeholder theory, and the corporate objective function", *Journal of Applied Corporate Finance*, vol. 22, no. 1, pp. 32–42.

33 Agle *et al.* (2008), op. cit.

34 Agle *et al.* (2008), op. cit.; Margolis and Walsh (2003), op. cit.; O'Higgins, E.R.E. (2009), "Corporations, civil society, and stakeholders: an organizational conceptualization", *Journal of Business Ethics*, vol. 94, pp. 157–176.

35 DiMaggio, P.J. and Powell, W.W. (1983), "The iron cage revisited: institutional isomorphism and collective rationality in organizational fields", *American Sociological Review*, vol. 48, pp. 147–10.

36 Scott, W.R. (2008), *Institutions and Organizations: Ideas and Interests*, Sage, Thousand Oaks.

37 Parsons, T. (1960), *Structure and Process in Modern Societies*, Free Press, Glencoe.

38 Aguilera, R.V. and Jackson, G. (2003), "The cross-national diversity of corporate governance: dimensions and determinants", *Academy of Management Review*, vol. 28, no. 3, pp. 447–466; Campbell, J.L. (2006), "Institutional analysis and the paradox of corporate social responsibility", *American Behavioral Scientist*, vol. 49, no. 7, pp. 925–938; Kondra, A.Z. and Hurst, D.C. (2009), "Institutional processes of organizational culture", *Culture and Organization*, vol. 15, no. 1, pp. 39–58; Matten, D. and Moon, J. (2008), "'Implicit' and 'explicit' CSR: a conceptual framework for a comparative understanding of corporate social responsibility", *Academy of Management Review*, vol. 33, no. 2, pp. 404–424; Scott and Meyer (1991), op. cit.

39 Powell, W.W. and DiMaggio, P.J. (1991), *The New Institutionalism in Organizational Analysis*, The University of Chicago Press, Chicago and London.

40 Scott (2008), op. cit.

41 Scott (2008), op. cit.

42 Powell and DiMaggio (1991), op. cit.

43 Birch, D. (2001), "Corporate citizenship: rethinking business beyond corporate social Responsibility". In J. Andriof and M. McIntosh (eds), *Perspectives on Corporate Citizenship*, Sheffield, Greenleaf Publishing; Goddard, T. (2005), "Corporate citizenship: creating social capacity in developing countries", *Development in Practice*, vol. 15, pp. 433–438.

44 Powell and DiMaggio (1991), op. cit.

45 Powell and DiMaggio (1991), op. cit.; Scott (2008), op. cit.

46 Hogue, C., 2010, "Trade secret anxiety", *Government and Policy*, vol. 89, no. 14, pp. 24–26.

47 Drayton, B. and Budinich, V. (2010), "A new alliance for global change", *Harvard Business Review*, vol. 88, no. 9, pp. 56–64.

48 Nattrass, B. and Altomare, M. (2002), *Dancing with the Tiger*, New Society Publishers, Canada.

49 Powell and DiMaggio (1991), op. cit.; Scott (2008), op. cit.

50 Scott (2008), op. cit.

51 Birch (2001), op. cit.; Goddard, T. (2005), "Corporate citizenship: creating social capacity in developing countries", *Development in Practice*, vol. 15, pp. 433–438.

52 Anderson, R.C. (2011), *Business Lessons from a Radical Industrialist*, St. Martin's Griffin, New York.

53 Kondra and Hurst (2009), op. cit.

54   Crane, A., Matten, D. and Moon, J. (2004), "Stakeholders as citizens? Rethinking rights, participation, and democracy", *Journal of Business Ethics*, vol. 53, pp. 107–122.

55   Powell and DiMaggio (1991), op. cit.

56   Scott and Meyer (1991), op. cit.

57   Deeg, R. (2007), "Complementarity and institutional change in capitalist systems", *Journal of European Public Policy*, vol. 14, pp. 611–630; Powell and DiMaggio (1991), op. cit.; Scott (2008), op. cit.

58   Kondra and Hurst (2009), op. cit.; Tichy, N.M. (1982), "Managing change strategically: the technical, political and cultural keys", *Organizational Dynamics*, vol. 11, pp. 59–80.

59   Buccholtz, R.A. and Rosenthal, S.B. (2001), "Pluralism, change, and corporate community", *Business and Professional Ethics Journal*, vol. 20, no. 2, pp. 63–83.

60   Jensen, 2010 (op. cit.); Wood (2008), op. cit.

61   Gibson (2000), op. cit.

62   Hoffman, A.J. (1999), "Institutional evolution and change: environmentalism and the U.S. chemical industry", *Academy of Management Journal*, vol. 42, no. 4, pp. 351–371.

63   Carroll (1993), op. cit.

64   Scott (2008), op. cit.

65   Agle *et al.* (2008), op. cit.; Jensen (2010), op. cit.; Sethi, P. (1975), "Dimensions of corporate social performance: an analytic framework", *California Management Review*, vol. 17, pp. 58–64.

66   Chia, J. and Peters, M. (2010), "Social capital initiatives: employees and communication managers leading the way?", *Journal of Promotion Management*, vol. 16, pp. 201–216.

67   DellaVigna, S. (2010), "Consumers who care", *Science*, vol. 329, July, pp. 287–288; Lee, K. and Shin, D. (2010), "Consumers' responses to CSR initiatives: the linkage between increased awareness and purchase intention", *Public Relations Review*, vol. 36, no. 2, pp. 193–195.

19 Enhancing the Care-based Resolution of CSR-related, Firm–stakeholder Conflict: Invoking the Counsel of Mary Parker Follett

SHELDENE SIMOLA*

Keyword

Care ethics, CSR, Mary Parker Follett, stakeholder.

Introduction

Both corporate social responsibility (CSR) and the stakeholder concept are contested notions in management thought. Not only do multiple scholarly definitions and conceptual frameworks exist within each of the two domains[1] but also, CSR proponents and critics alike often hold staunch but discordant views on the purpose that business should serve in broader society, and the nature and scope of practices that CSR should comprise.[2]

Despite the range of benefits associated with implementing CSR initiatives and "managing for stakeholders",[3] many business leaders still experience confusion about these processes, pointing to the need for clearer guidance on the pragmatics of such endeavors.[4] This is particularly true when extensive or frequently evolving sets of stakeholder claims[5] diverge with one another or with current corporate perspectives or practices.

The purpose of this chapter is to consider the implications of one particular theoretical perspective, care ethics, for the integrative resolution of CSR-related stakeholder conflict. Two goals will be accomplished. First, it will be demonstrated that care ethics can serve as a unified conceptual framework through which firms can respond to the diverse range of challenges associated with such discord. Secondly, this chapter will extend previous, more circumscribed research on care ethics when managing for stakeholders[6] by considering how the contributions of classic management scholar Mary Parker Follett can enlarge

*   Sheldene Simola, Business Administration Program, Trent University, 1600 West Bank Dr., Peterborough, ON, K9J 7B8, Canada. E-mail: ssimola@trentu.ca.

and enhance our practical understanding of care ethics as they pertain to managing CSR-related stakeholder conflict. Follett's work, though largely absent from the management literature for several generations, has recently not only resurged but also been heralded by leading business scholars as highly relevant for a range of contemporary management challenges.[7] Although Follett's work has received renewed attention during the last decade, including occasional articles directed toward ethics[8] and stakeholder theory,[9] application of her work in these realms has still been noticeably limited. This is unfortunate given the significant potential of her writing to enrich our understanding in these areas.

In order to accomplish its goals, this article will be structured in the following way. First, contemporary care ethics will be introduced and their defining features described, following which, a brief orientation to the perspective of Mary Parker Follett will be provided. Secondly, the nature of CSR-related stakeholder conflict will be reviewed, and five specific challenges for resolving such discord identified. Thirdly, the potential of care ethics to serve as a unified conceptual framework through which to respond to the aforementioned challenges will be described. The implications of Follett's work for enlarging and enhancing our understanding of care ethics and their practical implications for resolving CSR-related conflict will be elaborated.

Overview of Contemporary Care Ethics

Contemporary care ethics emerged from within several scholarly disciplines, including education, philosophy, political science and psychology.[10] Although specific definitions of care ethics vary depending on the theoretical perspective being used, business ethicists often understand care ethics in terms of Gilligan's path-breaking research on moral reasoning.[11] In reflecting on this research, Derry defined care ethics as a form of "moral reasoning that derives from a concern for others and a desire to maintain thoughtful mutual relationships with those affected by one's actions".[12] The processes through which mutual relationships are maintained in care ethics are several. They include forms of problem-solving that go beyond purely rational approaches to emphasize the value of emotion in ethical recognition and deliberation. Additionally, within care ethics the focus is *not* upon understanding the objective, general and abstract features of specific situations, but rather, on understanding the subjective, specific and concrete experiences, needs and feelings of others, including those who might be relatively disempowered or vulnerable in some way. Moreover, rather than adjudicating between conflicting rights, care ethics emphasize creativity in finding nonzero-sum solutions when responding to the seemingly conflicting needs of various parties.[13]

Although care ethics have been the subject of significant scholarly attention since the early 1980s, they have not been viewed uncritically. Four potential concerns are identified here. First, scholars have perceived that some conceptualizations of care are distinctively feminine in nature.[14] Although these conceptualizations have led to concerns that care ethics could be used to legitimize and reinforce gendered divisions of labour,[15] meta-analysis of empirical studies has demonstrated that care ethics are neither exclusively nor even disproportionately used by women relative to men.[16]

A second criticism of care ethics has been questions about the extent to which they are applicable beyond the parochial confines of the private (i.e., familial) sphere into the public (i.e., nonfamilial) domain. However, a number of researchers have demonstrated quite compellingly both the applicability and pliability of care ethics to broad public and organizational contexts.[17]

Thirdly, given the historic contrasting of care ethics to more conventional approaches such as justice, concern has been expressed about whether care could or would be used to try to supplant the substantial benefits of justice perspectives. However, it should be noted that although various accounts have been offered about the relationship between care ethics and other more conventional approaches such as justice, many scholars have highlighted that both approaches are important and that neither is expendable.[18]

Fourthly, because care ethics emphasize relatively nebulous goals such as maintaining or enhancing relationships, concern has been expressed that care ethics offer less concrete or clear guidance in terms of decision-making than that which might be obtained using other ethical frameworks.[19] Indeed, the work of Mary Parker Follett is quite relevant in responding to this criticism. As will be described subsequently, Follett's work was not simply prescient to the emergence of contemporary care ethics, but also sufficiently pragmatic in focus that it has significant potential to enlarge and enhance our practical understanding and application of care ethics.

Classic Management Scholar Mary Parker Follett

Mary Parker Follett (1868–1933) began her career as a scholar of politics and public administration, as well as a social worker specializing in community development. Throughout her career, she became a prolific writer, as well as an internationally recognized and much-sought-after speaker and consultant in business and management.[20]

Follett's influence in business and management emerged from the theory of democratic governance articulated in her book *The New State: Group Organization the Solution of Popular Government*.[21] Follett argued that the study of democracy had typically involved consideration of formal institutions, when it should have focused on the psychology of group interaction. Given its focus on group interaction, Follett's work was seen to have significant implications not just for higher level and formal political organization, but also for other forms, such as those which occur in business and management.

Drawing heavily on emergent research in social psychology, Follett[22] was intrigued by the difference between "crowd psychology" in which autonomous individuals undertake similar actions through the power of "suggestion and imitation", and the social psychological processes through which individuals interact to develop vibrant and powerful forms of democratic governance. Follett argued that democracy is much more than a remote, bureaucratic and hierarchical institution to which individual citizens passively respond. Rather, true democracy is that which requires active involvement of diverse citizens and groups working to identify, understand and integratively resolve conflicts and problems. Follett argued that power emerges in democracy not through the formalized structures through which it is conferred, but rather, through creative problem-solving in which both individuals and groups are simultaneously strengthened, developed and fulfilled.

Following completion of *The New State*, Follett continued to develop, test and refine her concepts not only through meticulous scholarship, but also through pragmatic activities including various forms of community development and managerial work. Follett's knowledge from this scholar-practitioner perspective was later presented in a series of speeches before the prestigious New York Bureau of Personnel Administration[23] as well as through her book *Creative Experience*.[24] These works focused on elaborating the theoretical foundations and practical applications of her key concepts involving conflict as a potentially health-enhancing relational experience; the development of genuine, co-active power formed through interaction with others rather than formal institutional appointment; the development of integrative (win–win) solutions to problems; and the notion of circular response involving the reciprocal influence of individuals existing in a constant state of relationship to one another. Each of these concepts will be elaborated in a subsequent section of this chapter on "Enhancing the care-based resolution of CSR-related stakeholder conflict: invoking the counsel of Mary Parker Follett."

Follett's work, like care ethics, has not gone uncriticized. Most notably, some of her concepts and approaches have been seen as relatively idealistic and somewhat naïve to the political realities of actual business practice.[25] Despite these criticisms, her orientation toward human interconnection along with the practical implications of her work are still highly valued among leading scholars[26] as worthy processes to undertake.

Prescience of Follett's Work for Contemporary Care Ethics

The prescience of Follett's work to contemporary care ethics has been noted by several. However, consideration of this observation has typically involved its peripheral and passing mention, or the use of circumscribed versus elaborated discussions.[27] Hence, the current chapter will describe the ways in which Follett's work can enlarge and enhance our understanding of care ethics, particularly in relation to their practical implications for managing CSR-related stakeholder conflict. We first consider the nature of CSR-related stakeholder conflict, following which five specific challenges to resolving such conflict will be elaborated. Subsequently, the potential of care ethics to serve as a unified framework through which to respond to these five challenges will be described. This discussion will highlight the ways in which Follett's work can expand and enhance our practical understanding of care ethics in resolving such discord. This information is summarized in Table 19.1, at the end of this chapter.

CSR, Stakeholders and Conflicting Views

Although a plethora of frameworks exist for understanding CSR[28] many popular conceptualizations define it in terms of five dimensions.[29] These include social, environmental and economic components, as well as both the stakeholder concept and notions of "voluntariness" on the part of the firm. Hence, despite disparate views about the exact nature and latitude of practices that CSR should encompass, CSR is commonly understood to comprise some group of discretionary activities directed toward advancing not simply economic objectives, but also social and environmental goals of relevance to a range of stakeholders.[30] So central is the consideration of diverse stakeholders to the development and implementation of CSR initiatives that the stakeholder concept has become a fundamental construct in this regard.[31]

In his classic work on the stakeholder approach, Freeman inextricably linked the concepts of stakeholder, CSR and conflict. While broadly defining stakeholders as "any group or individual who can affect or is affected by the achievement of the organization's objectives",[32] he also identified that a commonality among definitions of CSR is that they affirm as stakeholders those diverse parties whose social values and goals have historically been seen as antithetical to the economic objectives of the firm. Hence, CSR initiatives engage a range of stakeholders with or among whom contentious relationships could exist. Indeed, it has been noted that under conditions of perfect agreement among firms and their stakeholders, neither CSR nor stakeholder management would be necessary. Rather, entirely harmonious interests and views would obviate the need to attend to such issues.[33] Therefore, although its form and degree might vary, conflict is an integral part of managing for stakeholders in CSR.

Challenges in Resolving CSR-related Conflict

During the last two decades, examples of CSR-related conflict have been common. These conflicts reflect a range of challenges which are summarized below. Subsequently, the potential of care ethics as a unified conceptual framework through which to resolve these challenges will be described, including elaboration of the practical insights implied by the work of Follett.

IMPORTANCE OF ENGAGING IN RELATIONSHIP-BUILDING WITH DIVERSE STAKEHOLDERS

Successfully managing for stakeholders in CSR involves much more than instrumental decisions about which activities the firm should or should not undertake in order to meet its own CSR-related objectives.[34] Rather, it requires active engagement in relationship-building, not just as a means to a particular end at a specified point in time, but rather as part of an ongoing process of establishing positive connections through which value creation for a range of stakeholders can occur. This effort should focus not upon relationships in the abstract, but rather on a concrete "names and faces" approach in which a detailed understanding of particular stakeholder needs[35] as well as authentic dialog occur.[36] In this regard, Freeman and Velamuri[37] argued that communication with stakeholders needs to be both thorough and conscientious, and occur not just with those who are allies, but also with those who are critics. They emphasized that although not every critic will be legitimate nor able to be satisfied, an ongoing commitment to a dialogical process is still essential.

Examples of corporate failures in relationship-building are common. For example, when it comes to environmental contamination, an increased likelihood of dangerous toxic chemical disposal has been found in communities that are differentially populated by those with lower socioeconomic status.[38] Demographic profiling has reportedly been used to identify communities inhabited by those assumed to be less willing or able to protest. The use of demographic profiling indicates corporate failures to engage in proactive relationship-building. It is, therefore, unsurprising that cases involving such circumstances have reflected prolonged and intense conflict among corporations, governments, the media and various community groups.[39]

UNDERSTANDING AND MANAGING POWER DIFFERENTIALS

Noland and Phillips[40] noted the challenges firms face in managing their power in a morally principled, rather than an excessive or unjustifiable way. They identified that sometimes the power afforded to firms by their financial status can be greater than that of certain countries, enabling such firms to dictate the kinds of relationships they have with host communities. Power differentials among other stakeholders are also common, particularly where some relatively disenfranchised groups are involved. Firms can work to avert what might be prolonged adversarial interactions by attempting to recognize the vulnerability of various groups.

A sector in which power differentials have posed concerns both between the firm and its stakeholders, as well as among stakeholders themselves, is that of resource extraction. Historically, some companies have used resources to their own economic benefit, and fallen short in relation to their social, economic and environmental responsibilities to local communities.[41] For example, in his study of occupational health and safety practices in the South African mining industry, Eweje identified that despite pressure from various groups to address significant risks to workers, only limited amelioration has occurred.[42] Moreover, perceptions of double standards exist in terms of how disempowered workers in developing countries are treated relative to their counterparts in more developed countries.

AUTHENTIC ENGAGEMENT WITH CSR-RELATED STAKEHOLDER CONFLICT TO IDENTIFY NON-ZERO SUM SOLUTIONS

Drawing on Freeman's[43] petition against the "separation thesis" (i.e., the belief that business and social concerns can be managed separately) scholars have persuasively argued that effective strategic management involves focusing not only on economic goals, but also on the social and environmental concerns of a range of stakeholders.[44] Such discussions have emphasized that the financial success of firms need not be a zero-sum proposition. Rather, the creative kindling of innovative ideas while considering the idiosyncratic needs of a variety of stakeholders has been seen as an important source of value creation.[45]

However, despite the growing prominence of this perspective in academic thought, it still appears to be a relatively obscure notion in practitioner terms. For example, Pedersen[46] found that in spite of scholarly trends emphasizing the importance of financial, social and environmental success, managers in international firms still continue to conceptualize financial issues as distinct and separate from other responsibilities. Hence, economic goals may continue to take precedence over a range of social and environmental needs, also leading to conflict both with and among various stakeholder groups.

IMPORTANCE OF FOCUSING ON STAKEHOLDER INTERCONNECTIONS (SYSTEMS) AS OPPOSED TO JUST STAKEHOLDER CHARACTERISTICS

Early work on the stakeholder concept tended to focus on characteristics such as the urgency, legitimacy and power through which stakeholders could elicit attention from firms about particular concerns.[47] Subsequent research has indicated the importance of considering not only the attributes of stakeholders themselves, but also the relationships among them.

For example, building on Rowley's[48] network theory of stakeholder influences, Frooman and Murrell[49] identified two different perspectives through which firms could understand and manage for stakeholders. The first of these was a "demographic" approach in which firms located at the center of a hub and spoke model have dyadic links with a series of different stakeholders. Firms then assess the characteristics of each stakeholder in order to evaluate the risks (or opportunities) posed. The second of these was a "structural" perspective in which firms comprise one element in a network of actors that have reciprocal influences on one another. Within this perspective, firms evaluate the relationships among stakeholders at various levels of influence in order to assess how potential interconnections among seemingly diverse stakeholders or interests could be established or leveraged to apply pressure to the firm.

The latter of these perspectives has become increasingly important. For example, in their study of multi-stakeholder conflict in the Canadian forestry industry, Zietsma and Winn[50] identified a range of systemic influence tactics through which stakeholders and target firms attempted to gain advantage in CSR-related disputes. For example, environmentalists used "issue linking" to tie a matter of concern for one stakeholder group to a different matter of concern for a second stakeholder group, which enabled various parties with seemingly divergent goals to augment the pressure each was able to apply to the target firm. Similarly, both stakeholders and target firms attempted to gain advantage through the use of sophisticated influence chains in which the potential power of each party was leveraged sequentially to achieve a series of proximal goals aimed at obtaining a distal end.

FOCUSING ON THE PROCESSES OF CSR, AS OPPOSED TO JUST IMPACTS

Phillips and Caldwell[51] identified a number of problems associated with focusing specifically on the impacts or outcomes of CSR, as opposed to the processes by which CSR is implemented. For example, when evaluating CSR practices throughout supply chains, firms often focus on outsourcing reports in which existing CSR standards are documented. However, this approach can result in a multiplicity of discrete measures assessing compliance across a large number of diverse transactions. Phillips and Caldwell therefore suggested that the development of a potentially transformational discourse on value chain responsibility (i.e., *process* orientation) versus a focus on counting transactional accomplishments (i.e., *impact* orientation) could be much more fruitful in terms of enhancing CSR.

Similarly, in their research on CSR in Nigeria's oil industry, Idemudia and Ite[52] found that the small number of studies addressing CSR activities in Nigeria have focused almost entirely on the *impacts* of CSR practices, with extremely limited consideration of the *processes* through which CSR is carried out. They argued persuasively that it is shortcomings in CSR *processes* that are largely responsible for stakeholder conflict and that if CSR is to achieve its desired effects, then an orientation directed solely toward impacts is insufficient. Rather, a multi-stakeholder and process-oriented approach is needed.

Given this array of challenges associated with CSR-related stakeholder conflict, how might managers respond coherently? One possibility is through the use of an integrated framework that can guide decision-making. Consider the potential of care ethics as a unified conceptual framework. The work by Mary Parker Follett is used to enlarge and enhance our understanding of the practical applications of care.

Care Ethics as a Conceptual Framework for CSR-related Reconciliation

The potential usefulness of care ethics for CSR-related stakeholder management has long been noted. For example, Wicks et al.[53] demonstrated that care ethics question traditional views of the firm and its stakeholders, thereby providing a potentially fruitful alternative through which such relationships might be understood and managed. In particular, they identified that care ethics focus on maintaining stakeholder relationships versus emphasizing the separation and autonomy of a firm or its stakeholders from one another. In this sense, care ethics emphasize mutuality versus antagonism in such relationships, including the creative kindling of win–win solutions to conflict, rather than the win–lose arbitration of it.[54] Through these sorts of processes, care ethics are consistent with the needs implied by the five aforementioned challenges for managing CSR-related stakeholder conflict. Indeed, the relevance of care ethics to each of the five aforementioned challenges will be highlighted below. However, the work of Follett has significant potential to enlarge and enhance our practical understanding of care ethics in this regard, and advice gleaned from her writing is also provided.

Enhancing the Care-based Resolution of CSR-related, Firm–stakeholder Conflict: Invoking the Counsel of Mary Parker Follett

IMPORTANCE OF ENGAGING IN RELATIONSHIP-BUILDING WITH DIVERSE STAKEHOLDERS

A key feature of care ethics is that relationships with diverse others are established, maintained or enhanced through authentic efforts to understand one another's subjective, concrete and particular needs.[55] Indeed, within care ethics, a major ethical concern would be ignorance of or indifference to the needs of others, when one could demonstrate attentiveness and responsiveness.[56] Follett's work provides practical advice on this type of relationship-building.

Follett argued that in order to learn to work collaboratively, individuals need regular and proactive meetings rather than intermittent and reactive ones that are designed only to address discrete and emergent concerns. Such meetings should not be primarily focused on attempting to obtain certain agreements consistent with a self-interested plan, but rather on enhancing one's connection to a community within which the needs of each party will have a logical place.[57]

In order to present their particular needs to stakeholders, Follett[58] advocated that organizations use experience meetings through which officials could provide information to stakeholders. She argued that information should be provided in ways that demonstrate how specific proposals would relate to or have impacts on the daily lives of a range of individuals. Importantly, community participants would also contribute by conveying knowledge about their own concrete life experiences that could help illuminate concerns related to the issues at hand.

Follett[59] further recommended that debates be avoided. Debates not only preclude the kind of thoughtful discussion necessary to develop a deep understanding of the issues, they can further divide rather than unite stakeholders through an emphasis on winning and losing. Instead, accurate information should be sought and given on all sides not only to avoid misunderstanding and overcome bias, but also to ensure that the range of concerns are examined in a concurrent and integrated way, rather than a sequential and compartmentalized way.[60] Integrative efforts create more degrees of freedom through which nonzero-sum solutions can be derived.

A theme emerging from Follett's work[61] is avoidance of "crowd manipulation" or the use of emotional skills to incite ill-thought agreement or to smooth and obscure disagreement.[62] Follett argued that such manipulation is problematic not only because it fails to capitalize on difference as a possible source for developing innovative and value-creating solutions, but also because it primes those who have been silenced to be ripe for subsequent influence by persons who might be inclined toward agitation. Contrary to common thought, Follett[63] noted that it is not conflict that creates separation between parties but rather indifference that keeps individuals separate.

An example of efforts aimed at long-term relationship-building consistent with Follett's recommendations is that of the Canadian forestry company MacMillan Bloedel (MB). After having experienced nearly a decade of activist pressure relative to its logging practices in British Columbia, Canada, MB shifted to a relational approach with its stakeholders. In 1997, MB's incoming CEO, Tom Stephens, reached out to stakeholder groups by inviting them to his home so he could learn about their logging concerns. Stephens was reportedly concerned not just with MB's legal license to operate, but also, its "social licence to operate".[64] Following nine months of ongoing dialog with stakeholders, MB announced its intention to shift from clear-cut to variable retention logging. In 1998, when a new campaign aimed at forestry companies operating in the region was initiated, MB was not targeted.

UNDERSTANDING AND MANAGING POWER DIFFERENTIALS

It has been argued that situations involving power imbalances are a context in which care ethics have particular import.[65] However, discussion of care ethics in this context has been largely conceptual in nature. Follett's work provides practical advice in this regard.

Follett[66] argued that the fundamental challenge of all social relations, including those that happen in industry, is power. While defining power as "the ability to make things happen, to be a causal agent, to initiate change",[67] she argued that a range of mechanisms exist through which arbitrary power can be gained, including manipulation or sheer force. However, she emphasized that genuine power can not be taken by, appointed to, or conferred upon a decision-maker. Rather, genuine power "is always that which inheres in the situation". Therefore, she advocated following the "law of the situation" to resolve emergent concerns.

The law of the situation comprises a depersonalized approach in which it is not the position of one party over another, but rather the features of a given predicament itself that determine the correct course of action.[68] By assessing the situation itself and responding to the needs inhering that situation, harmony among parties can be achieved.

Although hierarchy might be an effective way of organizing operations within certain firms, it is situational needs rather than authority that should determine responses. Specifically, whereas pseudo or coercive power represents power *over* others, genuine or co-active power represents power *with* others. The latter of these protects the integrity of all individuals and contributes to the "enrichment and advancement" of all.[69]

Interestingly, Follett[70] argued that decreasing power differentials among parties is neither a useful nor even a viable approach. Rather, attempts to ensure equal power among parties was deemed problematic because it is directed only toward ensuring a "fair fight", which still has the potential to be divisive. Rather than trying to equalize power among parties in order to allow this fair fight, she suggested a shared approach to resolving difficulties in which co-active power would emerge through experience and practice. This co-active power would be directed not toward one another but rather toward the integration of a broad range of differences among parties in the form of win–win solutions to be described subsequently.

Contemporary examples consistent with Follett's advice exist. For example, although resource extraction is an industry in which power has sometimes been leveraged to differentially benefit the firm, Follett's notion of co-active power is also reflected in some cases. Drawing on examples supplied by Canadian Business for Social Responsibility,[71] Simola[72] offered several instances in the Canadian oil industry in which powerful private sector organizations as well as potentially vulnerable stakeholders were included in the development of shared power. In these cases, the oil companies refrained from trying to exercise "power over" potentially vulnerable stakeholders. Similarly, they abstained from trying to manage power through manipulation, force, or "fair fights". Rather, the oil companies worked to create opportunities for indigenous peoples to work collaboratively with them in a genuinely co-active way to meet the needs of all. For example, officials from Polaris Minerals Corporation and the Hupacasath First Nation described approaches taken during their joint venture aimed at developing a granite deposit located on land claimed by the First Nation. Although Polaris might have held greater power in terms of financial wealth, other resources and industry experience, Polaris personnel refrained from manipulation or other coercive exercises of power in relation to the First Nation. Instead, Polaris and Hupacasath personnel spent innumerable hours in unstructured time together, away from business concerns. Together with their families, they engaged in outdoor activities such as fishing and hiking in order to facilitate mutual understanding. Their interactions were characterized by openness and patience in information-sharing. Polaris provided financial support to the Hupacasath First Nation to enable its retention of independent, expert consultants to assess the opportunity. Moreover, rather than trying to assimilate the views of the Hupacasath First Nation into their own preexisting agenda, Polaris worked collaboratively with the Hupacasath in order to find innovative ways of responding to the needs of both. They began to conceptualize their predicament as "shared problems" and evolved such that they were "no longer working from opposite sides of the table ... we were bringing our very different perspectives, experiences and skills to bear on ... seeking and finding creative solutions".[73]

AUTHENTIC ENGAGEMENT WITH CSR-RELATED STAKEHOLDER CONFLICT TO IDENTIFY NONZERO-SUM SOLUTIONS

Within care ethics, conflict versus indifference is welcomed as an important element of authenticity in relationships[74] and creative problem-solving is used to develop nonzero-sum solutions for what on the surface might seem like conflicting responsibilities to different parties. Follett's work is instructive on the practical processes through which this might occur.

For example, Follett once famously commented on two letters she had seen in the London *Times* from two separate stakeholders in relation to an ongoing coal strike. The first letter argued that the coal strike was strictly an economic versus moral issue, while the second letter argued that the coal strike was a moral rather than an economic concern. In evaluating these sorts of positional approaches to conflict, Follett commented "I do not think we have psychological and ethical and economic problems. We have human problems with psychological, ethical and economic aspects and as many as you like, legal often."[75]

Follett indicated that because conflict represents an "interacting of desires" it has neither positive nor negative connotations. Rather, it can be managed in more or less constructive ways. However, when conflict emerges as "the moment of the appearing and focussing of difference" then it "may be a sign of health, a prophecy of progress".[76]

In particular, Follett[77] argued that when differing interests emerge, these need not remain opposed. Rather, four outcomes are possible. These include the voluntary submission of one or more parties to another; struggle followed by victory of one group such that it is able to dominate the others; compromise; and integration. It is apparent in considering these potential outcomes that the first two are zero sum. Some party's win is another party's loss. However, the third potential outcome involving compromise is also problematic in that no side attains its goals. Follett[78] was critical of those who still "glorify compromise". She argued that compromise is a situation in which all parties lose. Compromise is therefore quantitative in nature—it fails to create new value. Moreover, compromise is a form of suppression in which submerged desires will eventually re-emerge with potential to be incited or manipulated by others. Hence, compromise is a postponement rather than a resolution of concerns.

Follett[79] therefore advocated making a qualitative shift in thinking toward integration or nonzero-sum solutions. She argued that when integrative solutions are found for seemingly conflicting goals and desires, then new value can emerge. However, Follett noted that integration of diverse desires would not necessarily be easy to achieve. Rather, she identified several potential barriers that would need to be overcome.[80] These included lack of training in integrative methods; language uses that are inflammatory rather than conciliatory; tendencies to focus on conquest and domination rather than integration; and propensities to theorize versus take action.

Specific guidelines on the process of integration included efforts to discover the interests underlying whatever stated goals individuals might have. In particular, Follett[81] argued that in the business realm, a leader would need to

get underneath all the camouflage, to find the real demand as against the demand put forward, distinguish declared motives from real motives, alleged causes from real causes, and to remember that sometimes an underlying motive is deliberately concealed, and that sometimes it exists unconsciously.

She elaborated that it is critical to bring differences among parties into the open rather than evading or suppressing them because it is not possible to integrate interests that are unknown. Moreover, when one party's interests are suppressed or evaded, this could be a sign that another party wishes to dominate.

A corporate example consistent with Follett's advice would be MacMillan Bloedel's (MB) efforts to work co-actively with community and activist stakeholders, including conscious efforts directed toward the attainment of nonzero-sum solutions. Former VP of Environment for MB Linda Coady[82] identified that

we all began to put more time and energy into achieving a shared goal ... than into fighting with each other. That shared goal was a new outcome ... Not the product of consensus or compromise, it was ... a constant redefinition of the situation and options for dealing with it.

IMPORTANCE OF FOCUSING ON STAKEHOLDER INTERCONNECTIONS (SYSTEMS) AS OPPOSED TO JUST STAKEHOLDER CHARACTERISTICS

Because care ethics emphasize interconnection within webs of relationships, they are consistent with structural versus demographic stakeholder perspectives.[83] However, notwithstanding scholarly work on care ethics in which various levels of systemic influence including sociopolitical ones are identified[84] care ethics sometimes demarcate relationships to focus on a small number of more immediate or parochial factors as opposed to the local, regional, national or international levels of factors that can impact relationships among firms and their stakeholders.[85]

Follett[86] more explicitly and consistently identified the broad and dynamic context in which various parties exist. Not only did she recognize the reciprocal influence occurring among actors in a network (i.e., "circular response"), she also acknowledged levels of influence. In particular, Follett[87] argued that

[the] individual is the unification of a multiplied variety of reactions. But the individual does not react to society. The interplay constitutes both society on the one hand and individuality on the other: individuality and society are evolving together from this constant and complex action and reaction ... each has no value, nor existence without the other.

In this sense, Follett's work is consonant with both foundational perspectives on system theory generally,[88] and with contemporary system perspectives on CSR in particular.[89]

Examples of companies that have recognized the systemic nature of their relationships with stakeholders and begun to serve as "network convenors" within those systems include GlaxoSmithKline (GSK) and Nike. As documented by Svendsen and Laberge,[90] the international pharmaceutical firm GSK has worked for over a decade with a large and diverse range of industry, health, social service, community and activist stakeholders for the purposes of information-sharing, dialog and strategy formation with regard to palliative care issues in Canada. The network's strategy has received broad-based support and been highly successful at a number of levels, including addressing systemic service gaps, funding issues and confusion across various sectors. Similarly, after having previously tried to function either autonomously from or bilaterally with its stakeholders, Nike recognized that it needed to focus on multilateral networks. In the late 1990s, Nike decided to use organically grown cotton in its products, but after identifying that organic cotton growers were quite rare, Nike realized it would need to help facilitate the development of the global cotton market. Therefore, it worked with 55 other companies to establish the "Organic Exchange", a nonprofit organization aimed at enhancing organic cotton farming throughout the world and creating a global inventory for purchasers.

FOCUSING ON THE PROCESSES OF CSR, AS OPPOSED TO JUST IMPACTS

Within care ethics, there is an implicit emphasis on the underlying processes through which relationships are developed and enhanced.[91] When this care-based emphasis on underlying process is placed in the context of Follett's systems orientation, it has potentially powerful implications for harmonizing relationships among stakeholders and for achieving more responsive and sustainable forms of CSR.

In particular, Follett's systems orientation focuses on the underlying processes by which interactions occur. Indeed, Follett[92] argued that "progress then must be through the group process. Progress implies respect for the creative process not the created thing; the created thing is forever and forever being left behind us." In this way, Follett suggested that the content concerns or claims to be addressed through group process, as well as the outcomes of that group process (i.e., the "created things") will continually be evolving. Therefore, what is important for achieving progress is to refrain from becoming solely focused on the diverse range of overtly stated stakeholder claims (or efforts to obtain specific outcomes related to those claims). Rather, progress will occur by affecting the underlying interactional, relational and creative processes through which the entire firm–stakeholder system operates. Hence, Follett's arguments are consistent with subsequent writing on general system theory.

Specifically, within general system theory, the principle of equifinality dictates that the same final state (i.e., underlying process or form of a system) can be reached from a number of different initial positions (i.e., content concerns or claims).[93] Although there are several implications of this principle, one of particular importance to the current discussion is as follows. Within any system (e.g., firm–stakeholder system), the readily articulated content concerns or claims can be diverse and changeable. Hence, if one focuses solely and reactively on the diverse and ever-changing set of content concerns or claims emanating from various stakeholders in the system, one will also likely (and quite unwittingly) become so absorbed with responding to each of these in a sequential and isolated way that one will be unsuccessful in understanding and positively impacting the underlying systemic processes in any sustained way. On the other hand, if one focuses on influencing the underlying interactional patterns or processes by which the entire system operates, one would not only have a more parsimonious task, but also, a greater chance of success in establishing a truly transformational discourse on social responsibility as was advocated by Phillips and Caldwell.[94]

Therefore, to shift firm–stakeholder systems toward more responsive and sustained CSR-related foci, one should emphasize the underlying processes or patterns through which all of the elements in the system interact. Indeed, as one CEO identified, responding to the diverse and disjointed array of content concerns arising within movements such as the environmental movement would almost certainly ensure failure to resolve conflict with diverse stakeholders.[95] It is argued here that focusing on underlying relational issues or patterns with stakeholders would offer a viable alternative.

Summary and Directions for Future Research

The purpose of this chapter was to consider the potential one particular theoretical perspective, care ethics, for managing the array of challenges associated with CSR-related stakeholder conflict. It was demonstrated not only that care ethics can serve as a unified conceptual framework through which to respond to the diverse range of challenges associated with such discord, but also that the work of Mary Parker Follett is able to enlarge and enhance our understanding of the practical uses of care when managing for stakeholders in CSR.

The practical implications of Follett's work for enhancing relationships with stakeholders, for better understanding and managing issues of power and for the integrative resolution of conflict were elaborated. In particular, she argued that true power emerges from coactive effort and responsibility, rather than through formal appointment. In keeping with this, Follett[96] admonished against trying to decrease power differentials among stakeholders as these would only lead to fair fights. Rather, she emphasized innovative and value-creating integration of stakeholder conflict instead of "crowd manipulation" to smooth over unresolved differences, or the use of compromise in which every party loses. [97]

However, perhaps the most uncommon and therefore useful implication of Follett's work for the care-based resolution of CSR-related conflict is the process orientation implied by her systems perspective.[98] As noted, to the extent to which firms focus on improving underlying "process" issues at the root of other problems, rather than on resolving a multiplicity of emergent "content" claims, this could result in a more parsimonious approach to harmonizing relationships.

Several areas for future research emerge. First, the scholar-practitioner and qualitative approaches to relationship-building and conflict resolution used both in care ethics and by Follett are pragmatically useful. However, research accounts of these efforts in firm–stakeholder relationships are often reported only in very general terms, such that it is difficult to discern and learn specific techniques that could be used in contemporary business settings. Hence, more micro-level research and reporting would be helpful.

Secondly, within the systems orientation alluded to in care ethics[99] and made explicit by Follett,[100] it would not be unusual to see certain relatively stable and predictable underlying interactional patterns in systems, many of which would not be unique to a single system of a particular type. Indeed, studies of systems within disciplines other than business and management have many well-documented examples of predictable underlying patterns of interaction that are commonly observed in many of the systems representing a given system type (e.g., family).[101] However, this sort of phenomenon has not been well-explored relative to firm–stakeholder relationships. Therefore, qualitative studies of the sort completed by Zietsma and Winn[102] that document common types of underlying interactions or influence strategies and techniques used in firm–stakeholder relationships would be helpful. This would shift managerial focus toward addressing the underlying interactional patterns or processes that are common in such disputes, and away from the infinite number of *seemingly* disparate problems through which these underlying process concerns are expressed. This would also allow the development of various interventions, including care-based interventions, for ameliorating these processes.

Finally, it is important to note that the approach toward resolving CSR-related, firm–stakeholder conflict reflected in this chapter represents one particular orientation, reflective of the norms, structures and therefore scholarship of North American society during the time periods in which stakeholder theory took root. In particular, the orientation here is one that reflects the challenges faced by managers who are looking at particular problems from their own vantage point within the firm and trying to identify potential solutions to these. Interestingly, in historic reviews of the stakeholder concept, Freeman and colleagues,[103] identified alternate perspectives that could be used as starting points, including systems theory (rather than a managerial or strategic approach). Freeman and colleagues noted that although systems theory took a holistic and far-reaching view on stakeholder relationships, considering these within the broader context of society generally or "total system design",[104] that research from within a systems perspective was also somewhat inconsistent with the narrower goals and problems of strategic management and planning per se. Hence, systems theory was not taken by many North American theorists as a viable starting point for stakeholder management. However, within critical management studies, system theory and "total system design" might well be seen as the more appropriate starting point from which to prevent and manage CSR-related stakeholder conflict and would be quite consistent with contemporary arguments that strategy should not be privileged over ethics.[105] Hence, future research might revisit systems theory to evaluate its viability and articulate its vision both as a general and care-based approach for preventing and managing CSR-related conflict.

Table 19.1 Enhancing the care-based resolution of CSR-related conflict: invoking the counsel of M.P. Follett

Challenges in resolving CSR-related conflict	Salient element of care ethics for resolving CSR-related conflict	Enlarging and enhancing our practical understanding of care ethics: invoking the counsel of M.P. Follett	Contemporary example of conflict resolution consistent with Follett's work
1. Importance of engaging in relationship building with diverse stakeholders			
Need for proactive and ongoing engagement with stakeholders for relationship-building versus occasional interaction as a means to a particular end[106]	Importance of activating, maintaining or enhancing relationships[107] and/or attentiveness, responsibility and responsiveness.[108] Including needs of both self and other[109]	Regular and proactive vs. sporadic and reactive meetings[110] Valuing of expert analysis and layperson experience[111] Abstaining from academic debate which precludes thoughtful discussion and is divisive, leading to winners and losers Use of authentic deliberation aimed at integrative solutions[112] Undesirability of crowd manipulation to incite agreement or smooth over unresolved differences[113]	After a decade of substantial activist pressure, incoming CEO of Canadian forestry company MacMillan Bloedel reaches out to range of stakeholder groups by inviting them to his home to learn about their concerns. Following nine months of ongoing dialog, shift from clear-cut to variable retention logging is announced. MB continues to engage in proactive relationship-building and is not targeted in subsequent campaign against forestry companies[114]
"Names and faces" versus abstract approach to stakeholders and their needs[115]	Attending the concrete, subjective and particular needs of others versus objective treatment of abstract others[116]	Experience meetings through which it is not only experts providing information to citizens, but also citizens providing information from their own concrete life experiences[117]	
2. Understanding and managing power differentials in a morally principled way[118]	Care as a practice that emerges in response to power differentials.[119] The pliability of systemic barriers such that they can be expanded to include practices of care[120]	Managing through the "law of the situation"[121] or the use of "power with" (i.e., genuine, "co-active" power) versus "power over" (pseudo, "coercive" power)[122] Avoiding efforts to decrease power differentials as these simply lead to "fair fights". Rather, practice use of co-active power aimed at integration versus each other[123]	Multiple examples from within Canadian oil industry of co-active power among powerful private sector organizations and potentially vulnerable stakeholders[124]

3. *Authentic engagement with CSR-related stakeholder conflict to identify nonzero-sum solutions.* Rejecting the "separation thesis" and refraining from the "privileging" of strategy over ethics or ethics over strategy[125]	Main ethical issue within care perspectives being relative "indifference" when one could authentically engage with conflict in order to creatively develop solutions for seemingly conflicting responsibilities[126]	Conflict as simply an "interacting of desires" which can enhance health and progress[127] Neither economic nor ethical problems but human problems with both economic and ethical aspects[128] Avoid domination, submission and compromise. Rather, use integration.[129] Distinguish demands put forth from real demands, declared from actual motives, alleged causes from real causes.[130] Explore what stated desires actually represent in terms of underlying interests.	Former VP of Environment for MB Linda Coady identified that "we all began to put more time and energy into achieving a shared goal ... than into fighting with each other. That shared goal was a new outcome ... Not the product of consensus or compromise, it was ... a constant redefinition of the situation and options for dealing with it."[131]
4. *Importance of focusing on stakeholder interconnections as opposed to just stakeholder characteristics[132]*	Recognition of "webs" of interconnections[133] and systemic levels of influence in relationships[134]	Recognition of both "circular response" among parties[135] as well as levels of influence on systems[136]	GSK network approach to "Living Lessons Strategy" on palliative care issues. Nike's multilateral network approach to the "Organic Exchange" for cotton[137]
5. *Focusing on the processes of CSR, as opposed to just impacts[138]* Importance of establishing a transformational discourse versus focusing simply on measures of transactional accomplishments[139]	Distinguishing characteristics of care ethics is focus on underlying relational processes[140]	Implications of process versus impact orientation to CSR-related firm–stakeholder systems[141] Progress occurring not through "created things", but rather through group and creative process[142]	Importance of focusing on underlying relational patterns with stakeholders versus responding to diverse and disjointed array of content issues arising within movements such as environmental[143]

Notes

1   Carroll, A.B. and Shabana, K.M. (2010), "The business case for corporate social responsibility: a review of concepts, research and practice", *International Journal of Management Reviews*, vol. 12, no. 1, pp. 85–105; Maon, F., Lindgreen, A. and Swaen, V. (2010), "Organizational stages and cultural phases: a critical review and a consolidative model of corporate social responsibility management", *International Journal of Management Reviews*, vol. 12, no. 1, pp. 20–37.

2   Idemudia, U. and Ite, U.E. (2006), "Corporate–community relations in Nigeria's oil industry: challenges and imperatives", *Corporate Social Responsibility and Environmental Management*, vol. 13, no. 4, pp. 194–206.

3   Freeman, R.E., Harrison, J.S. and Wicks, A.C. (2007), *Managing for Stakeholders: Survival, Reputation and Success*, Yale University Press, New Haven, CT; Lindgreen, A. and Swaen, V. (2010), "Corporate social responsibility", *International Journal of Management Reviews*, vol. 12, no. 1, pp. 1–8.

4   Freeman, R.E. and Velamuri, S.R. (2006), "A new approach to CSR: company stakeholder responsibility". In A. Kakabadse and M. Morsing (eds), *Corporate Social Responsibility: Reconciling Aspiration with Application*, Palgrave MacMillan, Hampshire, UK, pp. 9–23; Kotler, P. and Lee, N. (2005), *Corporate Social Responsibility: Doing the Most Good for Your Company and Your Cause*, John Wiley and Sons, Inc., Hoboken, NJ.

5   Maon, F., Lindgreen, A. and Swaen, V. (2008), "Thinking of the organization as a system: the role of managerial perceptions in developing a corporate social responsibility strategic agenda", *Systems Research and Behavioral Science*, vol. 25, no. 3, pp. 413–426.

6   See, e.g., Wicks, A.C., Gilbert, D.R. Jr. and Freeman, R.E. (1994), "A feminist reinterpretation of the stakeholder concept", *Business Ethics Quarterly*, vol. 4, no. 4, pp. 475–497.

7   Drucker, P. (1995), "Introduction: Mary Parker Follett: prophet of management". In P. Graham (ed.), *Mary Parker Follett: Prophet of Management*, Harvard Business School Press, Boston, MA, pp. 1–9; Kanter, R.M. (1995), "Preface". In P. Graham (ed.), *Mary Parker Follett: Prophet of Management,* Harvard Business School Press, Boston, MA, pp. xiii–xix.

8   Melé, D. (2007), "Ethics in management: exploring the contribution of Mary Parker Follett", *International Journal of Public Administration*, vol. 30, no. 4, pp. 405–424.

9   Schilling, M.A. (2000), "Decades ahead of her time: advancing stakeholder theory through the ideas of Mary Parker Follett", *Journal of Management History*, vol. 6, no. 5, pp. 224–242.

10 Gilligan, C. (1982), *In a Different Voice*, Harvard University Press, Cambridge, MA; Noddings, N. (1984), *Caring: A Feminine Approach to Ethics and Moral Education*, University of California Press, Berkeley, CA; Ruddick, S. (1984), "Maternal thinking". In J. Trebilcot (ed.), *Mothering: Essays in Feminist Theory*, Rowman and Allanheld, Totowa, NJ, pp. 213–230; Tronto, J.C. (1993), *Moral Boundaries: A Political Argument for an Ethic of Care*, Routledge, New York.

11 Gilligan (1982), op. cit.

12 Derry, R. (2005), "Care, ethics of". In P.H. Werhane and R.E. Freeman (eds), *The Blackwell Encyclopedia of Management*, 2nd ed., *Business Ethic*, Blackwell Publishing Ltd., Malden, MA, pp. 65–68.

13 Gilligan (1982), op. cit.

14 See, e.g., Gilligan (1982), op. cit.; Noddings (1984), op. cit.; Ruddick (1984), op. cit., which are sometimes perceived as promoting a distinctively feminine or even essentialist view.

15 Broughton, J.M. (1983), "Women's rationality and men's virtues", *Social Research*, vol. 50, pp. 597–642; Calhoun, C. (1988), "Justice, care, gender bias", *The Journal of Philosophy*,

vol. 85, no. 9, pp. 451–463; Grimshaw, J. (1986), *Philosophy and Feminist Thinking*, University of Minnesota Press, Minnesota.

16   Jaffee, S. and Shibley-Hyde, J. (2000), "Gender difference in moral orientation: a meta-analysis", *Psychological Bulletin*, vol. 26, no. 5, pp. 703–726.

17   McLaughlin, J. (1997), "An ethic of care: a valuable political tool?", *Politics*, vol. 17, no. 1, pp. 17–23; Sevenhuijsen, S. (1998), *Citizenship and the Ethics of Care: Feminist Considerations on Justice, Morality, and Politics*, Routledge, New York; Tronto (1993), op. cit..

18   Held, V. (1998), "The meshing of care and justice". In M. Gatens (ed.), *Feminist Ethics*, Ashgate Dartmouth, Brookfield, USA, pp. 537–541; Katz, M.S., Noddings, N. and Strike, K.A. (1999), *Justice and Caring: The Search for Common Ground in Education*, Columbia University Teachers College Press, New York.

19   Koehn, D. (1998), *Rethinking Feminist Ethics: Care, Trust and Empathy*, Routledge, New York.

20   Morton, N. O'R. and Lindquist, S.A. (1997), "Revealing the feminist in Mary Parker Follett", *Administration and Society*, vol. 29, no. 3, pp. 348–371.

21   Follett, M.P. (1998), *The New State Group Organization the Solution of Popular Government*, University Park, The Pennsylvania State University Press (original work published 1918, Longmans, Green and Co., New York).

22   Follett, M.P. (1951), *Creative Experience*, Peter Smith, New York (original work published 1924).

23   Follett, M.P. (1977a), "The psychological foundations". In H.C. Metcalf (ed.), *Scientific Foundations of Business Administration*, Hive Publishing Company, Easton, PA, pp. 114–190 (original work published 1926, The Williams and Wilkins Company, Baltimore).

24   Follett (1951), op. cit.

25   Nohria, N. (1995), "Commentary: Mary Parker Follett's view on power, the giving of orders, and authority: an alternative to hierarch or a Utopian ideology?" In P. Graham (ed.), *Mary Parker Follett: Prophet of Management*, Harvard Business School Press, Boston, MA, pp. 154–162.

26   Drucker (1995), op. cit.; Kanter (1995), op. cit.

27   Burnier D. (2003), "Other voices/other rooms: towards a care-centered public administration", *Administrative Theory and Praxis*, vol. 25, no. 4, pp. 529–544; Fletcher, J.K. (2001), *Disappearing Acts: Gender, Power, and Relational Practice at Work*, The MIT Press, Cambridge, MA; Morton and Lindquist (1997), op. cit.

28   Carroll and Shabana (2010), op. cit.; Maon, Lindgreen and Swaen (2010), op. cit.

29   Dahlsrud, A. (2008), "How corporate social responsibility is defined: an analysis of 37 definitions", *Corporate Social Responsibility and Environmental Management*, vol. 15, no. 1, pp. 1–13; Carroll and Shabana (2010), op. cit.

30   European Commission (2001), Promoting a European Framework for Corporate Social Responsibility. Green Paper, Luxembourg: Office for Official Publications of the European Communities; WBCSD (2002), *The Business Case for Sustainable Development: Making a Difference Towards The Johannesburg Summit 2002 and Beyond*, World Business Council for Sustainable Development, Geneva.

31   Matten, D., Crane, A. and Chapple, W. (2003), "Behind the mask: revealing the true face of corporate citizenship", *Journal of Business Ethics*, vol. 45, no. 1/2, pp. 209–120; Pedersen, E.R. (2006), "Making corporate social responsibility (CSR) operable: how companies translate stakeholder dialogue into practice", *Business and Society Review*, vol. 111, no. 2, pp. 137–163.

32   Freeman, R.E. (1984), *Strategic Management: A Stakeholder Approach*, Pittman, Toronto, p. 25.

33   Frooman J. (1999), "Stakeholder influence strategies", *Academy of Management Review*, vol. 24, no. 2, pp. 191–216; Frooman, J. and Murrell, A. (2005), "Stakeholder influence strategies: the

roles of structural and demographic determinants", *Business and Society*, vol. 44, no. 1, pp. 3–31.

34   Noland, J. and Phillips, R. (2010), "Stakeholder engagement, discourse ethics and strategic management", *International Journal of Management Reviews*, vol. 12, no. 1, pp. 39–40.

35   McVea, J.F. and Freeman, R.E. (2005), "A names-and-faces approach to stakeholder management—how focusing on stakeholders as individuals can bring ethics and entrepreneurial strategy together", *Journal of Management Inquiry*, vol. 14, no. 1, pp. 57–69.

36   Pedersen (2006), op. cit.

37   Freeman and Velamuri (2006), op. cit.

38   Berry, G.R. (2003), "Organizing against multinational corporate power in cancer alley", *Organization and Environment*, vol. 16, no. 1, pp. 3–33; Hamilton, C. (1994), "Women, home, and community: the struggle in an urban environment". In A. Jaggar (ed.), *Living with Contradictions: Controversies in Feminist Ethics*, Westview Press, Inc., Boulder, CO, pp. 676–679 (original work published in 1990).

39   See, e.g., Gibbs, L.M. (1998), *Love Canal: The Story Continues*, New Society Publishers, Stoney Creek, CT.

40   Noland and Phillips (2010), op. cit.

41   Calvano, L. (2008), "Multinational corporations and local communities: a critical analysis of conflict", *Journal of Business Ethics*, vol. 82, no. 4, pp. 793–805.

42   Eweje, G. (2005), "Hazardous employment and regulatory regimes in the South African mining industry: arguments for corporate ethics at workplace", *Journal of Business Ethics*, vol. 56, no. 2, pp. 163–183.

43   Freeman, R.E. (1994), "The politics of stakeholder theory: some future directions", *Business Ethics Quarterly*, vol. 4, no. 4, pp. 409–421.

44   Freeman and Velamuri (2006), op. cit.; Noland and Phillips (2010), op. cit.

45   McVea and Freeman (2005), op. cit.

46   Pedersen, E.R. (2010), "Modelling CSR: how managers understand the responsibilities of business towards society", *Journal of Business Ethics*, vol. 91, no. 2, pp. 155–166.

47   Mitchell, R.K., Agle, B.R. and Wood, D.J. (1997), "Toward a theory of stakeholder identification and salience: defining the principle of who and what really counts", *Academy of Management Review*, vol. 22, no. 4, pp. 853–887.

48   Rowley, T.J. (1997), "Moving beyond dyadic ties: a network theory of stakeholder influences", *Academy of Management Review*, vol. 22, no. 4, pp. 897–910.

49   Frooman and Murrell (2005), op. cit.

50   Zietsma, C. and Winn, M.I. (2008), "Building chains and directing flows: strategies and tactics of mutual influence in stakeholder conflicts", *Business and Society*, vol. 47, no. 1, pp. 68–101.

51   Phillips, R. and Caldwell, C.B. (2005), "Value chain responsibility: a farewell to arm's length", *Business and Society Review*, vol. 110, no. 4, pp. 345–370.

52   Idemudia and Ite (2006), op. cit.

53   Wicks, Gilbert and Freeman (1994), op. cit.

54   Gilligan (1982), op. cit.

55   Ibid.

56   Ibid.; Tronto (1993), op. cit.

57   Follett (1918/1998), op. cit.

58   Follett (1924/1951), op. cit.

59   Follett (1918/1998, op. cit.

60   Ibid.; Follett (1924/1951), op. cit.

61   Follett (1918/1998), op. cit.

62   Fox, E.M. (1968), "Mary Parker Follett: the enduring contribution", *Public Administration Review*, vol. 28, no. 6, pp. 520–529; Mattson, K. (1998), "Reading Follett: introduction to the new state". In M.P. Follett, *The New State Group Organization the Solution of Popular Government*, University Park: The Pennsylvania State University Press (original work published 1918, Longmans, Green and Co., New York).

63   Follett (1918/1998), op. cit.

64   Svendsen, A.C. and Laberge, M. (2005), "Convening stakeholder networks: a new way of thinking, being and engaging", *Journal of Corporate Citizenship*, vol. 19, Fall, pp. 91–104.

65   McLaughlin (1997), op. cit.

66   Follett (1924/1951), op. cit.

67   Follett, M.P. (1977b), "Power". In H.C. Metcalf (ed.), *Scientific Foundations of Business Administration*, Hive Publishing Company, Easton, PA, pp. 171–190; see p. 174 (original work published 1926, The Williams and Wilkins Company, Baltimore).

68   Follett, M.P. (1977c), "The giving of orders". In H.C. Metcalf (ed.), *Scientific Foundations of Business Administration*, Hive Publishing Company, Easton, PA., pp. 132–149 (original work published 1926, The Williams and Wilkins Company, Baltimore).

69   Follett (1924/1951), op. cit., p. xiii.

70   Follett (1926/1977b), op. cit., p. 189.

71   Canadian Business for Social Responsibility (2005), *Synergy: A United Perspective Between the Hupacasath First Nation and Polaris Minerals Corporation*, CBSR, Toronto.

72   Simola, S. (2007), "Pragmatics of care in sustainable global enterprise", *Journal of Business Ethics*, vol. 74, no. 2, pp. 131–147.

73   Canadian Business for Social Responsibility (2005), op. cit., p. 23.

74   Gilligan (1982), op. cit.; Tronto (1993), op. cit.

75   Follett, M.P. (1982), "The psychology of control". In E.M. Fox and L. Urwick (eds), *Dynamic Administration: The Collected Papers of Mary Parker Follett*, Hippocrene Books, Inc., New York, p. 149 (original work published 1927 in H.C. Metcalf (ed.), *Psychological Foundations of Management*, A.W. Shaw Company, New York)

76   Follett, M.P. (1977d), "Constructive conflict". In H.C. Metcalf (ed.), *Scientific Foundations of Business Administration*, Hive Publishing Company, Easton, PA., pp. 114–131; see p. 117 (original work published 1926, Baltimore, The Williams and Wilkins Company).

77   Follett (1924/1951), op. cit.; Follett (1926/1977d), op. cit.

78   Follett (1924/1951), op. cit., p. 159.

79   Follett (1924/1951), op. cit.; Follett (1926/1977d), op. cit.

80   Follett (1926/1977d), op. cit.

81   Ibid., pp. 120–121.

82   Coady, L. (1999), "Good stuff you mostly won't find on anybody's website", unpublished paper delivered as the Doug Little Memorial Lecture, University of Northern British Columbia, Prince George, BC; as cited by Svendsen and Laberge (2005), op. cit.

83   See, e.g., Frooman and Murrell (2005), op. cit.

84   See, e.g., McLaughlin (1997), op. cit.; Tronto (1993), op. cit.

85   See, e.g., Maon, Lindgreen and Swaen (2008), op. cit.

86   Follett (1924/1951), op. cit.

87   Follett (1918/1998), op. cit., p. 61.

88   von Bertalanffy, L. (1968), *General System Theory*, Braziller, New York.

89   Maon, Lindgreen and Swaen (2008), op. cit.

90   Svendsen and Laberge (2005), op. cit.
91   Porter, E. (1999), *Feminist Perspectives on Ethics*, Longman, New York.
92   Follett (1918/1998), op. cit., p. 98.
93   Foley, V.D. (1984), *An Introduction to Family Therapy*, Grune and Stratton, New York; von Bertalanffy, op. cit., p. 40.
94   Phillips and Caldwell (2005), op. cit.
95   Zietsma and Winn (2008), op. cit., p. 78.
96   Follett (1924/1951), op. cit.; Follett (1926/1977b), op. cit.
97   Readers wishing to explore the contemporary implications of Follett's work in more detail are referred to Graham, P. (1995), *Mary Parker Follett: Prophet of management*, Harvard Business School Press, Boston, MA.
98   Follett (1918/1998), op. cit., p. 98.
99   McLaughlin (1997), op. cit.; Tronto (1993), op. cit.
100 Follett (1918/1998), op. cit., p. 98.
101 Foley (1984), op. cit.
102 Zietsma and Winn (2008), op. cit.
103 Freeman (1984), op. cit.; Freeman, R.E., Harrison, S.S., Wicks, A.C., Parmar, B.L. and De Colle, S. (2010), *Stakeholder Theory: The State of the Art*, Cambridge University Press, Cambridge, UK.
104 Freeman (1984), op. cit., p. 38.
105 Freeman (1994), op. cit.
106 Freeman, Harrison, and Wicks (2007), op. cit.; Noland and Phillips (2010), op. cit.
107 Gilligan (1982), op. cit.
108 Tronto (1993), op. cit.
109 Gilligan (1982), op. cit.
110 Follett (1918/1998), op. cit.
111 Follett (1924/1951), op. cit.
112 Follett (1918/1998), op. cit.; ibid.
113 Follett (1918/1998), op. cit.
114 Svendsen and Laberge (2005), op. cit.
115 McVea and Freeman (2005), op. cit.
116 Gilligan (1982), op. cit.
117 Follett (1924/1951), op. cit.
118 Noland and Phillips (2010), op. cit.
119 McLaughlin (1997), op. cit.
120 Tronto (1993), op. cit.
121 Follett (1926/1977c), op. cit.
122 Follett (1924/1951), op. cit.; Follett (1926/1977b), op. cit.
123 Follett (1926/1977b), op. cit.
124 Simola (2007), op. cit.
125 Freeman (1994), op. cit.
126 Gilligan (1982), op. cit.
127 Follett (1926/1977d), op. cit.
128 Follett (1927/1982), op. cit.
129 Follett (1924/1951), op. cit.; Follett (1926/1977d), op. cit.
130 Follett (1926/1977d), op. cit.
131 Coady (1999), op. cit.
132 Frooman and Murrell (2005), op. cit.; Rowley (1997), op. cit.

133 Gilligan (1982), op. cit.
134 McLaughlin (1997), op. cit.; Tronto (1993), op. cit.
135 Follett (1924/1951), op. cit.
136 Follett (1918/1998), op. cit.
137 Svendsen and Laberge (2005), op. cit.
138 Idemudia and Ite (2006), op. cit.
139 Phillips and Caldwell (2005), op. cit.
140 Gilligan (1982), op. cit.
141 Follett (1918/1998), op. cit.
142 Follett (1918/1998), op. cit., p. 98.
143 Zietsma and Winn (2008), op. cit., p. 78.

20 *A Configurational Approach to Corporate Social Responsibility– financial Performance Empirical Research*

ROBERTO GARCÍA-CASTRO[*]

Keywords

Corporate social responsibility, financial performance, fuzzy sets, stakeholder management.

Introduction

Empirical research on corporate social responsibility (CSR) has addressed, to a large extent, a hypothesized relationship between CSR and financial performance. In these empirical studies, CSR has typically been measured as an aggregate of stakeholder relationships ranging from employees to local communities or governments. The results of these studies attempting to link socially responsible behaviors to either accounting- or market-based measures of financial performance have been ambiguous;[1] researchers have found positive, negative and neutral relationships.

CSR researchers have advanced some reasons to explain these inconsistent findings, such as ill-defined CSR constructs, lack of relevant control variables, sampling issues, time-horizon issues or endogeneity problems.[2] In this chapter we argue for a more general explanation related to the nature of the research methods used in the CSR field.

Methods based on lineal correlations such as regression analysis are very useful to discover statistically significant relationships between CSR practices and financial performance. However, these methods quite often force researchers to oversimplify the different CSR approaches found in firms, neglecting the fact that CSR can be bundled differently in different firms and that the impact of CSR on performance may be different for different firms depending on their specific attributes and organizational context.

* Roberto García-Castro, IESE Business School, Camino del Cerro del Águila, 3 28023 Madrid, Spain. E-mail: rgarcia@ iese.edu. The authors gratefully acknowledge financial support from the Ministry of Science and Innovation of Spain (Project reference ECO2009-08302-E).

In order to overcome some of the limitations of correlational methods we suggest qualitative comparative analysis (QCA)[3] as a method that is able to (1) identify empirically complex bundles or configurations of CSR practices; and (2) establish causal relationships between the identified CSR configurations and profitability based on sufficiency and necessary conditions by using set–subset connections between sets instead of correlations between variables.

The chapter has the following structure. First, we present a brief review of the literature on the CSR–financial performance link. Then we review some basic notions behind QCA methods. Next, we use a hypothetical example to illustrate how QCA can contribute to resolve and explain some previous inconsistent empirical findings in CSR research. A conclusion section completes the chapter.

The Corporate Social Responsibility–financial Performance Relationship

Over the last 40 years, numerous researchers have tried to provide a definitive and clear answer to the fundamental question of whether higher CSR leads to superior financial performance. However, according to the empirical evidence obtained, a unique answer to this question seems elusive. Some scholars have found a positive relationship[4] while others find more ambiguous or even negative relationships.[5] Moreover, following Preston and O'Bannon[6] and Allouche and Laroche,[7] we can identify up to seven hypotheses that have found some support in previous empirical literature (see Table 20.1).

Table 20.1   Seven hypotheses on the link between CSR and financial performance

Link		Positive	Negative	Neutral
CSR	FP	Social impact hypothesis (1)	Trade-off hypothesis (2)	Neutral association hypothesis (7)
FP	CSR	Slack resources hypothesis (3)	Opportunism hypothesis (4)	
CSR	FP	Virtuous circle hypothesis (5)	Vicious circle hypothesis (6)	

Sources: Preston and O'Bannon; Allouche and Laroche; Author[8]

The social impact hypothesis (hypothesis # 1) suggests that the better the firm performs from a social point of view, the better it performs in economic and financial terms. The rationale behind this hypothesis is the well-known argument that if a firm satisfies its stakeholder claims, then they will reciprocate by making firm-specific investments in the firm or by improving the firm global reputation, image, and so on. Contrary to the social impact hypothesis, the trade-off hypothesis (hypothesis # 2) posits that CSR investment imposes additional costs on the firm that cause a competitive disadvantage over those competitors whose competitive strategy is not constrained by those CSR-related investments.

The slack resources hypothesis (hypothesis # 3) postulates that the most opulent firms, with available slack resources and funds, are the ones that engage in socially responsible activities. On the other hand, the managerial opportunism hypothesis (hypothesis #

4) is rooted in the organizational economics literature and it postulates that managers pursue their own self-interested objectives and these may clash with the objectives of shareholders and other stakeholders.

The virtuous circle hypothesis (hypothesis # 5) integrates the social impact and the slack resources into one single argument. Some authors have advanced the hypothesis that there are synergetic forces in place that, in practice, mean that causation between CSR and profitability may run in both directions in firms. That is, better financial performance may lead to improved CSR and, at the same time, better CSR may lead to improved financial performance. Of course this synergetic relation between CSR and financial performance may also be negative, meaning that corporations displaying strong social credentials experience declining stock prices relative to the market average, and that this decline in financial performance will subsequently affect the social investments and activities in the next period, and so forth, creating a vicious circle between CSR and performance (hypothesis # 6).

Finally, proponents of the neutral association between CSR and financial performance (hypothesis # 7) posit that there are so many intervening variables between CSR and financial performance that there is no reason to expect a relationship to exist, except by chance. The neutral association hypothesis has found some empirical support in the literature.[9]

In the most comprehensive survey performed to date on the link between CSR and financial performance, Margolis and Walsh[10] review 127 studies published in articles and books since the early work of Moskowitz.[11] In 109 of the 127 studies, CSR has been treated as the independent variable, predicting profitability. Margolis and Walsh conclude that, of these 109 studies, just over one half (54) pointed towards a positive CSR–financial performance relationship, 20 showed mixed results, 28 studies reported nonsignificant relationships and 7 studies showed a negative relationship.[12] Other more recent meta-analyses of past research confirm the heterogeneity of the empirical results obtained to date on the relationship between CSR and performance.[13]

In light of these heterogeneous results, CSR scholars have started to search for several explanations. First, the mixed empirical evidence may be due to a lack of consistent and reliable instruments for measuring CSR,[14] and sampling-related problems. Early studies in the field used corporate reputation indexes, or distributed ad hoc questionnaires to measure the firm's commitment to certain stakeholders. More recent studies have tried to refine CSR measures and use more consistent and comparable cross-study measures such as the Kinder, Lydenberg, Domini (KLD) index of CSR.[15] However, although the more recent studies that use KLD to measure CSR tend to support a positive relationship between CSR and financial performance,[16] some contradictory results are still found.[17]

A second explanation for the heterogeneity of empirical results is that CSR and financial performance may have a relationship that changes with circumstances which may not yet be understood well enough to be embodied in control variables.[18] According to this view the inconsistent findings will disappear once we incorporate all the relevant control variables in the regression models.

A third aspect that must be better understood is the relationship between short- and long-run performance. Cross-sectional empirical studies tend to measure both CSR and profitability in the same single year and, therefore, the long-term consequences of certain decisions affecting stakeholders are left unexplored. Introducing the short- and long-term dimension can contribute to explaining the inconsistency of previous empirical findings.

For example, Ogden and Watson, in a longitudinal study of ten water supply companies operating in the UK, found that, whereas a high CSR had a negative impact on firm's current profitability—as managers typically had to incur certain expenses in order to attend to the needs of concrete stakeholders—it also had a significant long-run positive effect on shareholders' returns.[19] Similar conclusions to Ogden and Watson are reached by other researchers.[20]

Finally, a fourth reason proposed to explain the inconsistent findings may be related to endogeneity issues; that is, firms do not randomly choose to engage in CSR actions but rather there is a strategic rationale behind their decisions, thereby making invalid the basic assumption of randomness in econometric models. In order to address endogeneity problems, researchers need to find out whether the decision of a firm to engage in socially responsible programs is correlated with other firm-specific variables such as the organization's strategy or culture, the quality of its top management, decision-making style, management's ethical attitudes, external pressures by stakeholder groups or any other hard to observe firm-specific variables and include them in the econometric models when possible.[21]

Yet despite the four methodological problems identified above, there is still a more fundamental question, somehow related to these four issues, that has not been properly addressed and that has to do with the general methodology used in empirical studies. The bulk of empirical studies on the CSR–financial performance link measure CSR as the "sum" of relationships between the firm and its stakeholders with the implicit assumption that the more positive relationships, the higher the CSR performance of the firm.[22] Hence, under this approach, if a firm has a positive relationship with customers, environmental groups, employees and local communities it will get a higher score than a firm with a positive relationship with just local communities, for example. This "aggregative" approach blends all stakeholder relationships into a single variable and does not distinguish, for example, between industries that may be subject to different pressures from different stakeholder groups, nor does it allow for a systematic classification of CSR approaches depending on the industry, the country, strategy of the firm, organizational context, or the international scope of the firm, to name just a few a critical variables.

While the "aggregative" approach has the advantage of providing a relatively simple measure of CSR to be used in econometric models (e.g., regression analysis), it somehow tends to mix very different types of CSR practices and behaviors into a single category without discriminating which type of company we are analyzing in each case. For example, companies in the textile industry tend to focus their CSR practices towards their international supply chain, highly scrutinized by international corporate-watchers in this industry, whereas CSR in the energy sector tends to emphasize environmental and sustainability issues, as these are the issues that receive more public attention in this last sector and, hence, are more likely to have a significant effect on the bottom line. If a researcher just creates a CSR score to measure "how much" CSR a company is doing it is likely that they will overlook these subtle differences between supply chain-driven CSR activities or environmental-driven CSR policies. These different activities should be analyzed separately in the empirical tests.

If we add that some CSR policies will be more effective only in combination with other policies (e.g., strategy of the firm), then the complexity of the analysis only increases because we have to analyze the impact of a given CSR practice on performance in combination with all the other relevant firm, industry or country attributes. We state that this mixing of different CSR typologies into simplistic "aggregated" metrics, as well as the complementarities existing between CSR activities and other attributes of the firm, may be driving, to a large extent, the inconsistencies found in the empirical CSR–financial performance literature.

The question naturally becomes, how can we deal in empirical works with these different configurations of CSR practices and their complementarities? While some researchers have tried to decompose the CSR construct by distinguishing between single stakeholder groups—customers, employees, suppliers, etc.—or they have included in their regression equations control variables and interaction effects between CSR measures and other firm attributes such as size or industry (e.g., Waddock and Graves),[23] they have done so in a quite ad hoc fashion, without systematically mapping all possible configurations of CSR that may exist in their samples.

We define a configuration in this chapter as a bundle of attributes (e.g., CSR practices, policies, mechanisms, firm characteristics, etc.) that must necessarily be present in a firm in order to produce a given hypothesized effect. For example if positive employee relationships only lead to high performance in combination with a differentiation based competitive strategy, then we will say that these two attributes together conform a configuration.

In this chapter we posit that a relatively new methodology based on qualitative comparative analysis (QCA)[24] might allow researchers to identify different CSR configurations in firms and test in a systematic way whether some of the identified configurations lead to superior financial performance or not. Next, we will briefly review the main characteristics of QCA and show how QCA can help researchers to discover these CSR configurations in empirical research.

Basic Notions of Qualitative Comparative Analysis and Fuzzy Sets

As we explained in the introduction the purpose of this chapter is to present to CSR researchers a methodology, qualitative comparative analysis (QCA), that specifically focuses on firms' CSR configurations and the impact that these configurations have on the bottom line.

QCA has recently been used in management studies as a way to better understand configurations in firms, the complementarities existing between different elements of the configurations and their impact on financial performance.[25] It is a methodology based on set theory and Boolean algebra. It was developed primarily by Charles Ragin[26] in the late 1980s to solve a fundamental problem presented by cross-case analyses: preserving the integrity of cases as complex configurations of causal factors while allowing for a systematic examination of similarities and differences in causal factors across many cases.

In the last few years, QCA is increasingly being used in social sciences research. In plain words this methodology uses the de facto that if all—or most—of the members of a given population that satisfy a condition or a combination of conditions also satisfy an outcome, then it is said that this condition is a sufficient condition for the outcome to be present. To apply this methodology, the researcher starts with a phenomenon to be explained, called the outcome, and a list of possible conditions that might have an influence on that phenomenon. Next, for each individual it is assessed whether or not they satisfy the outcome and whether or not they satisfy each of the causal conditions.

A combination of qualitative reasoning and quantitative techniques are used to assess whether an individual belongs to a specific set or not. If the number of possible established causal conditions is k, then there exist 2^k possible combinations of causal conditions, also called configurations. Each individual belongs to one of the 2^k configurations, so each configuration is associated with a subset of the individuals. If a configuration, considered as a set of individuals, is a subset of the set of the population that satisfy the outcome, then it is said that this configuration is a sufficient condition for the outcome. Different configurations can be sufficient conditions for the outcome, so this methodology allows the researcher to identify different paths leading to a given outcome (i.e., equifinality).

A Generalization of QCA: Fuzzy Sets

A very powerful generalization of QCA allows for a relaxation of the conditions of membership of the individuals to the causal conditions and to the outcome, whereby individuals may have a *degree* of membership to a set. The membership of an individual to a set could be a number between 0 and 1; a membership value of 1 means full membership, while 0 means that the individual is fully outside the set. Degrees of membership between 0.5 and 1 mean that the individual is more in than out, while the reverse is true for degrees of membership between 0 and 0.5. Maximum ambiguity corresponds to a degree of membership of 0.5. The degree of membership of an individual to a set is assessed qualitatively, although it is enough to indicate a value for full membership, for full nonmembership and the point of maximum ambiguity. With these three anchors, an algorithm (to be outlined below) is used to assess the degree of membership in the intermediate cases. This generalization is known as *fuzzy set* analysis. In this context, a set is not made up of different elements that belong to the set. Rather, the degree of membership of each element is continuous; some of them have full membership and others have lower or null degree of membership. A fuzzy set A is contained in another fuzzy set B, if for every element x the membership of x in A is smaller than or equal to the degree of membership of x in B. So if a configuration is contained in an outcome we say that this configuration is a sufficient condition for the outcome.

    QCA and fuzzy-set analysis (QCA/fs) differs in several respects from conventional statistical methods.[27] First, fuzzy-set methods allow the researcher to address both quantitative as well as qualitative aspects of CSR policies. Therefore, we can calibrate differences in kind (e.g., a firm belongs to the set of socially responsible firms or does not) without *measuring* the attributes we are studying: we just need to *calibrate* whether a case is included or not in a given set.[28] Secondly, unlike correlational linear approaches that disaggregate cases into independent, separate aspects, QCA/fs uncovers bundles or configurations of qualitative and quantitative attributes leading to a given outcome and establishes causal relationships between the whole configurations and the outcome. Thirdly, rather than assuming linear causation and estimating the average effect of a given variable net of all other variables as in conventional regression analysis, QCA/fs analysis assumes that a given causal condition may be necessary or sufficient for an outcome, together with combinations of jointly sufficient causal conditions. This last point implies that a causal condition found to be related to an outcome in one configuration may even have an inverse relation in some other configuration, i.e., the effect of causal conditions is not necessarily symmetrical. In a regression model, an independent variable affects the dependent variable for good and bad, while in the proposed methodology the fact that a causal condition is sufficient for the outcome does not necessarily imply that the absence of that causal condition is sufficient to lead to the absence of the outcome.

Altogether, it seems that this methodology presents some advantages over more traditional methods. We are not saying that QCA/fs methodology is superior to regression techniques; only that under certain conditions it has some advantages. In Table 20.2 we highlight some differences between regression analysis and QCA.

Table 20.2   Differences between regression-like approaches and QCA

	Regression analysis approach	**QCA/fs approach**
Basic unit of analysis	Variables	Sets
Causality	Correlations	Set-theoretic connections
CSR measurement	Single CSR items	Configurations of practices
Sample size	Large sample	Small or large sample
Causal direction	Symmetric	Asymmetric
Tests	T-test, R-square	Consistency, coverage

Calibrating Fuzzy Sets

As we explained before, the transformation of normal variables into sets requires the specification of full membership, full nonmembership to the set of interest, and the crossover point of maximum ambiguity. Crossover point is the score that makes an element have a 0.5 degree of membership in the set of interest, and also, logically, a degree of non-membership of 0.5. Only for dummy variables (0,1) can this transformation be done directly from the original variable into a crisp set (where 1 indicates full membership and 0 indicates full nonmembership). For the construction of the fuzzy sets the researchers have to predefine some anchors according to the "direct method" described by Ragin.[29] The direct method transformation proceeds in two steps: in the first, once the full membership, full nonmembership and the cross-over point are specified, variables scores are translated into the metric of log odds as described by Ragin. Given the log odds of membership of each element, its degree of membership to the set of interest is calculated according to the formula:

Degree of membership = exp (log odds) / [1+exp (log odds)]

These final rescaled measures will range from 0 to 1 and the converted scores are firmly tied to the three qualitative anchors specified of full membership, cross-over point and full nonmembership.[30] In this way, scores with log odds values greater than 5 are translated to a degree of membership greater than 0.99, while scores with log odds values greater than 3 are translated to a degree of membership greater than 0.95. Scores with log odds values of 0 are translated to a degree of membership of 0.5, and so forth.

Consistency and Coverage

The key tool for analyzing causality using QCA/fs is the truth table. Truth tables list the logically possible combinations of causal conditions (e.g., CSR policies) and the empirical outcome (e.g., financial performance) associated with each configuration. The truth table allows the researcher to identify which particular configurations of CSR lead to superior performance in practice. Most fuzzy set empirical works have used the inclusion algorithm described by Ragin[31] to examine the relationship between membership in causal conditions and the outcome of interest.[32] One can use standard software such as fsQCA (www.fsqca.com) or the 'fuzzy' command in Stata[33] to construct a truth table. Sets calibration can also be done using the fsQCA and Stata software.

The truth table algorithm is based on standard methods of Boolean algebra and allows the researcher to calculate the consistency and coverage of the solutions obtained.[34] The consistency assesses the degree to which cases sharing a given condition or a combination of conditions agree in displaying the outcome in question. That is, consistency indicates how closely a perfect subset relation is approximated. The consistency goes from 0 to 1, where 1 would indicate a perfect subset relation. The coverage assesses the degree to which a cause or a causal combination accounts for instances of an outcome. The coverage also ranges from 0 to 1 and it can be thought of as a measure similar to an R-square in regression models, allowing the researcher to evaluate the empirical relevance of the solutions found. Researchers should aim at having highly consistent connections, higher than the often-used threshold of 0.75, while not losing too much coverage.[35] The calculation of fuzzy set-theoretic consistency and coverage is done as follows:

$$\text{Consistency } (X_i \le Y_i) = \Sigma \ [\min \ (X_i, Y_i)] \ / \ \Sigma (X_i)$$

$$\text{Coverage } (X_i \le Y_i) = \Sigma \ [\min \ (X_i, Y_i)] \ / \ \Sigma (Y_i)$$

where X_i is the degree of membership of individual i in configuration X and Y_i is its degree of membership in outcome Y.

Applying QCA/fs to the Study of the CSR–financial Performance Relationship

Now that we understand the basics of QCA/fs, the question is this: how can QCA/fs help CSR researchers? And more particularly: how can QCA/fs contribute to solving and explaining the inconsistent findings in the CSR–financial performance literature?

QCA/fs allows for a systematic exploration of different CSR configurations and a rigorous analysis of the complementarities and contingencies existing between CSR practices and other firm-specific attributes. For instance, a textile firm such as Inditex (Zara) is very active in its relationship with its suppliers because monitoring, supervising and auditing its supply chain is a critical task, given Inditex's large and complex supply chain of more than 2,000 apparel and garment manufacturers, most of them located in developing countries. Given Nike's earlier scandals with child labor and working conditions in developing countries, monitoring the supply chain and all the stakeholders involved has become a major concern for textile firms. At the same time, Inditex places relatively less emphasis on its activities regarding NGOs, minorities and the environment. However, because of the greater visibility of Inditex's supply chain, this CSR strategy is likely to lead to superior performance, given the critical importance of suppliers in Inditex's business model. Another company in a different industry or a different country with the same supplier-driven CSR strategy will not necessarily obtain the same results because the complementarities and contingencies in place are different. For example, BP's CSR strategy is more focused on environmental and sustainability concerns. It is likely that BP's efforts in pro-environmental policies pay off more than policies aimed at auditing and monitoring all the suppliers in their supply chain.

We see in the two examples shown above how adding CSR policies into single scores may hide the complex ways in which these policies lead to high performance. Under a configurational logic, unlike regression analysis, what counts are not the individual CSR scores obtained by each firm but rather the whole *configuration* of CSR practices that each firm adopts in combination with other firm-specific attributes. From this point of view more CSR is not always better.

In the next section we will use a hypothetical illustration to show how QCA/fs can lead to new discoveries about the CSR–financial performance link.

QCA/fs in Action: A Hypothetical Illustration

We show in Table 20.3 how a more systematic examination of the conditions under which CSR actions may lead to superior performance can be carried out in empirical studies. We use two simple hypothetical examples (A and B) to illustrate how QCA/fs works in practice.

In the illustration we use *stakeholder groups, legal system, industry* and *competitive strategy* followed by the firm, but researchers may use, of course, any other attribute they consider relevant for their research. The calibration of some sets, such as legal system or industry where the firm operates, is straightforward (0/1). Other sets, such as whether a firm has positive relationships with its employees, customers, suppliers, NGOs, etc., are more complex to calibrate and can be done using some well-known metrics such as KLD, SAM, ad hoc questionnaires sent to firms or just public information. One advantage of QCA/fs is that the researcher does not need to assign an exact number; all they have to do is to determine, for example, whether a firm belongs to the set of firms with positive employee relationships or not, combining qualitative and quantitative information. This is a great advantage when evaluating CSR activities. We do know if there is a democracy or not in a given country; however it is harder to assign a precise score to a democracy. The same happens with some CSR activities which are easier to observe and to *calibrate* than to *measure*.[36]

Finally, the outcome (financial performance) is a continuous variable and it can be calibrated, for example, using the percentiles of the distribution or using some benchmark as, for example, the cost of equity (e.g., a firm belongs to the set of firms with high financial performance if it earns a return on equity higher than its cost of capital).

In Table 20.3 we follow the notation recently introduced by Charles Ragin and Peer Fiss,[37] whereby full circles indicate the presence of a condition, while crossed-out circles indicate its absence. So, for example, a full circle in "Anglo-Saxon" indicates that the firm belongs to the set of firms whose headquarters are located in a country with an

Anglo-Saxon legal system and a crossed-out circle indicates that the firm belongs to a non-Anglo-Saxon country.

It is important to observe that, given the large number of variables considered (14 in total), there are up to 2^{14} (16,384) different possible combinations, assuming that the variables were dichotomous (0/1). It seems an overwhelming task to handle this many possible configurations using the traditional regression analysis template.

In Table 20.3 we just show five different configurations (1a, 2a, 3a, 1b, 2b) in order to illustrate how QCA/fs operates. Following the hypothetical illustration, out of all the possible 16,384 combinations, only two configurations (1a and 1b) are sufficient conditions leading to high financial performance because only these last two configurations show a consistency higher than 0.75. Each configuration has a unique consistency and coverage. For instance, configuration 1a has a consistency of 0.92 and a coverage of 0.14. We can use probabilistic criteria to determine whether a configuration consistency is statistically significant higher than a benchmark value (e.g., 0.75 consistency) with a given confidence level (p-value< 0.05).[38] If we set the consistency benchmark at 0.75, only configurations 1a and 1b can be said to be configurations that lead to high financial performance, while configurations 2a, 3a and 2b either never lead to high financial performance or sometimes lead to high performance and sometimes do not, and therefore they cannot be said to be sufficient causal conditions. The relatively high coverage of all five configurations indicate that they account for a high number of cases in our sample (i.e., they are empirically relevant).

EXAMPLE A (1A, 2A, 3A)

Let's suppose that a researcher finds that a positive relationship with NGOs leads to higher firm performance (1a). Configuration 2a (consistency = 0.54; coverage = 0.12) is identical to 1a (consistency = 0.92; coverage = 0.14) but in 2a the firm operates in a French legal system rather than an Anglo-Saxon one. The low consistency of 2a indicates that this configuration is not a sufficient causal condition leading to high performance. It may happen that having strong ties with NGOs stops being critical to achieving financial performance due to the fact that NGOs are less active in non-Anglo-Saxon countries because the pressure from outsiders on corporations are weaker in these countries. Finally, configuration 3a (consistency = 0.40; coverage = 0.10) is identical to 1a but now this type of firm does not operate in manufacturing but in the financial sector. The results in Table 20.3 suggest that the positive financial impact of having a positive relationship with NGOs found in 1a disappear when we only consider firms operating in the financial sector (configuration 3a). It may happen that NGOs positive relationships stop being effective in this case because financial services firms face less criticism and pressure from NGOs than manufacturing companies who are more exposed to corporate watchers due to pollution issues, child labor, working conditions and other social concerns related to their manufacturing activities.

By analyzing the configurations of CSR activities in combination with other firm-specific characteristics we observe how previous inconsistent CSR–financial performance empirical findings can be reconciled. For example, the same single CSR practice, involvement with NGOs, may have a positive impact on financial performance (1a) or just a neutral or even negative impact on financial performance (2a, 3a) depending on the boundary conditions imposed by configurations 1a, 2a and 3a depicted in Table 20.3.

Table 20.3   Configurations of CSR

	Configurations of CSR				
	(1a)	(2a)	(3a)	(1b)	(2b)
Stakeholders					
Employees				•	•
Customers					
Suppliers					
NGOs	•	•	•		
Environment groups					
Minorities					
Legal system					
Anglo-Saxon	•	⊗	•		
French	⊗	•	⊗		
German	⊗	⊗	⊗		
Industry*					
Manufacturing	•	•	⊗		
Financial	⊗	⊗	•		
Services (nonfinancial)					
Strategy					
Differentiation				•	⊗
Cost				⊗	•
Leads to superior financial performance	Yes	No	No	Yes	No
Consistency	0.92	0.54	0.40	0.94	0.42
Coverage	0.14	0.12	0.10	0.13	0.09

• Presence of conditions

⊗ Absence of conditions

* A firm may be diversified and be present, for example, in manufacturing and in the financial sector at the same time

EXAMPLE B (1B, 2B)

Configuration 1b (consistency = 0.94; coverage = 0.13) indicates that if a firm has strong employee relationships it will have a superior financial performance. This positive relationship has been reported in many previous empirical studies.[39] However, configuration 2b (consistency = 0.42; coverage = 0.09) indicates that this empirical result only holds when the firm follows a differentiation competitive strategy, and that firms with strong employee relationships following cost leadership strategies do not enjoy superior financial performance.

One may argue that, in the process of theory-building, researchers should advance the boundary conditions of their hypothesis. In this example, a researcher should state during the theory-building process that the hypothesized relationship between strong employee relationships and financial performance only holds when the firm pursues a differentiation strategy. Then the researcher can easily control for this last variable in their regression model. While this is true, it is also true that often the number of boundary conditions is simply too high in complex theories, especially while conducting exploratory research. Even in this relatively simple hypothetical illustration, with just 14 explanatory variables, we have 16,384 possible configurations. In these cases, QCA/fs helps to discover new associations between causal conditions and the outcome of interest, especially during the early stages of research (e.g., exploratory research).

Examples A and B are just two very simple applications of QCA/fs. Although real data configurations are more complex than the ones shown in Table 20.3, the main point is that QCA/fs allows researchers to systematically explore all the possible combinations for a given population of firms being studied, rather than using ad hoc control variables or randomly trying some interaction effects in the regression equations. This is especially relevant when the number of variables to consider is high. As the number of variables to study increases, the number of combinations grows exponentially. For example, if we deal with 5 variables then we have 32 (2^5) different configurations, with 6 variables 64 (2^6) and so on.

In addition, and more importantly, a researcher using regression analysis would likely conclude that having positive NGOs relationships or having positive employee relationships, after controlling for industry, size, legal system and so on, always leads to superior financial performance. However, QCA/fs clearly shows that this positive relationship only holds under a complex set of particular conditions (configurations 1a and 1b).

Finally, another important characteristic of QCA/fs is that it allows for the analysis of causal asymmetry as it takes into account the fact that the CSR configurations leading to very high performance are frequently different from those leading to merely high or average performance. This view stands in contrast to the common correlational understanding of causality, which assumes causal symmetry because correlations are by their very nature symmetric; for example, if we model the inverse of high performance, then the results of a regression analysis will be unchanged except for the sign of the coefficients. However, a causal understanding of necessary and sufficient conditions is causally asymmetric—that is, the set of causal conditions leading to the presence of the outcome may frequently be different from the set of conditions leading to the absence of the outcome.

So for example, configuration 1b shows that having strong positive relationships with employees lead to superior financial performance when combined with a differentiation-based competitive strategy. However, the opposite, that is, having weak or damaged relationships with employees and pursuing a cost-based strategy, does not necessarily lead to low financial performance. All that Table 20.3 indicates is that firms with configuration 2b do not belong to the set of firms with superior financial performance. In order to test if configuration 2b is a sufficient causal condition leading to low financial performance, the researcher has to build a new set of "firms with low financial performance" and then discover the causal conditions leading to this particular outcome. So far, causal asymmetry has for the most part been neglected not only in the CSR field but in organizational research more broadly. However, causal asymmetry is arguably pervasive in this field, and failing to take this causal structure into account is likely to lead to incomplete or incorrect conclusions from the data.

In sum, these are some of the reasons why we argue that configurational analysis and QCA/fs can contribute to explaining some of the previous inconsistent and contradictory findings on the CSR–financial performance link.

Discussion and Conclusions

The view of CSR based on the notion of stakeholder has made substantial progress in the last decades. One remaining challenge is that of identifying the salient stakeholders and their relative importance in the corporate agenda. This task is a hard one because stakeholder claims are often at conflict, their relative importance is hard to assess for managers and they are hardly universal, varying by business, by size, by sector, by legal system and by geographic region. Confronted by all these often conflicting claims managers ideally need to know *ex-ante* the impact in the bottom line of investing in one stakeholder group vs. another group so that their normative criteria can be complemented by instrumental considerations during the decision-making process. Thus, empirical research plays a major role in informing managers about the financial consequences of internalizing in their decision-making the claims of particular stakeholder groups.

A close examination of the CSR–financial performance empirical literature over the last 30 years reveals that several hypotheses are being tested at once and the results of those studies are inconclusive. Is there a positive, negative or neutral relationship between CSR and financial performance? Is it CSR that determines financial performance or vice versa? Is there a virtuous—or vicious—circle between the two?

In this chapter we argued that the theoretical developments of the last three decades in this field have not been matched by a similar improvement in the research methods used to test the relative merits of the different hypotheses. In the theoretical battlefront important advances have been made by conceptualizing CSR as the aggregate of stakeholder relationships.[40] However, the challenge for empirical researchers in the CSR field is, of course, to find out which of the seven alternative hypotheses posited in the literature[41] shown in Table 20.1 deserves more credit in the light of the empirical results obtained.

Disentangling the CSR–financial performance causality in an empirical setting is troublesome and a fine-grained analysis of the data requires the introduction of more sophisticated methods. As a result, some advanced statistical methods such as simultaneous equation models, panel data and meta-analysis have been proposed and used in some recent works.[42]

However, in addition—and complementary—to these improved correlation-based methods, QCA/fs-based methods can play an important role in the advancement of the field. Important issues such as small numbers sample, bundles of CSR practices, causality based on sufficient and necessary conditions, the direction of the causality between CSR and profitability or the asymmetry between causal conditions and outcomes can be explored more accurately by using QCA/fs under the conditions introduced in this chapter.

Researchers may, for instance, go back to their original samples and apply this new method in order to identify patterns of association or complementarities among different CSR practices and among different stakeholders that were systematically overlooked using correlational methods. In addition, it would be very interesting if researchers came up with several empirical studies in which the most relevant interactions between CSR policies and other firm attributes (size, industry, legal system, strategy and so on) are made explicit in order to identify which particular bundles of CSR policies constitute sufficient causal conditions leading to higher performance. Another intriguing possibility would be to use fs/QCA to check for equifinality: different CSR arrangements leading to the same outcome (e.g., financial performance).

In sum, in this chapter we argued that it is consubstantial to QCA/fs that a single CSR attribute has a positive, negative or neutral effect on financial performance, depending on the value of all other variables within the configuration. Thus, previous inconsistent empirical results may be reconciled when single CSR policies are studied in the broader context of CSR configurations using QCA/fs. Once interdependence and contingencies are fully incorporated into the empirical analysis, most of the apparent inconsistencies may disappear, as depicted in Table 20.3. While some CSR researchers have started to empirically explore some of the advantages of QCA/fs explained in this chapter,[43] we foresee a whole new avenue for future empirical research based on this relatively new method.

Notes

1   Griffin, J.J. and Mahon, J.F. (1997), "The corporate social performance and corporate financial performance debate", *Business and Society*, vol. 36, no. 1, pp. 5–31; Margolis, J. and Walsh, J. (2001), *People and Profits?*, Lawrence Erlbaum Associates, New Jersey; Margolis, J. and Walsh, J. (2003), "Misery loves companies: rethinking social initiatives by business", *Administrative Science Quarterly*, vol. 48, pp. 268–305; Roman, R., Hayibor, S. and Agle, B.R. (1999), "The relationship between social and financial performance", *Business and Society*, vol. 38, no. 1, pp. 109–125; Ullmann, A.A. (1985), "Data in search of a theory: a critical examination of the relationships among social performance, social disclosure, and economic performance of U.S. firms", *Academy of Management Review*, vol. 10, no. 3, pp. 540–557.

2   Waddock, S.A. and Graves, S.B. (1997a), "Quality of management and quality of stakeholder relations: are they synonymous?", *Business and Society*, vol. 36, no. 3, pp. 250–279; Waddock S.A. and Graves, S.B. (1997b), "The corporate social performance–financial performance link", *Strategic Management Journal*, vol. 18, no. 4, pp. 303–319.

3   For details on QCA, see Ragin, C.C. (1987), *The Comparative Method: Moving Beyond Qualitative and Quantitative Strategies*, University of California Press, Berkeley, CA; Ragin, C.C. (2000), *Fuzzy-set Social Science*, University of Chicago Press, Chicago, IL; Ragin, C.C. (2008), *Redesigning Social Inquiry: Fuzzy Sets and Beyond*, University of Chicago Press, Chicago, IL.

4   Berman, S.L., Wicks, A.C., Kotha, S. and Jones, T.M. (1999), "Does stakeholder orientation matter? The relationship between stakeholder management models and the firm financial performance", *Academy of Management Journal*, vol. 42, no. 5, pp. 488–506; Hillman, A.J. and Keim, G.D. (2001), "Shareholder value, stakeholder management, and social issues: what's the bottom line?", *Strategic Management Journal*, vol. 22, no. 2, pp. 125–139; McGuire, J.B., Sundgren, A. and Schneeweis, T. (1988), "Corporate social responsibility and firm financial

performance", *Academy of Management Journal*, vol. 31, pp. 854–872; Waddock and Graves (1997b), op. cit.

5   Alexander, G.J. and Buchholz, R.A. (1978), "Corporate social responsibility and stock market performance", *Academy of Management Journal*, vol. 21, no. 3, pp. 479–486; Aupperle, K.E., Carroll, A.B. and Hatfield, J.D. (1985), "An empirical examination of the relationship between corporate social responsibility and profitability", *Academy of Management Journal*, vol. 28, no. 2, pp. 446–463; García-Castro, R., Ariño, M.A. and Canela, M.A. (2010), "Does social performance really lead to financial performane? Accounting for endogeneity", *Journal of Business Ethics*, vol. 92, pp. 107–126; McWilliams, A. and Siegel, D. (2000), "Corporate social responsibility and financial performance: correlation or misspecification?", *Strategic Management Journal*, vol. 21, pp. 603–609.

6   Preston, L.E. and O´Bannon, D.P. (1997), "The corporate social–financial performance relationship: a typology and analysis", *Business and Society*, vol. 36, pp. 419–429.

7   Allouche, J. and Laroche, P. (2006), "The relationship between corporate social responsibility and corporate financial performance: a survey", in J. Allouche (eds), *Corporate Social Responsibility*, Palgrave Macmillan, New York, pp. 3–40.

8   Preston and O'Bannon (1997), op. cit.; Allouche and Laroche (2006), op. cit.

9   See for example, García-Castro, Ariño and Canela (2010), op. cit.; McWilliams and Siegel, op. cit.

10   Margolis and Walsh (2001, 2003), op. cit.

11   Moskowitz, M. (1972), "Choosing socially responsible stocks", *Business and Society Review*, vol. 1, pp. 71–75.

12   Margolis and Walsh (2003), op. cit., p. 278.

13   Orlitzky, M., Schmidt, F. and Rynes, S. (2003), "Corporate social and financial performance: a meta-analysis", *Organization Studies*, vol. 24, pp. 403–441.

14   Waddock and Graves (1997a, 1997b), op. cit.

15   Kinder, Lydenberg, Domini and Co. Inc., 129 Mt. Auburn St, Cambridge, MA 02138, USA.

16   Berman, Wicks, Kotha and Jones (1999), op. cit.; Hillman and Keim (2001), op. cit.; Waddock and Graves (1997a, 1997b), op. cit.

17   García-Castro *et al.* (2010), op. cit.; McWilliams and Siegel (2000), op. cit.

18   McWilliams and Siegel (2000), op. cit.; Waddock and Graves (1997a, 1997b), op. cit.

19   Ogden, S. and Watson, R. (1999), "Corporate performance and stakeholder management: balancing shareholder and customer interests in the U.K. privatized water industry", *Academy of Management Journal*, vol. 42, no. 5, pp. 526–538.

20   García-Castro, R., Ariño, M.A. and Canela, M.A. (2011), "Over the long run? Short-run impact and long-run consequences of stakeholder management", *Business and Society, Business and Society*, vol. 50, pp. 428–455.

21   García-Castro, Ariño and Canela (2010), op. cit.

22   See for example, Margolis and Walsh (2001, 2003), op. cit.; Waddock and Graves (1997a, 1997b), op. cit.

23   Waddock and Graves (1997a, 1997b), op. cit.

24   For additional details on QCA, see Ragin (1987, 2000, 2008), op. cit.

25   Fiss P.C. (2007), "A set-theoretic approach to organizational configurations", *Academy of Management Review*, vol. 32, pp. 1180–1198; Fiss P.C. (2010), "Building better causal theories: a fuzzy set approach to typologies in organization research", *Academy of Management Journal*, in press; Kogut, B., MacDuffie, J.P. and Ragin, C.C. (2004), "Prototypes and strategy: assigning causal credit using fuzzy sets", *European Management Review*, vol. 1, pp. 114–131; Kogut,

B. and Ragin, C.C. (2006), "Exploring complexity when diversity is limited: institutional complementarity in theories of rule of law and national systems revisited", *European Management Review*, vol. 3, pp. 44–59.

26   Ragin (1987, 2000, 2008), op. cit.

27   Fiss (2007, 2010), op. cit.; Ragin (1987, 2000, 2008), op. cit.

28   For an in-depth discussion on the differences between measurement and calibration see Ragin (2008), op. cit., pp. 71–105.

29   Ragin (1987, 2000, 2008), op. cit.

30   Ibid.

31   Ibid.

32   Kogut, MacDuffie and Ragin (2004), op. cit.; Kogut and Ragin (2006), op. cit.

33   Longest, K. (2008), "Fuzzy: a program for performing qualitative comparative analyses (QCA) in Stata", *The Stata Journal*, vol. 8, pp. 79–104.

34   Ragin (1987, 2000, 2008), op. cit.

35   Ibid.

36   Ragin (2008), op. cit., p. 71.

37   See Fiss (2010), op. cit.

38   For details, see Longest (2008), op. cit.

39   Waddock and Graves (1997b), op. cit.; Margolis and Walsh (2003), op. cit.

40   Waddock and Graves (1997a, 1997b), op. cit.

41   Preston and O'Bannon (1997), op. cit.; Allouche and Laroche (2006), op. cit.

42   Orlitzky, Schmidt and Rynes (2003), op. cit.

43   Jackson, G., Na, N. and Gao, J. (2010), "A configurational analysis of corporate social responsibility and corporate social irresponsibility among U.S. listed firms", paper presented at the Academy of Management Annual Meeting, Montreal, 9–11 August.

21 A Corporate Social Responsibility Decision Framework for Managers and Stakeholders

DUANE WINDSOR*

Keywords

Community and environmental investment, corporate social responsibility, decision framework, fair trade, organic agriculture.

Introduction

The purpose of this chapter is to help managers and stakeholders evaluate specific corporate social responsibility (CSR) decisions through using a heuristic framework integrating neutral CSR principles with managerial consideration of the preferences of salient stakeholders who may have conflicting views and interests. A salient stakeholder has influence or moral claim on the decision. There are two difficulties affecting CSR decisions. First, there is no broad consensus about CSR as corporate strategy. CSR is a contested concept among academics and business executives.[1] The contest is partly conceptual and theoretical, and partly ideological and political. One reason for a long-lived debate concerning CSR is that there are advocates for strong CSR (including environmental sustainability),[2] zero CSR (or nonresponsibility),[3] and lying between those two opposing poles of a theory continuum strategic CSR perspectives (including strategic philanthropy).[4] Theoretical debate can make it difficult for managers and stakeholders to get to the substance of specific decisions. A second difficulty is that CSR is a broad rubric including business ethics, corporate citizenship, corporate philanthropy, environmental sustainability, legal compliance, stakeholder management and sustainable development.[5] Academics, executives, nongovernmental organizations (NGOs) and governments use different specific elements of this broad rubric in constructing CSR arguments. Even within strong CSR and strategic CSR conceptions, there is disagreement on specific choices.

Norman A. Augustine, CEO of Martin Marietta and later of Lockheed Martin, emphasized that the hard cases concern not "right versus wrong" but "choosing among or balancing conflicting responsibilities—to the customer, to employees, to the

*   Duane Windsor, Rice University, Jesse H. Jones Graduate School of Business, MS-531, PO Box 2932, Houston, TX 77252-2932 USA. E-mail: odw@rice.edu.

community, and to the shareholders".[6] A heuristic framework is a conceptual aid to decision-making where the answer itself is not immediately known. Heuristic decision-making involves following procedures to find answers through reflection and judgment. Specific CSR decisions cannot be resolved theoretically. Managers must weigh strategy, values and stakeholder reactions. The zero CSR perspective counsels against undertaking any voluntary CSR activities beyond strict compliance with desirably minimal legal and ethical requires. The firm should do nothing but comply presently while lobbying to reduce requirements. Even in this perspective, however, lobbying involves a choice among stakeholder interests. The strategic CSR perspective counsels in favor of undertaking any voluntary CSR activities that seem likely to be profitable. Even in this perspective, managers have to consider reactions of key stakeholders and long-run sustainability. The strong CSR perspective counsels strong legal requirements and strong ethical responsibilities for managers and investors to undertake broad CSR activities, partly as substitutes for increased legal requirements in the future. Even a strong CSR perspective does not tell a manager how to balance two competing or conflicting projects. In all three perspectives, stakeholders have to judge how far to push managers, with discretion and values, on specific choices. It is unavoidable that managers must balance decisions that are difficult and always involve heuristic judgments and conflicting interests. This chapter takes the manager from contested theoretical perspectives to considerations bearing on specific CSR decisions.

The following set of definitions conveys the essential features of CSR. The European Commission (EC) defines CSR as "A concept whereby companies integrate social and environmental concerns in their business operations and in their interaction with their stakeholders on a voluntary basis".[7] The EC characterizes CSR as a contribution to sustainability and competitiveness. A legal counselor to businesses advises that CSR policies attempt "to encourage a positive impact through a company's activities on the environment, consumers, employees, communities, stakeholders, and other persons. CSR is a means to include the public interest in corporate decision-making".[8] The Carroll pyramid of multiple responsibilities, well established in the CSR literature, proposes that firms generate economic benefits to stakeholders while meeting legal requirements and the ethical and charitable expectations of society.[9] Drawing on these definitions, a socially responsible business should be concerned for all its impacts on society at large and other stakeholders. CSR entails not simply creating net benefits to society at large. Net benefits may embed wrong actions and negative impacts on specific stakeholders.[10] A business should ideally do nothing wrong, legally or ethically. Where this ideal standard proves impossible to meet in practice, then at least a business should minimize doing wrong.[11] This effort should thus avoid generating negative impacts for stakeholders, including society at large. A business also should do some social good beyond its direct economic contributions, even if this social contribution requires that the firm receive somewhat lower immediate profitability. The reasons are basically strategic: social contribution is a hedge against doing wrong; and social contribution may (not necessarily will) enhance reputation with key stakeholders, improving long-term profitability.

This chapter provides an integrative conceptual framework that combines a set of four neutral CSR principles with a basic five-stakeholder model that is scalable up and down for specific CSR decisions. The chapter provides references to key literature that is supportive of such an approach. The proposed "toolkit" for managers and stakeholders to aid in CSR decision-making and influencing[12] is a heuristic framework with options for how to make CSR decisions.[13] The chapter's contribution is to help managers and stakeholders understand how to make CSR decisions in a theoretically contested setting. The approach is also intended to help build theory as well as improve practice as follows.[14] This integrative approach should function, in principle, for any number of included stakeholders from one to N. (Complexity of analysis and decision increases.) The approach explained here focuses on the key instance of five stakeholders (external and internal), whether individuals or groups, other than management (directors and executives). The basic five-stakeholder model reasonably identifies the key considerations typically involved in CSR decisions. Although CSR is theoretically contested at an abstract level concerned with allocation of responsibilities among individuals and between markets and governments, the actual CSR decisions made by managers interacting with stakeholders generate a company's real CSR profile[15] from specific issue and conflict reconciliations. This real profile is the collection of CSR decisions over time.[16] Understanding how and why to weigh CSR decisions is thus of considerable practical importance to managers and stakeholders.

The chapter is organized as follows. This introduction explained the reason for the framework and this chapter's contribution. Because CSR is a contested concept, there is little agreement on theoretical perspectives or specific decisions. The second section explains four CSR decision principles that are neutral in not working for or against a particular CSR perspective (strong CSR, strategic CSR, or zero CSR). Regardless of CSR perspective, a specific decision should not violate these principles. The third section identifies and explains key literature supportive of an integrative framework combining neutral CSR principles with a stakeholder model. The fourth section explains a basic five-stakeholder model that can be scaled up and down as needed for specific CSR decisions. Each stakeholder must choose among six decision rules to determine how to "vote" on a specific CSR decision: market outcomes, prioritization of interests, aggregation or voting, concession, balancing of interests, or value principle. The fifth section illustrates how the framework can work for three CSR decisions: (1) fair trade with no domestic substitute; (2) organic trade with a foreign substitute; and (3) discretionary environmental and community investment. A summary section emphasizes managerial implications.

Four Neutral CSR Principles

Because CSR is a contested concept, there is little agreement on either theoretical perspectives or specific decisions. The integrative conceptual framework proposed here therefore begins with four neutral principles concerning CSR decisions. Neutrality means the principles do not automatically work for or against a particular CSR perspective. The set of principles constitutes a philosophical foundation from which all stakeholders can proceed concerning specific CSR decisions. One can construct within these principles an argument for any CSR position as the best approach to social welfare. The zero CSR argument is that over the longer run competitive markets, regulated for monopolies and negative externalities, will outperform further government intervention.[17] Any voluntary CSR activities will reduce profitability and social welfare. The strong CSR argument is that the likely combination of markets and governments will prove plainly unsatisfactory. Various CSR activities can increase social welfare and long-term profitability. The strategic CSR argument is that corporate reputation will lead managers to support some CSR activities improving social welfare and calculated to improve long-term profitability. Corporate social performance (CSP) can be defined as the outcomes of business activity in multiple dimensions of social welfare.[18] Strong CSP suggests zero to low CSR is reasonable. But weak CSP correspondingly suggests strong CSR or alternatively strong governmental intervention, advocated by Vogel over discretionary CSR.[19]

The author proposes the four principles as jointly constituting a reasonably neutral foundation for a conceptual framework that does not bias the decision-maker on specific issues. Regardless of one's CSR perspective, a specific decision does not violate any of the neutral principles. Support for each principle can be found in the literature cited below (including Adam Smith, not a proponent of CSR), but the reader should find the principles both neutral and reasonable. Table 21.1 provides a summary definition and interpretation of the four principles.

Table 21.1 Four neutral CSR principles briefly described

#	Principle	Interpretation
1	Firm behavior should improve social welfare as well as firm profit.	Ideally, firm profit and social welfare should increase jointly in a specific decision. At a minimum, greater firm profit should not damage social welfare. Higher profit at constant social welfare is thus acceptable.
2	A firm should obey law not by cost–benefit analysis but out of respect for law and community.	Legal compliance is not a matter of instrumental calculation of whether benefits outweigh costs in a specific decision. Legal compliance may require net loss to the firm.
3	A firm should practice business ethics and corporate citizenship seeking to advance the public or common interest.	Viewing business ethics as "do no harm" and corporate citizenship as "do some good", a firm should undertake to advance the public interest. This interest may involve net loss to one or more key stakeholders.
4	Management has sufficient discretion to make CSR decisions. (Managers are not automatically bound by the majority "vote" of the stakeholder advisory "committee" concerning specific CSR decisions. A strong "yes" or "no" vote must of course influence management choice.)	Managers must make forward-looking choices in changing conditions. They cannot be strictly fiduciary agents for investors operating on a short-term time horizon. Although investors are a key stakeholder group, managers have stewardship responsibility for the longer-term sustainability of the firm, and are individuals with moral values.

There are two reasons for identifying neutral principles.[20] The first is deficiency of adequate theory for resolving disputes about specific CSR decisions or more broadly stakeholder interest conflicts. Orts and Strudler argue that stakeholder theory is a useful heuristic for thinking about multiple interests but contains no convincing way to reconcile or balance conflicts among those interests.[21] In their view, the resulting philosophical problem is intractable. The same point is valid for CSR theory. The zero CSR literature asserts negative effects of all CSR activities on short-term corporate performance and long-term social welfare. The strategic CSR literature asserts positive effects of certain CSR choices on long-term corporate performance and likely on long-term social welfare. The strong CSR literature asserts positive effects of many CSR activities on social welfare and likely on long-term corporate performance.

The second reason is the weakness of empirical evidence resolving the CSR contest. There is disagreement over extent of market opportunities to "doing well by doing good" among distinguished scholars. Vogel thinks the "market for virtue" is very limited,[22] while Margolis and Walsh think that the market is likely extensive.[23] The limited condition suggests a view of CSR as altruism, unless some stakeholder is prepared to replace lost profit. If consumers might be prepared to pay a higher price for a CSR-good, investor return is not affected.[24] Consumers may be willing to pay a premium for environmentally friendly products or fair trade products.[25] The extensive condition suggests the possibility of a broad set of profitable opportunities, varying by firm and industry.[26] There is no strong evidence concerning the relationship between CSP or CSR and firm financial performance, despite multiple studies.[27] One possibility for this lack of evidence is that Vogel is correct. Another possibility is that the various cases across companies, industries and decisions reflect differing positive, neutral and negative relationships: CSR is highly situational and thus a matter for informed management judgment.

The first CSR principle is that ideally firm behavior should improve social welfare as well as firm profit.[28] This prescriptive principle should not be controversial, as distinct from the problem of defining social welfare. While profit may be a business goal, social welfare is the prerequisite moral and political condition and the socially expected outcome. The economic theory of markets and firms is that their functioning results overall in greater social benefits than social costs; and the opposite result would be peculiar.[29] The firm is an instrument for social welfare improvement. A minimum condition is that firm behavior should not worsen social welfare (i.e. "do no harm"). An illegitimate industry or company is one that worsens social welfare.[30] The burden of proof for profit maximization at the expense of social welfare is therefore on the proponent. Society should promote CSP that best improves social welfare. This exposition posits a simple two-dimensional model illustrating the relationship of social outcomes and firm outcomes. In Figure 21.1, social welfare is the vertical axis (reflecting the overriding condition); firm profitability is the horizontal axis (reflecting management's operational goal). Over a relevant range of change, rising firm profitability is associated with rising social welfare for legitimate businesses. Rising firm profitability is associated with falling social welfare for illegitimate businesses.

These three possibilities form a continuum from legitimate through "do no harm" to illegitimate business. Although resting on economic benefits and costs, legitimacy and illegitimacy are ultimately social judgments. Transportation industries (e.g. air, auto, rail and water) for moving people and goods are instances of presently legitimate business. While overall, social welfare effects are positive and greater than industry profits, there are negative environmental impacts. Legitimacy rests on broad social approval of net benefits such that positives clearly outweigh negatives and substitutes are difficult to provide. Illegal industries (e.g. certain drugs, prostitution and criminal organizations) are instances of presently illegitimate business. Although there are disagreements and

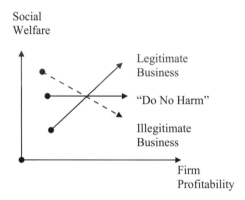

Figure 21.1 Relationship of firm profitability and social welfare

local variations (such as legal prostitution), illegitimacy rests on broad social disapproval of net harms such that negatives arguably outweigh positives. "Do no harm" businesses occur at the center of the continuum. Some financial transactions illustrate: speculation and hedging may fall toward the legitimate side, while insider trading and short selling (in some conditions) may fall toward the illegitimate side. Alcohol consumption, a social practice, has some negative effects (e.g. alcoholism, driving under the influence and vehicular homicide) but is acceptable by a long history. Tobacco consumption has more strongly negative effects (e.g. cancer, second-hand smoke, littering and health costs borne by society as a whole) that are under increasing scrutiny as socially unacceptable. For tobacco, a global ban and buy-out of farmers may become socially supported due to cancer, second-hand smoke, littering and health costs.

The second CSR principle is that a firm should obey law not by cost–benefit calculus but out of respect for law and community.[31] This normative principle in practice separates decision making into two levels.[32] At an overriding level, policy should be morally principled—the basis for respect for law and community. At a subordinated level, governed by such respect, specific choices can then consider cost–benefit analysis.[33] Respect for law and community does not mean, automatically, paying beyond definable liability. The principle is essentially "do no harm" which is illustrated in Figure 21.1 as not reducing social welfare in order to increase profitability. The ordering by level is important. A cost–benefit analysis works from the specific decision to the policy level to undermine respect for law and community. This principle is included because it can have broad implications beyond criminal statutes concerning deception and fraud. While generally competitors are not stakeholders of one another, there are limits on anti-competitive behavior for which the standard is social (not firm) welfare. Negative externalities ought to be handled by the firm without costly lawsuits and regulatory interventions. A peculiarity in Coase's social cost theory of market solutions is that the injured party could be the one paying to halt, for example, pollution.[34]

The third CSR principle is that a firm should practice business ethics and corporate citizenship seeking to advance the public or common interest.[35] The latter is not necessarily the same as social welfare; and the principle is not simply in favor of altruism. This principle is strategic (i.e. pragmatic) and concerned with management intentions and stakeholder expectations. One might argue for equating this principle to the simple "do no harm" criterion explained in the previous paragraph. Friedman assumes such a position in arguing against voluntary CSR so long as the firm obeys both laws and customary ethics.[36] In contrast, this principle is in favor of strategic practice as good reputational strategy reinforcing moral considerations.[37] The burden is on the proponent to demonstrate that a specific decision situation reduces to the "do no harm" criterion. There are several reasons for an expression going beyond "do no harm". First, influential stakeholders may demand higher standards of business ethics and corporate citizenship. Secondly, firms may cause harm (inadvertently or intentionally) and thus have special responsibility for helping to correct market failures they helped to cause. Excessive risk-taking by some executives and firms arguably helped precipitate the 2008–10 global financial crisis and economic recession.[38] Thirdly, firms ought not to lobby government for weak laws in their favor but adverse to the common interest.[39] Fourthly, the laws of some countries may not merit respect; and thus ethics and citizenship may require what amounts to civil disobedience in support of certain values—although such decisions are strategically difficult and thus fairly rare.[40]

The fourth and practical CSR principle is that management has sufficient discretion to make CSR decisions.[41] An executive uses judgment to make specific decisions. Discretion implies responsibility, and vice versa.[42] Informed judgment is here superior to following rules blindly.[43] Even legal compliance is in a sense a strategic choice. The net costs of compliance to the firm or executive might be lower than the net benefits of noncompliance.[44] Such choice violates the second and third CSR principles. There is considerable support for management discretion in both the U.S. and the European Union.[45] The U.S. legal framework for reasonable philanthropy is well established;[46] and over half of the states have corporate constituency statutes permitting deviation from stockholder interests in certain circumstances.[47] The European Union has advanced CSR as a voluntary discussion forum involving businesses and stakeholders.[48]

There are basically two different kinds of discretionary CSR decisions (or choices) that firms make. One kind involves direct trade-off among two or more key stakeholders.[49] Fair trade and organic trade illustrate differing kinds of trade-offs among customers, influencers and impactees. Investors are typically not affected negatively. Since some effects may be negative, management judgment is involved. The other kind of decision concerns collective responsibility and subsequent distribution of burden, as illustrated by environmental or community investments.[50] There are trade-offs among key stakeholders involved, and investors might be affected negatively depending on the options for handling distribution of burden. The benefits of the investment may be diffuse and going to secondary stakeholders. The firm's reputation may improve, depending on conditions affecting the decision to make the investment; but the financial benefits are likely postponed. Management judgment is even more clearly involved.

Key Literature Supporting an Integrative Approach

This section explains key literature supporting an integrative conceptual framework combining neutral CSR principles with a basic stakeholder model. The approach developed in this chapter is a pressure-adjusted market model in which managers and stakeholders may possess moral values and psychological perceptions in addition to economic interests.[51] The approach begins with a market model. Whether in the form of a capitalist market economy (illustrated by the U.S.) or a social economy (illustrated by Germany and Japan), as differing institutional settings, the basic regime is relatively free flow of capital (financial and human) to highest market-valued uses. That market regime may be more or less regulated by government. Given the particular institutional arrangements of market and regulation in a country, stakeholders may attempt to apply pressure to management and government in various ways.[52] Pressure and concession, within respect for law and public interest, are the essence of voluntary CSR decisions.

There is a very large literature bearing on CSP, CSR and stakeholders. Some of that literature has been referenced in the earlier sections of this chapter. Basic developmental histories and compendiums are in print.[53] The focus here is on identification and explanation of some key literature bearing on this development of an integrative approach.

One key debate concerns the objective function (or goal) of the firm. This debate occurs at two levels. One level concerns whether the objective function should be stated as strictly shareholder value maximization (in some form).[54] The other level concerns whether managers realistically can handle two or more objectives. Privately owned firms may behave as if individuals; but executives of publicly traded firms have fiduciary obligations to investors.[55] Neither type of firm is obliged legally to maximize profits. The business judgment rule affords reasonable discretion to executives concerning how rationally to operate a firm in shareholders' interest.[56]

At the level of the objective function, executives and investors do act primarily out of financial self-interest. Certain adjustments in that realism presumption are necessary and useful. First, agency theory expects separation between interests of executives and investors. Executives maximize corporate wealth under their control rather than shareholder wealth; and consideration of multiple stakeholder interests can be advisable in specific circumstances.[57] Secondly, short-run profit maximization is a dubious notion; longer-run wealth-seeking is a more accurate description of a corporate objective function.[58] Thirdly, executives have to be concerned with personal and corporate reputation, in the interest of investors as well as of themselves.[59] Self-preservation plays a role here. Executives do not wish to lose their positions and thus must play to the perceived desires of those with the most power to depose them.[60] Fourthly, executives and investors may choose to operate social enterprises or mixed-purpose enterprises; nothing theoretically or legally constrains executive or investor to maximize financial returns.[61] As a result of these adjustments, executives must think about strategy as distinct from profit maximization or share price maximization; the latter are resultants and not instruments.[62]

At the level of management, there are two competing theories. One theory asserts that managers cannot handle more than one objective at a time. Multiple objectives must be strictly hierarchical: CSR for example must be profitable. The empirical evidence over the past two centuries of capitalist economic development favors long-run wealth seeking (but not necessarily short-run profit maximization). Even in this theory, Jensen accepts that managers must consider the values of employees (concerning CSR, sustainability and other stakeholders), as ignoring their concerns may affect employee productivity adversely.[63] The competing theory is that firms can and ought to be multiple-objective organizations, and that managers handle difficult trade-offs all the time.[64] Not specifying objectives too precisely facilitates flexibility in performance. The difficulty of managing conflicts should not be underestimated.[65] While shareholder financial return is easy to measure, stakeholder and social welfare is more vague.[66] It may be the case that a CSR activity does not maximize future cash flows but still maximizes the firm's market value, which can be affected by investor sentiments and stakeholder reactions.[67]

Effective strategy integrates market and nonmarket dimensions of a firm's external environment.[68] Stakeholder salience theory is a broader version of executive self-preservation noted above. Mitchell, Agle and Wood[69] suggested that stakeholders' prioritized salience to executives reflects relationships among urgency, legitimacy and power.[70] Basically, a powerful and legitimate stakeholder with an urgent issue will receive attention; a powerless stakeholder without an urgent issue will not receive attention. Stakeholder salience has been subjected to empirical validation.[71] Strategic calculus is complicated rather than simple. For the long-run profitability of the firm, CSR and stakeholder salience judgments will likely be unavoidable; customer expectations and stakeholder activism are arguably rising. Salient stakeholders have influence or moral claims on the firm's choices.

Basic Five-Stakeholder Model

Narayana Murthy, a founding partner and as of August 2011 chairman emeritus of Infosys (India), explained corporate mission as follows:

> *The primary purpose of corporate leadership is to create wealth legally and ethically. This translates to bringing a high level of satisfaction to five constituencies—customers, employees, investors, vendors and the society-at-large. The raison d'être of every corporate body is to ensure predictability, sustainability and profitability of revenues year after year.*[72]

There is no incompatibility between business judgment and CSR; business executives make value and stakeholder salience judgments about that relationship.[73]

The key instance is a five-stakeholder setting (depicted in Figure 21.2). A "stakeholder" makes some contribution to or derives some net benefit or cost from an organization. Specific combinations of contributions, benefits and costs define different kinds of stakeholders. Three key stakeholders—customers, employees, and investors—contribute in exchange for benefits. Two other stakeholders in the basic model are any specific kind of influencer (e.g. government) and impactee (e.g. negative externality victim). The model can be scaled down (to one, for internal choice) or up (to N). A five-stakeholder version would appear to be the most suitable model for useful analysis of CSR decisions.

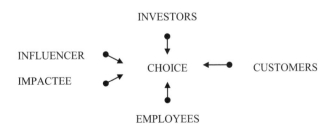

Figure 21.2 Basic model for five stakeholders affecting management choice

One can treat a "stakeholder" category as a representative actor or the weighted average of actors in the category. This form permits the framework to be treated as if a "committee" (or board) of representatives of different interests were addressing choices jointly.[74] Managers, while retaining decision discretion, consult this committee for advice and weight preferences according to perceived salience of stakeholders. That more committee members favor or oppose a decision is supporting but not binding information. The committee has two different kinds of choices to make. The first kind is how to make any decision given potentially conflicting interests. The second kind is what to do in a specific decision situation.

The first choice is effectively "constitutional": a stakeholder must adopt a decision rule, although it may not be possible to posit a single rule in advance (i.e. there might need to be a set of rules).[75] Alternatives for a decision rule are:

1. Market outcome (i.e., bidding using existing resources);
2. Prioritization of interests (i.e., defer to management judgment in a salience model);
3. Aggregation (i.e., voting), itself involving a choice of specific voting rule (i.e., majority, extra-majority, weighted voting) and subsuming coalition-building (i.e. management defers to the vote);
4. Concession (i.e., one or more stakeholders sacrifices);
5. Balance of interests (i.e., maximum satisfaction of multiple stakeholder demands); or
6. Principle (i.e., some value dominates the choice), including appeal to legal ruling.[76]

Stakeholder pressure (e.g. stockholder proposals, activism, or boycott) is an adjustment of the market outcome.[77] In specific decisions, the six rule alternatives might not be as strictly separable as suggested here.[78]

The other choice is issue-specific: what to do in variable situations, given a decision rule set as above. Any decision rule, other than pure market outcomes, involves management judgment and committee voting. Lankoski reported systematic differences in economic impacts of different CSR issues and influence of the content of CSR on economic impact. Generally, economic impacts are more positive for CSR issues reducing negative externalities and less positive for CSR issues generating positive externalities. A negative externality generates a cost for another party ignored by the externality generating entity; a positive externality generates a benefit for another party not captured by the externality generating entity. Generally, economic impacts are more positive for CSR issues in which the outcome benefits market stakeholders (e.g. customers) rather than nonmarket stakeholders (e.g. communities).[79] Empirical evidence suggests that while effective stakeholder engagement can benefit the firm, social issues tend to cost the firm.[80]

Three Illustrative Choice Problems

The framework logic is illustrated here by analysis of three specific choice problems from the manager's viewpoint: (1) fair trade with no domestic substitute; (2) organic trade with a foreign substitute; and (3) discretionary environmental or community investment. Each choice is designed as a voluntary decision. The choices vary in terms of affected stakeholders and management values and outcomes—so that the choices must be judged. The choices thus help illustrate variation in key considerations likely to occur in many CSR decisions. The market outcome is the benchmark not requiring specific illustration. The committee, and management, simply votes in favor of letting markets resolve issues as avoiding debate and study.[81] Each CSR problem involves variation from market outcomes due to a combination of stakeholder concession (reflecting values), management judgment (including values) and activist pressure (asserting values). Each problem involves combining several decision rules.

Table 21.2 presents a visual depiction comparing the three choice problems. The depiction provides a sense of trade-offs among interests and dynamics of interaction among salient stakeholders in making specific CSR decisions. The depiction is organized as a table used in discussion of the three choices. The table records what the manager understands about the economic condition and value satisfaction of each salient stakeholder. Economic condition is relatively objectives (prices, costs and volumes); value satisfaction is subjective (what the stakeholder feels). The text takes the reader through each decision in more detail, referring back to the table. The three choice problems are arrayed across the table. Stakeholders are arrayed down the table. The decision for each choice problem is separated into economic condition and value satisfaction of each stakeholder. The former is reasonably objective (i.e. measured by observable changes in market prices); the latter is subjective (i.e. as evaluated by the stakeholder). The lower portion of the table maps each choice problem into the six decision rules and suggests how the "committee" of salient stakeholders is likely to "vote" on the specific decision. The three choice problems have been selected as reasonably meeting the four neutral CSR principles, so specification of the four principles is not needed in the table itself. While effects for specific stakeholders may be negative, aggregate social welfare increases in each instance (depending on whether one's perspective of the relationship between the choice and social welfare). The decisions (whether for or against CSR) are legal, although the possibility of anti-trust collusion between retailers and producers may exist in fair trade and organic produce. Management can act in the public or common interest (again depending on one's perspective). Management has the discretion to make these particular decisions.

FAIR TRADE WITH NO DOMESTIC SUBSTITUTE

In Table 21.2, the left-hand column labeled Decision #1 concerns a management decision to provide some fair trade products at higher prices to customers willing to pay more. The decision involves CSR because a disadvantaged producer obtains price above market out of a value principle concerning fairness shared by managers, customers and employees and paid for voluntarily by customers. This kind of decision is characteristic of the zero CSR perspective: management will not act unless there is customer willingness to pay. Fair trade products typically have no domestic substitute. Activists drive the movement for fair trade. Management must decide how much of the product portfolio should be fair trade and conventional, what prices to charge with intention to transfer the increase to producers, and which producers to favor. So long as there is choice (i.e. a mix of fair trade and conventional products), then customers still decide which items to purchase at what prices. In Table 21.2, the manager can observe that the economic condition of purchasing customers declines (recorded as a negative change) but their value satisfaction increases (recorded as a positive change). These customers pay more willingly. The economic

Table 21.2 Trade-offs and dynamics in three specific choice problems

	Specific choice problems meeting the four neutral CSR principles					
	Decision #1 Fair trade with no domestic substitute		Decision #2 Organic trade with foreign substitute		Decision #3 Discretionary environmental and community investments	
Alphabetical order	Economic condition	Value satisfaction	Economic condition	Value satisfaction	Economic condition	Value satisfaction
Customers	−	+	0	+	− or 0	+
Employees	0	+	0	+	−	+
Impactee (domestic)	Indirect: loss of volume	−	Direct: loss of volume	−	+	+
Impactee (foreign)	+	+	+	+	0	0
Influencer	0	+	0	+	0	+
Investors	0	0	0	0	− or +	− if financial investor + if socially responsible investor
Decision rule						
1. Market	Higher demand		Lower cost		Legal requirement	
2. Salience	Activist influencer		Customer demand		Investors	
3. Voting	+ greater than −		+ greater than −		+ and − about equal	
4. Concede	Customers pay more		Customers pay more		Either customers pay more or investors accept loss	
5. Balance	Indirect impactees less important		Direct impactees less important		Direct impactees are important	
6. Principle	Fairness		Environmentalism		Citizenship	

Notes:

+ = a change positive from perspective of stakeholder: gain or satisfaction.

0 = a constant (no change) from perspective of stakeholder.

− = a change negative from perspective of stakeholder: loss or dissatisfaction.

condition of employees does not change (recorded as a zero change, although employees might receive slightly higher nominal tip amounts), but their value satisfaction may increase. Investors are indifferent in the sense that neither economic condition nor value satisfaction is affected. (Similar strategies of competitors and transfer of price increase to producers suggest that neither stock price nor dividend is likely to increase much.) The favored producer experiences both increased economic condition and value satisfaction. An excluded producer may experience the reverse (depending on whether selected by a competitor). A domestic impactee, if any, may suffer an indirect loss of volume and thus reduced value satisfaction; but this effect is likely to be very minor. In this instance, an influencer is most likely to be an activist organization promoting fair trade for producers in developing countries. The advisory "committee" of salient stakeholders is thus likely to vote in favor of this change in product portfolio: some customers support the change; employees are likely to support the change; investors are indifferent. Adverse domestic impacts are likely to be minor and thus can be disregarded. In terms of stakeholder decision rules, there is customer demand, activists have influence, there are more positive or zero impacts than negative and thus "committee" advises in favor, some customers are willing to concede higher payments to producers (not to the retailer), indirect impactees are not important, and the underlying value principle is fairness especially for small producers struggling in developing countries. This CSR decision is straightforward, so long as management maintains a portfolio of fair trade and conventional products. Serious difficulties can arise if management attempts to retain some proportion of higher prices and makes controversial choices among producers. There will be further pressure from customers for lower prices and from activists to help the more deserving countries and small producers.

The most common fair trade products are produced in countries of the south: the product typically has no significant domestic substitute in countries of the north.[82] The choice problem is the same however if there is a domestic fair trade product with no foreign substitute. There is no direct conflict in supply chain between domestic and foreign sources. Customer fair trade support might reduce customer spending on other products, but such effects are likely to be minor. Fair trade (or import preference) debates can occur for virtually any non-substitutable good produced in a developing country. A typical instance is coffee, where there are both small and large producers in developing countries. Bananas tend to be marketed as organic or conventional, as production is more typically controlled by large firms. If small producers become more prominent, then fair trade and organic marketing would likely be combined.

Fair trade is in effect a supply-side arrangement to promote customer tipping above market price motivated by ethical concerns for the producer's welfare.[83] The reason for using this choice problem is that a customer is influenced (by values or promotion) to act other than according to market signals.[84] The customer makes a concession passed through to producers by retailers. Management, under some pressure from activists, prioritizes in favor of certain suppliers. Value and salience judgments are involved. The arrangement overall arguably balances interests and promotes welfare of the investors, the customers and the suppliers. A fair trade arrangement is not a supplier cartel, like the Organization of Petroleum Exporting Countries (OPEC). In fair trade, an intermediary distributor or set of distributors does act to restrict customer options and influence consumer selections. A fair trade arrangement is not the same as a consumer buying directly from the original producer.

Coffee is grown in developing countries of the south and exported to developed countries of the north (U.S.-grown coffee is strictly limited). Specific companies can be used to illustrate this kind of CSR decision. Retail coffee providers (e.g., Seattle Coffee, Starbucks, or Whole Foods) must decide what mix of fair trade and other products to obtain from specific suppliers. The retailers affect suppliers on the one hand and customers on the other hand. Coffee suppliers are impactees (i.e. fair trade beneficiaries). The World Bank has promoted coffee farming in developing countries. One result has been a competitive struggle for quality reputation and branding.[85] Certain NGOs may advocate fair trade with the threat of boycott.[86] There was a running dispute with

Starbucks concerning Ethiopian coffee trade-marking. Recently, Starbucks announced it will work with Tata Coffee, an Indian firm part of the Tata Group and likely the largest integrated plantation firm in the world. Part of the decision involves the possibility of opening Starbucks outlets in India, which closely regulated foreign-owned retail chains.[87]

The coffee supply chain involves growers, roasters and distributors. Arrangements vary considerably. While Starbucks Coffee is a publicly traded corporation, Planet Bean is a worker-owned cooperative (Ontario, Canada). One comparative assessment concludes that while Planet Bean is more oriented toward the ethical dimension of fair trade, Starbucks is as the world's largest specialty coffee roaster likely increasingly dominant in the fair trade network through greater market reach.[88] Evidence for Nicaragua coffee production and Finland coffee consumption suggested that, although Finnish consumers paid much more for fair trade certification and producers in Nicaragua received a price premium, roasters and retailers in the consuming country received a larger share of retail prices than for conventional coffee. Both premium and share of premium must be assessed.[89] Part of the literature concerns impacts on coffee growers, which may be organized as agricultural cooperatives among relatively small landholders. A random sample of coffee growing households in southern Mexico suggests government subsidies and migration affect decisions concerning fair trade and also organic coffee.[90] Land and labor returns are higher for fair trade/organic production than for conventional production. However, yield differences outweigh price premiums. The coffee sector itself is dominated by education and labor opportunities outside that sector.

Retailers might provide a broad range of coffee options so that customers choose; but this range is likely pretty limited. If fair trade coffee sells at market price, then the choice is between one impactee (growers) and another impactee (fair trade groups). If fair trade coffee sells above market price, then the choice is between customers and impactees. Customers must decide whether to tip (in effect). Influencers, employees, and investors are apt to vote (in "committee") for fair trade; and some customers prefer to tip. Porter points out a limitation on passing costs forward to customers: long-term strategy involves relative cost reduction and relative non-priced benefit provision to secure customer loyalty.[91] Fair trade retailers benefit from higher reputation with some stakeholders and profitability is either unaffected or potentially higher.

ORGANIC PRODUCE WITH A FOREIGN SUBSTITUTE

More space was devoted to detailed explanation of the first choice problem, so that the reader can see how to work with the conceptual framework. In Table 21.2, the middle column labeled Decision #2 concerns a domestic organic product with a foreign substitute. The decision involves CSR because the value principle involved concerns environmental sustainability shared among managers, customers and employees and paid for by customers. Organics often involve foreign substitutes (especially in Europe). Here food or apparel are typical instances. Bananas do not have a significant domestic substitute in countries of the north. Organic production involves specialized farming systems, as for pest control as an example.[92] There are two differences from the previous choice problem. First, the customer has a consumption preference (for product quality) rather than a fair trade tipping value. This consumption preference may involve, however, concerns about CSR toward the environment (a value akin to the fair trade tipping value, where is there relatively less variation in perceived quality). Nature is treated by customers and managers as an impactee. Secondly, the existence of foreign substitutes involves customers and retailers in explicit choices between domestic and foreign suppliers. Foreign producers may in addition also resort to fair trade arrangements as in the first choice problem. If so, fair trade considerations are layered on top of organic considerations. (Organic and fair trade dimensions are analytically separable, although sometimes involved in a given product. The discussion here emphasizes the organic dimension.) The combination of decision rules involved is roughly the same as for fair trade products.

This kind of decision typically characterizes the strong CSR position. In Table 21.2, the economic condition of customers is basically unaffected: they pay more for higher-cost quality preference rather than tip a producer; their value satisfaction is higher. Although customers are willing to pay and often demanding organic produce, there are important environmental and sustainable development effects. Management might be prepared on a value principle to introduce organic produce at constant profit or even lower profit margin per item. The economic condition of employees is unaffected, but they may also experience higher value satisfaction. The investors remain unaffected, as price and cost for organic products adjust together. The stock price and dividend effects are unchanged if competitors adopt similar strategies. Influencers are again likely to be activists favoring organic produce—being indifferent to domestic or foreign sourcing in this instance. The "committee" of salient stakeholders is thus likely to vote in favor of this change in product portfolio: some customers support the change; employees are likely to support the change; investors are indifferent. In this instance, customers rather than activists are the most salient group. As management chooses domestic or foreign sourcing, domestic and foreign impactees are directly affected. In Table 21.2, the illustration is a choice for foreign sourcing such that domestic producers suffer a direct loss of volume and thus decreased value satisfaction, while foreign producers experience increased economic condition and value satisfaction. For the salient stakeholders, the market rule seeks lower cost sources among organic producers; customers demand organic produce; more stakeholders will favor organic production than oppose; again customers concede by paying more; the direct impactees are here less important. The value principle concerns environmentalism.

Consumers may be willing to pay a premium for organic apparel and food products. Labor and brand labeling can affect this willingness to pay.[93] One example is organic cotton sportswear introduced by Patagonia.[94] There are differential impacts on producers. A comparative assessment of agricultural cooperatives in Paraguay illustrates alternative strategies. A cooperative exporting organic sugar follows a strategy based on fair trade, independence of state bureaucracies and alliances with international buyers and NGOs. A cooperative exporting bananas to neighboring Argentina follows a strategy based on free trade, regional market liberalization (within South America) and dependence on state bureaucracies.[95] Food instances include fruit, coffee, tea, vegetables, rice, spices and sugar—among likely now hundreds of organically grown products.[96] Some customers are prepared to pay extra for organic, and the retailer can likely provide both organic and non-organic alternatives (e.g., Whole Foods).[97] Fruit is seasonal, so likely sourcing with present production technology is the U.S. in summer and Southern Hemisphere countries in winter.

In this instance, voting within a stakeholder advisory "committee" would be about the same as for fair trade items. A social issue arises when organic fruit can be sourced in the same season (or seasonal transition period) from domestic or foreign sources, and the latter is less expensive. Voting within a "committee" is more complicated, as there are two impactees with conflicting interests: domestic and foreign. The committee voting faces additional complications when fair trade considerations are layered on organic considerations. Management judgment is thus juggling at times with two value dimensions and more stakeholder conflicts.

DISCRETIONARY ENVIRONMENTAL AND COMMUNITY INVESTMEN

The third choice problem is discretionary environmental or community investment. In Table 21.2, the right-hand column labeled Decision #3 depicts this kind of choice. This decision is more typically what executives and academics mean by CSR issues. The CSR decision for management is to undertake voluntary investments that may affect corporate reputation but likely involve short-term reduction in profit. Management must assess the trade-off between short-term and long-term time horizons for the firm and its salient stakeholders. The decision is more difficult for investors; society at large is the beneficiary (whether at the local level of community or more broadly). The costs are concentrated on the firm and the benefits are more diffuse. Here, decision rules involve balancing and aggregation of interests, in conjunction with values concerning environment and community. Mandatory environmental investment is required by law or public policy; and the decision focuses on distribution of burden. If final product price can be raised, then the issue is how to distribute burden among other stakeholders. Airlines typically pass security taxes levied by government directly to passengers.[98] Airlines may provide an option for passengers to make a voluntary environmental contribution per trip. In a voluntary investment, once a CSR activity is selected then distribution of burden is also involved (as in mandatory investment). There is evidence for the UK FTSE 100 that companies closer to consumers will be significantly more active in environmental measures and furthermore are more likely to undertake environmental activities motivated by concern for reputation with consumers and society, even though there is no explicit cost-reduction benefit.[99]

In Table 21.2, customers may or may not bear the ultimate burden of the management choices depending on whether the firm can raise prices. Customers and employees are likely to enjoy increased value satisfaction. But employees may face a reduced economic condition if the burden is absorbed by the firm rather than passed to customers through increased prices. Impactees enjoy increased economic condition and value satisfaction through environmental and community improvements. There are no direct foreign impactees in this instance. Activists attempt to influence management toward environmental and community investments. What happens to investors depends on whether the burden is transferred to customers or employees or to investors, and investors may have different preferences concerning financial returns and social responsibility. The market rule would avoid voluntary investments and respond only to legal requirements. The most salient stakeholders are investors, but the decision depends on whether they bear the ultimate burden. Some stakeholder group will need to concede bearing the cost. Direct impactees (of environmental effects and community conditions) are important. The value principle involved is how to define citizenship, in the sense of being a good neighbor. In typical CSR decisions, the "committee" will divide in voting and voting depends on who bears the ultimate burden. More CSR-conscious customers, employees and investors will tend to vote with activists; more financially oriented stakeholders will tend to vote against CSR projects. Management must judge the reputation and long-term sustainability of the firm in making specific decisions. One community may be more important than another. One environmental issue may be more sensitive than another. A particular CSR issue may be more important to management values. These decisions are what typically define the strategic CSR perspective.

Community or more broadly social contributions can be addressed similarly.[100] Here the CSR decision is typically voluntary. The poorer the community, the stronger the CSR of a firm will arguably have to be. Developing community locations into premium-commanding brands may be more difficult. But one can imagine branding campaigns to help promote purchase of products from poorer regions of the U.S., or from particular developing countries.

A firm may be more sensitive to communities in which it operates. A particular concern may arise in health issues of the local population. For example, Marathon Oil Corporation operates on Bioko Island, off the coast of Equatorial Guinea, where the country's capital is located. Malaria is rampant. Marathon and partners, now providing much of the funding through the Global Fund for AIDs, TB and malaria, are engaged in an anti-malaria campaign expanded from the island to the mainland. Marathon estimates an economic return of 4 to 1 for every dollar invested in the campaign. Marathon is a member of the Global Business Coalition.[101] While some companies have reported considerable success with and return from community investment programs, particularly involving employee engagement and client relationship-building, reflecting a mix of altruistic and business motives,[102] reporting of community investment activities seems generally more difficult to articulate.[103] Data concerning employee participation and corporate philanthropy leaves vague corporate objectives. Management judgment of values, stakeholder salience and reputation effects is likely more important in such decisions.

Conclusions and Managerial Implications

This chapter aids managers and stakeholders in assessing decisions concerning corporate social responsibility (CSR) activities. It provides a conceptual decision framework emphasizing an integrative approach developed from a focused literature review. The heuristic framework is tested conceptually on three illustrative CSR decision problems: (1) fair trade with no domestic substitute; (2) organic trade with a foreign substitute; and (3) discretionary environmental or community investments. The three choice problems capture typical considerations affecting CSR decisions involving key stakeholders. Managers should search for opportunities to generate profits or market value. One kind of opportunity lies in consumer preferences, illustrated by fair trade or organic products. A different kind of opportunity involves environmental or community investments that while costly in the short term may affect longer-term profits or market value. Both kinds of opportunities can generate social benefits and firm value.

The conceptual framework proposed and illustrated in this chapter has certain strengths and limitations for managers and stakeholders. The basic purpose is to provide a structured approach by which managers and stakeholders can organize and assess information and interests bearing on CSR decisions. CSR theory is contested; empirical evidence is not determinative. The framework, provided in Figure 21.2 and illustrated in Table 21.2, is a desirable heuristic aid to decision-making in such circumstances. The framework rests on four neutral principles that should not bias a decision-maker for or against a particular theory of CSR. A prescriptive principle is that firm profitability should be associated with social welfare. A normative principle is that firms should obey law out of respect, not cost–benefit calculus. A strategic principle is that firms should engage in business ethics and corporate citizenship beyond "do no harm" as a means of building positive reputation. A practical principle is that managers possess discretion to make CSR judgments. Table 21.2 illustrates how the framework can work in three choice problems addressing variations in key CSR considerations. Firms are likely to engage in fair trade arrangements and organic produce provision, while dividing on voluntary environmental and community investments according to managerial judgments about values and stakeholder salience. The approach is limited in being a heuristic aid and not a computational algorithm. Judgment is required concerning values, salience and strategy. Space available for this chapter constrains illustrations to three choice problems. Fair trade and organic production are concerns for some but not all firms. Environmental and community investments are broad concerns. CSR issues may involve combinations of the six decision rules identified. The model does not provide a full set of all possible combinations of rules or stakeholder interests. There may be other rules and other stakeholders that affect other kinds of decisions. On balance, however, the approach here should help managers and stakeholders in thinking carefully about other CSR decision circumstances that cannot be addressed in detail here.

Notes

1   "Rethinking the Social Responsibility of Business: a *Reason* debate featuring Milton Friedman, Whole Foods' John Mackey, and Cypress Semiconductor's T.J. Rodgers", October 2005, http://reason.com/archives/2005/10/01/rethinking-the-social-responsi.

2   Carroll, A.B. and Shabana, K.M. (2010), "The business case for corporate social responsibility: a review of concepts, research and practice", *International Journal of Management Reviews*, vol. 12, no. 1, pp. 85–105.

3   Karnani, A. (2010), "The case against corporate social responsibility", *Wall Street Journal*, supports strong business ethics, government regulation, and stakeholder activism, August 23, http://online.wsj.com/article/SB10001424052748703338004575230112664504890.html.

4   Porter, M.E. and Kramer, M.R. (2006), "Strategy and society: the link between competitive advantage and corporate social responsibility", *Harvard Business Review*, vol. 84, no. 12, pp. 78–92.

5   Schwartz, M.S. and Carroll, A.B. (2008), "Integrating and unifying competing and complementary frameworks: the search for a common core in the business and society field", *Business & Society*, vol. 47, no. 2, pp. 148–186; Whetten, D.A., Rands, G. and Godfrey, P. (2002), "What are the responsibilities of business to society?" In A. Pettigrew, H. Thomas, and R. Whittington (eds), *Handbook of Strategy and Management*, Thousand Oaks, CA, Sage, pp. 373–408.

6   Paine, L.S., *et al.* (2004), "Martin Marietta: Managing Corporate Ethics (A)", Harvard Business School case 9-393-016, p. 9.

7   http://ec.europa.eu/enterprise/policies/sustainable-business/corporate-social-responsibility/index_en.htm.

8   Krivosha, T. (2011, May 14), "Social enterprise: a new way to enhance corporate social responsibility", ON Securities, published by Marty Rosenbaum of Maslon, http://www.onsecurities.com/2011/05/14/social-enterprise-a-new-way-to-enhance-corporate-social-responsibility/. Terri Krivosha is Chair of the Business and Securities Practice Group of Maslon Edelman Borman and Brand, LLP in Minneapolis, MN.

9   Carroll, A.B. (1991), "The pyramid of corporate social responsibility: toward the moral management of organizational stakeholders", *Business Horizons*, vol. 34, no. 4, pp. 39–48; Carroll, A.B. (1995), "Stakeholder thinking in three models of management morality". In J. Näsi (ed.), *Understanding Stakeholder Thinking*, LSR-Julkaisut Oy, Helsinki, pp. 47–74.

10   Mishina, Y., *et al.* (2010), "Why 'good' firms do bad things: the effects of high aspirations, high expectations, and prominence on the incidence of corporate illegality", *Academy of Management Journal*, vol. 53, no. 4, pp. 701–722.

11   Business ethics is explicitly counseled by the American Law Institute (1994), *Principles of Corporate Governance: Analysis and Recommendations*, St. Paul, MN, §2.01(b), cited by Orts, E.W. and Strudler, A. (2002), "The ethical and environmental limits of stakeholder theory", *Business Ethics Quarterly*, vol. 12, no. 2, pp. 215–233, at p. 220 (n. 36). One reasonable objection to adding business ethics to legal compliance is that there are multiple ethical perspectives and in some perspectives, at least, one's actions might have negative impacts but still be ethical: e.g. Aristotle's virtue ethics, Kant's rule-based ethics, Plato's consequentialist ethics and answerability ethics. See Louden, R. (1984), "Some vices of virtue ethics", *American Philosophical Quarterly*, vol. 21, no. 3, pp. 227–236; Merle, J.-C. (2000), "A Kantian argument for a duty to donate one's own organs: a reply to Nicole Gerrand", *Journal of Applied Philosophy*, vol. 17, no. 1, pp. 93–101; Holland, R.F. (1977), "Absolute ethics, mathematics and the impossibility of politics", *Royal Institute of Philosophy Lectures*, vol. 11, pp. 172–188; Kopf, D.A., Boje, D. and Torres, I.M. (2010), "The good, the bad and the ugly: dialogical ethics and market information", *Journal of Business Ethics*, vol. 94, Supplement 2, pp. 285–297. The author makes three answers to this objection. First, these perspectives properly apply to individual ethics—the ethics of natural citizens. Business executives are agents—in stakeholder theory and at law of multiple principals; and firms are socially licensed entities. Secondly, business ethics are defined here by reference to social expectations. A business executive should presumably have moral values, one of which is presumably concern with expectations of as well as impacts on others. Thirdly, the argument here is stated explicitly as a socially preferred ideal, which may have well to be relaxed in practice. The underlying difficulty is the absence of a widely accepted theoretical solution for CSR decisions and stakeholder interest conflicts backed by conclusive empirical evidence.

12   Barnett, M. (2007), "Stakeholder influence capacity and the variability of financial returns to corporate social responsibility", *Academy of Management Review*, vol. 32, no. 3, pp. 794–816; Frooman, J. (1999), "Stakeholder influence strategies", *Academy of Management Review*, vol. 24, no. 2, pp. 191–205.

13   Strong, K.C., Ringer, R.C. and Taylor, S.A. (2001), "The rules of stakeholder satisfaction (timeliness, honesty, empathy)", *Journal of Business Ethics*, vol. 32, no. 3, pp. 219–230.

14   Aoki, M. (1984), *The Co-Operative Game Theory of the Firm*, Clarendon Press, Oxford, UK.

15   Schwartz, M.S. and Carroll, A.B. (2003), "Corporate social responsibility: a three domain approach", *Business Ethics Quarterly*, vol. 13, no. 4, pp. 503–530.

16   As Porter points out, the actual trade-offs managers make constitute the firm's real strategy evolving through time. The CSR profile of this strategy may or may not fit neatly into theoretical perspectives (strong CSR, strategic CSR and zero CSR); the integrative conceptual

framework of this chapter is as a result a heuristic aid; Porter, M.E. (1996), "What is strategy?", *Harvard Business Review*, vol. 74, no. 6, pp. 61–78.

17   Jensen, M.C. (2002), "Value maximization, stakeholder theory, and the corporate objective function", *Business Ethics Quarterly*, vol. 12, no. 2, pp. 235–256.

18   Wood, D.J. (1991), "Corporate social performance revisited", *Academy of Management Review*, vol. 16, no. 4, pp. 691–718.

19   Vogel, D. (2010), "The private regulation of global corporate conduct: achievements and limitations", *Business & Society*, vol. 49, no. 1, pp. 68–87.

20   If the reader does not fully agree with the four CSR principles proposed here, then the vital point is still that some set of neutral principles is desirable. The Organisation for Economic Cooperation and Development (OECD) issued revised CSR principles for multinational enterprises (MNEs) in May 2011: http://www.oecd.org/dataoecd/43/29/48004323.pdf. The UN Global Compact (UNGC) asks businesses voluntarily to adhere to ten principles concerning labor rights, human rights, environmental practices and anti-corruption: http://www.unglobalcompact.org. The OECD principles and UNGC principles take specific positions on CSR issues.

21   Orts and Strudler (2002), op. cit., at pp. 215, 218.

22   Vogel, D. (2006). *The Market for Virtue: The Potential and Limits of Corporate Social Responsibility*, revised ed., Brookings Institution Press, Washington, DC.

23   Margolis, J.D. and Walsh, J.P. (2003), "Misery loves companies: rethinking social initiatives by business", *Administrative Science Quarterly*, vol. 48, no. 2, pp. 268–305.

24   McWilliams, A. and Siegel, D. (2001). "Corporate social responsibility: a theory of the firm perspective", *Academy of Management Review*, vol. 26, no. 1, pp. 117–127.

25   Thoergersen, J. and Olander, F. (2006), "The dynamic interaction of personal norms and environment-friendly buying behavior: a panel study", *Journal of Applied Social Psychology*, vol. 36, no. 7, pp. 1758–1780.

26   Drucker, P.F. (1984), "Converting social problems into business opportunities: the new meaning of corporate social responsibility", *California Management Review*, vol. 26, no. 2, pp. 53–63.

27   Orlitzky, M., Schmidt, F.L. and Rynes, S.L. (2003), "Corporate social and financial performance: a meta-analysis", *Organization Studies*, vol. 24, no. 3, pp. 403–441.

28   The strong CSR literature basically assumes such a relationship. See Carroll, A. (1999), "Corporate social responsibility: evolution of a definitional construct", *Business & Society*, vol. 38, no. 3, pp. 268–295.

29   This principle is not controversial except by being misconstrued. The zero CSR theory is simply an argument that the properly regulated market will maximize social welfare more effectively than voluntary CSR actions viewed as a tax on shareholders for the common good. Jensen (2002), op. cit., and Karnani (2010), op. cit., are fully explicit on this point. The debate is about whether markets, governments, CSR, or some specific combination of the three approaches most effectively increases social welfare.

30   Suchman, M. (1995), "Managing legitimacy: strategic and institutional approaches", *Academy of Management Review*, vol. 20, pp. 571–610.

31   Smith, A. (1759), *The Theory of Moral Sentiments*, London, VI.II.36; see Orts and Strudler (2002), op. cit., p. 215 and at p. 222 (n. 42) citing American Law Institute (1994), op. cit. As Orts and Strudler explain, the essence of the principle is that legal compliance ought not to be an economic cost–benefit calculation.

32   Strictly speaking, an outside observer cannot determine underlying motive or intention. This principle is normative: what one ought to do. It is sufficient however for observed behavior to conform to this principle.

33   Ghemawat, P. (1991), "Strategic choices demand cost–benefit analysis", *Commitment: The Dynamic of Strategy*, Free Press, New York, pp. 46–49; Kelman, S. (1981), "Cost–benefit analysis: an ethical critique", *Regulation*, vol. 5, no. 1, pp. 33–40.

34   Coase, R.H. (1960), "The problem of social cost", *Journal of Law and Economics*, vol. 2, no. 1, pp. 1–44. A polluter causes harm to an impactee. One possibility is for government regulation, including by courts, to halt the pollution. Coase points out a market solution in which one possibility is that the impactee pays the polluter to reduce the activity. This privatization of responsibility raises ethical issues, in that an impactee might have to act to induce abatement of pollution without government action. See McChesney, F.S. (2006), "Coase, Demsetz, and the unending externality debate", *Cato Journal*, vol. 26, no. 1, pp. 179–200; Terrell, T.D. (1999), "Property rights and externality: the ethics of the Austrian school", *Journal of Markets and Morality*, vol. 2, no. 2, pp. 197–207.

35   Krivosha, op. cit. (2011); Smith (1759), op. cit.

36   Friedman, M. (1970), "The social responsibility of business is to increase its profits", *New York Times Magazine*, September 13 1970.

37   A recent empirical study at the Harvard Business School and London Business School concludes that superior CSR (i.e. social and environmental) performance, rather than corporate governance, results in better access to finance (i.e., lower capital constraints). The cross-section study confirms results using instrumental variables and simultaneous equations approaches. Cheng, B., Ioannou, I., and Serafeim, G. (2011), "Corporate social responsibility and access to finance", May 19 2011, http://ssrn.com/abstract=1847085.

38   The argument is that badly designed executive compensation promoted a short-term profit orientation and excess risk taking, especially in financial institutions. See Committee on Economic Development (2007, June), *Built to Last: Focusing Corporations on Long-Term Performance*; "Regulating the Unknown: Can Financial Reform Prevent Another Crisis?", http://knowledge.wharton.upenn.edu/article.cfm?articleid=2516 (2010, June 9); Strine, L.E., Jr. (2009), vice chancellor of the Delaware Court of Chancery, "Why excessive risk-taking is not unexpected", October 5 2009, http://dealbook.nytimes.com/2009/10/05/dealbook-dialogue-leo-strine/. Lorsch, J., and Khurana, R. (2010), "The pay problem: Time for a new paradigm for executive compensation", *Harvard Magazine*, vol. 112, no. 5 (May–June), pp. 30–35, propose that a new compensation approach is desirable. There is an argument that while there is a positive relationship between bank CEO compensation and risk taking, that relationship is not causative because it was an implicit too-big-to-fail government policy that provided the underlying incentive. If so, then a credible no-bailout policy might prove more effective than directly controlling executive compensation at deterring excessive risk taking. See Matthews, K. and Matthews, O. (2010), "Controlling bankers' bonuses: efficient regulation or politics of envy?" *Economic Affairs*, vol. 30, no. 1, pp. 71–76.

39   Bebchuk, L.A. and Neeman, Z. (2010), "Investor protection and interest group politics", *Review of Financial Studies*, vol. 23, no. 3, pp. 1089–1119.

40   Hanson, K.O. and Rothlin, S. (2010), "Taking your code to China", *Journal of International Business Ethics*, vol. 3, no. 1, pp. 69–80; Kumar, R., Lamb, W. and Wokutch, R. (2002), "The end of South African sanctions, institutional ownership, and the stock price performance of boycotted firms", *Business & Society*, vol. 41, no. 2, pp. 133–165.

41   Phillips, R.A., *et al.* (2010), "Stakeholder theory and managerial discretion", *Strategic Organization*, vol. 8, no. 2, pp. 176–183.

42   Wood (1991), op. cit., pp. 696, 698–699. See Key, S. (1996), "Do managers matter? The role of managerial discretion in corporate social responsibility decisions", *Business & Society*, vol. 35, no. 2, pp. 247–249.

43   Bennis, W.M., Medin, D.L. and Bartels, D.M. (2010), "The costs and benefits of calculation and moral rules", *Perspectives on Psychological Science*, vol. 5, no. 2, pp. 187–202.

44   Di Lorenzo, V. (2006), "Does the law encourage unethical conduct in the securities industry?" *Fordham Journal of Corporate and Financial Law*, no. 11, pp. 765–805.

45   Holmstrom, B. and Kaplan, S. (2003), "The dangers of too much governance", *MIT Sloan Management Review*, vol. 45, no. 1, p. 96.

46   American Law Institute (1994), op. cit.

47   Orts, E.W. (1992), "Beyond shareholders: interpreting corporate constituency statutes", *George Washington Law Review*, no. 61, pp. 14–135.

48   The most recent CSR communications of the European Commission are *Implementing the Partnership for Growth and Jobs: Making Europe a Pole of Excellence on Corporate Social Responsibility*, COM(2006) 136 Final, March 22 2006; *A Renewed EU Strategy 2011–14 for Corporate Social Responsibility*, COM(2011) 681 Final, October 25 2011.

49   David, P., *et al.* (2010), "Do shareholders or stakeholders appropriate the rents from corporate diversification? the influence of ownership structure", *Academy of Management Journal*, vol. 53, no. 3, pp. 636–654.

50   Aguilera, R.V., *et al.* (2007), "Putting the S back in corporate social responsibility: a multi-level theory of social change in organizations", *Academy of Management Review*, vol. 32, no. 3, pp. 836–863; Campbell, J.L. (2007), "Why would corporations behave in socially responsible ways: an institutional theory of corporate social responsibility", *Academy of Management Review*, vol. 32, no. 3, pp. 946–947.

51   Ingebrigtsen, S. and Jakobsen, O. (2009), "Moral development of the economic actor", *Ecological Economics*, vol. 68, no. 11, pp. 2777–2784; Vanberg, V.J. (2008), "On the economics of moral preferences", *American Journal of Economics and Sociology*, vol. 67, no. 4, pp. 605–628; Wolman, L. (1921), "The theory of production", *American Economic Review*, vol. 11, March, pp. 37–56.

52   Baron, D.P. (2001), "Private politics, corporate social responsibility and integrated strategy", *Journal of Economics and Management Strategy*, vol. 10, no. 1, pp. 7–45; Baron, D.P. (2009), "The positive theory of moral management, social pressure, and corporate social performance", *Journal of Economics and Management Strategy*, vol. 18, no. 1, pp. 7–43.

53   Carroll, A.B. (2004), "Corporate social responsibility: a historical perspective". In M.J. Epstein and K.O. Hanson (eds), *The Accountable Corporation*, Praeger, Westport, CT, vol. 3, pp. 3–30; Carroll, A.B. (2008), "A history of corporate social responsibility: concepts and practices". In A. Crane, *et al.* (eds), *The Oxford Handbook of Corporate Social Responsibility*, Oxford University Press, Oxford, UK, pp. 19–46; Garriga, E. and Mele, D. (2004), "Corporate social responsibility theories: mapping the territory", *Journal of Business Ethics*, vol. 53, pp. 51–71; Phillips, R.A. and Freeman, R.E. (eds) (2010), *Stakeholders*, Edward Elgar, Cheltenham, UK.

54   Sundaram, A.K. and Inkpen, A.C. (2004), "The corporate objective revisited", *Organization Science*, vol. 15, no. 3, pp. 350–363.

55   Friedman (1970), op. cit.

56   Rosenberg, D. (2007), "Galactic stupidity and the business judgment rule", *Journal of Corporation Law* (University of Iowa) vol. 32, no. 2, pp. 301–322: the doctrine does permit

review of substance to determine whether judgment constitutes "galactic stupidity" and thus bad faith. The standard is simply what a rational director acting in good faith would do (at p. 322).

57   Ross, S.A., Westerfield, R.W. and Jaffe, J. (2002), *Corporate Finance*, 6th ed., McGraw-Hill, Irwin, New York, see pp. 15–17. Nyberg, A.J., *et al.* (2010), "Agency theory revisited: CEO return and shareholder interest alignment", *Academy of Management Journal*, vol. 53, no. 5, pp. 1029–1049, finds stronger alignment than typically asserted.

58   Jensen (2002), op. cit.

59   Hillenbrand, C. and Money, K. (2007), "Corporate responsibility and corporate reputation: two separate concepts or two sides of the same coin?", *Corporate Reputation Review*, vol. 10, no. 4, pp. 261–277; Roberts, P.W. and Dowling, G.R. (1997), "The value of a firm's corporate reputation: how reputation helps attain and sustain superior profitability", *Corporate Reputation Review*, vol. 1, pp. 72–75; Vergin, R.C. and Qoronfleh, M.W. (1998), "Corporate reputation and the stock market", *Business Horizons*, vol. 41, no. 1, pp. 19–26; Waddock, S. (2000), "The multiple bottom lines of corporate citizenship: social investing, reputation, and responsibility audits", *Business & Society Review*, no. 105, pp. 323–345.

60   Donaldson, T. and Preston, L.E. (1995), "The stakeholder theory of the corporation: concepts, evidence, and implications", *Academy of Management Review*, vol. 20, no. 1, pp. 65–91, at pp. 75, 79–80; Jagersma, P.K. (2009), "The strategic value of sustainable stakeholder management", *Business Strategy Series*, vol. 10, no. 6, pp. 339–344; Wrage, M., Tuschke, A. and Bresser, R.K.F. (2011), "The influence of social capital on CEO dismissal in Germany: an empirical analysis", Freie Universität Berlin, School of Business and Economics discussion paper: Economics 2011/5, http://hdl.handle.net/10419/45377; Xuan, Y. (2009), "Empire-building or bridge-building? Evidence from new CEOs' internal capital allocation decisions", *Review of Financial Studies*, vol. 22, no. 12, pp. 4919–4948.

61   The still understudied field of social enterprise concerns organizations deliberately combining mission and market-based strategies for social purposes, and organized alternatively for non-profit, for-profit, or hybrid objectives. Such enterprises seek investors with so-called "patient capital." See Krivosha (2011), op. cit.; Mair, J. and Noboa, E. (2003, September), "Social Entrepreneurship: How Intentions to Create a Social Enterprise Get Formed", IESE Business School, University of Navarra, Spain, IESE Working Paper no. D/521, http://ssrn.com/abstract=462283. An example is Panera's nonprofit café project—see Salter, J. (2011), "Panera pleased with nonprofit cafe idea: chain says its unusual concept sends a message", *Houston Chronicle*, vol. 110, no. 221, Sunday, May 22, p. D2 (Business).

62   Querrera, F. (2009), [Jack] Welch condemns stock price focus, *Financial Times*, March 12 2009.

63   Jensen (2002), op. cit.

64   Ethiraj, S.K. and Levinthal, D. (2009), "Hoping for A to Z while rewarding only A: complex organizations and multiple goals", *Organization Science*, vol. 20, no. 1, pp. 4–21; Lankoski, L. (2008), "Multiobjective firms and the management of trade-offs", University of Helsinki, Department of Economics and Management, Discussion Papers no. 26, Food Economics.

65   Pache, A.-C. and Santos, F. (2010), "When worlds collide: the internal dynamics of organizational responses to conflicting institutional demands", *Academy of Management Review*, vol. 35, no. 3, pp. 455–476.

66   Cho, K. (2010), "Idealism and business are not incompatible, says Banyan Tree [hotel group] founder [Ho Kwon Ping]", http:knowledge.insead.edu/csr-banyan-tree-100510.cfm?vid=413.

67 Mackey, A., Mackey, T.B. and Barney, J.B. 2007), "Corporate social responsibility and firm performance: investor preferences and corporate strategies", *Academy of Management Review*, vol. 32, no. 3, pp. 817–835.

68 Baron, D.P. (1995), "Integrated strategy: market and nonmarket components", *California Management Review*, vol. 37, no. 2, pp. 47–65.

69 Mitchell, R.K., Agle, B.R. and Wood, D.J. (1997), "Toward a theory of stakeholder identification and salience: defining the principle of who and what really counts", *Academy of Management Review*, vol. 22, no. 4, pp. 853–886.

70 Parent, M.M. and Deephouse, D.L. (2007), "A case study of stakeholder identification and prioritization by managers", *Journal of Business Ethics*, vol. 75, no. 1, pp. 1–23.

71 Agle, B.R., Mitchell, R.K. and Sonnenfeld, J.A. (1999), "Who matters to CEOs? an investigation of stakeholder attributes and salience, corporate performance, and CEO values", *Academy of Management Journal*, vol. 42, no. 5, pp. 507–525; Magness, V. (2008), "Who are the stakeholders now? an empirical examination of the Mitchell, Agle, and Wood theory of stakeholder salience", *Journal of Business Ethics*, vol. 82, no. 2, pp. 177–192.

72 http://www.infosys.com/investors. Friedman (1970), op. cit., stipulates legal and ethical "rules of the game".

73 Tetrault Sirsly, C.-A. (2009), "75 years of lessons learned: chief executive officer values and corporate social responsibility", *Journal of Management Inquiry*, vol. 15, no. 1, pp. 78–94.

74 Black, D. (1987), *The Theory of Committees and Elections*, Kluwer, Dordrecht, The Netherlands (1958, Cambridge University Press, Cambridge, UK). A corporate board of directors might be so composed (as suggested by German two-board governance); or the shareholders' board might act on behalf of multiple interests as suggested in corporate constituency statutes; Orts (1992), op. cit.

75 Bennis *et al.* (2010), op. cit.

76 Hosseini, J.C. and Brenner, S.N. (1992), "The stakeholder theory of the firm: a methodology to generate value matrix weights", *Business Ethics Quarterly*, vol. 2, no. 2, pp. 99–119. The present approach permits the weights to vary according to the specific decision issue depending on views of management and the voting "committee."

77 For an illustration, see Baker, D.R. (2011), "CEO to protesters: We share ideals, but ...: Chevron leader says their views of oil giant are totally wrong", *Houston Chronicle*, vol. 110, no. 225, Thursday, May 26, pp. D1, D5 (Business). Questions and shareholder proposals at the 2011 annual meeting included gas flaring in Nigeria, the lawsuit about oil-field contamination in Ecuador, election of an environmental representative to the board, linking executive pay to environmental sustainability, and reporting on financial risks from climate change. A proposal for a report on environmental risks of fracking (i.e. extracting natural gas from rock) reportedly received nearly 41 percent of shareholder votes.

78 As an example, Freeman's proposed approach to stakeholder theory is entrepreneurial value creation by management that reduces conflicts through win–win market solutions. This approach posits that it is not possible to separate strategy and ethics. In effect, proper strategic management inherently integrates rules one and six. Harris, J.D. and Freeman, R.E. (2008), "The impossibility of the separation thesis", *Business Ethics Quarterly*, vol. 18, no. 4, pp. 541–548.

79 Lankoski, L. (2009), "Differential economic impacts of corporate responsibility issues", *Business & Society*, vol. 48, no. 2, pp. 206–224.

80 Hillman, A.J. and Keim, G.D. (2001), "Shareholder value, stakeholder management, and social issues: what's the bottom line?" *Strategic Management Journal*, vol. 22, no. 2, pp. 125–139.

81   Friedman (1970), op. cit., and McWilliams and Siegel (2001), op. cit., advocate this approach: any voluntary CSR is a violation of market outcomes.

82   Long, J.C. (2008), "From cocoa to CSR: finding sustainability in a cup of hot chocolate", *Thunderbird International Business Review*, vol. 50, no. 5, pp. 315–320.

83   Kim, G.-S., Lee, G.Y. and Park, K. (2010), "A cross-national investigation on how ethical consumers build loyalty toward fair trade brands", *Journal of Business Ethics*, vol. 96, no. 4, pp. 589–611.

84   Adam Smith, *The Wealth of Nations* (1776), Book Four, Ch. 4: "Consumption is the sole end and purpose of all production; and the interest of the producer ought to be attended to only so far as it may be necessary for promoting that of the consumer. The maxim is so perfectly self-evident that it would be absurd to attempt to prove it. But in the mercantile system the interest of the consumer is almost constantly sacrificed to that of the producer; and it seems to consider production, and not consumption, as the ultimate end and object of all industry and commerce."

85   Petit, N. (2007), "Ethiopia's coffee sector: a bitter or better future?", *Journal of Agrarian Change*, vol. 7, no. 2, pp. 225–263.

86   Rehbein, K., Waddock, S. and Graves, S.B. (2004), "Understanding shareholder activism: which corporations are targeted?", *Business & Society*, vol. 43, no. 3, pp. 239–268.

87   Adamy, J. and Thurow, R. (2007, March 5), "Brewing conflict: Ethiopia battles Starbucks over rights to coffee names; chain's image rattled by trademark spat; hints of chocolate, rum", *Wall Street Journal*, Eastern ed., p. A1; "Starbucks to buy beans from Tata", *Houston Chronicle*, vol. 110, no. 93, Friday, January 14, p. D3 (Business).

88   Fridell, G. (2009), "The co-operative and the corporation: competing visions of the future of fair trade", *Journal of Business Ethics*, vol. 86, no. 1, pp. 81–95.

89   Valkila, J., Haaparanta, P. and Niemi, N. (2010), "Empowering coffee traders? The coffee value chain from Nicaraguan fair trade farmers to Finnish consumers", *Journal of Business Ethics*, vol. 97, no. 2, pp. 257–270.

90   Barham, B.L., *et al.* (2011), "Fair trade/organic coffee, rural livelihoods, and the 'agrarian question': southern Mexican coffee families in transition", *World Development*, vol. 39, no. 1, pp. 134–145.

91   Porter (1996), op. cit.

92   Zhengfei, G., *et al.* (2005), "Damage control inputs: a comparison of conventional and organic farming systems", *European Review of Agricultural Economics*, vol. 32, no. 2, pp. 167–189.

93   Hustvedt, G. and Bernard, J.C. (2010), "Effects of social responsibility labeling and brand on willingness to pay for apparel", *International Journal of Consumer Studies*, vol. 34, no. 6, pp. 619–626.

94   Casadesus-Masanell, R., *et al.* (2009), "Households' willingness to pay for green goods: evidence from Patagonia's introduction of organic cotton sportswear", *Journal of Economics and Management Strategy*, vol. 18, no. 1, pp. 203–233.

95   Vásquez-León, M. (2010), "Free markets and fair trade, collective livelihood struggles, and the cooperative model: two cases from Paraguay", *Latin American Perspectives*, vol. 37, no. 6, pp. 53–73.

96   Kortbech-Olesen, R. (1998), "Exporting organic foods", *International Trade Forum*, no. 3, pp. 4–7.

97   Pivato, S., Misani, N. and Tencati, A. (2008), "The impact of corporate social responsibility on consumer trust: the case of organic food", *Business Ethics: A European Review*, vol. 17, no. 1, pp. 3–12.

98   Additional taxes and charges then involve questions of adequate disclosure to facilitate price competition among carriers. The U.S. Department of Transportation fined Continental Airlines and US Airways Group for advertising ticket prices without insufficient disclosure concerning fuel surcharges that could almost double quoted fares. Martin, H. (2011), "Continental fined in pricing case: website didn't clearly disclose fuel surcharges, regulators say", *Houston Chronicle*, vol. 110, no. 233, Friday, June 3, p. D4 (Business). In January 2012, the U.S. Department of Transportation ordered greater disclosure of taxes and fees: see http://travel.usatoday.com/flights/story/2012-01-10/Government-forcing-full-disclosure-on-airfares/52486078/1.

99   Haddock-Fraser, J.E. and Tourelle, M. (2010), "Corporate motivations for environmental sustainable development: exploring the role of consumers in stakeholder engagement", *Business Strategy and the Environment*, vol. 19, no. 8, pp. 527–542.

100 Kramer, M.R. and Porter, M.E. (2002), "The competitive advantage of corporate philanthropy", *Harvard Business Review*, vol. 80, no. 12, pp. 56–69.

101 INSEAD (2009), "Combating malaria: how an oil company is helping to tackle the problem", http://knowledge.insead.edu/combatingmalaria090114.cfm.

102 Jenkins, C. and Baker, P. (200), "Engaging employees in community investment at Pfizer", *Corporate Reputation Review*, vol. 10, no. 4, pp. 305–311; Talbot, M. (2009), "Ernst and Young sees community investment as key to high returns", *Strategic HR Review*, vol. 8, no. 2, p. 49.

103 Tsang, S., Welford, R. and Brown, M. (2009), "Reporting on community investment", *Corporate Social Responsibility and Environmental Management*, vol. 16, no. 3, pp. 123–136.

Index

If you have found this book useful you may be interested in other titles from Gower

**A Handbook of Corporate Governance
and Social Responsibility:
Transforming Project Delivery**
Edited by
Güler Aras and David Crowther
Hardback: 978-0-566-08817-9
e-book: 978-0-7546-9217-1

**Advising Upwards:
A Framework for Understanding and Engaging
Senior Management Stakeholders**
Edited by
Lynda Bourne
Hardback: 978-0-566-09249-7
e-book: 978-1-4094-3430-6

**Finance at the Threshold:
Rethinking the Real and Financial Economies**
Christopher Houghton Budd
Hardback: 978-0-566-09211-4
e-book: 978-0-566-09212-1

GOWER

Global Perspectives on Corporate Governance and CSR
Edited by
Güler Aras and David Crowther
Hardback: 978-0-566-08830-8
e-book: 978-0-566-09185-8

Making Ecopreneurs:
Developing Sustainable Entrepreneurship
Edited by
Michael Schaper
Hardback: 978-0-566-08875-9
e-book: 978-1-4094-0123-0

Market Orientation:
Transforming Food and Agribusiness around the Customer
Edited by
Adam Lindgreen, Martin Hingley, David Harness and Paul Custance
Hardback: 978-0-566-09208-4
e-book: 978-0-566-09236-7

Visit **www.gowerpublishing.com** and

- search the entire catalogue of Gower books in print
- order titles online at 10% discount
- take advantage of special offers
- sign up for our monthly e-mail update service
- download free sample chapters from all recent titles
- download or order our catalogue